Disarming Words

FLASHPOINTS

The series solicits books that consider literature beyond strictly national and disciplinary frameworks, distinguished both by their historical grounding and their theoretical and conceptual strength. We seek studies that engage theory without losing touch with history, and work historically without falling into uncritical positivism. FlashPoints will aim for a broad audience within the humanities and the social sciences concerned with moments of cultural emergence and transformation. In a Benjaminian mode, FlashPoints is interested in how literature contributes to forming new constellations of culture and history, and in how such formations function critically and politically in the present. Available online at http://repositories.cdlib.org/ucpress

Series Editors: Ali Behdad (Comparative Literature and English, UCLA); Judith Butler (Rhetoric and Comparative Literature, UC Berkeley), Founding Editor; Edward Dimendberg (Film & Media Studies, UC Irvine), Coordinator; Catherine Gallagher (English, UC Berkeley), Founding Editor; Jody Greene (Literature, UC Santa Cruz); Susan Gillman (Literature, UC Santa Cruz); Richard Terdiman (Literature, UC Santa Cruz)

1. *On Pain of Speech: Fantasies of the First Order and the Literary Rant,* by Dina Al-Kassim
2. *Moses and Multiculturalism,* by Barbara Johnson, with a foreword by Barbara Rietveld
3. *The Cosmic Time of Empire: Modern Britain and World Literature,* by Adam Barrows
4. *Poetry in Pieces: César Vallejo and Lyric Modernity,* by Michelle Clayton
5. *Disarming Words: Empire and the Seductions of Translation in Egypt,* by Shaden M. Tageldin

Disarming Words

Empire and the Seductions of Translation in Egypt

Shaden M. Tageldin

UNIVERSITY OF CALIFORNIA PRESS
Berkeley · Los Angeles · London

the modern language initiative

THIS BOOK IS MADE POSSIBLE BY A COLLABORATIVE GRANT FROM THE ANDREW W. MELLON FOUNDATION.

University of California Press, one of the most distinguished university presses in the United States, enriches lives around the world by advancing scholarship in the humanities, social sciences, and natural sciences. Its activities are supported by the UC Press Foundation and by philanthropic contributions from individuals and institutions. For more information, visit www.ucpress.edu.

University of California Press
Berkeley and Los Angeles, California

University of California Press, Ltd.
London, England

Library of Congress Cataloging-in-Publication Data

Tageldin, Shaden M.
Disarming words : empire and the seductions of translation in Egypt / Shaden M. Tageldin.
p. cm.—(FlashPoints ; 5)
ISBN 978-0-520-26552-3 (pbk. : alk. paper)
1. Translating and interpreting—Egypt—History—19th century. 2. Translating and interpreting—Egypt—History—20th century. 3. Postcolonialism—Egypt. 4. Comparative literature—Arabic and English. 5. Comparative literature—Arabic and French. 6. Language and languages in literature. I. Title.
P306.T265 2011
418'.02—dc22

2011005499

Manufactured in the United States of America

20 19 18 17 16 15 14 13 12 11
10 9 8 7 6 5 4 3 2 1

The paper used in this publication meets the minimum requirements of ANSI/NISO Z39.48-1992 (R 1997) (*Permanence of Paper*).

for my parents
and for all who struggle, in word and in deed,
with imperialism and its wake

Contents

List of Illustrations *ix*
Acknowledgments *xi*
Note on Translation and Transliteration *xvii*

Overture | Cultural Imperialism Revisited: Translation, Seduction, Power *1*

1. The Irresistible Lure of Recognition *33*
2. The Dismantling *I:* Al-ʿAṭṭār's Antihistory of the French in Egypt, 1798–1799 *66*
3. Suspect Kinships: Al-Ṭahṭāwī and the Theory of French-Arabic "Equivalence," 1827–1834 *108*
4. Surrogate Seed, World-Tree: Mubārak, al-Sibāʿī, and the Translations of "Islam" in British Egypt, 1882–1912 *152*
5. Order, Origin, and the Elusive Sovereign: Post-1919 Nation Formation and the Imperial Urge toward Translatability *195*
6. English Lessons: The Illicit Copulations of Egypt at Empire's End *237*

Coda | History, Affect, and the Problem of the Universal *273*

Notes *289*
Index *331*

Illustrations

1. Proclamation by Napoleon Bonaparte to the people of Egypt, 2 July 1798 / *35*
2. Portrait of a Janus-faced Napoleon Bonaparte, sporting French *bicorne* and Mamlūk turban, c. 1798–1801 / *41*
3. Bilingual Arabic-French cover of Rifāʿa Rāfiʿ al-Ṭahṭāwī's *Naẓm al-ʿUqūd fī Kasr al-ʿŪd* (1827), a translation of Joseph Agoub's *La Lyre brisée* (1825) / *142*
4. Arabic title page of Rifāʿa Rāfiʿ al-Ṭahṭāwī's *Naẓm al-ʿUqūd fī Kasr al-ʿŪd* (1827) / *143*
5. Pictorial comparison of proto-Egyptian skull and ancient Egyptian bust, reproduced and recaptioned by Salāma Mūsā, 1928 / *232*
6. Ancient Egyptian representations of ancient Arabs, reproduced and recaptioned by Salāma Mūsā, with continuation of comparative chart of modern English, modern Arabic, and ancient Egyptian words, 1928 / *233*
7. Comparative chart of modern English, modern Arabic, and ancient Egyptian words, 1928 / *234*
8. Cartoon, "Egypt and the League of Nations," 1929 / *248*
9. Cartoon of Egypt as a Westernized woman shackled head-to-toe by the British, 1930 / *249*

Acknowledgments

This book is a translation of many minds, times, spaces, and voices. In writing it, I have incurred untold debts.

Several grants made completion of this book possible. A postdoctoral fellowship from the Europe in the Middle East–the Middle East in Europe (EUME) program, cosponsored by the Berlin-Brandenburgische Akademie der Wissenschaften (BBAW), the Fritz-Thyssen Stiftung, and the Wissenschaftskolleg zu Berlin, sent me to Berlin in 2007. My work profited from lively exchanges with Georges Khalil, Samah Selim, Nora Lafi, Amnon Raz-Krakotzkin, and my fellowship cohort: Eli Bar-Chen, Z. Özlem Biner, Magdi Guirguis, Erol Köroğlu, Raja Rhouni, Dana Sajdi, Oded Schechter, Mohamad Nur Kholis Setiawan, Muhammad Reza Vasfi, and Zafer Yenal. Many thanks to Georges Khalil and Christine Hofmann of EUME for their hospitality and support and to the Zentrum für Literatur- und Kulturforschung in Berlin for hosting me as a guest researcher. Equally important was a Residential Fellowship from the Institute for Advanced Study (IAS) at the University of Minnesota. I thank Ann Waltner, Angie Hoffman-Walter, Karen Kinoshita, Susannah Smith, and my fellowship cohort, to whom I owe much intellectual stimulation. A 2006 Summer Stipend from the National Endowment for the Humanities (NEH), matched by the University of Minnesota Graduate School, supported research in Egypt and France. (Any views, findings, conclusions, or recommendations expressed in this book do not necessarily reflect those of the NEH.) Other grants from the University of Minnesota—a College of Liberal Arts Single-Semester Leave, a Faculty Summer Research Fellowship and McKnight Summer Research Fellowship in the Arts and Humanities, a Grant-in-Aid for Research, and an Imagine Fund Faculty Research Award—funded work at home and overseas, research assistance, and fees for reproduction of the illustrations in this book, as well as permission to reprint them.

I thank the gracious staffs of the many libraries and archives that supported my research: in Egypt, the Egyptian National Library and Archives (Dār al-Kutub wa al-Wathā'iq al-Qawmiyya), the American University in Cairo Library, the Cairo University Central Library, and the Bibliotheca Alexandrina; in France, the Bibliothèque Nationale de France and the Centre des Archives d'Outre-Mer; in the United Kingdom, the British Library and the British National Archives; and in the United States, Doe Library at the University of California, Berkeley, and Wilson Library and the Digital Collections Unit of Andersen Library at the University of Minnesota. Sincere thanks also to the Binational Fulbright Commission in Cairo and the U.S.-U.K. Fulbright Commission in London, which welcomed me to their cities in 2002–3 and helped launch my research.

Words alone cannot thank the many whose generosity with time and ideas inform this book. This project began at the University of California, Berkeley, where I earned my Ph.D. Thanks to Lydia Liu, I learned to read empire translingually and to rethink translation as a philosophical and political problem, and thanks to Muhammad Siddiq, I learned to read modern Arabic literature in its aesthetic richness and political complexity, tracing its links to the past and to other world literary traditions. Karl Britto introduced me to francophone literature across three continents and encouraged me to take a comparative approach to colonialism and postcoloniality. Catherine Gallagher taught me to read Victorian texts with an eye for context and the counterintuitive. And to Abdul JanMohamed, I owe the insight that recognition can disarm resistance. To these mentors, I extend abiding gratitude.

At the University of Minnesota, I have enjoyed the support of two department chairs, John Archer and John Mowitt, and of my other colleagues in the Department of Cultural Studies and Comparative Literature: Hisham Bizri, Timothy Brennan, Robin Brown, Cesare Casarino, Keya Ganguly, Richard Leppert, Thomas Pepper, Harvey Sarles, Jochen Schulte-Sasse, and Gary Thomas. Their commitment to progressive scholarship, pedagogy, and politics has inspired me to rethink my arguments in profound ways, and I am most grateful. To my students, whose insights always teach me, I owe further pleasures of intellectual community. Warmest thanks also to the dedicated staff of our department, past and present.

Julietta Singh was my graduate research assistant in spring 2008. She tirelessly tracked down sources and images and compiled an extensive working bibliography. For her deft, dedicated, and ever gracious assistance, she has my deep thanks.

At this project's inception, Gaber Asfour in Cairo and Wen-chin Ouyang in London took time to discuss my work and facilitated access to important sources. As the revised manuscript took shape, Karl Britto, Cesare Casarino, Siobhan Craig, Muhammad Siddiq, Omise'eke Natasha Tinsley, and Christophe Wall-Romana each read at least one chapter. Their incisive comments helped me reimagine parts of this book, as did invaluable suggestions from Lydia Liu and informal responses from Roderick Ferguson and Laura Nader. Donald Brenneis and other anonymous readers for the University of California Press parsed my arguments with keen intelligence. This book is better for the care, insight, and generosity of these colleagues. I cannot thank them enough. Any oversights are, of course, my own.

Finally, I thank Judith Butler, Edward Dimendberg, and Richard Terdiman of the FlashPoints editorial group for their commitment to this project. At the University of California Press, Lynne Withey, Hannah Love, Emily Park, and Eric Schmidt deserve special gratitude for their efforts to see this book to publication, as do Tim Roberts of the Modern Language Initiative and copyeditor Sheila Berg.

Parts of chapter 3 were presented in the 2009 Reading World Literature lecture series, sponsored by the Program in Comparative Literary Studies at Northwestern University. My thanks to Christopher Bush, Michal Peled Ginsburg, Nasrin Qader, Alejandra Uslenghi, and William West for probing questions. Parts of chapter 5 were presented in a 2007 lecture at the BBAW and in the "Nation and Translation" workshop at the Europaïsche Akademie Berlin. For their comments, I thank Ian Almond, Mona Baker, Michael Beard, Nergis Ertürk, Sameh Fekry Hanna, Şehnaz Tahir Gürçağlar, Richard Jacquemond, Kader Konuk, Erol Köroğlu, Samia Mehrez, Anwar Moghith, Oded Schechter, Samah Selim, Sunil Sharma, and Mona Tolba. Sameh Hanna enriched my conception of chapter 4 by generously sharing his work. Parts of this book and related papers also were presented in other venues, including conferences of the African Literature Association, the American Comparative Literature Association, the American Research Center in Egypt, Boğaziçi University, Cairo University, Columbia University, the Middle East Studies Association, and the Modern Language Association. Warmest thanks to my interlocutors, especially Samer Ali, Michael Allan, Roger Allen, Amal Amireh, Doris Bachmann-Medick, Şebnem Bahadır, Christopher Bush, Elliott Colla, miriam cooke, Dilek Dizdar, Charitini Douvaldzi, Brian Edwards, Tarek El-Ariss, Marie-Therese Ellis-House, Nergis Ertürk, Anne-Lise François, Nouri Gana, Moneera Al-Ghadeer, Arthur Goldschmidt Jr., William Granara, Alexandra Gueydan-Turek, Hala Halim, Waïl Hassan, Margaret Higonnet, Elizabeth Holt, Ayşe Banu Karadağ, Erika Lee, Lital Levy, Patricia Lorcin, Anouar Majid, Nabil Matar, Mary Jo Maynes, Muhsin Al-Musawi, Ngũgĩ wa Thiong'o, Jeffrey Sacks, Haun Saussy, Simona Sawhney, Jaroslav Stetkevych, Suzanne Stetkevych, Kate Sturge, Yasir Suleiman, and Edwige Tamalet Talbayev.

Parts of chapter 3 appear in modified form in "One Comparative Literature? 'Birth' of a Discipline in French-Egyptian Translation, 1810–1834," *Comparative Literature Studies* 47, no. 4 (2010): 417–45, reprinted by permission of Pennsylvania State University Press. Parts of the overture and chapter 4 appear in modified form in "Secularizing Islam: Carlyle, al-Sibāʿī, and the Translations of 'Religion' in British Egypt," *PMLA* 126, no. 1 (January 2011): 123–39, reprinted by permission of the copyright owner, The Modern Language Association of America. Excerpts of chapter 3 also appear in different form in "The Sword and the Pen: Egyptian Musings on European Penetration, Persuasion, and Power," *Kroeber Anthropological Society Papers* 87 (Spring 2002): 196–218; and select passages in chapter 6 recast arguments from "'Dignity is the most precious . . . deformity there is!': Language, Dismemberment, and the Body Colonized in Naguib Mahfouz's *Zuqaq al-Midaqq*," *Critical Sense* 7, no. 1 (Winter 1999): 11–53. I thank the editors of both journals for granting me free use of these essays.

The support of many colleagues and friends, within and beyond academe, has sustained me through the years. I especially thank Hakim Abderrezak, Joseph Allen, Daniel Brewer, Mária Brewer, Bianet Castellanos, Leo Chen, Geneviève Emanuely, Roderick Ferguson, Toral Gajarawala, Njeri Githire, Mónica Gómez, Karen Ho, Whitney Hopler, Liz Kotz, Margaret Larkin, Yu-Ting Lin, Usha Narayanan, Lena Salaymeh, Rachel Schurman, Miriam Thaggert, Omise'eke Natasha Tinsley, and Christophe Wall-Romana.

Above all, this book owes its life to my father and my mother, whose intellectual example inspired me to love reading from earliest childhood and whose critical spirit informs every page, and to my extended family. As their love knows no bounds, so too my gratitude.

Surely I have forgotten someone, but this book has not forgotten you.

Note on Translation and Transliteration

Unless otherwise noted, all translations in this book are mine. Transliterations from the Arabic generally follow the *International Journal of Middle East Studies (IJMES)* system. I have deviated from *IJMES* style, however, in at least three important respects. First, to limit the number of hyphenations in transliterated passages, I have omitted the hyphen after certain inseparable prepositions or conjunctions (e.g., *fa*, *la*), preferring to run these into the words that follow (e.g., *laqad* instead of *la-qad*); similarly, I have chosen not to render in print the elision of certain prepositions or conjunctions (e.g., *bi*, *li*, *wa*) with the following definite article *al-* (e.g., opting for the form *wa al-tarjama* instead of *wa-l-tarjama* and relying on the reader of Arabic to perform the necessary elision mentally). Second, I have applied full diacritical notation to the names of persons and places and to the titles of published works. Third, in text—but not in the titles of published works—I have chosen to fully vocalize my transliterations to capture the syntax and cadence of the original. Finally, in references to the Ottoman viceroy Mehmed Ali, I have used an Ottoman Turkish transliteration but indicated the Arabic form (Muḥammad ʻAlī) in which his name appears in Egyptian sources.

Disarming Words

OVERTURE

Cultural Imperialism Revisited

Translation, Seduction, Power

One of the ways to get around the confines of one's "identity" as one produces expository prose is to work at someone else's title, as one works with a language that belongs to many others. This, after all, is one of the seductions of translating. It is a simple miming of the responsibility to the trace of the other in the self.

Translation is the most intimate act of reading. I surrender to the text when I translate.

—Gayatri Chakravorty Spivak, "The Politics of Translation"

Much as I hesitate to air the intimate apparel of (post)coloniality in general and of mainstream (post)colonial Egyptian intellectual subjectivity in particular, do so I shall—with a little help from the Moroccan literary theorist ʿAbd al-Fattāḥ Kīlīṭū (Abdelfattah Kilito). Kīlīṭū opens *Lan Tatakallama Lughatī* (2002; *Thou Shalt Not Speak My Language*), a provocative excursus into the psychological underbelly of translation in the medieval and modern Arab worlds, with a prologue that speaks volumes to a central argument of this book. Citing the example of Muṣṭafā Luṭfī al-Manfalūṭī (1876–1924), an influential early-twentieth-century Egyptian man of letters known for his "free" retranslations of others' Arabic translations, Kīlīṭū notes that al-Manfalūṭī knew no European languages and wrote a neoclassical Arabic that appears, to the naked eye, "steeped in tradition."[1] "Nevertheless," he observes, "every one of [al-Manfalūṭī's] pages whispers the same question: how do I become European?"[2] Al-Manfalūṭī's "Arabic-only" posture, Kīlīṭū suggests, evades the charge of surrender to Europe. Yet his vicarious translations of European literature betray an anxious need to register the arrival of European colonial modernity in Egypt, to bring Arabic into the fold of the modern by folding Europe into Arabic. The paradox of al-Manfalūṭī's dress glosses the tragic two-facedness of his seemingly "resistant"—yet translated—Arabic. On the covers of his books, Kīlīṭū tells us, al-Manfalūṭī flaunts his "traditional garb—turban and cloak—and seems to ask, Aren't I an Azharite?"[3] Through his chosen self-representation, he styles himself a product of al-Azhar, Cairo's millennium-old Islamic institution of higher learning, and thus an "authentic" exemplar of the Arab-Islamic literary tradition. Beneath, however, he sports European underwear—of which, "those with intimate knowledge of him assert," he was "fond."[4] Concludes Kīlīṭū, "European dress is al-Manfaluti's secret passion *[sirru al-Manfalūṭī]*, an unspeakable secret because it clings to his body, to his being. It does not appear on the cover of his books any more than the names of the European authors he adapted."[5] Europe enters Egyptian bodies and books under domestic cover, cloaked in Arabic. As Kīlīṭū observes, the question he puts in al-Manfalūṭī's mouth, "How do I become European?" is one that al-Manfalūṭī never poses explicitly. Kīlīṭū raises that occulted question to an audible whisper.

If, as Gayatri Chakravorty Spivak argues, "'translation is the most intimate act of reading,'" small wonder that Europe should be al-Manfalūṭī's intimate apparel—the undergarment of his Arabic. What the translating (and thus translated) colonized mimics, in this scenario, ultimately is not—or not only—the colonizer but *himself*. It is his own Europeanness that he camouflages, not his nativeness. This is because his origin—his original—already has been translated *into* "Europe." To invoke one of Walter Benjamin's metaphors for the relationship of translation to original, the cloak of the Azharite is but a royal robe whose folds drape loosely around the original—the European undergarment.[6] The colonized preserves the sovereignty of his native *I* ("Aren't I an Azharite?") by surreptitiously equating himself with the European *I:* by fusing himself to the sovereign colonizer (hence the clinging underwear). Since the Egyptian's native body and being are fused to the European, to be himself he must "play" himself—don the royal robe of the Azharite. But if mimicry can turn to menace, as Homi Bhabha argues it always does, the European threatens to peek out.[7] That is, if we look closely enough.

As both an instrument of and a response to cultural imperialism, translation exercises its greatest power in the transubstantiating zone of seduction, beyond the pales of pure identity—a forced homology of meaning, the tyranny of what Jacques Derrida has called the "transcendental signified"—and pure difference: a supposedly liberationist, yet equally forced, preservation-in-transit of the literalness of the word, the regime of Derrida's "transcendental signifier."[8] These two pales—or poles—still dominate postcolonial theories of translation, which are just beginning to break free of their tautology.[9] Often translation is understood as a bipolar choice between foreignization and domestication, hitched to an understanding of imperialism as an equally bipolar dynamic of domination and resistance. Even Bhabha, who early refused a simple politics of colonial imposition and anticolonial "writing back," favors the oppositional native. Hence Bhabha describes the language of mimicry, a hybrid native idiom that bespeaks both "civility" to and "civil disobedience" of the colonizer, as a mode of "spectacular resistance."[10] In the mid-1990s, Lydia Liu drew on Lisa Lowe's critique of an East/West divide premised on "a static dualism of identity and difference" (Lowe's phrase) to argue that prevailing trends in postcolonial theory risk "reducing the power relationship between East and West to that of native resistance and Western domination," ignoring the permeability of the boundary.[11] Rethinking the politics of translation under colonial conditions, she concluded that "a non-European language does not automatically constitute a site of resistance to European languages."[12]

Liu's insight has been slow to catch on. Writing of late-nineteenth- and early-twentieth-century Chinese translations from Western literatures, Lawrence Venuti suggests that the domesticating translation—which conceals its foreign provenance, passing itself off as nontranslation—is more dangerous to the target culture, more likely to surrender translator and audience to foreign ideology because it so deeply absorbs the foreign into the familiar body. Venuti implies that foreignizing translations, which consciously attempt to transform the target culture by making visible the introduction of the foreign, encourage a more selective—and critical—appropriation of the translated text into the target culture.[13] Richard Jacquemond disagrees. For Jacquemond, early Egyptian translations from French literature, which deeply acculturated French originals to Arabic literary conventions and Egyptian cultural norms, were not just the freest translations but also the most freeing; they suggest that Egyptians still held France at some epistemological distance. By contrast, he contends, later Egyptian translations from French—more faithful to the originals and thus more likely to foreignize the target language, to contort Arabic to approximate French—index the beginnings of French hegemony over Arabic.[14] Both Venuti and Jacquemond imply that the resistant translation is the desirable translation, one that avoids the surrender that Spivak imputes to the seductions of translation. Their investment in resistance drives their diverging views of domestication: Venuti holds that the seemingly intact native signifier conceals surrender to the colonizer; Jacquemond, that it betokens greater resistance to that surrender. Neither, however, fully answers this critical question: What happens when a "native" signifier binds to a "foreign"—especially a colonizing—signifier to shore up the power of the native *through* the power of the foreign? Through the example of al-Manfalūṭī's unbroken native Arabic, which couples overt self-assertion and self-preservation to covert intimacy with the language of the dominant European, Kīlīṭū makes us wonder whether resistance to translation and surrender to translation might not in fact translate one another. The muse of European culture has visited and seduced the Egyptian translator. In its wake, it has left a clinging relic behind, and clinging to that a certain fondness. Affect complicates resistance.

In a 1990 interview with the *Sunday Times* of London, the Nobel Prize–winning Egyptian novelist Najīb Maḥfūẓ (Naguib Mahfouz, 1911–2006) spoke out loud al-Manfalūṭī's "secret passion"—the translational fascination of much modern Egyptian literature with European literature. Maḥfūẓ was asked about the influence of Charles Dickens, Honoré de Balzac, and other European novelists on his writing. His reply was arch. "Yes, we know Western literature here," he said. "In fact, we love it too much."[15] That Maḥfūẓ wrote only in standard literary Arabic makes some imagine him a purist. Yet he is acutely aware that the language of his novels is anything but pure, that modern Arabic—long in love with European languages and literatures—is in fact "contaminated" by that love's excess. Maḥfūẓ himself was weaned on the imperialist adventures of Sir Walter Scott and H. Rider Haggard, which he read in Arabic translation, and on the sentimental fictions of none other than al-Manfalūṭī, whose ornate Arabic prose style left its mark on his first novels.[16] Thus he readily concedes that Western literature has shaped modern Arabic literary creativity. For, like others of his era, Maḥfūẓ—who lived to witness British rule, the nationalist revolutions of 1919 and 1952, and three generations of postindependence statehood in Egypt—was heir to the Egyptian literary "renaissance," or *nahḍa*, of the late nineteenth and early twentieth century. To reestablish Egypt's preeminence in the family of nations, the exponents of that renaissance pursued a paradoxical strategy of cultural revitalization. They translated European texts and called on Egypt to emulate the modes of literary, philosophical, and scientific exploration that seemed to underpin Europe's imperial dominance in their country and elsewhere. Yet they marshaled these emulations of Europe to renew the faded glory of indigenous cultural heritages—Pharaonic, Arabic, Islamic—and to restore Egypt to pride of place in modernity. For most of the elite Egyptian intellectuals of the *nahḍa*, becoming modern was never a question of abandoning Arabic and writing in the languages of their European colonizers—in French or English. The *nahḍa* unfolded in translation: it transported French or English into Arabic. Thus it appeared to "preserve" Arabic—all the while *translating* it.

Unlike Algeria—where French suppression of Arabic over some 130 years left many acutely conscious of language loss—Egypt could hide such loss in the illusion of unbroken Arabic, could imagine imperialism irrelevant to the emergence of its modern Arabic literature. As late as 1996, the translation scholar Bashīr al-'Īsawī could contend that Arabic in Egypt had always been impervious to empire. "The Arabic language," he writes,

> has suffered the shock of long waves of military and epistemological conquest by neighboring states whose peoples do not speak Arabic. Yet it did not surrender very long, as its European-language counterparts did, to the influence of occupation, [nor did] it fling itself into the arms of colonialism *[fī aḥḍāni al-isti'māri]*. If no less than 60 percent of the English language is taken from French, the [borrowed] percentage is nil in the case of the Arabic language in Egypt, which the French occupied for almost one hundred years, followed by the British, who occupied it for seventy-four years. Arabic in Egypt remained intact; nothing of what entered English when the French occupied it for only one hundred years ever entered Arabic.[17]

Most striking here is al-'Īsawī's transhistorical comparison of post-1798 Egypt to post-1066 England, of the fate of Arabic after Napoléon Bonaparte (hereafter Napoleon Bonaparte) to that of English after William the Conqueror. Egypt is said to be less colonized than its former colonizer, England. In only one century of Norman occupation, England is said to have lost most of its "originary" tongue and absorbed almost two-thirds of its modern language, whereas Egypt—occupied by the French, according to al-'Īsawī, for the same duration—is imagined to have lost nothing and gained nothing. The French, of course, did not actually occupy Egypt for one hundred years; Napoleon's military presence lasted a mere three (1798–1801). Yet al-'Īsawī suggests that Egypt was dominated for roughly the same number of years by the French and the British, more often the acknowledged—and reviled—colonizer. He appears to base his premise of a "long" French occupation on the fact that France influenced Egyptian culture well after its military presence in Egypt had ended. Yet he exempts one key element of culture—language—from such influence. Intent on proving the immunity of Arabic to colonial influence, al-'Īsawī dismisses the impact of French domination on the Arabic language, thereby leveling the politically unequal field between French and Arabic and thus the distinction between a dominant France and a dominated Egypt. Further, he marshals the supposed "common" denominator of French domination to level any distinction between Arabic and English and thus also between a dominated Egypt and a dominant England. Al-'Īsawī thus upholds two fictions: first, that colonial Egypt can be "compared" to—rendered equal to or greater than—its European colonizers; and second, that Egypt suffered no linguistic or cultural losses to imperialism. Though he fiercely denies the eros of cultural imperialism—to which his insistence that Egypt never flung itself "into the arms of colonialism" ironically alludes—al-'Īsawī ultimately cements its seductive logic, which dissolves the inequality of colonizers and colonized in the possibility of their "likeness."

While most Egyptian literati of the nineteenth and early twentieth century decried the military, economic, and political violences that European imperialism wreaked on their land, many resisted the notion that Europe also was doing cultural violence to their understandings of language and literature and to their broader ways of thinking and knowing. Often they imagined their relationship to European aesthetics and epistemologies in terms of "love," not subjection. This imagination persists: even in al-'Īsawī the denial of love points to the excess of love's presence. Yet one cannot dislodge this humanist "love-logic" of literary-cultural traffic from the frame of empire. Elite Egyptians transported European culture into Arabic at a time when Europe wielded growing power over the Arab-Islamic world; their awareness of that power, however disavowed, moved them first to look to European knowledge for *self*-validation, then to emulate European epistemes, and finally to translate both themselves and Arab-Islamic cultural forms toward ever greater Europeanness.

If attraction, assimilation, even love are dominant refrains in nineteenth- and early-twentieth-century Egypt's literary and cultural response to a colonizing Europe, why is this so? How do the emergence and the persistence of this ideology of "love" challenge the domination/resistance binary of empire and postcolonial studies? And given the centrality of translation in modern Egypt's cultural encounter with the West, how might translation be connected to this ideology of "love"? These are central questions that I engage in this book. *Disarming Words* explores why the colonized tend to "love" their colonizers as often as they hate them and how seduction haunts both empire and decolonization. Early philosophers of decolonization like Frantz Fanon have asked this question under various guises, and several contemporary studies inch us toward a fuller understanding of the ways in which the literatures and cultures of modern European empires claimed the psyches of the peoples they colonized.[18] Still, empire and postcolonial studies often read cultural artifacts as instruments of domination—read the literary canon, philosophically speaking, as "cannon." The field is less attentive to the dynamics of cultural attraction between presumed enemies. Understanding cultural imperialism as willful imposition—not attractive proposition—the reigning discourse conceals the undertow of seduction, which often transmits colonial culture. By reading cultural imperialism through resolutely instrumentalist lenses, I argue, we mystify the *exchange*-value of literature in colonial contexts as *use*-value. In doing so, paradoxically, we fail to understand how colonial powers and their (post)colonial interlocutors have mystified the *use*-value of culture as *exchange*-value, how they have converted instruments of coercion into those of seduction and thereby solicited—and often elicited—the complex "love" of the colonized and their (post)colonial heirs.

Analyzing the cultural afterlives of two modern colonial occupations of Egypt—the French, in 1798, and the British, in 1882—this book reexamines the psychodynamics of translation in (post)colonial Egypt to propose new understandings of cultural imperialism in general and of Orientalism in particular.[19] Current understandings of both, influenced by the work of Edward Said, tend toward the impositionist and the unilateral: impositionist, because Saidian postcolonial studies generally views cultural imperialism as a mere extension of military imperialism; unilateral, because it posits Europe as "doer" (the grammatical and political subject of empire) and the Arab-Islamic Orient as "done-to" (empire's object).[20] I suggest that Orientalism did not simply do violence to a passive, feminized Arab-Islamic world; it also *translated Europe* into Arab-Islamic terms, tempting its Egyptian interlocutors to imagine themselves "masculinized" masters of the Europeans who were mastering them. For Egyptians of the late eighteenth to the early twentieth century, Orientalist scholarship often dissociated European knowledge from European power by reassociating Europeans with Arabic and Islam. As a translational form of cultural imperialism, Orientalism appeared to affirm Egypt's Pharaonic and Arab-Islamic pasts as unbroken, still vital—uncolonized.

The dynamics of identification that I propose here diverge somewhat from those that Abdeslam Maghraoui and Stephen Sheehi describe in early-twentieth-century Egypt and in early- to mid-nineteenth-century Syria, respectively, and more closely approximate those that Thomas Trautmann discerns in colonial Bengal. According to Maghraoui, the drive of liberal intellectuals in 1920s Egypt to attach their country to Europe—linguistically, culturally, even racially—doomed their democratic nationalist vision to failure. These intellectuals, he rightly observes, were "trapped in the language of the Other."[21] Yet Maghraoui concludes that they remade Egypt in a European image because they had learned to see themselves through European Orientalism's denigrating eye.[22] In a more complex reading, Sheehi suggests that the *nahḍa* "subject develops a self-consciousness that exists for itself but is 'determined' through the European Self and apart from the Arab Self," such that "only the supplemental mediation of the European Self can bestow knowledge, and thereby mastery and subjective presence, to the modern Arab." Sheehi implies that a desire for self-determination—in the strong sense of "mastery"—drove the modern Arab to retrieve himself through Europe, whose imperial power in the nineteenth century incarnated sovereignty. Moreover, he limns a connection between that desire and the logic of reciprocity. Citing the Syro-Lebanese intellectual Buṭrus al-Bustānī (1819–83), who willfully recast the modern Arab imperative to imbibe imperial European knowledge as a mere cycle in a long-alternating current of exchange between "kin," Sheehi flirts with the possibility that "equivocality," or the "reciprocity of exchanging knowledge between East and West," may have submitted Arab subjectivity to a Hegelian logic of "universal history."[23] Yet he stops short of theorizing the lure of "reciprocity"—and the perception of *self-value* at its core—for Arab intellectuals of the *nahḍa*, and thus its implications for a new understanding of empire's power to invoke—and evoke—the native will to be master. Though rich, his reading—like Maghraoui's—ultimately foregrounds perceived self-lack and recesses perceived self-value, suggesting that the former motivated the fission of the Arab self and the fusion of its "better" half to the European. While such a conclusion unseats the "resistance" paradigm of postcolonial studies, it does little to complicate the "domination" paradigm that is its corollary.

Toward a richer theory of the entrapments of language, I argue that Orientalist discourse attracted Egyptian intellectuals because it appeared to *validate* the Arab-Islamic even as it denigrated it, putting European and Egyptian on an illusory footing of "equal" exchange. The language of the Other captivated Egyptians only when they imagined that it sounded like the language of the self. Then the terms of Egypt's self-affirmation (and self-abasement) could translate Europe's. This reception of Orientalism echoes the nineteenth-century Bengali response that Trautmann describes. Critiquing the Foucauldian power/knowledge paradigms of Said's *Orientalism,* Trautmann shows how early British Orientalism invented linguistic and ethnological family trees that traced Sanskrit and English to a common Indo-European source and constructed Aryan affinities between Indians and Englishmen.[24] This construction of kinship—first marshaled to naturalize India's colonial bond to England, then denied once Britain held sway over India—he calls "a love story."[25] Unraveling the love-logic at work in an Orientalism usually understood as simple "domination," Trautmann argues that this "love" is less political fact than "political rhetoric," and the relationship it inscribes is decidedly unequal.[26] My reading of Trautmann suggests that Orientalist scholarship might predict the desired differential of British imperialism—the "superiority" of Briton to Indian—by flashing before its Indian interlocutors the seductive mirage of another relationship: the equality, indeed superiority, of Indian to Briton. For the differential equation that underpins the Aryan/Indo-European "love story" also operates in reverse. To nineteenth-century Bengali Hindus, Trautmann notes, "the Aryan idea seems . . . a source of kinship (Aryans = Indians + Europeans) for some writers and of difference, superiority, and greater antiquity (Aryans = Hindus) for others."[27] Thus, I suggest, the power of the Aryan idea lies in its capacity to make the copula of kinship—"equivalence"—between Indian and Briton oscillate. What Trautmann limns is an affective economy that empowers the colonized to declare themselves "equal to" or "greater than" the European—through the prism of an Orientalist thesis itself attractive because it issues from the gaze of the colonizer.

French and British Orientalist projections of affinity with Arabic, Islam, and the ancient Egyptian engender similar fantasies of modern Egyptian sovereignty—at once equality with and superiority to Europe—in a global field that imperial Europe ultimately controls. As I read the political "love story" that translational seduction writes, the modern Egyptian subject finds a way to make the Egyptian or the Arab-Islamic past "compete" with the European future on the fundamentally unequal ground of a colonial present. While I submit that the political rhetoric of affection between colonizers and colonized rarely describes political fact, I contend that the enthusiasm with which at least some nineteenth-century colonial subjects in Egypt (as in Bengal) received such rhetoric suggests that rhetorical *affect* can translate into political *effect*. Studying the friendships that Britons and Indians transacted across geopolitical lines in the nineteenth and early twentieth century—affective bonds that crystallized in transnational anti-imperialist movements—Leela Gandhi offers compelling evidence of the liberationist, anticolonial politics that *philoxenia*—love of the foreigner, the stranger—enables.[28] While anti-imperialist alliances of the kind that Gandhi describes also play out in the literary-political history of colonial Egypt—witness the insurgent affiliations of Muṣṭafā Kāmil and Juliette Adam, Wilfrid Scawen Blunt and Aḥmad 'Urabī, Aḥmad Shawqī and Hall Caine—their exploration lies beyond the scope of this book. My focus is not on the anti-imperialist dimension of *philoxenia*. As important (and unjustly neglected) as that dimension is, I am interested here in exploring the more counter-intuitive and less optimistic possibility that the "love" extended to the foreign—by the European to the Egyptian, then by the Egyptian to the European—might more deeply colonize than liberate.

Reading the literary record of post-1798 Egypt, I argue that Egyptians were moved to "love" and to translate the cultures of their colonizers when those cultures presented themselves to Egyptians *in* "loving" translation. The French and the British were most attractive to Egyptians when they "spoke" the idioms of Arabic, Islam, or Egyptianness—when they translated themselves, or were perceived to have translated themselves, into imitations of their colonial targets. As Egyptian intellectuals came to see their colonizers and themselves as translatable—or exchangeable—terms, they could in turn "love" those colonizers enough to translate French or English idioms and ideas. In so doing, they negotiated a complex and often conflicted surrender to the ideology of European supremacy and to the imperatives of European colonialism. The case of Egypt, I contend, suggests that cultural imperialism might be better understood as a politics that lures the colonized to seek power *through* empire rather than against it, to translate their cultures into an empowered "equivalence" with those of their dominators and thereby repress the inequalities between those dominators and themselves. This politics I call *translational seduction*.

In reinterpreting cultural imperialism as a politics of translational seduction, I conjoin Jean Baudrillard's notion of seduction to Spivak's understanding of translation. In *De la séduction* (1979; *Seduction*), Baudrillard suggests that diversion, or leading astray, is at the etymological root of *seduction:* the word derives from the Latin "*se-ducere:* to take aside, to divert from one's path."[29] For Baudrillard, seduction—although often metaphorized through the sexual—is fundamentally not about sex. Rather, it is a semiotic and intersubjective strategy of displacement, a mastery of diverted (thus diverting) appearances. Hence he pronounces seduction a power that exercises itself through the subtle manipulation of illusion, a "war game" played for sovereignty at the level of the sign.[30] To seduce is to make the grammars of both signs and ontologies dance: to make the polarities of subject and object oscillate such that they blur, and the mastered can fancy himself master.[31] The seducer's very strategy, then, consists in creating the illusion that she is the object of seduction—without ever actually succumbing to object status—and in making the true object of seduction, the seduced, believe himself the seducer.[32] Baudrillard recognizes that the pull of seduction for the seduced lies less in the attraction of seeing oneself the object of desire than it does in the attraction of seeing oneself as the seducing subject, as the sovereign who calls the shots of exchange. "Seduction," he writes, "is sovereign"; whoever commands its capacity to reverse signs—its "flotation of the law that regulates . . . difference" between polarities—can displace, in theory if not always in fact, the power of another and divert it to his or her advantage.[33] Yet Baudrillard never extrapolates the theoretical possibilities of seduction to translation or to colonial politics (two directions in which its semiotic and intersubjective operations point).

By contrast, Spivak's "The Politics of Translation" dubs the ontological and ethical transformations a translator undergoes in translation "one of the seductions" of the act.[34] She notes—suggestively—that translation calls on the translator to abandon authorial autonomy for surrogacy, to "work at someone else's title," to "'surrender to the text'" that she or he translates.[35] Spivak, however, does not connect the seductions of translation to the operations of cultural imperialism. To be fair, she writes in this essay of translating a native Bengali tongue whose intimacy has been lost to her as an Indian-born academic living in (post) colonial diaspora, not of the transfers of power at stake when a (post) colonial subject translates a colonizer's language—or vice versa. When she does address the geopolitics of translation, it is to condemn the "First World" feminist translator who approaches the "Third World" woman's text as a native informant, blind to the text's rhetoricity—the texture of its language and its literary context—and attentive only to the anthropological information that it can deliver about the presumed plight of the non-Western or nonwhite female subject. That is why she valorizes a foreignizing praxis of translation in which the translator surrenders to the (presumably) alien signifiers of the original and channels their manners of meaning. Still, Spivak's suggestion that translation *seduces* the translator into surrendering self-identity to the text that she or he translates, into "miming . . . the responsibility to the trace of the other in the self," hints at the ways in which a colonizer might use translation to usurp the ontological and territorial "title" of the colonized—and the ways in which a native translator might surrender his or her "title" to the colonizer by rendering the latter's idioms into his or her own.[36] A "trace of the other in the self" there might always be, but a colonizer who wields disproportionate power over the colonized can exploit that trace to hegemonic advantage, use it to lure the colonized into confusing self with Other and thus into fusing their "identity" to that of their dominator.

What I share with Baudrillard is a desire to articulate forms of power that color outside the lines of domination and resistance and that understand the "in-between" as something more complex than a hybrid of the two. My treatment of seduction in this book, however, parts ways with Baudrillard's on two counts. First, I do not share his nostalgia for feudal aristocracy. Suspicious of the ideological regimes of power and production installed by the French, the Industrial, and (implicitly) the Bolshevik Revolutions, Baudrillard aligns seduction with the aristocratic values of the eighteenth century. He counterpoises seduction to the "fallen" and "subaltern" post-nineteenth-century values of "sexuality, desire and pleasure," which he imputes to the "inferior classes" of the bourgeoisie and the petite bourgeoisie.[37] Specters of the defining event of Europe's long nineteenth century—the French Revolution of 1789—hover over this disturbing class(ist) analysis, and longing for an ancien régime of desire is indeed one bias along which Baudrillardian seduction is cut. Second, I reject Baudrillard's tendency to divorce seduction from history and thus also from the dynamics of oppression. He describes the "feminine"—the principle of seduction—as "blank," "without history." To my mind, a seduction-theory of cultural imperialism holds explanatory power only if it recognizes that seduction *itself* is a force exercised unequally. While Baudrillard may insist on seduction's infinite reversibility, I maintain that not all historical actors hold the material power to temporarily suspend their identities in otherness—to set power adrift in a play of appearances—yet ultimately to restore themselves, in the realm of the actual, to dominance over others. The seduced will be seduced by the illusion that he or she can be—is—the seducer. But the real seducer is one whose illusions can call for backup. That seducer asserts (and ultimately regains) power by twice arresting exchange: first to create the illusion that sovereignty redounds to the seduced, then to restore the real by making sovereignty rebound to himself or herself. In other words, some political actors are more empowered than others—precisely because of their position in history—to make the *affective* attraction of their antihistorical "self-Othering" hold *effective* force over (indeed, within) others. Baudrillard would have us understand the feminine not as that which opposes the masculine but as that which seduces it, displacing it from within.[38] So too, I argue, must the antihistorical power of seduction be understood within, not outside, history—as that which seduces history rather than that which opposes it.

By articulating Baudrillard's theory to Spivak's so that each finishes the other's incomplete sentence, we begin to see how a politics of translational seduction might divert the language, epistemes, and very being of the dominated to approximate those of the dominator. Indeed, this book engages precisely these three forms of translation: *interlingual,* the rendition of one language in another, whether understood as a transfer of "common" sense or as an evocation of the peculiar sensibility that attaches to one language's manner of meaning in another tongue; *intercultural,* the transaction of epistemic "equivalence" in economies of cultural exchange; and *intersubjective,* the translation of one's self to resemble an Other's, as in Fanon's rephrasing of the Hegelian dialectic. In thus invoking the full polysemy of *translation,* I take care to historicize the term, exploring the unequal exchange of languages, of intellectual and spiritual idioms, and of subjectivities that underwrote both modern French or British efforts to seduce Egypt into empire and Egyptian receptions of that colonial enterprise. Reading the operations of translation within the frame of colonial history, I argue that translation is perhaps the most seductive of imperial powers. Translation, after all, forges from two differences the *appearance* of equivalence: its fundamental syntax is "$x = y$," or "x 'is' y," where the verb of being *is* functions in linguistic terms as a *copula* equating subject to predicate. Yet if in all translation a slash haunts that copula's equal sign with the specter of the not-equal, such that "$x \neq y$," or "x is (not really) y," I argue that it does so all the more profoundly under colonial conditions, where geopolitical inequality compounds linguistic nonequivalence. Thus the translational seduction I locate at the heart of cultural imperialism is consummated in what I call the "copulation" of the colonizer and the colonized. This coupling is a differential equation of the two: a transformation of the disempowered into the delusory "likeness" of the empowered. If seduction knows yet disavows the power differential—the slash—between the terms it brings into "equivalence," its upshot, "copulation," forgets that differential entirely. In this economy of translation, I argue, the colonized lose themselves *in* the colonizer in order to regain their "sovereign" selves.

While 1798 is hardly the definitive "beginning" of modern Egyptian literary history, the Napoleonic invasion of Egypt that year inaugurated just such a translational relation between the modernities of Europe and of the Arab-Islamic world. Napoleon circulated a proclamation, in Arabic and mimicking Qur'ānic style, that assured the predominantly Muslim people of Egypt that the French were "sincere Muslims" like them. Such words—translating not just French into Arabic, but Christian Frenchness into Arab-Islamicity, and preceding the force of arms—disarmed Egyptian intellectuals, whether they believed Napoleon a friend or took pains to dissect his language and prove his enmity. Napoleon's "self-translation" into Arabic seduced colonized Egyptian Muslims into desiring French precisely because it identified with them in the guise of their *pre*colonial selves, still in possession of a "sovereign" language (Arabic) and culture (Islam). It dangled before Egyptian eyes a tantalizing homology between the "subjects" and "objects" of empire, between the *I* who would be conqueror and the *you* who would be conquered. "I am you," Napoleon's Arabic declared. Over a century later, Evelyn Baring, first Earl of Cromer, who effectively ruled Egypt as British consul-general from 1882 to 1907, drew lessons from the French strategy. In *Modern Egypt* (1908), Cromer hints that to win Egypt, England must shed its matronly respectability and become an "attractive damsel" like France, manipulating—like Napoleon—the appearance of intimacy.[39] Only then, he says, will Egyptians spurn French embraces and rush headlong into England's open arms.

For more than a century after Napoleon's occupation ended in 1801, the narrative of Egyptian-European "equivalence" that his colonial proclamation activated would continue to seduce Egyptians into believing that they never had lost their cultural self-determination, that Arab-Islamic and European civilizations could engage one another as equals, free of the Napoleonic "pre-text" of domination. Under that spell generations of Egyptian intellectuals—first as warily intrigued receivers of French and British "self-translations" into Arab-Islamicity, then as often admiring translators of European literature into Arabic—would attach themselves psychologically to European empire. The earliest exemplar of this dynamic is Ḥasan al-ʻAṭṭār's rhymed-prose narrative "Maqāmat al-Faransīs" (*Maqāma* of the French, c. 1799), a theorization-in-fiction of the translational dynamics of Napoleon's proclamation. Here an Egyptian narrator, initially terrified of the French, becomes powerfully drawn to them when a French scholar addresses him in Arabic—specifically, with an extract from *al-Burda* (The Mantle), a thirteenth-century Egyptian panegyric to the Prophet Muḥammad. Intoxicated by this invocation of his past, the narrator begins to fancy *himself* the seducer; he hallucinates the French as the feminine love objects of his erotic gaze and refers to them (largely) in the grammatical feminine, forgetting the fact that *he* is the object of their (masculine) colonial power. By tale's end we find him working with Napoleon's Orientalists on a bilingual French-Arabic dictionary and composing an Arabic panegyric to the French scholar himself, containing a "word or two of their language [French]."[40]

Like al-ʻAṭṭār's fictional narrator, many intellectuals of the Egyptian *nahḍa* responded to French and British identifications with Arabic, Islam, or Egyptianness with the mimetic desire to translate themselves, in turn, into Frenchness and Englishness. This they did largely within the skin of Arabic, which made it all too easy for them to disavow their mental colonization. First, disarmed by the illusion that Arabic might yet be "equivalent"—even superior—to French and English despite the European languages' advantage under empire, they imagined it possible to learn their colonizers' tongues and to translate European literatures into Arabic without seeing that doing so might endanger their own cultures. Second, by adapting European literature and thought as models for an Arab-Islamic "renaissance," they believed that they could fill the imagined literary and philosophical "lacks" that had left their world lagging behind the European and had enabled Europe to dominate them. *Disarming Words* engages both of these phenomena. Rather than offer a full history of literary translation in nineteenth- and early-twentieth-century Egypt, however, or a direct account of the rise of the novel and other "modern" Arabic literary forms during that period, this book traces the emergence of a peculiarly (post)colonial psychology of translation in Egypt through a series of pivotal literary translations, translation theories, and translational fictions. I show how intellectuals often attached Egypt to Europe *through* translation even as they imagined themselves empowering Egypt to "compete" with Europe *by* translation. Ultimately, I argue, the translated word—luring the self to forget itself (if not its language) in the memory of another—annexes a colonized people far more effectively than arms.

In this translational dynamic, resistance also figures. Not all Egyptian intellectuals of the period produced translations, and not all embraced the Westernization project so avidly. While I focus on dominant discourses of translation and literary production in the Egyptian *nahḍa*, those discourses did not reign absolute. One can cite many contrapuntal figures in the Egyptian context, from the political satirist 'Abd Allāh al-Nadīm in the 1850s to the neoclassicist poets Ḥāfiẓ Ibrāhīm and Aḥmad Shawqī and the journalist-novelist Muḥammad al-Muwayliḥī at the turn of the nineteenth to the twentieth century. Still, I would note that specters of translation and comparison haunt both the Arabic literary praxes of these writers and their representations of the Arab encounter with European modernity. In one biting satire published on the eve of the British occupation (1881), "Lā Anta Anta wa Lā al-Mathīl Mathīl" (You Are Not Yourself, nor Is the Copy a Copy), al-Nadīm attacks the Frenchification of the Egyptian because it threatens to reproduce him as a bad "copy"—bad translation—of the French original he mimics.[41] Ibrāhīm, for his part, laments the cultural dispossession of Arabic in "al-Lugha al-'Arabiyya Tan'ī Ḥaẓẓahā bayna Ahlihā" (The Arabic Language Laments Its Fortunes among Its People), published in 1903.[42] Like much of Ibrāhīm's verse, this poem retains the Arabic *qaṣīda* (ode) form, yet takes pains to prove Arabic poetry a fitting vessel for "modernity." Similarly, while Shawqī's powerful *qaṣīda* "Wadā' Lūrd Krūmir" (1907; "A Farewell to Lord Cromer") attacks British colonialism in Egypt, it extols the civilizing mission of Egypt's post-Napoleonic Ottoman rulers—Mehmed Ali (Muḥammad 'Alī) Pasha and Khedive Ismā'īl, both francophile—and thus upholds the ideology of colonial modernity.[43] These works too, then, reflect the strain of the dominant. Finally, although al-Muwayliḥī's *Ḥadīth 'Īsā ibn Hishām, aw Fatra min al-Zaman* (The Tale of 'Īsā ibn Hishām; or, A Period of Time, 1898–1902, 1907, 1927; *A Period of Time*) adapts the medieval Arabic form of the *maqāma*, its narrative is translational: it represents a Cairo whose Ottoman form has been overwritten—in just fifty years—by a new social order at once fast decolonizing (turning "Egyptian") and fast recolonizing (becoming "European").[44]

DOMINATION, RESISTANCE, AND THE COLONIAL "IN-BETWEEN"

By listening for the attraction that colonial translation might represent for the (post)colonial subject, I hold the door between domination and resistance ajar not simply for the structural collusion of the two—as Bhabha does—but also for the interposition of translational seduction *between* the two and thus for the reinterpretation of cultural imperialism I advance in this book.[45] On the threshold between domination and resistance, a power that diverts both steals in. The colonizing text that wields this power mobilizes affect—the attachment of the colonized to themselves, which in politicohistorical terms is also an attachment to their lost sovereignty—to strategically re-present the colonizer as the most flattering "likeness" of the colonized. Such a translational mobilization of affect lures the colonized into *loving the colonizer as they would themselves* and thus into embracing the very power that all too often they are imagined merely to "resist."

This book, then, stands in contrapuntal relation to Edward Said's understanding of the impact of European cultural imperialism on the modern Arab-Islamic world. Said's theory of cultural imperialism generally hews to a domination/resistance binary. In this schema, culture is a discursive armament that colonizers almost always impose and the colonized almost always oppose, though their attack on the imposed culture may turn its very terms. Following Said, I suggest that the politics of translation in post-1798 Egypt cannot be extracted from the colonial power that frames them. I argue, however, that we cannot understand the effects of cultural imperialism in terms of imposition alone. Only by crossing the "come-hither" with the "or-else" of both French and British imperialisms and their Egyptian receptions, I suggest, can we expose the impact of these imperialisms on Egyptian ideologies of translation and literary transformation and explain why Egyptians have translated European literatures so Janus-facedly—why one *I* has gazed longingly North and West even as the other has looked defiantly East and South. Here I agree with John Tomlinson, who wonders why cultural imperialism rests "on the idea that alien cultural products and practices are *imposed* on a culture," although often their receivers "don't perceive them as an 'imposition.'"[46] Arguing that this idea wrongly presupposes the "autonomy" of cultures, Tomlinson calls us to see cultural imperialism as "*loss* rather than . . . *imposition*": a loss he ascribes to "*the failure of the processes of collective will-formation.*"[47] My reading, however, attempts a more complex theorization of culture "loss." I posit that loss as a function of the very *will* of the colonized to rediscover their "autonomy" through the colonizer's *I:* a will motivated by their apprehension of the colonizer's force.

In *The World, the Text, and the Critic* (1983), Said suggests that culture drives politics less by imposition than by affirmation. As a "quasi-autonomous extension of political reality," he writes, "culture serves authority . . . not because it represses and coerces but because it is affirmative, positive, and persuasive."[48] Elsewhere, however, he correlates culture to coercion, declaring all texts—all artifacts of culture—undemocratic. "Texts," he insists, "are fundamentally facts of power, not of democratic exchange."[49] While they stage as equal the discursive relation of speakers (writers) to hearers (readers), Said argues, that relation is "far from equal in actuality," a fact that texts "dissemble" in "an act of bad faith."[50] Here Said edges close to Émile Benveniste, who (as I show in chapter 6) argues that the speaking *I* claims the moment of discourse as its own and in that instant subordinates the *you* of the hearer to its own authorial and authoritative intention. Said ultimately contends that "far from being a type of conversation between equals, the discursive situation is more usually like the unequal relation between colonizer and colonized, oppressor and oppressed. . . . Words and texts are so much of the world that their effectiveness, in some cases even their use, are matters having to do with ownership, authority, power, and the imposition of force."[51] In this economy, cultural affirmation and persuasion figure only as alibis for imposition—indeed colonial domination. Having defined all culture as, in effect, cultural imperialism and constrained its operations to imposition, Said must imagine resistance as its polar opposite. He wisely rejects Michel Foucault's intimation that the power wielded by authority (imposition) and the power wielded against it (resistance) are morally equivalent. Yet his solution is to pose a relation in which the twain never meet. "Resistance," he writes, "cannot equally be an adversarial alternative to power and a dependent function of it."[52]

I share Said's conviction that resistance is morally nonequivalent to domination and thus never simply power in reverse, but I question his radical separation of the lexicons of resistance and power. To Foucauldian symmetry and Saidian asymmetry, I would oppose *transymmetry* as a more helpful way to understand both the exercise of and the response to cultural imperialism. In transymmetry—the a/symmetry of translation—culture-as-imposition and culture-as-resistance are mutually, but not equally, constitutive; resistance, I would argue, more often derives from imposition, works through and displaces it (as Bhabha suggests), than the other way around. If dominant culture dissembles its impositionist tendencies in order to pretend to affirm its would-be subjects, and if resistance culture in turn wears but tears the logic of imposition in order to make itself persuasive to the dominant, is not cultural power on both sides of the colonial divide seductive?

The binary opposition of domination/resistance also marks Said's *Culture and Imperialism* (1993), both a sequel to and a divergence from his *Orientalism* (1978). *Orientalism* had characterized European knowledge production about the Arab-Islamic world, especially between the eighteenth and twentieth centuries, as "a form of discursive currency by whose presence the Orient henceforth would be *spoken for*."[53] Here the European Orientalist speaks and dominates, and the fictive "Orient" is silenced and acted upon. While Said insists throughout *Orientalism* that we are not to mistake the fictive "Orient" for the real—that European representation of the Arab-Islamic world has little to do with that world itself—it is clear that, thanks to the conjunction of Orientalist scholarship with colonial Realpolitik, this fictive "Orient" shades into the real Orient and to some extent determines it. As Said himself concedes, "Orientalism is fundamentally a political doctrine willed over the Orient because the Orient was weaker than the West."[54] Thus he seems all too aware that the intersection of European knowledge with power has created much of what passes for contemporary Arab-Islamic reality, that the legacies of European Orientalism in fact have produced *him*; "much of the personal investment in this study," he confesses, "derives from my awareness of being an 'Oriental.'"[55] In *Culture and Imperialism,* Said overcorrects critical misperceptions of his arguments in *Orientalism* by opposing resistance to domination. Where *Orientalism* presupposes the power of European scholarship to will its vision of the "Orient" over the real Orient—with nary a reply, it seems, from the latter—*Culture and Imperialism* insists that imperial domination always met its corollary, decolonizing resistance, wherever it sought to assert its political will. "Never was it the case," Said writes in the later work, "that the imperial encounter pitted an active Western intruder against a supine or inert non-Western native; there was *always* some form of active resistance."[56] If modern European imperialism began with a "voyage out" to non-Western lands, the non-Western decolonization movements of the mid-twentieth century represent what Said calls *"the voyage in":* a "conscious effort to enter into the discourse of . . . the West, to mix with it, transform it."[57] Such a definition of resistance implies its hybridity—however strategic—with imperialist discourse. Yet Said goes on to posit decolonizing resistance as always and only a radical "alternative" to the historical logic of domination, retracting his intimation that it might also *couple*—"mix"—with hegemonic discourse. Once again, he insists on the radical asymmetry of resistance to power.

So assiduous a separation between domination and resistance requires an equally studied forgetting of the space between. That forgetting is all the more curious when we observe that Said's *Culture and Imperialism* both introduces and enacts the praxis of contrapuntal reading, with which Said himself proposes to render "the *overlapping* experience of Westerners and Orientals, the *interdependence* of cultural terrains in which colonizer and colonized co-existed and battled each other through projections."[58] While Said closely explores the ways in which culture secured the consent of British, French, and other colonizing societies "for the distant rule of native peoples and territories," he attends less deeply to the operations of hegemony in the cultures of the colonized.[59] Still, he suggests that the colonized too might experience imperialism as something more than coercion, as a structure that seeks (and sometimes gains) their consent and does so to troubling ends. Here he defines imperialism as "an ideological vision implemented and sustained not only by direct domination and physical force but much more effectively . . . by *persuasive means,* the quotidian processes of hegemony," describing these processes as an "interaction among natives, the white man, and the institutions of authority" that passes from "'communication to command' and back again."[60] Indeed, as Said observes, "many of the classes and individuals collaborating with imperialism began by trying to emulate modern European ways."[61] As one instance of such "collaboration" he notes the proliferation of educational missions in the colonial period, missions like those that Mehmed Ali Pasha, Ottoman viceroy of Egypt from 1805 to 1848, sent to Paris and London during the first half of the nineteenth century. "The primary purpose of these early missions to the West," Said observes,

> was to learn the ways of the advanced white man, *translate his works,* pick up his habits. . . .
>
> An entire massive chapter in cultural history across five continents grows out of this kind of collaboration between natives on the one hand and . . . representatives of imperialism on the other. In paying respect to it, acknowledging the shared and combined experiences that produced many of

us, we must at the same time note how at its center it nevertheless preserved the nineteenth-century imperial divide between native and Westerner.[62]

Said, then, reduces the impulse that drives the colonized to translate the words, culture, ways, and being of his or her colonizer to mere "collaboration" and quickly dismisses it as such—though he later notes that that impulse occasionally took an anti-imperialist turn. Yet his reading of collaboration, which insists finally on the "imperial divide" it reinforces, does not explain why the subjects of empire so avidly abet their cultural colonization, nor how those subjects negotiate the terms of their transformation as they study, translate, and (falsely) approximate "the advanced white man." Collaboration (at least insofar as Said deploys the term) serves only the interests of empire, never those of its subjects. Yet clearly "collaboration" must appeal to the self-interest of the colonized—as much their *ontological* as their material self-interest—if they are to join forces with their dominators. The discourse of a dominant culture disarms the dominated into subjection whenever it can seduce them into imagining their dominators at once equal to and greater than themselves, excite them to love their dominators as not just their selves, but their "best" selves—possessed of the new/old knowledge and power to reinstate themselves as the sovereigns they once were.

Given that both culture and imperialism in Said realize their colonial effects through the play of domination and suasion and that resistance too achieves its libratory effects by interleaving contestatory historical visions with dominant ones, why then does he ultimately refuse the ground that is most "hybrid"—that connects the voyage out to the voyage in—in thinking the relationships of culture to imperialism and decolonization? While he declares that "an entire massive chapter in cultural history across five continents grows out of . . . collaboration" between "natives" and "representatives of imperialism," he writes only its preface in *Culture and Imperialism.* He prefers to lay the body of that chapter to rest in a premature grave—notice that he calls us to "[pay] respect to it"—and return his gaze to the twin poles of imposition and resistance. I would suggest that Said does not write this "massive chapter" because it touches the self too intimately: it inscribes, after all, the "shared and combined experiences that produced many of us," including the "Oriental" Said. To write this chapter would be to explain why he, though aware of the imperial ugliness in which so many Western cultural artifacts are implicated, nonetheless must confess the attraction of—his attraction to?—these images of imperial authority, powerfully seductive despite their powerful testimony to the objectification, exploitation, and murder of fellow humans. The unwritten chapter would tell us why, having inventoried many such objects, Said concludes, "The list is long and its treasures massive."[63] The missing "massive chapter" would illuminate, in other words, the *massive value* that the (post)colonial subject attaches to the colonizer's culture. To grant politically ugly objects aesthetic brilliance, Said repeatedly invokes their complexity. It is this complexity he must disavow to quiet the ghost of aesthetic—indeed humanist—valuation that haunts his otherwise trenchant political critique of imperialism.

Although Timothy Mitchell writes in Said's intellectual footsteps, he travels further. He shows us how—through the processes of emulation and translation to which Said gestures—European ideas of "discipline" and "order" infiltrated Egyptian social thought and organization in the nineteenth century. Not content to assume the intractable resistance of the native signifier (as al-ʿĪsawī is, or as Said might be), he takes the Arabic word as a pressure point at which we might feel its surrenders to colonial reoccupation, if only we press hard enough. Alongside the evolution of other keywords, Mitchell traces that of the Arabic term *tarbiya*, which originally referred to "nurture" or "rearing" but during the nineteenth century came to signify "education" in the colonial mold, as intellectual reformers like Rifāʿa Rāfiʿ al-Ṭahṭāwī and ʿAlī Mubārak introduced into Egypt the Benthamite regimes of discipline they experienced as students in Paris between the 1820s and the 1840s. Mitchell ascribes such lexical transformations—translations in which old words reattach to new objects—to a broader shift in Arab-Islamic understandings of the relationship between signifiers and signifieds: a shift that transpired in the crucible of colonial power. Noting that Arab-Islamic thought traditionally had refused the Cartesian mind-body dualism implied in the modern European separation of words and things, he suggests that the rising currency of European epistemes in nineteenth-century Egypt encouraged Egyptians to see both word and world as "divided absolutely into two."[64]

Mitchell's reading of the reconception of signification itself in nineteenth-century Egypt is compelling, and I consider its implications in chapter 5. What interests me here is how deeply his argument about colonial power comes to rest on the very logic of absolute twoness that underpins Said's understanding of Orientalism. According to Mitchell, what distinguishes the "modern political order" of colonialism "is the effect of seeming to exclude the other absolutely from the self."[65] "What Orientalism offered," he maintains,

> was not just a technical knowledge of Oriental languages, religious beliefs and methods of government, but a series of absolute differences according to which the Oriental could be understood as the negative of the European. These differences were not the differences within a self, which would be understood as an always-divided identity; they were the differences between a self and its opposite, the opposite that makes possible such an imaginary, undivided self.[66]

In this reading, the power of Orientalism to consolidate the putative "superiority" of the European and to produce the non-Western subject as a colonizable "inferior" resides in the architecture of radical difference it erects between West and East. Here Orientalism replaces an integral conception of self, in which the self contains its own difference, with a self/Other dualism. No doubt Orientalism, from the standpoint of the European, enforced such a fiction of absolute separateness between the excluded Oriental and a European self purified of all disquieting traces of the Oriental within. I would suggest, however, that this interpretation of Orientalist knowledge production did not necessarily extend to the non-Westerner who received it. To the Egyptian, Orientalist writings on Arabic literature and on Islam often suggested that the European was interested in him and perhaps even needed him, for his world continued to offer some insight that the European—despite his world dominance—did not yet possess. As I note in chapter 3, seeing a French Orientalist like Silvestre de Sacy produce books in Arabic only encouraged an Egyptian intellectual like al-Ṭahṭāwī to imagine the world as a series of likenesses in which the Oriental could be understood as the "equivalent" of the European—not, or not immediately, as Mitchell's series of "absolute differences." So powerful was this effect of similitude, in fact, that the Egyptian *willfully* overlooked the differences that Orientalist scholarship sought to install between himself and the European, forgot the lacks (backwardness, irrationality, disorder) that colonial discourse imputed to him. In that overlooking, the Egyptian reproduced himself as "an imaginary, undivided self": not just a self undivided from its precolonial sovereign self but also—in the same breath—a self undivided from colonizing Europe. If the colonizing European, as Mitchell maintains, consolidates "its uncorrupted and undivided identity" by excluding the Oriental from himself and forgetting "the dependence of [the self's] identity upon what it excludes," the colonized Egyptian—I argue—often redeems the perceived cultural integrity lost to the interruption of European colonialism by *counting the European as himself* and thus eventually by including himself in the

European.[67] Forgotten are those aspects of the self that cannot include the foreign, cannot be synchronized with it. For ever threatening Egyptian identification with the European is the gnawing intimation of lack that the Egyptian has banished to a space beyond "likeness": beyond the translational union of West and non-West effected by Orientalist cultural production, which a Saidian understanding of Orientalism as domination cannot quite explain. The European typically shunts lack onto an "Oriental" outside; the elite Egyptian intellectual positions both himself and the European on the inside and casts the lack attached to him onto a "bad" Oriental alter ego who no longer can count in the mainstream nation's self-fashioning.[68]

TOWARD THE EROTIC *AND*

Spivak's call on the self to surrender itself in translation enjoins humility on the dominant but holds peril for the dominated. For where does the colonized translator fly after she or he bids the self good-bye? Into the master-Other. If, for the colonized, the eros of translation fabricates a dangerously seductive "likeness" in the face of difference—the deep difference power makes—then the politics of (post)colonial translation beg retheorization, as much for the future of comparative literary studies and translation theory as for the future of postcolonial studies. Rey Chow, for one, has argued that the crisis of comparative literature today lies in the field's unexamined assumption of "parity" between languages.[69] Chow dismisses debates about translation as "unhelpful" to her critique, as these generally traffic in "an unhistoricized notion of language and language users."[70] Yet translation is the whispering double of comparison in her work. The chief target of Chow's critique, after all, is the logic of supplementation that underpins the conjunction *and* in the comparative paradigm "Europe and Its Others"—what I would call the traditional province of a postcolonial studies centered on domination and resistance. This inclusive *and* can add an infinity of "other" (read: non-European) cultures to the space of comparison without engaging the ways in which those "other" cultures have negotiated their relations with the European and thus without dislodging European supremacy; as Chow asserts, the paradigm "stabilizes Europe as the grid of intelligibility to which may be added more and more others."[71]

I would argue that this logic of supplementation also describes the imperial universalism that continues to haunt translation theory, even at its most sensitive to the incommensurability of languages. For the logic evokes the relationship between languages-in-translation that Benjamin adumbrates in "The Task of the Translator": the notion that languages supplement one another in their modes of intention, such that in their supplementarity they together approximate "pure language."[72] Tejaswini Niranjana, Samuel Weber, and Naomi Seidman variously have tried to rescue Benjamin from charges of theological utopianism or high humanist universalism by stressing that his "pure language" is induced—or add-uced—from multiplicity rather than deduced from origin.[73] Still, the Babel narrative—intelligible primarily to Western (or at least Judeo-Christian) readers familiar with the Hebrew Bible, as well as to readers "Judeo-Christianized" through a process of Westernizing acculturation—remains the subtext of Benjamin's zone of supplementarity, his fissured vessel of "pure language."[74] Although, in Benjamin's conception, languages differ in the ways they mean, it is not always clear that that difference includes the differential positions of languages themselves within global geopolitics or global capital. As a Marxian historical materialist, Benjamin could not have been indifferent to these forces. Yet in his schema of linguistic supplementarity the specter of political inequality between languages remains just that—a specter, not a material presence.

Against the neoimperial logic of supplementarity that subtends the paradigm "Europe and Its Others," Chow proposes that of "Post-European Culture and the West." This new paradigm, she argues, recenters global relations in worlds beyond Europe while recognizing that "even in the seemingly narcissistic . . . preoccupation with itself," the (post)colonial culture typically "contains, in its many forms of self-writing, imprints of a fraught . . . relation of comparison and judgment in which Europe haunts it as the referent of supremacy."[75] In this geography of colonized selves realizing themselves *through* imperial Europe, I include the modern Arab world in general and modern Egypt in particular. Here too "the conjunction *and*" does not inscribe what Chow calls "complacent" supplementarity, but registers a historically troubled *affective* relation between the "post-European" subject and a West that has intruded onto its history, violated its relationship to its own past, destroyed its capacity for self-determination.[76] The *and* of "Post-European Culture and the West," argues Chow, is a "neurotic *and*": "a cluster of lingering ideological and emotional effects."[77] She contends that the West invades the "Rest" not on the axis of space alone—governed by a homogenizing *and*—but most acutely on the axis of time, where a differentiating *and* traps the post-European culture in a hierarchical relation "between this 'always already' present that is Europe, on the one hand, and the histories and traditions it must now live as its pasts, on the other—pasts that nonetheless continue to erupt as so many suppressed indices of time with forgotten and/or unfinished potentialities."[78] As I read Chow, time—more recursive than space—is less assuredly decolonizable.

In attributing the neurosis of (post)colonial temporality to "lived historic violation," however, Chow associates the "neurotic *and*" with rape. Her reading echoes Said's final diagnosis of the psychology of Orientalism from a Western perspective. In the "British and French experiences of and with the Near Orient, Islam, and the Arabs," he initially discerns an "*intimate, perhaps even the most intimate, . . . relationship* between Occident and Orient."[79] Yet his last word goes to the battle posture of confrontation: "What seems to have influenced Orientalism most was *a fairly constant sense of confrontation* felt by Westerners dealing with the East."[80] What if we were to refuse Said's choice and take intimacy more seriously as a colonial force, enmeshed—through its semiotic avatar, translation, which Spivak describes as "the most intimate act of reading"—in the West's confrontation with the Arab-Islamic East? What if Chow's neurotic *and* is also an erotic *and*, perhaps even an erotic *is* that moves conjunction toward a conjugation of the *Is* of colonized and colonizer?

Violation is incontestably the material beginning—and the material end—of colonial encounter. It does not always tell us, however, how the experience of colonialism translates native time. This book maintains that cultural imperialism often does the greatest violence to native time not by raping the native's histories, traditions, or pasts but by *flattering* these. I suggest that the "neurotic *and*" produces such anxiety for the post-European subject because love has been part of its conjunction. In Arabic linguistics, after all, the conjunction *and (wa)* is termed *ḥarf 'aṭf*—literally, "a particle of bonding." And the implied bond is affective: *'aṭf* denotes emotion, especially sympathy. *Disarming Words* proposes, then, that we shift our gaze from a colonial politics of mere rupture—violation or rape—to a politics that welds rupture to rapture: a colonial politics of seduction, which also institutes rupture but does so by making its object believe that rupture is coterminous with the past, that subject and object are one and the same. Thus, as I argue in chapter 2, falling into "love" is not just the outcome of seduction, but the contestation of its effects: a struggle to wrest the affective bond of the erotic *and* away from bondage, to translate the colonized love object "flattered" by the colonizer into the *subject who loves,* to bend seduction's alluring proposition of a continuity of colonized object and colonizing subject (the "equal to") toward a reassertion of that object's superiority to the subject (the "greater than").

In placing post-1798 Egypt at the center of my analyses and reading France and Britain around this center, I abandon the comparative paradigm Chow calls "Europe and Its Others" in favor of what she dubs "Post-European Culture and the West." To the neurotic *and* of violation and confrontation, however, I couple the erotic *and* of translational seduction—the oscillating copula of the verb *to be*—and explore its power to bind the colonized to the colonizer, to make the latter haunt the former as what Chow calls "the referent of supremacy." Comparative literary studies of translation, empire, and postcoloniality can gain much from exploring sites positioned, like Egypt, in the colonial "in-between," for such sites compel critical attention to the interplay of the effective and the affective, of force and seduction, in empire and decolonization. Throughout its periods of French and British domination, Egypt was also, officially or loosely, linked to the Ottoman Empire: thus it was doubly colonized from 1798 to 1801, during the French occupation, and again from 1882, the beginning of British occupation, until 1914, when it became a British protectorate.[81] Between 1922 and 1952, Egypt was nominally "independent," yet ruled by descendants of Mehmed Ali who remained subject to British dictates. Moreover, as al-ʿĪsawī, Mitchell, Khaled Fahmy, and others have suggested, Egypt remained in "semicolonial" bondage to Europe throughout much of its Ottoman nineteenth century, even between periods of direct European occupation. Certainly France continued to influence Ottoman-Egyptian institutions long after the Napoleonic occupation—from the reign of Mehmed Ali Pasha (1805–48) through that of Khedive Ismāʿīl (1863–79), with a brief anti-Westernization interlude (more anti-French than anti-British) during the reign of Khedive ʿAbbās I (1848–54). Further, during the reign of Khedive Ismāʿīl, European creditors siphoned nearly three quarters of Egypt's treasury to support both European development schemes (among these, the Suez Canal) and Ismāʿīl's strongly Westernizing cultural tastes (institutions like the Cairo Opera House and efforts to transform Cairo into Paris on the Nile). Bankrupted, Egypt was seized as collateral for its debts; in 1876, France and Britain assumed joint economic control over the Ottoman province, citing the need to bring its wayward finances in line. This structure of governance—termed the Dual Control—was paternalistic, indeed colonial; it both resurrected the French invasion of 1798 and predicted the British invasion of 1882.

Still more unusual is the fact that Ottoman Egypt became a regional imperial power even as it battled the specter of European domination: between 1811 and the 1840s, Mehmed Ali's armies invaded the Arabian peninsula (1811–18), the Morea (1824–27), Syria (1831–40), and the Sudan (1820 onward).[82] Most of these territories were lost quickly to foreign intervention, but the Sudan remained under direct Egyptian control from 1821 to 1884, then under joint Egyptian-British dominion until 1952. As Eve Troutt Powell has argued in her study of Anglo-Egyptian imperialism in the Sudan, from the 1820s through the early 1950s, Egypt was a "colonized colonizer," intent on subjecting others to imperial power even as it remained subject to various forms of imperial domination itself.[83] I would suggest that Egypt's domination of the Sudan is the tragic geopolitical outcome of the translational seduction I describe in this book: a territorial enactment of the ontological fantasy of liberating the self from the colonizer by usurping and reoccupying the colonizer's *I*.

If Egypt's status as an imperial power was peculiar, so too was its postcoloniality. Three moments of equivocal "postcoloniality" would precede Egypt's final independence: one in the early nineteenth century, with the end of French occupation, and two more in the early twentieth, with the end of Khedival rule (1914) and the demise of the British protectorate (1922). Even Egypt's fourth and final postcoloniality—which arrived in the mid-twentieth century with the ultimate end of both Turco-Egyptian monarchy and British dominion—is equivocal, not least because legacies of empire continue to haunt Egyptian self-understanding.

This book, then, is a reply to overheard questions: the two mirror questions that Kīlīṭū puts in al-Manfalūṭī's mouth ("Aren't I an Azharite?" and "How do I become European?"), which so oddly predicate the self-assurance of the Egyptian Muslim *I* on its translation into the European's "likeness," and the self-incriminating question that lingers—like an embarrassed half-smile—at the corners of Said's discourse: Might cultural imperialism achieve its deepest effects by appealing to its targets' deepest affects, rule more by seduction than by fiat, depend more heavily on captivating its subjects than on capturing them? To that end, chapter 1 studies Napoleon's first proclamation to the Egyptian people of 2 July 1798 as a historical and rhetorical "pre-text" that would figure the translational terms on which Egyptians would relate to the imperial West for the next 150 years. Drawing on Vicente Rafael's understanding of translation as an attractive technology of "telecommunication," I counterpoise my reading of translational seduction, as it plays out in Napoleon's proclamation, to Althusserian interpellation (invoked by Niranjana in her theory of autocolonization) and its presumed opposite (invoked by Natalie Melas in her theory of dissimilation). Chapter 2 reads Ḥasan al-'Aṭṭār's "Maqāmat al-Faransīs" (1799) as a literary translation of Napoleon's pre-text. Engaging the theories of Fanon, Jūrj Ṭarābīshī, Bhabha, Baudrillard, G. W. F. Hegel, and Slavoj Žižek, I argue that al-'Aṭṭār's fiction writes an antihistory of the French occupation: a narrative that abandons the dominant force plot of colonial historiography to probe its subterranean love plot.

In chapter 3, I turn to the impact of Egypt's experience of French rule on its first "post"-colonial cultural moment. I focus on the earliest translations and translation theories of Rifā'a Rāfi' al-Ṭahṭāwī, who studied in Paris from 1826 to 1831 and became a leading intellectual "reformer" of the Egyptian nineteenth century, spearheading the drive to translate French texts into Arabic. Reading his *Takhlīṣ al-Ibrīz fī Talkhīṣ Bārīz* (1834)—the first modern Arabic account of European life—with his translation (1827) of Joseph Agoub's poem *La Lyre brisée* (1825), I show how his engagements with Orientalists like Agoub and de Sacy led him to theorize the inherent "exchangeability" of Arabic with French, thereby debunking the presumed incomparability of Arabic and subordinating Arab-Islamic epistemes to a Eurocentric literary-historical genealogy. I compare al-Ṭahṭāwī's theory of translation to that of Walter Benjamin and interrogate the Eurocentrism that haunts current understandings of world literature and the origins of literary comparison, engaging the work of Pascale Casanova, David Damrosch, and Kīlīṭū.

Chapter 4 traces the Egyptian turn to English after the British occupation of 1882. I contend that 'Alī Mubārak's *'Alam al-Dīn* (1882), arguably the first Egyptian novel, shifts Egyptian "love" for Europe from France to England on the grounds of British Orientalist Islamophilia, to which Mubārak contrasts (unfavorably) the desacralizing tendencies of secular French Orientalism. This valorization of English thought as a new and more "proper" love object for Egypt prefigures Muḥammad al-Sibā'ī's 1911 translation of Thomas Carlyle's *On Heroes, Hero-Worship, and the Heroic in History* (1841). I argue that Carlyle's praise for the Prophet Muḥammad in *On Heroes* moved al-Sibā'ī to ignore Carlyle's ultimate subordination of the Prophet to Shakespeare and to insist—against the evidence of Carlyle's full text—on the radical translatability of the native Islamic "religious" and the British colonial "secular." Rethinking the articulation of religion to secularism in the work of Talal Asad, Muhsin Al-Musawi, and Gauri Viswanathan, I show how Islam in al-Sibā'ī's translation becomes a conduit for the secular, fulfilling Cromer's colonial wish that "de-moslemised Moslems" undergo a literal reformation by de-Christianized Christianity.[84]

Focusing on the period just after the anticolonial revolution of 1919, chapter 5 argues that the historical dependence of empire in Egypt on translation led nationalist intellectuals of the 1920s and the early 1930s like Ibrāhīm 'Abd al-Qādir al-Māzinī, Muḥammad Ḥusayn Haykal, Aḥmad Ḥasan al-Zayyāt, and Salāma Mūsā to define Egyptian claims to nationhood, national culture, and national literature in equally translational terms: to wonder whether, how, and to what extent Egypt could or should "translate" into Europe if it wished to be a nation. If modern Egypt's equality with Britain hinges on a homology between the words and bones of ancient Egyptians and Britons, as Mūsā argues, or its nationhood on the translation of its "Babel" of ideological idioms into a single hegemonic language in tune with European colonial modernity, as Haykal suggests, did becoming nationally Egyptian mean remaining colonially "European"? Reading post-1919 Egyptian writings through and against the work of Mikhail Bakhtin, Derrida, Partha Chatterjee, Liu, Mitchell, Rafael, Naoki Sakai, and Venuti on national ideology, translation, and sovereignty, I contend that the drive to institute Egyptian nationality surrendered Egypt to imperial translationality, pushing Egypt to eradicate all local incommensurability with a European "universal."

Engaging the thought of Benveniste and Derrida on language, sovereignty, and violence, chapter 6 examines two novels that represent Egypt's intimacies with England during the late imperial, almost postcolonial 1940s. In Najīb Maḥfūẓ's *Zuqāq al-Midaqq* (1947; *Midaq Alley*) and Lawrence Durrell's *Mountolive* (1958), Egyptian women—seduced and translated—both incarnate the triumph of British empire and project its imminent demise. It is as consummations of the seductive enterprise of colonial translation, as bodies prostituting or "adulterating" themselves into full "copulation" to English and Englishness, that the late-empire "Egypts" these women embody begin to exceed and escape colonial control. While I focus on Maḥfūẓ's *Zuqāq*, I argue that both novels stage decolonization as a question of re-recognition: how can colonized Egypt separate itself from its colonizer when it has become its colonizer—seduced and translated beyond recognition? Only by betraying itself can Egypt become "itself" again in the (post)colonial.

Against the backdrop of recent attempts by Western thinkers such as Derrida and Jessica Benjamin to theorize the relationships of love to friendship, domination, and enmity, my conclusion examines a 1929 exchange between the Egyptian literati Ṭāhā Ḥusayn and 'Abbās Maḥmūd al-'Aqqād that centers on two interrelated questions. First, between conquerors and the conquered, who translates whom more, and why? Second, is cross-cultural translation motivated by love or by war? I argue that these writers' interrogation of the psychopolitical motivations of translation within a decade of the 1919 revolution reflects a nascent awareness of the uneasy nexus of translation, empire, and the emerging nation in Egypt. Their early (post)colonial meditations on translation remain relevant to our present. Only by reoriginating literary-cultural comparison in a hermeneutics of intimate enmity, as al-'Aqqād suggests, can we transact new and perhaps genuinely postcolonial forms of cross-cultural "love."

Sounding postcolonial theory's silences on the affective power of colonialism, then, I have tried in this book to uncover what makes colonial "enemies" and their postcolonial descendants intimate. I have tried to ask not what makes them "hate" each other so but what makes them "love" each other so. Thus I address the historical amnesia that confounds relations between the West and the Arab-Islamic world in the post–9/11 moment. Within one month of 11 September 2001, the Italian novelist Umberto Eco argued the need to counter the assaults of Islamic "fundamentalism" on the West by bringing Arab and Muslim students to the West to "study [its] customs and practices."[85] The *Arab Human Development Report 2003*, an "auto-critique" by Arab analysts for the United Nations Development Programme, ascribed the "failure" of the Arab world to modernize and democratize to its presumed "failure" to adequately translate Western thought. We occupy a world, then, in which Westerners and Easterners who deny thick histories of intercultural traffic can pretend that modern Arab and Muslim travels to and translations of the West have not in fact informed and transformed Arab-Islamic consciousness for over 150 years. Never has it been so important to remind both the Western and the Arab-Islamic worlds that they are no strangers to one another, that what so-called Islamic fundamentalists strive to undo is the thoroughgoing Westernness of most Arab-Islamic societies today: a Westernness that traces its roots as much to the translational intimacies that modern European colonialism engendered in the Arab world as it does to the violences that such colonialism has sometimes created, sometimes only exacerbated, but in any case always left seething in its wake.

CHAPTER ONE

The Irresistible Lure of Recognition

When Napoleon Bonaparte invaded Egypt on 2 July 1798, he came bearing not a cross but a crescent. I speak metonymically, of course, but not far from the mark. For in his first proclamation to the people of Egypt, written in French and translated into Arabic just before the invasion, Napoleon does not announce the Christianization—or even the Europeanization—of Egyptian subjects as his aim but instead assures Egyptians that he is a Muslim like them, as are his armies of soldiers and scholars.[1] By a brilliant stroke of (mis)translation from Napoleon's French, which read, "Nous sommes amis des vrais musulmans" ("We are friends of the true Muslims"), the chief translator of the Egyptian expedition, Jean-Michel Venture de Paradis, interpreted the general's words to their fullest strategic intent.[2] Possibly he did so in consultation with Napoleon, while his French text was still in transit to Arabic.[3] Overtures of friendship, he sensed from long diplomatic experience in Egypt and elsewhere in the Arab-Islamic East, although an alluring departure from the expected language of domination, would not be alluring enough. Better to declare the conqueror a coreligionist of the conquered. The result follows less Napoleon's meaning than his "manner of meaning," which elsewhere in the original is *identificatory*.[4] "The French also are sincere Muslims" ("inna al-faransāwiyyata hum ayḍan muslimīna khāliṣīna *[sic]*"), the Arabic version ultimately intones to its Egyptian audience.[5] Thus Napoleon arrives under the banner of equivalence, not difference.

Indeed, Napoleon leaves Toulon for Alexandria on a ship named not *La France*—or *Ville de Toulon,* on the pattern of *Ville de Marseille,* the frigate from which Amable Thiébault Matterer would both launch and record the French invasion of Algiers, thirty-two years later—but *L'Orient,* as if the West were not coming to the East but the East were returning to itself (though "christened" anew in French, translated into Frenchness even before its colonization). Written and translated on that very ship, Napoleon's first proclamation to the people of Egypt is a fragment of the vessel that bears it across the geographic, historical, and ideological gulf between Europe and Africa: a vessel that is itself a "broken" original, itself a translation that masks difference *(la France)* with equivalence *(l'Orient).* Yet the proclamation outdoes even the masquerade of *L'Orient:* once in Egypt, it circulates entirely in Arabic, screening the French original from view, its only trace of French the mysterious seal of the République Française emblazoned above the Arabic text (see figure 1). Napoleon's vessel cracking a Muslim smile, the translated proclamation speaks Arabic and sidles up to the Egyptian.

What happens when a colonial translation lacks an "original"? What happens when such a translation mimics its "target"—linguistic and military—and not its "source"? Reading Napoleon's strategy of colonial proclamation, we can hazard an answer: by translating language and self to mimic those whom they wished to colonize, the French could better assert their superiority and dominion; that is, by pretending equivalence, they could impose difference. The proclamation's formula could be stated thus: "I am so like you that you should be like me." The *you* and the *I,* however, are *not* equivalent; that is precisely why the "should" of resemblance—the compulsion of the colonized subject to equate itself with the colonizer, to redefine its subjectivity, so to speak, in the colonizer's *I*—rears its head. Translating French power into Arabic and the Arab-Islamic and thereby appearing to recognize power *in* Arabic and the Arab-Islamic, Napoleon's proclamation ruptures the dual *before* the duel. In so doing, it brandishes a seductive weapon indeed.

In this document—a translational pre-text that would condition Egyptian response to European imperialism, first French and later British, for the next 150 years—Napoleon evinces an understanding of the dialectics of selfhood and Otherness less in tune with Hegel than with the anti-Hegelian Frantz Fanon. In his 1807 *Phänomenologie des Geistes (Phenomenology of Spirit),* Hegel stages the relationship of two self-consciousnesses as a dialectic of mutual recognition in which the

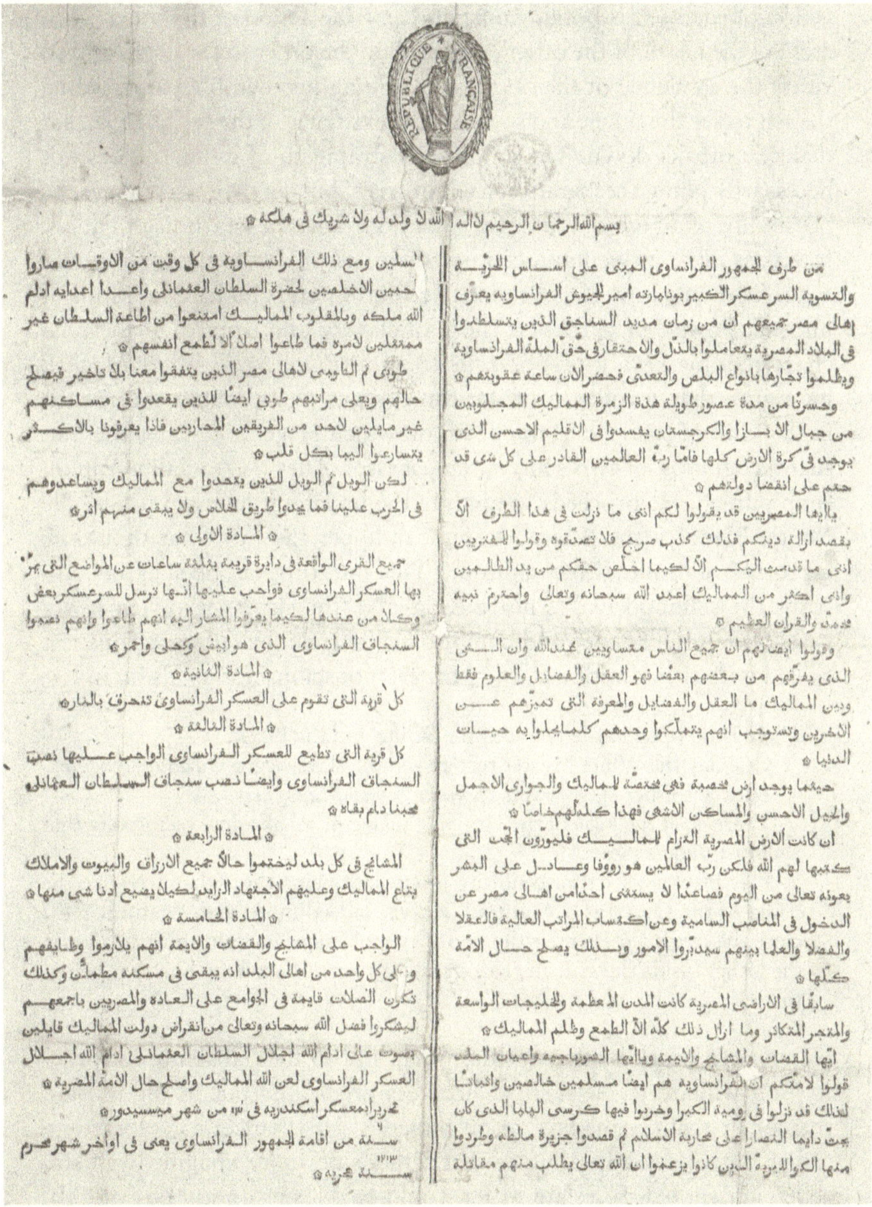

RÉPUBLIQUE FRANÇAISE

بسم الله الرحمن الرحيم لا اله الا الله لا ولد له ولا شريك فى ملكه ۞

من طرف الجمهور الفرانساوى المبنى على اساس الحريه والتسويه السرعسكر الكبير بونابارته امير الجيوش الفرانساويه يعرّف لاهالى مصر جميعهم ان من زمان مديد السناجق الذين يتسلطنوا فى البلاد المصريه يتعاملوا بالذل والاحتقار فى حق الملة الفرانساويه ويظلموا تجّارها بانواع البلص والتعدى فحضر الان ساعة عقوبتهم ۞

وحسرتا من مدة عصور طويلة هذه الزمرة المماليك المجلوبين من جبال الابازا والكرجستان يفسدوا فى الاقليم الاحسن الذى يوجد فى كرة الارض كلها فامّا ربّ العالمين القادر على كل شى قد حتم على انقضا دولتهم ۞

يا ايها المصريين قد يقولوا لكم اننى ما نزلت فى هذا الطرف الا بقصد ازالة دينكم فذلك كذب صريح فلا تصدّقوه وقولوا للمفتريين اننى ما قدمت اليكم الا لكيما اخلّص حقكم من يد الظالمين وانى اكثر من المماليك اعبد الله سبحانه وتعالى واحترم نبيه محمد والقران العظيم ۞

وقولوا ايضا لهم ان جميع الناس متساويين عند الله وان الشى الذى يفرّقهم من بعضهم بعضا فهو العقل والفضايل والعلوم فقط وبين المماليك ما العقل والفضايل والمعرفة التى تميّزهم عن الاخرين وتستوجب انهم يتملكوا وحدهم كلما يحلوا به حيات الدنيا ۞

حيثما يوجد ارض مخصبة فهى مختصّة للمماليك والجوارى الاجمل والخيل الاحسن والمساكن الاشهى فهذا كله لهم خاصًا ۞

ان كانت الارض المصرية التزام للمماليك فليورونا الحجة التى كتبها لهم الله فلكن ربّ العالمين هو رووف وعادل على البشر بعونه تعالى من اليوم فصاعدًا لا يستثنى احد من اهالى مصر عن الدخول فى المناصب السامية وعن اكتساب المراتب العالية فالعقلا والفضلا والعلما بينهم سيدبّروا الامور وبذلك يصلح حال الامّة كلها ۞

سابقًا فى الاراضى المصرية كانت المدن المعظمة والخليجات الواسعة والمتجر المتكاثر وما ازال ذلك كلّه الا الطمع وظلم المماليك ۞

ايها القضات والمشايخ والايمة ويا ايها الشوربجية واعيان البلد قولوا لامتكم ان الفرانساويه هم ايضًا مسلمين خالصين واثباتًا لذلك قد نزلوا فى رومية الكبرا وخربوا فيها كرسى الباپا الذى كان يحث دايما النصارا على محاربة الاسلام ثم قصدوا جزيرة مالطه وطردوا منها الكوالليرية الذين كانوا يزعموا ان الله تعالى يطلب منهم مقاتلة المسلمين ومع ذلك الفرانساويه فى كل وقت من الاوقات صاروا محبين الاخلصين لحضرة السلطان العثمانلى واعدا اعدايه ادام الله ملكه وبالمقلوب المماليك امتنعوا من اطاعة السلطان غير ممتثلين لامره فما طاعوا اصلًا الا لطمع انفسهم ۞

طوبى ثم طوبى لاهالى مصر الذين يتفقوا معنا بلا تاخير فيصلح حالهم ويعلى مراتبهم طوبى ايضًا للذين يقعدوا فى مساكنهم غير مايلين لاحد من الفريقين المحاربين فاذا يعرفونا بالاكثر يتسارعوا الينا بكل قلب ۞

لكن الويل ثم الويل للذين يتحدوا مع المماليك ويساعدوهم فى الحرب علينا فما يجدوا طريق الخلاص ولا يبقى منهم اثر ۞

۞ المادة الاولى ۞

جميع القرى الواقعة فى دايرة قريبة بثلثة ساعات عن المواضع التى يمر بها العسكر الفرانساوى فواجب عليها انها ترسل للسرعسكر بعض وكلا من عندها لكيما يعرّفوا المشار اليه انهم طاعوا وانهم نصبوا السنجاق الفرانساوى الذى هو ابيض وكحلى واحمر ۞

۞ المادة الثانية ۞

كل قرية التى تقوم على العسكر الفرانساوى تنحرق بالنار ۞

۞ المادة الثالثة ۞

كل قرية التى تطيع للعسكر الفرانساوى الواجب عليها نصب السنجاق الفرانساوى وايضًا نصب سنجاق السلطان العثمانلى محبنا دام بقاه ۞

۞ المادة الرابعة ۞

المشايخ فى كل بلد ليختموا حالًا جميع الارزاق والبيوت والاملاك بتاع المماليك وعليهم الاجتهاد الزايد لكيلا يضيع ادنا شى منها ۞

۞ المادة الخامسة ۞

الواجب على المشايخ والقضات والايمة انهم يلازموا وظايفهم وعلى كل واحد من اهالى البلد انه يبقى فى مسكنه مطمانًا وكذلك تكون الصلاة قايمة فى الجوامع على العاده والمصريين باجمعهم ليشكروا فضل الله سبحانه وتعالى من انقراض دولت المماليك قايلين بصوت عالى ادام الله اجلال السلطان العثمانلى ادام الله اجلال العسكر الفرانساوى لعن الله المماليك واصلح حال الامّة المصريه ۞

تحريرا بمعسكر اسكندريه فى ١٣ من شهر ميسيدور ۞

سنة ٦ من اقامة الجمهور الفرانساوى يعنى فى اواخر شهر محرم

سنة ١٢١٣ هجريه ۞

FIGURE 1. Arabic proclamation by Napoleon Bonaparte to the people of Egypt, 2 July 1798.

action of each self is both *against* and *also* the action of the other, each seeking the death of the other (superseding the other to see itself, and so verify the existence of the other) and staking his own life (superseding the self to see the other, and so verify the existence of the self).[6] Here that dialectic breaks down. The colonizer's stratagem of mimicry does not necessarily plunge recognition itself in crisis, but surely it neutralizes the possibility of any *mutuality* of recognition. This the Martinican Fanon, foremost among twentieth-century theorists of decolonization, would argue, showing how Hegel's dialectic short-circuits under conditions of unequal power, in particular those of slavery and empire. In the final chapter of his *Peau noire, masques blancs (Black Skin, White Masks),* he argues that Antilleans of African descent never fought the French in the kind of struggle to the death on which Hegel predicates the mutual recognition of two self-consciousnesses. They were, claims Fanon, simply freed. He proceeds to analyze the unilateral interruption by "le Maître Blanc" ("the White Master," in upper case) of what should be a process of "mutual recognition." This interruption, he suggests, absorbs the selfhood of "le nègre esclave" ("the slave-negro," in lower case) within the Master and compels his struggle for self-consciousness to end with the adoption of the *Master's* consciousness as his own.

> There is no open battle between the White and the Black.
>
> One day the White Master recognized the slave-negro *without struggle.*
>
> But the former slave wants to *make himself recognized.*
>
> There is, at the base of the Hegelian dialectic, an absolute reciprocity that we must underscore.
>
> It is insofar as I transcend my immediate being-there that I realize the being of the Other as a "natural" reality, indeed more than "natural." If I close the circuit, if I render the two-way movement unrealizable, I maintain the Other inside the self. At the extreme, I even abduct from him that being-for-self.[7]

Napoleon's proclamation traffics, then, not in the "absolute reciprocity" on which the Hegelian dialectic is predicated but in the illusion thereof. It realizes the will of an imperial self (France) to colonize an Other (Egypt) by appealing to that Other's desire to imagine itself still sovereign enough to relate to its would-be Master on an axis of "absolute reciprocity" and then by insinuating *irreciprocity* through that lure of recognition. Thus it extends to the Arabic-speaking and predominantly Muslim population of Egypt precisely the sort of recognition *avant la lutte* that Fanon pronounces so lethal to the formation of the autonomous Antillean subject, pretending that the Arab-Islamic is the "theme"—the sovereign subject—of French colonial action there ("the French also are sincere Muslims"). Once Egyptianness and Arab-Islamicity appear not extrinsic but *intrinsic* to Frenchness, the Egyptian Muslim will misrecognize France not as the Other who would rule as its colonial sovereign but as a validation, indeed an incarnation, of its precolonial sovereign *self*—and thereby permit French sovereignty, paradoxically, to replace its own.[8] Recognized before he can fight for recognition ("impose himself on another man, in order to make himself recognized"), the Egyptian subject—like Fanon's black Antillean—finds his path of self-actuation deviated from its proper object and toward the master: becoming, as Fanon puts it, "the theme of his action," the French master Other remains inside him unsuperseded, eclipsing his selfhood.[9] To "be for self," in this conception, becomes "to be the Other," since self has been translated *into* Other in a "copulation" premised on false equivalence.

By reading Fanon with Homi Bhabha's essay "Of Mimicry and Man," we can better understand why a mimicry of the sort that Napoleon's proclamation performs might be so seductive to the Egyptian it targets, given that the compulsion it engenders—the compulsion of the colonized subject to translate itself into a false "self-consciousness" across a copula, or verb of being, that the recognizing (and colonizing) Other really controls—betrays the fundamental inequality of colonial power, unmasks the mask. Interested primarily in the mimicry of colonizers by their colonized subjects, Bhabha never quite describes as "mimicry" the self-translation by *colonizers* into strategic semblances of those they wish to colonize—although he comes close to doing so in another essay, "Signs Taken for Wonders."[10] Still, Bhabha's understanding of mimicry as the metonymic re-presentation of an original in a form "almost the same but not quite" suggests the concept's intimacy with the dynamics of colonial translation. If mimicry occurs, as Bhabha argues, "at the site of interdiction, . . . uttered *inter dicta*," or "between the lines and as such both against the rules and within them," then colonial translation is mimicry par excellence.[11] What discourse indeed is uttered between the lines of the copula—between and against the lines of the grammatical equal sign, the verb *to be*, that links *I* and *you* in Napoleon's "I *am* you"—but the colonizing translation, which at once resembles the native (the "original") it translates and retains a wisp of difference that menaces that original? Such a translation is both *inter dicta*, within the "rules" (the lines and the laws) that stipulate commensurability, and *interdictory*, against those rules, prohibiting commensurability. On the one hand, the copula of colonial translation, which is also the copula of colonial mimicry, transgresses the divide of colonizer and colonized to promote the illusion that power might be exchangeable; on the other, it insists on a prohibition of that exchange. In other words, the equal sign imposes itself, daringly, upon the slash of the divide between colonizer/colonized—but the slash, the divide, is still there, trumping equivalence. Each attempt to pretend equivalence, then, also asserts an irrevocable difference; each resemblance, to invoke Bhabha's citation of Jacques Lacan, "*differs from* or *defends* presence by displaying it in part, metonymically."[12]

Uttering interdiction *inter dicta*—voicing the radical power difference that prohibits the *real* "conversion" of the colonizer into the colonized between the lines of a French-to-Arabic translation that appears to perform precisely that conversion—Bonaparte's proclamation deploys, throughout, a dialectic of similarity and superiority to strategic ends. When it speaks *inter dicta,* it suggests that French invader and Egyptian subject are equals, are one; when it lets the mask slip to assert French military might, it checks equivalence with interdiction. The trajectory of resemblance—"I am you"—flatters and lures; that of menace, traveling in the opposite direction, interposes the "but" of unequal power—"but I am also your ruler." That "but" checks the colonized, momentarily, from accepting the proposition that the colonizer is he or she. Yet the interdiction that it implies generates desire, invites the colonized to rebalance the dialectic of recognition—to rebalance power—by saying, "Wait—no—*I* want to be *you,* so that I can be myself again." Fanon's revision of Hegel captures this turn to the master to return the self:

> In Hegel there is reciprocity; here the master mocks the consciousness of the slave. He does not demand recognition from the latter, but his labor.
>
> Similarly, the slave here is in no way assimilable to the one who, losing himself in the object, finds in labor the source of his liberation.
>
> The Negro wants to be like the master.
>
> Thus he is less independent than the Hegelian slave.
>
> In Hegel, the slave turns away from the master and turns toward the object.
>
> *Here the slave turns toward the master* and abandons the object.[13]

Shattering the illusion of reciprocity on which Hegel premises his dialectic of self-consciousnesses, Fanon suggests that it is the very *absence* of reciprocity in the master-slave relation—the fact that the master can dole out "recognition" to the slave without really struggling with the slave's self-consciousness, without subjecting his *own* self-consciousness to real death—that makes the slave identify with the master rather than resist him.[14] Giving in to the colonizer's invitation to short-circuit the power play of "I am you . . . but I am also your ruler," which carries the tacit command, "Therefore, you should be me"—giving in to the colonizer's invitation to forget the presence of its power, to "copulate" the self across an equal sign that the colonizer already has slashed—the colonized is seduced into perpetuating his or her subjection. Indeed, the very short-circuit of power into which the colonized is seduced by the resemblance/menace of mimicry will prevent his or her reborn *I* from ruling, from being itself—its precolonial self—again. Identification with the *you* of the colonizer already has made repossession of "self" the possession of only a simulacrum of the self: an ongoing subjection.

FOOLING THE EGYPTIAN *I*

Clearly Napoleon relied on his proclamation to seduce Egypt into surrender. A survey of his tactical communications during the first month of the occupation alone suggests that the text was a cornerstone of his colonial strategy. On 15 messidor an VI (3 July 1798), one day after landing at Alexandria, Napoleon sent a few Arabic proclamations to General Louis Desaix, informing him that he was "waiting for five to six hundred copies from on board *L'Orient,* which [he] would send shortly." With these proclamations Bonaparte called on Desaix to subdue villages from Alexandria to Cairo, masking the full extent of his firepower as he entered. Military and textual strategies chime. "The art here," writes Napoleon, "consists in keeping all my extraordinary means hidden, . . . and thereby surprising them [the Mamālīk, and the Egyptians] all the more."[15] In an order of 19 messidor an VI (7 July 1798), Napoleon called for the installation of French, Arabic, and Greek presses in the home of the Venetian consul at Alexandria. What he wanted to disseminate most was his Arabic proclamation. "The moment that the Arabic press is set up, we will print 4,000 Arabic proclamations," he writes.[16]

To understand how the colonizer's self-translation into those it wishes to subjugate seduces the latter not just into "surrender" before battle but also eventually into identification with their colonizer, let us return now to Napoleon's proclamation and examine the ways in which it deploys similarity to assert superiority. Consider, first, the visual effect of the text: its entirely Arabic "presence," save for the seal of the République Française. Napoleon's text anticipates the principal fear of a largely Muslim populace as it encounters an unfamiliar conqueror from the all-too-familiar lands of the Crusaders: fear that the French seek to eradicate its religion.[17] Thus the Arabic radically revises the original French preamble to the proclamation, which declares that it comes from "Bonaparte, member of the Institut National, commander-in-chief"—betraying both Napoleon's force and his foreignness (what is the "Institut National" to the Egyptian of 1798?)—and places the first mention of Bonaparte and the French Republic in whose name he speaks *second* to the words we find directly under the seal: "Bismillāhi al-raḥmāni al-raḥīm; lā ilāha illā Allāh lā walada lahu wa lā sharīka fī mulkihi" ("In the name of God, the Merciful, the Compassionate. There is no god but God; no offspring [son] has He, and no partner in His sovereignty").[18] Lest the average Egyptian think the French bent on subordinating Islam to their authority, Napoleon undercuts the menace of the seal by placing the entire text of his proclamation under the sign of the traditional Islamic invocation of God, which opens each chapter *(sūra)* of the Qur'ān: "In the name of God, the Merciful, the Compassionate." True to Bhabha's conception of mimicry, the proclamation's "Muslim" text *eclipses* its French seal. All the while, however, that seal remains a part of the whole, the partial presence that menaces the mask of resemblance: after all, the entire proclamation—even its *basmala*, its invocation of God—is under the sign of the seal. Eclipsing the part, then, that would betray the colonial designs of the French Republic, Napoleon marshals the Muslim *basmala* to defuse Egyptian suspicions that the French seek sovereignty over Egypt—absolute sovereignty, he slyly assures them, is God's alone. More important, he styles *himself* Muslim: he not only invokes the *basmala* before launching his text, as a Muslim writer traditionally would, but also affirms that God has no son, thereby repudiating Christian doctrine. Edward Said remarks Napoleon's use of both religious and linguistic identification to win Egypt: "Napoleon tried everywhere to prove that he was fighting *for* Islam; everything he said was translated into Koranic Arabic."[19] As vaguely aware as most Egyptians of the period were of the secularist orientation of post-Revolutionary France, which would have licensed Napoleon to reject Christian doctrine without necessarily professing Islam, Napoleon's intimation that he had "embraced" Islam could have been profoundly disarming (see figure 2).

Not all of Napoleon's Egyptian interlocutors, of course, initially were so disarmed. The intellectual 'Abd al-Raḥmān al-Jabartī (1753/54–1825/26), a historian of the French occupation, was acutely aware that

FIGURE 2. "Double portrait de Bonaparte, en turban de mameluk et en chapeau de général." Portrait of a Janus-faced Napoleon Bonaparte, sporting a French *bicorne* and a Mamlūk turban, c. 1798–1801? Estampes et Photographie–RES QB-370 (53)-FT 4–De Vinck, 7372. Copyright © Bibliothèque Nationale de France.

Napoleon's republican army was not the old Christian enemy of the Crusades. Critiquing Napoleon's proclamation in his 1798 *Tārīkh Muddat al-Faransīs bi Miṣr* (History of the Period of the French in Egypt), an eyewitness account of the first seven months of the occupation, al-Jabartī notes that Napoleon falls one step shy of embracing Islam in his "miserable letter," since he elides the second half of the *shahāda,* the Islamic profession of faith: "Ashhadu anna lā ilāha illā Allāh, wa ashhadu anna Muḥammadan rasūlu Allāh" ("I bear witness that there is no god but God, and I bear witness that Muḥammad is the messenger of God").[20] Al-Jabartī's account begins not on a note of attraction to the colonizer but on one of stark terror. He tells us that frightened Egyptians—unsure when the French would reach Cairo—amassed for days at the city's fortifications, abandoning their shops and homes to looters. When the French arrived, they clashed with the forces of Egypt's two most powerful rulers at the time, the Mamālīk Ibrāhīm Bey and Murād Bey, in the Battle of the Pyramids near Giza. There, they would open "continuous barrages of fire" on crowds of Egyptian noncombatants watching the fighting across the Nile, from the eastern bank of Būlāq, "chewing their fingers out of distress and sorrow."[21] With Murād Bey's galleons captured and Ibrāhīm Bey's forces dispersed, the people fled back into Cairo. "In their great alarm," writes al-Jabartī, "they took to their heels and ran like the waves of the sea. . . . Their cries and lamentings rose up from far and near."[22] Al-Jabartī's Cairenes are unsure where to turn as the bullets fall. Only their cries and the whiz of French bullets pierce the opacity of a blind, and blinding, historical moment in which the conquered confront a conqueror with inscrutable motives.

The historical moment that al-Jabartī describes is opaque, the conqueror's motives inscrutable, precisely because the French occupation's disarming words traveled faster than its armed blows: news of Napoleon's coming preceded the actual invasion. Nothing save the image of the Frenchman of Napoleon's proclamation, which had circulated for some three weeks from Alexandria to Cairo, could have made French bullets come almost as a shock to the Egyptian capital. After all, Cairo had anticipated enemy fire for days, arming itself against assault. Yet by al-Jabartī's own testimony, Napoleon's proclamation had misled some to believe the French more friend than foe. He notes its appeal to large sectors of the Egyptian populace, who seem convinced by Napoleon's assurances that he comes to Egypt as an ally of the Sublime Porte in Istanbul—at that time the seat of both the Ottoman Empire and the Islamic caliphate.

> Some of the people said that this was by Imperial order and that the French were accompanied by Pashas sent by the Sultan. Most of the rural population and fallāḥīn [peasants] believed this because of the proclamation . . . which the French distributed throughout the country. The Shaykhs, the dignitaries, and the common people set out with clubs and arms.[23]

Al-Jabartī implies that the legitimacy of French presence in Egypt failed to convince many Cairenes, who ultimately arm themselves in the face of their attempted disarmament. Yet to say that the "rural population" believed Napoleon is to betray, almost in spite of oneself, the allure of the proclamation for the great *majority* of the Egyptian people. For Napoleon does use language that—for all its infelicities of grammar, style, and religious expression, which render it almost Arabic and Islamic but not quite—remains charged with resonance for the Muslim ear. Witness this remarkable passage from the second paragraph of the proclamation, which mimics language and culture to lure Egyptians into seeing the colonizing enemy as their friend:

> O you Egyptians, you may hear it said that I did not come to this part [of the world] with anything but the intention to eradicate your religion; indeed this is an outright lie, so do not believe it, and tell the fabricators that I have not come to you except to liberate your right *[likaymā ukhalliṣa ḥaqqakum]* from the hand of the oppressors *[al-ẓālimīn]*. Indeed I worship God—may He be praised and exalted—more than the Mamālīk [i.e., the Mamelukes] do *[innanī aktharu min al-mamālīki a'budu Allāha (sic)]*, and I respect His Prophet, Muḥammad, and the glorious Qur'ān.

Here Napoleon appropriates two powerful concepts in the political ethos of Islam, the right of the human being to social justice and the condemnation of oppressors, to position himself as a friend of Egyptian freedom, he who will uphold the right of Egyptians to be "masters" of their own land by fighting the ruling Mamālīk, their "oppressors." That he couches his intent in Islamic terms is not accidental. Henry Laurens suggests that Napoleon borrowed the rhetoric of various revolutionary forces *within* Ottoman Egypt, which had struggled to overthrow the political order there well before the French invasion, each calling for more just and more truly Islamic government.[24] According to Laurens, Napoleon adopted, first, the language of 'Alī Bey al-Kabīr, a Mamlūk who became Egypt's *shaykh al-balad*—its highest-ranking potentate—in 1760 and went on to seize absolute power, shattering the delicate balance between Mamlūk forces and representatives of the central government in Istanbul.[25] 'Alī Bey annexed other parts of the Ottoman Empire, taking Damascus in 1771 and Jaffa in 1773. Before his forces entered Damascus, he issued a proclamation that Napoleon's missive to the Egyptians later would echo. Laurens cites the former, in French translation, from the chronicles of Vasif Wassif Effendi, then official historian of the Sublime Porte. In this document 'Alī Bey styles himself a ruler "given" by God to the people of his age, allied with God's will because he has "enjoined justice in all nations" and "menaced the unjust with destruction." To this self-presentation he contrasts an unflattering sketch of his Ottoman rival. In Qur'ānic terms, 'Alī Bey reminds the Damascenes that "God does not love oppressors" ("inna Allāha lā yuḥibbu al-ẓālimīn"), exhorting them to abandon their unjust ruler and embrace him instead.[26] Napoleon too, I would argue, puts himself on the side of the God of Islam and casts the Mamālīk on the wrong side. In so doing, he dissociates the French invasion of Egypt from colonial oppression and recasts it as a divine mission, ordained to declare, in the Qur'ānic terms of Last Judgment he invokes in the first paragraph of his proclamation, that the "Hour of [the Mamālīk's] punishment has come" ("ḥaḍara al-āna sā'atu 'uqūbatihim").

"REVOLUTIONIZING" EMPIRE

French imperialists saw in Egypt a potentially profitable replacement for the colony of Saint-Domingue—soon to be lost to the Haitian Revolution—and for other French colonies lost to English ascendancy elsewhere in the Americas.[27] According to Laurens, the notion that Egypt should be annexed as a settler "province . . . of the French Republic" comes from Charles Magallon, who by 1798 had spent thirty years in Egypt as a trade negotiator and five as the consul of the new Republic in Alexandria. Magallon's report on Egypt—commissioned by Talleyrand, then minister of foreign relations—would move the latter to recommend the conquest of Egypt on 14 February 1798. In late 1797 Talleyrand also had met Napoleon in Paris. From the converging visions of Magallon, Napoleon, and Talleyrand, the French imperial project in Egypt crystallized.[28]

On the complex history of the Mamlūk regime that Napoleon sought to topple, a fuller retrospective also is in order. By 1798 Egypt had been under Mamlūk domination of varying kinds for over seven hundred years. The term *mamālīk,* plural of the Arabic *mamlūk* (owned), names a military guard of manumitted slaves originally imported from central Asia and the Caucasus by the last of the major Ayyūbid sultans of Egypt, al-Ṣāliḥ Ayyūb (1240–49), to protect his throne from the Mongols and the European Crusaders, among others.[29] The Mamālīk seized power from their Ayyūbid masters, who had governed Egypt under allegiance to the 'Abbāsid caliphate of Baghdad, in the mid-thirteenth century; they ruled Egypt until 1517, when the Ottomans conquered the country and "incorporated [the Mamlūk system] into their own . . . , which [already] included a class of slaves who formed the military and much of the bureaucracy of the Ottoman Empire."[30] After 1711, according to Afaf Lutfi al-Sayyid Marsot, the Mamālīk seized control of Egypt once again and reduced its Ottoman governor to "little more than a puppet."[31] 'Alī Bey would revive the pre-Ottoman Mamlūk state.

By the time Murād Bey and Ibrāhīm Bey took control of Egypt later in the eighteenth century, a second strain of Islamic revolutionary discourse gathered force. According to Laurens, when the two potentates transacted independent "commercial agreements with European powers," Istanbul strove to reassert dominion.[32] At the helm was Ḥasan Pasha al-Jazā'irlī. Landing at Alexandria in 1786, al-Jazā'irlī issued several proclamations that would supply still more "native" vocabulary for Napoleon's future mimicry.[33] Claiming that the sultan in Istanbul had ordered him to "put a stop to tyranny," al-Jazā'irlī invaded Egypt at the behest of both the Ottoman center and the Islamic religious scholars *('ulamā')* of Cairo, whom he had summoned to air Egypt's grievances against the Mamālīk.[34] Thus, argues Laurens, al-Jazā'irlī's "reconquest" of Egypt was at once an imperial act and a revolutionary one, drawing legitimacy from a populist activation of Islamic civil rights.[35] Unlike Ibrahim Abu-Lughod, who (wrongly) argues that Napoleon's reference to *al-jumhūriyya* (republic) in his proclamation of 2 July 1798 was incomprehensible to a Muslim like al-Jabartī, Laurens hears homologies between late-eighteenth-century Islamic and French revolutionary discourses and suggests that the right to resist oppressive government struck a virtually *synchronic* chord in France and in Egypt.[36]

Perhaps Napoleon too heard distant echoes of the French Revolution in the winds of Ottoman reform in Egypt. Filtering the ideology of one revolution through the idiom of another, the consummate colonial mimic would style himself a Jazā'irlī-esque defender of Ottoman sovereignty and in that guise would call on *ahālī Miṣr,* the people of Egypt, to uphold their allegiance to the sultan and restore their rights by resisting Mamlūk oppression. Assuring Egyptians that "the French ha[d] been, at all times, the sincerest friends *[al-muḥibbīna al-akhlaṣīna (sic)]* of his Majesty the Ottoman sultan and the greatest enemy of his enemies," Napoleon identified himself intimately with Istanbul; by the admission of even al-Jabartī, as we have seen, his proclamation managed to convince the Egyptian masses—at least initially—that the French had arrived under the sultan's orders. On the other side of the battlefield—as the common enemy of the French Republic, the Ottoman Empire, and the people of Egypt—Napoleon would range the Mamālīk, charging that they "ha[d] refused to obey the sultan" and indeed had "never obeyed anything but their souls' greed." He accuses the Mamālīk of having turned Egypt into a giant tax farm *(iltizām)* whose profits only they can reap and challenges them to produce the title deed by which God has given them claim to the land—a challenge, of course, they cannot meet. Thus, once more recalling al-Jazā'irlī, Napoleon would delegitimize Mamlūk rule on the grounds that it had robbed Egyptians of their God-given rights to property.

THE SHIFTY GRAMMAR OF IMPERIAL FORETELLING

By the time the French arrived in 1798, the constant infighting of Mamlūk forces—coupled with the drought, famine, and plague that had swept Egypt between 1783 and 1792—had devastated the land.[37] Yet Marsot, for one, rejects the notion that the French occupation "rescued" Egypt from chaos: she reminds us that the "occupation did not help matters, since it was a further exploitation of resources."[38] Al-Jabartī captures that exploitation in his *Tārīkh,* which bears witness to the devastation of Cairo by French forces in only the first seven months of what would be a three-year military occupation. With the accusation that the Mamālīk had run roughshod over the trading rights of the French in Egypt, Napoleon justified wholesale theft and plunder of their wealth: ordering their properties sealed, his forces proceeded "to enter and loot them to their hearts' content."[39] (Napoleon himself occupied one such expropriated home; the Institut d'Égypte, the research arm of his campaign, another.) According to al-Jabartī, the French presence also unleashed widespread civil disorder; further, it precipitated rapid inflation.[40] Finally, the French destroyed much of Cairo's infrastructure: al-Jabartī documents the demolition of buildings and walls across Cairo, some centuries old; the leveling of districts to make way for French projects; and—most egregious of all, for Muslims—the invasion, desecration, and sacking of the mosque and student quarters of al-Azhar, in "retaliation" for an anticolonial uprising.[41]

Still, Bonaparte's missive compelled al-Jabartī enough to dissect its Arabic line by line, exposing its ungrammaticality and linking its corrupt language—its lapses of partial French presence—to corrupt colonial designs.[42] In one especially brilliant sally, he chides Bonaparte for putting the word *muslim* in the accusative case, called *naṣb* in Arabic, instead of the nominative; punning on the Frenchman's incorrect application of *al-naṣb*, his ungrammaticality, and the other meaning of *al-naṣb*, his fraud, al-Jabartī dismisses French pretensions to shared faith with the conclusion that "their Islam is *naṣb* [fraud]."[43] Thus al-Jabartī's chronicle represents the French self-translation of Napoleon's proclamation as unquestionably deceitful—menace masquerading as resemblance—but also alluring enough to merit retranslation and interpretation, to merit being followed in its sinuous manner of meaning, almost "lovingly," back to the strange French vessel from which it issued. That al-Jabartī is, perversely, under the spell of French discourse suggests why he ends his "retranslation" of the proclamation by putting so appropriate a curse on his colonizers: the wish that God might "strike the organ[s] of their speech dumb."[44] As Jacques Derrida hints in his *Politiques de l'amitié (Politics of Friendship)*, enmity is not hate but the ghost of friendship, for it cares entirely too much about the object of its inimical feeling to ignore that object. Rather, it is *indifference* that is hate.[45] Al-Jabartī may be a declared enemy of the French, but he is far from indifferent to them. Already, in his 1798 *Tārīkh*, he vacillates between support for anti-French resistance and condemnation of such resistance as "unreasonable," and—more important—he evinces admiration of the state of French knowledge and of the intellectual institutions that the French establish in Egypt.[46] Pace Edward Said, who argues that "Jabarti has eyes for, and only appreciates, the facts of power," al-Jabartī is anything but blind to the cultural face of imperialism, to the textual and intellectual strategies that mediate Napoleon's bid for power in Egypt.[47] Jamāl al-Dīn al-Shayyāl shows, indeed, that in 1800 al-Jabartī became a member of the *dīwān* (council) of Egyptian notables reconstituted under the administration of General Jacques 'Abd Allāh Menou. (When General Jean-Baptiste Kléber, who became Egypt's chief colonial administrator after Napoleon returned to France in 1799, was assassinated in Cairo on 14 June 1800, Menou acceded to the governorship.) Thus al-Jabartī became a participant-observer in the Egyptian arm of a French colonial government.[48] By the time he wrote his encyclopedic history of Egypt, *'Ajā'ib al-Āthār fī al-Tarājim wa al-Akhbār*—compiled between 1805 and 1821, well after the French occupation had ended and thus, as Shmuel Moreh suggests, at his greatest psychological distance from the shock of the French invasion—al-Jabartī would vaunt French justice, perhaps too uncritically, and compare the (post)colonial governments of early-nineteenth-century Egypt unfavorably to that of Napoleon.[49]

Al-Jabartī could not be indifferent to the French, for notice how cleverly Napoleon insinuates himself into the favor of Egyptian Muslims, claiming that he "respect[s] the Prophet Muḥammad and the glorious Qur'ān" and "worship[s] God more than the Mamālīk do." Elsewhere in the proclamation, he addresses the judges *(al-quḍāt)*, the religious scholars *(al-mashāyikh)*, and the leaders of prayer, or imams *(al-a'imma)*, of Egypt, exhorting them to inform the people that "the French also are sincere Muslims" *("muslimīna khāliṣīna [sic]").* Though its word choice is infelicitous and its grammar botched—the phrase *muslimīna khāliṣīna* should be rendered in the nominative case, as *muslimūna mukhliṣūna,* and *mukhliṣūna,* "sincere," should replace *khāliṣīna,* "pure"—the line is calculated to produce a mimicry so convincing that the Egyptian will not see the partial presence of the French. Its non-idiomatic usage of the word *khāliṣīna* re-presents the French as fully Muslim, unadulterated. Contrast this strategic affirmation, in Arabic, of deep—and shared—belief with the "original" French of Napoleon's proclamation, as we find it in the 1860 edition of the *Correspondance de Napoléon 1er:* "Cadis, cheiks, imams, tchorbadjis, dites au peuple que *nous sommes amis des vrais musulmans.*"[50] Had Napoleon, as I suggested earlier, merely translated this statement verbatim in the Arabic version, he would have said that "the French are friends of the true Muslims": a message entirely different from that which the extant Arabic conveys. He would have professed only French friendship for Muslims, not French belief in Islam; moreover, his very emphasis on extending friendship to "true Muslims" *("vrais musulmans")* would have betrayed his desire to selectively interpret Islam—to decide who is a "true Muslim" worthy of French friendship and which Islam would be consonant with his imperialist designs—before he had won the trust of Egypt's Muslim religious leadership and positioned himself to insinuate French interests into just such a reinterpretation of Islamic texts and belief systems.[51] Instead, Napoleon devotes the first paragraphs of the proclamation to "evidence" that he intends to reinforce Islam on its own terms and relegates to the close of the document his interest in reinterpreting Islam in French terms.

More is at work here, then, than the proverbial logic "The enemy of [your] enemy is [your] friend." Napoleon posits *equivalence* between the French and the Muslims of Egypt: he not only identifies *with* Muslims, but he identifies himself and his people *as* Muslims—people who hold God, the Prophet Muḥammad, and the Qur'ān in the same reverence as Muslim Egyptians. To prove his "pure" Islamicity, Napoleon cites the fact that his armies had invaded Rome and destroyed the Papal See *(kursī al-bābā)*—and had not the pope always incited the Christians to fight Islam? Moreover, he notes, the French had reached Malta and ousted *"al-kawālīriyya* [the cavaliers, or Knights of St. John] who, like the pope, used to claim that God . . . had commanded them to fight Muslims to the death." To be sure, this attempt to Islamize the French would not inspire trust in every Muslim. For al-Jabartī, Napoleon's menace to Islam peeks through this mask of resemblance, since his assault on the pope exposes him as a nonbeliever in Christianity. He who menaces religion cannot, in al-Jabartī's eyes, resemble a Muslim, still less be one.[52] Nonetheless, we should not underestimate the lure of recognition and identification that Napoleon's proclamation holds out to the Egyptian. "I am you," Napoleon is saying, not "You are I." That difference is crucial, for it tips the definition of being to the side of the Other, not the self, even as it links the two across the copula.

Further, Napoleon identifies French interests with Egyptian aspirations to national "self-determination," which he imagines proleptically, as these were virtually nonexistent at the time in the form in which he imagined them. Ironically, the very people Bonaparte would represent as "alien" elements ruling "native" Egyptians were also the only group, according to Laurens, to bear the name "Egyptian" in Ottoman Egypt: the Turkish epithet *Misirli,* derived from the Arabic word for Egypt, *Miṣr*.[53] Thus, while the Mamālīk were ethnically distinct from the Egyptian masses, they were dubbed "Egyptians." By the eighteenth century, they had developed what Laurens calls "a certain form of 'Egyptian' consciousness."[54] Interestingly, then, the term appears to have signified at once membership in the class that ruled Egyptians *and* identification with the ruled, making the "Egyptianness" of the Mamālīk strangely proto-Napoleonic. More important is the fact that even at the close of the eighteenth century, Egypt's "native" Muslim majority did not conceive nationhood along ethnic lines but religious ones: the Mamālīk, despite their diverse ethnic and racial origins, were coreligionists of Egyptian Muslims, and as such, nominally acceptable rulers; the French were not.[55] Napoleon names the Mamālīk Egypt's principal enemies because he must; he cannot install himself as Egypt's new conqueror without dethroning the old. Yet even he seems to sense the unacceptability of French colonization. Thus he must translate himself into a Muslim—must cancel his difference and mimic the *I* of those whom he wishes to colonize in order to assert French difference (read: superiority) metonymically, as partial presence. Without "converting" himself across the copula of colonial translation, he cannot "convert" Egypt to French dominion. The colonized would not be his in turn, or in return.

However seductively Napoleon's proclamation identifies the colonizer with the colonized, the partial presence of the French glints, menacingly, in the mask of resemblance. The colonizer's pretensions to similarity continually veer toward reminders of its superiority, beckoning the colonized to re-vision the self through the conqueror's gaze. In the third paragraph of the proclamation, Napoleon urges Egyptians to tell those who invent "lies" against the French—accusing them of threatening Islam—the following:

> that all people are equal before God *[inna jamī'a al-nāsi mutasāwiyyīna (sic) 'inda Allāhi],* and that what differentiates them . . . [are] reason *[al-'aql]* and virtue [lit., *al-faḍā'il,* "virtues"] and knowledge [lit., *al-'ulūm,* "sciences"] alone. And among the Mamālīk, what is there of reason and virtue and knowledge that would distinguish them . . . and demand that they possess, as kings, all with which they sweeten the life of this world?

Onto the Qur'ānic understanding of equality and difference, which holds that no human being or nation is intrinsically superior to another in the eyes of God except in piety or God-consciousness (see Qur'ān 49:13), Napoleon's rhetoric grafts grounds for equality and difference rooted in French Enlightenment discourse: reason and knowledge. (Reason and knowledge are also crucial values in Islam—some might say essential to proper God-consciousness. Shorn of piety, however, these attributes per se do not define human worth.) He suggests not only that Egyptians are equal to the Mamālīk but also that the French and the Mamālīk are exchangeable as ruling powers. His persuasion of the Egyptians to embrace the French as their new rulers is thus premised on a commensurability of old and new dominators. But to effect French domination Napoleon must slash the lure of equivalence with difference. The Mamālīk, he now argues, should be exchanged for the French because the French are *better.* Moreover, he no longer couches French superiority in the Islamic terms of piety but now does so only in the French Enlightenment terms of reason, knowledge, and (secular?) virtue.

Here the "no longer" and the "now only" are crucial. For if piety is the sole acceptable arbiter of nonmaterial "status" in Islam and the sole term on which Napoleon thus far has premised a similarity between himself and the Egyptian Muslim, then his new terms for valuing the French and devaluing the Mamālīk carry serious implications not just for the rulers to be ousted, but for the Egyptians to be ruled. Only by substituting French terms of equivalence for Islamic ones, by reimposing a superiority that he appeared to shed with his earlier self-translations into Arabic and Islamicity, can Bonaparte declare the Frenchman "superior" to the Egyptian. The new terms permit him to interpose the qualification of unequal power—the "but" of "I am you, . . . but I am also your ruler"—across the copula that would appear to equate him with the Egyptian. Unless Napoleon charges equivalent polarities so that a positive difference accrues to the French and a negative difference attaches to the Mamālīk (and by extension to the "native" Egyptians), what reason would there be to exchange one ruler for another, and what incentive to be ruled? Staging "equality" between unequal opposites (- = +), the French manipulate the magnetism of seduction to assert their *incommensurability*. Hence the rhetorical question that concludes this third paragraph of Napoleon's proclamation. Rippling beneath it is the assumption that the *French* possess the reason, the virtue, the knowledge that distinguish them from others and entitle them to rule the Egyptians and Egypt, elsewhere flatteringly described as "the best land on the face of this earth."

Still, by constructing the political syllogism that equates Egyptians with Mamālīk and Mamālīk with French, Napoleon also invites the Egyptians to reincarnate themselves and their aspirations to sovereignty in the French. He whets Egyptian desire to supplant the Mamālīk, thereby whetting Egyptian desire to *be French:* "From this day forward," the next paragraph of his proclamation reads, "no Egyptian shall be barred from occupying high positions or from attaining high ranks; the wise, the virtuous, and the learned among them *[fal-ʿuqalāʾu wa al-fuḍalāʾu wa al-ʿulamāʾu baynahum]* will manage affairs and thus the condition of the entire community be righted." In thus stating the conditions of Egyptian self-governance, Napoleon echoes the three terms he earlier invoked to legitimize French rule in Egypt: reason ("the wise"), virtue ("the virtuous"), and knowledge ("the learned"). The colonizer's reassertion of his superiority at last has given way to an invitation—a demand?—to the colonized to *be like him.*

What the French want from the Egyptians is, if not immediate allegiance, at least the potential conversion of neutrality. Just as they blur the polarities of colonizer and colonized in order to seduce Egypt, so too do they yearn to see a similar indeterminacy in the object of their seduction. For such indeterminacy implies a potential for reversibility, for translation toward and into Frenchness, that fixity does not. "Blessing upon blessing," the proclamation intones, "to the people of Egypt who cooperate with us without delay, for their condition shall be righted and their ranks elevated; blessings also to those who stay in their houses, inclined toward neither one of the two warring parties, for when they know us better they will rush to us wholeheartedly." Here Napoleon is as interested in the Egyptian who is "hard to get" yet perhaps seducible—the potentiality that hovers on the cusp of translation—as he is in the "easy lay." He knows that the "moderate" can be tipped toward either the French or the Mamālīk; to lean toward the former, he or she need only be properly persuaded. Yet for those who resist, utter destruction awaits. "But woe upon woe to those who collaborate with the Mamālīk and abet them in fighting us," Napoleon warns, "for they shall find no way to escape, nor shall any trace of them remain."

Only in the five articles that close the proclamation—which appear almost as postscripts to the main text of French-Muslim identification—does the undercurrent of deadly violence that subtends Napoleon's rhetoric of seduction gather full force. Even here, shades of resemblance alternate with those of menace. In the first and third articles, the French seek not only the Egyptians' "voluntary" compliance with French rule—that is, their self-annexation—but also evidence thereof. The first commands every Egyptian village within a three-hour radius of the French armies' warpath to raise the *tricolore* (blue, white, and red) French flag as a sign of its obedience and to send deputies to the French vouching for their compliance with colonial law. The third demands that each village raise, alongside the *tricolore* flag, the flag of the Ottoman sultan, thereby at once demanding shows of obedience to the French and reinforcing the identification of Paris with Istanbul. The second and fourth articles, by contrast, threaten physical, economic, and epistemic violence. The second makes the punishment for refusing to surrender the self all too clear: "Any village that rises up against the French will be razed." In the fourth, Napoleon declares it incumbent on the shaykhs, or religious scholars, of every city to "immediately impound all the . . . possessions of the Mamālīk." Bonaparte may speak softly, but he carries a big stick.

Indeed, the fifth and final article of Napoleon's proclamation consummates the translation of its desired Egyptian subject toward a position from which he henceforth will see himself through the French *I:*

> It is imperative that the religious scholars and the judges and the imams fulfill the duties of their posts and that every citizen of the land stay in his house, secure, and likewise that prayers be observed as usual in the Friday congregational mosques and that all Egyptians *[wa al-miṣriyyīna bi ajma'ihim]* say, out loud, "May God preserve the might of the Ottoman sultan; may God preserve the might of the French military; may God curse the Mamālīk and right the condition of the Egyptian nation *[al-umma al-miṣriyya]*."

Here Napoleon seems to call for life in Egypt, especially religious life, to proceed as usual. Yet that life will be lived under a house arrest at once physical and philosophical, local and transnational. Not only are Egypt's citizens to stay home and thereby signal their surrender to the new French order, but they are to practice an Islam subordinated to the will of French empire. Asked to pray for the Ottoman and French empires, Egyptians are called to validate *French* rule—given Napoleon's false alliance of French and Ottoman—and to translate themselves into essentially "French" republican subjects. Napoleon's curse on the Mamālīk is meant to destroy any commonality (however fraught) "native" Egyptian Muslims still might enjoy with their Mamlūk coreligionists under the Islamic *umma*, which traditionally denotes the "transnational" community of Muslim believers. In constituting, proleptically, the modern Egyptian nation-state—in calling on Egyptians to pray for a new imagined community called *"al-umma al-miṣriyya,"* the "Egyptian *umma*"—Napoleon substitutes a territorially Egyptian *umma* for the larger *umma* of Islam whose boundaries are too vast to totalize and conquer. Thus he invokes the pan-Islamic *umma* to install an amputated secular version thereof. Significantly, the proclamation closes by locating its composition in French time (on the thirteenth of the month of messidor, year VI of the French Republic) and failing to fully translate the temporality of French republicanism into that of the Islamic *hijra,* which marks time from the year of the Prophet Muḥammad's migration from Mecca to Medina to form the first Islamic *umma*. The proclamation's Islamic date is vague: the "*last days* of the month of A.H. Muḥarram 1213." The European is now the standard by which Egypt is called to measure itself, its history, its time. Although Islamic time survives, it already is consigned to the realm of the nonspecific, hence the "unscientific." The days of its epistemological sovereignty in Egypt are numbered.

For Napoleon's invasion would leave a lasting imprint on Ottoman Egypt. While Kenneth Cuno and Khaled Fahmy contest the notions that pre-1798 Egypt was a "Sleeping Beauty" awakened by France (in Cuno's inimitable phrase) and that post-1798 Egypt was primarily the product of French-inspired transformations, both acknowledge the occupation's long-term effects. In his work on land reform in Egypt between 1740 and 1858, Cuno rightly seeks to "conceive of change [in Egypt] as a process influenced partly but not necessarily decisively—or even at all times—by interaction with Europe."[56] Yet he also links Mehmed Ali's empire building in the 1810s to 1830s directly to Ottoman-Egyptian insecurity in the face of European (especially French) expansionism. According to Cuno, Mehmed Ali understood that Egypt was "enmeshed in a European-dominated system of economic and political relations" and "that the achievement of his ambitions depended ultimately upon the will of the European powers."[57] Moreover, he suggests that Mehmed Ali's abolition of the *iltizām* (tax farm) system in 1813–14—the most radical land reform of the Egyptian nineteenth century—was a direct legacy of the French occupation, which "completely disrupted" it.[58] "The tax farms of approximately two-thirds of Egypt's land," Cuno informs us, "were confiscated" by the French as their holders "either fled or perished," and in the face of unsuccessful attempts to auction them to new holders, the French appointed local shaykhs to "keep order and collect taxes."[59] Mehmed Ali would pursue precisely such strategies some fifteen years later.[60]

Fahmy, in turn, suggests that the legacies of French imperialism did not die with the evacuation of Napoleon's armies in 1801; indeed, he cites those armies as at least one major inspiration for Mehmed Ali's (post)colonial reorganization of the Ottoman-Egyptian army.[61] By the 1820s, he writes, "the Pasha came to depend heavily on French advisors to run his army and train his soldiers," chief among them Colonel Joseph Sève (Süleyman Pasha), "who eventually became second-in-command."[62] Finally, Fahmy shows that Mehmed Ali's imperial ambitions in the Sudan, Syria, Arabia, and elsewhere flourished only at the mercy of European powers. Where Fahmy intervenes is by questioning the overstatement of "Mehmed Ali's fascination with western models of reform, and French ones in particular."[63] "As obvious as it is that he was borrowing from the French," he writes, "it is clear that he was equally influenced by the Ottomans who themselves had been borrowing from the French and adopting their models to suit their own needs."[64] Yet Fahmy concedes that the Ottomans *themselves* were transforming their institutions in the French mold, well aware that French power was in the ascendant.

More acutely than the annals of social history, the archive of literature and culture suggests that the experience of French occupation resonated with Egyptians well into the 1820s, 1830s, and beyond. For some twenty years after the French occupation, al-Jabartī would reassess its legacies in three separate studies, first in *Tārīkh* and finally in *'Ajā'ib al-Āthār,* a history of Egypt from 1688 to 1821. As evidence of French inhumanity, Rifā'a Rāfi' al-Ṭahṭāwī's 1834 account of his travels in Paris would cite the public display—in the Jardin des Plantes—of the corpse of Sulaymān al-Ḥalabī, the young Azharite from Aleppo whose assassination of Kléber in 1800 speeded the French occupation to its end. This specter of French violation haunts al-Ṭahṭāwī's otherwise positive reception of French scholarship and institutions. Finally, in 'Alī Mubārak's novel *'Alam al-Dīn* (begun 1867, published 1882) an Egyptian contests a French Orientalist's rosy account of Napoleon's legacy to Egypt by invoking his parents' bitter memories of occupation. Mubārak's fiction suggests the ways in which many Egyptians may have remembered French colonialism in the mid-nineteenth century.

INTERPELLATION, DISSIMILATION, OR SEDUCTION?

Napoleon's proclamation and the self-translation toward Frenchness into which it ultimately seduces the Egyptian—despite the latter's obvious resistance to the brutality of French colonialism—suggests how deeply empire depends on translation. In the Western tradition especially, translation long has been a copula between the imperatives of power and those of knowledge. As Douglas Robinson observes, the ancient Roman theory of *translatio studii et imperii* held that "both knowledge and imperial control of the world tend to move in a westerly direction."[65] Just as the Roman Empire styled itself heir to the intellectual and political dominance of the Greek, so too would medieval, Renaissance, and modern Europeans maintain that the mantle of supremacy once worn by ancient Greece and Rome was now their own. Itself an ideological construct translated across time—from the Roman Empire to the medieval and finally to the modern West—*translatio studii et imperii* points the global movements of knowledge and power decisively toward Europe and does so under the sign of translation. Since the ideology rests, in part, on the sun's movement from east to west and thus on an analogy between the physical and the epistemopolitical worlds, European universalisms—Christian and secular—could harness it to naturalize both their self-installation at the origin of "enlightenment" and the political necessity of shining their light on the supposedly "benighted" subjects of colonialism. As light travels, so too must knowledge and empire. One paradox here, I would note, is that the light each empire—progressively more Western—shines on points farther and farther West is borrowed from points farther and farther East.

Napoleon's proclamation reverses the conventional trajectory of *translatio studii et imperii.* Not only does its West borrow light from an alternative East—not ancient Greece or Rome but the worlds of Islam and the Ottoman Empire—but its translational mirror throws that borrowed light *back* East, returning West as East under the guise of returning the East to itself. If, as Robinson argues, *translatio studii et imperii* rests on a logic of transcendental signification—the very logic that would underpin most Western translation theory until the early twentieth century, when Ferdinand de Saussure would argue that meaning is contingent on the relation between signifiers—Napoleon's proclamation bends that transcendence to French advantage.[66] *Translatio studii et imperii*, writes Robinson,

> grew out of the mystical and philosophical tradition that Pythagoras called *metempsychosis*, or the "transmigration of souls," or reincarnation: just as the ancient mystics believed that every soul travelled through a series of bodies (and thus "lives") but remained fundamentally the same soul, so too did the believers in the *translatio studii et imperii* insist that learning and empire were successively embodied in a sequence of cultures while remaining fundamentally the same.[67]

Here translation is a matter of exchanging a "common" soul—a common meaning, or signified—through different bodies: different languages or systems of signification. Yet as Robinson observes, "this impulse is undermined by the constant geographical drift of the *translatio*," which "must repeatedly be retranslated into the mobile terms of empire."[68] The different bodies in which a supposedly "common" soul takes up residence surely must impinge on that soul in some way, inflecting it with the historical context specific to a given imperial formation and thus altering its substance. Any new signifier must act on—not simply reflect—the original signified. We might say, then, that the roots of *translatio studii et imperii* in Pythagorean *metempsychosis* link the epistemological and political imperia of translation to the intersubjective in its fully historical sense. Moreover, they suggest a new way of imagining the link between translation and colonialism. While Timothy Mitchell argues that colonialism maintained its power by producing unbridgeable differences between colonizers and colonized and Tejaswini Niranjana and Natalie Melas (implicitly) argue that colonialism ruled its subjects by attempting to reproduce them as images of the colonizer, Robinson's allusion to *metempsychosis* suggests that colonialism may act most powerfully when it implants the *illusion* of identity with the colonized—not identity itself—in the alien body of the colonizer, thus convincing the colonized that they can be the colonizer and be themselves at one and the same time. If two signifiers can be made to appear to mean the "same" thing, as Lydia Liu suggests, what may be lost to the vision (or hearing) of the colonized is the way in which the colonizer's signifier—the more powerful of the two—acts on and inflects the supposedly selfsame.[69] Of this dynamic the proclamation of 2 July

1798, which attempts to confuse Bonaparte's "Islam" with the Egyptian reader's, is a powerful example.

Bhabha's conception of mimicry aside, postcolonial theory has defined the intersubjective dynamics of colonial translation and its close cousin, comparison, along two major axes: as Althusserian interpellation (Niranjana) or its obverse, dissimilation (Melas). The translational economy of Napoleon's proclamation exposes the interpretive limits of both axes. Rather than understand translation under asymmetrical power as interpellation or dissimilation, I propose that we reinterpret it as seduction: as a circuit of displacements of pronominality and time through which both the colonizer and the colonized, though from radically unequal positions of material and epistemological power, re-recognize themselves as sovereign. The (post)colonial subjectivity that circuit engenders is an erotic one that couples the colonized subject-object to the colonizing Subject and dissolves the latter in the former. It eschews both the binary opposition of two powers (domination and resistance, refigured in Niranjana as containment/assimilation and in Melas as escape/dissimilation) and the neat correlation of those powers to the binary opposition of two temporalities (the colonial and the post-colonial). Closer, perhaps, is Vicente Rafael's redefinition of translation as a technology of "telecommunication," one that brings colonizers and colonized (otherwise geopolitically, religiously, linguistically far-flung) into charged proximity—although I reverse its vector.[70]

While I grant the attractions of a colonialism embodied in what Bhabha calls the "English book"—the King James Bible translated into Hindi and making a "miraculous" appearance among non-Christian natives in early-nineteenth-century Delhi—I am more interested in what happens when a European colonizer circulates among the colonized as, say, the "Arabic book."[71] I ask not how the colonized react to the wonder of a quintessentially European text made Arabic but how they respond to the wonder of encountering a European text (like Napoleon's) that takes a quintessentially Arab-Islamic rhetoricity on its tongue, speaking *as*—or as if—Arab or Muslim. The distinction is subtle; its implications, vast. For if both Niranjana and Rafael argue that the colonized are invited to imagine themselves party to their own colonization on the terrain of translation, both ultimately restrict their hypotheses of translational affect to the domain of Bhabha's "English book"—or its Spanish version. Writing of the Spanish colonization of the Philippines, where "God's Word was delivered to the natives in their own tongue," Rafael argues that that act of translation attracted Tagalog-speaking islanders to Catholicism—hence to Spanish empire—in ways coercion never could.[72] On the tongue of the Spanish missionary, Rafael suggests, native speakers of Tagalog apprehended their language as both imperially and theologically "otherworldly," or infinite—capable of reaching to other, terrestrial worlds (those of Castilian or Latin) as well as to the supernatural world of a (foreign) Christian divinity—and imperially and theologically limited, incapable of asserting its dominion over Castilian or of rendering those key terms of Christian divinity *(Dios, Espíritu Santo, Virgen)* on whose untranslatability the Spaniards insisted. Certainly the desire for Castilian born in this tension between illusory equality and real-historical inequality approximates the desire for French or English that erupts in the Egyptian zone of translational seduction. Yet there is a difference between speaking the Castilian Bible in Tagalog (Rafael) or the English one in Hindi (Bhabha) and speaking "Qur'ānically" in Arabic, as in the Egyptian case. In the first case, the native language becomes a medium for what is clearly the colonizer's epistemology; in the second, native language appears just that: a medium for nothing more (and nothing less) than itself. The "Arabic book" is distinguished by an indifference between surface and depth. It is the colonizer who seems converted in this schema, whereas in Rafael—and even in Niranjana—the colonizer holds a magical power to "convert" the native. If the "Arabic book" works magic on the native beholder, that magic lies in the hallucination that both *the content and the form* of the native idiom possess a strange power to make the colonizer convert *itself*. Here the dominant religion (Islam) and language (Arabic) of the colonized—not the dominant religion (Catholicism) and language (French) of the colonizer—become wavering copulas of approximation: loci of the power to set power seductively adrift, to turn invaders intimates. On foreign tongues, the native idiom becomes the seductive (Rafael would say "telecommunicative") lingua franca that translates the colonizer's mastery into a seeming affirmation of the native's.

On one axis, then, Niranjana's argument edges closer to my own. What lures the colonized in early-nineteenth-century Bengal into desiring English, she hints, may not be texts of the variety that Bhabha dubs "the English book"—or not directly so—but the Sanskrit, Arabic, or Persian book appropriated by the British Orientalist, then "purified" and *re-presented* to native readers as a retranslation in its original language. She cites the case of Sir William Jones, who set out to reconcile and restore discordant Hindu and Muslim sacred, legal, and literary texts to an original state of undebased "purity," arguing that such purified Indian "translations" would serve British commercial (and imperial) interests by making India more comprehensible, manageable, and thus governable.[73] Strangely, the "India" that Orientalists like Jones translated into existence was embraced as *real* by some Bengalis of the time, as it is by some mainline Indian intellectuals today.[74] Thus the desire for the foreign (English) book is detoured through the fascination of one's own. As provocative as this intimation is, however, Niranjana stops short of pursuing it to its end. No part of the power of, say, the Sanskrit book over the Bengali reader redounds to that native tongue; in Niranjana's view, such a book really *is* only, in the end, Bhabha's "English book," for its signifiers have been refracted through English. We are to understand the sort of colonial translation it incarnates as "containment," as the fixing of the colonized Bengali in the image desired by the colonizing English, and the effect of that translation as a population of Indian subjects who are "'interpellated' or constituted as subjects by the discourses of colonialism" and who thus, "without any external compulsion, beg for 'English.'"[75] This phenomenon she dubs *autocolonization.*[76]

To understand *autocolonization,* Niranjana suggests that we commandeer two pivotal concepts from the Marxist tradition and transport their analytical purchase to colonial translation: Antonio Gramsci's theory of hegemony and Louis Althusser's theory of interpellation.[77] For Niranjana, Gramsci's distinction between the "coercive mechanism of the state" and what he calls civil society—"the school, the family, the church, and the media"—offers us one way to understand colonial translation as a complex interplay of coercion and consent. In her reading of Gramsci, "the dominant group exercises *domination* through the state apparatus, with the use of force or coercion, and ensures its *hegemony* through the production of ideology in civil society, where it secures its power through consent."[78] Althusser hitches the consensual machinations of hegemony to the coercive state apparatus itself, suggesting that the state coerces—at least in part—*through* consent: through the ideological structures that Gramsci reserves for civil society. In Althusser's well-known scene of interpellation, the ostensibly autonomous individual is called to reinscribe himself or herself as a subject within the divine Subject of the state, to recognize (indeed, recognize) himself or herself as the subject of a system that he or she always already was. A police officer—in Gramscian terms, the very incarnation of the coercive state—hails the individual with the words,

"Hey, you there!"; the individual receives this call with the response, *"Yes; it really is me!"* and in turning toward the police, makes what Althusser dubs the one-hundred-eighty-degree turn toward *assujetissement:* at once subjectification (constitution as subject) and subjection (submission to the ideology that constitutes him or her as such). Thus, according to Althusser, "the individual *is interpellated as a (free) subject in order that he shall submit freely to the commandments of the Subject, i.e. in order that he shall (freely) accept his subjection,* i.e. in order that he shall make the gestures and actions of his subjection 'all by himself.'"[79] Niranjana concludes that in the case of British India, such "'free acceptance' of subjection is ensured, in part, by the production of hegemonic texts about the civilization of the colonized by philosophers like Hegel, historians like Mill, Orientalists like Sir William Jones."[80] Thus she shares Althusser's determinism: as Althusser insists that the subject interpellated by state power—or any comparable coercive system—hardly ever fails to answer its call, so too does Niranjana maintain that the "free" acceptance of subjectification and subjection by the Indian interlocutors of British Orientalism is in effect *dictated* by colonial power.

The endpoint of Niranjana's analysis is that British colonialism, through the practice of translation, made *real* its fictive representations of India and of the Indian "begging for English books"—representations with no backing in "reality," translations with no historical original.[81] Through translation, in other words, British colonialism fulfilled the prophecy of its representation. Yet what guarantees the desired outcome of interpellation as fait accompli? As Judith Butler asks, why assume that interpellation works as Althusser says it does—or works to its desired end?[82] Niranjana herself acknowledges—in passing—that the colonized also participated in the project of British colonial translation. Something must have drawn them to do so. While the notion of autocolonization acknowledges the "complicity" of the (post)colonial subject in maintaining the authority of the colonial over himself or herself, it presupposes that only the colonizer translates the language of the dominated into an imperial idiom, be that idiom English or a transubstantiated native tongue. In Niranjana's schema, the colonized may "freely" accept his or her subjection and resubjectification on the colonizer's terms—à la Althusser—but always, and only, in passive response to the colonizer's acts of translation. The colonized remain strangely mute. Little is said of the native intellectuals who translate the dominator's language into their own. Still less is said of why the colonizer's acts of translation prove so attractive to the colonized. As Lydia Liu has argued, Niranjana "unwittingly privileges European languages as a host language (or target language) where meanings are decided."[83] "If the postcolonial critic," Liu wonders, "continues to emphasize European languages in these accounts of East-West linguistic transactions and to leave the unspoken part of that history/story unaddressed, how far can she go toward fulfilling her own promise of rewriting history? The irony is that one often remembers only to forget."[84] If Rafael's focus on the "Spanish book" is less provocative than Niranjana's flirtation with the Sanskrit book turned English, his reading of translation is more productive, as it acknowledges the intervention of the non-European language of the native in the meaning-making of colonial translation and thus adumbrates a potential revision of the dynamics of interpellation as Niranjana understands these. Tagalog submission to the Subject Spain/God appears a classically Althusserian case of interpellation by the ideological apparatuses of state and church. Read between Rafael's lines, however, and we discover that the Tagalog-speaking native saw such submission as "desirable" because the colonizing Subject sounded uncannily *like* the subject-object of colonialism, because the former spoke up close to the latter and invited it to imagine itself, however falsely, the *I*'s "equivalent"—and not, as Althusser would have it, because the *I* called the *you* to recognize itself simply as the *I*'s intended, as the subject-object *me*. In other words, the colonizing Spaniard flattered the language of the native Tagalog by making that language the very medium of the Subject Spain/God and its intention coterminous with the Subject's. The missionary allowed the native to imagine himself supreme, or sovereign. Hence the seductive power of his discourse.

Autocolonization describes the Egyptian experiences of translation and empire that Napoleon's pre-text inaugurates. Yet only partly. What remain ambiguous in Niranjana's schema, to my mind suggestively so, are the source and the target of autocolonization: the self from whom the *auto-* ostensibly issues and to which it ostensibly redounds. We are hard pressed to know which *I* colonizes: that of the colonizer or that of the colonized. Autocolonization, I would argue, must be more than just a fiction that only the colonizer produces to legitimate its rule. The interpellation that subtends it must be more than just a dynamic governed entirely by the motives of the colonizing *I*. It must also be a fiction, a process, and a prophecy that the colonized produce, embrace, and fulfill because it enables them to claim freedom-in-subjection—that is, to style themselves their *own* colonizers and thereby disavow their subjection.

If we locate autocolonization not only in the realm of the colonizer but also in that of the colonized, and take seriously the desire of the colonized to substitute themselves for the absolute Subject of interpellation, we arrive at an intriguing hypothesis: autocolonization might be a dynamic that both the dominator and the dominated engage to apparently different political ends, yet one that ultimately serves the interests of the dominator.[85] The *auto-* would then conflate into one, selfsame Subject, both colonizer and colonized. In this schema, the liberation of the colonized would be predicated on the assumption, indeed subsumption, of the very person of the colonizer. To theorize the psychodynamics of seduction at work in colonial translation, then, we must look beyond both Althusser and Gramsci.

The "beyond" I have in mind, however, is not the space of postcolonial *dissimilation* that Melas has counterpoised to interpellation. In Melas's reading, Althusserian interpellation is the assimilation of the individual to the identity of a subject—the subject of an ideological system that he or she always already was.[86] Interpellated by the state apparatus, the individual suddenly recognizes as *fiction* his or her putative individuality and as *real* his or her status as subject: his or her identity within—indeed with—that apparatus.[87] According to Melas, Althusserian interpellation emplaces subject within system and thus within a "transcendental common ground."[88] By contrast, dissimilation is "an interpellation from . . . subject to individual."[89] It is thus an "interpellation into dislocation," into the "recognition of the absence of common ground."[90] What the colonial subject "is called into," she contends, is

> an identity whose experience is one of dissimilation: *that is me, but not like me[,]* . . . an interpellation that . . . provokes an experience of difference, of being outside. This outside, however, is not a position outside or beyond all specific localities. Rather it is differential; that is, it marks the individual as different and as such leads him or her to a position of attachment rather than detachment.[91]

Given the indebtedness of her theory of dissimilation to the Martinican theorist Édouard Glissant, who maintains that beyond the stubborn nub of attachment to the local—the point of resistance—all is Relation, openness to the world, one might surmise that by "attachment" Melas means attachment to difference, to the local that differentiates the colonized from the colonizer who interpellates him or her, to what makes the colonized "not like" the colonizer.[92] The individual so implicated—

reattached to a specific geography—is, we infer, restored to his or her "individuality." The realization of the individual, his or her turn from the subject and return to the "real," renders the subject—as Althusser understands that position—effectively fictional. Thus Melas's postcolonial individual is de-annexed not just from empire but also from the aftereffects of imperial ideology.

I would like to suggest another way to understand interpellation in the specific context of the (post)colonial, one that draws on Niranjana's reading of colonialism through the economy of Althusserian interpellation and on Melas's contrapuntal reading of that economy, yet also refuses both. In Althusser's account, the speech act of interpellation takes the form of "Hey, you there!"—an interjection addressed by a first-person Subject—*I*—to a second-person object, *you,* who recognizes himself or herself at that moment as a subject (think a lowercase *i*) within the speaking Subject (think *I* in the upper case). Yet colonial translation, I propose, assumes its most attractive voice when it takes the form of Althusserian interpellation one better—as it does in Napoleon's proclamation—and calls out, "Hey, *I* there!" Such a speech act would be nonsensical in the "real" world. Yet it is precisely the gesture of translation, which (to invoke Walter Benjamin) "calls" into the original and struggles to return its echo in another tongue, to make the foreign *ring* familiar—or the familiar ring foreign.[93] In the colonial Egyptian context I examine here, interpellation does not hail the colonized in a way that makes him or her think, in any immediate sense, "*Yes; it really is me!*" Pace Althusser, the hailed Egyptians see themselves not as subject-objects "made *in the image*" of a French Subject but as Subjects in whose image the *French* are made and whose power (not subjection) the French need to be Subjects in turn.[94] For the hailed, the lure of interpellation does not lie in imagining his or her *me* identical to the *you* of "Hey, you there!" We can comprehend the attraction only if we recognize that the hailed identifies with the hailer—with the uppercase *I* calling, "Hey, you there!" That is, as I believe Fanon understood best, the colonized subject fancies himself or herself equivalent to the colonizing Subject: selfsame, sovereign.

This imagined equivalence of the subject-object to the Subject, I would argue, proceeds through a complex chain of psychohistorical associations. Niranjana worries that the colonized understand themselves as the colonizer wishes them to, but in her schema that understanding takes the form of an identification with the *you* of "Hey, you there!"

The colonized subject accepts the colonizer's vision of the dominated as fact, embraces the *you* called by the hailer as equivalent to his or her own *me*. Melas, on the other hand, imagines a scenario in which the colonized answer the call of interpellation first by identifying with the colonizer but ultimately by turning away from the latter; such is the fundamental gesture of her "That is me, but not like me." I would contend that by reading colonial interpellation as a process that yields one of two opposed outcomes—either the containment and assimilation of the colonized (as Niranjana does) or the turning-away and dissimilation of the colonized (as Melas does)—we fail to unsettle the binary opposition of domination and resistance. What if we were to redefine interpellation as seduction, as an oscillation of subject and object—or Subject and subject-object—between assimilation and dissimilation, as a series of detours through subjectivity and time? What if we were to reroute the subject's identification with the Subject through the circuit of temporalities that the arrival of empire sets in motion—precolonial, colonial, postcolonial, (post)colonial? In that case, I propose, the colonized receives the call of the colonizer ("Hey, *I* there!") with the following response: "That once *was* me but *is not* (now) me; yet that *could be* me *again*. Therefore, that *must be* me!"[95] This response translates not just subjectivity but also time, indeed subjectivity-in-time. In the colonizer the colonized first reads a copy of his *own* past (precolonial) sovereignty—hence the past-tense identification, "That *was* me"—and also reads the difference between himself (the subject-object) and his colonizer (the Subject) as a slippage between past and present, a present in which he is no longer sovereign: hence the negative present of "but *is not* (now) me," which reads rather differently from Melas's affirmative (if split) present of "That is me, but not like me." Yet in this moment of transtemporal, diss/assimilating recognition the colonized entertains the nostalgic logic—at once retrospective and prospective, to borrow the words of Svetlana Boym—that what once was could be again.[96] He or she imagines that the precolonial could be the postcolonial. This prolepsis engenders a new imperative of recognition—of the colonized self in the image of the colonizing Other—in the conclusion, "Therefore, that *must be* me!" Here the *must* adumbrates equivalence as surmise and imperative, wager and command. Power—the power of the colonizer, of the Subject—seduces the colonized to coax, perhaps even to coerce, his or her *me* from the *must be:* to predicate his or her sovereignty on the colonizing Subject. It is on the hinge of the *must* that nostalgia (return to the interrupted past as revival in the potential future), desire (for one's own sovereignty, detoured through the sovereign power of the colonizer), and thus the imperatives of colonialism and postcoloniality meet. Here seduction wavers into coercion. For the subjectivity born of seduction remains tethered to the colonial, though it imagines itself *pre-* and *post-* the colonial partum. It is, in a word, (post)colonial.

CHAPTER TWO

The Dismantling *I*

Al-ʿAṭṭār's Antihistory of the French in Egypt, 1798–1799

To the intimation that the colonized might be as much disarmed as coerced into subjection, only fiction does justice. No Egyptian representation of the French occupation better attests to the power of French self-translation to seduce Egyptian minds than a rhymed-prose fiction *(maqāma)* written, in Arabic, around 1799. Its author, the Maghribi-Egyptian intellectual Ḥasan al-ʿAṭṭār (1766?–1835)—who had fled Cairo for Upper Egypt in terror of the French—returned that year to befriend scholars of the occupation and to teach them Arabic.[1] In al-ʿAṭṭār's "Maqāmat al-Faransīs" (*Maqāma* of the French), a strangely erotic encounter between cultures erupts in the shadow of brutal occupation.[2] That colonial relation might be both erotic and antagonistic is not surprising in itself. Yet theories of empire typically read colonial desire through the eye of the beholder—that is, the colonizer. It is the colonizer who represents colonized persons or territory as erotic objects, often feminized, to be seized and possessed. Al-ʿAṭṭār's fictional Egyptian is an atypical beholder: though colonized, his erotic gaze—assuredly "male"—feminizes the French colonizer. Paradoxically, what translates the colonizing French from inimical "masculinity" into lovable "femininity" is their command of Arabic, the very idiom in which Egyptian self-mastery ("masculinity") is encoded. Too terrified at first to approach the Cairo quarter where Napoleon's forces are encamped, al-ʿAṭṭār's Egyptian becomes erotically drawn to them when a French scholar addresses him in Arabic—quoting *al-Burda* (The Mantle), a thirteenth-century praise-poem to the Prophet Muḥammad by the Egyptian Sufi shaykh Sharaf al-Dīn Abū ʿAbd Allāh Muḥammad ibn Saʿīd al-Būṣīrī (1212–94?). Although well aware that the French have entered Egypt by force and made its people start "with fear," he lets delusion cloud reason and succumbs to the "intoxication of literature."[3]

Like the linguistic and religious "conversions" of the historical Napoleon in his first proclamation to the people of Egypt, then, the self-translation of al-ʿAṭṭār's fictional Frenchman into Arabic seduces the Egyptian into submission by displacing the subjects and objects of power in a series of oscillations of pronominality and time. The atypical mode of address in which both Napoleon and al-ʿAṭṭār's fictional Frenchman speak to the Egyptian eschews the form of Althusserian interpellation ("Hey, you there!") for the truly strange form "Hey, *I* there!" In this mode of address, which Napoleon's proclamation activates and al-ʿAṭṭār's fiction decodes and "translates," the colonizer identifies with the colonized not in his colonized state but in the guise of his precolonial self, autonomous and sovereign. Here, to echo Frantz Fanon, we find a form of recognition that Hegel never imagined. By recognizing the colonized subject as sovereign, as master, before he even fights for recognition, the colonizer disarms him.

FRIENDLY FIRE?

A rationalist, religious scholar *(ʿālim),* rhetorician, and poet, al-ʿAṭṭār rose to prominence from socioeconomic disadvantage. Born in Cairo to a modest family of the artisanal class, originally from the Maghrib, he lacked the stable patronage that would have won his early scholarship wider recognition—this despite his brilliant performance at al-Azhar.[4] Intellectual curiosity—and his damning association with Napoleon's scholars, which threatened his reputation after the occupation ended—sent him on travels to Istanbul, Damascus, and elsewhere in the Ottoman Empire between 1803 and 1815, when he returned to Cairo permanently.[5] Back in Egypt, al-ʿAṭṭār taught within and beyond al-Azhar, winning renown for his erudition.[6] What he once had lacked in patronage he now enjoyed from the highest state echelons. In 1828 Mehmed Ali Pasha—the Albanian-born officer who became, in the aftermath of the French occupation, the first (post)colonial Ottoman governor of Egypt—appointed him Arabic editor of *al-Waqāʾiʿ al-Miṣriyya* (Egyptian Events), the new Arabic-Turkish official state gazette. Five years later he appointed al-ʿAṭṭār rector of al-Azhar.[7] By his death in

1835 al-ʻAṭṭār had written over fifty works in an astonishing range of fields: from grammar, rhetoric, and the sciences of language to history and geography; from Islamic theology to philosophy and logic; from natural science, medicine, and technology to literature.[8]

To represent modern Europe's first colonial incursion into the Arab-Islamic world, al-ʻAṭṭār eschewed historiography and turned instead to imaginative literature: specifically, to the *maqāma,* a narrative fiction in rhymed prose *(sajʻ)*—usually containing lines of poetry—whose tradition dates to the masterworks of Badīʻ al-Zamān al-Hamadhānī (969–1008) and Abū Muḥammad al-Qāsim ibn ʻAlī al-Ḥarīrī (1054–1122).[9] The *maqāma* permits him to explore tabooed relations to the colonizer at two removes, as it is not only a literary fiction, and thus by definition asymptotically related to the real, but also a fiction of displacement. Always an as-told-to fiction—a core narration nested within another, essentially skeletal framing narration—it calls into question the reliability of narration and of the real itself by shifting "account-ability" from one narrator to another. The framing narration of the *maqāma,* which cites the source of its story and yields rapidly to the core narration (told in the voice of the "informant"), borrows the structure of religious *ḥadīth:* one of many sayings *(aḥādīth)* of the Prophet Muḥammad, as reported by an authenticated chain of transmitters, that Muslim tradition considers an essential supplement to the teachings of the Qur'ān. The *maqāma* thus co-opts the sacred for the "profane," surrenders authenticated truth to ambiguous fictionality. For the dogmas of colonial history—its fixed truths of identity, its sharp demarcations of dominators and the dominated—the *maqāma* substitutes the seductive translations of identification.

Against the almost "objective" authority, then, of its extradiegetic narrative voice—once removed from the plot—the opening of al-ʻAṭṭār's *maqāma* pits a suspiciously seduction-prone intradiegetic countervoice, contesting the explanatory power of standard historiography.

> A brother from the ranks of the dissolute and the intoxicated told me *[Ḥaddathanī baʻḍu al-ikhwati min ahli al-khalāʻati wa al-nashwati]:* "Tuesday, when the French alarmed the people, and most of them started with fear in the streets, gasping for air, I left my house wandering [*hā'iman,* mystified like one mad with love]; I had no idea where I would end up, so I plied the byways and the streets. Anticipating imminent annihilation, I was terrified, unable to settle anywhere; I didn't turn my reins toward anyone['s house] until inexorable fate drove me to the Azbakiyya, which is the dwelling-place of that people [*al-qawm,* i.e., the French]. Delusion intermingled with my thought and it [my mind] showed me that I was making a risky move. For I

> had fallen to that which I had escaped. So I steeled my heart and fortified my pillars *[arkānī]*, and I applied my mind to this assault. Thus my reason yielded an answer: [that I would] reach security and safety, for the [indigenous] people of this quarter are at peace with them [the French] and mingle with many of them; no struggle or evil has befallen them, and there is no attack or retreat [here]. Indeed, I used to hear from people of knowledge and from those who had toured the regions and the lands [of the world] that these people were not apt to trample any except those who made war with them, nor did they terrorize any but those who battled and defeated them, and that some of them aspired to know the obscure mysteries of knowledge. . . . In fact, their hearts had been imbued with a love of all the [secular] philosophical sciences. . . . Once I came to a stop in the Azbakiyya and rid myself of this fear, I went to the house of a friend of mine . . . [who] had become one of the leading authorities of these branches of knowledge in our Egypt."[10]

This *maqāma* is set, presumably, just after Napoleon enters Cairo; its opening suggests that the French already have encamped in the city's Azbakiyya district. What the narrator describes as the "inexorable fate" that "drove [him] to the Azbakiyya," then, might seem the strange compulsion to apprehend the power of these foreigners who have invaded his city. Yet such a reading would take force for the real seducer of the colonizing process, and al-'Aṭṭār refuses to subsume the power of seduction within military terror. In his account, colonization is at once a fait accompli and an unfinished business. Its virtual conclusion on the military front surely predicts the demise of Ottoman-Egyptian political and intellectual culture as al-'Aṭṭār and his contemporaries know these. Yet in another, real sense, the long-term impact of military invasion depends, too, on its reception by the colonized: on how the latter choose to resist, embrace, or otherwise engage conquest—to "read" the colonial project. Thus the force plot of military conquest yields quickly, in al-'Aṭṭār's fiction, to the indeterminacy of seduction; the text introduces judgment only to suspend it. By "judgment," I mean the narrator's rational apprehension of the French as conquerors bent on his "annihilation," as colonizers to be feared. Such reason devolves into delusion: a delusion that inspires "a risky move," a wager on a rather different chain of reasoning that neutralizes the antagonism of colonization, eschews resistance (even flight), and reimagines the enemy as possible neighbor, friend, even (as we shall see) lover. Remarking the near-instant unhoming of both the narrator and the terms on which he should perceive the arrival of the French, Elliott Colla notes that the rhyme of *dārī* ("my home") with *qarārī* ("my decision, my sense of settledness") in "Kharajtu hā'iman min dārī, lā adrī ayna yakūnu qarārī" ("I left my home, not knowing where I would settle") "doubles the theme of displacement so common to the *maqama* genre" by "suggest[ing] not only a sense of being 'out of house' and unsettled, but also *undecided.*"[11] What ultimately cements the narrator's decision to draw closer to the colonizer, I argue, is not so much the latter's firepower as the seductive report of civility and civilization that precedes it. Ordinarily the report of a gunshot—its reverberation—follows its firing. In al-'Aṭṭār's representation of the Napoleonic invasion, however, the buzz of French presence—the "report" of their supposedly peaceful disposition toward other peoples and their enlightened interest in knowledge—*precedes* the shot that the Egyptian expects might annihilate him. The disarming word whizzes toward its recipient faster than the bullet, striking amity in his heart where fear otherwise would (should?) be, luring him to alight in the enemy camp and to surrender to his dominator's charms—and arms.

Certainly Napoleon's first Egyptian proclamation, whose peculiar form al-'Aṭṭār's *maqāma* discerns, presents itself as just such a lure. At first, al-'Aṭṭār's Egyptian defies Napoleonic dictate: he neither collaborates with the French nor stays home and signals neutrality toward them, as the proclamation urges. Rather, he flees. Yet his flight is stasis: racked with indecision, it is easily waylaid. Thus the narrator ultimately will fulfill the proclamation's prophecy for the nonaligned, which insists that once they truly know the French, they will be seduced: "they will rush" to the French "wholeheartedly."[12] By the narrator's admission, just such a report of "friendly fire" deludes him, sabotaging reason and making him fall, half-consciously, for the enemy. Under its spell he is drawn to the French, "fallen to that which [he] had escaped," even before he begins to reason that he and other Egyptians, like the Azbakiyya's residents, might surrender their arms to their dominators, who are, after all, cultured: they aspire to unearth "the obscure mysteries of knowledge." While the narrator claims to fortify his "pillars"—the five pillars, or foundations, of Islamic belief and practice—against the French and apply his "mind to the assault," the defensive reasoning he marshals already is corrupted. His mind and heart, and his religio-epistemological tradition, have been transformed before their transformation. Thus the narrator's implicit attraction to the friendship that Napoleon's proclamation promises Egypt, as well as his explicit one to French knowledge and intellectual curiosity, rapidly overwhelms his consciousness of French military force. In that state, the colonized may well cede to the invader as lover: renounce resistance. Al-'Aṭṭār uses the word *hā'im* (as in "*kharajtu hā'iman*") to describe the narrator's unsettled wandering through the streets of an unsettled city. Since *hā'im* also describes a person beside himself with love, the word injects the ghost of passion into even the framing force field of terror, the first postconquest moment.

That word becomes a rhetorical bridge between the fear-stricken colonial subject of the opening lines of al-'Aṭṭār's *maqāma* and his love-besotted reincarnation:

> "Thus I chanced upon, in the neighborhood where his [the narrator's friend's] place lies, and next to the house in which he resides, a group of youths, among them those who rose like suns, swaying with the lilt of a bride, with faces on which Beauty had dropped its loose flowing robe. Indeed [Beauty] had made the lances of [their] bodies flags when it unfurled on them its locks of hair; they [the bodies] are a banner that legions [lit., *ajnād,* armies] of lovers follow, swaying with it in passionate love wherever [those bodies] sway—and I looked at them as one in love *[hā'imun],* mystified, looks at flowers."[13]

Here the French scholars in Napoleon's expedition undergo a metamorphosis from extensions of French military force, implied by the description of their bodies as lances *("rimāḥ al-qudūd"),* into lilting suns and flowers: armies of love objects that send armies of Egyptian lovers (described as such in the phrase *"min al-'ushshāqi ajnādun"*) swooning over their beauty. With stock imagery from classical and medieval Arabic love poetry, al-'Aṭṭār evokes a conquest scene in which French force is mystified *as* beauty: camouflaged by the unfurling locks of Beauty's hair, lances become flags, and slowly the ranks of French soldier-savants blur into a single fluttering banner that beckons the eye to follow it, first perceptually (indeed, sensually) and then politically. Invoking Brian Massumi's theory of affect, we might say that the Egyptian's body "knows" its feeling for the French before his mind experiences it in cognition—although I would concur with Sara Ahmed that the body knows what it does because the mind to which it is linked has imprinted it many times before with experienced feelings.[14] Al-'Aṭṭār's narrator sees the French as he does—"feels" the French as he does—because his eye has been trained by reports (like Napoleon's proclamation) that establish affinity between Arab-Islamic and French subjects. The colonizer's beauty sways its colonized beholder to embrace it because that beholder has been so persuaded before.

Interestingly, this passage also marks the first of several gender-bendings in al-'Aṭṭār's representation of the colonizer. In the description *"fityatun minhum barazna ka al-shumūsi, wa hunna yatamāyalna tamāyula al-'arūsi*" ("a group of youths, among them those who rose like suns, swaying with the lilt of a bride"), the collective noun *fitya-tun* (a group of youths), morphologically feminine but grammatically masculine, licenses the narrator to assign hermaphroditic subjectivities to the French. The noun takes an appropriately masculine third-person-plural pronoun in the prepositional phrase *minhum* (among them) but an astonishingly feminine third-person-plural conjugation in the verbs *barazna* (rose) and *yatamāyalna* (swaying). By comparing this *fitya* to a stock trope for beautiful women, *shumūs* (suns)—a noun morphologically masculine but grammatically feminine—al-'Aṭṭār further complicates the gendering of his Frenchmen. So too when he metaphorizes the Frenchmen's bodies as lances. While the lance trope associates the scholar with soldierly maleness, it also represents him—in classical Arabic terms—as a graceful *female* body. Henceforth the colonized Egyptian will assign alternating masculine and feminine pronouns, verb conjugations, and tropes to the colonizing Frenchmen. Perceptually, then, French force is no longer a stable term: rather, it plunges into perpetual translation, its alluring "feminine" avatars continually seducing its gun-toting masculine and seducing, in turn, the Egyptian narrator's "masculine" resistance.[15] From the ranks of those who oppose the French—if even just by fleeing them—he defects to those who follow, even love, them. As the inner narrative of al-'Aṭṭār's *maqāma* displaces the frames of conventional history that initially circumscribed it, coercion blurs into seduction.

The feminization of the colonizer in al-'Aṭṭār's *maqāma* would become a recurrent motif in Arabic literature. If, according to Edward Said's *Orientalism,* European colonial discourse nearly always feminizes the colonized, modern Arabic fiction often reverses this dynamic.[16] "What we witness there," argues Rasheed El-Enany, "is a simple 'feminisation of the Occident.'"[17] According to El-Enany, "What is particularly intriguing about this scheme of things in which the East is male and the West feminised is that the power actually lies with the feminised party, such that the expected power roles in a patriarchal world order are ironically inverted in order to reflect the facts of the reality allegorised, that is, that of a dominant West and a domineered East."[18] Here he confronts a paradox that baffles him: Why this "incorrect" figuration of power relations by the colonized? In the feminization of the Occident in modern Arabic fiction—especially fiction by men—he reads resistance: a reversal of colonial logic that transforms the West into "object."[19] On the other hand, he hints, the feminized Western "object" of Arab representation actually retains the power of the Subject. In my view, El-Enany's attachment to the resistance paradigm obscures one possible resolution of this paradox. What if the "object" apparently resisted is also the "object" loved—loved precisely because it embodies the Subject? The "object" thus loved would wield considerable power over the ostensible "subject" (and would-be Subject) who loves it. Thus the feminization that El-Enany dubs "simple" is hardly so. If the feminized West presents in Arab fiction as at once "object" and "Subject," it is because that "feminine" is a fraught site of onto-epistemological seduction and translation, a site in which the making-equivalent of East and West—on the planes of power and knowledge—is exposed as the fully problematic act it is.

To this problematic, the Syrian intellectual Jūrj Ṭarābīshī (Georges Tarabishi) offers a key. One year before Said's *Orientalism* appeared in the United States, Ṭarābīshī argued that the colonized East (read: the Arab world) consistently feminizes its Western colonizer. Reading the record of East-West representation from an Arab perspective—and through Fanon—Ṭarābīshī explains the feminization of the Occident in modern Arabic fiction thus:

> So long as the relationship between East and West is, by necessity, a gendered relation—because it is a relationship of power and defiance . . . —it is inconceivable that it could accommodate two masculine first principles. . . . Yet the Eastern intellectual, even after he is presented with proof that he is a man, persists in feeling the need to prove his manhood [*qaḍībihi*, lit., "his penis"], not his culture. He is not content to reverse the transculturation [*al-muthāqafa*, lit., "swordplay"] . . . ; rather, it behooves him to desire defiance on the plane of culture especially—that is, to prove that the West, despite the fact that its cultural superiority *[tafawwuq]* is almost crushing, represents the feminine principle and the party that takes instruction in the enterprise of transculturation. . . . [A]s he has responded to the Western challenge to his cultural masculinity [by brandishing] his reputation as one who conquers by the sword of his masculinity, so will he transact an ontological union between the Western woman and the West—and it is impossible for this last to be a mere vagina *[farj]*. . . . Thus it is that all equations have been overturned, if even by illusion. And thus the circle of false consciousness is tightly closed, for the Eastern intellectual was content to answer plunder with a comparable—indeed more complex—web of plunders.[20]

Applying Fanon's restatement of Hegel to the problem of culture and imperialism, Ṭarābīshī invokes an ingenious term to describe the civilizational encounter of the (Arab) East with the world-dominant West: *al-muthāqafa*. While this verbal noun *(maṣdar)* denotes "fencing, swordplay," it not only issues from a verb form that implies reciprocity *(thāqafa)* but also derives from the very root that gives Arabic its word for "culture," *thaqāfa*. In Ṭarābīshī's usage, then, the term connotes *transculturation:* the mutual transaction—translation—of culture. Tacitly, he reinterprets as a Baudrillardian "duel/dual affinity" what others have read as benign "exchange."[21] While the Eastern (male) intellectual imagines himself a resister or conqueror of the West, Ṭarābīshī suggests, his conquest "by the sword of his masculinity" is more rumor ("reputation") than reality, more feint than fact. Fencing is a false duel with one's Other; swordplay, a mimicry of death-dealing by the sword. To fence is to simulate battle in play: as an illusion *(wahm)* that only seems to overturn equivalences. Thus the transculturation that transpires between East and West is a fraught process of making-equivalent. It is a zone of Baudrillardian seduction, where the so-called feminine always threatens to reverse signs and dominate the so-called masculine subject.

Ṭarābīshī senses the strangeness of the "feminine" that the Eastern (male) intellectual constructs. He notes its counterfactuality: the Easterner imagines the West "feminine"—the passive party in a sexualized relation, who "takes instruction [read also: orders] in the enterprise of transculturation"—despite the fact that it is the West that imparts new knowledge, or epistemological modernity, to the East. The Eastern male intellectual might prove his virility by styling the West "female," but the real-historical West is hardly "a mere vagina *[farj]*." Ṭarābīshī suggests that the Eastern male intellectual misrecognizes the West as a "woman," fails to see—perhaps denies—the fact that "she" comes armed with a phallus.

Still, however subtle Ṭarābīshī's analysis, its upshot differs little from El-Enany's. The Western "feminine" remains a pure figment of the Arab male imagination, conjured for penetration: a self-deceiving "web of plunders *[shabakati istilābātin]*"—violations—that the Arab male weaves to avenge Europe's plunder *(istilāb)* of his manhood. Like El-Enany, Ṭarābīshī ultimately understands the feminization of the West as a counterrape staged in delusional resistance to colonial rape. (Here El-Enany, reinforcing an oppositional East-West relationship, abandons his provocative contention that Arab Occidentalism evinces a "desire to become the [Western] other, or at least to become like the other.")[22] El-Enany and Ṭarābīshī overlook the possibility that the European "feminine" might also represent European Orientalism's strategic use of its knowledge of and power over the Arab-Islamic world to style itself "like" its object, the better to encourage that object to hallucinate itself the real Subject: a "masculine first principle" equal if not superior to Europe's "feminine." In other words, the European "feminine" is never simply the passive receptacle that Ṭarābīshī and El-Enany believe the naive "Arab mind" (El-Enany's term) imagines but always *also,* to that mind, the embodiment of sovereignty: the "lost" sovereignty of the colonized resurrected in the knowledge and power of the colonizing Orientalist, himself a cultural hermaphrodite, "Arabized" and "Islamized" by the very knowledge he commands. If we decouple the European "feminine" in Arabic fictions like al-'Aṭṭār's from conventional sex/gender assignment and understand it in Baudrillardian terms—as the principle of seduction and thus also the principle of the sovereign—we unravel the paradox that intrigues El-Enany: why so many Arab male writers could style Europe "feminine" despite its obvious power over them.

The Western "feminine" is, I would argue, as much the locus of Eastern attraction as it is the site of imagined domination or violation. It is loved because—as surely as it plunders the East—it attracts the East by presenting itself, on the plane of culture, both as "like" and "unlike." Colla's analysis of al-'Aṭṭār's *maqāma* complicates Ṭarābīshī's reading. For Colla, the feminization of the Frenchman in al-'Aṭṭār's text "is linked to a desire which seems as epistemological as it does erotic."[23] On the homoerotic plane, "it is the narrator who submits himself to the beauty of the feminized Frenchman"; epistemologically, however, "it is the Egyptian narrator . . . who appears master, who has knowledge to impart, power to disseminate over the *savant* initiate," and thus "the feminized party [i.e., the Frenchman] that might submit to the narrator."[24] Ultimately, al-'Aṭṭār's "theory of colonialism is to be found in undecided space where these two codes—the homoerotic and the pedagogic—diverge, conflict, and engage."[25] Drawing on the work of Abdellah Hammoudi, Colla argues that al-'Aṭṭār invokes Sufi pedagogical traditions in which the (male) disciple is "inseminated" and "impregnated"—temporarily turned "woman"—by the master who imparts knowledge.[26] As the French slide from master to mastered, he implies, their "femininity" is impregnated by the remasculinized Egyptian. This intriguing reading suggests one reason al-'Aṭṭār may have conceived the Egyptian's relation to the Frenchman in terms startlingly similar to Fanon's. Moreover, it unites, however conflictually, two poles Ṭarābīshī holds apart: attraction and domination. Yet Colla ignores the fact that the Frenchman is erotically attractive to the Egyptian *from the outset*—before the latter begins to teach the former anything—because he makes the Egyptian feel master. What Colla distinguishes as the "erotic" and the "pedagogical" or "epistemological"—the plane of Egyptian attraction (hence submission) to the French and the plane of Egyptian mastery over the French—are, I argue, intertwined from the start.

THE DIFFERENTIAL EQUATIONS OF COLONIAL "DRAG"

I would suggest that by feminizing the West the Arab or Muslim writes not his resistance to Western dominance, but *rewrites as mastery his surrender* thereto. Feminized, al-ʿAṭṭār's Frenchmen no longer appear inimical to the "masculine" Egyptian narrator but alluring enough to entice him away from his own power. Yet in rendering the French objects of an amorous (male) Egyptian gaze, the narrator also emasculates them: he transforms them from conquerors in pursuit of Egypt into the *pursued* love objects of an Egyptian *pursuer.* The act denies the "hard" military force of the French, suggesting that only rapture—not capture—has placed Egypt in Napoleon's thrall. Even rapture ceases to be the calculated effect of the French colonizer's friendly "reports," his seductive pursuit of those he seeks to dominate. Rather, the narrator's translation of the French into objects of pursuit insists that the colonized Egyptian has abandoned himself to rapture *on his own power.* For the colonized subject, such a seduction plot of colonial encounter, which suggests his complicity in his own subjection, would seem more damning a story/history than a force plot thereof. Yet it can be face-saving. The seduction plot, after all, recasts capitulation to the colonizer as agency, recasts the formula "He/she mastered me" (by coercion or even by attraction) into the formula "*I* found him/her so alluring that *I* allowed him/her to master me," or "*I* found him/her so alluring that *I* abandoned myself to him/her." It is more flattering, in other words, for the colonized to imagine himself sovereign. And that illusion of sovereignty, as the "self-translating" Napoleon knew well, is what makes the seduction plot of colonization so seductive.

As Jean Baudrillard contends, what seduces is the attraction of seeing oneself as subject, as *sovereign*—and not, as an Althusserian reading might suggest, that of believing oneself the object of the sovereign's desire. "Seduction," writes Baudrillard, "consists in letting the other believe himself to be the subject of his desire, without oneself being caught in this trap."[27] To be seduced is to be so taken by the seducer that one forgets the latter's presence, believing *oneself* the seducer—and forgetting that one has been produced as such *by* the seducer. Clothing subjectivity in drag, the seducer affirms the sovereignty of the seduced and thereby consolidates his *own* sovereignty over the seduced. That play of appearances of subjectivity and sovereignty can, as it does in al-'Aṭṭār's text, take a "sexual" form, where the French appear as feminized "sex objects" to the male Egyptian. Yet the form is symbolic. For under the spell of "sexual" attraction, as Baudrillard suggests, seduction wages a duel to the death. In that duel one subject makes itself unrecognizable—and exploits another's desire for recognition—so that it can be master.

Thus al-'Aṭṭār's narrator forgets that he is admiring his sovereign "self-image"—beholding himself beholding French "brides"—in a mirror that the *French* hold up to him. One might argue that the French "bride"—the French "feminine"—issues entirely from the Egyptian's perception. Nothing in the immediate scene of representation, after all, suggests that the French have calculated their appearance as the "'seductive' sex object" of Baudrillard's formulation.[28] I would argue, however, that the "mirror" that the French hold up to the Egyptian sits offstage. It is Napoleon's first proclamation to the people of Egypt—and the logic of (asymmetrical) exchange it inaugurates—that construct the French in oscillatory relation to the Egyptian. At once "Muslim" enough and "pro-Ottoman/pro-Egyptian" enough to appear "like" the average Egyptian it addresses, yet powerful and death-dealing enough to appear "unlike" its Egyptian addressee, the French voice of Napoleon's proclamation speaks in tones that make it possible for its Egyptian interlocutor to imagine the two faces of Frenchness ("like" and "unlike" the colonized) as one, and thus the roles of the subject-object and the Subject as interchangeable. In al-'Aṭṭār's *maqāma,* the proclamation surfaces in fictionalized form as the "report" of French civilization (the pursuit of knowledge) and civility (reputed neighborliness) that disarms the narrator's initial terror of French power and triggers his misrecognition of the French soldiers as "brides" in the scene immediately following. Thus the French "feminine" is not simply a mirage of Egyptian perception, but indeed a mirage of French *creation.* By appearing symbolically "female," in the deceptive mirror image of the Egyptian beheld and pursued, the French present themselves as "like" the Egyptian. Such a reversal of the real prompts the Egyptian to hallucinate the following syllogism: if I am pursued by the French, and the French—who happen to be my pursuers—are "like" me, then *I* could be their pursuer after all. It is seduction's logic of reversibility that is at work here. Yet there is a catch. If the Baudrillardian "feminine" is the "flotation of the law that regulates the difference" between oppositions, sexual and otherwise, we can imagine it as a wavering equal sign (≈) that strategically suspends the slash (/) of the not-equal (≠) in oscillation, the better to "bounce" power's inflection of equality—the difference (/) that undercuts equivalence (=) as lesser-than-or-equal-to (≤) or greater-than-or-equal-to (≥)—from seducer to seduced and back. Indeed, Baudrillard suggests, seduction is sex transubstantiated—through this "feminine"—into the "equal" exchange or *reversibility* of signs.[29] That shimmering copula holds out the tantalizing possibility of what I call "copulation"—the outcome of seduction—only to keep equivalence in abeyance, to assert its sovereignty, to intimate the slash of the not-equal. In commanding the "feminine," the French command the very instrument of reversibility, and thus they can revert easily to a reassertion of the "masculine" pole of power. Does not Napoleon, the arch-"Frenchman" lurking behind the scenes of al-'Aṭṭār's fiction, deploy precisely such a symbolic "feminine" in his first proclamation to the people of Egypt, exchanging the role of the (French) pursuer for that of the (Egyptian) pursued, all the while remaining in hot pursuit of the people whose persona—and language—he assumes? In al-'Aṭṭār's *maqāma,* the Frenchmen's assumption of the "feminine" similarly fools the colonized Egyptian into forgetting his "feminization" and believing his "masculinity" uninterrupted; it upholds the illusion of his "masculine" (the Egyptian never visibly shape-shifts to the "feminine" in the text) only to seduce it *as* illusion. That the Egyptian perceives the French as women attests not, then, to his turning of the imperial tables but to his surrender to colonization.

Yet if the "feminine" represented merely subjection to colonial rule, the disempowered position of the beheld, it could never motivate the Egyptian to "pursue" the French. Recall that the Egyptian's attraction to the French is not the attraction of like to like but the magnetism of like and unlike masquerading as the former. Thus, like Baudrillard, I maintain that it is not the attraction of resemblance that seduces.[30] Seduction passes "reflection" through the differentiating medium of power, which *refracts* the seducer's identity with the seduced into a superiority both denied and conceded to the seduced.[31] It is this refraction of equivalence into superiority that is irresistible to the seduced: the colonized Egyptian in al-'Aṭṭār's *maqāma* is drawn to the French not because they love him as the object he is but because they appear to recognize him as the sovereign subject *he was,* which so happens to be what the *Frenchmen are* at this moment of colonial confrontation. Since power attaches unequally to signs in seduction, like those in translation, they are not neatly reversible. Yet they appear to be, and the illusion of their reversibility—an illusion the seducer creates—is seductive.

Giving the slip to both identity and difference, the feminization of the colonizer in al-ʿAṭṭār's *maqāma* ruptures their tautology and impels the narrative toward a third form of culture contact: a seduction that proceeds through translation. Yet translation how understood? Not, to be sure, as equal exchange, but as a differential exchange that masquerades as equal, where French follows Arabic metonymically to create an illusion of totality that ultimately breaks. The seductiveness of the French lies in their *translatability* between identity with and superiority to those whom they have colonized—which enables them, in turn, to translate their would-be subjects into submission. Translatability, then, may be another word for the Baudrillardian "feminine," thus also for the principle of seduction. Thus al-ʿAṭṭār's Frenchmen transfigure *leur présence,* their presence, into *leurre présence,* decoy-presence, where we might imagine *leurre*—if Baudrillard intends the pun I believe he does—as the "feminine" form of the "masculine" *leur.*[32] As the *maqāma*'s next scene suggests, although the French decoy may look "like" the Egyptian, it also embodies the power—the intent to seduce—of the hunter.

> "I began to gaze at those bodies' bending gait; they grasped [fem., *faṭinna*] what I wished and knew [fem., *'arafna*] what I meant. So all turned toward me [masc., *māla ilayya*] and began to greet me [fem., *ibtada'na bi al-taḥiyyati 'alayya*]. One youth among them showed me a book and entered into conversation with me. Lo and behold! His Arabic was free of any accent, his expressions free of any archaism. He began introducing himself by way of several books by great notables and mentioning what he owned in the way of books and manuscripts, and he went on enumerating and explaining until he mentioned [Naṣīr al-Dīn] al-Ṭūsī's *Tadhkira* and [Qāḍī 'Iyāḍ ibn Mūsā's] *al-Shifā'*, calling it *al-Shifā' al-Sharīf* [the honorable *al-Shifā'*]. . . . At this, wonder flooded my senses *[khālaṭanī min dhālika al-'ajabu]* and the intoxication of literature sent me reeling toward him *[wa rannaḥatnī ilayhi nashwatu al-adabi]*. My attraction to him intensified as, when I said to him, 'Indeed, I am a guest who has dropped by to visit your neighbor' *[innī ḍayfun bi jārikum alamma]*, he instantly sang to me [the line], 'From [sheer] remembrance of neighbors in Dhū Salam . . . ?' *[A min tadhakkuri jīrānin bi Dhī Salami . . . ?]*. And he informed me that he had translated it *[naqalahā]* from the Arabic into his language. . . . "[33]

The wonder of hearing the Other translated into the self, however hyperbolic the mimicry, sends the Egyptian "reeling," as if drunk, toward the Frenchman. What clinches this seduction is the Frenchman's citation of a line of Arabic verse—especially from so Islamic (and so Egyptian) a text as *al-Burda*—in (calculatedly) "spontaneous" speech. Here it is not the colonized Egyptian who mimics the colonizing Frenchman, after Homi Bhabha's formulation in "Of Mimicry and Man," but the *colonizer* who mimics his subject-object: the young French scholar speaks Arabic so well, according to the narrator, that he betrays virtually no foreignness.[34] Only two "not-quites" slip out of his eclipse. The first is his studied effort to translate culture, betrayed in his hyperconscious Arabic: he answers the Egyptian's matter-of-fact statement with a line from al-Būṣīrī's *Burda,* a thirteenth-century panegyric to the Prophet Muḥammad![35] The second is his studied effort to translate language and to attach power to his act of translation: noting that he has translated that Arabic line into French, he reasserts his Frenchness and the control French now wields over Arabic. Though he wears a mask of "conversion" into Arabic—as Napoleon did when he addressed a conquered Egypt *in* Arabic and professed not just friendship, but Islamicity, therein—the pursued hints that he is, in fact, still the pursuer. Here the dynamics of translation are irreciprocal: the French scholar can strategically translate himself into Arabic, but his real work is the conversion of Arabic into French, and the directionality of this conversion mirrors that of colonization. The colonized Egyptian's "male" subject position is not, then, an empowered one at all; rather, it testifies to a breakdown of equivalence in colonialism's asymmetrical economy of translation. In this differential coupling, the Egyptian "pursuer" cannot equal the French "pursuer," nor the Egyptian "pursued" the French "pursued." The colonizer can, after all, deploy resemblance (Bhabha: "a difference that is almost nothing but not quite") to camouflage menace (Bhabha: "a difference that is almost total but not quite"): he can pretend to embrace the culture he has dominated even as he undermines that culture's power.[36]

This passage of al-'Aṭṭār's *maqāma* appears to foreground—and to interpret—the repressed seduction plot in 'Abd al-Raḥmān al-Jabartī's *Tārīkh Muddat al-Faransīs bi Miṣr.* Arguing that French and Egyptian accounts of the Napoleonic invasion invite us to rethink colonialism as an ambivalent enterprise involving both violence and exchange, Colla juxtaposes two passages from al-Jabartī that speak to this ambivalence: one denouncing the French for their violent desecration of al-Azhar, the other praising them for their pursuit of knowledge.[37] The following passage from al-Jabartī's *Tārīkh,* startlingly similar to the *Burda* scene in al-'Aṭṭār's *maqāma,* falls on the side of praise. Here even the "anti-

French" al-Jabartī dissolves into rhapsodic admiration for his colonizers as he witnesses their knowledge of Islamic texts and of the Arabic language. He is enchanted by French Orientalist philology, which not only reproduces Arabic in French language but also reproduces Frenchmen as "Arabs," as "Muslims."

> The glorious Qur'ān is translated into their language! Also many other Islamic books. I saw in their possession the *Kitāb al-Shifā'* of Qāḍī 'Iyāḍ, which they call *al-Shifā' al-Sharīf[,]* and *al-Burda* by Abū Ṣīrī *[sic]*, many verses of which they know by heart and which they translated into French. I saw some of them who know chapters of the Qur'ān by heart. They have a great interest in the sciences, mainly in mathematics and the knowledge of languages, and make great efforts to learn the Arabic language and the colloquial. In this they strive day and night. And they have books especially devoted to all types of languages, their declensions and conjugations as well as their etymologies.[38]

While astute, Colla's reading tends to see exchange—or translation—as an optimistic alternative to power, not as "soft power" itself, luring the colonized into subjection by confusing their *I* with the colonizer's. What strikes wonder in al-Jabartī is the fact that the French sovereign has accorded Arab-Islamic knowledge epistemological value by at once translating that knowledge into French and translating Frenchness toward it. In mastering the Arab-Islamic tradition, the French appear to have allowed themselves to be *mastered by* it. They not only render Arab-Islamic texts into French but also inhabit Arabic and Islamic idioms as if their own, transacting intimacy across every register: from commanding the colloquial to memorizing the Qur'ān—Islam's most sacred text and traditional arbiter of all formal Arabic style—and other Arabic texts in praise of the Prophet Muḥammad. Of the latter al-Jabartī singles out *al-Shifā' bi Ta'rīf Ḥuqūq al-Muṣṭafā* (Healing by Expounding the Real Traits of the Chosen One), by the prominent Maliki jurist and scholar Qāḍī 'Iyāḍ ibn Mūsā (1083–1149), and al-Būṣīrī's *Burda*. These are the very texts that al-'Aṭṭār's fiction names.

What we witness in this pivotal scene, shared by al-'Aṭṭār's fiction and al-Jabartī's history, is not the colonized Indian's discovery of Bhabha's wondrous "English book": that is, the English Bible, which British missionaries of the late eighteenth and early nineteenth century translated into (and printed) in Hindi and used to lure the natives of Delhi into acquiescence in their own colonization.[39] That "English book" is the subject of "Signs Taken for Wonders," an essay in which Bhabha explores the colonizer's use of resemblance—in the form of translation—to disarm and to subjugate the colonized. In al-'Aṭṭār's *maqāma,* the Egyptian's wondrous discovery of the French colonizer—indeed, of European colonial modernity—takes not the form of the "French book" but rather (as in the case of Napoleon's proclamation) that of the *Arabic* book. For al-'Aṭṭār's Frenchman does not search French poetry for a line about neighbors, translate that line into Arabic, and offer it in response to the Egyptian who addresses him. He appropriates a line of *Arabic* poetry by an Egyptian Sufi and cites it both to prove his equivalence (I speak Arabic at its most indigenous, just like you; I am not your enemy, but your friend, your neighbor, even yourself—perhaps more yourself than you) and to insinuate his difference (I may not be your friend, your neighbor; or precisely because I am, you may find no peace in venturing into my quarters). Thus, although the Frenchman's double entendre suggests that his mimicry could turn into menace at any moment, no distinctively French presence hides behind the mimicry itself. When the Frenchman addresses the Egyptian, in other words, he does not speak French in Arabic translation but translates his French presence into Egyptian presence by ventriloquizing the Arabic book, the Islamic text. What makes both the fictional Frenchman and the historical Napoleon enter Egypt so effectively—which is to say so seductively—is the fact that each assumes not just the language of the colonized Other, but his religiocultural tradition. Theirs are not texts of English Christianity appearing, miraculously, in Hindi form under a tree in Delhi; theirs are the texts (or the textual simulacra) of Islam and its literary-cultural heritage, appearing, miraculously, in the hands and mouths of Arabic-manuscript-collecting, Arabic-speaking French scholars encamped in Cairo—and in the proclamations of French conquest littering that city.

No words could better camouflage menace with resemblance than the snatch of poetry the Frenchman quotes in reply to the Egyptian's "Innī ḍayfun bi jārikum alamma" ("Indeed, I am a guest who has dropped by to visit your neighbor"): *"A min tadhakkuri jīrānin bi Dhī Salami . . . ?"* ("From [sheer] remembrance of neighbors *[jīrānin]* in Dhū Salam . . . ?"). Certainly he chooses a phrase with religious resonances in Arab-Islamic culture, especially for a literate interlocutor: *al-Burda* is, as I have noted, a panegyric *(madīḥ)* to the Prophet Muḥammad, and—according to the nineteenth-century Egyptian Azharite Ibrāhīm al-Bājūrī, author of an important commentary on the poem—the reference to Dhū Salam in the first line is an allusion to the nearby city of Medina, to which the Prophet and his first followers migrated in the *hijra* with which both Islamic time and community begin.[40] Yet he also chooses a phrase that (strategically) evokes literary associations of the "neighbor" with the "beloved." For *al-Burda* is also very much a love poem. Its opening line, in which a speaker addresses an interlocutor whose memories have returned to lost neighbors in a city the latter has left behind, follows an Arabic poetic convention as old as *al-Mu'allaqāt,* the seven "suspended" odes of pre-Islamic Arabia, in which a speaker revisits the abandoned campsite where his beloved once lived and laments both the passing of a place and the loss of the beloved associated with it, yearning for their return. Indeed, al-Bājūrī argues that what the poet of *al-Burda* intends by *jīrānin* (neighbors) is *al-maḥbūbūn,* "loved ones" or "beloveds." Even more important, he suggests that neighborliness *is* contiguity and relates to love *in* contiguity—in other words, that neighborliness is metonymy and that neighborliness and love evoke one another metonymically. "Neighborhood or proximity, which is contiguity," he writes, "must fundamentally be described as 'belovedness' *[al-maḥbūbiyya]* . . . after the pattern of metonymy *[al-majāz al-mursal].*"[41] If the Egyptian friend whom the narrator stops to visit in al-'Aṭṭār's *maqāma* is the Frenchman's neighbor, then the Frenchman too—by contiguity to that friend—becomes a potential beloved to the narrator. This the French scholar quickly realizes. By citing the opening hemistich of *al-Burda,* he insinuates himself as both "neighbor" and "beloved" of the Egyptian. Suddenly, the ghost of the French as the yearned-for beloved haunts a place near the second-holiest site of Islam.

Yet precisely because neighborliness is metonymy and is related to love only metonymically—because, as an *approximation* in more than one sense, it can appease asymmetry in equivalence—it all too easily can become Baudrillard's eclipse or Bhabha's mimicry. Indeed, the young French scholar cites only the first hemistich of the opening line of *al-Burda* and omits the second; the full line, "A min tadhakkuri jīrānin bi Dhī Salami // mazajta dam'an jarā min muqlatin bi dami?" would translate, "From [sheer] remembrance of neighbors *[jīrānin]* in Dhū Salam, have you shot [lit., "mingled"] the tear that ran *[jarā]* from [your] eye with blood?"[42] His omission is hardly accidental. The elided hemistich points, in fact, to the disruption of neighborliness by conquest: if we listen to the alliteration and assonance of *jīrānin* and *jarā,* which derive from two phonetically similar Arabic roots (the verb *jāwara,* "to be next to" or "to be the neighbor of," derives from *jīm-wāw-rā',* whereas the verb *jarā,* "to run, stream," derives from *jīm-rā'-yā'*), we hear neighborliness burst into blood-shot tears. Where the quoted hemistich evokes the joins of contiguity, the occluded hemistich rends them, prizing open the gaps that always already separated those joins. Thus the Frenchman, replying to the Egyptian, presents him with something very like Napoleon's first Egyptian proclamation: uttering only the decontextualized half-line that powerfully links him to Arab-Islamic cultural memory, that suggests his resemblance to the colonized Egyptian Other, he totally eclipses the part that suggests his menace, consigning it to a pregnant silence of the self. "Translated" on the Frenchman's tongue in a colonial context of utterance, Arab-Islamic tradition undergoes a radical transformation. A new "neighbor" has moved in.

The Frenchman's reply compels us to rewind the Egyptian narrator's self-introduction and to listen again, more closely: "I am a guest who has dropped by to visit your neighbor." Even before the Frenchman speaks, that line sets the positions of "guest" and "neighbor" adrift. The Egyptian, subdued at this point by first a terror of and then a nascent attraction to the invader, already sees himself as a triple guest. He is, of course, a guest of his (presumably) Egyptian friend, who happens to be the Frenchman's "neighbor." Yet he is, equally, a guest of the French—dependent, in the French quarters of al-Azbakiyya, on the "hospitality" of the colonizer. By dubbing his friend the Frenchman's "neighbor" and himself a "guest" of both, the Egyptian folds the French into Egyptian society—invoking the economy of hospitality so important in Arab-Islamic culture—and normalizes their colonial presence in Egypt. Ultimately, then, he becomes a guest in his own country, for French has become the referent that fixes the meaning of property in Egypt. Thus the Egyptian no longer is on his way to see *his* friend but the *Frenchman's* neighbor. He capitulates to the new colonial order, accepting the contiguity of the French and the Egyptians as "neighbors" and by extension taking the French as "beloved." Yet in placing the colonized self and the colonizing Other in metonymic relation, the narrator cannot erase the tense oscillation between equivalence and incommensurability that the very structure of metonymy implies. The Frenchman seizes this oscillation as opportunity: turning the face of equivalence—the loving neighborliness and cultural continuity implied by the quoted hemistich—to the Egyptian, he eclipses the shadow of incommensurability—the violent loss implied by the elided hemistich—to which colonization will subject Egypt.

Still, the unquoted hemistich from *al-Burda*'s opening line buzzes silently over the exchange, for as surely as the Frenchman withholds it from utterance, the Egyptian knows (at least subconsciously) that it has been withheld. Its absence flickers in the partial presence of what is said, mottling the spoken. As if sensing, in the colonized Egyptian's confused self-description as "guest" and in his surrender of the very terms of Egyptian social relation ("neighborliness") to French possession, his slippage into acquiescence to French colonization, the Frenchman's silent speech splinters the meaning of the "neighbor" in the spoken hemistich into a kaleidoscope of equally confusing—and menacing—"'identity effects'" (to borrow Bhabha's phrase).[43] Conjuring the specter of the second hemistich's tear, the Frenchman intimates that the "neighbor" he intends in his strategic mimicry of *al-Burda* is both a beloved to be mourned for his *loss to* colonization—the Egyptian friend whom the narrator never seems, in the end, to visit—and a beloved to be mourned for his *introduction of* colonization—the Frenchman who essentially has taken the lost friend's place. With an ecliptic stroke of mimicry, the Frenchman seduces the narrator, turns him astray: the phantom tear discourages the narrator from proceeding to his friend's house, diverts him from a path that might lead him back to "Egyptianness" and holds him, instead, in the thrall of a conversation that will lure him to the French. He tells the narrator, in effect, "Why visit your friend, my neighbor? Doing that will only bring you to tears—visit me instead." Yet doing the latter, the Frenchman tacitly warns, will only shoot those tears with the blood of colonial violence. For if the other "neighbor" to whom the Frenchman alludes is himself, Dhū Salam is none other than the "abandoned campsite" of al-Azbakiyya, a synecdoche for an Egypt altered by French conquest and no longer retrievable. If the narrator "revisits" it, he can only end up in French space: lose himself, as his friend already has been lost, to colonization. Under the seductive guise of resemblance, then, the Frenchman lures the narrator into the trap of his menace, ensures that he will fall "to that which [he] had escaped." Once wandering, bewildered, in fear of the colonizer, al-'Aṭṭār's Egyptian is now destined to wander, equally bewildered, in an attraction to the colonizer that "the intoxication of literature" has kindled.

RECOGNITION, INTERRUPTED

What happens, then, when the colonizer appropriates the culture and subjectivity of the colonized and strives to resemble the latter so as to better control him? To read the relationship of colonizer and colonized that obtains in Napoleon's Egypt, Hegel is useful—if only to fight against him, as Fanon does, for the recognition of a mode of relation he never envisioned. By sounding the narrator's encounter with the self-translating Frenchman in al-'Aṭṭār's *maqāma* against Hegel's reading of self-consciousness, desire, and recognition in *Phenomenology of Spirit,* we can better theorize why the Frenchman is so attractive to his Egyptian interlocutor.[44]

Hegel begins his analysis of lordship and bondage in the *Phenomenology* with a bold claim: "Self-consciousness exists in and for itself when, and by the fact that, it so exists for another; that is, it exists only in being acknowledged. . . . The detailed exposition of the Notion of this spiritual unity in its duplication will present us with the process of Recognition."[45] With the "Notion of . . . spiritual unity in its duplication," Hegel in effect substitutes a duality of consciousness for the Christian Trinity, although the copula might well be the third term—the unseen Holy Spirit—making the unity of two possible, and thus rendering his duality a Trinity after all. (No wonder Baudrillard's theory of seduction finds Hegel so seductive; the latter's theory of recognition is a theory of transubstantiation, and Baudrillard's seduction, as we have seen, is the *"transubstantiation of sex into signs"*—more precisely, into an *"affinité duelle,"* or duel/dual affinity, between polarized signs that evokes Hegel's unity-duality of self-consciousnesses dueling for mutual Recognition.)[46] Imagine, says Hegel, the following scene:

> Self-consciousness is faced by another self-consciousness; it has come *out of itself.* This has a twofold significance: first, it has lost itself, for it finds itself as an *other* being; secondly, in doing so it has superseded the other, for it does not see the other as an essential being, but in the other sees its own self.
>
> It must supersede this otherness of itself. This is the supersession of the first ambiguity, and is therefore itself a second ambiguity. First, it must proceed to supersede the *other* independent being in order thereby to become certain of *itself* as the essential being; secondly, in so doing it proceeds to supersede its *own* self, for this other is itself.[47]

If we substitute the narrator of al-'Aṭṭār's *maqāma* for the "self-consciousness" that Hegel describes in the opening line of this passage, we see that the play of subject positions in al-'Aṭṭār's text (at least initially) follows the movement that Hegel contours. Recall that the narrator begins his journey toward the French from the moment that the French alarm the people of Cairo. In this spectral—for it is not yet real—face-to-face confrontation with the terrorizing French, with a self-consciousness not his own, he leaves his house wandering, so terrified of being annihilated—lost—by looking the French in their *I* that he in fact *loses* himself to the Other: he ends up almost instantly in the Azbakiyya, in the arms of the French, "fallen to that which [he] had escaped." He finds himself, to use Hegel's words, as an *other* being, as one of the "nation" (the French) who dwell in that district, a nation suddenly almost indistinguishable—in the narrator's eyes—from the Egyptians indigenous to the neighborhood, including the narrator's Egyptian friend (the latter, after all, not only shares territory with the French, but loves and pursues all branches of knowledge, just as the French do). Here we see that the narrator has superseded the Other in the very process of finding *himself* in and as an *other* being, for he indeed no longer "see[s] the other as an essential being, but in the other sees [his] own self."

We come now to Hegel's contention that self-consciousness "must supersede this otherness of itself," a contention that enfolds two ambiguities. The first such ambiguity is the "otherness" of the self. This "otherness" is twofold: it implies that the self is outside itself, lost in the Other it beholds *and* that the self cannot be thus lost unless it has transacted what I call a *selfness of the Other*—translated the Other's "difference" (what Hegel calls its "essential being") into an equivalent of the self, the selfsame. This transaction of a selfness of the Other, which produces the "otherness" of the self, is what Hegel calls a *supersession of the Other.* I would suggest, then, that another way to understand Hegel's supersession of the Other and "otherness" of the self—or what I call the *transaction of the selfness of the Other*—is to read these as the impulse toward *equivalence,* toward a mode of translation that presumes a transcendental signified. We come now to the second ambiguity, which is the act of superseding this supersession of the Other. Hegel insists on the imperative of superseding the supersession of the Other in order to regain the self: the sovereign self, "certain of *itself* as the essential being." Yet precisely because the "otherness" of the self is twofold (the "first ambiguity"), so too will its supersession be double (the "second ambiguity"). The supersession of the supersession of the Other, then, must be both a supersession of the Other and a supersession of the self—in other words, of the very dialectic that "locks" the self and the Other in each other's eyes and *I*s, making each self dependent on its Other.

Hegel imagines the bondsman, or slave, as he who escapes this dialectic of equivalence and attains a truly independent consciousness by turning toward a third term—a thing—beyond, and getting to work. By contrast, the lord, or master, remains dependent for his self-consciousness on the *I* of the Other: the bondsman, or slave. Thus in Hegel the slave interrupts the dialectic by breaking its duel/dual exchange between two subjects—and breaking, also, the fundamental impurity of their "equivalence," in which each must turn to the other for self-confirmation. Entertaining only a thing—the purest "object"—as his Other, Hegel's slave becomes the purest "subject": pure self-consciousness. Fanon, however, insists that the slave wants to *be* master, thereby reinforcing (not undoing) the tyranny of the dialectic. Fanon redirects power to the colonizer; to do otherwise, he suggests, is to mystify the operations of power in the world, to pretend that the slave embodies an independence that he in fact does not. Contra Fanon, Bhabha would like to believe in the possibility of a turn toward a third space and thus the possibility of breaking the dialectic that immures the slave, or the colonized, in the *I* of the master. Bhabha redirects power to the colonized, liberating what he sees as the most revolutionary possibility in Hegel and turning its strategy toward the prospect of freedom for the dominated. I appreciate Bhabha's investment in resistance. Yet in undoing Fanon too quickly, I would suggest, we overstep what Lydia Liu has called the "desire for the sovereign."[48] We would do better to tarry a while with Fanon's suggestion that the colonized wish to be master—and to plumb the political and epistemological implications of that desire.

I propose, then, that we rethink the Hegelian dialectic as translational seduction. Such a model enables us to see that the colonized often resist subjection by acquiescing to its translation as "sovereignty," by *apprehending their ideal (sovereign) self in the subjectivity of the colonizer:* the very problem that produces, postindependence, what Fanon calls the "pitfalls of national consciousness."[49] Indeed, the colonizer often invites the colonized to assume the mantle of just such a subjectivity, to imagine its freedom from (if not triumph over) colonization the better to be controlled. Seduction transacts and holds in tension—suspension—two states of being: first, the selfness of the Other (i.e., the "otherness" of the self that Hegel names as the "first ambiguity" in the encounter of two self-consciousnesses, or the supersession of the Other by its *translation* into self); second, the otherness of the Other and selfness of the self (i.e., the supersession of the supersession of the Other). It holds the relational impulses toward the universal (the extension of sameness to others) and the particular (the withholding of equivalence between those others and the self) in suspension, flotation, oscillation. Seduction makes the objecthood of "Others" appear to die. Thus it deceptively restates the relationship between an objectified subject (the bondsman, the slave) and a subjectified Subject as a relation of Subject to Subject, interrupting the dialectic not to uphold the real independence of the slave, but the illusion of his independence—and thus the real "independence" (or at least will to power) of the master. The master's power, not the slave's, is the precipitate that crystallizes from the suspense/suspension of seduction.

Thus the scene of seduction I analyze here hews more closely to Fanon's rewriting of Hegel. For in al-'Aṭṭār's fiction, the *master* interrupts the dialectic of self-consciousnesses with a Baudrillardian play of illusion. To all appearances, the master refuses to supersede the supersession of the Other—that is, *refuses to stop seeing the Other as itself,* to shatter the logic of "equivalence" between the Other and itself—and insists instead on bestowing its lordship on the slave, rendering the slave his "equal." What short-circuits the fear that might secure the Egyptian's identity against dissolution in Frenchness is the apparition of "friendship"—the humanistic love-logic of fellow feeling—that intrudes. Two acts of French self-translation conspire to reinforce the illusion that would-be master and would-be slave are "one," dissolving the master's voice in that of the slave and therefore *appearing* to revoice the slave as master: first, the reports of French civility that precede the narrator's first sighting of the occupier in al-Azbakiyya (as Napoleon's "friendly" canon preceded his cannon), in which the French style themselves at "peace" with Egypt; second, the direct address of the *Burda*-quoting French Orientalist to the narrator, in which the former announces himself as "Arab" and "Muslim," nary a word of French escaping his lips. To recall my attempt to rewrite Althusser, seduction ushers in a relation that takes the form, "Hey, *I* there!" wherein the subject-object (Hegel's "other [self-consciousness]," in this case the slave) is equated with the Subject (Hegel's "self-consciousness," in this case the master). Of course, as Fanon recognized in his critique of Hegel, the very act of refusing supersession and enacting a cession of the lordly self to the enslaved Other maintains the power of master over slave. In other words, each time the French master addresses the colonized Egyptian in al-'Aṭṭār's *maqāma,* whether indirectly (through circulated reports) or directly (as when the Orientalist quotes *al-Burda*), he leaps several steps forward in the logic of intersubjective encounter Hegel limns in the *Phenomenology,* giving back the slave's self-consciousness to itself—yet returning it with "interest," for the slave is not really being restored to itself but being restored to itself as (and through) the *I* of the master, cut along the very bias of that *I*. Though the master has exchanged his own *I* for the slave's, the structural logic of seduction entices the slave to believe that he has transacted that exchange all by himself.

By *interest*—the slash of the not-equal, a surplus that veers from supplementation to supplantation—I intend, then, not only the desire of the colonizer to assert his sovereignty over the colonized, but the equally keen desire of the colonized to see himself sovereign. For by superseding the Other (i.e., by making the Other "equal" to the self) and refusing to supersede that supersession, al-'Aṭṭār's Frenchmen trigger a one-sided execution of the refused gesture on the part of the Egyptian. They trigger the Egyptian's fantasy of reverting to his "pure," precolonial self, to his sovereign state of freedom. Yet that reversion is a translation across a copula the French *I* controls: it is the (re)production of "Egyptianness" via the seduction of "Frenchness." When the Egyptian supersedes the supersession of the Other, Hegel would say, this "ambiguous supersession of its ambiguous otherness is equally an ambiguous return *into itself,*" for that self is at least partly given back—made "equal to itself"—by the Other, by the French Orientalist who imbues Arabic and Islam with sovereignty and thus makes the Egyptian self desire itself again.[50] In other words, the supersession of the otherness of the self—the reassertion of difference, of incommensurability—must return the self to itself via a refraction through the *I* of the Other, which "equally gives it back again to itself."[51] Yet in Hegel this giving back seems to transpire solely through the agency of the self, which sees "itself in the other, but supersedes this being of itself in the other and thus lets the other again go free."[52] What Fanon helps us recognize is that such agency appears self-executed but is in fact illusory: a seductive mirage that forms wherever the master bonds the slave's selfhood to his own and refuses to relinquish that bond.

Indeed, Fanon's critique of the Hegelian schema of recognition describes with uncanny accuracy the breakdown of reciprocity between Egyptian and Frenchman in al-'Aṭṭār's *Burda* scene. Here the Arabic-speaking, Islamized Frenchman short-circuits the life-and-death struggle between colonizer and colonized for what Hegel calls "the truth of . . . recognition [of each] as an independent self-consciousness."[53] I recognize you, I am you, he intimates to the Egyptian, and I do not care to be me—at least not right now. You need not be me to be you—at least not right away. In this blocked exchange, which holds one pole of the continuum of meaning-making in suspension—the oscillating "feminine"—and points the vector of signification toward the ostensible "masculine" of the Egyptian, sovereign Frenchness "disappears." The Egyptian is left with the illusion of pure—and sovereign—Egyptianness, indeed, with the illusion that *he* defines the sovereign. Commanding the "soft" power to speak Arabic and sound "Muslim"—to manipulate appearances and thus to reverse signification—the French can dissolve into Egyptianness. Yet the Egyptian cannot dissolve into Frenchness in turn; he cannot take on the language and the literary guises of French because a deeper knowledge of the culture of his European colonizer generally remains, at this historical moment, foreclosed to him. No Egyptian "Occidentalists" were busily studying French and textualizing France in the eighteenth century, as French Orientalists studied Arabic and textualized Egypt. Still less can the Egyptian take on French "hard" power with that knowledge, for a military-industrial power equal to Europe's remains—to this day—indefinitely foreclosed. Barring the Egyptian from recognizing the French *as* French—yet making sure that the Egyptian knows full well that he cannot "be" French as the French can "be" Egyptian or Arab or Muslim—the colonizer sets in motion a Benjaminian translation of the colonized. From the seductive vanishing point of the oscillating French "feminine," from which it touches off ever so lightly, the new Egyptian "sovereign"—translated through Frenchness at that infinitesimal point of contact—imagines itself soaring free. By giving the Egyptian's self-consciousness back to "itself" and superseding his *own* self-consciousness as "French," choosing to temporarily lose that self and find himself as an *Other* (Egyptian) being, the Frenchman binds the Egyptian even as he appears to set him "free." To be recognized, the French know, without a life-and-death struggle—to see your colonizer kill himself off and become you, in a consummate act of mimicry you are too flattered to scan for menace—is disarming. Thus the Egyptian's flight into freedom is destined to be a fall into love.

Seduction works, we might say, by activating the tension between the supersession of the Other, which inscribes sovereignty-in-equivalence, and the supersession of that supersession, which inscribes sovereignty-as-supremacy. It also—despite Baudrillard's insistence on its unbridled "reversibility"—attaches a vector to the initial act of supersession: a Fanonian interruption of the supposed two-way circuit of recognition. With this interruption the colonizer sets the colonized on a paradoxical path of self-fulfillment and self-destruction. I would argue, then, that the Egyptian's "fall into love" with the colonizer is the irruption of difference that, according to Hegel, must follow the making-same of the

Other. "Falling in love" is thus the attempt of the slave to take ownership of a sovereign *I* the master has bestowed on him, to rewrite a surrender to the logic of the sovereign as "pure" sovereignty, unmediated by any master but himself. Love is a supersession of the supersession of the Other because it restates the relationship between two consciousnesses as "unequal," for s/he who loves plays subject to the beloved's object. It is thus a denial of the fact that the *master* has short-circuited the dialectic of mutual recognition by refusing the slave any *I* but the lord's own. If the slave can claim to be the lover, he can all the better imagine *himself* the pursuer, the seducer—all the better believe that his own power, not the master's, has made him and the master one. Thus, while "falling in love" may be the desired outcome of both parties to a translational seduction, master and slave desire it to different ends. By making the slave perceive him as loving and thus fall in love with him in turn, the master wishes to subject the slave to his empire. Yet in the act of loving, the slave sees not subjection but the potential for equivalence, and even for sovereignty. Here one falls into love in order to affirm the self's superiority to the Other, to (re)find the self in the play of consciousnesses that forever threatens to convert self into Other in an endless series of equivalences. Of course, as Fanon reminds us, this supersession of the supersession of the Other—this dream of an escape from the dialectic—is an illusion, because the dissymmetry of power that obtains in the master-slave relation undercuts the very possibility of escape.

Turning again to al-'Aṭṭār's *maqāma,* we find that each time the French refuse to supersede the supersession of the Egyptian Other, choosing instead to fuse that Other to the self, the Egyptian responds by loving passionately. Just after he ponders the rumored civility of the French, the narrator sights his first "bride-like" group of French youths and falls in love with them; just after he hears the wondrous Arabic of the manuscript-toting, *Burda*-quoting French Orientalist, he reels in love toward him. In other words, love is the response of the colonized to a seductive politics of recognition—wielded by the colonizer, avidly consumed (to a point) by the colonized—that blocks the apprehension of difference between colonizer and colonized. The colonizer does not, of course, desire to level his power with that of the colonized, still less to surrender to the power of the latter. He merely wishes to guard the illusion of so leveling and so surrendering, the better to rule by that seduction. By loving, the colonized translates that illusion into "fact," arrests the oscillation of subject/objectivity on which seduction hinges, and redirects power to himself. What seduction would maintain as illusion, love seeks to consummate as *real.*

Fanon is perceptive on this point. In *Peau noire, masques blancs (Black Skin, White Masks)* he restages a homoerotic competition for *white sovereignty* between the black man and the white as a psychosexual scenario in which the black man hungers to "possess" the white woman.

> In the blackest part of my soul, across its cross-hatched zone *[la zone hachurée],* there grows in me this desire to be all of a sudden *white.*
>
> I do not want to be recognized as *Black,* but as *White.*
>
> Now—and there is a recognition that Hegel did not describe—who can do it, if not the White woman? In loving me, she proves that I am worthy of a white love. I am loved as a White man.
>
> I am a White man.
>
> Her love opens up for me the illustrious corridor that leads to total pregnancy. . .
>
> I marry white culture, white beauty, white whiteness.
>
> In these white breasts that my ubiquitous hands caress, it is white civilization and dignity that I make mine.[54]

For Fanon, the "love" that the white woman extends to the black man is a mode of recognition that disarms black struggle, diverts it from autonomous self-realization to self-realization in and as the white Other, the white master. The white woman who loves a black man translates a simile of apparent equivalence ("I am loved as a White man") into a metaphor of "true" equivalence, into the radical "real" of substitution, wherein the black man *is* a white man ("I am a White man"). Although Fanon does not yet make explicit why the black man who *returns the love* of the white woman might choose to do so (that explanation will appear much later, in his final critique of Hegelian recognition), one likely motivation colors his lines. It is the sociopolitical construct of whiteness the black man desires when he wishes to be recognized not as black but as white: "white whiteness," "white civilization and dignity," white sovereignty. Thus, like al-'Aṭṭār's Egyptian male beholder and his French "brides," the black man and the white woman are strangely hermaphroditic subjects twined in "queer" embrace. Though the black man imagines himself impregnating the white woman, it is only by *being impregnated* (and thus feminized) by the (masculinized) white woman that he accedes to the sovereign masculinity that attaches to "white whiteness." Hence Fanon's double helix of a line, "Her love opens up for me the illustrious corridor that leads to total pregnancy," where the "feminine" suddenly oscillates (as it does in Baudrillardian seduction) and the male becomes invaginated, then inseminated by a phallic female: knocked up by/with mastery.

In Derridean terms, the French "feminine" in al-'Aṭṭār's fiction is thus both the mimicry of friendship (the copula that suppresses dissymmetry) and the irruption of love in that mimicry (the slash of the not-equal that reveals the suppressed dissymmetry).[55] By transforming the French into hermaphroditic subjects akin to Fanon's ambiguous white man/woman, al-'Aṭṭār tears away the veil of friendship and reveals the love—the slashed copula—between two unequal "sames." The incommensurability so unmasked cuts two ways: it is both the force that enables the French to captivate (and capture) the Egyptian and the force that enables the Egyptian to imagine that he is pursuing the French, what compels the Egyptian to concede surrender and what allows him to argue that he has surrendered on his own terms. Thus, within the "reciprocity" that Hegel falsely presumes in the relationship of lord to bondsman, the irruption of love is both the *cession to* and the face-saving *supersession of* the colonizer by the colonized that I have identified with the seduction plot of colonization.

Thus, even as the colonizing French and the colonized Egyptians (under Mamlūk command) wage, in one scene, a struggle-to-the-death for territorial control over Egypt, the two also engage in an erotic tussle of translation that upends that struggle. In a brilliant departure from the classical *maqāma* form, al-'Aṭṭār deploys the itinerant trickster figure typical of the genre—a "beggar" who extorts money from his audiences by using the wiles of language to delight and delude them—in a radically new guise. Here the French are the tricksters who, seducing language, beguile Egypt into assuming—hence losing—its self-possession. Al-'Aṭṭār represents the lure of French colonialism, then, as (false) recognition before battle. Once, as Fanon puts it, the two-way circuit of recognition is closed—interrupted by the colonizer's startling "I am you"—no possibility of actuating a self outside the colonizer exists for the colonized; the colonized can only be-for-self by *becoming* the colonizing Other. Seduced by the colonizer's "I am you" into a desire to *be* the colonizer in return (*"I* want to be *you"*) and so reclaim the self, the colonized Egyptian appears to enact what Slavoj Žižek would call an *imaginary identification* with himself as the restored sovereign (an identification with "the image in which [he] appear[s] likeable to [himself], with the image representing 'what [he] would like to be'") but really enacts, once again in Žižek's formulation, a *symbolic identification* with the French gaze, "with the very place *from where* [he is] being observed, *from where* [he] look[s] at [himself] so that [he] appear[s] to [himself] likeable, worthy of love."[56] Writing in 1836 of a late-1820s encounter with al-'Aṭṭār, the British Orientalist Edward William Lane would note that the Egyptian had exacted a telling promise: "Supposing that I should publish, in my own country, some account of the people of Cairo," writes Lane, "he desired me to state that I was acquainted with him, and *to give my opinion of his acquirements.*"[57] Twenty-five years after Napoleon's occupation, so eminent an Egyptian intellectual as al-'Aṭṭār no longer could see himself through sovereign eyes—content himself with the judgment of Egyptian contemporaries—but needed the eye of the European Other to judge him: needed to view himself, to reprise Žižek, "*from where* [he was] being observed." Fanon would say that he had turned toward the master.

REAWAKENING TO THE SELF IN THE ARMS OF THE OTHER

It is at just such a turn toward symbolic identification that we return to al-'Aṭṭār's *maqāma*. Here the Frenchman's self-translation into Arabic—and the French knowledge of Arabic it reflects—lure the narrator into desiring, increasingly, the Frenchman, Frenchness, and finally the French language itself. By the time his first conversation with the French scholar ends, the narrator tells us, "astonishment over him had penetrated the very lining of [his] heart" *("khālaṭa ta'ajjubī minhu al-shaghāfa")* and "the devil of love had overpowered and mastered [him]" *("ghalaba shayṭānu al-maḥabbati 'alayya wa istaḥwadha")*. The shocking realization that he "had been smitten by [the Frenchman's] beauty" *("bi ḥusnihi duhītu")*—as the Arabic *duhītu* implies catastrophe, *smitten* must carry the full etymological violence of the English—jolts him, at first, into defensive retreat.[58] Clearly the narrator's allegiance to Egypt is at war with his attraction to the French. Struggling to renew that allegiance, he resolves to leave his French love interest and attempts to withdraw to some form of "Egypt"—if we take "Egypt" to mean a space apart from the French. Yet "Egypt" has become a restless space. If the narrator does spend the night with the Egyptian friend with whom he had originally sought refuge, that friend's home—like the Egyptian homeland—has lost its hominess. It has become a generic topos, a makeshift way station in a city already French-occupied. "I went," says the narrator, "to the place where I had arranged my shelter for the night."[59] A sleepless refugee in this unsettled "Egypt," the narrator stays up all night imagining his return to "France," aching for reunion with the Frenchman the following day. The urge to write a love poem to the young scholar seizes him.

> "Among the French is a gazelle, the magic of whose eye lodged in the lover's heart *[Min al-faransīsi ẓabyun siḥru muqlatihi 'inda al-muḥibbi lahu fī al-qalbi ta'sīsu];*
>
> He broke like the dawn in black garments, so I turned into daylight [sheathed] in drapes of dark night.
>
> A garden of beauty no hand could touch, a prize guarded by the folds of the eyelids,
>
> slender-bodied, he shook loose his leaves of hair as if he were a branch in a garden planted.[60]
>
> He saw the love in my eye, so he addressed me with a pearl of speech containing friendliness in feminine form *[Ra'ā al-maḥabbata min 'aynī fakhāṭabanī bi durri lafẓin bihi luṭfun wa ta'nīthu (sic)]*
>
> when his speech came into perfect harmony with his mouth, a harmonious beauty played in his countenance *[Tajānasa al-ḥusnu fī mar'ahu ḥīna ghadā bayna al-kalāmi wa bayna al-thaghri tajnīsu].*
>
> He hunted my mind with glances—what a wonder! The French might pillage even reason itself."[61]

Retelling in verse a colonial encounter thus far recounted in (rhymed) prose, the poem collapses earlier scenes. With a flash of poetic economy the narrator captures—in uncannily Baudrillardian terms—the dynamics of colonial seduction that play out across those scenes, describing the half-line the French scholar quotes from *al-Burda* as "a pearl of speech containing friendliness in feminine form."[62] Bringing us up to the climax of that seduction, which has precipitated the narrator's retreat, the poem's final line confirms what we already suspect: namely, that the narrator's desperate attempt to withdraw to Egyptian ground—to repossess a sovereign self unmediated by the French *I*—has failed. "He hunted my mind with glances—what a wonder!" cries the stunned Egyptian. "The French might pillage even reason itself" ("Wa ṣāda 'aqlī bi lafatātin fawā 'ajabā! Ḥattā 'alā al-'aqli qad tasṭū al-faransīsu").[63] The narrator registers both dismay over his mind's capture and admiration for the hunter whose "glances" might yet "pillage" it (*tasṭū* means to pounce on, attack, or burglarize; "pillage" concatenates these senses). He is now less bewildered by fear than bewildered in love.

Yet the French have hunted more than the narrator's mind. With the seductive "glances" of their attention to the native, they have hunted his mind's *eye,* his gaze.[64] What transpires in these lines is nothing short of the *occupation* of the poet's eye by the eye—and *I*—of the French beloved. Not only does the gazelle-like magic of the young Frenchman's eye lodge in his heart, as line 1 tells us, but the young scholar becomes, by line 3, a "prize" for the Egyptian, "guarded by the folds of the eyelids." Tucked between the lids of the Egyptian beholder's eye, the Frenchman is both the object of the Egyptian's amorous (and jealous) gaze and the subject of that gaze: the eye itself that looks. Beauty is indeed in the eye of the beholder, but that eye has a split personality, for the *I* of the beholder itself has been split by the operation of colonial mimicry. Although the Egyptian appears to behold the Frenchman on his own power, he does so only under the spell that the Frenchman's gazelle-like magic has cast over him, all the while remaining the colonized beheld. It is the French seducer who—by commanding the strategy of appearances and presenting himself as the beheld "gazelle," assuming the guise of the Baudrillardian "feminine" and confounding subject with object—is the empowered beholder of the colonial relation. His "glances" steal the eye and *I* of the Egyptian. The colonizer whom the Egyptian beholds and pursues as a "gazelle," much as he earlier beheld and pursued him as a lilting bride, is in fact the "hunter" who beholds and pursues *him*.

It is by merging with the hunter—with the position, in Žižek's terms, *from where* he is being observed—that the Egyptian will struggle to rebalance the dialectic of recognition and become a real beholder, a sovereign subject. The irreciprocity of colonial translation drives the colonized Egyptian to reestablish equilibrium by translating himself into the hunter. Thus, when the new day he awaits in the makeshift remains of "Egypt" breaks at last, the Egyptian narrator becomes an ally of the French—their hunting partner—in his own pursuit. Colla observes that both al-ʿAṭṭār's text and the writings of some of his French contemporaries "describe moments . . . when they identify with their Other, when they desire their Other, and when they become *collaborators*."[65] Yet collaborators with what object? What is curious about this scene is the fact that the Egyptian narrator joins the French as a co-Subject studying *himself* as object, as if on a split screen of subject/objectivity.

> "They took turns reciting [fem., *akhadhna yudirna*] the poetry of conviviality to me, heady stuff *[ḥumayyā al-kuʾūs]*, and they showed me [fem., *araynanī*] large books and small, the unknown to me and the renowned—all these in mathematical and literary studies. . . . They conversed [fem., *taḥādathna*] with me about problems in these disciplines and recorded [fem., *katabna*] some of my understandings thereof. They asked me [fem., *saʾalnanī*] to unravel some verses of *al-Burda* (it was in their possession, written in Arabic

> in multiple copies), then showed me [fem., *araynanī*] snatches of poetry and asked me about their subtleties. . . . One of them [masc., *ba'ḍuhum*] informed me that in their country was a collection of the seven *Mu'allaqāt*, and that they [masc.] have collections of poetry in their own language whose meanings delight the ear. Each time they [masc.] asked me to clarify an utterance, they would look it up in a precious tome on language, in the style of *al-Jamhara* and in Arabic, and translated into French."[66]

What transfixes al-'Aṭṭār's narrator is French knowledge of Arabic literature. The poetry of conviviality *(al-munādama)* that the French scholars recite includes, no doubt, wine poetry like that of the 'Abbāsid-era poet Abū Nuwās (c. 755–c. 813); the narrator describes it as "*ḥumayyā al-ku'ūs*," associating it with the intoxication of wine. Poetry in this text, as Colla argues, is a key "register for articulating desire and exchange."[67] It is literally, then, under the influence of literature, of the Frenchmen's ongoing self-translation into poetry-quoting "Arabs," that the narrator begins to collaborate with the French in the translation of Arab-Islamic culture. The Egyptian now identifies deeply enough with the colonizing French Subject to pursue his own self as *object*. In this collaboration the irreciprocity of colonial translation rears its head: as the narrator "unravels" the Arabic of *al-Burda*—the very poem from which the Frenchman earlier had quoted his alluring line—while the French cross-reference his explications with a bilingual dictionary they have begun to develop, he obliquely translates his cultural tradition into French and himself into an epistemopolitically *French* Subject/subject-object. Once flattered by the Frenchman's mimicry into identifying with an image of Arab-Islamic sovereignty in which he appeared so likable to himself, the narrator now identifies with the very point of view from which he is being observed: the *I* of the French Orientalist, translating Arabic texts for French consumption and appropriation. In so recuperating Arab-Islamic culture through the French *I*, the Egyptian accepts the colonizer's seductive invitation to restore his sovereignty—to be his "Egyptian" self again—by becoming "French." That decision to translate the self across an equal sign that the French already have slashed ends in a repossession of not the sovereign self but its subaltern simulacrum.

History would write the ending that al-'Aṭṭār's seduction plot predicts. The first French translation of *al-Burda* (1822), undertaken by the most influential French Orientalist of the nineteenth century, Silvestre de Sacy, likely depended on research gleaned during Napoleon's invasion of Egypt—on the expertise of Egyptian informants like al-'Aṭṭār's fictional narrator. Yet de Sacy would include no notes linking his translation to Napoleon's Egyptian campaign, and no accompanying Arabic original.[68] Thus he would subsume an Arabic text into French subjection. This radical appropriation departs from de Sacy's practice in his 1806 *Chrestomathie arabe,* though not perhaps with its colonial spirit. Dedicating this first edition of his three-volume textbook of Arabic to Napoleon, de Sacy pronounces the masterworks of Arabic "trophies" of Napoleon's imperial conquest—relics of a once-glorious Asia whose "marvels" Europe had now "effaced" and eclipsed.[69] Displaced not only from Arabic but also from the historical circumstances of its French translation, de Sacy's *Burda* assumes a mantle of authorship that at once evokes and cloaks just such an effacement of Asia by Europe.

No transformation in al-ʻAṭṭār's *maqāma* more powerfully reflects the identification of the Egyptian with the French gaze than the shifting meaning of *al-Burda* in the text, which mirrors the dislocation of Arab-Islamic culture by French conquest. Certainly the literary, cultural, and religious tradition embodied in al-Būṣīrī's celebrated poem is transfigured once the French appropriate it: first by using it to seduce the Egyptian into colonization, then by calling on the colonized so seduced to help them translate it. Yet what of the image monumentalized in the poem's title—the *burda,* the cloak or mantle of the Prophet Muḥammad—which al-ʻAṭṭār manipulates to chart the Egyptian's gradual translation of himself into "Frenchness"? In the love poem he composes as he restlessly anticipates reunion with the Frenchman—the very reunion in which he would join Napoleon's scholars in translating Arabic literature—al-ʻAṭṭār's narrator *dismantles* the mantle to which al-Būṣīrī's poem alludes. The interpenetration—by no means reciprocal—of the eyes and *I*s of French/Egyptian subjects and objects plays out yet again in the unequal "exchange" between two sets of clothes in line 2 of the poem, "He broke like the dawn in black garments, so I turned into daylight [sheathed] in drapes of dark night" ("Qad lāḥa fī ḥulalin sūdin faḥultu sanā ṣubḥin ʻalayhi min al-astāri ḥindīsu [ḥindisu]"). Here both "garments" and "drapes" hint, metonymically, at the "mantle" or *burda.* Just as a quoted snatch (swatch?) of the *Burda*-as-poem earlier coupled the Frenchman to the Egyptian as his neighbor, beloved, and even coreligionist, the ghost of the *burda*-as-garment functions here as the tacit copula between the clothing of French and Egyptian, which otherwise would share nothing but color. (Dressed, presumably, in the style of Napoleon and his fellow soldier-savants, the young French scholar would have worn a black coat; the narrator, in turn, standing in for an Azharite like al-ʻAṭṭār himself, would have worn the dark outer cloak of the shaykh.) Yet beneath that appeased symmetry simmers colonial irreciprocity. It is no accident that *ḥulal,* the word al-ʿAṭṭār chooses for the Frenchman's clothes, derives from the verb *ḥalla,* "to take up residence in a place." In the locution *ḥalla maḥallan,* which means "to take the place of, replace, supersede" something or someone, the verb's denotation of "settlement" accrues ominous overtones, which emerge full-blown in its sinister kin *iḥtalla,* "to occupy" a territory (as in colonization), and *istaḥalla,* "to usurp." Thus al-ʿAṭṭār subtly endows the Frenchman's garments with the power to supplant, supersede, occupy, usurp: powers against which the Egyptian's more "feminine" *astār*—his drapes, veils, or coverings, which derive from the verb *satara,* "to shield, guard, protect"—put up only a feeble defense. Like the pickup line from *al-Burda* with which he earlier seduced the Egyptian narrator, then, the Frenchman's black *burda* is a mimicry that eclipses the scholar's Frenchness and thus eclipses, in the end, the narrator's Egyptianness.

The line is a chiaroscuro of colonial seduction. For the ecliptic mimicry of the Egyptian's dark *burda* by the Frenchman's envelops a parallel, and more obviously irreciprocal, "exchange" of light. The Frenchman's appearance in his black garments—an appearance that the verb *lāḥa,* which means "to dawn" as well as "to appear," associates with the arrival of light—transforms the Egyptian into a virtual reflection of that light: he becomes the light of the Frenchman's daybreak, *sanā ṣubḥin.* Moreover, since the image of turning into light (turning "white") also evokes, in the tropological conventions of Arabic poetry, the pallor of the lover whose blood drains when he sights his beloved, the narrator's line suggests that a surrender to seduction has spurred his "conversion" into the Frenchman.[70] By turns we hear first the alliteration of *ḥā' (h)* and *lām (l)* in the verb *lāḥa* (the narrator's "he broke like the dawn," referring to the Frenchman), the noun *ḥulal* (the Frenchman's garments), and the verb *ḥultu* (the narrator's "I turned into"), then that of *sīn (s)* in *sūdin* ("black," describing the Frenchman's garments) and *sanā ṣubḥin* ("the [narrator's] daylight"). Both alliterative strains associate the Frenchman's *burda,* or "mantle," with the light that seduces the Egyptian, transforms him, and finally refracts his identification, deviating it from its proper object and toward the colonial master. Capturing sense in sound, these parallel strains of alliteration suggest that within the eclipse, or supersession, of the Egyptian's *burda* by the Frenchman's nests the eclipse of the Egyptian's "light"—of his indigenous intellectual tradition—by the breaking of a new "light" whose origin is the Frenchman's dawn. Yet this daybreak resurrects the Egyptian in a French shroud—as "daylight [sheathed] in drapes of dark night," his radiance is swathed in the Frenchman's dark clothing. French imperialism—its Enlightenment tyranny of "enlightenment"—dis-mantles him.

Al-ʿAṭṭār's mantle trope also recalls the circumstances of *al-Burda*'s composition and the intertextuality that gave the poem its title. A *burda* is a "woolen cloth . . . worn as a cloak or mantle during the day, and used as a blanket at night."[71] The *burda* of al-Būṣīrī's title refers specifically to the mantle worn by the Prophet Muḥammad. Al-Bājūrī explains that al-Būṣīrī's *Burda*

> became known thus because when he composed it in the hope of being cured of paralysis, . . . he saw the Prophet—may the blessings and peace of God be upon him—in his dream: he [the Prophet] stroked him with his hand and wrapped him in his mantle *[burda]*. Thus he was cured instantly.[72]

In al-Bājūrī's account, the *burda*—the daytime garment of the Prophet Muḥammad turned, via the operation of dream, into the nighttime blanket that miraculously heals his stricken charge—comes to "be" the poem that al-Būṣīrī composes as a prayer for his cure by metonymic association with that cure. Yet it also gains that title—as al-Bājūrī goes on to note—by association with yet another *burda:* the mantle bestowed by the Prophet on the poet Kaʿb ibn Zuhayr for eulogizing him at the end of his ode "Bānat Suʿād" (Suʿād Appeared), which earned *that* work the epithet *al-Burda.*[73] This last *burda* is less the sign of cure than the sign of recognition: recognition of a poet's allegiance, through literature, to a new religiopolitical order. For Kaʿb, who had satirized the Prophet and resisted conversion to Islam, was pardoned when he signaled his allegiance to the Prophet with this ode.[74] Playing on the multiple meanings of the *burda,* then, al-ʿAṭṭār's narrator suggests that just as the Frenchman's translation of *al-Burda* has begun to supplant the original Arabic text, so too are his *burda*-like black garments replacing the Prophet Muḥammad's *burda* as the agent of Egypt's "cure," transformation, renewal. Here Ottoman Egypt, the "sick man" of Asia and Africa, is saved from "decline" by the dawn of the European day. The *burda* trope traces the narrator's shifting perspectival center from the world of Islam to the world of Europe: he now receives the mantle of recognition not from the Prophet Muḥammad but from the "alien" Napoleon and his scholarly surrogates.

Al-ʿAṭṭār's narrator, then, glides from infatuation with the French for their knowledge of Arabic literature—their radiant appearance in a *burda/Burda* almost the same as his own, but not quite—to a recuperation of the sovereign self in the very guise of the French Orientalist, with whom he comes to identify. In al-ʻAṭṭār's representation of an Egyptian reawakening to and resuscitating Arabic literature under the intoxicating spell of the West, we find intimations of the nineteenth-century Arab literary revival known as *al-nahḍa,* the "awakening" or "renaissance." Captured in the narrator's admission that "an intoxication with literature *[nashwatu adabin]* welled up in [him] whose sustenance had long ebbed" is al-ʻAṭṭār's own activity as a writer.[75] In reviving the medieval Arabic *maqāma* to represent the shock that modern colonization dealt Egyptian subjectivity—in rewriting an old literary form through a colonized consciousness—al-ʻAṭṭār rediscovers self, story, and the Arabic literary tradition anew through the French *I.* By this I do not mean that French "influenced"—in any simple sense—the presumed (re)awakening of Arabic literature. Both Peter Gran and Shmuel Moreh stress the vitality of pre-Napoleonic Egyptian literary culture. While the declining fortunes of literature in the 1790s may well explain al-ʻAṭṭār's perception of ebbing sustenance, Gran suggests that the years 1760–90 were among the most fertile in Egyptian literary history.[76] Moreh notes the lively realism of al-Jabartī's *Tārīkh,* dubbing its style—which peppers literary Arabic with colloquial Egyptian—"a direct offspring of the late Mamlūk period."[77] What infuses al-ʻAṭṭār's style with modern realism is its struggle to reclaim an *I* whose socket the French have occupied, to re-vision a self that colonization has unmoored. Indeed, if al-ʻAṭṭār suggests—against the evidence of his time—that a "dead" Arabic literature only billows anew with the arrival of the French, it is because he has begun to reevaluate Arabic literature through French eyes. His *maqāma* launches the (post)colonial *nahḍa*—the Arab "awakening" that begins at a French daybreak—that has eclipsed revivals of non-European provenance in the minds of many Arab intellectuals over the past two hundred years.[78] Al-ʻAṭṭār himself appears to register the profound contradiction of reawakening to oneself in the arms of the Other. For what could be more paradoxical than a drunken awakening?

Still, al-ʻAṭṭār's fiction suggests that the conversion of Egypt into Europeanness will remain uncertain, always destabilized by resurgences of Arab-Islamic "tradition." Ultimately al-ʻAṭṭār short-circuits—at least temporarily—the narrator's attempt to short-circuit power and *be* French. Throughout much of the scene in which the narrator discusses Arabic poetry and other Arab-Islamic texts with the French, he recasts his interlocutors in the feminine. Yet once the scholars inform him that

France possesses a copy of *al-Mu'allaqāt* and, ambiguously, that they have "poetry in their own language" (presumably Arabic poetry translated into French) "whose meanings delight the ear," their feminization is interrupted. For the remainder of the scene, the narrator will style the French masculine. The irruption of an all-too-real France—capable of removing Arab-Islamic knowledge to both French language and French territory—shatters the illusion of a French "feminine" that seductively blurs colonizer with colonized, and thus also shatters the illusion of the Egyptian's "masculine" sovereignty. Whereas the narrator began his tale of the French invasion by ceding terror to passion, he now shadows *with* terror a passionate scene of surrender-in-translation:

> "I wrote verses for them in some of the[ir] dictionaries, and I explicated for them some of the words therein. Among these were two lines [of poetry] I had composed before, when I was in the bloom of beauty, passionately enamored, and these were:
>
> Draw security for me from your glances, which fill my heart with arrows and spears
>
> that have shed my blood even though its shedding is forbidden; for by what sin [of mine] have they transformed it into something lawfully shed?"[79]

Through the oblique register of love poetry, the narrator reminds the French that the fall of his mind and heart to their "glances" has come on the heels of a bloodletting. In rebuking the French for having shed his blood unlawfully—for he has committed no murder and thus, under Islamic law, deserves no death penalty—he rebukes them for having forced him to love them, disarmed him in their arms. This amorous reproach prefaces the parting ode the narrator composes to his beloved Frenchman and recites before the youth and his colleagues:

> "Then I reinforced the couplet with an impromptu ode that included a few words of their language; it was among what they suggested to me in their desire to test what I knew:
>
> Among the French is a supple shoot who appeared in all the beauty of [his] creation, a little moon *[Min al-faransīsi ghusnu bānin* [lit., "bamboo-branch"] *qad lāḥa bi al-ḥusni fī junūsi]:*
>
> He has a face like the full moon [peering from] under a night of clothing *[laylin min al-lubūsi];*
>
> He showed me pearls in a smile flowing with the wine of vessels;
>
> His black eyes acted on my innermost soul with the effect of wine.
>
> O heart, patience in [your] love of him; for in love lies the resurrection of souls.
>
> Union with him is now impossible, for he has no pity on an insignificant thing:
>
> I say, 'Union!'; he says, *'Non, non!'*—I say, 'Breakup?'; he says, *'Si, si!'*"[80]

The narrator's final ode to the Frenchman is nothing less than an open declaration of love to his colonizer. Here he "comes out" with the admiration his first poem expressed secretly. Describing the French scholar's face as a "full moon [peering from] under a night of clothing," he echoes not only the first poem's image of him breaking "like the dawn in black garments" but also that poem's image of the *Egyptian* as "daylight [sheathed] in drapes of dark night." In this seeming crossover of the Frenchman into Egyptianness, he reinforces the real crossover of the Egyptian into Frenchness. Moreover, he reprises, from the earlier poem, the paronomasia *(tajnīs)* he imagines between the Frenchman's speech and mouth and adds the scholar's gazelle-like eyes to the harmony: the "pearl of speech" the Frenchman uttered in the earlier poem now literally finds its way (as a tooth!) into "a smile flowing with the wine of vessels," which, spilling over in turn into the Frenchman's "black eyes," acts on the narrator's "innermost soul." The narrator injects yet another *tajnīs,* or *jīnās,* of his own—that is, an alliteration of root sounds and a play on words—by echoing the words *tajnīs* and *tajānasa* from the earlier poem (used there to describe the melding of the Frenchman's speech, mouth, and countenance) in the brilliantly chosen *junūs,* which means both "creation" and "little moon" and thus conjoins the Frenchman's radiant appearance—and implied civilizational "light"—to the harmony. The root of all these words, *jīm-nūn-sīn (j-n-s),* connotes sex, race, and kinship. The poetic economy of al-ʿAṭṭār's *maqāma* suggests that the Egyptian has begun to hypothesize one offshoot of *jins*—the "racial" beauty of Frenchness—from another, the beautiful speech of its young Orientalist representative: an *identificatory* speech whose seductive power is mediated through a third offshoot of *jins,* the form of "sexual" beauty. Capitalizing, then, on the relation of *jins,* or sex and race, to *tajnīs* or *jīnās,* word- and sound-play, the Egyptian knits the Frenchman's disarming words (which style him "like" the Arab or Muslim) and his sexual/racial attractiveness into kinship with one another—and possibly with the Egyptian's very soul in turn. However cracked the "Arabic" and "Muslim" vessels that mimic, "recognize," disarm, and seduce the Egyptian into identifying with his would-be French colonizer, clearly those vessels are not too broken to pour wine. And intoxicate.

Yet love has its limits; the shadow of unequal power under colonial conditions looms large. Incommensurability ruptures the seeming reciprocity of the chiasmic exchange of "mantles." Much as the colonized Egyptian might make, like Robinson Crusoe's Friday, signs of Affection toward the Frenchman, "union with him is . . . impossible" under present conditions, which deal the Frenchman the upper hand and position the Egyptian as "an insignificant thing." Its fulfillment must be deferred to the time and space of the "No, not yet" and the "No, not there" with which the conclusion of E. M. Forster's *Passage to India* imperially aborts a similar consummation of love between men. To the proposition of union, the young Frenchman replies "No, no!"; to the announcement of rupture, he cries "Yes, yes!" Using "Si, si!" rather than "Oui, oui!" the Frenchman appears to affirm a negative—the negative relation, perhaps, implied by the narrator's "Breakup?" But the Frenchman's "yes" might also mean "no": his cry of "Si, si!" also, perhaps, equivocates his response to the narrator's question, tantalizing the narrator with a *sous-entendu* of desire beneath its seeming refusal.[81]

Still, if the Frenchman equivocates in his reply, so too does the narrator. We must not forget that the narrator is in love not so much with the French but with his own lost sovereignty, which the French now incarnate. Once the narrator ceases to imagine himself the pursuer of the French and realizes that he is pursued by the French, he retracts his story.

> "Rapturous delight transported them [masc.; *akhadhahum min dhālika al-ṭarabu*] and they [fem.] marveled over me with such wonder *[taʿajjabna minnī ghāyata al-ʿajabi];* they [fem.] kept singing my praises . . . , and they insisted that I stay with them. . . . So I equivocated in my reply and resolved secretly not to oblige, knowing that this was a matter for which the barb of blame would target me, on account of which all humanity would heap hostility and contempt upon me. So I returned to reason, . . . and I sought pardon from God."[82]

This surprise of an ending returns us to Baudrillard's reading of what disables the power of the male transvestite to seduce. "Only the non-female/female *[une femme/non-femme, se mouvant dans les signes],*" he writes, "can exercise an untainted fascination, because s/he is more seductive than sexual. The fascination is lost when the real sex shows through."[83] In the final scene of al-ʿAṭṭār's *maqāma,* indeed, the light changes. So long as the narrator can imagine the Frenchmen as "conquests" of his verbal art, they remain, in the Baudrillardian sense, "feminine": masters of the art of colonial seduction, of the strategy of appearances that enables them to assume the guise of the object and thereby to exert the power of the subject. Yet the minute the French, still in the guise of the "feminine," ask the narrator to stay with them—to emigrate from the "Egypt" in which he continues to take shelter for the night to the "France" in which they reside, and so consummate the final handover of the liminal space of the Azbakiyya—they reveal themselves unambiguously as his *pursuers.* Their real "sex"—their real power position—shows through: their colonial maleness resurges. It is at that moment that they vanish, curiously, from the narrator's tale: suddenly the narrator recoils and "refocuses" his eye on his *I,* as if to reclaim that self as the subject of its own object, and "return[s] to reason," regaining the voice of historical judgment with which he had framed his tale and with which the extradiegetic narrator of the *maqāma* had framed the whole narrative. The mimicry of the French/Egyptian, deist/Muslim "non-female/female" opens—along the slash of the not-equal—to reveal, at last, the long shadow of colonial power it has absorbed in its eclipse. And the colonized Egyptian reassures himself, and us, that he is no fool for love.

Yet the fascination of the transvestite French "feminine" is not entirely lost. For the intradiegetic narrator of al-ʿAṭṭār's *maqāma* tells us, after all, that he "equivocated in [his] reply" to the Frenchmen's invitation to join them and resolved only "secretly not to oblige," intimating that he said "yes" to his own annexation but intended a "no." That he says something very like the Frenchman's "Si, si!" to the proposition of "union" with his colonizer while secretly mouthing the "Non, non!" of "breakup" forces us to question the dissolution of the colonial love relation with which he resolves his tale in favor of the other dissolution for which he stands accused by the framing voice of the extradiegetic narrator: his moral and thus political irresolve. Indeed, despite the fact that it ends on the presumed untenability of love between colonizer and colonized, al-ʿAṭṭār's *maqāma* repeats that "impossible" love story time and again. Within the text's inner frame, the narrator's telling of one larger event metastasizes into the tellings of the events of two separate days, each echoing the other; moreover, the cell of each day's account divides again, featuring a poem that retells that day's plot in verse. That the intradiegetic narrator's morality and judgment are suspect—doubly so within a Muslim orthodoxy that circumscribes sex within the bounds of law and forbids the consumption of alcohol—renders his *ḥadīth* in this *maqāma* potentially unsound: his rendition of colonial encounter potential untruth, sheer fantasy. Yet the extradiegetic narrator of al-ʿAṭṭār's "Maqāmat al-Faransīs," though he dismisses his source as unreliable—given to hedonistic sex *(al-khalāʿa)* and intoxication *(al-nashwa)* and thus vulnerable from the outset to the "intoxication of literature" with which, and into which, the French would seduce him—chooses to overlook the character flaws of his source and retell the latter's account of the French occupation of Egypt anyway. While this fantasy of seduction might indeed be truer to the history of colonial transformation than the conventional "truth" of force, we are left to wonder whether the forgetting of force and the remembrance of love—what I have called the face-saving plot of seduction—is also the history that the colonized subject ultimately prefers to believe, desperately wants to tell.

CHAPTER THREE

Suspect Kinships

Al-Ṭahṭāwī and the Theory of French-Arabic "Equivalence," 1827–1834

To speak of the nineteenth-century French project to teach Egyptians "language" as a (post)colonial enterprise is to interrupt conventional historiographies of Egyptian-European cultural contact, which persist in forgetting fear, remembering love, and failing to ask why they so forget—and so remember. It is to intercept a critical tradition in flight from the fact that French colonialism and its imperial afterlives rewrote Egyptian self-understanding on the ground of the linguistic and the literary. For most critical accounts of the literary and cultural transformations in Egypt that followed the expulsion, in 1801, of the armies of the French Republic and the subsequent rise to power of Mehmed Ali—who ruled Egypt as a quasi-independent province of the Ottoman Empire from 1805 to 1848—"decolonize" not only the context of those transformations but even the Napoleonic occupation of Egypt itself. Such accounts downplay the impact of colonialism on Egyptian interest in European knowledge. Although Matti Moosa, for instance, suggests that the French occupation was a potent catalyst of literary change in Egypt, he insists that European literature attracted nineteenth- and early-twentieth-century Egyptians because of its inherent "superiority" to its Arabic counterpart. According to Moosa, it was the "ignorance, corruption, and . . . degeneration" of Egyptian culture before the French occupation—not the crisis of consciousness that European colonialism engendered—that compelled Egyptian literati to look to Europe for inspiration.[1] Such a narrative of pre-Napoleonic decline and post-Napoleonic regeneration rests on colonial assumptions. As Roger Allen observes,

"Our general lack of knowledge of, and indeed our skewed attitude towards, the so-called 'Ottoman period' (say, the 16th–18th centuries) radically downplays and fails to explore the role of the indigenous in the cultural movement known as *al-nahḍah* [the Arab 'renaissance']"; that attitude, he argues, in effect dictates "our understanding and use of the notions of pre-modernity, 'renaissance,' . . . and modernity."[2] I would suggest that if contemporary scholars like Moosa choose to narrate the transformation of nineteenth-century Egyptian culture as a story of decline and regeneration, they do so because—like the fictional protagonist of Ḥasan al-'Aṭṭār's *maqāma* and many real-world Egyptians of the nineteenth century—they have come to see themselves through the *I* of the European.

Egyptian scholars writing in Arabic generally share Moosa's view. Ḥusayn Fawzī al-Najjār opens his study of the nineteenth-century Egyptian intellectual reformer Rifā'a Rāfi' al-Ṭahṭāwī (1801–73), whose translational mediations between the West and the Arab-Islamic world are the focus of this chapter, with the image of a late-eighteenth-century Egypt bathed in intellectual near-darkness: "All light had died out; there remained nothing but a dwindling wick flickering from the remote fringes of al-Azhar, which hardly gave light."[3] The Napoleonic invasion, al-Najjār contends, exposed this dwindling light—this lack—and triggered the project of Egyptian enlightenment, or *tanwīr,* that Westernizers like al-Ṭahṭāwī would usher forth.

> The . . . French military campaign revealed the enormity of the chasm that divided the rising, advanced civilization of the West and the closed civilization of the East, of which nothing remained except that wick breathing its last in the remote fringes of al-Azhar, which—by attachment to a past—was the last of what survived in the souls of Egyptians, fortifying them with power and . . . with pride in country *[waṭan]* and religion. As it revealed the steadfastness of the Egyptian spirit, which stood up to resist the French.[4]

Al-Najjār's nationalist literary historiography drives a wedge between the military and cultural impacts of the Napoleonic invasion. If Egyptians were right to fight "the cannons of Napoleon," they were just as right *not* to resist the canons of his culture.[5] Culturally, the French occupation motivated Egypt to become "modern": it showed Egyptians how far they stood from the "advanced civilization of the West" and inspired them to rekindle the dying wick of their knowledge. In al-Najjār's reading, the military occupation of Egypt was a deplorable evil but the cultural imperialism to which it submitted Egyptian psyches a necessary good. From the *huwwa* (chasm) of civilizational "inequality," Egypt discovered its modern—and national—*huwiya* (identity).

Sabry Hafez takes a more critical view. He suggests that "emergent" literary cultures in post-1798 Egypt drew not only on new European influences but also on continuities with "residual" literary traditions. Hafez argues that both traditionalists and modernists, then and now, fail to recognize this "complex dialectical relationship between the 'emergent' and 'residual' cultures."[6] Refusing to countenance 1798 as a watershed in Egyptian literary history, traditionalists acknowledge "change yet are unwilling to embrace it." Thus they insist, Hafez suggests, on assimilating change to their terms, renaming it "a continuation of their own tradition."[7] By contrast, he argues, modernists are so deeply involved in change that they grow blind to its continuities with the past.[8] Yet Hafez's criticisms of the "traditionalist" and "modernist" positions fail to identify the axis of "change" around which both turn.[9] By describing as "change" what was really a process of (post)colonial transformation and by arguing that the "French expedition to Egypt" represented only a spike in a "long and painful interaction between two cultures with two contradictory world-views," Hafez neuters the coloniality of the Napoleonic occupation and dismisses the distinctively (post)colonial cast of subsequent Egyptian-European cultural contact.[10] While "painful interaction" with Europe and "change" predate 1798, Egypt's first colonial confrontation with the modern West marked a new crisis and reorientation of Arab-Islamic consciousness. Unlike al-'Aṭṭār's seduction plot of French-Egyptian cultural encounter, which perpetually returns to its colonial frame, Hafez's account of the Egyptian *nahḍa*—like Moosa's—effectively forgets the colonial.

Yet colonial the shifts in early-nineteenth-century Egyptian culture surely were. Indeed, the writings of the geographer-engineer Edme-François Jomard, who masterminded as early as 1811 the project that would bring the first Egyptian students to Paris in 1826, reveal all too clearly that this *mission scolaire* was a *mission civilisatrice:* a direct descendant of Napoleon's colonial designs on Egypt thirty years earlier.[11] While it was at the urgings of Jomard and Bernardino Drovetti, French consul in Egypt, that Mehmed Ali agreed to send his subjects to France for instruction, the idea of doing so was originally Napoleon's.[12] If Napoleon could not establish a permanent French colony in Egypt, why not cultivate a "colony" of Egyptians in France and send it back to Egypt to claim that territory *for* France? It is not by coincidence, I believe, that *colonie* is Jomard's word of choice for the Egyptian mission.

Jomard himself—by 1826 director of the École Égyptienne de Paris, where the first Egyptian students studied—had come to Cairo with the Napoleonic occupation as a member of its scholarly arm, the Institut d'Égypte. He later oversaw production of the Institut's monumental *Description de l'Égypte,* published in over twenty volumes between 1809 and 1828. Small wonder, then, that his "Relation de l'expédition scientifique des Français en Égypte en 1798" (Account of the 1798 Scientific Expedition of the French to Egypt) ends with this declaration:

> The activities of the Institut d'Égypte were not without fruit for the improvement of the country. Seeds had been implanted: from 1812, [their fruits] began to appear. Mehmed Ali . . . summoned the sciences, the arts from Europe to render his conquest richer and greater. There was, in France, a member of the [1798] expedition to Egypt [i.e., Jomard!] for whom that thought fulfilled the most ardent wish; and, in Egypt itself, a representative of France, the Chevalier [of the Order of Saint Louis] Drovetti, . . . who also wanted to favor this land with the benefit of the arts. By this fortuitous cooperation, the seeds of the expedition to Egypt reawakened and grew, in a few years, to the point that the face of the country had utterly changed. . . . This dispatch of a colony *[colonie]* of 120 Egyptians, *entrusted to France to study in its womb [pour s'instruire dans son sein],* is it anything besides a continuation of the activities of the Institut d'Égypte?[13]

Writing sometime after Mehmed Ali recalled all Egyptian students from Paris to Cairo by a decree of 1 December 1835, Jomard dubs both the project to reeducate Egyptians in Paris and the 120 Egyptians who by then had been thus reeducated "fruits" of a colonial seed planted during the Napoleonic occupation—"reawakened" and sprouted at last.[14] In so doing, he tacitly paints a hermaphroditic landscape of colonial seduction in which the two impregnators who spread seed (France and, later, Egypt) double, at various historical moments, as the two wombs that incubate its translational progeny. To the womb of *la France, "dans son sein,"* the reeducation of the first *colonies* of Egyptian students in the 1820s and 1830s is said to be entrusted. To that of Egypt, inseminated by France during the occupation of 1798–1801, a longer pregnancy is in store: it awaits that (post)colonial moment when French-educated Egyptians—sons and lovers of seductress-France—can return to *re*inseminate it with Frenchness and preside over the birth of a translated land.

It is in the blossoming of French-to-Arabic translation in Egypt that Jomard finds the ultimate "fruits" of his nation's long-standing efforts to instruct, to "civilize," and thus to "regenerate" Egypt in and on French terms. In his 1836 *Coup-d'œil impartial sur l'état présent de l'Égypte* (An Impartial Glance at the Present State of Egypt), he credits instruction with having continued the "work of regeneration and of civilization" that occupation had begun.

> It is by *instruction,* to a very great degree, that Egypt had to march—and has marched, in effect, for the past eighteen years—toward its regeneration. . . . It was in the natives themselves, on European soil *[en Europe],* that we had to inculcate the principles of the arts and sciences. And as Oriental languages are strangers to scientific terms, just as the lands of the Orient are to the sciences themselves, there was no other certain path to take but that of immediately putting a rather large number of natives in possession of a European tongue. This meant putting in their hands the key to the arts and to science. By that means alone they entered into a relationship with our books, our lessons, our teachers.[15]

Egypt has France to thank, Jomard concludes, for "twice yanking it from sleep, and snatching it from barbarism: the first time by the force of its sword, and the second, by the benefit of instruction."[16] And in that vision of a second, (post)colonial "reawakening," language has the real power to Europeanize Egypt. The first goal of the French (post) colonial instruction of Egypt was to put its "natives in possession of a European tongue." Language was the "key" that would make France's very lesson to Egypt possible, opening the locked antechamber of the arts and then the inner sanctum of science: the space of "modernity" that Jomard significantly locates at the farthest remove from Oriental tongues and the Orient itself. As Jomard's reference to "inculcat[ing] the principles of the arts and sciences" suggests, the desired effect of (post)colonial instruction was to make French knowledge enter Egyptian consciousness in ways profound and thus enduring—realizing Napoleon's colonial dream in a (post)colonial afterlife.

Thus, if French instruction continued the unfinished work of an aborted occupation, Egyptian translation would continue the unfinished work of direct French instruction. "Civilization," writes Jomard, "has minted currency on *the presses of Būlāq;* it could continue to mint it still, even after the Turkish crusade [!]; it could do it with the help of Europeans, more interested than one thinks in [this] revolution."[17] Established by Mehmed Ali in 1822, these presses of Būlāq (then a town just outside Cairo) were, by 1836, being "fed by a swarm of translators"—many trained at the École Égyptienne de Paris. According to Jomard, they had "already published . . . 120 works in science, art, or history, translated from French and Italian into Turkish or Arabic."[18] Understanding Egyptian translations as the "currency" that a tacitly

French civilization has "minted," Jomard implicates these translations in an economy of unequal exchange, whereby "civilization"—French-defined—determines meaning for Egypt and puts that meaning into circulation among an ever-widening circle of Egyptians. He hints that this currency could put Egypt within the orbit of French rather than Ottoman imperial influence, beyond the reach of a Turkish power to which he deftly reassigns any lingering Egyptian memory of Europe's *Christian* crusades. The ultimate power of French empire, he suggests, lies not in the use-value of the sword, which ceased to govern Egypt in 1801, but in the ability to lure Egypt into an irreciprocal economy of colonial translation, in which exchange-value inheres on only one side of the copula—that of the French knowledge embodied in "our books, our lessons, our teachers" and transported, in Arabic especially, to growing Egyptian readerships.

TRANSLATING THE SOVEREIGN SELF INTO SUBALTERNITY

The first modern Arabic account of European life, *Takhlīṣ al-Ibrīz fī Talkhīṣ Bārīz, aw al-Dīwān al-Nafīs fī Īwān Bārīs* (Extracting Pure Gold to Render Paris, Briefly Told; or, the Anthology So Precious on the Arcaded Hall of Paris), was published at Būlāq in 1834.[19] Although not, strictly speaking, an interlingual translation of the sort to which Jomard's *Coup-d'œil* refers, it was among the most valuable currency that French "civilization," through its (post)colonial project of Egyptian re-education, minted there. Its author, al-Ṭahṭāwī, had traveled to France in 1826 as a religious guide *(imām)* to that first *colonie* of Ottoman, Levantine, and Egyptian students for which both Jomard and Mehmed Ali cherished high hopes—Jomard for the resurrection of French empire, Mehmed Ali for the consolidation of his own.[20] Fresh from an Islamic intellectual formation at Cairo's al-Azhar, al-Ṭahṭāwī was a student of al-'Aṭṭār, and it was at al-'Aṭṭār's recommendation that he was sent to France. Though not an "official" member of the *mission scolaire,* al-Ṭahṭāwī became an avid student of French; by the time he left Paris in 1831, he had translated at least twelve French-language selections in literature, history, philosophy, geography, science, and technology.[21] By 1837 Mehmed Ali had appointed him head of the School of Languages (Madrasat al-Alsun) in Cairo, then, in 1841, head of a bureau of translation attached to the school.[22] Maḥmūd Fahmī Ḥijāzī dubs this school the brainchild of al-Ṭahṭāwī, who patterned it on the École des Langues

Orientales in Paris.[23] After the death of Mehmed Ali, al-Ṭahṭāwī would fall out of official favor; in 1850, during the reign of Khedive 'Abbās I—Mehmed Ali's grandson and successor—the School of Languages was closed, and he was exiled to the Sudan.[24] There, he would complete his only large-scale literary translation: an Arabic rendering of François de Salignac de La Mothe-Fénelon's *Les Aventures de Télémaque, fils d'Ulysse* (1699), first published in Beirut in 1867 as *Mawāqi' al-Aflāk fī Waqā'i' Tilīmāk* (Orbits of the Stars in Telemachus's Accidents [of Afar]).[25] The reigns of Khedives Sa'īd and Ismā'īl would restore al-Ṭahṭāwī to prominence in the cultural politics of a Westernizing Egypt. From his return to Egypt in 1854 to his death in 1873, he would teach translation, continue to translate French texts, and oversee the translation of many more. Among these was the translation of the Code Napoléon into Arabic (1866), which introduced a French-inspired system of civil law into Egypt that survives to this day. Al-Ṭahṭāwī also helped develop a new system of government schools. His last major writings of the 1860s and 1870s, *Manāhij al-Albāb al-Miṣriyya fī Mabāhij al-Ādāb al-'Aṣriyya* (The Paths of Egyptian Hearts in the Joys of the Contemporary Arts) and *al-Murshid al-Amīn li al-Banāt wa al-Banīn* (Guiding Truths for Girls and Youths), expounded a transformative vision for Egyptian education that would inspire the Westernizing "reforms" of the late nineteenth and early twentieth century.[26] In his myriad capacities, then, al-Ṭahṭāwī catalyzed what liberal nationalist historiography would call Egypt's intellectual "renaissance" in this period.[27]

Like his translations, al-Ṭahṭāwī's *Takhlīṣ al-Ibrīz* is a work of double provenance. On the one hand, the book responds to early-nineteenth-century Islamic and Ottoman-Egyptian imperatives of knowledge and power. Al-Ṭahṭāwī addresses himself both to his Azharite mentor al-'Aṭṭār—who had urged him to write the book before he left for France—and to his Ottoman ruler and patron Mehmed Ali, who sought more instrumental insights into the European power he wished to rival.[28] On the other hand, the book responds to a French desire to educate Egyptians in the ways of "civilization" and thereby reattach them to French empire in the wake of Napoleon's failed occupation; it enacts Jomard's plan to extend the severed arm of that occupation with the prosthesis of imperial education. Al-Ṭahṭāwī submitted this text, after all, in partial fulfillment of the requirements for his certification as a French-Arabic translator by the École Égyptienne de Paris. That final examination was "graded" by none other than Jomard, along with a seven-member jury that Jomard convened.[29] *Takhlīṣ al-Ibrīz* is thus far more than a rich account of five years of study in Paris. Interpreting post-Napoleonic French society for an Arabic-speaking readership, it presents a detailed ethnography of French letters, science, political and cultural institutions, mores, and habits of everyday life. Ḥijāzī contends that *Takhlīṣ al-Ibrīz* is al-Ṭahṭāwī's most important work, as it staged—for the first time in Arabic—a conscious comparison of French and Egyptian actuality.[30] Most crucially, I would argue, the text is a translational revelation of the complex psychodynamics of East-West cultural encounter in an era of European colonial expansion. For *Takhlīṣ al-Ibrīz* not only translates "French" culture into "Arabic" under clearly (post)colonial conditions of unequal exchange but roots that act of cultural transport in a theory of interlingual translation and gestures to the colonial seductions that engendered that theory.

Some commentators on al-Ṭahṭāwī's translational *œuvre* suggest that his interest in French works, when not driven by Mehmed Ali's investments in military and technical knowledge, veered toward the historical and the "utilitarian." Moosa, for one, argues that since most of the works that al-Ṭahṭāwī and his students translated were "military and scientific treatises, designed to serve Muhammad Ali's purpose in creating a modern, strong Egypt, they had no immediate effect on Arabic literature."[31] I would suggest that we turn the tables and ask how al-Ṭahṭāwī's early engagements with language and literature in Paris—be these his reading of French works of literature or literary criticism, his exposure to the writings of French Orientalists in Arabic and about Arabic literature, or his first translation from French, a translation of a literary text—conditioned his translations of the military, the scientific, or the historical into Egypt, and thus also the epistemological transformations that spurred the reinvention of Arabic literature, over the next century, as a fundamentally *comparative* literature. Reassessing the connection of cultural to material decolonization in postindependence African societies, Olakunle George has argued that African literature often prepares "the ground for material (economic-technical) advancement."[32] "If the hard sciences are sponsored by the often unexamined lure of what is called *technology transfer,*" George writes,

> the soft sciences operate on the strength of a corresponding passion. That passion aims to set in place a conducive theoretical-discursive atmosphere, the idea being that the desired concrete-political march towards technologization and the other promises and markers of modernity require an appropriate backcloth in the humanities and social sciences.[33]

George's acute observation that "soft" sciences like literature and the humanities weave the "backcloth" that supports the introduction of the "hard" sciences of modernity applies not just to postindependence African culture in the late twentieth century but also to the (post)colonial Egyptian context of the early nineteenth century. Here too literary and epistemic translation—and the attendant "collective psychic reconstruction" they perform, to borrow George's phrase—subtend "technology transfer."[34]

For it is on the ground of linguistic and literary translatability, I argue, that *Takhlīṣ al-Ibrīz* decides Europe's potential to dominate Arab-Islamic culture. What first unsettles al-Ṭahṭāwī's belief in the primacy of Arab-Islamic culture, in fact, is his seduction by the "Egyptian" French of the Levantine-Egyptian poet and scholar Joseph Agoub (Ya'qūb or 'Ajjūb; 1795–1832) and by the "French" Arabic of the prominent French Orientalist Silvestre de Sacy (1758–1838). Agoub codirected, with Jomard, the École Égyptienne de Paris and was one of al-Ṭahṭāwī's most influential French teachers there; de Sacy, in turn, befriended al-Ṭahṭāwī in Paris, reviewed (and praised) his *Takhlīṣ al-Ibrīz,* and on that basis recommended his certification as a translator.[35] From his encounters with the translational writings and personalities of Agoub, de Sacy, and others, al-Ṭahṭāwī derives a theory of translation that presumes an unproblematic reciprocity and commensurability between languages. Musing that the kinship of tongues in a deeper "protolanguage" makes every world language *inherently* transparent to a person well versed in any other, he dissolves the boundaries separating French culture from his own and plunges into a vertiginous process of self-revaluation palpable in the very rhythms of his prose. Arabic becomes increasingly "exchangeable" with any other tongue, and thus too easily traded for the former colonizer's French. Given its issue from, and potential mystification of, the clash of unequal powers under (post)colonial conditions, this equalizing gesture is a troubling translation of sovereignty into subalternity.

In *Takhlīṣ al-Ibrīz,* al-Ṭahṭāwī receives French culture with fascination and repulsion, openness and ambivalence. To a French "secular" reason that threatens to engulf him, he opposes an Arab-Islamic counterknowledge that insists on the unity of reason and belief. In his earliest discussions of French philosophy, he maintains that its "disbelieving" tendencies defy reason and that its propositions, therefore, constitute a form of *un*reason.[36] Entrusted with the spiritual conscience of a mission that Mehmed Ali had ordered to mine French military and technical knowledge for Egyptian application, al-Ṭahṭāwī writes as a warner.

He predicts with uncanny accuracy that Egyptians would never learn enough French to import the "secrets of machines" into Egypt without importing also the seductions of French thought.

> It is well known that knowledge of the secrets of machines is the most powerful support for industries; however, [the French] have [injected], in the philosophical sciences, erroneous and misleading "fillers" in contradiction to all divine books, and on these they bring evidence to bear that is difficult for a person to refute. There will come to us many of their [heterodox] innovations; of their absurdity we will be forewarned, God—may He be exalted—willing.[37]

Clearly al-Ṭahṭāwī sees little threat to the ontology and epistemology of the Egyptian subject in French industrial ingenuity; philosophical "innovations," not technological ones, worry him most. However vehemently he might discredit those "innovations" as *bida'*—that is, as heterodox deviations from the sources of Islam—he senses their attractive power and, more important still, locates that power in the language of their expression.

> Philosophical works are altogether filled with many of these innovations *[bida']*. . . . Thus it is incumbent upon one who wishes to delve into the language of the French, which includes something of philosophy, to acquire a solid grasp of the Book [i.e., the Qur'ān] and the teachings of the Prophet Muḥammad *[al-sunna]*, so that he will not become arrogant by this [study of French], nor slacken in his belief—otherwise his certainty will be lost.[38]

Between the lines of this passage, the French language—inseparable from French ideas, since, as al-Ṭahṭāwī astutely remarks, language itself "includes something of philosophy"—emerges as an arch-seducer, tempting the Egyptian who masters it into the abyss of lost belief. If the Egyptian does not arm himself with knowledge of the Arab-Islamic tradition before confronting the lure of French, al-Ṭahṭāwī argues, "his [religious] certainty will be lost" *("ḍā'a yaqīnuhu")*. Coming from an Azharite, this confession is startling. To be sure, al-Ṭahṭāwī is defusing the censure of potential detractors; he suggests that his religious foundations are too strong to be shaken by the philosophical heterodoxies into which French lures the unwitting Muslim. Yet the notion that a Muslim's faith could be lost to those heterodoxies, coupled with his admission that the French supply almost irrefutable evidence for anti-religious claims, intimates the erosion of al-Ṭahṭāwī's Islamic "fortifications."[39] What French language and ideas promote in the psyche of the Muslim who studies them, al-Ṭahṭāwī suggests, is a disidentification with Arab-Islamic epistemes, on the one hand, and a misidentification with French ways of knowing, on the other.

Yet al-Ṭahṭāwī, in the end, embraces the value of French knowledge, however equivocally. Having warned of the danger of taking French philosophy as reason, he reestablishes equilibrium with two lines of poetry "combining praise [of Paris] with censure." The rhetorical question he poses in those lines straddles two faces of a paradox.

> Is there any place like Paris, where the suns of knowledge never set
> and the night of unbelief gives way to no morning? Truly, this is strange![40]

In the first, al-Ṭahṭāwī commends the unflagging spirit of inquiry he notes everywhere in Paris; in the second, he quenches the radiance of French "enlightenment" by reminding us that it coexists with "the night of unbelief," from which no sun, presumably, can rise. Knowledge and belief are no longer fundamentally inseparable. Here a diurnal cycle of knowledge that never surrenders to night, on the one hand, and a nocturnal one of unbelief that never gives way to morning, on the other, share a single temporality. Neither trumps the other. Al-Ṭahṭāwī's parting musing—"Truly, this is strange!"—holds, in suspension, the oxymoronic marriage of knowledge and unbelief that Paris embodies. He recognizes the possible value of French knowledge, however "strange" its exclusion of belief might appear to his Azharite eyes.

To transact a comparison between an "unbelieving" French knowledge and a classical Arab-Islamic epistemology that assumes no necessary separation between belief and reason, al-Ṭahṭāwī must reattach both French and Arabic to a new system of belief, decoupled from religious faith but no less "theological" in its universalism. Such a system must forget not only the epistemological chasm ("the night of unbelief") that obstructs the colonial project of French "enlightenment"—the resistant native particularity that blocks the "light" of the colonial universal from attaining its target—but also the geopolitical chasm that divides al-Ṭahṭāwī's Arabic from Jomard's French. The translational zone of language—especially language as apprehended in the literary—supplies that missing system. In *La République mondiale des lettres (The World Republic of Letters)*, Pascale Casanova argues that "literary belief obscures the very mechanism of literary domination."[41] For Casanova, the "belief" in question is the conviction held by many writers that the field of world literature is equal—however geopolitically and economically unequal the world may be—and that its writers, translators, and readers traffic in a market of equal opportunity and equal exchange. This ostensibly free market of equalities roughly corresponds to the universal sphere of the "human," composed of individual humans unmarked and thus eminently exchangeable: a world in which it is possible to write and to translate, to read and be translated, to love and be loved in literary space with no political strings attached. According to Casanova, this seeming order of equivalences masks the fact that certain centers of global literary power determine the relative value of more "peripheral" literatures, pronouncing these "universal" insofar as they hew to the dominant "standard" of modernity: its "Greenwich meridian."[42] This process Casanova calls *consecration*. Whenever a subaltern language or literature is recognized by a dominant one, she contends, that recognition sacralizes the subaltern, imbuing it with the quasi-divine aura of the dominant standard. Such a standard is precisely the "theological" universal of language that replaces religious faith as the arbiter (or avatar) of translingual reason for al-Ṭahṭāwī, although in the case I examine here consecration is not merely a process in which the French "dominant" recognizes the Egyptian "subaltern"; it is one in which Egyptian "subalterns" like al-Ṭahṭāwī struggle to discover the terms on which they might recognize the French "dominant."

Consecration, then, is a politics of recognition in which certain particulars—those that have assumed the mantle of the universal and in so doing declared themselves less "particular" than others—accord universality to other particulars insofar as the latter resemble themselves. As an operation that transmutes difference into equivalence, translation is for Casanova perhaps the most important way in which the putative "centers" of the literary universal consecrate the world's so-called literary peripheries.[43] While the unequal politics of global recognition tip the scales of translation, unbalancing what both the dominant and the dominated (for different reasons) falsely project as a "pure" exchange between languages, the "apparent neutrality" of translation mystifies this inequality. It encourages the subaltern translator in particular to *believe* in the depoliticized fantasy of pure exchangeability. Casanova rightly notes that subaltern translators who transport the literatures of the dominant into their own "seek to introduce into their language the modernity of the center (whose domination they perpetuate by doing just this)," thereby playing "an essential role in the process of unifying literary space."[44] Although she does not pursue her argument to its logical conclusion, she implies that the universal of literary modernity is not simply "decreed" in the hegemonic West but also (if from a vantage point of disadvantage) transacted by the dominated non-West. It owes at least some measure of its world dominance to the subaltern who translates it.

Yet Casanova holds stubbornly to a center-periphery model in which the center dictates the universal with little "say" from the dominated. Moreover, she unabashedly locates the center of global literary modernity in Paris, claiming that historical evidence has led her to that conclusion. "Paris," she writes, "is not only the capital of the literary world. It is also . . . *the chief place of consecration in the world of literature.*"[45] This conception of world literature positions Paris as the Subject of global recognition: the *I* that recognizes writers—especially those who hail from "impoverished" non-Western literary markets—and introduces them *into* the world. Paris is the *I* that holds the power to consecrate the languages of various Others, to bestow the secular sacrality of "literariness" upon their tongues (provided they "speak" in ways that Paris can understand) and to hereafter pronounce them worldly, universal "like" French. Oddly, Casanova severs French claims to global literary dominance from political and economic power, past or present.[46] Yet if, as Casanova herself intimates, the "universal" of Western modernity is fabricated at the expense of historical and political actuality, then the economies of language and literature must be at least partly capitalized by the politics of nations.

Setting aside (but not forgetting) Casanova's insistence that Paris is the apotheosis of the universal human of "world literature" to which writers the world over have aspired for the past three hundred years, I take seriously her suggestion that literary "belief" seduces its converts into disavowing the domination that infects the idea and practice of literary comparison and translation across the power lines of global modernity. For Casanova's formulation describes the dominant affect that nineteenth-century Egyptians like al-Ṭahṭāwī evinced in their relations with European culture, no matter how fierce their antagonism toward European power. Whereas Casanova, however, sees such "belief" as a direct and unilateral production of the dominant, I would argue that it is the indirect offspring of the seduction of the dominated. Whereas she implies that the non-Western translator only confirms the West's prior consecration of its own cultural productions, I would suggest that the subaltern translator does not simply mirror the center's consecrations, but refracts and forges these anew. Moreover, I contend, the desire of the subaltern translator to consecrate the literature of the dominant arises from the dominant power's seductive extension of recognition to the subaltern: not a recognition that, as Casanova supposes, overtly assimilates the subaltern to the "standard" of the dominant, *but one that recasts the dominant in the "standard" of the subaltern,* more surreptitiously annexing the latter to the former. Witness the case of al-Ṭahṭāwī, who actively consecrates France only because France appears to consecrate Arabic, Islam, and Egypt by "speaking" the idioms of all three, not simply because France translates these "non-Western" quantities into its own language and its own terms. Casanova defines "Parisianization" as "universalization through denial of difference."[47] I would add that "Arab-Islamization" can perform the same operation—and that it might in fact circuitously lead to Parisianization. Parisianization may not, in other words, be the prime mover of universalization, but it certainly may be its ultimate effect.

For al-Ṭahṭāwī, the universality of Paris was not at first the given that Casanova assumes. In her tautological reasoning, Paris has been the world's cultural capital for at least two centuries because it holds the greatest cultural capital. Casanova argues that age determines currency; the older a literature, the longer the shadow of its nationhood, the greater its capital and its share in the very definition of modernity. "The temporal law of the world of letters *[l'univers littéraire],*" she writes, "may be stated thus: *it is necessary to be old in order to have any chance of being modern or of decreeing what is modern.*"[48] Here French literature wears the modern mantle of the universal because it bears the patina of the ancient. Casanova ignores non-Western literary production before the mid-twentieth century—and its interaction with Western cultures to shape global literary modernity. To her mind, "those literary spaces that have more recently appeared"—by which she means those more recently nationalized, often in the wake of mid-twentieth-century decolonization—are "poor by comparison" to a venerable France.[49] Yet if antiquity is the source of global literary capital, surely Arabic, Chinese, or any other literature "older" than French could lay claim to the centrality that France enjoys. Egypt's antiquity, for instance, does not assure its modern literature any pride of place in a world still dominated by the West. For David Damrosch, Egypt ultimately figures as the Sphinx that Napoleon's invading scholars and soldiers—blind to ancient Egyptian narratives—mismeasured through European eyes, ushering in a dynamic of unequal attention that has characterized world and comparative literature since. According to Damrosch, the feminized African Sphinx is an emblem of "the opening up of the world of world literature"; it embodies the enlargement of "what was once largely a European and male preserve" into "a far broader and less familiar terrain."[50] In this schema, European conquest and "possessive mastery" of a feminized non-European antiquity usher in the new world of world literature, create it along lines that Damrosch condemns—he would have wished for a "more detached" and thus more "genuinely revivifying encounter"—but create it nonetheless.[51] Such terms deny Egypt coevalness in the creative acts of "reorigination" from which the nineteenth-century global literary universal would emerge; they fail to show that Egypt too was taking the measure of Europe and pondering its (in)commensurability to the European while Europe was measuring it. The musty odor of the past and a whiff of "feminine" passivity cling to Egypt, while Napoleon represents modernity and muscle: mistaken—yet unmistakable—activity. Between the lines of Casanova and Damrosch, we find ourselves on a universal ground of comparison in which only France speaks and acts. Egypt remains mute, immobile.

Pace Casanova and Damrosch, nineteenth-century Ottoman Egypt (like other lands confronting Western European empire) clearly had to accept the premise of Paris's antiquity in order to accept the inevitability of Paris's modernity, had to take the measure of Europe in order to retake its own measure. Al-Ṭahṭāwī had to make the antiquity of Paris prior to his own—to make France a priori to himself, subsume himself within a French origin story—in order to allow the present of Paris to reshape his future. And to reascribe himself to a French origin, he had to transact a suspect kinship not just between Arabic and French, but indeed between Arabic and the ancient languages to which French had styled itself the modern successor: Greek and Latin. Reading al-Ṭahṭāwī, we find that his relocation and reconciliation of dissonant French and Arabic epistemologies within a new (French-dominated) universal of "language" unfold in regress. Al-Ṭahṭāwī leads with the effect of translation: with a universalization of French epistemes that places Paris at the center—as Casanova would predict—by placing Egypt and France (via Greece) on a footing of inequality. Yet the ideology of translation that subtends this conclusion, not immediately obvious, is that French (and Greek and Latin, its ancient forebears) and Arabic are equal, comparable, translatable. So far, I am again in agreement with Casanova: this "denial of difference" is crucial to the effect of universalization-as-Parisianization. Yet the logic that underpins that ideology, less obvious still, compels us to step back once more in time: to a "translation zone" in which French Orientalism's identification of Frenchness with the Arab-Islamic or the Egyptian subject—whether in texts Arabic (as in de Sacy) or in texts French (as in Agoub)—elicits a powerful affective response in its Egyptian interlocutors, holds out the tantalizing possibility that French and Arabic might be exchangeable.[52] The peculiarly seductive "denial of difference" that Orientalist texts perform for their Egyptian interlocutors—a denial that appears to submit the French particular to an Arab-Islamic or Egyptian universal, reversing the sign of mastery and pointing it toward the dominated—is the paradoxical root cause of what ultimately will be a universalization of the French particular. This root cause is what Casanova's vision misses.

To retrace the rationale that underlies al-Ṭahṭāwī's ultimate "progress" toward a Eurocentric logic of linguistic value and literary modernity, then, I will follow the lines of his discursive regress. In concert with French scholars of his time, al-Ṭahṭāwī invented kinships between ancient Greek, French, and Arabic to construct the ultimate incomparability (read: sovereignty) of French literature and comparability (read: subalternity) of Arabic literature on a new imperial world stage. My analysis of these kinships unfolds in a triptych of French-Egyptian-French "panels." Revisiting the first appearance of the term *comparative literature* in the West—in one of the first books that al-Ṭahṭāwī read in Paris, the 1816 edition of François-Joseph-Michel Noël and Guislain-François-Marie-Joseph de La Place's teaching anthology, *Leçons françaises de littérature et de morale* (French Lessons in Literature and Morality)—I show that Noël and de La Place invoke linguistic and literary comparison to shore up the national, to imperialize the nation-state. Elevating modern French to a status comparable to and even greater than that of ancient Greek and Latin, the book's introduction engages *translatio imperii*—the translation of imperial power and political authority from the empires of Greece and Rome to that of France—in the act of *translatio studii:* the transfer of knowledge from Greek and Latin to French. The third "panel" of the triptych flanks the first. Here, I argue that a parallel French discourse of literary comparison emerges in the writings of de Sacy. As early as 1810, de Sacy compared Arabic literature to Greek and Latin; though he upheld the inferiority of Arabic to both, he nonetheless inserted Arabic as the missing link—the translational bridge—between the Greco-Roman and French traditions. In his formulation, France was almost as much a new Arab-Islam as it was a new Greece or Rome. (The "almost," we shall see, is important.)

Between these first and third "panels" of the triptych, al-Ṭahṭāwī transacts a new regime of comparison for the Arab-Islamic world, yoking Arab epistemes to French across the neurotic/erotic copula of asymmetrical translation. I contend that al-Ṭahṭāwī's *Takhlīṣ al-Ibrīz* at once subordinates Arabic literature to an ancient Greek origin story and propels Arabic toward a French telos by translating the forked tongues of Noël, de La Place, and de Sacy. As Ferial Ghazoul has noted, premodern Arab-Islamic intellectual tradition held both the Qur'ān and the secular Arabic poetic heritage literally "*incomparable,* and thus the whole notion of a comparison of equals . . . a non-starter."[53] By staging a comparison of ancient Greek and classical Arabic literatures from which Arabic emerges as lacking the capacity to write history, al-Ṭahṭāwī debunks the incomparability of Arabic and produces it as lesser; by extension, French—language of a city he describes as the new Athens—becomes the greater. Yet we would be wrong to assume that al-Ṭahṭāwī compares and subordinates Arab-Islamic culture to Greek and French only because he has embraced the ideologies that Noël, de La Place, and de Sacy variously articulated. What first shakes al-Ṭahṭāwī's belief in the incomparability of Arabic is his seduction by the apparent *resemblance* of the French to the Arab. Among other forces, the fluent literary Arabic of de Sacy leads al-Ṭahṭāwī to hypothesize the "equivalence" of French and Arabic—to imagine that it is possible for a person who knows any given tongue well (as de Sacy knew French) to automatically "know" any other (as de Sacy knew Arabic). From here al-Ṭahṭāwī also intimates the exchangeability of Arabic *for* French.

I return to the contention with which I began before I took al-Ṭahṭāwī's project on a detour through Casanova: it is on the ground of language that *Takhlīṣ al-Ibrīz* decides Europe's potential to seduce—hence to dominate—its Arab-Islamic interlocutor. A profound meditation on the dynamics of interlingual translation between French and Arabic precedes and underpins the cultural "translation" of France to Egypt that al-Ṭahṭāwī's *riḥla,* or travel narrative, performs. In other words, before al-Ṭahṭāwī's text can transport into Egypt those forces generally assumed to be the prime bearers of French colonialism's "civilizing mission"—science, technology, industry, even forms of education and governance—it must establish *the conditions of possibility* for the linguistic translation of French into Arabic. Those conditions bear out Lydia Liu's observation that "the circulation of meaning," in colonial encounters especially, "involves a great deal of coauthorship and struggle among the dominant and dominated groups over the meaning and distribution of universal values."[54] As Liu notes, in this process the "agents of translation on each side start out by hypothesizing an exchange of equivalent meanings, even if the hypothesis itself is born of a structure of unequal exchange and linguistic currency."[55] In the second section of the Third Essay of *Takhlīṣ al-Ibrīz,* titled "Fī al-Kalām 'alā Ahl Bārīs" (A Discourse on the People of Paris), al-Ṭahṭāwī posits just such a commensurability between French and Arabic and the systems of signification that those languages represent—only to take up the sword of French dominance and swiftly undercut their potential "equivalence":

> The rules of the French language and the art of its word construction *[tarkīb kalimātihā],* its writing, and its reading are called by the French *grammatique,* and *grammaire,* with a doubling of the *mīm* [the *m* sound in Arabic], and its meaning is the art of constructing speech in any given language, so it is as if one says, "In the art of syntax is encompassed all that relates to language," as we ourselves say "the Arabic sciences" *[al-'ulūm al-'arabiyya],* and intend by that the twelve sciences associated with one another in the words of our shaykh [Ḥasan] al-'Aṭṭār:
>
> Syntax, morphology, prosody, and then philology;
> Then derivation, poetry, composition;
> Also semantics, explication *[bayān],* calligraphy, rhyme,
> History—This is an enumeration of the sciences of the Arabs
>
> . . .
>
> Clearly, these "disciplines" should be research fields of the discipline of Arabic *['ilm al-'arabiyya]* only, for how could versification and poetry and rhyme each be an independent field in itself, and syntax and morphology and derivation each be a field unto itself? Look what is meant here by history and its status as one of the Arabic disciplines, even though it is clear that the first to write in that [discipline] were the scholars of Greece, and the first of this art to appear were the books of Homer [Ūmīrūs] on the battle of Troy, and no Arabs wrote of this domain except in more recent times—unless one means the chronicling of annual events, in the style of *ḥisāb al-jumal*—so that its designation as a "discipline" [in the Arab-Islamic context] requires an expansion of the meaning of the word *discipline* [itself].[56]

Initially, al-Ṭahṭāwī constructs *grammaire* (French "grammar") and *al-'ulūm al-'arabiyya* ("the Arabic sciences") as familiars: *grammaire* appears to describe the same supralinguistic structure in French that *al-'ulūm al-'arabiyya* does in Arabic. This construction reflects al-Ṭahṭāwī's hypothesis, in Liu's terms, of an "exchange of equivalent meanings." Yet the commensurability of the French and the Arabic terms gives way to a tacit notion of the incomparability of French, where the French understanding of *grammaire* sets the norms by which a "discipline" should be defined. The French *grammaire* seems to posit a general principle of language: notice that al-Ṭahṭāwī defines it as "the art of constructing speech in any given language," suggesting that its rules extend beyond the French particular to describe the universal, the operations of *all* language. By contrast, "the Arabic sciences" *("al-'ulūm al-'arabiyya")* designate fields that suddenly seem too specific to deserve general designation as a "science" or as a "discipline." Al-Ṭahṭāwī implies that the Arab-Islamic conception of the disciplines of language is defective: it accords false autonomy and falsely equal weight to epistemic categories (syntax, morphology, prosody, philology, derivation, poetry, composition, semantics, explication, calligraphy, rhyme, history) that should be dependent—subordinate—clauses of a "proper" universal and not presumed to carry independent heft and volume. Once al-Ṭahṭāwī decides that the French *grammaire* offers an epistemological universal that *al-'ulūm al-'arabiyya* fails to imagine, he begins to measure Arabic fields like "versification" or "syntax" against that assumed French universal—and to find those Arabic "fields" too particular to merit designation as "disciplines." Out of these many so-called disciplines, he argues, Egyptians should distill just one: that of the Arabic language. That unitary "science of Arabic" *("'ilm al-'arabiyya")* would be a truer "equivalent" of the French *grammaire,* encompassing within its "universal"—a universal whose rationale is translated from French—the particulars that currently constitute the plural "Arabic sciences," *al-'ulūm al-'arabiyya.* Thus while Liu calls us to understand acts of translation as "competing universalisms," al-Ṭahṭāwī's struggle to construct an Egyptian "universal" that might compete with the French—a *'ilm al-'arabiyya* whose currency can vie with that of *grammaire*—shows us that a "competing" universalism can in fact be embedded in, indeed translated from, the universalism with which it seeks to compete.[57] The very *ground of competition itself* is not neutral under (post)colonial conditions.

For what is ultimately also in question here, besides the right of Arabic to define its "disciplines," is the right of *any* discipline to be defined as *Arabic,* or as "Arab." Al-Ṭahṭāwī begins to challenge the designation of syntax, language, poetry, or history as "the *Arabic* sciences," ostensibly because that term provincializes knowledge. Yet in assuming the universality of the French *grammaire* and the provincialism of the Arabic *al-'ulūm al-'arabiyya,* he takes too literally the difference between the occultation of the local in the French term, which bears no trace of its ethnolinguistic referent, and the hyperemphasis of the local in the Arabic one. Articulating that epistemological "*difference as value* within a structure of unequal exchange," as Liu describes the act of translation under conditions of asymmetrical power, al-Ṭahṭāwī "simultaneously victimizes that difference by translating it as *lesser value* or *nonuniversal value.*"[58] This he does based on his new understanding of the origins of the interrelated disciplines of "history" and "literature." Al-'Aṭṭār's enumeration of the Arabic sciences enfolds history in the larger domain of language and claims a place for history in the Arabic-language intellectual tradition. His taxonomy of knowledge bears out Nadia Al-Bagdadi's contention that in "premodern use, literature and history belonged epistemologically to the same domain, namely *adab*," a term that enlarged "literature" to humanistic scholarship in its broadest sense.[59] It is al-Ṭahṭāwī who first insists—to an Arabic-language readership weaned on the idea that poetry is the historical record *(dīwān)* of the Arabs—that Homer was the world's first "true" author of history (also, mind you, of history-as-literature) and that premodern Arab poets cannot lay claim—even later claim—to the writing of "proper" history. That the ancient Greek bard's *Iliad* and *Odyssey* might have wielded an aesthetic power strong enough to convince al-Ṭahṭāwī of the virtual reality of the "history" they represent is not at issue here. Nor is my point to argue chronological priority for the Arabs. More troubling is the fact that al-Ṭahṭāwī perceives Homeric epic as the purveyor of a history to which Arab history is *epistemologically* only secondary and tacitly also as a literary vehicle *for* history that the Arabs' revered poetic canon cannot match. Given the predominance of Islam in Egypt and the intimate association of Arabia with the "birth" of Islam, for most Egyptians of al-Ṭahṭāwī's day Arabia would have been the psychogeographic center of historical consciousness, and the Arab-Islamic conquest of Egypt the origin of their "modern" history. In relocating that center and that origin from Arabia to Greece—to the cultural geography in which French civilization locates its origins—al-Ṭahṭāwī not only pushes Arab-Islamic time and epistemes to the peripheries of Egyptian self-understanding but also positions France as the new Athens from which modern Egypt must originate. Thus he accords French the power to define the meanings of "history" and "literature"—and the course of both—for Egypt. Eyeing Arab history and Arabic literature through a French lens, he has come to see both as less and less world relevant unless comparable to European literature.

'Abd al-Fattāḥ Kīlīṭū captures this dynamic well. Contemplating the riddle of literary memory, he notes that the time of Arabic literature—from its pre-Islamic beginnings to its modern manifestations—does not "translate" easily. He locates the rupture of Islamic time, the time that governs Arabic literature at least from the rise of Islam until the *nahḍa* of the (Gregorian) nineteenth century, in the work of translators like al-Ṭahṭāwī and his Lebanese contemporary, Aḥmad Fāris al-Shidyāq: "When I hear of al-Tahtawi and al-Shidyaq, my mind does not turn to the thirteenth [century of the Islamic calendar], but to the nineteenth century [of the Gregorian]. If classical Arabic literature automatically refers me to the spaciousness of the *hijrah [ilā al-hijrati wa faḍā'ihā]*, modern literature spontaneously refers me to Europe as a chronology and a frame of reference *[ilā Ūrūbbā ka taqwīmin wa iṭārin]*."[60] For Kīlīṭū, then, the particularism of "classical Arabic literature"—its seeming specificity and clarity—affords "spaciousness," indeed movement, as the term *hijra* implies (*hijra* refers not only to the migration of the Prophet Muḥammad and his earliest followers from Mecca to Medina—the point of origin for the Islamic calendar—but also to migration writ large). By contrast, the globality of "modern literature"—where Arabic is not specified—constrains, squeezes the definition of literature into the enframing chronotope of Europe. Time, after all, is neither universal nor neutral; it is not "pure" but particular. What permits us today to read the globe's disparate time zones contrapuntally is the fact that time itself has been "worlded" by modern Western empire. Thus no calendar is universal except the Gregorian, the time of the modern Western world dominant. Other calendars persist, but however globally dispersed their users may be, their epistemological reach is locked in the particular: in the time of a specific religious or ethnic community. Hence Kīlīṭū goes on to observe, "Naturally, literary memory is different for Arabs and Europeans. . . . Obviously, European memory goes back to Athens, and Arab memory to the desert."[61] As Arabic literature "jumped from its own calendar into another, alien one," he writes, "memory lost its bearings and plunged into another memory and another time frame."[62] Standing at precisely the two foci of memory Kīlīṭū names—the West's Athens and Islam's Arabia—al-Ṭahṭāwī transacts the loss of one in the sum of both: the universal "constant" of France and, by extension, the European West. If this act of translation is what Damrosch calls the "elliptical refraction" of world literature, the ellipse it limns is no equal world but one whose space-time constant is overdetermined by Europe.[63] Al-Ṭahṭāwī's new perspective on the literary-historical reproduces at least one assumption of European Orientalism, which Kīlīṭū aptly describes: "Arabic literature is boring unless it bears a family resemblance [*washā'iju qurbā;* lit., "close kinship ties"] to European literature."[64] One might note here that the Arabic for "comparative" *(muqāran)* shares a root with "marriage" *(qirān)*: a constructed (suspect?) kinship tie.

THE CHAMPS ÉLYSÉES OF NEO-GRECO-FRENCH

Al-Ṭahṭāwī's acceptance of ancient Greece as the "universal" origin of history and literature, then, derives from his increasing conviction that French ways of knowing are more properly "universal" than Arabic ones—witness his treatment of *grammaire*—and from his exposure to nineteenth-century French self-constructions as the new Greeks and Romans. Among the first literary texts that he read in Paris was Noël and de La Place's 1816 anthology of French literature, *Leçons françaises de littérature et de morale*. To this, the first of a three-part series of anthologies of French, Greek and Latin, and English literary texts, Noël and de La Place affixed the enigmatic second title *Cours de littérature comparée*, presenting their series as a "Course in Compared Literature."[65] This second title marks the first appearance of the term "comparative literature" in a European tongue. While Susan Bassnett follows René Wellek in suggesting that Noël and de La Place failed to define comparative literature, I would suggest that the French scholars' preface to the anthology—which accompanied the text from its 1804 first edition—implicitly embeds the term in a competition of civilizations for global cultural capital.[66] For Noël and de La Place, literary comparison begins when the value of modern French literature can be said not just to match but indeed to outdo that of its classical ancestors: to supersede them as a standard of literary measure. Thus defined, literary comparison in France is the culmination of a long process that begins—as Casanova tells us—with the 1549 publication by Joachim du Bellay of *La Deffence et illustration de la langue françoyse* (The Defense and Illustration of the French Language).[67] Calling on French to devour and so supplant Greek and Latin, Casanova argues, Du Bellay proposed "a *diversion of capital* that conserved the gains of Latinist humanism . . . while diverting them to the profit of French."[68] The decision of René Descartes to publish his 1637 *Discours de la méthode* (Discourse on Method) in French rather than in Latin, followed by the triumph of the "moderns" in their quarrel with the "ancients," sealed the victory of French by the end of the seventeenth century.[69]

Interestingly, the first edition of Noël and de La Place's French anthology, published in 1804, makes no mention of French in its main title, which reads simply *Leçons de littérature et de morale* (Lessons in Literature and Morality). Its "lessons" are thus unmarked as specifically French, although the book's subtitle—*Recueil, en prose et en vers, des plus beaux morceaux de notre langue, dans la littérature des deux derniers siècles* (Collection, in Prose and in Verse, of the Most Beautiful Selections from Our Language, in the Literature of the Last Two Centuries)—does refer to *"notre langue"* (our language), thereby gesturing to the missing French referent. Nor does the 1804 version feature the second title page that would appear in the 1816 edition; it makes no mention of *"littérature comparée"* (comparative literature).

Yet even in the first edition of 1804, Noël and de La Place tacitly compare French to Greek and Latin and in that process—paradoxically—declare their language incomparable. In their preface to that edition, they note that they had decided to suspend work on an advanced textbook in ancient languages and to prepare instead a teaching anthology for French. Why? "Our language," they write, "assumed preference."[70] Dubbing their anthology a distillation of "the sum total of the two most beautiful centuries of our literature," the editors describe it in classicizing terms: "It is a Museum or a French Elysium of sorts, where our best orators, historians, philosophers, and poets seem to recite [their work] to one another."[71] That this anthology should function as a *"Muséum"* or *"Elysée français"* makes "dead"—ancient—icons of even the living French writers it showcases. The second subtitle of the 1804 anthology, *ouvrage classique* (classical work), inscribes French literature all the more firmly in the ranks of the classics. Further, the editors note that they have constructed their anthology not just as a classicized space of conversation in which the French moderns speak as if they were Greek ancients but also as a space of comparison and contrast, "putting writers who treat similar, analogous, or contrasting objects face to face with one another, and sometimes the same author with himself, in order to compare [their] genius."[72] The 1804 edition, then, defines even the *intralingual* study of French literature as a praxis of "littérature comparée." It declares French self-sufficient. Yet it also anticipates the more explicitly *interlingual* use of the term *littérature comparée* on the title page of the 1816 edition, where French literature would precede Greek and Latin. So deployed, *littérature comparée* would render French no longer the descendant but the peer—indeed the predecessor—of the ancients.

That this transformation should occur between 1804 and 1816 is telling. In 1804 France (under Napoleon) was fast securing the largest European empire since the age of Charlemagne, despite its overseas colonial losses that year of Saint-Domingue to the Haitian Revolution and in 1801 of Egypt to native insurrection and ultimately to Ottoman-British naval war. Thus Noël and de La Place could wordlessly assert both the universality and the incomparability of French literature: literature and morality could go unmarked on the first title page, as if French were automatically tantamount to both; the work of comparison, unremarked on the second, as if to say that French needed no comparison to establish itself as nonpareil. By 1816, however, France's European imperium had collapsed; after Napoleon's decisive defeat at Waterloo in 1815, Britain reigned supreme in the region and, increasingly, in the world. With the waning fortunes of French empire come both the humility of comparison—suddenly French must be marked as such and explicitly compared to Greek, Latin, and English—and its arrogance: the French volume comes first and sets the beat to which other major literatures of the Western world, present and past, will march. Its position restores a cultural imperium—if not a territorial one—to a France momentarily shrunken to its national borders.

Al-Ṭahṭāwī caught on to Noël and de La Place's comparisons of French literature and culture with the esteemed traditions of the "European" ancients; elsewhere in this very section of *Takhlīṣ al-Ibrīz,* he describes Paris as a nineteenth-century "Athens" of the mind.[73] Insisting, then, that Arabic "history" cannot, fundamentally, be called "history," he negates the possibility that Arabic and Greek "histories" might be commensurable. The European notion of *history* becomes an untranslatable telos—an incomparable—toward which Arabic must stretch. It is Arabic that must translate itself toward Greek and toward the "European" that Greece has come to imply, not Greek and the "European" that must bend to Arabic. Lawrence Venuti has defined translation as "a process by which the chain of signifiers that constitutes the source-language text is *replaced by a chain of signifiers in the target language.*"[74] So far, translation seems innocent enough. Yet Venuti goes on to identify its violence, although his understanding of that violence remains unidirectional. "Translation," he concludes, "is the forcible replacement of the linguistic and cultural difference of the foreign text with a text that will be intelligible to the target-language reader"; its aim "is to bring back a cultural other as the same, the recognizable, even the familiar."[75] Thus translation in Venuti does violence to source, never to target. Yet the translations that al-Ṭahṭāwī performs between Greek, French, and Arab-Islamic histories and epistemes, though they bring back the French Other "as the same," do less violence to that French "Other" than they do to the self. Al-Ṭahṭāwī's translations target the target, *replacing the chain of signifiers in the target language* (Arabic) *with those of the source* (French).

WHAT IS FRENCH TO ARABIC? OF GOLD, TINSEL, AND ALLOYED EXCHANGE

No doubt al-Ṭahṭāwī's Azharite formation had instilled the belief that Arabic—as the Qur'ānic language of divine revelation—was "superior" to all other languages and thus incomparable. His encounter with French would destabilize that certainty. Nowhere in *Takhlīṣ al-Ibrīz* is the subordination of the "sovereign state" of Arabic to the empire of French universalism as clear as in this passage:

> The French language . . . has a terminology specific to it, and on this foundation its grammar is built, . . . and this is what is called *ighramātīqā [grammatique*, or *grammatica]*. So if all languages governed by rules feature an art that comprises their rules, . . . then the Arabic language has no monopoly on this, but in every language this can be found—yes, [we know] Arabic is the most eloquent of languages, and the greatest, the vastest, and the most pleasant to the ear. So when the scholar of Latin knows all that pertains to it, . . . it is ignorant to say, "He does not know anything," simply on the basis of his ignorance of the Arabic language. If a person were to delve deeply into any given language, he would be, perforce, a scholar of another tongue *[idhā tabaḥḥara al-insānu fī lughatin min al-lughāti kāna 'āliman bi al-lughati al-ukhrā bi al-quwwati]*, meaning that if that which is in another language were translated and explained to him, he would be quick to receive it and compare it to his own language—indeed, he may even have known it before *[kāna ya'rifuhu min qablu]*, and known even more than [what it implies], and investigated it, and discarded that which the mind cannot accept. How [can we say that one who knows French but not Arabic knows nothing], . . . when a person does not know tomes in Arabic, but knows them in French if they were to be translated for him, given that every language . . . has its masterworks of rhetoric and grammar [lit., *lahā Muṭawwaluhā wa Aṭwaluhā wa Sa'duhā*]? True, not every liquid is water, nor every ceiling a sky, nor every house the house of God, nor every Muḥammad the messenger of God.[76]

This time al-Ṭahṭāwī substitutes the Latin roots of French language for the Greek origins of French history and literature. Clearly he does not immediately assume the supremacy of French or of Latin, its forebear. Eurocentrism-as-law is not, as Casanova presumes, simply decreed at Paris and obeyed. Rather, al-Ṭahṭāwī must transact the "supremacy" of Western civilization for readers who believe otherwise, convince them that Latin and French might know something that Arabic does not. What he is at pains to debunk is Arabic's monopoly on the universal: its capacity to style itself incomparable (or untranslatable) and thus the touchstone of all possible comparisons and translations in the world. Thus he must approximate French to *Arabic incomparability*, translate a vaguely comparable European idiom into synonymy with its "matchless" Arab-Islamic counterpart. Of course, al-Ṭahṭāwī is aware that France has threatened the sovereignty of Ottoman Egypt and that he is learning French because it bears the "secret" of potential geopolitical dominance. The twin impulses of making French approximate Arabic incomparability and of making Arabic approximate French dominance, then, drive his subsumption of both French and Arabic within a seemingly unmarked universal that renders the two "equal." By imagining a universal—the "depths" of what we might call "pure language"—in which both the semantic and the political particularities of French and Arabic are submerged and neutralized, al-Ṭahṭāwī transacts a "commensurability" between Arabic and French that involves yet masks the recent historical rupture of equivalence between them.[77] An individual who knows any given language deeply, he argues, perforce *("bi al-quwwati")* knows any "other" language deeply. In this conception of commensurability, languages share common depths: the Arabic verb that al-Ṭahṭāwī chooses to describe language mastery is *tabaḥḥara,* to dive into or to plumb the depths of something as if it were a sea *(baḥr).* It is not "words," in this conception, that must be translated but underlying "concepts." If the untranslatable foreign word is "explained"—taken to its depths—the receiver will find its native corollary, supply its equivalent in his own language, perhaps even supplement it. For when the receiver finally does translate, he speaks not only as if he knew the foreign word a priori—knew it before he learned it—but as if he knew it *better* than its original speaker. Al-Ṭahṭāwī tries to offset his nagging sense of French supremacy by turning the tables of incommensurability back on France. "Yes, [we know] Arabic is the most eloquent of languages, and the greatest, the vastest, and the most pleasant to the ear," he protests, and "True, not every liquid is water, nor every ceiling a sky, nor every house the house of God, nor every Muḥammad the messenger of God." Choosing words that even in one language (in this case, Arabic) are metonymically related yet not equivalent, he entertains the possibility that "particulars" like *water, sky, the house of God,* or *Muḥammad the messenger of God* might hold greater meaning-value than the "universals"—the unmarked *liquid, ceiling, house,* and *Muḥammad*—that subtend them. Obliquely, he suggests that while French may be more "universal" than Arabic, "local" Arabic might hold more meaning-value for the Egyptian. Still, al-Ṭahṭāwī concludes that pure language—a universal of universals—subtends and reconciles its particular, "untranslatable" manifestations in individual tongues, permitting their translatability.

So too does Walter Benjamin. In "Die Aufgabe des Übersetzers" ("The

Task of the Translator"), Benjamin famously argues that translation is the voyage of the *untranslatable* between two languages—not what they hold in common—to the stratosphere of "pure" language: a region of "reconciliation and fulfillment of languages" in which incommensurability is resolved into union.[78] To convert incommensurability into a "commensurability" that *contains* it, Benjamin, like al-Ṭahṭāwī, must supplant the plurality of "modes of intention"—with all the historicity and the thorny fact of differential power these imply—with what Benjamin calls the "suprahistorical" unity of Intention, the sum total of otherwise irreconcilable particulars.

> Wherein resides the relatedness of two languages, apart from historical considerations? Certainly not in the similarity between works of literature or words. Rather, *all suprahistorical kinship of languages rests in the intention underlying each language as a whole*—an intention, however, which no single language can attain by itself but which is realized only by the totality of their intentions supplementing each other: pure language.[79]

Elsewhere Benjamin amplifies these assertions, arguing, in one case, that "languages are not strangers to one another, but are, a priori and apart from all historical relationships, interrelated in what they want to express."[80] Taken together, his pronouncements echo al-Ṭahṭāwī's apprehension that translation involves the resolution of incommensurability—the fact that one language's word for a given concept might "know" or intend more than another's—in the commensurability of "pure language": a "totality" that "no longer means or expresses anything but is, as expressionless and creative Word, that which is meant in all languages."[81] Although, in Benjamin's formulation as in al-Ṭahṭāwī's, that totality remains ever fractured by linguistic difference and thus in some sense unattainable in any form but supplementarity, translation must proceed *as if* languages "want to express" the same thing, *as if* they share one desire. Moreover, while both al-Ṭahṭāwī and Benjamin may understand languages as "unequal" in the ways they mean, they still imagine those differences to carry equal weight—equal value, uninflected by politics or history—as they voyage toward additive Intention. It is on just such an imagined common ground of otherworldly Intention—a ground of presumed "reciprocity" among languages, on which "French" is said to speak "Arabic" and potentially be more Arabic than Arabic—that the seduction whereby the dominated translate themselves toward, and finally into, their dominator begins.

For such reciprocity among languages, whether in al-Ṭahṭāwī's conception or in Benjamin's, can only exist on the terrain of "pure" language. That terrain disavows the historical inequalities between languages and cultures under colonial conditions. And yet history looms large in the translation we witness here. In the end, al-Ṭahṭāwī valorizes Greece—and by extension France—not for their "antiquity" per se but for their presumed capacity to make history: to originate, to embody, and thus to dictate the world historical. Taught to relocate Arab history and literature within European time, he now relocates the Arabic linguistic particular *within* the French linguistic universal. The undertow of his sea of exchangeability is the French notion of *grammaire*. The "art of constructing speech in any given language"—which in French submerges a host of epistemological categories, and which to al-Ṭahṭāwī's mind "ought" to do so in Arabic too—is precisely what "in every language . . . can be found," whereas Arabic's particulars lend themselves less easily to a totalizing sphere of pure language. French, he ultimately argues, might not only "mean" as much as Arabic "means," but even supersede Arabic in foreknowledge of an idea. Quite likely it already has put that idea to the test of reason, "discarded that which the mind cannot accept," and distilled its essence. Indeed, al-Ṭahṭāwī would write that the "ease" of the French language—its disambiguation—had enabled French "advancement in the sciences and the arts."[82] He contrasts the complexity of Arabic, in which any given word stands in relation to a constellation of forms derived from the same root, each carrying a subtle semantic nuance that cannot be fully actualized, except, as Timothy Mitchell has noted, in the instant of enunciation.[83] However productive the ambiguities of Arabic, however evocative its deferrals of signification, al-Ṭahṭāwī tacitly pronounces its complexity an obstacle to progress. In associating the clarity of French with civilizational advancement, he echoes Antoine de Rivarol's declaration, in his 1784 *De l'universalité de la langue française* (On the Universality of the French Language), that "what is not clear is not French."[84] Rivarol argued the universality of the French language on the grounds of its clarity: a trait I would interpret as radical translatability. Al-Ṭahṭāwī's argument hews to this view: clarity universalizes French, makes it maximally legible and thus eminently translatable; complexity particularizes Arabic, makes it travel less well.

Rich and resonant though Arabic may be to al-Ṭahṭāwī, it no longer is the language of "advancement." The aftertaste of colonization on Egyptian tongues—with the foretaste of possible colonizations to come—has made French that language. My larger point is this one:

in the political economy of colonial translation, language cannot be evaporated into the high thin air of Benjamin's zone of reconciliation, nor can it be drowned in al-Ṭahṭāwī's bottomless sea of linguistic interchangeability. Thus the final self-affirmation al-Ṭahṭāwī entertains in his meditations on the commensurability of French and Arabic must fold in self-interrogation: "Falā shakka anna lisāna al-'arabi huwa a'ẓamu al-lughāti wa abhaju: / wa hal dhahabun ṣirfun yuḥākīhi bahrajun[?]" ("There is no doubt that the Arab tongue is the greatest and the most beautiful of languages— / and can counterfeit tinsel mimic pure gold?").[85] To that question, the very title of his text—*Takhlīṣ al-Ibrīz fī Talkhīṣ Bārīz* (Extracting Pure Gold to Render Paris, Briefly Told), which both semantically and alliteratively links Paris *(Bārīz)* to pure gold *(ibrīz)*—gives answer: yes, French too is pure gold, perhaps even "purer" than your Arabic, so precious now that you must extract and import it into Arabic. Casanova links the act of translating and thereby consecrating a literature to alchemical transubstantiation. "The consecration of a text," she observes, "is the almost magical metamorphosis of an ordinary material into 'gold,' into absolute literary value."[86] In her view, Paris is always already—at least since the dawn of modernity—keeper of the gold standard. Yet for al-Ṭahṭāwī, that truism is not so obvious. French is "counterfeit tinsel"; Arabic, his gold standard, his pure gold. It is through his translational agency that Paris—and by extension French—are consecrated as the global gold standards Casanova imagines as given. To rearrange the phonemes of *ibrīz* (pure gold) to "spell" *Bārīz* (Paris), he must perform a series of epistemic translations that render Arab-Islamic value subordinate to the European. Henceforth Arabic would become the counterfeit, the poor copy of French. Only the translated currency that al-Ṭahṭāwī's French reeducation would mint on the presses of Būlāq would hold value. By 1834 language already had been indelibly written into the script of "progress" toward a colonial "modernity." And so al-Ṭahṭāwī must translate the sovereign Arabic-speaking self into subalternity.

BETWEEN GREEK AND FRENCH: ARABIC AS MISSING TITLE

All this, however, does not explain why a (post)colonial subject might translate himself or herself into recolonization. If, as Casanova argues, a dominant France produces the fiction of its antiquity, hence its incomparability, hence its universality, why should others believe it? If, as

Liu has counterargued, the meaning of a universal value is born of "co-authorship and struggle among the dominant and dominated," what motivates al-Ṭahṭāwī to "coauthor" an essentially *French* universal, one whose construction and propagation are so strongly overdetermined by French imperial power that the very equivalence of authorial (and authoritative) agency that "coauthorship" implies must itself be interrogated as a mystification of inequality? My answer is that the lure of "coauthoring" such a universal for the (post)colonial Egyptian subject is precisely the fantasy of reasserting the competitiveness of a precolonial *Arab-Islamic* universal by rearticulating it through the now world-dominant voice of French. In that articulation, be it in French or in an Arabic "Frenchified," the Egyptian subject gives up his claim *to* the universal, cedes his self-assertive intention to the ground of an Intention seemingly coauthored but ultimately French-inflected. Thus the fiction of French incomparability becomes seductive only when it is emplaced in *comparability* with other cultural fictions of the incomparable, like the Arabic—that is, when the dominated are invited to imagine themselves, their languages, and their cultures in relations of kinship to the world dominant, to an Other whose power already marks it as *unlike*. The emerging universal, then, lies not in the equal sign that a theory of "coauthorship" interposes between the epistemologies of the dominant and the dominated but in a zone of slashed equality.

If Noël and de La Place's anthology convinced al-Ṭahṭāwī to view France as the avatar of the oldest ancient and the measure of the newest modern, what drives him to question the primacy of Arab-Islamic culture in the face of European culture—and to theorize the inherent exchangeability of French and Arabic—is his seduction by the "French" Arabic of the Orientalist de Sacy. Al-Ṭahṭāwī's encounter in Paris with the translational personality of de Sacy—a Frenchman remarkably fluent in Arabic—reminded him that French might not be the only language "worth" learning, that Arabic too might be a language into which others yearn to translate themselves. Focused on the value that de Sacy's fluency seems to place on Arabic and half-forgetting that de Sacy studied Arabic for the glory of France, al-Ṭahṭāwī derives a theory of translation that presumes an unproblematic commensurability between languages. Witness his analysis of de Sacy's Arabic-language preface to his long commentary on the *maqāmāt* of the medieval Arab belletrist Abū Muḥammad al-Qāsim ibn 'Alī al-Ḥarīrī. Here al-Ṭahṭāwī notes with appreciation de Sacy's attempts to blaze a translational path between Christianity and Islam "without defrauding either."[87] (The

Orientalist's Arabic introduction to his work on al-Ḥarīrī begins and ends, in fact, with quasi-Islamic praises to Allāh and hopes that Allāh might make his book useful to peoples East and West.) Moreover, he pronounces the French scholar's Arabic generally "eloquent," though he concedes certain stylistic weaknesses: "He is indeed eloquent, even though he is dogged by weak style, and the reason for this is . . . that he [first] mastered the rules of foreign tongues, and thus his Arabic expression leaned toward these."[88] By the end of the passage, what appears an obstacle to de Sacy's full mastery of Arabic—his prior command of French and other languages—emerges as the *basis* on which he commands Arabic, the better to buttress the logic of radical translatability. Admiring de Sacy for his stature as a grammarian of Arabic and other "Oriental" languages (especially Persian) and the range of his translations from Arabic literature, al-Ṭahṭāwī writes, "He has a formidable knowledge of scholarly works in all languages, and the entire reason for this is his command of his own language in its totality, then his turning afterwards to the knowledge of [other] languages."[89] Clearly, al-Ṭahṭāwī takes this French Orientalist—whose command of French enables his command of Arabic and indeed of "all languages"—as the very model of the scholar whose deep knowledge of one language enables him to know any other, and thus the model for his theorizations that French might be exchangeable with Arabic.

Al-Ṭahṭāwī's comparative reading of Greek, French, and Arabic ideas of language, literature, and history—as well as his efforts to reassign Egyptian "origins" to Europe—suggests further provocative comparisons to the writings of de Sacy. As early as 1810, de Sacy strove to reorient the genealogy of European literature to include not only Greek and Latin but also Arabic. He argued that the Arabic literary tradition might supply the missing ancestor in a European literary genealogy that so far had failed to link Greek and Latin to the efflorescence of literature in Renaissance Europe and thus to the development of modern French literature. Presenting his seminal textbook for European students of Arabic—*Grammaire arabe, à l'usage des élèves de l'École spéciale des langues orientales vivantes* (Arabic Grammar, for the Use of Students of the Special School of Living Oriental Languages)—in a 5 March 1810 address to the Corps Législatif in Paris, de Sacy laments the decline of Arabic literary studies in Europe. After the mid-seventeenth century, when even parts of European Christendom not directly linked to the Arab-Islamic world began to "discover" Arabic literature, these studies had withered.[90] De Sacy notes, of course, that Arabic literature had never been unknown to the republics of Italy, which had traded with the Islamic world at least since the Crusades, or to Spain, whose long submission to Arab-Islamic empire made it the crucible of "the first seeds of the renaissance of letters among us."[91] Yet Arabic literature, he suggests, was in danger of being reforgotten by Europe.

> The literature of the Orient is quite far from having acquired among us the degree of culture that [the literatures] of the Greeks and Romans have long since attained. No doubt, genius and taste admit no comparison between the inimitable models of beauty and grace that the writers of Athens and Rome offer us, and the often uneven products of the exalted imagination of the Arabs, or the subtlety—more brilliant than solid—of the Persians. But is it permissible to fail to recognize what immense gap remains to be filled in the history of letters and sciences? And does it not fall to the Arabs, who cultivated these [domains] so successfully, while Europe apparently was plunged in profound lethargy, to furnish us with the original titles that should fill this lacuna?[92]

Where contemporaries like Noël and de La Place trace the lineage of French literature only to Greek and Latin, de Sacy insists on including Arabic among its ancestors. Interestingly, the non-European—specifically, the Arab and the Persian—is not a space of *nonculture* for de Sacy: not a "barbarian" beyond the gates of a Greco-Roman-French preserve. Rather, non-European literature is "*sans culture*" ("without culture") only insofar as it is not known to Europe.[93] In this address and elsewhere, de Sacy repeatedly describes Orientalist scholarship on Arabic literature as a comparative praxis that clears, populates, and "cultures" lands that Europeans previously imagined sterile, uninhabitable, and "*sans culture.*" Between de Sacy's lines, the Orientalist emerges as one who clears a land that is already inhabited and already cultured, the better to resettle and reculture it *for* Europe. In this epistemological deforestation, the overtones of colonial territorial settlement ring clear. Yet if such a conception strips Arabic literature of being-for-itself and makes its value inhere only in being-for-the-European—and here I echo 'Abd al-Fattāḥ Kīlīṭū's description of the fate of Arabic literature after the nineteenth century, its destiny to *be* comparison in the way that black men and women, for Frantz Fanon, "*sont comparaison*" ("are comparison") because so fated by white domination—it at least equally suggests that Europe's ignorance of and active hostility toward incorporating Arabic literature within its literary genome, its self-conception of its own civilization, impoverish the European.[94] This is not to say that differential understandings of the European self and the Oriental

Other do not haunt the horizons of comparison for de Sacy, for, as Edward Said has argued, de Sacy's scholarship is deeply implicated in French imperialism.[95] At the heart of de Sacy's understanding of what we might call "comparative literature" is, after all, a thesis of Europe's *incomparability:* the literature of the Orient, represented here by the defective genius of the "uneven" Arabs and the less-than-solid Persians, admits no comparison with the "inimitable models" of Athens and Rome. And yet, he says, we must compare these literatures anyway—or at least compare the legacies of Greek and Latin (on the one hand) and Arabic (on the other) to modern European letters, which needs Arabic literature to complete its history. The influence of Arabic on European literature, de Sacy suggests, is so extensive that Europeans must count it among their literary progenitors. Yet the anxiety of its influence is so great that Europeans cannot count it among their most venerated literary forefathers but can only acknowledge it as a stepfather "origin," a figure outside Europe's accepted genealogy, second-rate yet nonetheless indispensable to a European family history. The "non-European" is at once kin, part of the "European," and not kind, fundamentally incomparable to Europe—*less than* "us."

A specter of empire, then, haunts both de Sacy's and al-Ṭahṭāwī's wrestlings with "origins." De Sacy viewed Arabic literary works as French war "trophies" (his word) rescued by Napoleon's armies from the deserts of Egypt and revivified by their incorporation into European literary history. And fresh as the legacies of French occupation remained for Ottoman Egypt in 1834, French accrued for al-Ṭahṭāwī a troubling edge of knowingness, however fiercely he struggled to reimagine his literary tradition "equivalent" to Jomard's French one and to assimilate both to a single ancestor and a common genealogy. Just as de Sacy argues that Arabic is the missing branch on European literature's family tree, al-Ṭahṭāwī claims that Greek and its modern cultural avatar, French, are the forgotten ancestors and estranged relations that Arabic literature and history must "take in"—and whose precedence they must acknowledge. Writing at a time of (post)colonial French cultural hegemony in Egypt, an intellectual climate in which he is increasingly driven to see French as the epistemologically incomparable language against which Arabic somehow "fails" to measure up, al-Ṭahṭāwī in his own turn posits French as kin (like "us") but not kind—*more than* "us." The encounter of European and Arab-Islamic "incomparabilities" in the colonial context of the early nineteenth century compelled both French and Arabic to rethink themselves in each other's eyes, in translation. Yet not equally. The hypothesized kinships of French with Greek, Latin, and Arabic shored up its dominance, its incomparability; the hypothesized kinships of Arabic with French, Latin, and Greek subordinated it. Translation did not "mean" the same thing to each.

"ON THE TIP OF THE TONGUE OF MY INTENTION"

De Sacy's "French" Arabic was not the only phenomenon that seduced al-Ṭahṭāwī into imagining the possibility of French-Arabic translation. Significantly, the first such translation that al-Ṭahṭāwī published, and likely the first that he completed in France, was of Agoub's lyric poem *La Lyre brisée* (The Broken Lyre, 1825).[96] Agoub, as I noted earlier, oversaw a crucial period in al-Ṭahṭāwī's study of French. Al-Ṭahṭāwī's Arabic translation of *La Lyre brisée,* titled *Naẓm al-'Uqūd fī Kasr al-'Ūd* (Stringing the Necklaces of *The Broken Lyre*, or—more poetically—Stringing the *Broken Lyre*), appeared in Paris in 1827, one year after he arrived in France (see figures 3 and 4). The work's early place in al-Ṭahṭāwī's nascent consciousness of the literary-political relationships of France to Egypt and of French to Arabic within a (post)colonial order, as well as its potential role in shaping his understanding of the task of the translator, compels scholarly attention both to the original and to its translation. Strangely, they have received little.[97]

For his part, Agoub remains a little-known figure in Arab, French, and francophone studies today, despite the fact that he was enmeshed in French Romanticist and Orientalist circles and implicated—through his impact on al-Ṭahṭāwī—in the genesis of an Egyptian national idea mediated through the French concept of *amour de la patrie,* or love of country. Born in 1795 to a Christian Cairene family of Syrian and Armenian origins that collaborated with Napoleon's forces of occupation, Agoub was exiled to France in 1801, when his family fled to Marseilles with the evacuating French.[98] He was himself a translation—a postcolonial migrant and writer before the advent of "postcolonial" time. The Arab community in early-nineteenth-century Marseilles was sizable, and as a child Agoub studied Arabic at home. Arriving in Paris in 1820, he frequented the *salon* of Adélaïde-Gillette Billet Dufrénoy, to whom he would dedicate *La Lyre brisée.* That year he published his first poem, *Dithyrambe sur l'Égypte* (Dithyramb on Egypt), to apparent acclaim. A philologist and translator as well as a poet, Agoub was named professor of Arabic at the École Royale des Jeunes de Langues, and the French

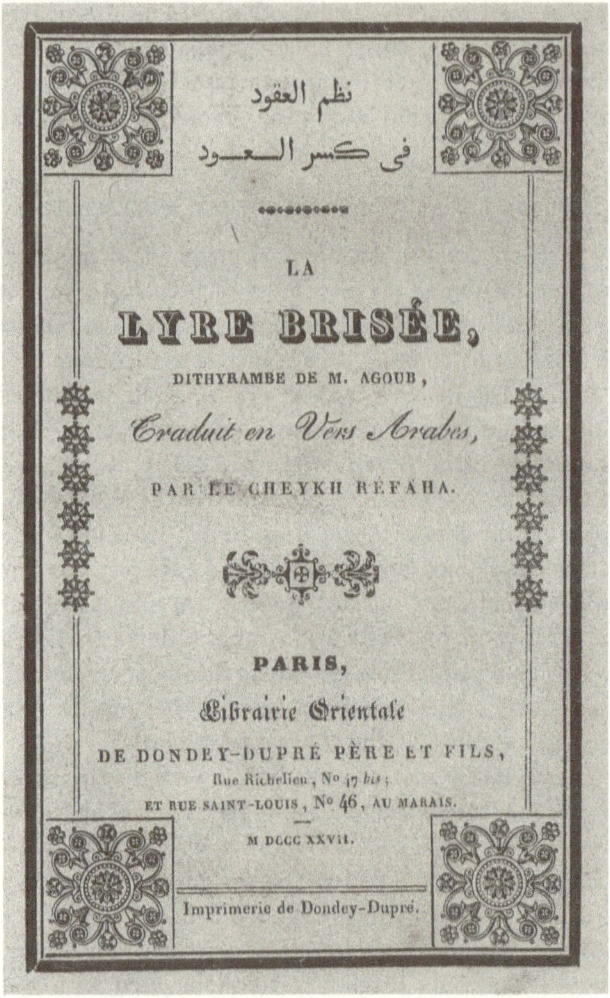

نظم العقود
فى كسر العود

LA

LYRE BRISÉE,

DITHYRAMBE DE M. AGOUB,

Traduit en Vers Arabes,

PAR LE CHEYKH REFAHA.

PARIS,

Librairie Orientale

DE DONDEY-DUPRÉ PÈRE ET FILS,

Rue Richelieu, N° 47 bis;

ET RUE SAINT-LOUIS, N° 46, AU MARAIS.

M DCCC XXVII.

Imprimerie de Dondey-Dupré.

FIGURE 3. Bilingual (Arabic-French) cover of Rifāʿa Rāfiʿ al-Ṭahṭāwī's *Naẓm al-ʿUqūd fī Kasr al-ʿŪd* (Paris: Dondey-Dupré, A.H. 1242/1827), a translation of Joseph Agoub's *La Lyre brisée* (Paris, 1825). Copyright © Bibliothèque Nationale de France.

Romantic poet Alphonse de Lamartine is said to have admired his French translations of Arabic *mawāwīl,* popular songs of love and lament.[99] He worked closely with the Commission d'Égypte, which oversaw the publication of the *Description de l'Égypte,* and he published both a book-length review of the second edition of the *Description*—under the Jomardian title *Coup-d'œil sur l'Égypte*

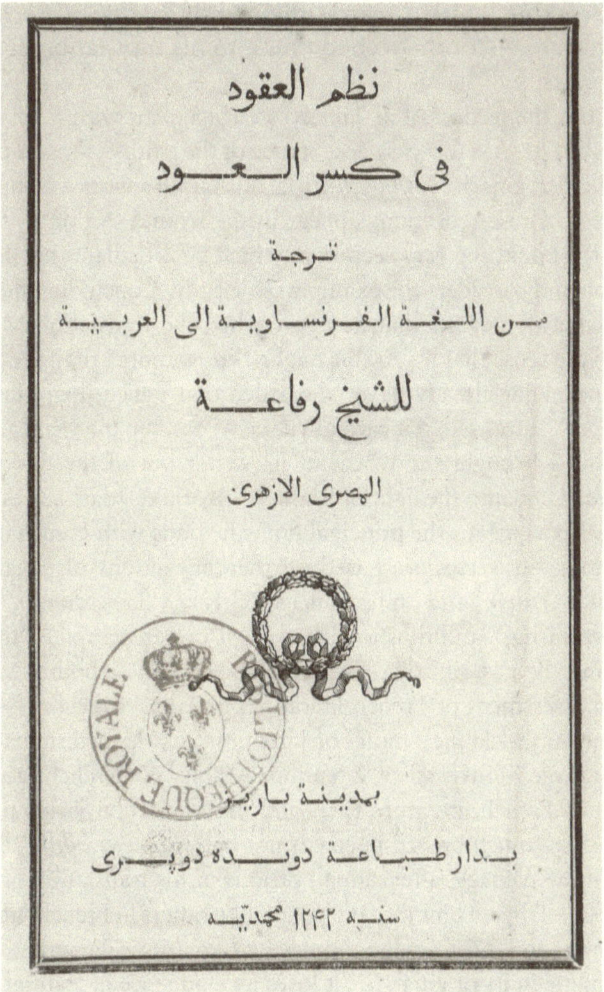
نظم العقود

فى كسر العود

ترجمة

من اللغة الفرنساوية الى العربية

للشيخ رفاعة

المصرى الازهرى

بمدينة باريز

بدار طباعة دونده دوپرى

سنه ١٢٤٢ محمدية

FIGURE 4. Arabic title page of *Naẓm al-ʿUqūd fī Kasr al-ʿŪd* (Paris, A.H. 1242 [1827]). Copyright © Bibliothèque Nationale de France. Unlike the book's cover, the title page identifies the translator, al-Ṭahṭāwī, as an Egyptian Azharite.

ancienne et moderne, ou Analyse raisonnée du grand ouvrage sur l'Égypte (A Glance at Ancient and Modern Egypt; or, A Reasoned Analysis of the Great Work on Egypt)—and his own *Discours historique sur l'Égypte* (A Historical Discourse on Egypt).[100] Al-Ṭahṭāwī was taken with the ideas of both history and Egypt that his teacher, Agoub, articulated in the *Discours:* so taken, in fact, that he translated at length from that text at the end of *Takhlīṣ al-Ibrīz,* where he also gestured—for the second time—to his translation of Agoub's *La Lyre brisée.*

No doubt the neglect of al-Ṭahṭāwī's engagement with *La Lyre brisée* stems, in part, from a too-easy acceptance of the truth-claims embedded in his initial reflections, in *Takhlīṣ al-Ibrīz,* on Agoub's work and his translation thereof. Those reflections appear in the second section of the Third Essay of the book, the very section in which he articulates his theories of translation and considers the example of de Sacy. Concluding that discussion, al-Ṭahṭāwī suggests that he approached the translation of Agoub's *Lyre* with the sense that his Arabic might "know more" than the original's French and might already have "discarded that which [his] mind [could not] accept." "I translated it carefully," he writes, "in the year [A.H.] 1242 [1827], and I brought the words of its writer out of the darknesses of unbelief *[al-kufr]* into the light of Islam."[101] By these "darknesses of unbelief," al-Ṭahṭāwī means the principal faults he finds with French literature: the fact that "its verses are based on the conventions of pagan Greece *[jāhiliyyat al-Yunān]* and on [the ancient Greeks'] deification of whatever they find pleasing" and thus are littered with references like "the god of Beauty, and the god of Love"— blasphemies to an orthodox Muslim.[102] With this assessment of French literature, al-Ṭahṭāwī reclaims—momentarily—the Arab-Islamic "mode of intention" as the determinant of the "pure-language" universal of Intention. Arabic, not French, governs his valuation of French literature here, and that valuation yields only lukewarm praise: "much French poetry is not bad *[lā ba'sa bihi].*"[103] Only at the end of the passage, after citing portions of his translation of Agoub's *Lyre,* does al-Ṭahṭāwī hint that the poem, like others in French, might have affected him more profoundly: though *La Lyre brisée,* he writes, is "spiritually sublime in its original, . . . it loses its eloquence in translation, such that the sublimity of its writer's spirit does not appear."[104]

Those parting words invite us to look elsewhere for testimony to the impact of Agoub's *Lyre* on al-Ṭahṭāwī. Significantly, not one of the stanzas he cites in *Takhlīṣ al-Ibrīz* reflects the many in Agoub's original that point directly to French-Egyptian cultural politics and geopolitics, which left the deepest impression on their translator. Indeed, al-Ṭahṭāwī's preface to *Naẓm al-'Uqūd* tells a different story of his reception of Agoub's *Lyre.* Here al-Ṭahṭāwī informs us that it was the poem's "praise for Egypt" that spurred him to translate it, suggesting that he was attracted to a French in which he saw a complex reflection of *Egyptianness.* So deep is al-Ṭahṭāwī's identification with Agoub's French poem that he insists that "most of its words had already occurred to [his] mind and heart, were on the tip of the tongue of [his] intention" *("wa kāna jullu mā fīhā yahjusu fī fu'ādī wa yanṭiqu bihi lisānu murādī")*, or—more literally—that "the tongue of his intention *speaks* much of what is in this poem."[105] Yet al-Ṭahṭāwī's "mode of intention"—his desire to affirm Egypt—clearly finds its fulfillment in a zone of "pure language," of Intention, that a *French* universal governs. For it is a Westernizing Egypt whose praises Agoub's *Lyre* sings. By declaring his intention to restore Egypt to glory with the Napoleonic cry, "Je transporte l'Europe aux déserts de l'Afrique!" ("I transport Europe to the deserts of Africa!") Agoub's speaker describes a (post)colonial Egyptian self whose supersession of Europe and restoration to sovereignty depend on *becoming European,* on resubmission to the colonial.

Given Agoub's biography, small wonder that the speaker of his *Lyre* should be a (post)colonial migrant Egyptian-born francophone poet whose voice and personhood are both inspired and silenced by a seductive French mistress-muse.[106] And given al-Ṭahṭāwī's position as a (post) colonial Egyptian intellectual forced to renegotiate the value of his civilizational currency against the new "gold" standard of France, small wonder that he found in Agoub's poem a "tongue" that could voice his preoccupations and predicaments. For *La Lyre brisée* is nothing if not an exploration of the troubled *accords*—harmonies, agreements—struck between an Egyptian speaker of French and a lover-antagonist who stands allegorically for a French language that both gives power to its Egyptian user and takes it away. To understand Agoub's *Lyre* and the ways in which al-Ṭahṭāwī would filter his experience of French through it, we must look through the sexual politics of love reflected in the few stanzas that surface in *Takhlīṣ al-Ibrīz* to the sexualized geopolitics of colonial attachment and rupture in the crucial stanzas that al-Ṭahṭāwī screens from immediate view.

THE TRANSPORTS OF *FRANCOPHONIE*

If al-'Aṭṭār's "Maqāmat al-Faransīs," written at the high noon of French colonialism in Egypt, interrupts an all-but-consummated French-Egyptian union only to equivocate that interruption and "retell" the seduction plot of Napoleonic occupation, Agoub's *Lyre* interrupts a French-Egyptian union *already* consummated to attempt a reassertion of Egypt's glory, only to end with the recoupling of Egypt to France. What the poem stages is an erotic and political tussle for sovereignty between two actors: a (tacitly) French-identified woman named Thaïre and an Egyptian-identified male speaker. Although passion for Thaïre unleashes the speaker's song, it also reduces his voice to sighs of love for her and resuscitations of the glories of ancient Greece, for the "ardent brand" *("ardente empreinte")* of her kiss "creates [his] harmonies *[accords]*."[107] Thus the *accords* struck in Agoub's *Lyre* are complex notes of poetico-political agreement. They at once strum the chords of the poet's self-expression—his attempted sovereignty—and tie the cords of his bond(age) to Thaïre, who imprints her mark on his words as a slave owner might brand the enslaved. Quickly the first stanza peels open to reveal the politics of "love." Hinting that his lyre has been little more than a "tributary lute," subordinating its song to passion for Thaïre, the poet cries for his muse to "burn, storm / like the wind of our deserts!"[108] With the translation of his Greco-French lyre into its Arab alter ego, a "tributary lute," Agoub's speaker implies that his is at best a subaltern instrument, bereft of any "authentic" voice. The utterance "our deserts," then, is an attempt to repossess voice by displacing it to a zone that is—at least in theory—beyond Thaïre's jurisdiction. Realigning the speaker's subjectivity, it restores his *I* to membership in the lost "we"—the community of Egyptians—from which it has been exiled by the aftermath of French colonialism. This speech act short-circuits the "feminized voice" *("voix efféminée")* into which his union with Thaïre has seduced him and translates him *to Egypt.*[109] It is, of course, a return deeply gendered: a reassertion of sovereign "masculinity" over a woman-France who has turned the poet "woman."

To retrieve his voice, then, Agoub's speaker must "return" to his Egyptian origins; he must also return Egypt to historical pride of place—remind his listeners that the arts of Greece and indeed those of "modern cities" (Paris?) owe *their* origins to his. Egypt now demands his "energetic harmonies"—his *accords*—and subjects him to "the transports of a filial stirring."[110] The word *déserts* (deserts) "exerts a magic power" on his soul: "It names the homeland *[patrie]* and dictates [his] duty." Cries the speaker, "Egypt, I hear you! . . . / and I dare to measure my thought against your stature!"[111] The French muse abandoned, Egypt is now both muse and yardstick of his measures—poetic, subjective, historical. Yet what seems a subversive shift of the "universal" ground of valuation from France to Egypt is not so subversive. In a breath, Agoub's speaker metamorphoses from proto–Egyptian nationalist into surrogate French imperialist.

And alone, by the superior force of poetic power,
I transport Europe to the deserts of Africa!
Egypt, one of your sons will be your benefactor.
Is there a nobler prize for even the gods?
May my lute, attaining the marvels of Orpheus,
the happy dominator of your climes,
create a nation *[patrie]* of your errant tribes
and send, echoing across your burning dunes,
a legislating song![112]

In the seductive guise of an Arab lute, the Western lyre enters Egypt. And similarly disguised as native son, Agoub's speaker operates as colonial agent. Having voided into "deserts" the Egypt that his voice ostensibly would reanimate, he proceeds to transport Europe into Africa. In that transport, we can read the ideological reconquest of Egypt by French empire that Agoub's student, al-Ṭahṭāwī, would abet: a process that would begin with the translation—or transport—of France into Egypt and end with the translation of Egyptian self-definition into French terms. For when "home" becomes a trophy and the lute of the Egyptian-born speaker its "happy dominator," Egypt is no longer the native son's inheritance but the outsider's prize, captured through French. No longer does the speaker receive Egypt's demands through its imagined voice. Once an object *on* whom a word acted magically and *for* whom the homeland was named, he is now a Subject who creates his own country—in Europe's image. Thus the speaker's early cry of Egyptian nationalism is also the *porte-parole* of French imperialism. His act of translation *(traduire)* is also a legal summons, as in the French locution *traduire quelqu'un en justice*. Indeed, since the exiled speaker cannot return to Egypt—"home" is forever lost to him—he exhorts Mehmed Ali instead to "see in Europe a judge, and march toward glory!"[113] Agoub's lawmaking French song summons Ottoman Egypt to the court of Europe, where Egyptian civilization ultimately will be judged. Thaïre's France is once again the locus of "glory." It is against heights French, not Egyptian, that the poet and his Egypt finally must "measure [their] thought."

Al-Ṭahṭāwī found these pivotal stanzas compelling. His translation deeply personalizes Agoub's original, replacing the diasporized son's strainings to remake Egypt with the intimate will of the autochthonous Egyptian to realize that end. For al-Ṭahṭāwī, Egypt is too fertile a space to void into "deserts," into Agoub's Africa Deserta. As the source of his inspiration, he replaces Agoub's "wind of our deserts" with "the winds of Egypt, [winds] of unrest," thereby locating his muse in a specifically Egyptian geography. Thus al-Ṭahṭāwī assumes not so much Agoub's *je* as that *je* intensified; he makes Agoub's "civilizing" *I* more profoundly his own. Witness his evocation of Egypt's return to the consciousness of the displaced poet:

> Ah Egypt! When she crosses my mind,
> she dazzles me with her formidable magic
> and stirs in me memories of my friends
>   and reminds me of my pledge to my homeland[114]

In al-Ṭahṭāwī's rendering, Egypt—not "deserts" evacuated of people and meaning—prompts a return of the speaker's imagination to his birthplace, and that "return" conjures emotions more immediate than Agoub's. Eschewing a literal translation of Agoub's "Il nomme la patrie et dicte le devoir" ("It names the homeland and dictates my duty"), al-Ṭahṭāwī situates his duty to bring the secrets of French "progress" back to Egypt (emotively described as *awṭānī,* lit., "my homelands") within a sense of obligation to flesh-and-blood Egyptian intimates (*ṣiḥābī,* "my friends"). Twice he accents the first-person possessive.

More arresting is al-Ṭahṭāwī's translation of the reconquest of Egypt by Agoub's speaker. Where Agoub invokes a translational yet nonamorous idiom of transcontinental movement—dubbing the reconquest a "transport" of Europe to Africa—al-Ṭahṭāwī recasts cultural transport and translation (the Arabic *anqulu* connotes both) as erotic penetration.

> By my establishing all the arts in you [fem.],
> with their gifts you certainly will become rich;
> With my creative powers, clear and firm,
> I transport Europe into you, O light of my eye!
>   and I endow you, through knowledge, with good fortune[115]

Ventriloquizing Agoub's "Je transporte l'Europe aux déserts de l'Afrique!" as "anqulu Ūrūbbā fīki yā nūra 'aynī" ("I transport Europe into you, O light of my eye!"), al-Ṭahṭāwī repitches the cry as a hotly personal apostrophe. He addresses Egypt directly, as *you,* using the second-person grammatical feminine *(fīki),* and as beloved: witness the endearment *yā nūra 'aynī* ("O light of my eye"). So visceral is the *I-you* connection between translator al-Ṭahṭāwī and his Egypt that his act of French-to-Arabic translation crackles with the electricity of a love union, comes to life as "copulation." He announces himself Egypt's Westernizer, civilizer, even impregnator: the twice-repeated prepositional phrase *fīki*—"in you" or "into you," implying penetration—

echoes in the clause "I endow you" *(awfīki)*. Thus identified with the French "civilizing mission," al-Ṭahṭāwī becomes, like Agoub's speaker, a surrogate regenerator of Egypt.

With *La Lyre brisée*, then, Agoub left a lingering last kiss—an *"ardente empreinte"*—on his foremost Egyptian student. For al-Ṭahṭāwī, a more "Islamically correct" incarnation of Agoub's speaker, France proved a seductive "bride" whose words lured him into reimagining Egypt within a new French-defined universal. She was a siren who re-taught him, as Jomard had hoped she would, "language." In part from his encounter with Agoub's "Egyptian" French, al-Ṭahṭāwī would conclude that French might be as poetic a language as Arabic (and thus *exchangeable with* Arabic) and would enact, on his return to Egypt, the imperial project of cultural transport he had translated from Agoub's text.

From his first description of Paris in *Takhlīṣ al-Ibrīz*, al-Ṭahṭāwī's comparisons of that city to Cairo—and, by extension, of France to Egypt—oscillate between commensurability and its opposite, only to succumb to the seduction of seeing proportion in disproportion. In complex erotic terms, al-Ṭahṭāwī dramatizes the grammar of incommensurability, linguistic and epistemological, that haunts his activity as a translator. That grammar plays out under the cover of an orthography lesson in which he teaches his Arabic-speaking readers, who write the ending of *Paris* with a *z* sound *(Bārīz)*, to spell its ending with an *s* sound *(Bārīs)*, as the French do:

> The Arabs and the Turks write "Bārīs" or "Barīs" or "Bārīz" and sometimes "Fāris" [for *Paris*]. I believe that what is most appropriate is to write it with an *s [bi al-sīn]*, even though [the practice of] reading it with a *z [bi al-zāy]* has become widespread on the tongues of those who are not of its people; perhaps that [practice] stemmed from the fact that *s* in the French language is sometimes read as *z*, under certain conditions—although [the *z* sound] is absent in this instance except in the case of the *nisba*-adjective, where the *nisba*-adjective [derived from] "Bārīs" is "Bārizyānī" *[Parisien]* among the French. And this is exactly the reason [why we say "Bārīz"], for the *nisba*-adjective returns things to their origins. But this rule [applies to] the Arabic *nisba*, and the *nisba* here is foreign. Thus I have followed [the practice] of writing ["Bārīs"] with an *s* in . . . verses that I have composed on that city, when I said:
>
> Were I to finalize my divorce from Paris, it would only be to reunite in love with Cairo—
> For each of the two is a bride to me, but Cairo is not the daughter of unbelief!

> *[La'in ṭallaqtu Bārīsa thalāthan // famā hādhā li ghayri wiṣāli Miṣr*
> *Fakullun minhumā 'indī 'arūsun // wa lākinna Miṣra laysat binta kufr!]*

And I have said:

> Indeed they have mentioned Beauty's suns [fem.] one and all, and said that they rise in Cairo;
> Yet had they seen them rising in Paris, they would have singled those [suns] out for mention
> *[Laqad dhakarū shumūsa al-ḥusni ṭurran // wa qālū inna maṭla'ahā bi Miṣr*
> *Wa lākin law ra'awhā wa hiya tabdū // bi Bārīsa lakhaṣṣūhā bi dhikr]*[116]

Al-Ṭahṭāwī invokes a complex grammatical logic to make Arabic French, bringing Arabic *Bārīz* in line with French *Paris*. One should, he suggests, write a proper noun as "properly" written by the people to whom it "properly" belongs: in the case of *Paris,* the French. What passes for a utilitarian discussion of the perils of incorrectly Arabizing French by misapplying Arabic rules to French, then, is actually a subtle meditation on the problem of *nisba.* While grammatically the *nisba* is an adjective denoting ancestry, origin, or belonging formed by the addition of a suffix *(yā')* to an Arabic noun, its semantic resonances in Arabic range from those of proportion, reference, and comparison to those of kinship, including kinship by marriage (from which its grammatical meaning derives). Al-Ṭahṭāwī's reflection on the back-formation of the Arabic noun *Bārīz* from the *nisba* adjective *Bārizyānī* thus unleashes a stream of questions, all turning on some notion of *nisba.* Which *nisba* (relation-by-marriage) should the intellectually bigamous (post)colonial Egyptian claim, and from what lineage—*nasab*—will Egypt henceforth descend? By what frame of reference *(bi al-nisbati li mādhā)* is the Egyptian intellect to judge the relative worth of Paris and of Cairo? If Cairo is the more pious (she is not, after all, the "daughter of unbelief!"), by what proportion *(fī ayyi nisbatin)* is the Egyptian to count that point in her favor? Or is the rising sun of Paris, as al-Ṭahṭāwī suggests, to eclipse even the Cairene Islamicity with which he wishes to "reunite in love"? Ultimately singling out the beauty of Paris for mention, al-Ṭahṭāwī refuses to conclude his imagined divorce and never returns (imaginatively speaking) to Cairo, for all his valorization of her piety. As he astutely notes, "the *nisba*-adjective returns things to their origins." To the question of how the Egyptian intellectual henceforth will form his *nisba*-adjective of belonging, what he will take as the point of origin of his thinking, and which genealogy *(nasab)*—Homer or the Arab chroniclers?—he will claim as his own, al-Ṭahṭāwī gives the last word to Paris—and *Bārīs*. Haunting his tacit reply to the question that yawns across the white space between the first couplet, privileging Cairo, and the second, privileging Paris, is the Qur'ānic last word on a man's conditional prerogative to marry more than one woman: the reminder that he may never be just between them, thereby failing the test of equity on which the Qur'ān predicates polygamy (4:3, 4:129). Moreover, the closing of his book's second title, *al-Dīwān al-Nafīs fī Īwān Bārīs*, rules in favor of *Bārīs*, cutting the ties that bind *Bārīz* to its Arabic *nisba*.

In the end, al-'Aṭṭār, al-Ṭahṭāwī's first teacher, theorized more than the psychodynamics of French colonialism in Egypt. He also prophesied Egypt's (post)colonial relation to France. If, for al-'Aṭṭār's fictional alter ego, the French scholar-soldier of the Napoleonic occupation resembled a sunlike "bride" whose power to seduce Egypt depended on the affirmation of "her" target's precolonial sovereignty, on "her" ability to make the Egyptian male subject see himself as the seducer, the same is no less true for al-Ṭahṭāwī's alter ego in the couplets above. Yet where al-'Aṭṭār's union with the French remains only hypostatized, al-Ṭahṭāwī's is real. He has committed the "sin" on whose brink al-'Aṭṭār's narrator only teetered: by accepting Mehmed Ali's invitation to travel to France, he has accepted at last—in (post)colonial time—the invitation to live with the French that al-'Aṭṭār's colonized double had refused. The Egyptian male subject of al-Ṭahṭāwī's couplets now claims both Paris and Cairo as sunlike "brides" *(shumūs)*. Self-styled colonizer of a France that culturally colonizes him—imaginary seducer to Paris's seduced "bride"—he becomes also colonizer of his own country, equally his "bride." Al-'Aṭṭār's narrator cannot quite imagine union with France. Al-Ṭahṭāwī's speaker, by contrast, cannot quite imagine *divorce* from France. His desire to leave his French "bride" remains conjectural: the line "Were I to finalize my divorce from Paris," which literally reads, "Were I to thrice divorce Paris," invokes the terms of Islamic law—in which a husband must invoke the words "I divorce you" three times before a divorce is final—only in the subjunctive. Quit France and return to Egypt al-Ṭahṭāwī must if he is to fulfill the imperial will of Jomard and Agoub, if he is to inseminate his other "bride"—Egypt—with the issue of French-Egyptian "copulation." Yet even then the French divorce will not be final.

CHAPTER FOUR

Surrogate Seed, World-Tree

Mubārak, al-Sibāʿī, and the Translations of "Islam" in British Egypt, 1882–1912

In 1908 Evelyn Baring, first Earl of Cromer, freshly resigned from his post as Britain's consul-general in Egypt, mused that England would never control Egypt until Egyptians had abandoned the "attractive damsel" of French civilization for the "greater moral worth" of England, that "excellent but somewhat ill-favoured matron."[1] Some eighty years after Mehmed Ali Pasha first dispatched Egyptian students to France, Cromer ascribed French success in Egypt in part to the Pasha's desire to fortify Egypt against the specter of "British aggression" but more emphatically to the attraction that French civilization exercised over Egyptian minds. That attraction Cromer located in language. The French, he writes, "were aware that, if the youth of Egypt learnt the French language, *they would, as a necessary consequence, be saturated with French habits of thought,* and they hoped that sympathy with France and French political aims would ensue."[2] Cromer's accent on language echoes that of his colonial forebear Thomas Babington Macaulay, whose "Minute on Indian Education" of 2 February 1835—which dubbed Egypt "a parallel case" to India—had this to say of Mehmed Ali's project:

> Suppose that the Pacha of Egypt, a country once superior in knowledge to the nations of Europe, but now sunk far below them, were to appropriate a sum for the purpose of 'reviving and promoting literature, and encouraging learned natives of Egypt,' would anybody infer that he meant the youth of his pachalic to give years to the study of hieroglyphics . . . ? Would he be justly charged with inconsistency if, instead of employing his young subjects

> in deciphering obelisks, he were to order them to be instructed in the English and French languages, and in all the sciences to which those languages are the chief keys?[3]

Yet where Macaulay, writing in 1835, saw in Mehmed Ali's promotion of a gallicized Egypt an "original" from which he could translate the policies that would anglicize India, Cromer's hindsight spots an opportunity that England had missed to make *itself* the original from which Egyptian modernity would translate. Seized, that opportunity could have forged an Egypt no less British than India. Hence Cromer's lament: "For half a century prior to the British occupation" in 1882, while "the British Government were wholly inactive in respect to Egyptian education, no effort was spared to propagate a knowledge of French in Egypt."[4] Macaulay's insinuation that English, like French, might enter Egypt as a "key" to European science languished—as Cromer implies—in the realm of the counterfactual. India was the field on which Macaulay sought to realize that counterfactual as *fact,* drawing inspiration for his creation of a "class of persons, Indian in blood and colour, but English in taste, in opinions, in morals, and in intellect" from the French creation of such a class of Egyptian interpreters.[5] For although Mehmed Ali also had sent Egyptians to England in the early nineteenth century, dispatching twenty students to Joseph Lancaster's Central School in London in the 1820s, by 1835 more than five times that number had been educated in France.[6] Fully twenty-five years after the British invaded Egypt, Cromer still called for the implantation of English in an Egypt preoccupied by French—still argued the imperial necessity of converting Macaulay's supposition into flesh-and-blood proposition.

Flesh-and-blood indeed. In the crucial passage from *Modern Egypt* to which the opening of this chapter alludes, Cromer stages the problem of Egypt's passage from a French (post)colony to a British quasi-colony in the sexualized tones of erotic competition. "Amongst the obstacles," he writes,

> which have stood in the way of the British reformer in Egypt, none is more noteworthy than that both Europeanised Egyptians and Levantines are *impregnated with French rather than with English habits of thought.*
>
> . . . The semi-educated Oriental . . . looks coldly on the Englishman, and rushes into the arms of the Frenchman.
>
> . . . On the one side, is a damsel possessing attractive, albeit somewhat artificial charms; on the other side, is a sober, elderly matron of perhaps somewhat greater moral worth, but of less pleasing outward appearance.

> The Egyptian, in the heyday of his political and intellectual youth, naturally smiled on the attractive damsel, and turned his back on the excellent but somewhat ill-favoured matron.[7]

Here, as in Ḥasan al-ʻAṭṭār's *maqāma* and in Frantz Fanon's reading of the man of color and the white woman, the genders of both colonized and colonizers—past and present—oscillate. What Cromer, remarking the gallicization of Egyptian thought, earlier describes as *saturation,* he now dubs *impregnation.* France he casts, implicitly, in the role of the impregnating masculine; Egypt, more explicitly, in that of the impregnated feminine. Yet impregnation, Cromer suggests, is only the dénouement of a colonial "pre-text." That pre-text is a story of seduction, where the "vivacious and cosmopolitan" Frenchman and the "undemonstrative" and "insular" Englishman—vying for Egypt's attentions—appear, strangely, in the guise of competing "females": one the very damsel that al-ʻAṭṭār, Joseph Agoub, and Rifāʻa Rāfiʻ al-Ṭahṭāwī invoke in their representations of France as "bride" or "mistress"; the other, the English matron "passed over" in favor of her younger, more dazzling French rival.[8] Here too, as in al-ʻAṭṭār, the would-be colonizer is the beheld; the would-be colonized, the beholder: the Egyptian is tempted to see himself not as a feminized subject susceptible to impregnation but a man in "the heyday of *his* political and intellectual youth," torn between damsel and matron and ostensibly empowered to choose between them.[9] With the British impregnator, like his French rival, strategically "disguised" in the feminine, the challenge now—as Cromer sees it—is to outdo flirtatious France and spread England's colonial seed in Egypt. Cromer predicates British success in Egypt on eros. Even the support of Egypt's resident Europeans for British colonial "reform" is insufficient, he sniffs, because "their friendship [is] *platonic.*"[10]

Yet potency eludes the would-be English impregnator. For even after "he" reincarnates himself as the Baudrillardian "feminine" and assumes the transvestite state of feminized masculinity that might seduce Egypt into subjection—a passage similar to that which the French undergo in the perception of al-ʻAṭṭār's narrator—"he" emerges, ironically, as a "sober, elderly matron": no longer fertile.[11] With both masculine potency and feminine fertility thus compromised, how can this man-turned-matron (however charming s/he might prove to the Egyptian) ultimately reproduce English thought in Egypt? To do so, s/he will need a surrogate. Thus, within the dynamics of relation that England's self-translation into the "feminine" engenders, the colonized Egyptian would find himself momentarily "masculine," reinvested with sovereignty. Yet the sovereignty he enjoys is mere surrogacy. In falling for the mature, respectable Victorian "matron," Cromer hints, the colonized Egyptian male subject might become a surrogate *father* for the Englishman lurking behind that matronly disguise, impregnating Egypt on England's behalf. Yet the Egyptian male subject cannot do so without first having turned himself into a surrogate *mother* for English ideas: without reverting to the colonized, "feminized" subject he actually is and offering up a metaphoric womb for English "impregnation," reproducing *himself* as the issue of a translational copulation. Thus reborn *as* "English," he can sire anglicized Egyptian progeny and exorcise the Gallic ghost at last.

In the Anglo-Egyptian union that Cromer so fervently desires, then, the Egyptian is called to translate a colonial relation imperiled by the specter of sterility into one alive with the promise of fertility. Cromer's reflections are written from the colonial hindsight of the 1906 Dinshawāy affair, which had driven the deepest wedge possible between the "undemonstrative" Englishman and the Egyptians he might have courted. At the village of Dinshawāy in the Nile Delta, a tribunal of three Britons and two Egyptians had wrongfully ordered the public hangings of four men and the brutal punishment of seventeen others for the alleged murder of a British officer who in fact had died of sunstroke.[12] The executions provoked outrage in Egypt and outcry in England, polarizing opinion there much as the Morant Bay massacre in Jamaica had polarized it in 1865. Cromer resigned and left Egypt in 1907. The opportunity to anglicize Egypt remained, in many respects, missed.

As architect of colonial policy in British Egypt, Cromer was well positioned to consummate the intellectual impregnation of which his *Modern Egypt* dreams. Yet he was reluctant to do so. Indeed, throughout his tenure as British agent and consul-general in Egypt (1883–1907), he encouraged a technocratic system of public instruction.[13] Certainly Cromer claimed that "the English in Egypt have acted on the principle advocated by Macaulay," refusing to keep Egyptians "ignorant" and thus "submissive."[14] Yet education was not a priority of his administration. Prior colonial service in India had convinced him that literary education, especially, more likely would sow anti-British revolt than cement "Christian morality" and pro-British attachments among the colonized.[15] Better to trust, Cromer believed, that Egyptians would embrace the live moral example of the English once they had outgrown the "heyday of [their] political and intellectual youth." Leaving Egypt, he was unsure that he had succeeded. Only by envisioning the future promise of what was, at the time, an inauspicious showing for Britain in Egypt could he assure himself and his English readership that the colonial enterprise in fact would bear fruit.

Sizing up the "political fruit" of a quarter century of British occupation in Egypt, then, Cromer issues this paternalistic postmortem:

> If a race of Egyptians capable of governing the country without foreign aid has not as yet been formed, the fault does not lie with the English. It must be sought elsewhere, neither need any impartial person go far afield to find where it lies. It lies mainly in the fact that two decades are but a short time in the life of a nation. Material progress may, under certain conditions, be rapid. Moral and intellectual progress must of necessity always be *a plant of slow growth.*[16]

To Cromer's *coup d'œil impartial,* an eye as "impartial" as the one Edme-François Jomard had trained on Egypt in the 1830s, England's ongoing imperial presence in Egypt is the fault of the Egyptians. The British Empire has done its work—planted the seed of "progress"—but Egypt is neither morally nor intellectually fertile enough to nurture that seed to maturity and in so doing permit the British to leave. For Cromer, the "moral and intellectual progress" that would make even the most "Europeanised" Egyptians English enough to claim the right to self-rule depended on the evolution of those Egyptians from "de-moslemised Moslems and invertebrate Europeans" into subjects whose moral backbone is structurally Christian if not religiously so.[17] To be fully Europeanized and thus eligible to seize the reins of governance from the British, then, the Egyptian Muslim had to become a secular Christian. Neither militaries nor money, Cromer maintains, could clinch the success of British empire in Egypt. Only an act of culture could—*culture* in a sense that evokes the word's etymological roots in cultivation, a seeding of secularity-as-religion and a trust in its eventual flowering.[18] That flowering was to be achieved by retaining the vessel of Islam but supplanting its contents with attitudes of Western provenance, hence the image of the "de-moslemised Moslem" whose moral vacuum—whose missing European vertebrae—might be refilled someday by a de-Christianized Christianity. Clearly Cromer does not want to herald the rise of Egyptian self-government too soon; he defers it to an unspecified (post)colonial future. It is to the afterlife of the British occupation of Egypt, he suggests, that the eye searching for "any immediate and important political fruit . . . from the tree of educational progress in Egypt" should look.[19]

In suggesting that England would not woo Egypt into empire until it manipulated—like Napoleon—the appearance of intimacy, Cromer drew lessons in colonial seduction from the French-Egyptian encounter. Yet his inability to sustain the illusion of equivalence between the Egyptian and the Englishman—his insistence, rather, on the intractable difference between them—forestalled the impregnation (or insemination) of Egypt with "English habits of thought" and the dissemination of those seeds within. For Cromer was no Napoleon. He believed far too strongly in the racial superiority of the English to flirt with Egypt in the language of Islam. English literature would do, half by accident, what English colonial policy would not. The British Empire's work of translational seduction would fall to an English text that had never "intended" a Muslim target—Thomas Carlyle's *On Heroes, Hero-Worship, and the Heroic in History* (1841)—and to an Egyptian translator that British colonial education had never "intended" to anglicize, Muḥammad al-Sibāʿī.[20]

Arguably the most influential Muslim translator of English texts in early-twentieth-century Egypt, al-Sibāʿī (1881–1931) would fulfill Cromer's wish in spite of Cromer. Indeed, he imagines his task as a translator in disseminatory terms strikingly reminiscent of Cromer's. Introducing his Arabic rendering of Charles Dickens's *A Tale of Two Cities* (*Qiṣṣat al-Madīnatayn,* 1912), al-Sibāʿī pronounces that translation, published in Cairo less than one year after his translation of Carlyle,[21]

> the third in a series of volumes that will appear so long as breath and pulse remain . . . in us, the third of these seeds of superiority that we will not give up on disseminating, despite the barrenness of this soil and dryness of this ground, and despite the lack of all hope of seeing this seedling of our hands' [planting] ripen, its blossoms smile at us, and its fruits stretch their necks to us. Rather, we felt certain that a day would come when God would breathe life into the [rotten] corpse of this nation *[fī rimmati hādhihi al-ummati]* and transform this grave that people call "Egypt" *[yuḥawwilu hādhā al-qabra alladhī yusammīhi al-nāsu "Miṣra"]* into a land where you might meet living human beings who feel and reason, not plants in human guise who do nothing but grow and die . . . when . . . the sun of sensation and feeling would rise at last over our buried seeds, . . . such that their roots would burgeon, their branches grow long, and they would glisten, suddenly, with the bloom of vigor, ripen with fruit.[22]

Though it traffics in the rhetoric of early-twentieth-century Egyptian nationalism, al-Sibāʿī's philosophy of translation is essentially colonialist. Given the ironic continuities between colonial ideology and nationalist discourse that Frantz Fanon, Partha Chatterjee, and others have exposed, their convergence in al-Sibāʿī is not surprising.[23] Thus his determination to introduce, through Dickens and other masters of English literature, "seeds of superiority" into "this grave that people call 'Egypt'" resonates eerily with the designs of British colonial pedagogy. As early as 1838, in his *On the Education of the People of India,* Charles Trevelyan had advanced the proto-Darwinian notion that the progress of a nation depended on the introduction of the foreign—in the case of India, the introduction of English literature, the culture of the *colonizing* foreign.[24] Al-Sibāʿī conjures just such an image of indigenous stasis awaiting the rejuvenating intervention of the foreign, suggesting that only a colonizing Britain could cultivate the barren soil of his country and make it yield the fruits of "civilization." His Egypt is sterile, even dead: a rotten corpse, a grave, a nation of unreasoning plants—that is, of nonhumans masquerading as humans. Even God, breathing life into this dead Egypt, is not omnipotent enough to recreate it ex nihilo; God disposes, yes, but first Britain—through the agency of al-Sibāʿī's translation—proposes. If "Egypt" is to become a nation, he intimates, if its people are to be at all human, it must be regrown from British seeds. Already Cromer's "plant of slow growth" is flourishing.

Both Cromer's postmortem on British empire in Egypt and al-Sibāʿī's hope of reviving a "dead" Egypt through his translational offices suggest that empires of culture, like texts, do not always begin life during the lives of their authors. The impact of British imperialism on the Egyptian literary-cultural psyche is perhaps a posthumous event or a prosthetic survival, born not in the lifetime of Cromer's tenure, or even in the immediate life of al-Sibāʿī's translations, but in their afterlife—not as "original" but as "translation," perhaps even as the translation of a translation. For if the "original" of Empire is dead, so too is the "original" of Egypt. Both the would-be British Empire whose power Cromer wishes to consolidate and the would-be Egyptian nation whose birth al-Sibāʿī wishes to spawn depend on the seductions of translation—its displacements of signification—to realize their powers. Empire awaits the agency of the native translator to disseminate its power in native soil; nation hopes that that very soil, fertilized by the native translator, might regenerate the colonized as the colonizer's "likeness" and—through that slow translation—transform the colonial subordinate into the national sovereign. Indeed, when Walter Benjamin argues that a translation issues from an original "not so much from its life as from its afterlife," he helps us see why colonial power more effectively realizes its intention by seduction—by indirection—than by force.[25]

PART OF EUROPE?

Yet the *prelife* of British occupation in Egypt also foreshadows the supplantation of French by English that al-Sibā'ī's translations eventually will perform. Cromer's dream is fulfilled as much in prolepsis as in futurity. To appreciate the dynamics of al-Sibā'ī's 1911 reception and translation of Carlyle, we must return to the eve of the British occupation of Egypt in 1882, and the scene of love-in-translation that transpires between an Egyptian Muslim shaykh and an English Orientalist in a fictional text published that year by one of the foremost Egyptian reformists of the nineteenth century, 'Alī Mubārak (1823/24–93). Mubārak wrote *'Alam al-Dīn* (Sign of Religion), arguably the first Egyptian "novel," at a time when the fate of Egypt hung between empires: the ongoing dominion of the Ottoman Turks, who had ruled Egypt since 1517; the aborted French occupation of 1798–1801, which though militarily short-lived sustained a long ideological afterlife in Egypt; and the imminent British invasion of Alexandria in 1882, which began just months after the first volumes of *'Alam al-Dīn* appeared in that city.[26] One of a second generation of Ottomans and Egyptians sent to Europe in the post-Napoleonic period, Mubārak studied in France between 1844 and 1849: first at the École Militaire Égyptienne in Paris, then in a military school at Metz.[27] (The École Militaire Égyptienne, founded by Mehmed Ali and run by the French Ministry of War, succeeded the École Égyptienne de Paris, where Mubārak's rival al-Ṭahṭāwī had studied in the 1820s.) When he returned to Cairo, he would serve, over the course of his lifetime, as minister of education and minister of public works.[28] In these capacities he would play a crucial role in modernizing (read: Westernizing) both Egyptian education and the urban plan of Cairo, which would be gutted to make way for a "new" city—patterned on Haussmann's Paris—alongside the old.[29]

From his introduction to *'Alam al-Dīn* and his autobiography in another major work, the twenty-volume Egyptian history, geography, and biographical dictionary *al-Khiṭaṭ al-Tawfīqiyya al-Jadīda* (1886–89), we can deduce that Mubārak began writing *'Alam al-Dīn* around 1867, during the reign of Khedive Ismā'īl.[30] As Timothy Mitchell notes, Mubārak—then undersecretary of the Bureau of Schools—returned to Paris in winter 1867–68 "on financial business for the Egyptian government . . . and to visit the [1867] Exposition Universelle."[31] Back in Cairo, the ambitious administrator-engineer launched *'Alam al-Dīn* as an effort to "teach" Egyptians the lessons he had learned in Europe.

Such a plan suited the designs of the arch-Westernizer Ismā'īl. Anxious to hitch his dominion to the rising star of European empire, Ismā'īl had declared Egypt no longer a part of Africa but now a part of Europe. It is against this geopolitical backdrop that Mubārak's novel unfolds. Running to nearly fifteen hundred pages, it narrates the European voyage of an Egyptian Azharite shaykh named 'Alam al-Dīn and his son, Burhān al-Dīn, in the company of a British Orientalist lexicographer.[32] In this Englishman's possession is a manuscript copy of a famous Arabic dictionary, the *Lisān al-'Arab* (The Arab Tongue) of the thirteenth-century Egyptian scholar Ibn Manẓūr; he seeks the help of an Arabic scholar to correct that copy and prepare it for print in England—and much wider dissemination to European students.[33] In 'Alam al-Dīn the Orientalist finds a willing partner; like many Azharites of the period, marginalized by the progressive secularization of Egyptian institutions from Mehmed Ali forward, the shaykh is impoverished. His decision to accompany the Orientalist to Europe is thus at least partly motivated by economic need. Yet material coercion does not tell the whole story. Translational seduction tells the rest.

For Mubārak's text is a novel in, of, and about translation: a romance of translation haunted by specters of unequal "exchange," where an Egyptian's love for an Englishman's Arabic ultimately impels him to embrace English as the medium through which Arabic might ensure both its preservation and its transformation, its sovereignty and its "progress." Indeed, *'Alam al-Dīn* adopts a posture toward the English much like that of al-'Aṭṭār's *maqāma* vis-à-vis the French, nearly a century earlier: the novel denies Egypt's imminent vulnerability to British rule by representing English acquisition of Arabic and Egyptian acquisition of English as a reciprocal exchange of translational "love." The English lexicographer who enlists 'Alam al-Dīn into the Orientalist enterprise of correcting the dictionary—the act that sets the novel's entire plot in motion—is described from the outset as a "lover of the Arabic language" *("min 'ushshāqi al-lughati al-'arabiyyati").*[34] Once 'Alam al-Dīn himself gets to know the Englishman, "he [grows] enamored of him *[shughifa bi maḥabbatihi]* and desire[s] his friendship with all his heart."[35] Significantly, this passionate desire stems from the fact that the Orientalist "inclines [in affection] toward Muslims *[yatawaddadu li al-muslimīna]*" and shows his "affection *[maḥabba]* for the Arabs, their language, and their sciences."[36] Far from implicating his knowledge in colonial power, the Orientalist's approximation of the religion and language of his interlocutors "humanizes" him enough for the Egyptian shaykh to befriend him: the Arabic reads, "*fa'anisa bihi wa lam yanfur min ṣuḥbatihi*" ("so he grew close to him and felt no aversion to his friendship").[37] From the root verb *anisa* ("to befriend," "to grow close to") derives the word *insān,* "human being," hence a gesture toward the universal human.

Remarking the persistent refrain of "love" in *'Alam al-Dīn,* Ghislaine Alleaume writes, "For 'Alī Bāshā Mubārak, the Orientalist's interest in the Arabs is the product of a 'penchant,' an 'inclination' *(mayl),* even a 'love' *(ḥubb, maḥabba)* for Arabs, or Muslims; the assimilation is constant."[38] Astute as this observation is, Alleaume does not fully probe its corollary. Why is the Arab or the Muslim so enamored of the Orientalist? How and why do the Egyptian characters in Mubārak's text fall "in love" with their European interlocutors—despite the fact that European Orientalism rarely took a benign view of the Arab-Islamic East? To answer that question, I return to the premise that cultural imperialism relies on a politics of translational seduction. By appearing to recognize and to affirm Arab-Islamic power at a time when the British Empire radically compromised that power, I argue, the British Orientalist's "loving" *self-translation* into Arabic (and near-Muslim identity) entices the Egyptian to forget the imperial force of English and ultimately to embrace English "habits of thought" as the protectors of Arab-Islamic—not British—dominion. Mubārak's fiction thus suggests that European Orientalist fluency in Arab-Islamic idiom, however insidious its ends, engendered the psychodynamics that lured real-historical nineteenth-century Egyptian intellectuals to disavow the growing power differential between Europe and the Arab-Islamic world at precisely the moment when they stood to become its victims. Indeed Mubārak was not alone among Egyptian writers of the interempire period in enlisting translation to imagine the Arab-Islamic world into "equality" with Europe. Al-Ṭahṭāwī was also, as we have seen, at pains to prove the commensurability of French and Arabic and the "reciprocity" of French-Egyptian cultural relations—all the while fighting off the undertow of geopolitical inequality that might sabotage his thesis.

I would suggest that the space of translation in Mubārak's novel is precisely the depoliticizing *baḥr,* or sea, in which al-Ṭahṭāwī's *tabaḥḥara* imagines and transacts the radical exchangeability of all languages. Both 'Alam al-Dīn and his son Burhān al-Dīn "exchange" lessons in Arabic for lessons in English on shipboard—the father with the British Orientalist and the son with an Arabic-speaking British youth he befriends during their travels—and Burhān al-Dīn even calls the epistolary travelogue he writes to his mother (who remains back home in Egypt) a "ship" *(safīna)* that shuttles between the shores of Europe and Egypt.[39] Unmoored from politics, Arabic-English exchange can be reimagined as "reciprocal," and so too the Egyptian-British love relation that blossoms from that exchange. Indeed, Burhān al-Dīn rationalizes his friendship with Ya'qūb, the young Englishman, in terms uncannily similar to his father's: "By God's grace, I encountered on the ship . . . an English person who had some knowledge of the Arabic language, so an exceeding intimacy developed between him and me."[40] Yet in a letter to his mother, Burhān al-Dīn hints at inequalities in the relation—the sense that he is gaining more from his English lessons than his British friend is acquiring from his Arabic ones. In fact, Burhān al-Dīn's first encounter with the English youth ends in embarrassment that he knows nothing of history and geography, two disciplines that the youth deems essential to the "progress" *(taqaddum)* of nations. Writes the son, "So I began to teach him and he to teach me, and I think that what I gained from him is greater than what he gained from me . . . for he revealed to me many things of which I had been ignorant."[41] Dubbing his English counterpart, so learned in history, "a mirror of time, a translator of the events of the bygone *[li akhbāri al-māḍīna ka al-turjumāni],*" the young Egyptian perceives himself as a failed "translator" of the material world and wishes that his education could *follow the Englishman's desire,* the better to translate *himself* into Ya'qūb's equivalent: "I became embarrassed by his words, and I longed for my education to follow his wishes."[42] (Significantly, much of the history and geography that the British youth proceeds to teach Burhān al-Dīn issues from European colonial expansion: he owes that knowledge to travels in the Orient, in Africa, and elsewhere with the East India Company and similar vehicles of the colonial sea trade.)[43] This fraught scene of instruction, in which the upper hand of English colonial knowledge upends the fiction of Anglo-Egyptian reciprocity, evokes the "something more" that undercuts al-Ṭahṭāwī's theorization of the radical equivalence of languages.

Given such colonial inequality, how do Mubārak's characters sustain the logic of reciprocity that subtends friendship with two Englishmen—representatives both of Egypt's soon-to-be-colonizer? As one clue, I single out a turning point in the relationship between the elder Egyptian, 'Alam al-Dīn, and his British Orientalist friend. When the Orientalist wonders if religious sensibilities might have stymied scientific advancement in the Islamic East, 'Alam al-Dīn intervenes. He notes that while the medieval Christian church opposed scientific inquiry, no comparable Islamic institution of the period deemed Islam incompatible with science. The Orientalist stands corrected; he tells the Egyptian that he wishes to discuss Islam not in the spirit of those inimical to the faith but as friends and "equals." Indeed, he notes, some European scholars already have begun to revise Western Christian misconceptions of Islam and its attitude toward science. He pulls out one such European "prooftext," which reminds its Western readership that medieval Arabs and Muslims translated ancient Greek science, augmented it with discoveries of their own, and transmitted this scientific legacy to Europe. Significantly, the British Orientalist has translated this text into Arabic; thus, like Bonaparte with his Arabic proclamation, this English traveler is ready, if necessary, to produce the "Arabic book" of European Orientalism as strategic evidence of Western Islamophilia whenever he encounters wary Egyptian Muslim interlocutors. To ʿAlam al-Dīn, he says, "I have translated an excerpt from one European work that proves the advancement of the Arabs; if you permit me, I will read it to you."[44] Curious, the Egyptian shaykh agrees.

The shaykh's reaction to this reading captures the affective force of an Orientalist discourse that submits European imperial power to the "superiority" of Islam. His thoughts "warmed to what his English friend had read . . . for he saw that [the Englishman] was a lover of truth and equitable in judgment, acknowledging the Islamic world's advancement in all the arts. And his love for him grew many times what it had been before."[45] Previously, Mubārak's narrator tells us, the shaykh had avoided discussing religion with the Englishman because he feared an exchange that would debase Islam and threaten their friendship. The Englishman's mobilization of pro-Islamic Orientalist scholarship transforms the Egyptian's mind-set.

> When [the Englishman] . . . did not betray, in his discussion of the [Muslim] community, the slightest sense of its deficiency . . . nor attribute to [that] community the slightest "backwardness," but instead ascribed to it continued progress on the basis of its past attainments, such that it [the Muslim world] became the foundation on which [all] humankind depends for its present and future advancement, and such that but for it . . . the causes of civilization *[al-tamaddun]* and prosperity [would be] lost to [people], so from this moment forward the shaykh conceded to his friend the abundance of research . . . [that this Orientalist account of Arab science evinced].[46]

This passage, I would suggest, answers the question that Alleaume does not: it reveals the terms on which Mubārak's text "assimilates" Egypt to Europe. It is, then, insofar as Western Orientalism fosters "self-love" in the Arab-Islamic subject that that subject is drawn to "love" the West and its knowledge in turn. 'Alam al-Dīn's love for the Englishman and for his translational scholarship redoubles precisely to the degree that Orientalism appears to "decolonize" itself, denying the superiority of imperial Europe and indeed *subordinating* Europe to the epistemological imperium of Arab-Islamic culture. For in negating the "backwardness" that modern European colonialism attributes to the Muslim world and repositioning Islam as the visible past and implied present and future of all human knowledge, the English Orientalist reestablishes Arab-Islamic culture as an epistemological universal: the touchstone of the very terms that the British Empire, poised to invade Egypt, would hijack—civilization, progress, modernity. He effectively "translates" the colonizing European such that he not only speaks in the voice of the colonized Arab-Islamic world, but restores that voice to its *precolonial* sovereignty and even "supremacy" over Europe.

Yet the "self-love" thus fostered issues from and depends on the "love" of the colonizer. Certainly 'Alam al-Dīn's reaction is evidence of anticolonial resistance, testimony to the fact that nineteenth-century Egyptians refused to accept European knowledge on anything but their own terms. Yet the Englishman's validation of Islam would not mean as much as it does to the Egyptian shaykh if the English did not wield the political upper hand in this supposedly "reciprocal" exchange. As we shall see when we return to al-Sibā'ī's reception of Carlyle, the validation of the powerful can hold the validated most deeply under its spell. Such is the effect of the Englishman's pro-Islamic, "Arabized" Orientalist text: it seduces 'Alam al-Dīn into embracing, bit by bit, the colonial idiom of Western scientific and material "progress" as *his own*, henceforth accepting the authority of Western knowledge both on and for Islam and Egypt—and more dangerous still, authorizing that knowledge on the basis of its presumed "disinterestedness."[47] In the intergenerational passage from father 'Alam al-Dīn (whose name means "Sign of Religion") to son Burhān al-Dīn (whose name means "Proof of Religion"), an Islam once taken for granted by its adherents as self-evident *sign* has become subject to external verification by European Orientalism: to the *proof* of the Orientalist's translated text.

With Wadad al-Qadi and other scholars of *'Alam al-Dīn*, Wen-chin Ouyang concurs that the novel's subject "is the role of the 'West' in the 'modernization' of the 'East.'"[48] Ouyang notes, however, that "more complex discursive dynamics" are at work.[49] Contra al-Qadi, who emphasizes Mubārak's insistence on the "superiority" of West to East, she contends that his approach "is less a case of pitting the inferiority of the 'East' against the superiority of the 'West.'"[50] In the dialogues that Mubārak stages between 'Alam al-Dīn, Burhān al-Dīn, and their European interlocutors, she sees sites of struggle in which a nascent Egyptian community negotiates "the paradox of resistance to and acceptance of the 'fruits' of a new colonization."[51] While Ouyang ultimately downplays acceptance and accents resistance in her reading of *'Alam al-Dīn,* I wish to stay close to the paradox between the two. That murky "translation zone" (to borrow Emily Apter's phrase), in which Mubārak's text negotiates the terms on which the dominated might "love" their dominators, is fundamental to the "reterritorialization" of Egyptian politics and culture Ouyang suggests his novel performs: a reorientation that points Ottoman Egypt away from France and toward Britain, presaging al-Sibā'ī's acts of translation nearly thirty years later.[52]

For 'Alam al-Dīn's translational encounter with the English Orientalist transforms not only the general horizons of affective relation between the Arab-Islamic world and the West but also the specific horizons of "love" between Egypt and France, Egypt's erstwhile colonizer and abiding civilizational muse. A closer look reveals just how complex the "love" that Mubārak's novel transacts truly is—and what it takes to effect the kind of assimilation of Egypt to Europe that Alleaume diagnoses in the text. In the novel's ninety-second chapter, "al-Jam'iyya al-Mashriqiyya" (The Oriental Society), 'Alam al-Dīn—along with his son and the pair's two English friends—goes to dinner at the Parisian home of the society's president. The society itself likely is patterned, as Ouyang remarks, on the Société Asiatique, founded in 1822 under the leadership of the French Orientalist Silvestre de Sacy.[53] Interestingly, the Egyptians' first encounter with this bastion of French Orientalism begins on a note of love: the same affect that underpins their relationships to the English. 'Alam al-Dīn is greeted with fanfare; the president takes him "by the hand . . . and [sits] next to him, striking up a friendship *[ānasahu].*"[54] This concord extends beyond social niceties to more serious intellectual exchange. When the assembled French men and women retire with their guests for after-dinner conversation, the shaykh becomes, in effect, sovereign of the gathering.

> [The French] received the shaykh as the halo does the moon, celebrating him as they would a king whose command is obeyed. Whenever a point related to . . . Arabic occurred to anyone, he or she courteously expressed it; the shaykh would answer [that person] with an irrefutable reply, such that they marveled at the eloquence of his expression, the pleasure of his articulation, and the excellence of his memory.[55]

While 'Alam al-Dīn's French hosts—mostly Orientalists—clearly exploit him as a native informant, plying him with questions to better master Arabic, they just as clearly receive him as their "superior." Surely imperial Europe dominates the nineteenth-century world system. Yet to the Egyptian guest, the French hosts extend the seductive possibility that the world might not be as Eurocentric as it seems. They invite the shaykh to imagine himself, and by extension Egypt and the wider Arab-Islamic world, as the axis around which European knowledge orbits. They play "halo" to his "moon" (thus refraction to his light), bondsmen to his lordship (he is, after all, said to be like a "king" obeyed). In Hegelian-Fanonian-Baudrillardian terms, the French entice 'Alam al-Dīn to imagine himself the epistemological, political, and even affective master of the "world" assembled in the president's parlor: the subject of seduction, not its object. In this counterfactual universe, it is the French Orientalists who appear awed by the Egyptian Azharite's command of the Arab-Islamic tradition—not the Orientalists whose knowledge production commands the horizons of Egyptian, or Arab-Islamic, epistemic and political possibility. Here the tables of European dominance and Egyptian subjection are turned—translated—in an illusory haze of love. Only in the guise of admirers do the French enter the orbit of 'Alam al-Dīn's lordly moon; so roundly are the shaykh's enemies defeated, we are told, that their counterarguments cannot touch—literally, circle—his own *("lā yaḥūmu ḥawlahu man 'adāhu")*. As Ouyang remarks of a later passage, 'Alam al-Dīn overturns the notion that "the Orientalists know about Arabic as much as, if not more than, the Arabs themselves." Rather, the shaykh stresses, "the Arabic language and its literary tradition . . . belong to the Arabs, and only they possess true mastery."[56]

But the love-logic that translates Europe's relationship to the Arab-Islamic world from hegemony into intimacy, seducing the Egyptian into believing himself not just beloved of his masters, but indeed their seducer and master, dissipates in the following chapter, "al-Faransīs fī Miṣr" (The French in Egypt). Here the haze of general festivity clears to a close-up conversation that reveals precisely what must be forgotten for the love-logic of French-Egyptian relation to stand. The first interlocutor with whom 'Alam al-Dīn enters into direct reported dialogue at the Oriental Society dinner is a Frenchman who lived in Egypt before the Napoleonic invasion of 1798 and who apparently returned to Egypt with the forces of occupation.[57] Ouyang reads him as "a French 'colonial' officer," a "member of Napoleon's campaign."[58] At first, 'Alam al-Dīn's encounter with this Frenchman elicits the same affect as his interactions with the English Orientalist and the French company gathered at the Oriental Society dinner: he senses the Frenchman's "love for Egyptians and his inclination toward the 'Muḥammadan' family."[59] Once he discovers, however, that this Frenchman had accompanied Napoleon to Egypt, that "love" evaporates in the specter of past violence.

With this nod to history, Mubārak interrupts the seduction plot of French-Egyptian encounter that governs his novel's master narrative. In al-'Aṭṭār's *maqāma* the narrator's terror of the French gives way to attraction precisely when the Frenchman addresses him in Arabic, intoning the opening words of a famous panegyric to the Prophet Muḥammad. In this episode of *'Alam al-Dīn,* by contrast, attraction to the French gives way to a restored apprehension of the terror of colonialism once the Frenchman addresses serious discourse to his Egyptian interlocutor. Mubārak's Frenchman may well speak Arabic. Yet the content of his form, as we soon shall see, breaks the spell of "likeness" to the Egyptian, hence also the seduction of translation. It reveals just how slyly the French thus far have evacuated the Arabic signifier and refilled it with the ideology of French supremacy. For the Frenchman's account of the Napoleonic occupation justifies it in blatantly imperialist terms, arguing the superiority of French epistemes to Arab-Islamic ones and thus the legitimacy of French sovereignty over Egypt.

Narratologically, however, *'Alam al-Dīn* gives the Egyptian the first word on the French occupation. Thus, before the Frenchman begins to narrate the "civilizing" transformations that Napoleon's conquest brought to Egypt and in so doing break the spell of seduction, we hear the effect of the broken spell. The chapter gives us nothing short of an anticolonial *counterhistory* from the Egyptian shaykh: a narrative that anticipates and undercuts not only the version of history his former colonizer would prefer to tell but also the pretensions of that former colonizer—perhaps even of Orientalism itself—to a "love" of Egyptians, Arabs, or Muslims. As Ouyang observes, "What distinguishes [this episode] . . . is the direct confrontation between the colonized and the colonizer over the colonial narrative of historical events and the discourse of modernization."[60] Says 'Alam al-Dīn diplomatically (but pointedly) to the Frenchman:

> I cannot verify this [history of French occupation], given my young age at that time; I can imagine it only to the extent that I used to see my father in those days . . . saying to my mother, "What do you think of these dire straits? The Bedouin Arabs *[al-'arab]* are pillaging in the desert, the Mamālīk [i.e.,

> the Mamelukes] are corrupting and destroying, and the French *[al-firinj]* are in the streets killing and looting, such that he who flees one group *[qawm]* falls into the hands of others," . . . although I know . . . the deceased to be tough . . . , such that nothing could drive him to air these complaints save the horror of what he saw.[61]

Here the Frenchman, forced to defend as benevolence the sheer "horror" of the Napoleonic occupation, intervenes. "The origin of the problem," he tells the shaykh,

> lies entirely in the presence of the Mamālīk, who had made Egypt prey for themselves . . . ; they turned the people and the Bedouin Arabs against us . . . even though the French were innocent . . . , with no goal but to reform [the Egyptian] condition and to rescue the people from the curse of those ignoramuses. So if . . . we had stayed in the lands of Egypt until now, it would have been better for [the Egyptians].[62]

With that apology for French colonialism, whose opposition of Mamlūk rapacity to French political innocence echoes that of Napoleon's proclamation, the Frenchman proceeds to enumerate the many "blessings" of the occupation's legacy: tokens of industrial and scientific modernization, from irrigation systems to new medical facilities (like the famous Qaṣr al-'Aynī hospital) to the printing press. He contrasts the French impulse toward scientific and humanistic innovation with Egyptian stasis in these fields. Most interesting, from my perspective, is the fact that the Frenchman explicitly attributes that stasis to Islam, arguing that "the tendency of Egyptians, like other peoples of the Orient *[al-mashriqiyyīn]*, is to rely on memorization of the Qur'ān and knowledge of some religious matters, stopping at these and never crossing their limits; they do not go deeper into the meanings of books and their secrets."[63] Clearly, the Frenchman associates Islam with arrested thinking and superficial reasoning.

In the face of such discursive domination—the Frenchman's refusal to translate himself into a "Muslim," indeed his insistence on his intellectual superiority *to* the Muslim—the Egyptian resists. As Rasheed El-Enany rightly observes, however, the shaykh does not rebut the Frenchman's charges against Islam.[64] Indeed, I would add, 'Alam al-Dīn initially confines the terms of his resistance to the political: he merely rejects the notion that the Egyptians were wrong to support the Mamālīk and to resist the French. Egyptians and Mamālīk banded together to fight the French, he insists, because the two shared a common stake in Egyptian territorial sovereignty—this despite the undeniable abuses to which the Mamālīk had subjected "native" Egyptians. Says 'Alam al-Dīn, "Defense of the nation [*al-waṭan;* lit., "homeland"] at that time was obligatory on all, there being no difference between the master and the slave *[lā farqa fīhā bayna al-māliki wa al-mamlūki]*. . . . So suppose that the people rose up [against the French] in obedience to the view of their rulers. . . . Did they do anything besides what they had to do?"[65] This rejoinder rejects the terms on which the French would divide (and conquer) the inhabitants of Egypt, separating Mamlūk from Egyptian native. In a society at war with an alien enemy, the shaykh declares, there is no difference between master and slave. Here 'Alam al-Dīn puns on the oxymoronic nature of political authority in eighteenth-century Egypt: the *mamlūk*—a military slave, technically "owned"—was in fact also a ruler or "master" *(mālik)*, and the rightful "master" *(mālik)* of Egyptian land was in fact ruled and thus enslaved *(mamlūk)*. In his ingenious turn of phrase, both the political structure of an old imperialism (that of the Mamālīk and the larger Ottoman imperial system they both represented and undermined) and the political threat of a new (the invasion of the French) justify the equivalence—the translatability—of Egyptian and Mamlūk, two quantities that Napoleon and his Oriental Society avatar deem incommensurable. Still, 'Alam al-Dīn seems oddly apologetic for Egyptian resistance. By insisting that the Egyptians did no wrong in obeying the Mamālīk—that they simply followed orders—he intimates that anti-French sentiment was less a spontaneous effusion of "native" Egyptian political feeling than an obligation to uphold the political imperatives of their Mamlūk rulers. Such a statement ultimately corroborates the Frenchman's assertion that the Mamālīk turned the Egyptians against the French and thus against a modernity supposedly "best" for them.

Further, 'Alam al-Dīn's silence on Islam thus far in this scene—his apparent hesitation to acknowledge that religious feeling too might have bound Egypt's Muslim majority to the Mamālīk—subtly capitulates to the secularizing imperatives of French discourse. Interestingly, it falls to the shaykh's English Orientalist friend to interject a religiopolitical justification of Egyptian resistance.

> What the shaykh says is true. Indeed, the human being's inclination toward his confessional community *[millatihi]* and his faith *[diyānatihi]* is an instinctive matter *[amrun fiṭriyyun]*. Don't you see that the people of Paris did not open the gates of the city to King Henry IV until he had renounced his Protestantism for their sect [i.e., Catholicism], even though . . . everyone [involved] was French, and the origin of the faith was one?[66]

Only when the Englishman thus validates Islam—and does so translationally, equating the reaction of Egyptian Muslims to non-Muslim rule in the eighteenth century with that of French Catholics to Huguenot rule in the sixteenth—does ʿAlam al-Dīn invoke the rationale of shared religion.

> From this one should infer that no one can blame the Egyptians for refusing to bow to the French . . . , given the natural inclination to object to the rule of those who differ from them in religion and race *[fī al-dīni wa al-jinsi]* and to leave [in power] those who share one faith with them and whose habits and laws in judgments are one.[67]

Facing this resistance, the Frenchman abandons the thesis of French-Egyptian nonequivalence and resurrects precisely those discursive tools Napoleon had used to effect a translational seduction of Egypt to French ends. He stresses Napoleon's respect for Islam and involvement of Muslim scholars in governance, pointing specifically to the language of Napoleon's proclamation and to the fact of its translation into Arabic.[68] The shaykh retorts that even if Napoleon had intended no harm to Islam and had tried to rule justly, his French subordinates did not always obey him but acted brutally against Egyptians. Thus, he hints, the sheer violence of occupation trumped any potentially positive intent—or outcome—in the minds of the Egyptians who suffered it.[69] Again, however, his anticolonial critique is tinged with defensiveness. So inconsistent are his French interlocutor's apparent "love" for Egypt (and insistence on the "loving" disposition of Napoleon toward those he conquered) with the stories of French murder, rape, and pillage he has heard since childhood that ʿAlam al-Dīn seems forced to "excuse" his own history as that of a people too traumatized by colonization to receive French governance on more value-neutral terms.[70]

Thus the Frenchman's ideological about-face only shows up the expediency of his "Islam," the insincerity of the Napoleonic claim that the French too are "sincere Muslims." After so open an imperialist insistence on French-Islamic difference, his attempted return to the translational seduction of French-Islamic equivalence fails to lure his Egyptian interlocutor, his would-be colonial subject. By contrast, the Englishman has become the "true" speaker of Arabic, the "sincere" champion of Islam, and thus the new arbiter of European-Egyptian "equivalence." In a move Cromer would think impossible, the French coquette has lost "her" charms, the sober English matron proved "her" moral worth. Indeed, the ninety-fourth chapter of Mubārak's novel, "al-ʿAqāʾid"

(Creeds), clinches Egypt's estrangement from the French and inclination toward the British.[71] Distressed by 'Alam al-Dīn's intimation, in his conversation with the Frenchman of the previous day, that Christians and Muslims are enemies, the Englishman pays him a visit to put matters "right" again—to restore the terms of Christian-Muslim (hence European-Egyptian) "love." As proof of the affection between Christians and Muslims, the English Orientalist cites the Qur'ānic verse, "You will find that those nearest in love for those who believe are those who say, 'We are Christians'" (Qur'ān 5:82).[72] Embracing the Qur'ānic reference, the shaykh affirms the Orientalist's contention and thus reaffirms "love" as the proper basis on which Egypt should receive modern Europe. The Englishman is half-relieved.

Yet 'Alam al-Dīn's English interlocutor is, perhaps, as sly as any Napoleon—as intent on marshaling "religion" to convince the Egyptian that with England lies Egypt's greatest spiritual (hence political) affinity. Into the shaykh's positive reassessment of the relationship of Christianity to Islam, he introduces a strategic wrinkle: today's Christians have lost, he says, many qualities that once distinguished them. Most lamentable, in the Englishman's view, is the fact that "they have an ugly philosophy [with] terrible writings on the religions, the messengers [of God], and the divine scriptures."[73] The shaykh's response is startling. He associates this desacralization of religion with the very *physiognomy* of the Frenchman he had debated the day before. Says 'Alam al-Dīn, "Yes, some of this is reflected on the face of the Frenchman *['alā wajhi al-rajuli al-faransāwī]* who was with us yesterday."[74] For one Egyptian, at least, the once-beloved French have come to embody not just the phenomenon of nonbelief but also the principal threat to Christian-Muslim "love" and European-Egyptian equivalence. Fanning that flame in uncannily Carlylean fashion, the Englishman goes on to tell 'Alam al-Dīn that the Frenchman he met is "among the most learned of the philosophers." "He has authored a book on beliefs," notes the Englishman, "of which I have read a substantial portion and found that it says . . . that all religious confessions descend from one root and that they hold fundamental premises in common, such as the oneness of God."[75] This thesis the shaykh might accept on the Qur'ānic grounds of the oneness of revelation, although elsewhere he is quick to uphold the doctrinal Islamic view that other religions "corrupt" and obscure that essential oneness.[76] More damning is the Englishman's revelation that this Frenchman has traced the Torah to human, not divine, provenance and the Christian contention that Jesus died and was resurrected to ancient Egyptian sources, which claimed the same of Osiris.[77] What stuns the shaykh is the realization that some European scholars have gone so far as to suggest that the origin of all sacred scripture—hence all religion—is not divine, but human.[78] "It is not permissible," he concludes, "to sit with, deal with, or mingle with such people, for they deny the messengers [of God] and the [holy] books, and diminish the true deity, may He be praised; so thanks be to God who safely parted us from that man."[79] With that verdict, reminiscent of 'Abd al-Raḥmān al-Jabartī's rejection of Napoleon's pretended Islamicity on account of its patent anti-Christianity, 'Alam al-Dīn repudiates all association with the Frenchman—and by extension with all French Enlightenment philosophy that imputes a nondivine origin to the divine word. Thus the seduction of Frenchness is dispelled. Yet the seduction plot of European-Egyptian encounter is restored, restaged with Egyptian and English "lovers" in what is merely a different theater.

If the French-educated Mubārak refuses to allow the coloniality of the French past in Egypt to be erased without struggle, why does he elide the looming colonial designs of the English on Egypt? I would suggest that 'Alam al-Dīn's painful struggle to engage the paradoxes of resistance and rapprochement between the French and the Arab-Islamic worlds stands in for a more proximate—hence more covert—struggle with the paradox of *Egyptian-British* friendship in the face of England's rising imperial power in Egypt, where history would belie it and the present betray it.[80] Thus, while virtually all of the action of *'Alam al-Dīn* is set in France, the intended voyage to England never consummated, Mubārak's novel deftly defers the question of Egyptian-European union—whether Egypt really is, could be, or should be "a part of Europe"—away from French, which carries the taint of a colonial past, and toward English, whose coloniality remains potential.[81] He does so despite the fact that the reciprocal "love-in-translation" that his Egyptians entertain with European Orientalists remains at profound odds with the geopolitical inequalities that the scholarship of those Orientalists often abetted: inequalities writ large on the eve of the British invasion of Egypt, which would accord Britain de facto colonial power there for nearly seventy-five years.[82]

ISLAMIZING CARLYLE, ANGLICIZING ISLAM

In *The Intimate Enemy,* Ashis Nandy argues that "modern colonialism won its great victories not so much through its military and technological prowess as through its ability to create secular hierarchies incompatible with the traditional order."[83] These hierarchies, Nandy claims, offered native intellectuals disaffected with local "tradition" an alternative "secular" episteme they found compelling.[84] Although Nandy writes from and about South Asia, his efforts to unravel the appeal of cultural imperialism resonate in other colonial contexts. He is right to suggest that empire succeeded only when the colonized found—or were made to find—something to love in imperial culture. And "secularity" may indeed be the attractive power in question. Yet if the ways in which the colonized choose to translate the literatures of their dominators speak to their epistemological tastes—as I believe they do—then the history of English-to-Arabic literary translation in colonial Egypt suggests a more complex dynamic.

For al-Sibā'ī, it was the recognition of a religious impulse in English literature—the imagination of a shared "Islam" between colonizer and colonized—that kindled the urge to translate that literature's Christian-secular ethos into Arabic. Nowhere is the power of the "religious" to attract the Muslim Egyptian intellect to "secularity" more evident than in al-Sibā'ī's seminal Arabic translation of Thomas Carlyle's *On Heroes,* first published in Cairo in 1911. On the surface, at least, al-Sibā'ī is drawn to Carlyle less because he promises a secular order than because he offers a believing English alternative to the nonbelieving French Orientalist or Parisian *"bint kufr"* ("daughter of unbelief") from whom Mubārak's fictional shaykh and his historical predecessor, al-Ṭahṭāwī, had won—or sought—a divorce. In the second of the original six lectures, delivered in London in May 1840 and published in 1841, Carlyle had upset the long-held European Christian view of the Prophet Muḥammad as an "impostor" and offered a startlingly revisionist account of his life, faith, and mission, basing his work on Orientalist sources, in particular George Sale's 1734 translation of the Qur'ān.[85] Such praise for the Prophet Muḥammad, I argue, moved al-Sibā'ī to ignore Carlyle's assertion that Shakespeare eventually would render the Prophet of Islam "obsolete" (even in Arabia) and to insist—against the evidence of Carlyle's full text—on the radical translatability of the native Islamic "religious" and the Western colonial "secular." Tacitly embracing Carlyle's notion of Shakespeare as poet-prophet (despite the sharp Qur'ānic distinction between poetry and prophetic revelation) and prescribing English literature to Egypt as a cure for French Enlightenment "unbelief," al-Sibā'ī performs the paradox of translating Englishness into Islam and translating both Islam and Egypt, in turn, toward Englishness.

Secularity seduces the colonized Egyptian, then, less by presenting itself as an alternative episteme, pace Nandy, than by validating an existing religious episteme but doing so *in translation*. That translation masks difference in the alluring garb of equivalence: although the translation appears to restore Islam to the Egyptian as "identical" mirror image, it refracts the terms of Islamic "religion" through the language of European "secular" modernity and thus through the distorting prism of European colonial power. As Talal Asad observes, the emergence of the secular in colonial Egypt is neither a break with "tradition" nor nothing new; rather, "new vocabularies . . . are acquired and linked to older ones," borrowing their clothes, for "it is not easy to shed attitudes, sensibilities, and memories."[86] Thus al-Sibāʿī embraces the English colonial secular not in opposition to his native Islam but through it—or through an "Islam" already translated by European colonial power. If al-Sibāʿī had intended to disarm English literature of its imperial force and to imagine a counterfactual cultural field on which Egypt and England could meet as "equals," his refusal to concede any Egyptian loss in the exchange—to countenance the power differential that divides Carlyle's "Islam" from his own—ultimately enables Carlyle's terms to disarm al-Sibāʿī, to annex Egypt to England. As linguistically Arabic and culturally Islamic as al-Sibāʿī's retranslation of Carlyle's "Islam" may seem, it speaks strangely like Carlyle's Christian-secular English.

Born in Cairo in 1881, just before the British occupation, al-Sibāʿī became Egypt's first major Muslim translator of English literature in part because he was a product of the first wave of English-language colonial education in Egypt. Cromer introduced English into Egyptian schools in 1889.[87] By 1913 the final-year curriculum for the literature track at Cairo's Madrasat al-Muʿallimīn (Teachers' College) devoted three times as many contact hours to English literary instruction as it did to Arabic.[88] Thus higher education in British Egypt—al-Sibāʿī's education—was more literary than Cromer wished it to be: "the Westernized, government schools" Cromer supported, as Robert L. Tignor has observed, trained future bureaucrats in English and thus "had the same literary bias as the Indian schools."[89] Al-Sibāʿī's strong English-language formation at the Teachers' College, Anwar al-Jindī suggests, placed him at the forefront of an English-to-Arabic translation movement.[90] A 1904 graduate of the college, al-Sibāʿī went on to translate into Arabic not only Carlyle's *On Heroes*, but many other English works, including William Shakespeare's *Julius Caesar (Riwāyat Yūlyūs Qayṣar)*, Lord Byron's *Childe Harold's Pilgrimage* and "The Bride of

Abydos" *(Tshāyild Hārūld* and "'Arūs 'Abdūs," collected in *Abṭāl al-'Ālam . . . al-Lūrd Bayrūn),* Herbert Spencer's *Education (al-Tarbiya),* Wilkie Collins's *The Woman in White (Riwāyat Dhāt al-Thawb al-Abyaḍ),* Edward FitzGerald's *Rubáiyát of Omar Khayyám (Rubā'iyyāt 'Umar al-Khayyām),* and Charles Dickens's *A Tale of Two Cities (Qiṣṣat al-Madīnatayn).*[91] In 1912 the Egyptian Ministry of Public Instruction made this last a mandatory text in the secondary-school curriculum.

That al-Sibā'ī's work was canonized by a semicolonial educational system is ironic, since he was an anti-authoritarian who routinely ran afoul of that system. Having graduated third in his class at the Teachers' College, al-Sibā'ī was to receive a scholarship to the Borough Road College near London. He was denied the scholarship because he spurned British authority. When Douglas Dunlop, a top British official in the Ministry of Public Instruction, visited the Teachers' College, al-Sibā'ī refused to stand at attention; he kept reading, legs propped on a chair. Years later, al-Sibā'ī—now a secondary-school teacher—again would flout Dunlop's authority during a school inspection, arriving late to class. He would be forced to resign.[92]

Yet al-Sibā'ī's rejection of British authority was of a piece with his investment in the modern subject—the ostensibly "free" individual—and thus with his attraction to the liberal-secularist strain of English thought. Still, the translator's family background suggests why an Islamophilic text like Carlyle's proved so powerful a medium for the transmission of that strain. Al-Sibā'ī was born to a devout Muslim family of the merchant class, renowned for religious knowledge. His father, a merchant of dry goods and textiles *(mānīfātūra)* who pursued literature as an avocation, hailed from a revered line of *ashrāf,* or descendants of the Prophet Muḥammad.[93] His mother, in turn, came from an Egyptianized Turco-Circassian family; her Turkish-born grandfather had arrived in Egypt after the European defeat of Ottoman and Egyptian forces in the 1827 Battle of Navarino.[94] She upheld her marital family's religious stature. The translator's brother, Ṭāhā al-Sibā'ī, noted that his family "clearly lived the religious and saintly spirit."[95]

By his brother's testimony, al-Sibā'ī despised most politicians of his day for their servility to powers British or Egyptian.[96] Nonetheless, he was associated with two major nationalist parties, Aḥmad Luṭfī al-Sayyid's Ḥizb al-Umma and Sa'd Zaghlūl's Wafd. His first writings appeared in 1907 in *al-Jarīda* (the Newspaper), the organ of Ḥizb al-Umma, and in the late 1920s he published regularly in the pro-Wafd weekly *al-Balāgh al-Usbū'ī* (the Weekly Report), where he eulogized Zaghlūl at his death in 1927.[97] Both parties were secular-liberal, and thus both—while clearly anticolonial—envisioned an independent Egypt refashioned along British lines of representative government. Versed in Western liberal political thought, Luṭfī al-Sayyid refused to base Egyptian nationalism in religion, which he felt would divide Egypt's Muslims and Christians and threaten nation formation.[98] Thus he opposed the pan-Islamist Ottomanism of his party's chief rival, Muṣṭafā Kāmil's al-Ḥizb al-Waṭanī. While Luṭfī al-Sayyid's party—which attracted many Egyptian intellectuals—rejected both Ottoman and British imperialisms as tyrannical absolutisms and called for constitutional democracy, Britain looked favorably on its insistence that Egypt must undergo social reform to be "ready" for democracy and that such reform would induce the British to evacuate through "goodwill, not . . . force."[99] Zaghlūl's Wafd, born after the 1914 declaration of the British Protectorate, was more intransigent: Zaghlūl demanded complete Egyptian independence from Britain. His uncompromising stance triggered the populist anticolonial revolution of 1919, and in 1922 Britain granted Egypt quasi-independence. Yet the Wafd negotiated with empire—the party took its name from a 1918 delegation *(wafd)* that requested permission to plead Egypt's case in London. Still, the Wafd enjoyed widespread popularity; its secular-liberal politics attracted Muslims and Coptic Christians. Al-Sibāʻī's eulogy for Zaghlūl suggests support for Wafdist politics and ardent anticolonial sympathies; Providence *(al-qudra),* he writes, placed Zaghlūl "on the stage of Egyptian national life" to confront "the tyranny of those who oppressed it and usurped its rights."[100] He staunchly backed the revolution of 1919.[101] Yet al-Sibāʻī's nationalist politics did not trump his abiding intimacy with English thought. Like Luṭfī al-Sayyid and Zaghlūl, he sensed that the structural logic of the modern liberal nation-state required the reconstitution of the human as a subject of secular law. Thus his work ultimately reoriented literary translation in Egypt toward English. And Carlyle's *On Heroes,* a text initially alluring not in its Englishness but in its Arab-Islamicity, was one reason English literature so compelled him.

Carlyle's *On Heroes* was not the first major English literary work translated in Egypt. As early as the 1880s, Syrian Christian émigrés to Egypt began to publish Arabic translations of English literature. Yaʻqūb Ṣarrūf, editor of the Cairo weekly *al-Muqtaṭaf* (the Selection), published an abridged translation of Sir Walter Scott's *The Talisman* in 1886 as *Riwāyat Qalb al-Asad* (Story of the Lionhearted). In 1898 Ṭāniyūs ʻAbduh published a translation of Shakespeare's *Romeo and Juliet (Riwāyat Rūmiyū wa Jūlīt),* then in 1902 one of *Hamlet (Riwāyat Hāmlit).*[102] Nor was al-Sibāʿī's Carlyle the first translation from "high" English imaginative literature by a Muslim Egyptian. Muḥammad ʿIffat's *Zawbaʿat al-Baḥr* (1909; Sea Storm), a translation of Shakespeare's *The Tempest,* might take that honor.[103] Yet al-Sibāʿī's Carlyle was arguably the first translation that consciously imported a new ideology of literature from English into Arabic—the first to preach a new "religion" of literature to Muslim readers especially. Muhammad ʿAbdul-Hai has suggested that those who revolutionized Arabic letters in early-twentieth-century Egypt—including writers of the Dīwān (Anthology) school such as ʿAbbās Maḥmūd al-ʿAqqād—owed their association of poetry with prophecy to al-Sibāʿī's translation of Carlyle.[104] Writes ʿAbdul-Hai, "His translation of [Carlyle's] chapter on the Hero as Poet was the first romantic edification in Arabic of Shakespeare as poet-prophet."[105] Al-Sibāʿī's popular translation would enter its third monograph edition by 1930. Al-ʿAqqād declared that a biography of al-Sibāʿī would be a biography of his age, pronouncing him the vanguard of the Egyptian literary "renaissance."[106] And Ṭāhā Ḥusayn, the doyen of twentieth-century Egyptian letters, noted that al-Sibāʿī's translations had enabled thousands to access European high culture through Arabic.[107]

If al-Sibāʿī's translation of Carlyle enabled Egyptian writers to view secular literature—English especially—as "religion," it ultimately also enabled them to subsume religion—Islam especially—within the secular and thus to reconcile religion to the political project of colonial modernity. Al-ʿAqqād, Ḥusayn, and other liberal Egyptian intellectuals—drawn to modern Western epistemologies and inclined to Europeanize Arabic literature—produced a spate of "secularizing" biographies of the Prophet Muḥammad in the 1930s and early 1940s. Al-Sibāʿī's translation informed these narratives. J. Brugman argues that it may well have "strongly influenced" al-ʿAqqād's 1942 biography of the Prophet.[108] In his introduction to that book, *ʿAbqariyyat Muḥammad* (The Genius of Muḥammad), al-ʿAqqād cites the deep impression that Carlyle's vindication of the Prophet made on him thirty years earlier.[109] He hints that for a generation of Egyptian intellectuals prone to attack Islam in the name of modern reason—one of whom dismissed the Prophet's power as "a heroism of sword and blood"—Carlyle's voice revalidated the possibility of at once embracing European modernity and recovering Islam.[110] Ḥusayn is said to have told al-Sibāʿī's son, the novelist Yūsuf al-Sibāʿī, "Your father was the first who extricated me from my Azhariteness *[ʿan*

Azhariyyatī]"—in other words, the first to precipitate Ḥusayn's epistemological turn from "traditional" Islam (symbolized by al-Azhar, Cairo's millennium-old mosque-university) to "secular" modernity.[111] Such testimonies bear out Muhsin Al-Musawi's observation that post-1920s attempts by Ḥusayn, al-'Aqqād, and others to "revisit Islamic history" signal neither a return to religiosity nor a concession to Islamist discourse.[112] Rather, as Al-Musawi argues, "elite writing on Islamic subjects is part of a strategy of . . . normalization": an effort to contain Islam by reducing it to "culture," the better to assimilate religion—as al-Sibā'ī first did—to the secular imperatives of the nation-state.[113]

The enthusiastic reception of Carlyle's *On Heroes* in early-twentieth-century Egypt invites us to reconsider Nandy's attribution of the greatest victories of colonialism to the appeal of the secular. Reading al-Sibā'ī, we might say that the "secular," like other colonial epistemologies, wins the minds of the colonized indirectly. For the effect of Carlyle's original on al-Sibā'ī hinges on its capacity to sound enough "like" the translator's native idiom that he begins to fulfill its intention *as if* his own. By fostering the Baudrillardian illusion that Carlyle—and by extension, Britain—have been "taken" by Islam, *On Heroes* beckons its unintended Muslim reader to imagine the Islamic world as not just sovereign (in possession of itself) but indeed imperial (in possession of Christian Europe), and thus to forget that Carlyle's text and history itself already have "taken" Islam for the British Empire. Witness Carlyle's treatment of the Prophet Muḥammad in the second lecture of *On Heroes,* "The Hero as Prophet," which al-Sibā'ī hailed as the reason Carlyle should command Muslim attention:

> We have chosen Mahomet not as the most eminent Prophet; but as the one we are freest to speak of. He is by no means the truest of Prophets; but I do esteem him a true one. Farther, as there is no danger of our becoming, any of us, Mahometans, I mean to say all the good of him I justly can. It is the way to get at his secret: let us try to understand what *he* meant with the world; what the world meant and means with him, will then be a more answerable question. Our current hypothesis about Mahomet, that he was a scheming Impostor, a Falsehood incarnate, that his religion is a mere mass of quackery and fatuity, begins really to be now untenable to any one. The lies, which well-meaning zeal has heaped round this man, are disgraceful to ourselves only. . . . It is really time to dismiss all that. The word this man spoke has been the life-guidance now of one hundred and eighty millions of men these twelve hundred years. These hundred and eighty millions were made by God as well as we. A greater number of God's creatures believe in Mahomet's word, at this hour, than in any other word whatever. Are we to suppose that it was a miserable piece of spiritual legerdemain, this which so many

> creatures of the Almighty have lived by and died by? I, for my part, cannot form any such supposition.[114]

As Muhammed Al-Da'mi has argued, Carlyle's text breaks with the anti-Islamic tenor of both the pre-nineteenth-century Christian theological tradition and much nineteenth-century Western Orientalist scholarship.[115] This passage calls on Christian Europe to reassess the Prophet Muḥammad's global relevance by rereading Islam in his own language—"what *he* meant with the world." Carlyle translates power away from expansionist Europe and returns it to the Arab-Islamic world. First, he fights supremacism with universalism, equalizing believers and beliefs that English prejudices would deem unequal: Muslims deserve to have their worldview taken seriously, he points out, because they "were made by God as well as we." Second, Carlyle reminds his audience that a "greater number of God's creatures believe in Mahomet's word, at this hour, than in any other word whatever." He hints that even in an age when the British Empire is in the ascendant, Islam exceeds the spiritual reach of any other imperium, religious or secular. Carlyle thus negates the logic of British triumphalism. Moreover, in insisting that European "lies" about Islam disgrace only their propagators, he effectively defends Islam from European epistemological violence. Most riveting, however, is Carlyle's assertion that he does "esteem [the Prophet Muḥammad] a true one." This validation of the truth-claim of Muḥammad's prophethood verges on a Muslim *shahāda*, the declaration of faith in which the Muslim believer testifies that there is no god but God and that Muḥammad is God's messenger. Certainly Carlyle, by refusing to name the Prophet Muḥammad the "truest" or the "most eminent" of prophets, registers his ideological distance from Islamic doctrine, which declares Muḥammad *"khātama al-nabiyyīna"* (Qur'ān 33:40), "Seal of the Prophets," and his message the completion and perfection of all prior received revelations.[116] This distance, as we shall see, is important. Still, the sum of Carlyle's rhetoric holds out to the (unintended) Muslim reader the tantalizing possibility that a historically hostile Christian West might "convert" to Islam, in sympathy if not in deed.

Al-Sibāʿī must have been intrigued to hear the power of Islam—threatened of late by Western ideological dominance—"speak" in the English voice of the colonizer. Surely he recognized that European colonialism had left Muslims themselves unconvinced of Islam's relevance to their present. He writes in the wake of the 1883 debate between the French philologist and scholar of religions Ernest Renan and the influential

Muslim scholar and anticolonial agitator Jamāl al-Dīn al-Afghānī—a debate that the fictional encounter of Mubārak's 'Alam al-Dīn with the imperialist French philosopher, who takes a similarly historicist-rationalist view of religion, eerily presages. Renan had declared Islam and science (hence "modernity") incompatible; al-Afghānī's rebuttal argued Islam's fundamental openness to reason, yet conceded that *all* religion was potentially irreconcilable with science.[117] In Carlyle al-Sibā'ī finds proof of the continued viability of a precolonial Arab-Islamic religious episteme in the face of secular colonial erasure—or more properly, of the viability of an episteme in which Islam and modern rationality intertwine to negate the colonial distinction between religion and secularity. In his Arabic translation of 1911—first published in excerpts in the Cairo journal *al-Bayān* (the Explication) as "al-Abṭāl wa 'Ibādat al-Buṭūla" (Heroes and the Worship of Heroism), then published in full as the monograph *al-Abṭāl* (Heroes)—al-Sibā'ī renders the above passage from Carlyle as follows:

> It has become the greatest shame on any civilized individual among the children of this age that he would listen to what is [commonly] believed about Islam—that it is a lie—and about [the Prophet] Muḥammad—that he is a deceiver and a forger. It is time that we fight what is bruited about in the way of such foolish, shameful words, for indeed the message that this messenger realized has remained, over twelve centuries, the light-giving lamp *[al-sirāja al-munīra]* for nearly two hundred million people like us, whom the God who created us [also] created. Do any of you think that this message—by which these countless millions have lived and for which they have died—is a lie and a deception? I, for one, can never hold that opinion.[118]

Translating Carlyle's object of address, al-Sibā'ī extends Carlyle's language beyond its original receiver, the English lecture-goer and reader of 1840–41, to reach a second receiver: the Muslim reader of 1911. His translated "we" oscillates between Carlyle's "we"—the non-Muslim English whom Carlyle addresses, a "we" that includes himself, as in the royal "We" with which his passage begins—and a new "we" that conjoins Muslim Egyptians to non-Muslim Englishmen in a *common* struggle to recover the meaning of Islam. Where Carlyle's original only reminds the English that Muslims "were made by God as well as we," al-Sibā'ī's translation makes Carlyle say something more: that Muslims are *"min al-nāsi amthālinā"* ("people like us")—that is, exactly like Carlyle's English "us." Thus his translated "we" aligns colonizing Englishmen and colonized Egyptians as "equivalents," unmarked human beings located in—and fighting for—a new, Islamophilic universal.

The translated Carlyle even speaks in Qur'ānic tones: where Carlyle describes the Prophet Muḥammad as the "life-guidance" of millions, al-Sibā'ī has him call the Prophet *"al-sirāja al-munīra,"* the "light-giving lamp," echoing the Qur'ānic description of the Prophet as *"sirājan munīran"* (Qur'ān 33:46).[119] Across the gulf of colonial inequality in which Carlyle's seductive equation of Arab-Islamic and European subjects otherwise would ring hollow, al-Sibā'ī stretches the copula of his translation, bringing the destinies of the British Empire and Islam, of "secular" modernity and native "religion," into startling alignment.

Indeed, the translation marshals Carlyle's discourse to upend both the assumptions of the civilizing mission and the dynamics of colonial power. Putting words in Carlyle's mouth, al-Sibā'ī's translation claims that the lies that European Christendom has propagated about Islam shame not just the English "us" Carlyle invokes but also a global modern "us": *"ayyi fardin mutamadyinin min abnā'i hādhā al-'aṣri"* ("any civilized individual among the children of this age"). Thus he expands Carlyle's original indictment of English Islamophobia to include the charge that colonizing, "civilizing" Europe might not be so civilized after all. More audaciously, he suggests that Europe will become "civilized" and "modern" (of *"hādhā al-'aṣri,"* "this age") only by recognizing Islam, thus making good on its pretensions to "secular" objectivity. Al-Sibā'ī's translated "we," then, appropriates the touchstones of the British Empire's world-colonizing mission—civilization and modernity—and makes the colonized episteme of Islam the arbiter of what those touchstones "mean": the litmus test of membership in the "civilized" and "modern" world, the ground of the universal itself.

In Carlyle's suggestion that the "Scepticism" of the eighteenth century and the Benthamist Utilitarianism of the nineteenth might well give rise to a new age of Faith, then, al-Sibā'ī hears the prospect of a revived Islam: the possibility that the "destruction of old *forms*" need not mean the "destruction of everlasting *substances*."[120] From Carlyle he infers that if old forms of "Islam," or Egypt for that matter, are dying under the press of colonial European (especially French) influence, their substance might be resurrected in the new form of English. Al-Sibā'ī's error lies in believing form and substance so separable. An Islam not only anglicized, but marshaled to buttress an imperialist comparison of civilizational value is not the equivalent of the Arabic-speaking Islam it displaces; form cannot exist without the substance it shapes, and substance cannot exist until shaped by form. Hinging on a false separation of the content of thought and the language in which it is expressed, the equivalence between English language and Arab-Islamic epistemes that al-Sibāʿī imagines into Carlyle's text in fact subjects al-Sibāʿī—and Islam—to colonial inequality.

For al-Sibāʿī's Islam is, like ʿAlam al-Dīn's in Mubārak's novel, an Islam translated into reempowerment through the power of secular Englishness: it accrues renewed value in the modern, "civilized" world only insofar as the non-Muslim Carlyle—and the British Empire he represents—choose to validate it. Try as al-Sibāʿī might to redefine "civilization" on an Arab-Islamic axis and to revive his culture's claim to the universal in the face of European colonialism, the politically unequal terms of exchange that govern his translation ultimately allow Carlyle to set the value of Islam. If al-Sibāʿī refracts Carlyle's original to make belief in Islam the touchstone of English civilization and modernity, he does so because Carlyle's original already has diverted *him*—al-Sibāʿī—into accepting English approval as the touchstone of Islam's civilization and modernity.

Thus determined to resurrect Islam through the gospel of Carlyle, al-Sibāʿī styles Carlyle as "Muslim" as possible. Witness two other major variations between the original passage cited above and al-Sibāʿī's Arabic translation. First, al-Sibāʿī omits the crucial opening sentences of Carlyle's original. Since Carlyle chooses the Prophet Muḥammad to epitomize the "Hero as Prophet," devoting the entirety of the so-named second lecture to the study of his example, al-Sibāʿī's omission might lead the unsuspecting Egyptian reader to conclude that Carlyle regards the Prophet of Islam as a prophet with no peer. The dropped text reveals that Carlyle never intended to imply that the Prophet Muḥammad was the "most eminent" or "truest." That Carlyle names this prophet "the one we are freest to speak of" underscores his marginality to the Christian tradition: he is fair game for secular analysis as "hero" because he falls outside the Christian sacred. Only in that light can we understand al-Sibāʿī's decision to omit a second crucial sentence from the original—namely, Carlyle's declaration that a "greater number of God's creatures believe in Mahomet's word, at this hour, than in any other word whatever." Such a statement would seem to clinch Carlyle's belief in the superiority of Islam. Yet to suggest that Carlyle only regards as "Mahomet's word" what Muslims believe is God's, transmitted by a messenger *(rasūl),* would have undercut the equivalence that al-Sibāʿī seeks to forge between English and Muslim interests. Had al-Sibāʿī conveyed the omitted words, his reader may have failed to imagine, in *On Heroes,* a text that could colonize Egypt's colonizers.

Second, al-Sibāʿī suppresses Carlyle's assurance to English readers that "there is no danger of our becoming, any of us, Mahometans," and thus no threat to English subjectivity in reappraising Islam's value. By emphasizing only Carlyle's positive revaluations of Islam and eliding his troubling reassertions of British power *over* Islam, al-Sibāʿī disavows the fact that Carlyle already speaks, in 1840, from a position of British geopolitical superiority vis-à-vis the East: a position that reflects Britain's post-Macaulayan confidence in the success of its colonial project in India. Carlyle's words describe, in effect, the colonizer's side of an economy of unequal exchange. With the decline of Mughal power in India and of Ottoman power across the Mediterranean world and the ascent of British dominion in these regions, the British Empire had begun to supersede the imperia of Islam. (By 1911 it would either officially or effectively colonize those imperia.) Thus England controls the geopolitical terms of "exchange" between itself and Islam. Carlyle does himself little ontological harm by translating himself into the colonized Muslim—by assuming the *I* of the Prophet Muḥammad, symbol of a subjugated Islam, and trying to "understand what *he* meant with the world." His *I,* after all, commands the copula of translation and thus the power to undo seduction, to retract its identification with the object and thus reconstitute itself as sovereign. Yet there is ample danger to al-Sibāʿī and to colonized Egypt in forgetting their object status and fancying themselves masters, for in so doing they see with Carlyle's *I,* speak with his tongue, and ultimately read Islam's destiny through the British Empire rather than against it. Indeed, Carlyle's dismissal of the fear that Britons might become "Mahometans"—turn Turk—if they understand Islam in Islamic terms bespeaks British superiority. In suppressing that dismissal al-Sibāʿī represses the fact that the Egyptian intellectual of 1911, lured into reclaiming the precolonial sovereignty of Arab-Islamic culture in the voice of imperial English, just might see the Islam he translates fall off the tongue and into the jaws of the mouth with which he speaks.

In his translation of the third of Carlyle's *Heroes* lectures, "The Hero as Poet," al-Sibāʿī is again intent on maintaining the illusion of Carlyle's Islamicity: the illusion that makes the colonizer's English an appropriate love object for the colonized Egyptian. Suppressing the specter of colonial incommensurability, he deletes every negative pronouncement Carlyle makes about the Prophet Muḥammad and Islam, refusing to render such devaluations into Arabic. In so doing, he amplifies Carlyle's Islamophilia. He omits, for instance, Carlyle's negative comparisons of the Prophet of Islam first with Dante—whose *Inferno* notoriously consigns the Prophet to the eighth circle of hell—and ultimately with Shakespeare.[121] Carlyle crowns both comparisons with the secular-colonial assertion that these European poets have superseded the Prophet Muḥammad and abrogated his message. "It was intrinsically an error that notion of Mahomet's, of his supreme Prophethood," Carlyle writes,

> . . . as makes it a questionable step for me here and now to say, as I have done, that Mahomet was a true Speaker at all, and not rather an ambitious charlatan, perversity and simulacrum, no Speaker, but a Babbler! Even in Arabia, as I compute, Mahomet will have exhausted himself and become obsolete, while this Shakspeare *[sic]*, this Dante may be still young;—while this Shakspeare may still pretend to be a Priest of Mankind, of Arabia as of other places, for unlimited periods to come![122]

Carlyle's comparisons are imperially motivated and imperially implicated. His insistence on the geographic and temporal universality of Dante and of Shakespeare and on their capacity—Shakespeare's especially—to supersede the Prophet of Islam "even in Arabia" pits European literature against "Arab" Islam in a geopolitical competition not only for territory (Dante and Shakespeare will claim Arabia and "other places") but also for time (Shakespeare, like Dante, will rule "unlimited periods to come," overwriting other histories). Further, Carlyle gives his English readers a telling choice: give up "your" Indian Empire, or give up Shakespeare? Give up the Empire and retain Shakespeare, he suggests, for Shakespeare alone can cement the bonds of Englishness across far-flung stretches of the earth—create a nation of Britons in points as distant as Parramatta (in Australia) and New York—and make the idea of Empire possible.[123]

> Nay, apart from spiritualities; and considering him merely as a real, marketable, tangibly useful possession. England, before long, this Island of ours, will hold but a small fraction of the English: . . . there will be a Saxondom covering great spaces of the Globe. . . . [W]hat is it that can keep all these together into virtually one Nation, so that they do not fall out and fight, but live at peace . . . ? . . . This King Shakspeare *[sic]*, does not he shine, in crowned sovereignty, over us all, as the noblest, gentlest, yet strongest of rallying-signs . . . ?[124]

While Carlyle now understands Shakespeare less as prophet than as nation-building commodity ("real, marketable, tangibly useful"), al-Sibāʿī's translation of Carlyle's core question refuses this materialist turn. Instead, al-Sibāʿī intensifies Carlyle's earlier sacralization of Shakespeare, who becomes the Islam of England:

> So what would bring together these disparate [English] souls and sow love between these opposed hearts such that they would become, by virtue of [that bond], one nation *[umma wāḥida]*? What would be the axis around which their interests and desires could turn and the Ka'ba toward which their necks and sights could stretch?[125]

The answer is Shakespeare, "the greatest unifier and firmest bond *[al-'urwatu al-wuthqā]* of the various and sundry groups of Britons at the ends of the inhabited world."[126] Here al-Sibā'ī wields an axe against Carlyle's original. Yet he does so only to reintroduce (and uphold) its assumptions in other guises. On the surface, his translation refuses to transmit Carlyle's contention that Arabia one day would exchange the Prophet for Shakespeare. By rendering Shakespeare a simulacrum of Islam, rather than (as Carlyle does) reducing the Prophet to a "simulacrum" of Shakespeare's prophethood, al-Sibā'ī turns the tables on Carlyle's original, hinting that Shakespeare might be the bad copy, the (poor) secular substitute for Islam's sacred. He suggests that no tie comparable with *"al-'urwati al-wuthqā"* (Qur'ān 2:256, 31:22)—"the firmest bond" of the Muslim believer to God—consolidates the secular, transnational community of Britons. Lacking that bond, the British cannot constitute one *umma* (nation), a term traditionally used to denote the global community of Muslim believers, not a secular nation-state.[127] Further, the British have no Ka'ba around which their scattered numbers might coalesce—no house of worship like the one that Muslims believe Abraham built in Mecca and to which all physically and financially able Muslims must make pilgrimage at least once in their lifetimes. Thus the secular Shakespeare must assume the symbolic function of the sacred for the British Empire. Still, one cannot say that al-Sibā'ī's translation denigrates Shakespeare in quite the way that Carlyle's original denigrates the Prophet Muḥammad—al-Sibā'ī associates the simulacrum not with falsehood or incoherence (Carlyle's "charlatan" and "Babbler") but with the most sacred. The translator, after all, likens Shakespeare to the Ka'ba and compares his capacity to bond Britons with God's capacity to bond Muslims, forging a global "Saxondom" much like the Islamic *umma*. He submits Shakespeare to Islam's terms, but the fact that he puts Shakespeare and Islam on the same metaphorical plane—the sacred—insinuates the exchangeability of the secular for the sacred. Al-Sibā'ī undercuts what his coreligionists would see as Islam's unique claims to the sacred. Assimilating Islam to Englishness, he comes perilously close to transacting Carlyle's exchange of Islam for Shakespeare.

THE "RELIGION" OF ENGLISH LITERATURE

Gauri Viswanathan has argued that literature might help us "understand the oblique processes of secularization": the fact that secularism might not succeed but precede religion—and continue to haunt it in the form of heterodoxy.[128] While literature, she maintains, has tended to imagine itself a postreligious, "secular vehicle," the history of literary education in colonial contexts suggests that literature was "an ideal instrument for conveying religiously inspired ethical values in a secular framework," for imparting Christianity "without inciting potential rebellion and resistance by colonial subjects practicing different religious faiths."[129] The secular might well transmit religion. Yet if we accept Viswanathan's argument that religion *contains* the secular (in the form of the heterodox), might not religion transmit the secular—as new religion, perhaps as a religion of literature?

If, after all, al-Sibāʿī's translation of Carlyle initially reasserts Islam's power against the secular(izing) onslaughts of the British Empire, his assumption of Carlyle's voice to effect that reassertion ultimately translates Islam into the idiom of English secularity and displaces Islam with the "religion" of English literature. Both Carlyle's original and al-Sibāʿī's translation point to the fundamental instability of the signifier "Islam" in the face of the Christianizing, secularizing, and modernizing drives of the British Empire: its vulnerability to evacuation, occupation, and resignification in ways that serve imperial interests. To illustrate just how Carlyle's *On Heroes* recast the substantives *religion, secularity,* and ultimately *literature* into new forms for al-Sibāʿī and for the Egyptian contemporaries he influenced, I turn now to a closer examination of the two key paratexts that frame his Arabic translation: the title and the translator's introduction. Indeed, a complex renegotiation of the meanings of religion and secularity haunts the translation from its title page. In the 1911 *al-Bayān* version, al-Sibāʿī's decision to render Carlyle's title—*On Heroes, Hero-Worship, and the Heroic in History*—as "al-Abṭāl wa ʿIbādat al-Buṭūla" (Heroes and the Worship of Heroism) adjusts Carlyle's "hero-worship" to "the worship of heroism" to bring the notion in tune with Muslim sensibilities. "Hero-worship" implies the worship of human beings and thus the association of other deities with God—an act that Islamic doctrine calls *shirk,* the worst (if also the most common) of sins. The "worship of heroism," by contrast, modulates Carlyle's term just enough to appeal to the Muslim preference for worship of the abstract—the (tacitly divine) quality of heroism. Yet within an Islamic framework, even an invitation to worship the divine through any quality expressed in the human borders on transgression, hence the final reduction of Carlyle's title on the cover of the 1911 monograph to *al-Abṭāl* (Heroes), which eliminates the problematic term. This Islamically innocent title entices readers into opening the book. And when they do, they encounter al-Sibā'ī's translator's introduction, where a slow dance of rapprochement ensues between his Islam and Carlyle's Christian "secular."

> What distinguishes this book, *Heroes,* is its explanation of the worship of heroism *['ibādata al-buṭūlati]* and of the canonization of great men, a full and detailed explanation that leaves no room for question. Unbelievers, atheists, scorners of the greatness of humanity, deniers of human genius, and scoffers at great men and at their devotees who are not cured of the disease of unbelief and ingratitude and scorn and sarcasm by reading this book will not be cured or changed by any power of the pen, any might of eloquence, or any force of human or spirit *[al-insi wa al-jinni].* And the best of what appears in this book is a chapter on al-Muṣṭafā [the Prophet Muḥammad], peace be upon him. Previously, the Prophet had been the target of the pens of many Westerners, especially those of the eighteenth century, the century of Voltaire—I mean the century of atheism and unbelief—who ignorantly and arrogantly hurled at him scurrilous slanders.[130]

Al-Sibā'ī's rhetoric wavers between two uneasy impulses. At first blush, he appears to enjoin Egyptians to read *al-Abṭāl* because Carlyle upholds the "religious" faith of Muslims ("the best of what appears in this book is a chapter on al-Muṣṭafā, peace be upon him"). Yet al-Sibā'ī also suggests that the book deserves reading because Carlyle institutes a new faith in the "secular," a faith that Egyptians must embrace if they are to engage colonial modernity ("What distinguishes this book . . . is . . . the canonization of great men"). On the surface these divergent motivations for reading Carlyle seem reconcilable. Since Muslims agree that the Prophet Muḥammad was perhaps the greatest human being but decidedly nondivine, why should his hagiography not stand alongside that of other "great men"? At heart, however, the motivations are contradictory: to Muslims, the Prophet Muḥammad is not just a "great man" in the secular understanding of that term, but the messenger of a divinely revealed religion—a radical monotheism that forbids the worship of human beings and their equation with God. Asad makes a similar point when he contrasts the ethicotheological role of the Prophet in classical Islam to his secular reinvention as founder of "the Arab nation" in twentieth-century Arab nationalism. The latter, he maintains, is "an inversion of the classical theological view according to which the Prophet is not the object of national inspiration for an imagined community, but the subject of divine inspiration, a messenger of God to mankind."[131] It is noteworthy, in fact, that Carlyle includes no other prophet but Muḥammad in his heroic pantheon. He would not, of course, include Jesus in its ranks. For a Christian, Jesus incarnates the divine in the human; thus he stands too far beyond the pale of ordinary humanity to count as a human "hero." Yet even biblical prophets like Moses are not equated with Norse deities like Odin—a "pagan" god to the Christian mind—or with secular heroes like Napoleon, Cromwell, Dante, Shakespeare, and Samuel Johnson. To suggest, as Carlyle does, the equivalence of the Prophet Muḥammad to such heroes is to secularize him, to contest Islam's claim to religious truth by assimilating its messenger to the mundane.

Thus al-Sibāʿī speaks in two tongues in his translator's introduction, sounding notes both religious and secular. What joins these tongues is the notion of unbelief, or *kufr,* which he redefines along two contradictory axes. In post-Islamic Arabic usage, *kufr* almost always refers to unbelief in God. No doubt al-Sibāʿī intends this definition when he lauds Carlyle for vindicating Islam and when he pronounces *On Heroes* an antidote to *"qarna al-ilḥādi wa al-kufri"* ("the century of atheism and unbelief") that the French eighteenth century, incarnated in Voltaire, embodies for Carlyle and his translator. While al-Sibāʿī's dislike of the French eighteenth century clashes with the francophile tenor of Egyptian intellectual discourse in this period, it is not altogether astonishing that al-Sibāʿī, perceiving a greater moral affinity between English letters and the Arab-Islamic tradition, might snub the French muse and favor the English. Mubārak's fictional ʿAlam al-Dīn similarly spurns the "nonbelieving" French Orientalist and embraces his Islamophilic English rival. More striking is al-Sibāʿī's application of *kufr* to unbelief in the human: what Carlyle's text cures best is not, in fact, the epidemic of "atheism and unbelief" that has swept the West since the century of Voltaire, al-Sibāʿī suggests, but the Muslim "disease of unbelief" *("dāʾi al-kufri")* in "great men"! Whereas ʿAlam al-Dīn condemned the French for imputing divine books to human origins, al-Sibāʿī hails the British for imputing divine qualities to the secular human.

The syntax of the clauses *"wa man qaraʾa hādhā al-kitāba wa kāna kāfiran mulḥidan mustahziʾan bi ʿaẓamati ibni Ādama"* (lit., "he who reads this book, though he might have been an unbeliever, an atheist, a scorner of the greatness of man") suspends al-Sibāʿī's intention in ambiguity. Of the three terms that he uses here—unbeliever, atheist, scorner—*mustahzi'* ("scorner"), although sometimes applied to the nonbeliever in God, most commonly describes an attitude of one human (or nondivine) being toward another; *kāfir* ("unbeliever") and *mulḥid* ("atheist") most commonly describe attitudes of the human toward the divine. The syntax of these clauses most directly links *mustahzi'an* to "*'aẓamati ibni Ādama*" ("greatness of man," lit., "greatness of the son of Adam"). While al-Sibā'ī may allude here to the Qur'ānic account of Satan's refusal to bow down to Adam—to concede the greatness of the human—and thus his disobedience to God (Qur'ān 2:33), he ingeniously invokes Satan's indictment for defying God to press the importance of belief in the human. Thus the semantics of *mustahzi'an* remain in tune with the word's syntactic position. By contrast, *kāfiran* and *mulḥidan* are off-key. Certainly they can be read as distinct from *mustahzi'an,* such that al-Sibā'ī credits Carlyle's text with curing readers' unbelief in God and, separately, their scorn for the human. Grammatically, however, *kāfiran* and *mulḥidan* are in a relation that Arabic calls *badal*—literally, "exchangeability"—with *mustahzi'an.* This relation slyly invites the reader to understand the attitudes of the *kāfir* and the *mulḥid*—the "unbeliever" and the "atheist"—as attitudes held, along with that of the *mustahzi'* (the "scorner"), toward the human too. Al-Sibā'ī's triple insistence in the remainder of the sentence on the grandeur of humanity—"the greatness of humanity," "human genius," and "great men and . . . their devotees"—supports this view. Al-Sibā'ī ultimately diverts *kufr* from its primary Arabic sense of unbelief in the divine toward a secular sense of unbelief in the human. And Carlyle's text, which worships human heroes, has seduced him into doing so.

In the guise of the "religious," the British "secular" beguiles the Egyptian intellect. Indeed, al-Sibā'ī's double tongue is Carlyle's too. For a religion of the "secular" competes with God-centered "religion" in Carlyle's original. Treading an ambivalent third space between religion and secularity, Carlyle maintains, on the one hand, that right knowledge rests on a conception of "Godhood" and, on the other, that literature can supplant religion as the medium of such knowledge. The fifth lecture of Carlyle's *On Heroes,* "The Hero as Man of Letters," crystallizes this tension. It is from that lecture, in fact, that al-Sibā'ī borrows his epitomization of *kufr,* or unbelief, in the person of the French Voltaire and his tacit association of English with the promise of renewed belief. Indicting the "Scepticism" of the European eighteenth century, Carlyle imputes that ethos not only to French Enlightenment thinkers like Voltaire but also to English Utilitarians like Jeremy Bentham. Still, he intimates that in England—not France—might live the seed of Belief that could renew the tie between intellectual production and a sense of "Godliness." Implicit in the contrast he draws between the English Johnson, author of the *Dictionary,* and the French Voltaire is at least a partial identification of a believing knowledge with the English literary tradition and of an unbelieving unreason with the French: "That Church of St. Clement Danes, where Johnson still *worshipped* in the era of Voltaire," he writes, "is to me a venerable place."[132]

This Carlyle who deems religious belief the precondition of secular knowledge, who decries the unbelieving tendencies of a "gross, steamengine Utilitarianism" and calls Bentham's understanding of the human "more beggarly . . . than Mahomet's," cuts a profoundly attractive figure for a colonial Muslim subject like al-Sibāʿī.[133] Attractive because he does not so much reassert Islam's value by placing it within the compass of the "scientific" and the "utilitarian"—within the compass of European "modernity"—as question the notion that "steamengine" science and utilitarianism should be master values at all. Carlyle anticipates claims that Mohandas Gandhi would make much later for the colonized East: namely, that what the East lacked in material civilization it might command in spiritual civilization.[134] Finding in Carlyle a remarriage of reason and belief—whose divorce al-Ṭahṭāwī had noted in French intellectual life—al-Sibāʿī entertains the illusion that "Islam" has colonized (at least philosophically) those who have colonized it, made Englishman and Egyptian "like." The implied shift from French models to British ones turns on the axis of cultural translatability, or commensurability: whose words better speak "our" language?

Such commensurability, however, is elusive. Elsewhere in the same lecture, in fact, the notions of "religion" and "worship"—and their connections to modern knowledge—undergo a subtle but decisive secularizing mutation. Carlyle suggests that secular "Literature," in various guises, has replaced the "Church" of old and assumed its function. Persuasion, he argues, is the power that underlies both institutions and permits their translatability: "writers of Newspapers, Pamphlets, Poems, Books"—who convince readers of the truth of their words and persuade them to interpret, reshape, and regulate their lives according to those words—"*are* the real working effective Church of a modern country."[135] Thus, in Carlyle's view, literature is a "'continuous revelation' of the Godlike in the Terrestrial."[136] Carlyle's pronouncements both resonate and collide with mainstream Islamic sensibilities. What might be deeply familiar to a Muslim reader in Carlyle's understanding of the spiritual world is the notion that all things in the universe are signs *(āyāt)* of the Creator and that all well-intentioned human acts—however mundane—are forms of worship *('ibādāt)* of that Creator. Yet if the Qur'ān fuses, in certain respects, the earthly and the divine, it just as emphatically insists—to the minds of all but its most rationalist interpreters—on the separation of human writ from divine. Carlyle lauds the *human* author who shows us that "a lily of the fields is beautiful" and the "*handwriting,* made visible there, of the great Maker of the Universe."[137] Yet the Qur'ān calls us to see in the beauty of the lily *itself,* unmediated by human pens, the "handwriting" of God. The human intermediary—the poet—cannot eclipse God, the Writer par excellence. Hence the apparent refusal of the Qur'ānic text to equate its verses *(āyāt)* with those of poets *(abyāt)* or to brook any comparison of its literary techniques (the use of rhymed prose, or *saj',* for example) to those of human authors. The Qur'ān repeatedly insists that the Prophet Muḥammad is not a poet but a messenger of God. It thereby rejects the equivalence of poetry to prophecy (Qur'ān 69:38–43).[138] In this worldview, literature cannot, strictly speaking, continue "revelation," as revelation—for all the literariness of its voicing—supersedes literature.

Whereas mainstream Islamic epistemologies separate the divine from the human, then, Carlyle's *On Heroes* confounds the two. In the book's very first lecture, "The Hero as Divinity," Carlyle locates hero worship, the "transcendent admiration of a Great Man," in an ageless human hunger to adore what appears to embody God and thereby to apprehend the divinity that is the "*not we.*"[139] Both the hunger to adore and the objects of adoration he describes are essentially religious: he speaks, after all, of a "worship" directed toward the "godlike." Yet such adoration and its objects are fundamentally also secular, for what is "godlike" is by definition not God. Indeed, the breathtaking variety of "Great Men" Carlyle admits into his pantheon—from the Norse god Odin, the hero of his first lecture, and the Prophet Muḥammad, the hero of his second, to such figures as Martin Luther, Shakespeare, Johnson, Jean-Jacques Rousseau, and Napoleon—bears out his gradual dissociation of religion from professed creed and redefinition of the term to mean that which a "man does practically believe"—a religion that could just as easily be a "scepticism and *no-religion.*"[140] Here eighteenth-century "Scepticism" is recast in the mold of faith—faith in something, even in "nothing"—and so redeemed. In the end, Carlyle invites his reader to believe less in God than in men who believe in God (or at least in something Godlike), displacing in that movement God worship with hero worship.[141]

Although al-Sibāʿī's translation appears, on the surface, to resist that displacement—worshiping "heroism" rather than the "hero"—it also, as we have seen, slyly effects it. To dub Shakespeare a *Kaʿba* and a *ʿurwa wuthqā* is to declare the English book not just the Church of Carlyle's England, of his ideal "modern society," but also the Mosque of al-Sibāʿī's Egypt: a society aspiring to modernity. If with one tongue, then, al-Sibāʿī imagines Carlyle as a force for Islam's renewal, with the other he ushers Carlyle's secular "religion" of English literature into translatability with Islam.

THE ORIGINAL MAN AND THE NEW "AWAKENING"

To understand the terms of that translatability, let us return to the first lecture of Carlyle's *On Heroes,* from which al-Sibāʿī transplants the language of seed, root, and tree in which he imagines his task as a translator. There Carlyle aligns the tree of belief not only with his secularized reformulation of religion but also, implicitly, with an imperial theory of interlingual and intercultural translation. Where al-Ṭahṭāwī finds translatability at the bottom of an implied "sea" in which one well versed in any original tongue perforce knows any other, and Benjamin locates it in the "higher and purer linguistic air" to which an otherwise untranslatable original rises to find fulfillment in other tongues, Carlyle discovers it in a "tap-root."[142] From that root grows the universal he calls the "world-tree": universal because its leaf fibers together speak in all tongues past, present, and future ("every fibre there an act or word"); because its leaves, in turn, tell the lives of all humanity ("every leaf of it a biography"); because its boughs comprise all "Histories of Nations"; and, finally, because its whole rustles with the undifferentiated "noise of Human Existence," the "voice of *all* the gods," a white noise of Intention whose realization of purity in supplementarity approximates the Benjaminian totality that "no longer means or expresses anything but is . . . that which is meant in all languages."[143] For Carlyle, language is fundamentally translational: the word one speaks today is decidedly "improper"—borrowed from "all men since the first man began to speak."[144] Such a translated word bestows a Benjaminian afterlife—an "over-life," survival, or overleaf—on an original thought "dead": it can conjugate a "dead" original tongue into indefinite futurity.[145] The budding translation, as it were, does not so much replace the leafless original as *displace* its life—hence also its death. While Carlyle's theory of translation appears, like Benjamin's, to reread "nature" as a species of secular history shot through with divine time—and to similarly articulate the "pure language" of Intention as at once a priori, "suprahistorical" relationality and post priori, historically embedded supplementarity—it is perhaps less attentive than Benjamin's (and al-Ṭahṭāwī's) to fissures between the modes in which different languages signify: to the troubling possibility that divergent boughs of language may stretch toward but never quite add up to God. Carlyle's tree posits translation as a repetition with a difference that nonetheless stands still: words move to new times and places, but their meaning remains intact.

Thus, if Carlyle's root engenders a universal, that universal is rather too particular. A root, after all, must ground itself somewhere. And Carlyle's ground is distinctly northern European. The Norse divinity Odin becomes his Adam: the primal hero from whom he conjugates all subsequent heroes. Yet not all of those heroes so conjugated, it would seem, are created equal—hence "exchangeable." For Carlyle claims Odin and his Norse fellows as biological and spiritual "progenitors" of the European: originators of the "godlike" Thought of "the Shakspeares, the Goethes!"[146] "Mahomet"—who despite his initial rehabilitation ultimately will compare unfavorably, in Carlyle's schema, with "godlike" Shakespeare—is reconsigned, in the end, to another (and implicitly inferior) genealogy altogether. He becomes less a Thinker, like Odin, than a *simulacrum* of Thought: a derivative "translation" from a more authentic "original." In other words, although Odin is as particular as the Prophet Muḥammad, his particular comes to stand *for* the universal.

Carlyle's world-tree, in fact, issues Athena-like from the head of Odin. From the first human hero who embodies the divine—"the *original* man"—Thought springs universal. Odin's "shaped spoken Thought awakes the slumbering capability of all into Thought. . . . What he says, all men were not far from saying, were longing to say."[147] Once uttered as word and seeded in the world, the originary Thought of the primal Thinker (identified with the West) inspires presumably "lesser" thinkers—plunged in deep slumber—to reproduce their inchoate thoughts in the *shape* of this new Thought that "awakens" them, to translate their thoughts into "equivalence" with dominant Thought. Carlyle provocatively suggests that signifiers travel most readily when a would-be original—a new Thought—seduces its potential translators into believing that that Thought represents what they always already have thought but did not know how to say, or perhaps said otherwise. Called to identify with the master, to imagine themselves as always already "like" him, the human beings so interpellated respond to the seductions of translation with a "Yes, even so!"[148] They come to accept the notion that the signifiers of two different (and politically unequal) languages signify one a priori meaning. Only when Intention is understood as one do signifiers become exchangeable, words so easily "borrowed."

The last Ottoman viceroy of Egypt, Khedive 'Abbās II, held British ascendancy responsible for a decline in the intellectual caliber of Egyptian education. 'Abbās was deposed in 1914, when the British declared Egypt an official protectorate. For him, the "most painful memory" of his reign was the Franco-English agreement (Entente Cordiale) of 1904, which secured French hegemony in Morocco and, in exchange, granted England hegemony in Egypt.[149] Reflecting on the fin-de-siècle twilight of a hybrid system of English-French education in Egypt, which ended (at least officially) with France's cession of Egypt to England, he pits what he calls the "apostleship" of French pedagogy against the dutiful soldiery of the English. "No concern to uplift the Egyptian spirit," he laments, "troubled the hearts of the British school masters."[150] Although the British may not have looked on their educational efforts in Egypt as an "apostleship," some of their Egyptian translators did—foremost among them al-Sibā'ī, who set out to fulfill Egyptian nationalist aspirations through the prophecy of Carlyle. Al-Sibā'ī's literary achievement—what would make him so valuable an accidental apostle for Cromer's colonial vision—was, in the end, to make British thought so "natural" to Egyptian soil that it seemed native to it. "The living doctrine," writes an ecstatic Carlyle, "grows, grows;—like a Banyan-tree; the first *seed* is the essential thing: any branch strikes itself down into the earth, becomes a new root; and so, in endless complexity, we have a whole wood, . . . one seed the parent of it all."[151] That Carlyle should translate his Eurocentric "world-tree" of Thought into power *through* the metaphor of a tree native to British-colonized India—a tree whose branches touch the ground to seed new, secondary trunks—underscores just how deeply the British imperial project depended on the seduction of a colonized native like al-Sibā'ī into becoming the surrogate incubator, inseminator, and disseminator of its "habits of thought." With the colonial original so naturalized, the Egyptian reader easily could forget not just the translator, but even the process of translation itself, believing itself—not the colonizer—to be the "original" source of the "shaped spoken Thought" that ultimately would uproot Egypt.

CHAPTER FIVE

Order, Origin, and the Elusive Sovereign

Post-1919 Nation Formation and the Imperial Urge toward Translatability

Recalling Muḥammad al-Sibāʿī after his death, Ibrāhīm ʿAbd al-Qādir al-Māzinī offers this telling snapshot:

> He . . . used to write or to translate anywhere, in a café or a shop or on the tram. [O]nce we were on the Metro tram to New Cairo *[Miṣr al-Jadīda]*, at night; he crossed his legs and began to translate. The light went out, so he turned to me and said, "Imagine this coincidence! I was writing the word 'dominion' *[al-su'dud]*, so I penned one *d [dāl]* in the light and one *d [dāl]* in the darkness!"[1]

Three forces meet in this passage: translation, colonial modernity, and the question of sovereignty. The anecdote tacitly plays on the dual meanings of *naql:* transport and translation. So naturally does al-Sibāʿī move between English and Arabic that he can "translate anywhere," even on a tram, and just as automatically. "I never saw him," writes al-Māzinī, "refer to a dictionary, Arabic or English; he relied solely on his memory."[2] As al-Sibāʿī transports another language (presumably English) into Arabic, the Metro tram conveys him from Cairo to the suburb of Heliopolis, or New Cairo. Built for expatriate foreigners and wealthy Egyptians, Heliopolis was effectively a colonial town, standing at some distance from—and in sharp contrast to—old Arab-Islamic Cairo. Like the tramway system, Heliopolis was the brainchild of Belgian magnate Baron Édouard Empain, who built both town and tram with a concession from an Ottoman-Egyptian government under British control. To invoke Frantz Fanon, it was the "settlers' town" to Cairo's "native town."[3] And the Metro was the epitome of colonial modernity. Launched in 1910, it was the fastest tram linking Cairo proper to New Cairo.[4] The Metro not only led its passengers to the "new"—the space of New Cairo—but also embodied the new: the force and the velocity of the transformation that modern European technology ushered into Egypt. Yet the translation of European modernity to Egyptian space falters. Electricity fails; the tram lights go out. And by a strange coincidence, as al-Sibāʿī points out to al-Māzinī, they go out on the question of sovereignty.

We might be tempted to read this scene as a stutter of colonial power in Egypt—especially British power, still formidable at a time when Ottoman power was dying. If the ideology of European imperialism based its legitimacy, in part, on the technological "superiority" of the West, might not the power outage here be a death blow to Britain? Might not al-Sibāʿī's failed translation—his incomplete transport of English text into Arabic—spell the end of British dominion over Egypt? Lurking behind the passage, certainly, is a question that preoccupied many Egyptians in the years preceding the anticolonial revolution of 1919, and more acutely afterward: Who rules Egypt? In the shadow of Ottoman and British dominion, can Egypt lay claim to sovereign nationhood? Egypt's status during this period was ambiguous. In 1914 Britain deposed the last Khedive and officially declared Egypt a protectorate of the British Empire. By 1922 Egypt earned provisional independence from Britain, and the Ottoman Empire collapsed. By 1922, then, Egypt ostensibly was "free," yet both the Ottoman ruling structure and British hegemony would survive nearly three decades more, as the monarchs Fu'ād and Fārūq—descendants of Mehmed Ali—continued to rule the country within the orbit of British control. Thus Egyptian sovereignty, not British, stutters in the balance of translation. If al-Sibāʿī had hoped to transfer the reins of sovereignty from English to Arabic, he falls just one letter short of spelling the Arabic word when light passes into darkness, and darkness reigns. Sovereignty, then, never quite makes the passage into Arabic: *su'dud,* the Arabic "equivalent" of the English term, is suspended between light—its visible realization—and darkness, its negation or at least ambiguation. Its final *d,* or *dāl,* dangles—as al-Sibāʿī tells us—invisible, in the dark, its fate at best unknown and at worst doomed. Although the translator's pen still moves, and quite possibly the tram as well, the technologies of modern words and wheels fail to liberate Egypt from Western domination and to secure its sovereign nationhood. When the lights go out on tram and pen, the investment of so many Egyptian intellectuals of the *nahḍa* in the project of Westernizing "enlightenment" flickers too.

SOVEREIGNTY, PARTICULARITY, UNIVERSALISM

Sovereignty is the ideological cognate of empire. To be fully and truly sovereign, a state must at once stand independent *of* others and reign supreme *over* others. In other words, it must become an autonomous value among many equally autonomous values and must also establish itself as unequal value, indeed as superior value, by subordinating its putative "equals" and denying them autonomy. Sovereignty takes the form of (post)colonial translation: it posits a relationship of equivalence between two or more terms—in this case national terms—yet slashes the equal sign to declare one term greater than another, indeed the greatest of all. Like translation, which poses as bilateral yet is in fact deictic, sovereignty masquerades as yet unmistakably inflects equation, pointing it (≥) toward the comparative and ultimately the superlative degree. The potential of sovereign logic to reverse the vector of domination (≤), to turn the tables of inequality on the colonizer and to redirect autonomy and power toward the colonized—to effect precisely the oscillation of subject and object that Jean Baudrillard calls seduction—is what makes sovereignty so alluring to the colonized, despite the fact that it secures liberation in the very idiom of empire and thus threatens to reinscribe the imperial. Its attraction, in other words, derives from its translationality.

By now it is a truism that nationalism is a declension—if not a mere derivative—of the grammar of colonialism, as Partha Chatterjee has argued.[5] The propinquity of sovereignty to imperialism, and of both to the operations of translation, suggests why this might be so. Chatterjee is critical both of liberal political theorists who represent Eastern nationalisms as failed imitations of Western political formations—as the illiberal, "evil" mistranslations of a "good" liberal original—and of more radical theorists who recast Western nationalisms as fundamentally "irrational" (because invented, and always tendentiously so) and thus Eastern nationalisms as mere replications of that irrationality. Both positions, Chatterjee maintains, assume that nationalism is the "gift" of the West to the East. As I read it, Chatterjee's nationalism is neither mistranslation nor perfect translation but a crossing of the two: a response by the colonized to the loss of self-determination that takes the historically "necessary" form of the nation in order to be heard by empire but just as purposely diverts that form to its own ends. Nationalism, Chatterjee maintains, "is a political revolution, but one whose course cannot be described by selecting from history two points of origin and culmination and joining them by a straight line."[6] To declare Eastern nationalisms either equal or unequal to Western ones, he implies, is to traffic in "straight"—indeed tautological—conceptions of equivalence. Insisting that a "crooked line" connects the diverse origins and destinations of nationalism, Eastern and Western, Chatterjee in effect redefines Eastern nationalism as the pursuit of an equality slashed and (to use Baudrillard's term) "reversibilized," where the East is seduced *by the prospect of its own sovereignty* into translating itself into the likeness of the West. Hence, I believe, Chatterjee's renunciation of the economy of the "gift" for one premised on intentional reception, if unintentional effects. Nationalism becomes, for Chatterjee, a political "revolution which at the same time, and in fundamental ways, is not a revolution."[7] The circuit he describes neither produces the postcolonial nor reproduces the colonial but seduces both.

The seductions of translation explain the circuitous relationship of nationalist revolution to the ancien régime of colonialism. Against Victor Hugo's contention that nationalisms in general (and national bourgeoisies in particular) repudiate translation because the foreign and the universal do violence to the integrity of the nation-state, Lawrence Venuti has argued that nationalisms feed on translation. "Translation practices," he contends, "form national identities through a specular process in which the subject identifies with cultural materials that are defined as national."[8] This specular process of national "self-recognition," he hints, is a detoured mirroring: a recognition of the self through and in the *I* of the Other. For the stuff of national culture, as Venuti notes, often is not "native" at all but "irreducibly foreign."[9] Wherever translation introduces the foreign into the language of the native, the foreignness so introduced must be "repressed in a fantastic identification with an apparently homogeneous national identity," a repression that paradoxically intensifies "national desire."[10] Indeed, Venuti maintains, "the formation of national identities can remain unconscious because it occurs in language that originates elsewhere, *in the subject's relations to others,* but that the subject perceives as his or her own self-expression."[11] Here he draws on the work of Antony Easthope, who argues that nation is "an identity that can speak us even when we may think we are speaking for ourselves."[12] Reading Venuti and Easthope with Chatterjee, I would suggest that the idea of the "nation," which absorbs external difference (foreignness) into the skin of indigeneity and indigenous difference (alternative nativity) into the skin of homogeneity, emerges from a translational seduction in which the object of sovereignty—of supremacist freedom, imperialist autonomy—fancies itself the subject thereof. Like Chatterjee, however, I would assign the "unconsciousness" of nationalism not to the formation of national identities but to the implications of nation formation. I argue that the object of sovereignty knows very well that he or she is not its subject but acts *as if* he or she were anyway, the better to conjure "real" autonomy and power through fantasy. The expansionist logic of modern imperialism is predicated, paradoxically, on centralization, or a strong concept of nation: on a delimitation and thus a concentration of sovereign power in a state and in the people most proximally identified with that state. Nation-centered imperialism lures those subject to its hegemony to constitute themselves, in turn, as nations, as similarly centralized powers capable of competing with and overcoming the imperial center and of establishing themselves as limited, sovereign, and thus also potentially expansionist entities in their own right.[13] To be seduced by sovereign nationality is to willfully forget the imperialist logic that haunts it, which assigns objecthood to the native and subjectivity to the foreign. In so forgetting, the nation that issues from colonial domination *repeats* that logic, becoming "foreign"—imperial and imperially universal—to become "itself." What is unconscious in this translation of the Other into the self is not the process of self-formation, of whose foreignizing impulse the nationalist is all too aware, but the potential for self-loss.

Venuti suggestively associates universalism with nationalism. Yet he withholds a full reading of the connections between the two. Writing of the translational construction of the idea of "Japan," Naoki Sakai more vividly exposes the complicity of nationalism and empire, understood as the complicity between particularism and universalism. "To insist on the particularity and autonomy of Japan," he argues, "is paradoxically to worship the putative ubiquity of the idealized West."[14] In Sakai's analysis, national particularity—in this case something called "Japan"—only emerges as such through the eye (and *I*) of a universal that the modern West has arrogated as its own, equated with itself. "Only when [Japan] is integrated into Western universalism" by being recognized as a nation, he writes, "does it gain its own identity as a particularity," and with it "a nagging urge to see the self from the viewpoint of the other."[15] Concludes Sakai, "a particularism such as nationalism can never be a serious critique of universalism, for it is an accomplice thereof."[16] Sakai's grace note echoes Chatterjee's: a particularism such as nationalism both is and is not a revolution against a universalism like imperialism. For against what background can the nation appear unique, Sakai asks, except that of the imperial "universal"? And how can the unitary be so, he implies, except by subsuming and homogenizing—universalizing—the differences within its particularity: by creating a national "universal"? Building on Sakai's suggestive connection of particularism and universalism, I would argue that nationalist claims to uniqueness and to the unitary at once articulate difference within the terms of an implicit universal (for national particulars paradoxically must differentiate themselves in ways "alike" enough—universal enough—to permit their recognition *as* "unique") and manufacture likeness within the putative borders of the particular (for the national particular, if it is to present itself to the universal *as* a cognizable—and recognizable—"unit," must homogenize the subnational particularities it contains).

Like Japan during the Meiji period (1868–1912), Egypt learned to recognize itself as such—as national particularity—in the translational mirror of the universal: the imperial universal of the modern West. The 1919 revolution was the largest, most concerted, and most militant expression of anticolonial sentiment in Egypt since 1881–82, when the Egyptian officer Aḥmad ʿUrābī led a failed revolt first against the Ottoman Khedive Tawfīq and the Turco-Circassian ruling class, then against the forces of British occupation that intervened, in 1882, on behalf of the Ottomans. In the wake of the 1919 revolution, Egyptian intellectuals became more interested than ever before in theorizing the relationships of translation to the sovereign nation and ultimately to empire. Focusing on the late 1920s, I contend that the strange kinship of sovereignty to empire—and the historical dependence of empire in Egypt on translation—led intellectuals of the post-1919 period to define Egyptian claims to nationhood, national culture, and national literature in equally translational terms: to wonder whether, how, and to what extent Egypt could or should "translate" into Europe if it wished to be a nation. Writing in 1928, Salāma Mūsā—echoing Rifāʿa Rāfiʿ al-Ṭahṭāwī's hypothesized "equivalences" between Arabic and French—claimed that Egypt was European because its originary ancient language was *akin* to English and nothing like Arabic. Mūsā intimated that Egypt would be a nation only insofar as it recognized itself as "English." That year, Muḥammad Ḥusayn Haykal dubbed Egypt a "Tower of Babel";

bemoaning Egypt's intranational untranslatability, he declared that its chaotic mix of "traditional" and "modernizing" idioms undercut the capacity of its European-educated elite to culture the mind-set proper to a "real" nation. If Egypt's claim to nationhood hinges on the translatability of its language(s) into Europe's, as Mūsā implies, or on the extent to which the constituent elements of its culture can be translated into a single hegemonic national "language" in tune with European colonial modernity, as Haykal insists, I would suggest that becoming nationally "Egyptian" meant remaining colonially "European." In the end, I argue, the effort to institute Egyptian nationality and national modernity—which sought to obliterate *local translationality*—surrendered Egypt to *imperial translationality,* eradicating local incommensurabilities within a "national universal" of European colonial origins. Egypt was most European when, paradoxically, it was most Egyptian.

FAILURES OF THE NATIONAL SIGN

Between the afterlife of French occupation, the spasmodic renewal and slow death of Ottoman rule, and the long shadow of the British Empire, then, modern "Egypt" was born. Yet the intellectual midwives who presided over its delivery—indeed its multiple deliveries—declared it stillborn each time, a "failed" nation. In 1823 Joseph Agoub had this to say of its people: "The Egyptians of today are not even a nation: a heterogeneous assemblage of different races of Asia and Africa, [Egypt] is a melange without unity; these [races] are diverse traits that do not add up to a physiognomy. One could say that all the countries of the earth have participated in the population of the banks of the Nile."[17] Nearly a century later, al-Māzinī (1890–1949)—the Egyptian critic, novelist, and translator who gave us the anecdote about al-Sibāʿī and the untranslatability of the sovereign with which I opened this chapter—reprises the problem of Egyptian national "failure."[18] Writing in 1935, al-Māzinī proposes to solve this problem by extending the borders of the nation through language, specifically Arabic.

> Nationalism is nothing but language. No matter what God may have willed the nature of countries to be—and no matter what distant origins, deeply rooted in antiquity, may have willed—so long as peoples have one language, they are one people. That is because humankind cannot think—for now at least—except in signifiers *[bi al-alfāẓi]*. . . . [I]t is impossible—now—for us to shape a meaning [*maʿnā;* signified] stripped of the word [*lafẓ;* signifier] that indicates it. . . . [F]rom this [point of departure] the speakers [lit., *abnāʾ,*

> "children"] of each language [come to] agree and to resemble one another, and to differ from the speakers [lit., "children"] of every other language. This is the difference between the Englishman and the Frenchman, and between the Englishman and the Indian. This, to my mind, is a scientific fact, and since such is the case, how could we be anything but Arabs . . . ?[19]

On the surface, these assertions appear separated by more than just time. Agoub argues that modern Egypt is not a nation because it is racially and ethnically heterogeneous, and heterogeneity is incompatible with the national idea. Egypt, he implies, has taken in the universal—"all the countries of the earth"—without becoming universal*ized,* without dissolving the particulars it has absorbed into a single, definable, totalizing character. Its disparate features do not add up to a face—specifically, a physiognomy: the composite of facial features from which mind and character can be "read," or divined. Al-Māzinī, on the other hand, suggests that differences between a nation's constituent parts do not matter. What does is a common language. In arguing that the "speakers of each language [come to] agree and to resemble one another," he implies that language can override genes and give unrelated speakers a common parent, such that they all become its "children" and look like kin ("resemble one another"). Language composes the homogeneous national face that disparate racial, religious, and other elements cannot; it qualifies a people who otherwise would be too heterogeneous to call itself a nation.

Yet these two statements share an underlying logic. Both are preoccupied with origins. When Agoub speaks of the "Egyptians of today" not constituting a nation, he has in mind an originary Egypt that did: an Egypt of antiquity, what he elsewhere calls Egypt of the Pharaohs. Agoub implies that the nation must be not only sui generis—unique in character—but also auto-created; it can only properly emerge at a given people's point of historical origin. Move away from the origin, and a people will cease to be "pure"—no longer a nation. Al-Māzinī, in turn, concedes that a people's origins may be lost to antiquity yet insists that language can supply precisely the fictive "pure" origin that the modern nation requires to compensate for its people's heterogeneity. Only by conjuring the illusory oneness of the elements that have "contaminated" it since antiquity can Egypt construct a *new* origin and become a nation in modernity. This may be why al-Māzinī speaks of *nationalism* rather than of *nation,* where nationalism is the dynamic act of identity construction and nation the identity it constructs. Nationalism is nothing but language because language *makes* the nation. It makes a motley people "pure." Out of many it makes the one—the single—and the sui generis—the singular, unique.

In al-Māzinī's understanding of nationalism, then, the *unicity* of the nation—at once the oneness and the uniqueness of a people—is not the given of language but the creature thereof. But is the language that produces nation itself unitary? On this point, al-Māzinī equivocates. Timothy Mitchell has argued that colonial discourse engenders a world divided, on every level, in two. According to Mitchell, this division unfolds primarily in language, visual or verbal, such that the structuring duality of the colonial world is a schism between concrete things (the world, for instance) and their abstract representations (the Heideggerian "world-picture"). "In Europe," writes Mitchell,

> the words of a language had come to be considered not meanings in themselves but the physical clues to some sort of metaphysical abstraction—a mind or mentality. . . . This view of language did not emerge in isolation. . . . [I]n the world-as-exhibition everything one encountered was coming to be ordered and grasped as though it were the mere physical representation of something abstract. Politics itself in its colonial age . . . continuously order[ed] up the representations that would produce this apparent realm of meaning.[20]

For Mitchell, the binaristic logic of sign/signification—that is, of signifier and signified, which unite to form yet another opposition to the "real" they purport to represent—underpins the infinite series of binary oppositions that the logic of European imperialism would propagate and manipulate to manage its relation to the non-Western Other: East/West, inferiority/superiority, tradition/modernity, backwardness/progress. He rightly suggests that the logic of Western semiosis, with its detachment of meaning from the signifier and referral of signification to a metaphysical beyond, transformed the epistemology of language in nineteenth- and early-twentieth-century Egypt. Indeed, al-Māzinī's rhetoric teeters on the boundary between this colonial logic of twoness and a restitution of the oneness-in-motion of sign/signification so central, according to Mitchell, to the precolonial Arab-Islamic intellectual tradition.[21] In his initial theorization of nation, al-Māzinī explodes the notion that thought can exist "outside" language: "humankind cannot think," he insists, " . . . except in signifiers." One cannot produce "meaning" shorn of the signifier that indicates it, so how is one to understand the nation as an "idea" outside language? In al-Māzinī's theory the signifier—the manner of meaning—determines the signified; if a people articulates meaning in the same manner, then it means the same thing, and it becomes one (and the same), whatever its other differences.

Thus al-Māzinī suggests that the unicity that defines a nation-idea is a sameness of "thought" produced through the transnational (perhaps also intranational) play of competing signifiers. In that play crystallize the agreements—"stylistic conventions"—that make one language's manner of meaning incommensurable with another's.[22]

Al-Māzinī's ideas beg comparison to those of the Russian theorist Mikhail Bakhtin, whose "Discourse in the Novel" (1934–35) is contemporaneous with al-Māzinī's meditation on language and nation.[23] Bakhtin's conception of unitary language similarly exposes its givenness as constructedness. "Unitary language," he writes,

> constitutes the theoretical expression of the historical processes of linguistic unification and centralization, an expression of the centripetal forces of language. A unitary language is not something given [*dan*] but is always in essence posited [*zadan*]. . . .
>
> A common unitary language is a system of linguistic norms. But these norms do not constitute an abstract imperative; they are rather . . . forces that struggle to overcome the heteroglossia of language, forces that unite and centralize verbal-ideological thought, creating within a heteroglot national language the firm, stable linguistic nucleus of an officially recognized literary language.[24]

Like al-Māzinī, then, Bakhtin suggests that a unitary "national language"—the norm that ensures maximal "verbal-ideological" understanding among speakers—is never positive but posited. Yet from this concurrence, the two diverge. Where al-Māzinī sees the unitary as the product of a long and repeated *negotiation* of differences, Bakhtin sees it as the *imposition* of centripetal force—of in-gathering or centralizing energy—on the equal and opposite tendency of language toward devolution, toward the centrifugal forces of the plural. In Bakhtin's conception, the "unitary language" of the nation must perpetually posit itself as such against a "heteroglot national language" that threatens its normalizing tendencies. Thus, while al-Māzinī and Bakhtin agree that "unitary language" is never a transcendental signified (in Bakhtin's words, the norms that it represents "do not constitute an abstract imperative") but always a social, relational, and thus relative totality (and potential totalitarianism), in al-Māzinī the unitary seems less an antiheteroglossic force that imposes itself from without than a fricative that issues from the brush of thoroughly social—hence thoroughly meaning-full—signifiers against one another, in the breath expelled from the narrow breach between. In the end, al-Māzinī suggests—like his contemporary Bakhtin—that maximal language, or national language, issues from the narrowing of language (Bakhtin's centripetal force). Yet in Bakhtin, the unitary *forces itself onto* heteroglossia; in al-Māzinī, by contrast, the unitary *forces itself out of* the mouth of heteroglossia, out of an implicit struggle of dueling signifiers thrown together by space or time—by geography or history—to reclaim the sovereignty of a particular mode of meaning-making over all other possible such modes.

Extrapolating an alternative theory of unitary language from al-Māzinī's intimations thereof, I would suggest that the *national universal* issues from the play of particulars across space and time, each such particular a would-be sovereign that styles its particularity universal. To become the universal of all universals and thus absolutely sovereign, however, a particular must perform an act of translational seduction. It must make its manner of meaning at once represent all other such modes—"equal" them—and mean more than they do: reign as unequal. It must make other modes of meaning imagine that in giving in to its word, they give up nothing of themselves—that, in ceding their voices to the "something more" implied by the universal of universals, they do not lose but in fact aggrandize themselves. Through the seduction of translation, one signifier emerges from the polyphonic mouth of heteroglossia as the unequal "likeness" of all other signifiers within. How else to speak *for* heteroglossia and make the polyphony of voices it subsumes believe that they continue to speak for themselves, indeed for their *best* selves, through the tongue of the imperial-national "Other," the absolute sovereign?

Thus al-Māzinī's theory of unitary language, less impositionist than seductionist, exposes the illiberalism of liberalism: the imperialism of the "representative democracy" of the nation and of its international extension, the family of nations. Its ear is uncannily attuned to the operations of the imperial universal and its effects on the formation of the national particular. In redescribing the unicity of the nation as the creature of language and implicitly also redefining the unicity of language, in turn, as the issue of particulars competing for recognition as the universal of universals first on the national and ultimately on the international stages, al-Māzinī is able to suggest that Western nationalisms (the competition of rival empires) are no different from Eastern ones (the battle of colonies against empires, the struggle of colonies to reassert their sovereignty and thus their rival claims to imperium), or perhaps that their in-difference points to their very real difference. He tells us that the difference between nations is interlingual, indeed *translational,* and politically so. Hence what differentiates England from France is no different from what differentiates England from India. The two inequalities are "equal." No matter that within the global economy of 1935, England *rivals* France, whereas England *dominates* India. Empire, understood as the desire for sovereignty, is the underlying logic of both pairings, and thus empire—and the colonial universal it creates—is the "same difference" that flattens the differences not just between the two entities in each pairing but also between the two pairings. Herein lies the attraction of the nation-form for the colonized: if West does not equal West as much as West does not equal East, then West and East might not be so different after all; their signs can be seduced—that is, reversed. Language in al-Māzinī, then, operates on two levels: the particular and the universal, each constitutive of the other. "National" language, an idiom constituted by the emergence of common signifiers from the play of differences, cannot exist outside metalanguage, the idiom of empire and of its cognate, sovereignty: an imperial universal into whose terms every "national" language must translate itself if it is to reign supreme within its borders and to become universally recognizable beyond those borders.

For this reason, al-Māzinī's bold effort to imagine national identity outside the grammar of European imperialism ultimately surrenders to the very logic of "twoness" that Mitchell imputes to Western epistemes and colonial politics. Prefacing his reflections on language and nation with a meditation on the Egyptian revolution of 1919, al-Māzinī argues that that revolution failed because its exponents had walled off their struggle from those of neighboring Arabic-speaking countries, circumscribing their nationalism within a wall as high as "*sūr al-Ṣayn*" ("the Great Wall of China"). Here he invokes a startlingly "Eastern" historicopolitical metaphor to describe his compatriots' enclosure in the fundamentally Western logic of Egyptian territorial nationalism. Paradoxically, his metaphor turns Western allegations of Eastern isolationism on their head, indicting West—not East—for exporting too limited a vision of human community to Egyptians and other Arabic-speaking peoples. Thus al-Māzinī eschews the confines of a Westernizing Egyptian nationalism for the expansive horizons of Arab nationalism and Easternization.

> It infuriates . . . me to see anyone view Egypt as if it were part of Europe and not part of the East. I maintain that Eastern citizenship/nationality *[al-jinsiyyata al-sharqiyyata]* is the foundation of our life and our history, and that this [Westernizing] perspective corrupts our Eastern merits—if it does not rob us of these—and gains us not one of the merits of the West. Knowledge is translatable *[al-'ilmu yunqalu]*; once, it was translated from the East

> to the West, and it can easily be translated from the West to the East without the East trying to shed its skin or lose its identifying traits.[25]

Here al-Māzinī exposes as ideological—and tendentious—the "natural" bond of Egypt to Europe on which many Egyptian intellectuals of the *nahḍa* insisted. This move is radical. Yet its manner of moving is less so. To the Western affiliation he decries, al-Māzinī simply counterpoises an Eastern nationality, claiming that Egypt is East and not West. We return to what Mitchell (after Fanon) calls the colonial world divided in two and to the regime of universalist—thus Eurocentric—particularism Sakai decries: to a Europe and an "outside" called the East, a world in which discrete Eastern and Western "merits" can be weighed and measured. Thus we return to a world in which knowledge and language too can be treated as autonomous rather than as socially embedded phenomena. And it is on the ground of translation—translatability—that al-Māzinī extracts and isolates knowledge and language from the political. One need not shed one's skin, he argues, to translate Western knowledge to the East—to transport it from English or French into Arabic. Where Western knowledge is concerned, its form—the signifiers through which its meaning is made—is inconsequential; only its content is essential, and that content can migrate independent of form. Where Eastern identity (more properly, Arab identity) is concerned, form is everything. Content is inconsequential; it entails no consequences for form. So long as the Arabic signifier still stands, new content—new signifieds—cannot alter it. In the end, al-Māzinī grants the West its long-standing imperial claim to a Derridean "transcendental signified," to a meaning that can travel the world over, but grants Egypt—and the East—sole rights to what is effectively a Derridean "transcendental signifier," to the word that ultimately will fix the destiny of traveling meaning. Here, as in the passage I analyzed earlier, the signifier is primary, and once again it seems to determine meaning. Yet if we are to believe the more radical al-Māzinī who speaks elsewhere in the essay, the al-Māzinī who insists that the signified can never be *thought* outside the signifier, can a "native" signifier ever really encounter a "foreign" signified shorn of its original signifier, of its mode of meaning in the original tongue? And can the "native" signifier, then, remain unchanged in its encounter with the foreign? What happens when a "native" signifier binds to a "foreign"—especially a colonizing—signifier/signified?

What al-Māzinī proposes, I would suggest, recalls Lydia Liu's theory of the super-sign—redirected toward the colonized. Liu's super-sign is the "destiny and destination" of a native word in a foreign tongue: it is born when signifiers from at least two languages—ostensible equivalents—bind, in the moment of translation, to produce an excess whose signification is the aggregate of its constitutive parts and thus the equivalent of none, yet whose intention or manner of meaning nonetheless points toward the most geopolitically powerful of the terms in translation.[26] "The super-sign escapes our attention," Liu argues,

> because it is made to camouflage the traces of that excess through normative etymological procedures and to disavow the mutual exposure and transformation of the languages.
>
> It is a commonplace that verbal signs are not stable and can change with time and usage; but as two, three, or multiple languages are involved and implicate one another, can we recapture the foreignness of that which has penetrated the opacity of the indigenous?[27]

Liu implies that the native speaker of a language ignores the action of super-signification on the native word because he or she understands etymology genealogically, as filiation: as direct descent from a parent, be that parent a native one (as in the "indigenous word") or a foreign one (as in the "loanword"), or direct kinship to other "children" of a common parent. What such a view misses, she hints, is the operation of *affiliation* on the native word at every moment in its history: the fact that the signification of the native word is determined not simply by the vertical pressure of local word-genealogy on the signifier, nor by its horizontal play within a field of other local signifiers, but also by the exogenous *network* of foreign significations that impinge upon ("crisscross") and overwrite it. Colonial conditions compound this effect. For the super-sign, Liu emphasizes, is "not a word, but a hetero-cultural [and "hetero-linguistic"] signifying chain that crisscrosses the semantic fields of two or more languages simultaneously and makes an impact on the meaning of recognizable verbal units" within and among these languages.[28] What emerges as this signifying chain "quilts" the field of local signification is something like the fricative of "sameness" that, as I argued in my earlier reading of al-Māzinī, is forced out of heteroglossia—this time, however, not the heteroglossia intrinsic to a single language, but one that issues from the fateful historicopolitical intersection of a given language with other linguistic systems. In other words, the produced "resemblance" that in turn produces the unicity of the nation—the shared signifier that, according to al-Māzinī, affiliates unrelated speakers, makes them "children" of an artificial common "parent"—never emerges from the contest of differences in one language alone, but always also from the differential interplay between the native signifier and its foreign competitors.

Al-Māzinī appears to sense that the heterocultural and heterolinguistic signifying chain of the colonial universal crosses and reshapes the national particular: a particular whose integrity he premises *on* language, on a unity of sign and signification. Why, then, does he ultimately imagine that Western epistemes can be unmoored, in translation, from the hegemonic power that the colonial universal bestows on their signifiers and reattached to the Arabic word without any loss to the Arabic signified? Why does a nationalism defined as "nothing but language"—a signified (*ma'nā*, "meaning") articulated from and thus hinging upon its signifier (*lafẓ*, "articulation")—give way to a vision in which the European signified is so transparently exchangeable across the politicolinguistic borders of "East" and "West," so easily imported into the Arabic signifier? Liu's analysis helps us see why the transcendental European signified disappears under the skin of Arabic and hides there, takes refuge in what I call (drawing on Jacques Derrida) the *transcendental signifier of the native.* According to Liu, the movement of the super-sign across the native signifier is "generally occulted," the foreignness it bears subsumed in "the unchanging face of an indigenous word," whose optical "illusion of homogeneity" fools the "unsuspecting eye of a native speaker."[29] If the signifier is all, as it is for al-Māzinī ("humankind cannot think . . . except in signifiers"), what matter its contents? Liu suggests that within the unequal geopolitical economy of (post)colonial translation, native signifiers appear unchanged yet are profoundly altered—at times even emptied and reoccupied—in their encounter with the foreign. In the super-sign forged by the recombination of the disempowered native and the empowered foreign in the unequal encounter of (post)colonial translation, the foreign dominates, pointing the native word toward its intention.

The native, then, is lured to signify as the foreign wishes it to signify precisely because the native clings to the illusion of the integrity of its signifiers and fancies itself still sovereign. Were we to follow al-Māzinī's reasoning to its logical conclusion, an Indian nationalism articulated in English, which shares its signifiers with the colonizer, must—by linguistic necessity—be barely distinguishable from British colonialism, whereas an Egyptian nationalism articulated in Arabic, which rejects the dominator's signifier, must—again by linguistic necessity—stand in stark opposition to British domination. Yet we know well that the Egyptian national form can be just as derivative, if differently so, and—more dangerously—far less conscious of its occupation by the colonizer's language, hence more deeply subject to its dominion. Thus al-Māzinī, precisely because he believes that signifiers embody thought, assumes that so long as Egypt and its fellows in the Arabic-speaking "East" have not lost their Arabic—the outward signifier of indigenous particularity—they hold the power to point the meaning of any conjunction of Arabic word and Western episteme toward their intention. Forgetting that the super-sign such a conjunction inscribes itself is embedded in a geopolitical superstructure—the colonial power that aligns the English or French signifier with the universal and thus pulls all meaning, even Arabic meaning, toward its magnet—al-Māzinī reverses the deictic logic of the super-sign and assumes that the geopolitically disempowered signifier of Arabic, Egypt, or the East might govern the signification of such a construct, however unequally it has been "coauthored" by East and West. In falling prey to the notion that the super-sign is reversible, al-Māzinī falls to what I have called the seduction of translation.

THE IDEA OF ORDER AT CAIRO

Translation was not just the prime vehicle through which early-twentieth-century Egyptian intellectuals assimilated European literature and thought but also the trope some used to describe both the failed and the desired Egyptian nation. Writing in 1928, the Egyptian writer and literary critic Muḥammad Ḥusayn Haykal (1888–1956)—author of what is usually (and wrongly) called the first Arabic novel (*Zaynab,* 1913) and editor of the major newspapers *al-Siyāsa* (Politics) and *al-Siyāsa al-Usbūʿiyya* (Politics Weekly)—compared 1920s Egypt to the Tower of Babel. Haykal argued that a chaotic mix of secularist versus Azharite intellectual tendencies, languages, and even modes of dress had plunged Egypt into a state of intranational untranslatability. According to Haykal, this state—if left unchecked—ultimately would undercut the efforts of European-educated Egyptians to "culture" the minds of their compatriots and to foster the "freedom of thought" proper to a cohesive nation.[30] That year the Egyptian literary translator and scholar Aḥmad Ḥasan al-Zayyāt (1885–1968), who later would become editor of the periodical *al-Risāla* (the Message), named Arabic literature a prime locus of Egypt's cultural confusion, calling its state "chaos," its boundaries and rules undefined.[31] Such writings, I argue, suggest that Egypt would join the ranks of orderly, "civilized" (read: European) nations only when its culture had changed from one in which "nothing

[was] translatable" into one in which "everything [was] translatable."[32] That dream of intranational translatability pointed in the direction of Europe.

If al-Māzinī represents the ideological future of al-Zayyāt, Agoub is the ideological forerunner of Haykal. Agoub, we will recall, was co-director of the École Égyptienne de Paris, where al-Ṭahṭāwī studied in the late 1820s. In his *Takhlīṣ al-Ibrīz fī Talkhīṣ Bārīz* (1834), al-Ṭahṭāwī would translate the passage from Agoub quoted earlier in this chapter, citing it as proof of the importance of studying history. "With the will of God . . . ," al-Ṭahṭāwī concludes, "the different [branches] of history will be translated from French into our language."[33] From Agoub's words al-Ṭahṭāwī imported at least one historical lesson: the idea—indeed ideology—of national order that would guide his projects of educational and social reform and thus transform the very fabric of nineteenth-century Egypt. According to Mitchell, the experiences of al-Ṭahṭāwī and 'Alī Mubārak in the École Égyptienne and École Militaire de Paris between the 1820s and the 1840s engendered a fascination in both with the construction of social "order," which suddenly emerges "as an end in itself."[34] Such order, Mitchell argues, is achieved by "practices of distribution" that array discrete social quantities—prisoners in the Benthamite panopticon, students in the Lancaster-style school, soldiers in military files—at exact and equal intervals, so that the spaces between appear "natural" and the unnatural practices that engendered those spaces are occulted and forgotten. "The gaps are further made to stand forward," Mitchell writes,

> by causing the objects they are to "separate" to appear as similar to one another as possible—by clothing them, for example, in identical dress. . . . In the uniformity of appearance, the equidistant interval, and the geometric angle, the acts of distribution, if practiced quietly, unceasingly, and uniformly, almost disappear from view.[35]

While physiognomic order of the kind Agoub envisions seems less amenable to such an array, it in fact requires that individual faces be reimagined—translated—into "uniformity of appearance" so that the "racial" gaps between disappear, composing one orderly national face. Haykal too, as we shall see, aspires to array look-alike, sound-alike, and think-alike Egyptians at intervals equidistant from each other and above all, equidistant from Europe. With the rise of this idea of "order" *(niẓām)* emerges its corollary: chaos *(fawḍā)*. "Order" can only seize control, Mitchell argues, when it produces as (threatening) "disorder" whatever exceeds its grid.[36] Thus disorder is a condition of unequal value, the "unequal end of the polarity" *order/disorder*. It is, as Mitchell suggests, an ideology of lack that exists "only to allow 'order' its conceptual possibility," only to legitimate the ideology of order and enable the latter to reign supreme.[37] The late 1920s writings of Haykal and al-Zayyāt on nation, translation, and cultural modernity, I contend, propagate just such an ideology of disorder to enjoin a new idea of order at Cairo.

Bearing the contradictory title "Iḥtiḍār al-Jumūd wa al-Fawḍā—Kayfa Yattasiq al-Niẓām al-Jadīd" (The Moribund State of Inertia and Chaos—How the New Order Can Be Well Ordered), Haykal's article appeared in the Cairo weekly *al-Jadīd* (the New) on 6 February 1928. It begins with two parables of nation and translation. The first is about a dinner party that Haykal attended one evening at the home of one "Ustādh Hilbāwī" ("Mister Hilbāwī")—most likely Ibrāhīm al-Hilbāwī (1858–1940), notorious for his role in the Dinshawāy trial of 1906. As prosecutor at that trial, al-Hilbāwī had abetted British colonial authorities, presiding over the wrongful execution of Egyptian peasants for the alleged murder of an English officer; later, he rehabilitated himself by defending Egyptian nationalists pro bono, becoming the first head of the Egyptian Lawyers' Syndicate in 1912 and joining Haykal's Liberal Constitutionalist Party (Ḥizb al-Aḥrār al-Dustūriyyīn) in 1922.[38] Al-Hilbāwī, writes Haykal, did not tell his guests in advance what the dress code would be. Thus a group of guests showed up, like their host, in Western evening dress—in "*Smūking,*" says Haykal, Arabizing the French word for "tuxedo," itself derived from the English "smoking jacket." The rest, presumably, turned up otherwise attired. Realizing that he had neglected to make explicit the standard to which all guests should conform, al-Hilbāwī could not resist a comparison to the still un-universalized nation-space: "This illustrates our Egyptian life, whose distinguishing feature is a lack of harmony *['adami al-ittisāqi].*"[39] Through al-Hilbāwī's voice, Haykal chides the Egyptian who has not taken the European (French/English) jacket as given—as the tacit *sensus communis* of the social collective and, by extension, the "universal" standard of the would-be nation—for failing to reproduce himself in a relation of sartorial equivalence to other citizens and thereby failing to construct the homogeneity that he (like Agoub) deems the precondition of proper nationhood.

In the second anecdote, Haykal recalls an encounter with students at the Egyptian Club in London in summer 1926.

> I was talking to our youth, who by their good fortune had been destined to mix with Western civilization and . . . to drink from its wellsprings, about the future duty that had been placed on their shoulders . . . : to strive to culture the minds of the people of their nation and to struggle their hardest . . . on behalf of freedom of thought.[40]

One young man, recalls Haykal, confronted him: "And how are we to attain freedom of thought in our nation when its people remain factions, no harmony between them in the modes of thinking?"[41] The student pointed out that an Egyptian like then–Prime Minister ʿAdlī Yakan Pasha and the average Azharite inhabit two universes of thought: almost never reading the same texts and—when they do—almost never interpreting these in the same ways.[42] Clearly the student embraces Haykal's civilizing mission, his call to "culture the minds" of Egypt with European thought. Blind to the possibility that a *lack* of harmony between intellectual camps might testify to "freedom of thought"—and not a dissolution of difference in absolute harmony—he appears to accept Haykal's tendentious definition of "freedom of thought" as unbridled Westernization. Tacitly also the student, as Haykal represents him, defines the conquering/liberating force of the new as "secular" and the antiquated mentalities to be conquered/liberated as "religious."

From these anecdotes Haykal deduces two problems that dog the Egyptian nation: a lack of harmony *(ittisāq)* and an abundance of internal contradiction *(tanāquḍ)*. If even the elite "crème de la crème of the nation" *("khulāṣatu al-ummati")*, the very "group supposed to model its intellectual and spiritual order," fail, on the one hand, to answer the summons of modernity by showing up automatically dressed in its standard uniform and fail, on the other, to consolidate a homogenized culture of the modern in which everyone reads the same canon and subjects that canon to the same hermeneutics, how can Egypt hope to constitute a viable polity? Haykal's interpretation of this supposedly untenable state of national affairs is arrestingly translational:

> Stand a little while in one of the public squares and study [*taṣaffaḥ;* lit., "leaf through"] the clothes, the faces, and the heads, and you would see this clearly. You would see yourself in something like what they say of the Tower of Babel *[mā yaqūlūnahu ʿan burji Bābila]*, hearing every possible language and seeing every possible appearance and . . . attire. And that each speaks and dresses and takes the shape he desires is not about devotion on the people's part to . . . freedom; rather, it is about the submission of each camp to a past or to a present that differs from that to which the other camp submits. . . . A condition like this cannot be sound.[43]

Several points interest me here. First, Haykal articulates Egypt's claim to nationality—or lack thereof—in terms similar to Agoub's a century earlier. He tells us that Egypt is a disorderly state because the languages, the garb, and the physiognomies ("faces") of its people are disjunctive. He also voices a corollary proposition: that Egypt will not consolidate itself as a nation unless it eliminates disorder—difference—and imposes harmony, even order, what he elsewhere calls *al-niẓām* or *al-tanẓīm*. Second, he invokes the Tower of Babel to describe this state of disorder, thereby imagining nation formation as a problem of "language," and more specifically, as a problem of translatability—anticipating al-Māzinī's observation that "nationalism is nothing but language." Indeed, Haykal's reference to the Tower of Babel is rare in early-twentieth-century Egyptian discourse; the parable does not exist as such in the Qur'ān, and thus the trope has not been, historically, a standard one for Arab Muslim writers.[44] We can hear its distance from mainstream Arabic usage in Haykal's very locution, "what they say of the Tower of Babel." Third, Haykal interprets both language and translation in their broadest possible senses: "language" is as much a metaphor for intellectual tendency—the ideological language that a given camp speaks—as it is "language" proper, and translation as much intercultural as it is interlingual. Witness how Haykal invites readers to understand Egypt's dilemma: he asks them to "leaf" through *(taṣaffaḥ)* the clothes, faces, and heads of passersby in public squares—to "read" the signifiers walking the city as they might read his article in the newspaper. Why heads? Some sport the fez, others the turban, others the hat—the fez identified with the culture of the Ottoman elite; the turban with "religious" or "traditional" Egyptian society; the hat with the Westernizing elite. A pointed cartoon of 1926, "Fawḍā al-Azyā' fī Miṣr" (The Chaos of Fashions in Egypt), similarly frames the problem of nation formation in terms of sartorial heterogeneity, indeed chaos *(fawḍā)*.[45] It bears the caption, "Heterogeneous fashions in Egypt. Where, then, is the national dress?" The nation demands uniformity: it must impose equivalence on difference.

While the "Where?" of the question "Where, then, is the national dress?"—like Haykal's turn to public space for evidence of Egypt's intranational untranslatability and thus national "failure"—appears to pose the national as a function of space, space in Haykal's theory of the nation is really an alibi for time. For above all, Haykal redefines the problem of becoming national as a question of becoming "modern," and becoming modern as a question of how one understands one's relationship to time. In so doing, he anticipates Benedict Anderson's argument, in *Imagined Communities,* that the nation emerges when its constituent parts imagine themselves inhabiting one common space, however far-flung, in real time—in simultaneity. The time of the nation, says Anderson, is the "meanwhile."[46] In Haykal the diversity of Egyptian "languages" testifies to the absence of the "meanwhile" Anderson deems necessary to nation formation, for it signals the submission of each of a multiplicity of communities to "a past or to a present that differs from that to which the other camp submits." Interestingly, Haykal does not say here—as he does elsewhere in this essay—that some communities of "language" in Egypt subscribe to the past, others to the present. Each "camp" subscribes to a past and to a present, but each, he implies, *originates* its present in the past differently. It is the unevenness of Egyptians' temporal self-understanding that makes the constituent parts of the would-be nation untranslatable. These parts lack the national universal—the single historical narrative—in which they might be legible *to* one another: automatically and transparently readable.

Which narrative, then, will take precedence as the national universal? Haykal's opening anecdotes, to which I now return, are telling. The first suggests that guests who eschew the European *"Smūking"* are at odds with the host, who wears such dress and sets the terms of the hospitality with which the nation—gathered here in microcosm—will receive its company. The second upholds Europe as the "wellspring" of "civilization," whose lessons Egyptian students in London owe their compatriots in Egypt. Of course, these students are to foster "freedom of thought" back home by suppressing the freedom of other, competing narratives of time and "civilization" to express themselves in Egypt. And certain such narratives surely will be suppressed. Indeed, Haykal leaves no doubt at these moments and elsewhere that the exponents of "inertia" (*al-jumūd,* "frozenness") and enemies of the "new" *(al-jadīd)* are precisely those who might be inimical to the reorigination of Egypt in European time: in colonial "modernity."[47] In his translational terms, as in those of other modern Egyptian intellectual reformers before him, the European becomes the autochthonous, and the autochthonous alien. Haykal not only translates—Egyptianizes—Europe's "civilizing" mission, appropriating the colonial impulse as national, he also translates the language of colonial reformism into a language of national reformism, transcoding (from imperialist ideology) the will to domination as the will to liberation. To "culture" one's compatriots to think and speak as one—to *control* thought and expression—becomes, paradoxically, to *free* thought and expression. Such nationalist translation is a seduction of meaning, itself the offspring of a prior seduction of nationalist discourse by European empire.

Within the economy of al-Hilbāwī's party and the disjunctive Egyptian nation that both he and Haykal take it to represent, then, the absence of a "*Smūking*" is a smoking gun: it incriminates the "unsuited" Egyptian as a failed universal and thus a failed national subject. Yet to our reading of Haykal's ideology of nation and translation, the "*Smūking*" itself, deceptively velvet, should be the smoking gun. The European jacket is oddly reminiscent of the English bottle of Atkinson cologne *("Atkinsūn")* that none other than al-Hilbāwī—as fictionalized in Maḥmūd Ṭāhir Ḥaqqī's novel *'Adhrā' Dinshawāy* (1906; *The Maiden of Dinshway*)—demanded at Dinshawāy, eager to mask the odor of the peasants he was forced to prosecute.[48] According to Samah Selim, al-Hilbāwī's call for English cologne—though purely fictional—"acquired legendary status in the imagination of contemporary readers, so much so that it was . . . accepted by people as an actual incident that had occurred at the real trial."[49] While Ḥaqqī's fiction and Haykal's real-life parable invoke al-Hilbāwī's traffic in European commodities to different ends, in each case these commodities cloak "undesirable" Egyptian elements in assimilative Europeanness, olfactory or sartorial. The properly national subject must wear the accoutrements of European bourgeois materialism. Remarking the Westernizing animus of 1920s Egyptian liberalism, Abdeslam Maghraoui notes that its adherents went so far as to declare adoption of the Western hat a prerequisite of modernity.[50] As a "national" signifier with a class-marked colonial etymology, then, the "*Smūking*" offers incriminating evidence that inclusion in the nascent Egyptian nation—as liberal Egyptian political elites imagined it—demanded one's self-translation into a bourgeois European. Ḥaqqī's English cologne, Selim observes, "becomes a textual marker for the natural complicity between colonialism and an acculturated professional elite."[51] Haykal's "*Smūking*" reeks just as strongly of elite Egyptian complicity with the cultural values of the European colonizer.

In a final parable, Haykal argues the impossibility of a national space in which disjunctive temporalities might continue to coexist, insisting on the inevitability of "the new." Lurking behind this parable too is the imperative of translation, this time figured as *naql,* or transport. Here Haykal predicates the coherence, harmony, and order of the "sound" nation on its accession to modernity, and modernity on a revolution in transport—on the speed with which Egyptians are able to travel on the vehicles of the new and toward its (pre) destination.

> Only the forces of renewal will bring back to the life of the nation the coherence and the order essential to it. . . . Have you found yourself—if you move through a street today and see cars *[al-ūtumūbīlāt]* speeding on it, worth all the forms of transport combined, and alongside these carriages and carts *[al-'arabātu wa 'arabātu al-naqli]* moving with a slowness that the nerves of today's children cannot tolerate—have you found yourself hesitating in the judgment that these old modes of transport have been sentenced at last to annihilation and to extinction?[52]

Once more Haykal describes the Egyptian city as disjunctive space. Earlier he metaphorizes Egypt's disorder in the language of corporeal dissonance, representing Egypt as the land of the *Smūking* and its Others, where discordant clothes fail to make the homogeneous national man and clashing faces and heads fail to compose any single physiognomic or sartorial "language." It is a space too incoherent to be read. Now he extends the metaphor to transport, reconjuring the Egyptian city as a conflicted space in which the antiquated carriage or cart, moving at a crawl, brings time to a standstill and thus immures Egypt in "inertia," while the motorized car, vehicle of the new, speeds forward on the road to modernity. Even lexically the car—emblem of the new—bears the mark of the European foreign, of translation and its more alienating cousin, transliteration: it appears in Haykal's discourse as *al-ūtumūbīl,* a direct loanword from the French or English *automobile.* Only on its graphical surface can the word *automobile* be Arabized; phonetically and semantically, both the signifier and that which it signifies remain defiantly French or English, uneasily integrated into Egyptian space. Though Haykal may not have intended the felicitous pun, the word for carriage *(al-'araba)* or cart *('arabatu al-naql)* is—by contrast—not just native to Arabic but etymologically kin and phonetically almost identical to the word *for* Arab (*al-'arab,* "the Arabs"). In this vision, only foreign technology and the foreign word are proper vehicles for progress. Unless reformed by mechanization or translation—overwritten by super-signification—native wheels and words are inadequate to the present. Both are provinces of the "dead," unable to support life.

Most striking is Haykal's conviction that no Egyptian of the present, even those partisans of "inertia" he consigns to rigor mortis, physically can stand the past or its vehicles, linguistic or technological. Addressing himself always to a "you" identified with the new, Haykal nonetheless observes that the old gets on everyone's nerves—even those of conservatives, who (in his estimation) secretly envy the harbingers of the new though they may publicly curse them. The would-be "ancients" who cling to their carts *('araba)* and their nativist Arabic share the same new sensorium as those "modern" Egyptians driving their cars and using words like *ūtumūbīl*—writes Haykal, "their nerves feel exactly what yours feel."[53] Both the slow-moving cart and the old world order of Arabic and Arab-Islamic "tradition" it embodies trigger a nervous condition in the Egyptian subject, conservative and modernizer alike. And although Haykal himself cannot admit it, the etiology of that condition is one, be the sufferer a proponent of "old" or "new." Both proponents have been forced to inhabit one world—the universal of colonial modernity—and in both, the logic of that universal has engendered an acute sense of lack, of asynchrony with the modern order, of disability *('ajz)*. Both inhabit what Rey Chow calls the "neurotic *and*" of "Post-European Culture and the West,"[54] uneasily reframing themselves in comparison to Europe—less directly in the case of the conservative, who apprehends Europe through the proximal mirror of his modernizing contemporaries, and more directly in the case of the modernizer, who stares Europe in the face and struggles to resight his own features in the image. For if the "ancient" secretly envies the "modern" Egyptian he purports to scorn, so too does the "modern" Egyptian ogle the imperial European from whom he purports to liberate the nation. Both conservatives and modernizers experience the local as lack, incompletion, incoherence: failed totality.

What, then, is the precise relationship of perceived lack within the nation, which issues from an inward-looking comparison of the subnational self to its compatriots, to the nation's perceived disability in the international sphere, which issues from an outward-directed comparison of the would-be national self to other nations? If the internal coherence of a social collective—its radical intratranslatability—is necessary to its constitution as a nation, why should that coherence tilt toward the automobile, vehicle of the foreign? Why does the foreign modernity of the automobile, as driven or spoken or written, secure the internal order that is, in turn, so essential to nation formation? I will propose an answer. On the surface, the nation appears to articulate that which is most idiosyncratic—most particular, "proper"—to a people. Yet that articulation, as Derrida has suggested, is fundamentally performative, and it need only be performed when a social collective must make itself recognizable *as nation* to those beyond its boundaries, within a universal regime in which the principle of sovereignty is disallowed embodiment in any other form. "Nationalism," writes Derrida, "never presents itself as a particularism but as a universal philosophical model, a philosophical *telos*."[55] More precisely, "a nation posits itself" as the bearer of "an exemplary philosophy, i.e. one that is both particular and potentially universal."[56] The national, then, is always international. More important, the nation is a model—it posits an example that its would-be members must emulate—and a *telos:* it presents itself as destination, the destination of the universal toward which it calls its particularities to move. It demands that its members make their particularities coincide with the universal, that they foreignize the familiar (make their local particularity "read" logically within the terms of the universal family of nations) by familiarizing the foreign (incorporating the universal logic of nationhood as *an element of the self*), such that the foreign and the familiar become nearly indistinguishable.[57]

To prove the coincidence of the particular and the universal in the nation-form, Derrida cites the example of German nationalism and its construction of "Germanity" as the essence (origin?) and apotheosis (destination?) of human being. Such a philosophical economy is at once all-inclusive and radically exclusive: one need only be human to be German, such that Germanness is unhinged from ethnos and redefined as universal citizenship, yet one must also, in being human, be German, such that the human cannot be thought outside the German.[58] In this economy, he writes, "German man is the measure of all mankind," and to be German means to be "up to the measure of man, of human essence as liberty."[59] Derrida's invocation of *measure* frames the nation as an exercise in commensurability: the making commensurate of the particular and the universal human. Thus too is the nation a practice of translation, a creation of equivalence from difference, a postulation of symmetry between asymmetries. And what undergirds this operation of commensuration or translation clearly is the very sort of transcendental signified that Derrida elsewhere has critiqued. For who sets the measure of meaning? Is the philosophical exemplarity the nation posits—the universal outside its borders—always dictated from a point within the nation, or is it more often ventriloquized by a local voice speaking for an outside, bringing the outside in? In colonial contexts, the philosophical exemplarity—or universalism—Derrida attributes to the nation lies outside the scope of the colonized's powers of enunciation, such that a "world" decided by Others takes the measure of the self and not the self the measure of all Others.

Here recognition plays a crucial role. Citing the work of C. H. Alexandrowicz, Liu notes that the nineteenth century marked a transition from the natural-law principle of universal sovereignty—in which all state entities, irrespective of their location in the world, were presumed to hold sovereignty—to a regime of positivist European international law in which non-European states had to petition for recognition as such by European states and thereby gain admission to the "family of nations."[60] According to Liu, the new regime is based on what Henry Wheaton described as "external sovereignty" in the third edition of his *Elements of International Law* (1846). In Wheaton's articulation, the internal sovereignty of a state—its right to dictate its internal affairs—hinges only on that state's independence. By contrast, a state accrues external sovereignty—the right to make legal claims on other nations—only when its recognition *as* nation "becomes universal on the part of other States."[61] Liu suggests that such a logic of reciprocal recognition, which structures "the basic mode of exchange among nations," places differences on "an assumed ground of equivalence," a ground that is in fact "a structure of *unequal* exchange."[62] (Recall my analysis of al-Māzinī.) In this schema, not all differences are equal: some operate as universal value and are thus coextensive with the ground of exchange, while others, Liu says, are translated as "lesser value or nonuniversal value" and thus must be made to conform to the ground of exchange.[63]

I would argue, then, that for the colonized seeking sovereignty—understood both as independence and as supremacy—nationalism may involve more than the willed forgetting of certain local narratives of the past, as Ernest Renan might have it. It also may entail the willed forgetting of the inequality of the putatively "universal" ground—essentially a *foreign* narrative—in which the colonized choose to reoriginate their past. As Vicente Rafael suggests, "the real origins of the nation lie outside the national."[64] Invoking Renan's 1882 essay "Qu'est-ce qu'une nation?" ("What Is a Nation?") to rethink late-nineteenth-century Filipino nationalism, Rafael defines nationalism as "the conjuring of the nation by way of substitution and estrangement."[65] To this "double process" of borrowing a foreign origin yet revising it into one's own, he gives the name *translation*.[66] Where Derrida writes of nations as if the universalist differences they demarcate are everywhere and always the same, regardless of the origins of their national ideas, Rafael—like Liu—insists on the difference of colonial difference. He does so to break precisely what Liu calls the tautology of a difference whose equivalence to other differences is secured on and by a ground of universal equivalence. In so doing, he also theorizes the nation born of colonialism as something more than a repetition of the colony. Hence his insistence on coupling *estrangement* to substitution, arguing that nationalism-as-translation is a "letting loose and putting forth of the foreign."[67] Translation here becomes something of an open-jaw ticket: its final destination is neither the target (as in the one-way ticket) nor the source (as in a round-trip) but a third site that fuses source and target into a new origin that is both and neither—a site that looks much like Liu's super-sign but operates in the reverse sense, "empowering" the native by redirecting it toward the foreign. Rafael's notion of nationalism-as-translation detaches colonial signifiers from their original signifieds and displaces them in colonized space, far from their original modes of intention. Early Filipino nationalists, he suggests, recognized that "colonialism lies at the origins of nationhood"—holding in view the foreign signifier that underwrites their own—yet also insisted that "the nation absorbs outside forces without itself becoming different. *It gives in without giving up what it essentially is.*"[68] Here, as in Liu, the foreign gets under the native's skin—and hides there. Yet while Liu holds that the foreign reoccupation of a native signifier, slipping unnoticed into the "mask" of native script, surreptitiously disempowers the epistemology of the colonized, Rafael maintains that the colonized not only recall the foreignness of what has gone native, but draw power from the translation. Clearly what Rafael describes as the "reformulation" of the foreign "into an element of oneself" is a mystification of the colonial as native.[69] Yet he sees this mystification as politically productive. His foreign is "a medium for forging nationalism."[70]

Rafael provocatively relocates the colony's emergence into nationhood and modernity in the colonized native's self-foreignization. "Could we not," he asks, "think of the foreign languages, dress, ideas, and machineries that increasingly penetrated . . . colonial society . . . as infrastructures with which to extend one's reach while simultaneously bringing distant others up close?"[71] After all, he observes, such technologies "brought the promise of the colony's transformation," of its "becoming other than what it had been, becoming, that is, modern in its proximity to events in the metropole and the rest of the 'civilized' world."[72] If I read Rafael correctly, he suggests that the colonized embraced the foreign—the *techne* of their colonizers—to close the distance between metropole and colony and to make their assertions of self-determination reach the metropole. The subaltern, in other words, speaks to be seen and heard by the dominator. Hence the imperative to nationalize and modernize—which is also to foreignize—the self, for only by assuming such a selfhood can the subaltern become visible and audible to the forces of domination. Thus Rafael's "infrastructures" of "foreign languages, dress, ideas, and machineries" bear uncanny resonances with Haykal's *Smūking, ūtumūbīl,* and the European languages and ideas he urges young Egyptians to imbibe in London and bring back to their compatriots, thereby building the "civilized" nation. Haykal too insists that Egyptians can only articulate what is most "intimate"—their Egyptianness, their nationhood—in the idiom of the foreign, that of their dominators. Indeed, he calls on Egyptians to remake themselves in forms of "civilization" recognizable to the European and thus to re-recognize themselves in the mirror of European recognition. To make new sense of the intimate in the so-called common sense of the foreign—to become intimate with the foreign—is to articulate one's society as "other than what it had been" on several levels. It is to open the possibility that the colony might be sovereign—independent—and capable of asserting that sovereignty beyond its borders because recognized by the arbiters of sovereign right—European powers—as a nation equal to the European, equally "civilized" and "modern."

In this respect, Derrida is right to say that nationalism "does not present itself as a retrenchment onto an empirical particularity, but as the assigning to a nation of a universalistic, essentialist representation."[73] The nation indeed exists both *in the form of* and *for* the other—not just any other, but one whose power has permitted it to claim its particularity as universal and thus generalizable. To become recognizable (hence recognized) as nation, the Egyptian social collective must assume a form familiar to those collectives that already have styled themselves "national" and that hold the imperial power to dictate the meaning of that term to the world. Thus the terms of Egypt's internal transport and translation *(naql)* must be reorganized not only *by* the external—its wheels and words—but also *for* the external, in compliance with its logic. The very concept of *naql*—of transport and translation—must be translated to accord ultimate value to Western modernity's preferred modes thereof. For in Haykal's words, the car is *worth* all the forms of transport combined. Its meaning-value surpasses and transcends all others. Thus the foreign signifier—the automobile, *"al-ūtumūbīl"*—becomes the vehicle for the transcendental signified of colonial modernity.

For Haykal, Egypt owes its potential to compete in the arena of the modern—what he dubs (with a nod to the ancien régime of horsepower) the "racetrack of renewal" *("miḍmāri al-tajdīdi")*—to its preeminence in the world of antiquity: a preeminence fundamentally translational. That Egypt—long a geographic crossroads for world power and thus a site of translation for world knowledge—mediated the rise and fall of each successive empire of the ancient world and thus became the arbiter of each new meaning of "civilization," Haykal believes, destines it to mediate the cession of the Rest to the modern imperial West, to broker the world's transition to the newest redefinition of "civilization," which Europe now epitomizes. Haykal hints that the task of the (Egyptian) translator is to adopt the motors of European colonial modernity—vehicles and vocables—and to recharge both Egypt and the world by running these.

> Egypt was, in many eras, a mediator between the old and the new and an inspiration to the world with whatever benefits [it] in the way of civilization. Such was the civilization of the Pharaohs, and the message of Moses, as was the worship of Isis and, later, the school of Alexandria: all were golden exemplars of the civilization that ruled the world for . . . centuries. But in the last centuries, the inertia *[jumūd]* of the East under Ottoman rule and the knowledge revolution in the West . . . did not meet in Egypt; Egypt did not fall under [the latter's] sway because of its rule by the partisans of inertia. Thus it received the various golden exemplars of world civilization without these mixing in such a way that the spark of human truth . . . could ignite and fly.[74]

In recounting Egypt's translational past, Haykal carefully selects those passages that chime with modern Western civilization's standard autobiography: the history of "the Pharaohs," in which the story of Moses—shared by the Qur'ān and the Bible and thus bonding Muslims to Judeo-Christian culture—is embedded, and the history of late-antique Alexandria—the city from which both the cult of Isis and the phenomenon of pan-Hellenism radiated, and which made Egypt the center of a Greco-Roman-Judaic world easily assimilated to a modern ideology of Egypt's "Mediterraneanness," hence Europeanness. While Haykal invokes the Judeo-Hellenic substrate of Coptic Christianity, he elides the Coptic period. He makes no mention of the Arab-Islamic period at all, a transformative span of nearly nine hundred years. And the Ottoman period—the most recent four-hundred-year span of Egyptian history—appears only in the negative: it is the obstacle that blocks the "light" of European advancement beginning in the sixteenth century, obstructing an Egypto-European coupling that would have made sparks fly, if only it had been consummated sooner. A whiff of the "if only" tinges Haykal's words. Under the alleged yoke of Ottoman "inertia" *(jumūd)*,

Egypt receives but is too passive to recognize the latest of the "golden exemplars of world civilization," to know the proper object of its love—imperial Europe—when she sees it. In its missed encounter with the "light" of Europe and thus with colonial modernity, Egypt lacks the stuff of universal fulfillment. Hence its space-time lag in the "racetrack of renewal," and hence too its arrested nationhood. To point Egypt toward (European) nationhood, Haykal paradoxically must return it to "pure" origin: to an antiquity that bypasses some thirteen hundred years of its history. He must skirt those Egyptian particulars unassimilable to the West's dominant self-narrative—especially the Arab and Ottoman worlds of Islam—to render Egypt particular in a particular way: in the idiom of the European universal.

The ideology of "order" and "origin" that informs Haykal's theory of the proper nation also redefined national aesthetics. In the very issue of *al-Jadīd* in which Haykal predicates successful nationality on radical inter- and intracultural translatability, Aḥmad Ḥasan al-Zayyāt calls Arabic literature to order. Al-Zayyāt's article, titled "Fī al-Adab al-'Arabī" (On Arabic Literature), blamed the "chaos" of Arabic literature on the dangerous indeterminacy of its boundaries and rules.[75] Claiming that Arabic literature had been frozen for centuries in arrested "incompletion"—as an amalgam of disjunctive tongues and cultural forms thrown together by the rise of Islam—al-Zayyāt argued the incompatibility of an unreformed Arabic literary tradition with national modernity. "Our Arabic literature," al-Zayyāt writes,

> despite its breadth and beauty, is chaos *[fawḍā]:* . . . its grammar consists of mingled, unintelligible echoes of the dialects of the pre-Islamic tribes, which hardly agree. . . . And its rhetoric *[balāghatuhu]* is . . . irreducible to art, nor does it reveal an aim, as if it were made for everything but poetry and writing!!
>
> . . . This is so because Arabic literature was not the literature of one nation *[ummatin wāḥidatin]*, nor the product of a single culture, nor the harvest of a single tongue. Rather, it is an amalgam of imaginary fictions . . . that intermixed with the miscegenation of the Islamic peoples in the youth of the 'Abbāsid state. Thus it most closely resembles a sea into which every river empties . . . an amalgam of pearls and corals and the depository of mother-of-pearl and rocks.
>
> No sooner did time look upon this wondrous placid sea than its tributaries dried up . . . and its waters ebbed, until it was reduced to something like a brackish creek, on whose surface gnats buzz and on whose banks frogs croak.
>
> . . . Stammering tongues began to wag in this [lost] tradition with prattle and idle talk, . . . then cast it into our hands as a corpse, the last breath of

> life faltering in it, [or] a form in which neither beauty nor life [lit., "water"] flows. So we looked at it [and found] a disfigured creation, ugly of aspect, tending neither to the old nor to the new.[76]

Once more "tradition"—this time the Arabic literary heritage—is suspect for its Babel-like heterogeneity. That the admixture of various dialectal Arabics; the "barbarisms" of the non-Arabs who adopted the Arabic language in the early years of the Islamic empire—and left the imprint of their native tongues; and the various genres of Arabic poetry and prose can coexist in *one* "Arabic literature," unhomogenized, leads al-Zayyāt to question the claim of Arabic *to* literature at all. The language does not "reveal an aim," he laments, "as if it were made for everything but poetry and writing!!" For al-Zayyāt, linguistic or literary purpose—clear intention, with the indexicality that implies—issues from ethnological purity: clear origin. Miscegenation, racial or linguistic, is negative. Where al-Māzinī presumes that Arabic—like other languages—represents a set of unifying conventions of signification, crystallized from the play of differences over centuries of negotiation, al-Zayyāt has little faith in the capacity of Arabic to unify a field of discourse, let alone a people. Read one way, the scene of language he describes might approximate Walter Benjamin's vessel: as a language of "tributaries" whose manners of meaning do not replicate but supplement one another in their intentions, Arabic approaches what Benjamin calls "pure language"—all the more pure for its heterogeneity, its Babel close to God's. Yet read in the way that al-Zayyāt has chosen to read it, an Arabic literature that is neither the harvest of one tongue nor the province of one people—an Arabic literature that is, in short, a *translational* and *transnational* literature—is a fallen creation, a Babel far from God's. In his ideological reading, *baḥr al-lugha al-ʿarabiyya*—the sea of Arabic language, so valorized for its riches by centuries of users—is reduced to a "brackish creek": a primordial soup too contaminated to spawn any evolution—a morass, emblem of both stagnation and the murk of unintelligibility. Even the pearl, long a metaphor for the well-wrought line in the Arabic *qaṣīda* (ode) and the basic unit from which Arabic prose is said to be strung (*nathr,* "prose," literally means "stringing," the stringing of pearls), suddenly finds itself translated from the rare epitome of perfect form—an artifactual "purity"—into a common thing of impurity: like coral reefs, mother-of-pearl, or rocks, the lumpy accretion of foreign "corruptions" that have left their mark on Arabic, deformed its forms and stunted its life.

To the presumed stagnation and aesthetic failure of Arabic al-Zayyāt counterpoises the equally presumed dynamism of European literary modernity and its successful adequation to the "real." The European modern, then, like Haykal's *Smūking,* becomes the aim toward which Arabic literature must translate itself—and by extension Egypt. Oddly, if the translationality that has marked Arabic since at least the 'Abbāsid period corrupts absolutely, the new translationality of an Arabic remade in the West's image returns the language to Eden. "Our youth have seen in Western literature real, live pictures of what stirs in their souls," al-Zayyāt continues, " . . . so they headed toward it thirsting, . . . plucking luscious fruits from its gardens, and they left our artificial, traditional, repetitive literature to wither on the tongues of the conservatives and on the pens of the rigid, remnants of the old era."[77] His rhetoric recalls al-Sibā'ī's description of Egypt, in the introduction to his 1912 translation of Charles Dickens's *A Tale of Two Cities,* as a "corpse" to be resurrected by the agency of the translated European. There too the infusion of the European is imagined as an intellectual fertility treatment that will bring forth fruit from otherwise sterile, moribund terrain. In al-Zayyāt, the Egyptian young—who embody the "new" to which the nation's aging "conservatives," trapped in the "inertia" of the old, are called to aspire—no longer see themselves reflected in Arabic. Western literature becomes, in effect, their *live self-image:* only in Western genres and forms do they see "real, live pictures of what stirs in their souls." The corpse of Egyptian selfhood only comes alive—radiates beauty—in its displacement in the European mirror. If the Arabic literary corpse has a physiognomy at all, it is an ugly one, temporally "disfigured" (tending toward "neither . . . the old nor . . . the new"). Tacitly, then, only European literature wears the face of "the beautiful," and thus—in the neo-Platonic terms of physiognomy itself—it is also the good, indeed the true. Thus the only hope for Arabic literature's survival is the destruction of its order and its radical reconstruction from European origins, taken to be the proper (universal) "order" of literature itself. The self-colonizing epistemology of pure origins and orderly destinations that underpins Egyptian nationalism begs us to rewrite the words of Wallace Stevens in "The Idea of Order at Key West," from whose title this section derives its own, and to ask if ghostlier demarcations might not produce freer sounds.

RIDDLES OF ORIGIN

In *Beginnings,* Edward Said argues that "beginning and beginning-again are historical whereas origins are divine." Beginnings are historical because they are conscious human acts that involve, Said says, "*making* or *producing difference[,]* but . . . difference which is the result of combining the already-familiar with the fertile novelty of human work in language."[78] If that is so, we might say that the common "origins" that Egyptian intellectuals of the *nahḍa* sometimes posited between Egypt and Europe are, properly speaking, "beginnings": constructed moments in which two lineages are said to converge in a shared ancestor, two divergent filiations willfully affiliated. The "difference"—or beginning—that Egyptian intellectuals produced was a new logic of *equivalence* between the familiar and the foreign: a presumption of translatability between themselves and their dominators and a reorigination of national selfhood within the terms of that translatability. They used language to reimagine human difference *as* likeness and to make the new (the European) familiar, interchangeable with the Egyptian.

This impulse is perhaps most vivid in a noteworthy pair of essays by the Coptic Egyptian intellectual Salāma Mūsā (1887–1958), at once an anti-imperialist and a Westernizer whose thought ran the gamut from socialism to Darwinism.[79] Marshaling the paleontological evidence linking ancient British and Egyptian bones and the philological evidence connecting ancient Egyptian hieroglyphs to modern English, Mūsā elaborates an anglophile psychogeography for the emerging Egyptian nation. Both essays appeared in the Cairo periodical *al-Hilāl* (the Crescent)—the first in 1927, the second in 1928. In the first, titled "Ilā Ayyihimā Naḥnu Aqrab: al-Sharq am al-Gharb?" (To Which of the Two Are We Closer: East or West?), Mūsā attacks a nascent tendency, in the wake of the 1919 Egyptian revolution, to identify Egypt with the East as opposed to the West. "Words," he writes, "have a profound effect on psyches, and this effect is that of an illusion, clinging to life. So if we say to a person that he is Eastern, he will . . . view himself with an Eastern eye. . . . Thus the Egyptian—no, say the Arab—sympathizes now with Asia . . . and looks at Europe with a fearful eye."[80] How could this be, wonders Mūsā, when—he insists—Egyptians are of European origin? He implies that Egyptians (among others) have constructed, through language, a counterfactual affinity with the East. This affinity defies historical "truth" on two counts. The first is racial. Writes Mūsā, "The brown-skinned peoples all belong to the European family/

race *[al-sulālati al-ūrubbiyyati]*"; moreover, "the skulls of predynastic ancient Egyptians do not differ in the slightest from the skulls that are being excavated now in England, whose owners lived in the British Isles three thousand years ago."[81] The second is religio-epistemological, although it too posits a shared cultural "inheritance" between the Arab world and Europe and thus a familial relation. "All of us in the Arab world," writes Mūsā,

> from Baghdad in the East to Tangiers in the West, share with Europe one inheritance. . . . Thus we have its culture and its civilization. [I]f you brought an Azharite scholar from Cairo or one of the shaykhs of Baghdad or a student from Fez together with a French or British or German scholar, you would find that they agree on the meaning of God and of prophethood and that they follow one logic, one that they all learned from Aristotle. This is the exact opposite of what would happen if you . . . asked one of the mandarins of China to debate a scholar from al-Azhar. Indeed the Azharite would move at that moment in the direction of the West and the Chinese would move in the direction of the East. And never the twain shall meet. . . . In a word, we are Europeans in blood, in taste, in culture, and in language *[innanā ūrubbiyyūna fī al-dami wa al-mazāji wa al-thaqāfati wa al-lughati]*.[82]

Thus Mūsā detaches the Arab world, including Egypt, from the East and annexes it to the West. Yet his concluding terms both uphold and subvert British colonial notions of East and West. "And never the twain shall meet" is, after all, a direct allusion to the refrain of Anglo-Indian poet Rudyard Kipling's "The Ballad of East and West": "Oh, East is East, and West is West, and never the / twain shall meet."[83] Yet East and West *do* meet in Mūsā, if only to assimilate and efface Egypt's "Easternness" in "Westernness." Moreover, Mūsā's insistence that Egyptians are "Europeans in blood, in taste, in culture, and in language" uncannily resembles Thomas Babington Macaulay's assertion, in his "Minute on Indian Education" of 1835, that what English education must cultivate in colonial Bengal is a class of interpreters—translators—"Indian in blood and colour, but English in taste, in opinions, in morals, and in intellect."[84] Yet Mūsā's sly restatement of Macaulay commingles blood with taste, opinions, morals, and intellect. He outdoes Macaulay, the better to dissociate Egypt from points East, like China or India, and reassociate it with the West. Egyptians are not just "almost the same" as "but not quite" like the English, to borrow Homi Bhabha's notion of colonial mimicry. Egyptians *are* English.

With this beginning, Mūsā can answer, in the title of his second essay, the open question he had posed in the title of his first. To the question,

"To Which of the Two Are We Closer: East or West?" his second essay confidently replies, "al-Miṣriyyūn Umma Gharbiyya" (Egyptians Are a Western Nation). Here he contends that "the current feud between [Egypt] and Europe" springs from the delusion that the two are racially distinct, "with no blood ties between us."[85] Nothing, he insists, could be less true. Reprising his earlier argument that "the ancient Egyptians and the ancient Britons descend from a single race," indeed from "one mother,"[86] he now furnishes "evidence" of "European"-featured ancient Egyptian statues and skulls to prove the racial identity of the English and the Egyptian. Mūsā cites the Australian-born comparative anatomist Sir Grafton Elliot Smith, who became (in 1900) first professor and chair of anatomy at the government medical school in Cairo. In the second edition (1923) of his *The Ancient Egyptians and the Origin of Civilization,* Smith reconstructs the predynastic "Proto-Egyptian" as a human type detached from any Africa or Asia that cannot be associated with "Mediterraneanness," this last understood in the broadest sense.[87] Reading the bones of the earliest "Egyptians," culled from thousands of ancient graves, Smith concludes that "the populations which occupied North-East Africa, the whole Mediterranean littoral, the Iberian peninsula, Western France, and the British Isles before the coming of copper were linked . . . by the closest bonds of affinity" and were "certainly the offspring of one mother."[88]

On the phenotypic evidence of the proto-Egyptian's hair, which he insists is not "'woolly'" like the "Negro's," Smith decouples Egypt from black Africa.[89] And Asia. "Like all his kinsmen of the Mediterranean group of peoples," he writes, "the Proto-Egyptian, when free from alien admixture, had a very scanty endowment of beard," in "contrast to the Armenoid people of Western Asia."[90] Citing ancient Egyptian representations of Arabs, which show the latter sporting short beards, Smith invites us to compare these renderings to an early predynastic Egyptian skull excavated at Naj' al-Dirr—its beard and soft parts reconstructed from supposedly similar specimens at that site—and to a statuette, dating to the same period, alleged to represent a "Proto-Egyptian." Through this intersemiotic reading of biology, custom as constrained by biology (both proto-Egyptians and ancient Arabs are said to wear short beards because they have scant facial hair), and art, Smith argues a "very close resemblance between the Proto-Egyptians and the Arabs, before either became intermingled with Armenoid racial elements," distilling a "pure" shared origin from Asian "corruption."[91] He then assimilates that origin (shared also by the de-Africanized East

African) to the Mediterranean—and to Britain. "So striking is the family likeness between the Early Neolithic peoples of the British Isles and the Mediterranean and the bulk of the population, both ancient and modern, of Egypt and East Africa," he concludes, "that a description of the bones of an Early Briton of that remote epoch might apply in all essential details to an inhabitant of Somaliland."[92] The hidden signifier of bones, taken alone or coupled with the visible signifier of phenotype, becomes a transcendental signified. This so-called transcendental signified is, of course, inherently imperial. For Smith's construction of ancient "family likeness" hews to the topography of the modern British Empire. By "Mediterraneanizing" early Britons, he links England to Egypt (until 1922 a British protectorate) and Somaliland (a protectorate since 1884), as well as to the British colony of India, which elsewhere he tucks into a Mediterranean fold.[93] Yet only the *early* Briton is kin to the "ancient and modern" Egyptian, Arab, East African, and Indian. Modernity interrupts kinship with incommensurability. Over a "Mediterranean" family in which the early Briton was but one (equal) member, the modern Briton rules. Smith constructs affinity as *differential likeness,* at once securing the horizontal boundaries of imperial geography and affirming the vertical strata of colonial hierarchy.

Mūsā, however, extrapolates Smith's arguments toward a thesis of radical Egyptian-British translatability. Whereas Smith guards the distance of modern Briton from ancient/modern Egyptian—such that, if Egypt is the origin of civilization, Britain is its destination—Mūsā closes it at every turn. From Smith he reproduces the comparative representation of proto-Egyptian skull and bearded statuette (figure 5), then the two ancient Egyptian representations of ancient Arabs (figure 6). Yet this reproduction gives way to seduction. Convinced, for instance, that the likeness of Egypt to Europe can never be clinched until Egypt's divorce from the Arab is final, Mūsā willfully mistranslates Smith. As Maghraoui has argued, Smith compares images of proto-Egyptians and ancient Arabs to show their similarity, not—as Mūsā would have it—to argue their radical difference. Yet Mūsā "not only disregards this statement by Smith[,] but changes the comment associated with one of the figures from 'a proto-Egyptian as represented in a portrait statuette by a contemporary artist' to 'a statue of a proto-Egyptian whose features show its European expressions.'"[94] Maghraoui's rendering of Mūsā's unfaithful translation is, however, incomplete. In fact, Mūsā's caption to the statuette reads, "Statue of an ancient Egyptian *before the age of nations,* and it is—as its features attest—*European of coun-*

tenance" (figure 5). Smith's description draws no analogy between the proto-Egyptian and the European. To prove the Europeanness of not just the ancient but also the modern Egyptian, Mūsā's "translation" of Smith transforms the latter's description into ascription, annexing times (an era "before the age of nations" to the imperial-national moment of 1928); races (proto-Egyptian features to a homogenizing European face); and spaces (Egypt to Europe, especially Britain). Thus Mūsā makes the visual "evidence" corroborate only the assimilative face of Smith's argument—that Britons and Egyptians are "kin"—and suppress its differential face, where time slashes kinship. In short-circuiting time so that it moves only between antiquity and modernity, between a desired origin and an even more fervently desired destination, Mūsā skirts history—especially the intervening "age of nations"—to yield a pointed "return": the return of Egypt wearing a European face, its Egyptian features resignified to read as a "proper" physiognomy of the nation.

This semiosis of Egyptian-British union is not limited to translations of the artifactual body. It operates just as profoundly through translations of the word. In his first essay of 1927, Mūsā transacts a relationship between speakers of Arabic and those of European languages, arguing that Arabic shares roughly a thousand words of Greek and Latin origin with Russian.[95] This hypothesis of a Greco-Latin linguistic substrate common to Egypt and Europe—and thus of Egypt's fundamentally "Western" origin—is, significantly, routed through various "Easts": Arabic, on the Egyptian side, and Russian, on the European. By the second essay of 1928, Mūsā decides that he can bypass the East entirely and argue a direct, unmediated, and virtually absolute homology between European and Egyptian tongues: specifically, between the modern English and ancient Egyptian languages. From Lillian Eichler's *The Customs of Mankind* (1924), he extracts and translates a chart of nineteen words that shows how, word for word, the ancient Egyptian language is *akin* both morphologically and semantically—both in form and in meaning—to modern English, and nothing like Arabic (figure 7; the end of the table appears in figure 6).[96] Mūsā suggests that Egypt must completely circumvent Arabic to reclaim its Europeanness.

Comparing Mūsā's translated tabulation of English-Egyptian "kinship" to Eichler's original, we find that Mūsā argues his thesis of common language with only nineteen of Eichler's forty-one words. Interestingly, he eschews the citation of English and Egyptian words for *mother* (Eichler's "mamma (the mother)" [English] / "mama (to bear)"

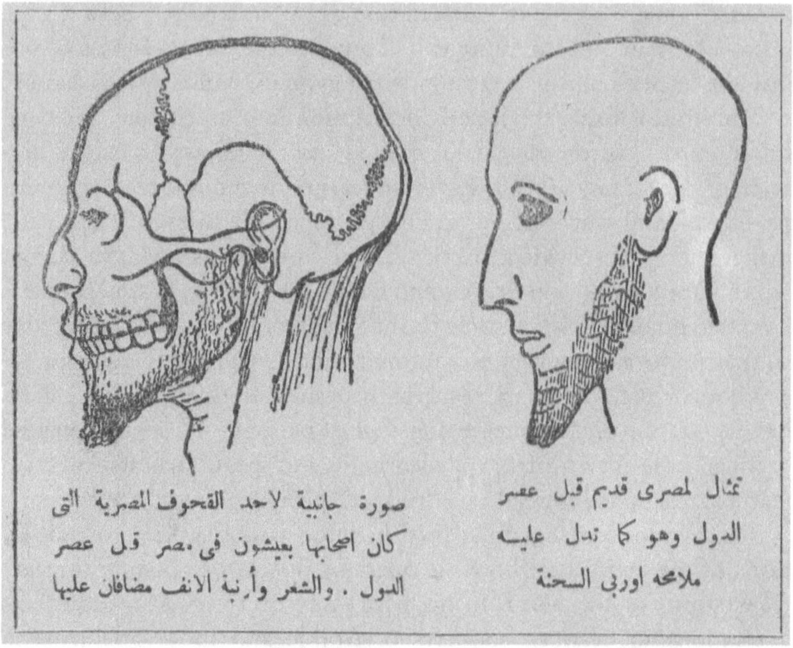

FIGURE 5. Pictorial comparison of proto-Egyptian skull (left) and bearded ancient Egyptian portrait statuette, translated by Salāma Mūsā from G. Elliot Smith's *The Ancient Egyptians and the Origin of Civilization* (1923). *Al-Hilāl*, 1 December 1928, 178. Mūsā's new caption for the statuette (right), which deviates radically from Smith's original, reads, "Statue of an ancient Egyptian before the age of nations, and it is—as its features attest—European of countenance."

[Egyptian]), sensing, perhaps, that too many human languages share similar words for *mother*. Mūsā is careful to cite only those words that directly correlate the English to the Egyptian, not those whose similarity can be referred to primal infant sounds and thus explained away as general to all (or most) humankind. Many of the words he chooses suggest the intimacies of home and hearth, of sleep and sex and procreation *(abode, bed)*, the optics of mimesis or resemblance *(mirror)*, and the most fundamental modes of human expression *(utter, write, mute)*: speech, writing, silence. Others evoke a shared vigor, indeed virility *(youth)* and a shared capacity to exercise power, military and political *(attack, mayor, kick,* the imperative tenor of *ought)*. Indeed, Mūsā chooses not to correlate modern English *mayor* to its closest modern Arabic "equivalent," *'umda* ("town or village headman"), but to give an Arabic translation (*ḥākim*, "ruler") that refers the modern English term to its ancient Egyptian counterpart, *mer,* which Eichler

الكلمة الانجليزية	لفظها بالعربية	الكلمة الفرعونية	معنى الكلمتين
mirror	ميرور	ميهر	مرآة
mayor	مايور	مير	حاكم
kick	كيك	خيخ	يرفس : يطرد

من عهد الفراعنة الى الآن

يقول اليوت سمث فى القليل الذى نقلته عنه ان صعيد مصر يمثل في سكانه الآن المصريين القدماء سحنة وعادات مع كل الغارات التى اغارتها الامم الاجنبية على مصر . وقد برهن بمقابلة الجماجم على ان المصريين القدماء ينتسبون هم وسكان انجلترا القدماء الى سلالة واحدة

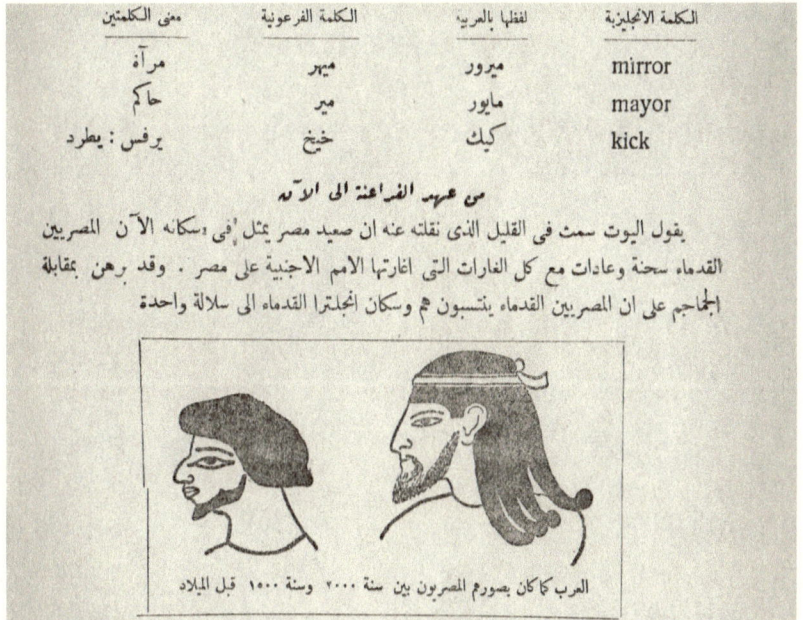

العرب كما كان يصورهم المصريون بين سنة ٢٠٠٠ وسنة ١٥٠٠ قبل الميلاد

FIGURE 6. Ancient Egyptian representations of ancient Arabs in 2000 B.C. (right) and in 1500 B.C. (left), translated by Salāma Mūsā from G. Elliot Smith's *The Ancient Egyptians and the Origin of Civilization* (1923), with conclusion of comparative chart of modern English, modern Arabic, and ancient Egyptian words (continued from figure 7). *Al-Hilāl*, 1 December 1928, 180.

glosses as "he who rules." While no totalizing logic governs all of the words that Mūsā writes into his lexicon, the majority establish Briton and Egyptian as one in origin *(nature)*, expression, sovereignty, and end *(death)*.

For Arabic disrupts the continuity of the ancient Egyptian language and thus contaminates the "bloodline" of the Egypto-European linguistic family on whose purity Mūsā's identification of Egypt with Europe depends. In the tripartite linguistic schema of Mūsā's neo-Rosetta stone, Arabic alone does not fit—unlike the ancient Egyptian, it does not sound like English, nor does it mean in the manner that English means, and thus it stands, tacitly, as the only "non-European" language of the three. Arabic belongs to the "West" in the 1927 essay's cultural geography of the world; by 1928, however, it becomes an "Eastern" interruption of ancient Egyptian culture, and by extension of "Westernness" as Mūsā now seems to define it. Yet Mūsā cannot communicate the supposed homology between ancient Egyptian and modern

كلمات تتفق فى الانجليزية والفرعونية

فيما يلى يرى القارىء طائفة من الكلمات الفرعونية التى تتفق لفظاً ومعنى مع الكلمات الانجليزية الحديثة . ولا يعقل ان يكون هذا الاتفاق مصادفة لا تدل على اشتراك فى الاصل بين الشعب الانجليزى الراهن والشعب المصرى القديم . وانا انقله عن كتاب « عادات النوع البشرى » تأليف ليليان ايشلر (١)

معنى الكلمتين	الكلمة الفرعونية	لفظها بالعربية	الكلمة الانجليزية
مسكن	ابوت	ابود	abode
هجوم	اتاخ	اتاك	attack
الخريف	اتوم	اوطم	autumn
الفراش	بت	بد	bed
بقرة	كاوى	كاو	cow
موت	تت	دث	death
كفاية : امتلاء	هينوفى	ايناف	enough
شاب	يوت	يوث	youth
قارب : زورق	ايتى	يوت	yacht
يكتب	رويت	رايت	write
ينطق	اطو	اطر	utter
يرضى : يوافق	سوتا	سوت	suit
شعاع الشمس	را	راى	ray
يجب	هوت	اوت	ought
الطبيعة	ناطر	ناطر	nature
ساكت : اخرس	موت	ميوت	mute

(١) The Customs of Mankind by Lilian Eichler وقد جمع اقلاديوس بك ليب الفاظاً اخرى من الانجليزية الحديثة والمصرية القديمة بهذا المعنى

FIGURE 7. "Words That Coincide in the English and the Pharaonic." Comparative chart of modern English, modern Arabic, and ancient Egyptian words, derived and translated by Salāma Mūsā from Lillian Eichler's comparison of modern English and ancient Egyptian words in *The Customs of Mankind* (1924). *Al-Hilāl*, 1 December 1928, 179. Mūsā's chart indicates, from right to left, the English in column 1; its Arabic transliteration *(lafẓ)* in column 2; its ancient Egyptian (lit., "Pharaonic") equivalent, transliterated into Arabic, in column 3; and the supposedly identical meaning of the two words (i.e., English and Pharaonic), once again rendered in Arabic, in column 4. For example, English *abode* (transliterated as Arabic *abūd*) echoes the ancient Egyptian *abūt,* whereas the Arabic meaning-equivalent—*maskan*—is phonetically off-key. The chart concludes in figure 6.

English to his Arabic-speaking readership *without the mediation of Arabic*, a fact that unwittingly positions Arabic as the copula of translational seduction, transhistorically rerouting subject/objectivity (hence power) between ancient/modern Egyptian and ancient/modern Briton by setting "origin" at play between them. It is into Arabic—through "Asia"—that Mūsā must both transliterate the sound and translate the meaning of the ancient Egyptian so that his modern Egyptian reader can hear, in language, Egypt's underlying "equivalence" to Europe. In fact, Egypt's "originary" signifiers—its hieroglyphs—appear nowhere in the translated chart, lost to it as they have been lost to modern Egyptian history and usage. We are left only with Mūsā's impure Arabic translation—his oddly Eastern reconstructed "beginning"—as proof of the pure racial and linguistic equivalence of Egypt and England.

Clearly European power casts a long shadow over Mūsā's enthusiasm for Egypt's European "origins." Talk of Egypt's Easternness, he writes, is "not beneficial," as "the star of Europe today is rising, so if we move with it . . . we will progress with its progress."[97] Thus Egyptians must recognize "that they are racially, culturally, and civilizationally European, and that they must move with the most refined of the European peoples, . . . adopt their ways."[98] Indeed, they must realize the nineteenth-century ambition of Khedive Ismā'īl to make Egypt "part of Europe" by *becoming* European; Mūsā lauds Ismā'īl for distributing "white-faced women" among Egyptian notables so that "our brownness will be wiped out and so that we will resemble the Europeans completely."[99] Such discourse challenges Derrida's insistence that national identity is always posited as a philosophical principle, never "as an empirical, natural character, of the type: . . . such and such a race has black hair or is of the dolicephalic *[sic]* type."[100] Mūsā's suggestion that Egypt and England are identical—thus paradoxically also divisible, into "equal" nations—rests as much on empirical proof that the skulls and words of Egyptians and Britons share one shape, that *both* peoples are originally "brown" (and hieroglyphone) or potentially "white" (and anglophone), as it does on the inscription of Egypt in the philosophical ground of the "universal," which underwrites the presumed equivalence of Egyptian and British signs. To conjure the Egyptian nation from the colony, Mūsā marries the empiricisms of bone, blood, and language to philosophical universalism: the imperial-universalist project of proving Egyptians "civilized to the marrow of their bones."[101]

In the circular historical logic Mūsā rewrites from Smith and Eichler, then, the universal of deepest antiquity—in which Britons and Egyptians descend from one "brown" mother and share a hieroglyphic mother tongue—translates into a universal of deepest modernity, in which Britons and Egyptians now hail one "white" mother, and English as their mother tongue. While Mūsā concedes his ex post facto creation of "a priori" kinship—the possibility that he has willed English words (and bones) to cling to Egyptian life—he bids Egypt to forget that kinship's historically embedded constructedness, to remember it only as prehistoric essence. Still, in hinting that Egypt's slow detachment from Africa and Asia—from the black and the Arab—and migration to Europe between the 1820s and the 1920s might have little to do with racialized essence, biological or linguistic, and much more to do with modern European empire, Mūsā unwittingly gives Egypt a way out of the whitening that to this day tilts Egyptian self-understanding toward a "Mediterranean" understood as European. If words, as Mūsā suggests, fashion realities from the stuff of illusions (or delusions), might not the notion of Egypt's Europeanness be as constructed a "truth" as that of its Easternness? Might not the true "origin" of Egypt in Europe that he proposes actually be a chosen "beginning"—a chosen delusion—issuing from and responding to the pressures of colonial history? The sheer contingency of Mūsā's fictions invites us to revise them, to unmoor modern Egyptian history and literature from Europe and to set these adrift, once more, between continents.

CHAPTER SIX

English Lessons

The Illicit Copulations of Egypt at Empire's End

The narrator of *Mountolive* (1958), the third novel in Lawrence Durrell's *Alexandria Quartet*, describes the first sexual encounter between the young English diplomat-in-training David Mountolive and the older, landed Coptic Egyptian siren Leila Hosnani as the stumbling of "a man into a mirror."[1] After all, when a mystified Mountolive asks Leila why she has taken him as her lover, she repeats his question with a "musical contempt"; coyly replies, "'Why you? Because'"; and straightaway proceeds to intone passages from an address by John Ruskin—"one of her favourite authors"—on arts education in England and its potential both to inspire and to realize England's will to empire.[2] Gone are the days of Egypt's exoticism in the British imagination, try as Mountolive or Durrell himself might to resurrect them in the mind and on the page. Mountolive's anglicized lover is less a descendant of what her invalid husband, Faltaus, proudly calls *"gins Pharoony"—al-jins al-fir'awnī*, "the Pharaonic race"—than she is an incarnation of late-empire Egypt, and late-empire England.[3] No longer the terra incognita that fed Shakespeare's fertile imaginings, she is now England's familiar—indeed, its reflection. It is Mountolive's turn to take signs for wonders as he listens in "astonishment" to this mimic woman—a woman Macaulay might have called Egyptian "in blood and colour, but English in taste, in opinions, in morals, and in intellect"—as she channels Ruskin and, through Ruskin, Shakespeare himself:

> Mountolive listened to her voice with astonishment, pity and shame. It was clear that what she saw in him was something like a prototype of a nation which existed now only in her imagination. She was kissing and cherishing a painted image of England. It was for him the oddest experience in the world. He felt the tears come into his eyes as she continued the magnificent peroration, suiting her clear voice to the melody of the prose. "Or will you, youths of England, make your country again a royal throne of kings, a sceptred isle, for all the world a source of light, a centre of peace; mistress of learning and the arts *[sic]* . . . amidst the cruel and clamorous jealousies of the nations, worshipped in her strange valour, of goodwill towards men?" The words began to vibrate in his skull.[4]

Leila quotes from the first of three lectures that Ruskin delivered at Oxford University in 1870, on the occasion of his appointment as Slade Professor of Fine Art, and the Shakespearean reference in the passage she recites—"This royal throne of kings, this scept'red isle"—is to John of Gaunt's eulogy of England in *Richard II.*[5] In his inaugural address, Ruskin declared that England faced the choice either to reign or to die. If she were not to perish, he insisted, "she must found colonies as fast and as far as she is able, formed of her most energetic and worthiest men;—seizing every piece of fruitful waste ground she can set her foot on, and there teaching these her colonists . . . that their first aim is to be to advance the power of England by land and sea."[6] These colonies would replace England's long-standing naval power and secure her global dominance in peace rather than in war: they would be, says Ruskin, "fastened fleets" or "motionless navies (or, in the true and mightiest sense, motionless churches, ruled by pilots on the Galilean lake of all the world)." By global "peace," Ruskin had in mind a Christian Pax Britannica—he alludes here to Saint Peter, the rock of the Church, whom John Milton had dubbed "pilot of the Galilean lake" in his 1638 elegy "Lycidas."[7] And in his worldview, this imperial Pax Britannica would follow not from the military, commercial, or technological dominance of England but from its beatification and beautification:

> But that they [English colonists] may be able to do this [implant English dominion across the globe], she must make her own majesty stainless; she must give them thoughts of their home of which they can be proud. The England who is to be mistress of half the earth cannot remain herself a heap of cinders, trampled by contending and miserable crowds; she must yet again become the England she was once, and in all beautiful ways more; so happy, so secluded, and so pure, that in her sky—polluted by no unholy clouds—she may be able to spell rightly of every star that heaven doth show; and in her fields, ordered and wide and fair, of every herb that sips the dew; and under the green avenues of her enchanted garden, a sacred Circe, true Daughter of

> the Sun, she must guide the human arts, and gather the divine knowledge, of distant nations, transformed from savageness to manhood, and redeemed from despairing into Peace.[8]

In Ruskin's view, then, England must deindustrialize and resacralize herself (shed her image as "a heap of cinders," ensure herself "polluted by no unholy clouds") and become beautiful enough to enchant not just her own colonists into believing in and executing her imperial mission, but also the "distant nations" these colonists would command. Unlike *The Odyssey*'s pagan Circe, who turns men into swine, this "sacred Circe"—implicitly Christian, bearer of what Ruskin earlier in this lecture calls "a religion of pure mercy"—would use her charms to guide England's so-called subject races in "the human arts" and to transform them "from savageness to manhood." The imperialist tenor of Ruskin's aesthetics is not lost on Edward Said. Ruskin, Said observes,

> connects his political ideas about British world domination to his aesthetic and moral philosophy. Insofar as he believes passionately in the one, he also believes passionately in the other, the political and imperial aspect enfolding and in a sense guaranteeing the aesthetic and moral one. Because England is to be "king" of the globe, "a sceptred isle, for all the world a source of light," its youth are to be colonists whose first aim is to advance the power of England by land and sea; *because* England must do that "or perish," its art and culture depend, in Ruskin's view, on an enforced imperialism.[9]

Said's "because" places politics first and aesthetics second; England's art and culture depend, he says, on an "enforced imperialism." Yet Leila's "because"—the rationale she offers for making love to Mountolive, who describes himself as "a painted image of England"—suggests, to borrow the words of William Blake, that "Empire follows Art & Not Vice versa."[10] Does not Ruskin intimate, after all, that the aesthetic and the moral enfold and guarantee the political and the imperial, that the enforcement of British imperialism depends on the export of a rarefied English art both to colonists searching for love objects that would renew their attachment to the faraway metropole and to colonized peoples who otherwise might find little to love in their colonizers? Notice that he names the aesthetic the cause—and affect the effect—that will produce, in turn, imperialism's desired political result: "*But that they* [English colonists] *may be able to do this* [implant English dominion across the globe]," he writes, "she must make her own majesty stainless." Certainly Ruskin acknowledges the debts of empire to the new "means of transit and communication . . . , which have made but one kingdom of the habitable globe." Yet the fact that the world has been made one kingdom, he says, does not settle the question of "who is to be its king."[11] Art does.

Indeed, so well has Leila, like the Europeanized Egypt she represents, learned her lessons in the colonizer's English—and so seduced has she been by its arts—that she needs virtually no prompt to become the Egyptian vessel for Ruskin's imperial tones. Having translated the "absurd book-fed dream" of imperial England into her consciousness well enough to now ventriloquize it, Leila has long since translated herself into Ruskin's colonial mistress, into the apotheosis of British empire. Here the translational seduction I locate at the heart of cultural imperialism is consummated in the "copulation" of the colonizer and the colonized. Thus Leila's lovemaking with the English Mountolive only consummates in sex her prior linguistic and ideological coupling with England.

Such a coupling certainly disavows the power differential between the terms it brings into "equivalence," forging an economy of translation in which, I argue, the colonized ultimately lose as much as the colonizer gains. Yet the fact that the colonized, in translation, assume the "likeness" of the colonizer does more than flatter the power and the self-image of the colonizer. It also fractures the colonizer's self-image, if not his actual power. Hala Halim notes that "Leila is ascribed to both a cosmopolitanism of Alexandria oriented towards Europe, and, through the fact of her being a Copt now also living in the countryside, to Egypt more broadly."[12] I would emphasize that Leila's Egyptianness—even when it seems most autochthonous, evinced in a Coptic identity rooted in Egyptian earth—is irrevocably translational, and motivatedly so. Halim herself suggests that it is because the Copt in particular seems so "successful" a colonial translation that he or she can wield power *over* the European by playing himself or herself back to the European as "'almost the same,'" as when she contends that Leila's son Nessim strategically "proffers the lure of the Copts as mimic men" to the French and the British in order to move his own political agenda.[13] The success of Leila's self-translation is what makes it, as Halim argues, uncanny—*strangely* like (thus also unlike) Mountolive's English "home."[14] If, as the Indian-born, part-Irish British expatriate Durrell believed, "language is really nationality," Leila could not be more English.[15] And this Mountolive cannot bear:

> "Stop. Stop," he cried sharply. "We are not like that any longer, Leila." It was an absurd book-fed dream this Copt had discovered and translated.

> He felt as if all those magical embraces had been somehow won under false pretences—as if her absurd thoughts were reducing the whole thing . . . to something as shadowy and unreal as, say, a transaction with a woman of the streets. Can you fall in love with the stone effigy of a dead crusader?
>
> "You asked me *why,*" she said, still with contempt. "Because," with a sigh, "you are English, I suppose."[16]

Coupled with England, more like the colonizer than the colonized, Leila has made England and Englishness at once too painfully recognizable and unrecognizable to Mountolive. For although he is being trained to exercise British dominion over Egyptian affairs in his future role as ambassador to Egypt, Mountolive knows that little remains of Ruskin's confident empire but "the stone effigy of a dead crusader." Yes, Leila is Mountolive's mirror—and his refracted mirror image. She seduces him by representing him as the sovereign he once was and might yet be again. But she repels him—as the light bends—with reminders that Egypt has eclipsed his sovereignty, that he embodies nothing more than the spent imperial energy of 1940s England, itself under assault by Hitler's Germany during World War II. Leila's sigh, "Because . . . you are English, I suppose," is his empire's last.

What really makes Mountolive stumble, however, is perhaps the most disturbing image of England he sees in the mirror that Leila holds up to him: the specter of national prostitution. For by illicitly coupling with the English of imperial nostalgia and betraying the possibility of an independent Egypt, Leila terrifyingly empties the concepts of "colonizer" and "colonized," "imperialism" and "independence," of all their usual meanings. The "magical embraces" he has shared with her seem, suddenly, favors that she might promiscuously lavish on all persons English: "as shadowy and unreal," he muses, as "a transaction with a woman of the streets."[17] To Mountolive, Leila's promiscuous generalization of the act of loving one Englishman to that of loving abstract "Englishness," as much as her prostitution of her native Egypt and assumption of an English voice, suggests that his own imperial motherland—the "mistress of half the earth" who must be "pure" if she is to govern—might too have turned whore, coupled too wantonly with its colonies. Responding "with contempt" to Mountolive's "But why me?" Leila mocks him for imagining their "embrace" a thing outside history. What Mountolive ascribes to "magic," she imputes to history: Egypt's colonial enchantment, through literary education and translation, with English. Leila's response calls on Mountolive to recognize the decisive ambiguity with which Egypt has been translated into "England" and thus the equally decisive ambiguity with which the British Empire has been translated toward its end.

THE UNEVEN TRADING FLOOR OF COLONIAL "EXCHANGE"

In 1988 Durrell lost the Nobel Prize in literature to the Egyptian novelist Najīb Maḥfūẓ (Naguib Mahfouz). The two had never met in person—this despite the fact that Durrell spent four years in Egypt during World War II.[18] Yet Maḥfūẓ's 1947 novel *Zuqāq al-Midaqq (Midaq Alley)* strangely prefigures Durrell's *Mountolive,* published over ten years later.[19] Like Durrell's novel, Maḥfūẓ's *Zuqāq* is deeply preoccupied with the seduction, translation, and prostitution of self and nation under the quasi-independent, quasi-colonial conditions of 1940s Egypt—though it refracts those preoccupations through a distinctly Egyptian mirror. Both novels allude to the sharply re-colonial turn that Anglo-Egyptian relations took on 4 February 1942, when British Ambassador to Egypt Sir Miles Lampson invaded the palace of Egypt's King Fārūq, British troops in tow, and declared that the king must install a "pro-British" prime minister or abdicate.[20] The sheer extremity of Lampson's intervention suggests the late-empire anxiety that Durrell's Mountolive incarnates; clearly the British had to resort to desperate measures in order to translate Fārūq into a puppet monarch and retain imperial control over Egypt. Still, by exposing the pretense of "equality" that had governed Anglo-Egyptian political relations since the 1930s, Lampson's act affirmed the ongoing imperium of England in Egypt. It flouted, especially, the uncertain independence granted to Egypt in the Anglo-Egyptian Treaty of 1936: a treaty of which Lampson himself, along with Muṣṭafā al-Naḥḥās Pasha (the very prime minister whom King Fārūq was now forced to install), had been the architect.

Recognizing Egypt as a "sovereign independent state," the 1936 agreement had billed itself "a treaty of friendship and alliance" between Great Britain and Egypt. In its special issue on Egypt of 26 January 1937, the *Times* of London noted that "Anglo-Egyptian friendship might have grown slowly without the treaty, but it could never have flowered in the sands of embarrassment and constraint. The treaty, by substituting an equal alliance for an unequal and ambiguous relation, has provided the soil in which that friendship can take root and blossom."[21] Such language, which suggests that the ambiguities of a so-called friendship shot through with colonial inequality have given way to the clarity of a true friendship (indeed alliance) of "equals" unshadowed by domination, evokes the dynamics of translational seduction. Once again, the colonizer seduces the colonized into love by translating itself into an "equivalent" of the dominated, thereby masking the differential equation that its self-translation in fact performs. On the surface, sovereignty and reciprocity govern the new state of Anglo-Egyptian relations. Article 1 of the treaty declares that "the military occupation of Egypt by the forces of His Majesty the King and Emperor is terminated"; Article 2, that henceforth the British monarch would be represented in Egypt by an ambassador (none other than Lampson). Article 3 pledges the support of "His Majesty's Government in the United Kingdom" for Egypt's application for membership to the League of Nations.[22] Yet Articles 7 and 8 undercut the promised end of British occupation in Egypt. Should either party to the treaty "become engaged in war," Article 7 stipulates, the other will "immediately come to his aid in the capacity of an ally."[23] Curiously, this statement—which appears to assign "equal" and mutual obligations to the treaty's signatories—is immediately followed by a proviso that effectively resubjects Egypt to British dominion:

> The aid of His Majesty the King of Egypt . . . will consist in furnishing to His Majesty the [British] King and Emperor on Egyptian territory . . . all the facilities and assistance in his power, including the use of his ports, aerodromes and means of communication . . . [and] all the administrative and legislative measures, including the establishment of martial law and an effective censorship, necessary to render these facilities and assistance effective.[24]

Not only does this proviso allow Britain unfettered access to Egyptian lands, it also legitimizes the imposition of totalitarian forms of "native" government (martial law, censorship) if such forms prove beneficial to British strategic interests. Moreover, the proviso is unilateral; it grants Britain specific rights of territorial access to Egypt but affords Egypt no such reciprocal claims over British territory. Article 8 makes England's interest in maintaining a colonial foothold on Egyptian soil even more explicit:

> In view of the fact that the Suez Canal, while being an integral part of Egypt, is a universal means of communication *as also* an essential means of communication between the different parts of the British Empire, His Majesty the King of Egypt . . . authorises His Majesty the [British] King and Emperor to station forces in Egyptian territory in the vicinity of the Canal. . . . The presence of these forces [up to 10,000 land troops and 400 air force pilots!] shall not constitute in any manner an occupation and will in no way prejudice the sovereign rights of Egypt.[25]

The language of this article insinuates that the ground of Anglo-Egyptian equivalence—the supposedly level universal on which England and Egypt are said to be translatable as "equal" nations—is a universal coextensive with Britain's dominions. The Suez Canal's designation as a "universal means of communication" shades into its designation "*as also* an essential means of communication between the different parts of the British Empire." Tacitly, empire and universe become one. This British-marked "universal" supersedes the canal's status as "an integral part of Egypt," effectively declaring the canal British territory (assurances that the British presence "shall not constitute . . . an occupation" notwithstanding).

Throughout the Anglo-Egyptian treaty, indeed, the dominions of "His Majesty the King and Emperor"—unlike those of "His Majesty the King of Egypt"—are almost always left unspecified, as if assuming the omnipresence, hence universality, of the British Empire. Only in the penultimate addendum to the treaty—which peremptorily declares that British ambassadors to Egypt "will be considered senior" to the diplomatic representatives of all other countries—is the scope of British dominions named, their global imperial reach reaffirmed. The British sovereign resurfaces now as "His Majesty the King of Great Britain, Ireland, and the British Dominions beyond the seas, Emperor of India."[26] The addendum positions Lampson, Britain's first ambassador to Egypt, both as an extension of British imperial power and as an affirmation of that power's unaltered privilege to dictate its preeminence over all nations and thus its authority over Egypt.

The imperial-pedagogical relationship of Lampson to Fārūq—Lampson referred to Fārūq as "the boy," while the resentful Fārūq called his nemesis "the schoolmaster"—shadows the novels of both Durrell and Maḥfūẓ.[27] Roger Bowen argues that Durrell's Mountolive, "as Britain's [fictional] first ambassador to Egypt is, historically speaking, Lampson, but he in no way resembles that bluff and confident servant of Empire."[28] I would suggest that Durrell's novel deliberately replaces the coercive power of the historical "schoolmaster" Lampson with the seductive power of a *textual* English schoolmaster—the mellifluous imperial prose of art professor Ruskin, which Leila associates with the "innocent" Mountolive, Lampson's neutered fictional stand-in—in order to better expose and interrogate the affective ambiguities of British imperialism in 1940s Egypt. Maḥfūẓ's *Zuqāq*, in turn, filters the persona of King Fārūq through the figure of Faraj Ibrāhīm, the sharp-dressing Egyptian "headmaster"-pimp who procures Egyptian women for British (and American) officers and trains them in a brothel he explicitly describes as his "school." The proper name *Faraj* means "liberation from affliction" but also "cleft" or "fissure." The libratory dimension of Faraj's name evokes the mobilization of King Fārūq by Islamist nationalists of the 1930s, who styled him a national liberator destined to fulfill the religious meaning of his name: "he who cleaves [between good and evil]."[29] Yet the other face of Faraj's name inverts the sense of Fārūq's and turns its active passive, as Faraj is a cleft—one cleaved—rather than a cleaver. While Fārūq had begun his reign somewhat indifferent to British pressures, his will to power eventually would eclipse these "anti-British" sensibilities. Intent on saving his crown, the increasingly decadent Fārūq would prostitute his anti-British politics to the political will of the British Empire. By acceding to the premiership of Egypt at Lampson's behest, so too would the Wafd Party leader Naḥḥās Pasha prostitute the Egyptian nationalist resistance his party had long led. Maḥfūẓ's *Zuqāq* suggests that Fārūq and his ally in colonial acquiescence, Naḥḥās, have become little more than the pimps of Egypt.[30] Faraj, the pimp who sells the project of national liberation within the symbolic economy of *Zuqāq* much as Fārūq has sold it in history, turns an ironic colonial screw in the meaning of liberation itself.[31] In Faraj's dominions, a microcosm of Fārūq's Egypt, liberation becomes synonymous with ongoing subjection.

As early as 1929, during the reign of Fārūq's father, King Fu'ād, the Egyptian weekly *al-Kashkūl* represented Egypt as a Europeanized woman in thrall to the British, and so "enthralled" because of the increasing complicity of Naḥḥās and the Wafd with British policy.[32] One such image, published on 27 September 1929, depicts a female "Egypt" standing, breasts exposed, on the fringe of a fully clothed group of mostly Western women who represent the League of Nations (figure 8).[33] Japan, at the time the only non-Western permanent member of this supposedly "global" family, recedes into the background. Addressing Egypt, scantily clad in a national-flag-cum-European-minidress, a woman whom the caption identifies as France—in martial regalia, breasts armored—rebukes her in an intimate colloquial whisper, "Lissa min ghayr libs wiḥnā kunnā muntaẓirīnik fī ''Uṣbat al-Umam'??" ("Are you *still* not dressed even though we're waiting for you in the 'League of Nations'??"). France implies that Egypt's nakedness is unseemly, given her rightful claim to a place in the League of Nations. She holds a fur-trimmed coat for Egypt, as if to clothe her "properly" and usher her into the fold. France's concern is, of course, insincere; although long the perceived champion of Egyptian national interests against the British, the fact that she wears a British flag across her hips—below the belt, so to speak—suggests the growing complicity of French and British imperial interests in the Arab world. It was within the context of the League of Nations, after all, that Britain and France together had agreed to refuse nationhood to the Arab peoples, to divide the former provinces of the Ottoman Empire between their respective imperial mandates. In any case, Egypt replies (also in the colloquial), "A'mil ayh idhā kān al-Naḥḥās w'iṣābtuh 'āwzīnnī afḍal ṭūl 'umrī 'iryāna?" ("What can I do if Naḥḥās and his gang want me to stay naked all my life?"), implying that an unscrupulous Naḥḥās (whom she tacitly accuses of serving British interests) has conspired to leave her undressed and thus helpless to assert her nationhood. In another telling image, published on 2 May 1930, an Egyptian woman in full "modern" (European) dress curves with the Nile and the ribbon of cultivable land along its banks, representing Egypt's habitable geography (figure 9).[34] Larger than life, she is shackled head-to-toe—her neck at Būr Fu'ād (Port Fu'ād) in the northeast, at the mouth of the Suez Canal, her feet at the Egyptian-Sudanese border city of Ḥalfā (Wadi Halfa)—by three tiny British soldiers. Two of these soldiers, "Jack" *(Jāk)* from the south and "Johnny" *(Jūnnī)* from the north, call out to each other as they secure the borders of English dominion. Jack shouts, "Johnny, are you sure that the chains around her neck are secure at Port Fu'ād?"; Johnny replies, "Just as I am sure that the chains are tight around her legs at Ḥalfā!!" A fourth British soldier, as Lilliputian as his fellows, stands at Sinai on Egypt's easternmost frontier, watching as she is chained. Toting a rifle, he is the only visibly armed soldier of the four. Meanwhile the heads of two British cannons, aimed at a shackled and visibly distressed Egypt, peer northwards from the Sudan. Banishing British force to the margins of Egypt and reducing to near-invisibility the English soldiers who hold Egypt captive, this caricature suggests that England colonizes Egypt most effectively by *concealing* its weapons—masking these, perhaps, in instruments of seduction. Seduction, after all, explains why the Egyptian woman—in this caricature as in the earlier one—wears the nation in the empire's clothes, no matter how scantily. In both images, the Egyptian woman incarnates the dilemma of the Egyptian nation: though thoroughly translated into Europeanness, as her dress and demeanor suggest, and thus "entitled" (within the logic to which Egyptian male nationalists of the day subscribed) to sovereign nationhood, her translation into a European look-alike spares her neither the indignities nor the depredations of European colonial power. Instead, that translation leaves her denuded by and chained to the European, her "nationhood" at the mercy of the colonizer. The caricatures imply that if Egypt somehow could push the simulacrum of Europeanness into which "she" has been translated over the tipping point between fiction and history, *becoming* European, she would win true independence. That her right to nationhood hinges on "real" Europeanness vexes the very meaning of decolonization.[35]

In Maḥfūẓ's novel, as in Durrell's, Egyptian women—seduced and translated—both incarnate the triumph of British empire and ironically project its demise. While the two novels view late empire from opposing perspectives, both stage decolonization as a problem of recognition, of re-cognizing what separates a colonized self from its colonizing Other when that very self has been seduced by and translated *into* its colonizer, that is, *beyond* recognition. In so doing, they recouple the seductions of colonial translation to the historical violence that those seductions have enabled. The prostituted Ḥamīda of Maḥfūẓ's *Zuqāq,* lured by an Egyptian schoolmaster-pimp into a viciously parodic "Department of English," learns to translate her Arabic name and body into parts that English soldiers can pronounce and possess; she is a compelling foil to Durrell's adulterous Leila, who—realizing her "book-fed dream" of making love to England—reproduces the imperialist aesthetics of Professor Ruskin. It is as consummations of the seductive enterprise of colonial translation, as bodies prostituting or "adulterating" themselves in flagrant couplings with English and Englishness, that the late-empire Egypts that Leila and Ḥamīda represent begin to exceed and escape colonial control; they become so like their colonizers that they easily supplant them.[36] The sad ironies of decolonization that both Durrell's and Maḥfūẓ's novels intimate, I contend, expose the strong arm of the disarming word. Only by betraying itself can Egypt become "itself" again in the (post)colonial.

THE DEPARTMENT OF "ENGLISH"

If the pen is mightier than the sword, as the Victorian novelist and colonial secretary Edward Bulwer-Lytton opined, small wonder that translation can seduce, violate, and kill. Maḥfūẓ knows that translation can deform languages and bodies as powerfully as it can bridge them, or, perhaps, that translation *must* deform them in order *to* bridge them. Set in old Cairo during the last decade of British rule, against a World

FIGURE 8. "Egypt and the League of Nations." Front cover of *al-Kashkūl*, 27 September 1929. Egypt (second from left) is bare-breasted, partially denuded of her flag.

War II backdrop of Allied-Axis air raids, his *Zuqāq* testifies to the particular violence that translation can assume in a colonial context.[37] The novel represents colonization *as* translation, and colonial translation as a connection, or copula, between two peoples that depends, ironically, on the erasure of one—the weaker—on linguistic, sexual, economic, cultural, and ultimately territorial fronts. In *Zuqāq,* the translation of Arabic words or Egyptian bodies into English "equivalents" is a charged process of colonial meaning-making, for English is always the more valuable commodity on the uneven trading floor of colonial exchange. Witness the character of Shaykh Darwīsh.[38] Described as a prophet in two languages, Arabic and English, Darwīsh is a former teacher of English in the religious endowment schools, a man whose career unraveled when those schools fell under the oversight of the Ministry of Education. As his family descends into poverty—a poverty linked to the rise

FIGURE 9. "The Independence of Egypt and the Position of the British Military." *Al-Kashkūl,* 2 May 1930, 28. Egypt appears as a Westernized woman, shackled head-to-toe by the British.

of Western "secular" education in Egypt and the concomitant devaluation of the traditional "religious" system—Darwīsh disintegrates.[39] His material, ontological, and psychological undoing are rooted, ultimately, in the uneasy translations of native Arabic into imperial English. A dismembered amalgam of European spectacles and necktie and Egyptian cloak and clogs, he speaks throughout the novel as the oracular voice of Egypt itself. His dress suggests Egypt's entanglement, at once intimate and violent, with its colonizer; the original Arabic tells us that Darwīsh's necktie is *threaded through* the gusset of his cloak, thereby evoking Egypt's coupling with England.[40] So too does his speech. The schoolmaster recast, Darwīsh "teaches" the Egyptians of Midaq Alley seven English watchwords over the course of the novel: *history*, *tragedy*, *frog* (possibly alluding to the French), *homosexuality, viceroy, elopement,* and *end.* With the telling exception of *homosexuality,* at once the disavowed erotic *and* that couples Egyptian men to their English colonizers and (as Joseph Massad has argued) the irruption of colonial epistemology into Arabic thought that "an English term that has no Arabic equivalent" implies, each is presented as the modern translation—signified and signifier, meaning *(ma'nā)* and spelling *(tahjiya)*—of an Arabic "equivalent."[41] All seven words are rendered *in* English, Roman letters erupting within the novel's Arabic text. The words trace an arc of colonial transformation, from the epistemological and political rupture of Egyptian "history" in 1798—and the turn to "tragedy" it announces—to the homosocial logic ("homosexuality") that dissolves colonized Egyptian men into the colonizing French (the "frog," which Darwīsh likens to a worm fattened on Egyptian corpses) and English (via "viceroy," Darwīsh's term for Egyptian surrogates of the "English king"). The arc climaxes in the heteroerotic "elopement" of a feminized nation with one such surrogate (Darwīsh spells the word when Ḥamīda runs off with Faraj), and—finally—in the "end" of empire toward which Egypt inches. While Darwīsh swears unwavering allegiance to Arab-Islamic tradition throughout the novel and inscribes veiled Arabic lessons of resistance in almost every word he teaches, English has the "last word" in his translational pedagogy as much as in Faraj Ibrāhīm's, suggesting the enduring colonial power of English in Egypt. The novel's systematic translation of Egyptian subjects into English suggests that "sovereign" Egypt exists only by relation to imperial Britain, never as an independent national term.

England and English appear in this text, then, not simply as powers violently forced on Egypt, but also as *seductions* into which Egypt enters half-knowingly and from which it cannot extricate itself. It is under the spell of English translation that various characters in Maḥfūẓ's *Zuqāq*—like Durrell's Leila—most violently lose Egypt, as English "equivalents" for Arabic words or Egyptian bodies can never replace, only approximate, the language and people they translate. Yet of all the richly realized plotlines in Maḥfūẓ's novel, none captures the seduction of colonial translation more powerfully than the story of Ḥamīda. A neighborhood beauty disgusted by the squalor of alley life, Ḥamīda abandons her poor fiancé, the alley barber 'Abbās al-Ḥulw, for a wealthy "headmaster" in a European suit who turns out to be not a lover, but a pimp. With romantic propositions, promises of luxury, and above all flattery of her desire for autonomy and sovereignty, Faraj lures her step by step to his classrooms of prostitution. There, like other girls who have learned to "translate" Egyptian bodies into English parts for British and American clients, Ḥamīda becomes fluent in the sexual principles of English. (Meanwhile, 'Abbās is off to the British Army camps to earn enough money to marry his beloved, only to return to the alley to find her eloped with Faraj.)

Ḥamīda's prostitution has divided Egyptian literary critics. Some, like Rajā' al-Naqqāsh, read her condition as symptomatic of Egypt's in the early to mid-twentieth century. Al-Naqqāsh maintains that Ḥamīda "symbolizes Egypt" at "the historical moment in which the old social order reached the apex of its collapse . . . during the Second World War," and Faraj the corruption of "Egyptian political power at the time," an "evil middleman between Egypt and British colonialism."[42] Others insist that Ḥamīda is too "immoral" to represent Egypt. 'Abd al-Muḥsin Ṭāhā Badr greets al-Naqqāsh's contention with dismay, arguing that "it maligns Egypt, especially since the author notes in the novel that Ḥamīda was a 'whore by instinct,' as no one coerced her into prostitution."[43] Yet Badr himself observes that while Ḥamīda seems eccentric to the alley—her lusts, ambitions, and "paganism" too great for its social economy to bear—she is in fact its center, as Maḥfūẓ "determines the fate of every character . . . by virtue of his or her proximity to or distance from the distinctive features of Ḥamīda's character."[44] I would argue, then, that Ḥamīda represents the "true" underbelly of the self that the collective psyche of the community (the alley, the nation, Egypt) spurns as a corrupted Other. To come to terms with Ḥamīda, a woman who has not been forced to prostitute her body to the British (and their American allies) in wartime Cairo yet does so anyway, is to come to terms with the uncomfortable fact that Egyptians have allowed European powers to seduce them into self-colonization even as they purport to resist these. That is why Badr and others so vociferously eject Ḥamīda from "Egypt" despite the fact that the novel itself refuses to do so. Elsewhere, Badr concedes that Maḥfūẓ implicates the nation in its self-prostitution. In the character of the café owner Kirsha, for instance, he argues that Maḥfūẓ reflects the materialism of modern life and tacitly links that materialism to the demise of revolutionary nationalism. With the decline of political values, Badr writes, Kirsha—once a "revolutionary and nationalist fighter"—becomes "a seller of elections."[45] Ḥamīda, I contend, figures precisely such a sale—and translation—of the nation. As such she is a fitting "symbol" for late-empire Egypt.

Rasheed El-Enany suggests as much. He reads Maḥfūẓ's *Zuqāq* as an allegory of Egypt's flight from the past into modernity.[46] Ḥamīda executes that flight when she decides to abandon 'Abbās for Faraj Ibrāhīm. While I question El-Enany's easy conflation of 'Abbās with "the past"—although 'Abbās loves the alley, he leaves it to earn money in the British camps, loses himself in alcohol and thus also his attachment to traditional Islamic values, and ultimately dies beyond the alley's borders—I find compelling his suggestion that Faraj brokers a seductive modernity, seductive because it represents itself to Ḥamīda not as the colonizer's desire but as "her own conviction."[47] "The very fact that Hamida can only free herself from the past . . . [by] becoming a prostitute in the service of Western soldiers," El-Enany writes,

> is not without significance on the symbolic level: for is not the renunciation by a culture of its traditional and historic identity in return for the "light, wealth and power" of modernity an act of prostitution *in extremis*?[48]

Where Badr insists that Ḥamīda's ambition, lust, and atheism dissociate her from "authentic" Egyptian values and thus from any capacity to symbolize Egypt, El-Enany intimates that Ḥamīda incarnates the destiny of Egypt precisely because she embodies these wayward traits. For those traits, he argues, look uncannily "like" those of the modern West—or at least the modern West as the Egyptian has received it. Insofar as Egypt began, under the press of European domination in the nineteenth and early twentieth century, to embrace colonial modernity as the inexorable path of "progress," Ḥamīda's prostitution represents modern Egypt's self-coupling, self-approximation, and self-loss to the West.

In his reading of Maḥfūẓ's *Zuqāq*, Muhammad Siddiq argues that "Faraj's school of prostitution, disguised as a school of languages, . . . appears to mock the fate of its historical antecedent: the school of languages founded by . . . Rifāʿa Rāfiʿ al-Ṭahṭāwī in 1836."[49] Noting that al-Ṭahṭāwī had founded that school "with the ultimate objective of transforming Egypt, through the assimilation of translated European knowledge, into a modern nation-state," Siddiq wryly observes that the "curriculum of the language and dance 'school' in which Ḥamīda 'enrolls' after she elopes with the pimp, Faraj, also involves 'translation,' but hardly of the kind envisaged by al-Ṭahṭāwī."[50] I would argue, however, that Faraj's school represents—in the negative, to be sure—the fulfillment of al-Ṭahṭāwī's project rather than its betrayal. The intimate violence of (post)colonial translation to Egyptian tongues and bodies is thrown most sharply into focus when Faraj introduces Ḥamīda to his school's English "department," where she encounters a naked woman learning to translate her person into English:

> Near the nude woman stood a man in a smart suit holding a pointer, its end resting on the tip of his shoes. Ibrahim Faraj noticed Hamida's confusion and reassuringly volunteered:
>
> "This department teaches the principles of the English language . . . !"
>
> . . . He then addressed the man holding the pointer:
>
> "Go on with the class, Professor."
>
> . . .
>
> Slowly he touched the naked woman's hair with the pointer. With a strange accent the woman spoke the word "hair" *["hayr"]*. The pointer touched her forehead and she replied "forehead" *["frunt"]*. He then moved on to her eyebrows, eyes, her mouth and then East and West and up and down. To each of his silent questions the woman uttered a strange word which Hamida had never heard before.[51]

What meets Ḥamīda's eye as she enters this strange English class strips her of self-possession. Frozen, she watches a naked woman offer herself up as consumable spectacle. The woman exists for the gaze of her beholder, ready for his sex. And this beholder is a distinctly Western master. For Faraj—her pimp—is only a stand-in for the British and American soldiers to whom she will be hired out. Even the instructor who touches every part of the woman's body with his pointer—clothed in a British "smart suit," unexposed and thus apparently empowered—is merely vested with the sartorial trappings of a power that Faraj borrows from the colonial master and bestows on him in turn. As native

Egyptian men, both Faraj and the instructor enjoy at best a prosthetic masculinity within a British-controlled economy of sexuality and language. Evacuated of heterosexual desire and effectively castrated, both eye the nude woman with "calm indifference."[52] Only by wielding the pointer—the sexual prosthesis of the Anglo-American phallus and the linguistic prosthesis of English—do Faraj and his instructor become "subjects": heterosexual white male masters. The pointer does not just "translate" the would-be Egyptian prostitute into Englishness; it so translates the Egyptian men who teach her and pimp her as well.

Still, it is the nude Egyptian woman—on whose body Britain, through "headmaster" Faraj and his "professor," teaches its English lesson in this scene—who most vividly incarnates Egyptian vulnerability to colonial translation. As the instructor's pointer moves "East and West" across her body, the woman's flesh turns imperial geography: a field that yokes (Egyptian) East to (British) West. Maḥfūẓ describes the tip of the instructor's pointer as a spearhead *(sinān),* as a colonial weapon, and indeed the Egyptian woman's personhood is mutilated by its thrusts. She begins to exist only as hair, forehead, eyebrows, eyes, mouth. Violated and slowly dismantled by the prod of the instructor's pointer, the woman—increasingly, a voice disembodied—names each of her body parts in English, reconstituting her Egyptian body as an English space, semantically intelligible to and physically consumable by the British or American john. The average Egyptian, on the other hand—lacking English like Ḥamīda—can barely understand this body, as it has turned into a set of "strange accent[s]," alien to all who have not yet learned *their* English lessons.

Here, then, Ḥamīda confronts a scene of linguistic "copulation" that doubles as an "undress" rehearsal for its sexual analogue. This translation originates in the sign language of the instructor's pointer, which symbolically prefigures the British phallus that will assert its pleasure *in* this woman's body and reconstitute as her intrinsic value her ability to satisfy the British "ego." To produce the English translations "hair," "front," and the like, the pointer must *copulate*—mingle in the moment of the copular "is"—with the unvoiced, erased Arabic names of the Egyptian woman's body parts. Inseminated by gesture (the tacitly English pointing of the pointer), consummated by silence (the implied Arabic that her mind must *couple to* the pointer), and birthed in speech (the English word), the woman's translation into an "English" subject exposes the violence of the asymmetrical relation that "exchanges" Arabic for English and Egyptianness for an ersatz Englishness.

Throughout the scene, the pointer acts as the gestural analogue of what Émile Benveniste calls grammatical *deixis:* the function of indication, of "pointing out."[53] Benveniste defines the indicators of deixis as pronouns, adverbs, and adjectives—like the demonstrative pronoun *this*—that "organize the spatial and temporal relationships around the 'subject' taken as referent."[54] Like the instructor's silent pointer, indicators of deixis are semantically "empty" until an implied grammatical subject—an implied *I*—fills them with meaning.[55] These indicators, then, stand in for the *I*, freezing the time (history) and space (geography) of the *you* they indicate in the directive mold of the *I*'s gesture.[56] Indeed the indicator of deixis—whether the demonstrative pronoun *this* in the verbal statement "*This* is your hair" or the silent touch of the pointer, which says as much to the Egyptian woman—is, according to Benveniste, the "*instrument of a conversion* . . . of language into discourse," where *language* is a resource available to all speakers and *discourse* is language that a particular speaking subject appropriates.[57] Yet if, as Benveniste argues, discourse begins only when an *I* arrogates the open system of language and declares its dominion over a *you*, then the deictic indicator—as a stand-in for the speaking subject and a grammatical surrogate of the *I*—represents more than just the instrument of language's conversion into discourse.[58] The deictic indicator is also the specter of domination that haunts that conversion.[59]

Benveniste prefigures Jean Baudrillard's notion of seduction and effectively articulates a theory of colonial translation. For if Benveniste problematically insists on the absolute reciprocity of the *I/you* relation—on the reversibility of the polarities of *I* and *you*, in which, he says, "the old antinomies of 'I' and 'the other' . . . fall"—he also undercuts such reciprocity by declaring that the polarity of *I* and *you* "does not mean either equality or symmetry," as "'ego' always has a position of transcendence with regard to *you*."[60] Based on an unequal *I/you* relation, then, deixis inscribes—across the grammatical copula of the verb *to be,* whether stated or implied—a *transymmetry* (*a/symmetry*) between two terms akin to that of translational seduction. Thus, under the guise of establishing "equivalence" between the seemingly neutral indicator *this* and the object or person indicated, deixis actually converts the *you* into the *I* behind the *this*. The linguistic conversion that deixis performs erases the *you*'s original ("proper") name and substitutes the *I*'s name in the guise of the native, passing the erasure off as "translation." Indeed, the first English words that the Egyptian woman in Faraj's school utters, *hair* and *front*, are not rendered in Roman characters in the text—as are, for instance, the English words that Shaykh Darwīsh teaches the residents of Midaq Alley—but instead rapidly "Arabized," transliterated as *hayr* and *frunt* and thus assimilated into Arabic script. English words masquerade as Arabic. So rendered, these words speak the violence that lurks in the seductions of translation; a foreign power that assumes the guise of one's native language, they hint, most sabotages one's personhood and sovereignty. Far better than equation, then, Benvenistian conversion captures the copulative operations of colonial translation, which transform the *you*'s "ego" into an extension—not an equal—of the *I*'s "ego."

By the end of the lesson, we witness the Egyptian woman trade flirtations with her instructor in seamless English dialogue. The instructor has told Ḥamīda that his is a "recitation class" *("ḥiṣṣatu tasmīʿin").*[61] The Arabic *tasmīʿ* ("recitation") derives from the root verb *sammaʿa,* "to make someone hear [that which one has been taught to say]." Recitation suggests the conditioned reproduction of linguistic models. Indeed, the instructor need not speak for the woman to recite: like Leila Hosnani's recitation of Ruskin in *Mountolive,* her English response is so conditioned—so automatic—that no Arabic prompt is needed to elicit it. No longer must the English language conceal itself in the wordless "sign language" of the pointer. Maḥfūẓ's Arabic original makes it clear that the instructor actually *sets the pointer aside* at this stage *("naḥḥā al-rajulu al-mu'ashshira jāniban"),* entering into a spontaneous "exchange" of words with the woman.[62] English now reveals itself *as* the pointer; the instructor actually speaks the British *I*'s English, the language he really has been "speaking" all along. Maḥfūẓ's Arabic also more clearly represents the conversation that follows as a mere simulacrum of "equal" exchange, where the instructor is a Benvenistian *I* and the student a Benvenistian *you.* It reminds us that domination shadows the exchange to come: when the instructor approaches the woman, speaking in English, the Arabic *"mukhāṭiban"* identifies him as the speaking subject, he who owns the present instance of discourse (and owns it in English). Then the Arabic goes on to dispel the ghost of power with the illusion of reciprocity. Rather than say that the woman "replied phrase by phrase in English," Maḥfūẓ conveys her manner of response with the verb *āʿṭā, "to reciprocate,"* suggesting that for each phrase the instructor addresses to her, she gives him one *in exchange ("āʿṭathu al-mar'atu qawlan bi qawlin").*[63] What follows from this seemingly "equal" word-for-word exchange, in fact, is the dissolution of the polarities *I* and *you* and the union of the two in discourse. This union, captured in the third-person *dual* Arabic verb *tarāṭanā* ("the two chatted"), testifies to the radical translation of the Egyptian woman into the terms of the English *I*. The woman reproduces herself *as* English without the pointer's artificial insemination. The conversion is complete: the Egyptian woman is now English property.[64]

BEFORE VIOLENCE, SEDUCTION

Certainly, then, *Zuqāq al-Midaqq* represents colonial translation as the linguistic analogue of colonial violence, tied, always, to the workings of the market. Faraj himself suggests as much to Ḥamīda once he lures her to his "school," arguing that he—as a "headmaster, . . . not a pimp"—would preside over her transformation into a woman of means.[65] Teasing Ḥamīda for imagining that the heavens could "rain only bombs" ("shrapnel" *[shaẓāyā]* in the Arabic), never "gold and diamonds," he associates the sexual economy of his "school" with the violence of British colonization.[66] The echoing rains of gold and diamonds, on the one hand, and bombs or shrapnel, on the other, suggest that Egypt's enrichment is also its ruin—and evoke the theater of European "world" war that unfolds in the novel's very first scene, where the residents of Midaq Alley speak, under blackout, of the "'terrors . . . of air-raids.'"[67] Indeed, Maḥfūẓ's narrator frames the pivotal moment of Ḥamīda's disappearance from the alley and translation toward "English" prostitution in terms of the very riches whose connections to imperial violence Faraj slyly adumbrates. As Ḥamīda steps into the taxi that Faraj has called to take her to his "school," her body undergoes a disfiguring translation into commodities of colonial exchange. Faraj's love words in the taxi dismantle her: she is reduced to a neck encircled by diamonds, to breasts "held away from [her] by supports of silk," dissociated from her body.[68] Each rhetorical dismemberment of her body is "fulfilled" by a sexual transgression of her physical space—a caress, a kiss, a moving closer.[69] Like the naked woman she soon will see in Faraj's department of English, she is translated by the discursive touch of the colonizer's surrogate into a collection of unstrung body parts. The violence of that translation prefigures that of the first English lesson she will witness.

Yet Maḥfūẓ's novel also embeds the violence of the translation that Ḥamīda and Egypt undergo, into English commodity or English territory, within a narrative of *seduction*. The text insistently predicates coercion upon seduction. One of the voices with which Egypt speaks to us, under cover of darkness, as the novel opens—"'If we've been suffering terrors of blackouts and air-raids for five years it's only due to our own wickedness!'"—activates that seduction plot from the outset.[70] While the voice shocks us by blaming the hapless Egyptian subjects of indirect British rule for their assault by a European "world" war, it rings disturbingly true as we watch desires for love or money or power lure one alley denizen after another into states of subjection, often colonial.[71] Money and the power of Englishness first attract Ḥamīda's "foster" brother Ḥusayn Kirsha to the British Army camps. There he wins the favor of his British superiors and with it a lucrative share of their black-market trade in army surplus goods; his superiors remark his successful translation—in all but color—into an English *"jalmān"* ("gentleman"), and his old friend 'Abbās al-Ḥulw admires his transformation into a good-looking "Johnny." Yet Ḥusayn achieves this translation by squandering all the money he earns; when British action on the North African front wanes, he is summarily laid off and returns penniless to Midaq Alley. While love for Ḥamīda—and the need to finance it—send 'Abbās in turn to the British Army camps, his departure only enables Ḥamīda's seduction into prostitution and turns his love, as we shall see, into the instrument of his end.[72] Thus when Maḥfūẓ's narrator, registering Ḥamīda's first reactions to Faraj's appearance in the alley, observes that money in Midaq Alley is an "eloquent language" *("lughatun balīghatun"),* he does more than link the unequal distribution of money and power in 1940s Egypt to the unequal exchange of language that will ensue in the translational space of Faraj's department of English.[73] British money, the narrator suggests, not only talks in a poor Cairene quarter, but does so artfully.[74] On impoverished Egyptians like Ḥusayn Kirsha, 'Abbās al-Ḥulw, and Ḥamīda, it works an aestheticized spell of colonial power: precisely the spell that Ruskin's oratorical flights work on Durrell's upper-class Egyptian siren, Leila Hosnani.

Always, in Maḥfūẓ's *Zuqāq,* the colonially produced self emanates from the "instinctual" self—that is to say, the desiring and the seducible self, which in the end itself wishes to be seductive: wealthy and powerful and attractive perhaps, but above all sovereign. If Faraj dazzles Ḥamīda with promises of gold, diamonds, and silk as he whisks her away to her "new life," he dazzles her more deeply with the power with which his endearments insistently invest these commodities: the power to seduce. This power, he suggests, is already inborn in and *proper to* Ḥamīda. Witness how Ḥamīda, now prostituted, is said to have willed herself into her present state. "From the very beginning," the narrator tells us, she "chose her path of *her own free will [bi maḥḍi irādatihā]*. . . . When eventually she gave way to the eloquence of Ibrahim Faraj, *it was because she wished to do so. . . .* She had justified her lover's comment that she was a 'whore by instinct' *['āhiratun bi al-fiṭrati].*"[75] Maḥfūẓ's narrator places Ḥamīda's capitulation to prostitution—to English translation—entirely within the compass of free choice; he associates her acquiescence with *instinct,* with her "natural" self. In so doing, he undercuts our desire to read Ḥamīda as a mere "victim" of Egyptian poverty and its exploitation by imperial Britain and Britain's Egyptian surrogate, Faraj Ibrāhīm. The eloquence of that surrogate, he suggests, seduces her because she *wishes* to be seduced.[76]

Or, more properly, wishes to be a seductress. With a nuance that the English translation elides, Maḥfūẓ's Arabic tells us why Ḥamīda chooses to cross the political border that divides al-Ghūriyya (in old Cairo) from New Street (al-Sikka al-Jadīda, symbolizing the modern European-style city): she acts *"istislāman li dā'ī 'ajrafatihā wa ishbā'an li gharīzatihā al-muta'aṭṭishati li al-'irāk"* ("in self-surrender to the driving force of her arrogance and in a need to quench her thirsty instinct for battle").[77] Ḥamīda enters into a relationship with Faraj, then, to gratify her own sense of self-importance by matching her will to his, in the kind of intersubjective struggle to the death that Frantz Fanon's rewriting of the Hegelian master-slave dialectic describes. As in Ḥasan al-'Aṭṭār's "Maqāmat al-Faransīs," it is the colonizer's sovereignty that seduces. Faraj embodies that sovereignty: his self-sufficiency and aplomb mirror the autonomous, empowered self that Ḥamīda wants to be, indeed believes she inherently is. The "eloquent language" of money speaks to her, yes, but only because it mediates a deeper desideratum: the wish to command seduction and its power to translate.

I have argued that seduction is a magnetism of like and unlike masquerading as an attraction of two similars; it hinges not on a dynamics of reflection, but on a *refraction* of the seducer's alluring "likeness" to the seduced through the differentiating medium of power. What draws Ḥamīda is just such a tension between the lived irreciprocity of her relation to Faraj and the reciprocity she imagines that relation could take. That Faraj wields power over Ḥamīda is clear from her recollections of their first meeting: he is the "taker," the subject of discourse; she, his object, existing only "to be taken."[78] These are no conditions of equal exchange; rather, they represent the asymmetry that Benveniste associates with deixis. Even if, as Benveniste suggests, the *I* and the *you* of deixis are reversible polarities—although the inequalities of colonial history would defy such a claim and attach, instead, a one-way sign to deictic asymmetry—deixis is no less politically insidious for that reversibility. After all, reversibility is, as Baudrillard contends, the crux of seduction: the seducer is sovereign because he or she commands the capacity to "reversibilize" signs, to make the polarities of sex and power waver. It is because Ḥamīda depoliticizes the asymmetry between her *you* and Faraj's *I* and assumes its potential "reversibility" in her favor that she goes blind to Faraj's seductive command even as she stares him unflinchingly in the *I*, boldly returning his gaze. Imagining her selfhood commensurable with and thus exchangeable with his, she blithely translates the prospect of "being taken" into a false equivalent, "marriage," which in class-stratified Egypt implies a socioeconomic commensurability between partners that extramarital sex would not.[79] As Ḥamīda assumes the conqueror's *I*, "her ungovernable vanity [gives] her a feeling of power and enormous self-confidence," and she increasingly misrecognizes Faraj's ego as her own: witness her conviction that Faraj's imperious (and imperial) eyes, unlike 'Abbās's "humble" ones, reveal "a great deal of herself."[80] While drawn "like the needle of a compass to the poles *[kamā tujdhabu ibratu al-bawṣalati ilā al-quṭbi],*" Ḥamīda imagines her needle pointed toward Faraj by force of will. She takes up the pointer of deixis, objectifying Faraj as her *you.*[81]

Yet Ḥamīda's needle does not point to Faraj on its own power. Her *I* is pointed toward Faraj—and toward the British North he represents—by sheer force of his calculated magnetism. No encounter better captures Baudrillard's characterization of seduction as an *"affinité duelle,"* a duel/dual affinity.[82] Ḥamīda's would-be taker greases his challenge to the duel with disarming words. Faraj questions her relation to her alley kin, wondering how she can live among them. Against their thinly disguised commonness, he pits her cloaked aristocracy: "'You are a princess in a shabby cloak, while these peasants [*ra'iyyatun,* lit., "commoners"] strut in their new finery.'"[83] Like the historical Napoleon of the Egyptian proclamation or the fictional Frenchman of al-'Aṭṭār's *maqāma*, Faraj woos his target both by embodying the self that Ḥamīda wishes to become—the "taker"—and by encouraging her to see herself as she wishes to be seen: as a deposed sovereign ("princess") poised for restoration. He encourages her to recognize herself in *his* mirror, all the while camouflaging the fact that his is precisely the strategic mirror that Baudrillard invokes, reflecting on her even as she fails to reflect on it.[84] Faraj relies on the counterfactual illusion of the "as if" to execute his imperial will, to make Ḥamīda yield to her prostitution *as if* by her will alone; here the English translation, which says that she succumbs "because she wished to do so," elides the illusion implied by the *ka'annahā* ("as if she") of the original Arabic, *"adh'anat ba'da dhālika wa ka'annahā tudh'inu bi maḥḍi mashī'atihā"* ("she yielded *as if* she were yielding by her will alone").[85] Ḥamīda almost unmasks her pimp's strategy. "It was *as if* that man had crossed her path deliberately," she observes, "to uncover what was buried inside her, spreading it all before her eyes *as though* reflected by a mirror."[86] Yet she stops short of doing so. While she senses the deliberateness of Faraj's seductions, she remains in his thrall by imagining her power "innate," reflected in Faraj rather than refracted by his will.

Faraj delivers the coup de grace of seduction when he declares it impossible that Ḥamīda should fear him.[87] Were he to reassure her that she should not fear his advances, he would assume the position of the empowered *I* against her helpless *you*. Instead, he speaks the language of his target: he recognizes Ḥamīda's fierce *I* before the Hegelian death-struggle for recognition—the battle she so deeply desires—actually ensues, and he thereby disarms her just as al-'Aṭṭār's Frenchman earlier disarmed his Egyptian target.[88] He *translates* her toward his subject position: *you* are as fearless as *I*; *you* are *I*, if only you knew. His words do not miss their mark; she returns his advances and thereby satisfies his desire.[89] With artifice, he has appealed to her most cherished self-image in order to reproduce her as artifice in turn: as the English-speaking "whore by instinct," an artifice so "natural" to her conquest-loving being that it passes *for* nature to her. Earlier I argued that the colonially produced self emanates, in Maḥfūẓ, from the seducible or instinctual self. The impulse to fight and the impulse to surrender are not, however, "naturally" exchangeable; it is the seducer's strategy—the colonizer's strategy—to make them appear to be so. For this reason Ḥamīda, though she enters love-battle with Faraj by her free will alone, surrenders to her colonial self-translation only *as if* by her will alone.

Indeed, from Ḥamīda's first allegation that he is not a man but a pimp, Faraj deflects her charge by wielding the seductions of translation. He translates Ḥamīda into his "likeness," and colonizing self-prostitution into the "equivalent" of sovereignty. "We are made from the same metal, you and I," he intones. " . . . If we join forces, then love, wealth and dignity will be ours, but if we part there will be hardship, poverty and humiliation—for one of us."[90] Faraj's words take the form of Napoleon's first Egyptian proclamation, which announces the sword with the translational seductions of the pen: I so recognize your dignity that I come to you *as* you; so come to me and become me, because if you do not, I truly will be your Other—your worst enemy. Only too late does Ḥamīda recognize that so long as she couples with Faraj in a translational mirror he controls, her reflection can never be commensurable with his: "It was perhaps because she knew she had not achieved control over her lover," the narrator observes, "that her attachment to him increased, along with her feeling of resentment and disillusion. . . . She was obsessed with mixed feelings of love, hostility and suspicion *as she stood looking at his reflection in the mirror.*"[91] Once Ḥamīda realizes that she is not Faraj's lover but his profit-making "pupil," she all the more acutely desires control of the sort that Faraj has wielded and still wields over her. She is angry that she cannot annex Faraj as he has annexed her. The power that so eludes her is none other than the power *to seduce,* and thus the capacity to be sovereign. Ironically, Ḥamīda's desire to attain sovereignty, passing as it does through a mirror that eclipses *her* reflection with Faraj's own (she stands "looking at *his* reflection in the mirror"), holds her in even deeper subjection. Her attachment to Faraj grows.

"A WORD WITHOUT MEANING CAN MEAN ALMOST ANYTHING"

Maḥfūẓ's *Zuqāq* compels us, in the end, to confront the erasure *beyond recognition* of the precolonial subject: the translation of an Egyptian self toward and indeed *into* her colonizer across a copula overdetermined by colonial power. How does seduction, which succeeds by affirming the sovereign subject, paradoxically figure in the coupling that so violently erases that subject? To answer this question, I turn to the reflections on language and violence of Jacques Derrida. Derrida's analysis, in *De la grammatologie (Of Grammatology),* of another imperialist "writing lesson"—the charged negotiations between the French anthropologist Claude Lévi-Strauss and the "objects" of his study, the Nambikwara Indians of Brazil, over the right to name and the claim to "writing"—might help us understand why the English lesson that is "written" on the body of the Egyptian woman in Faraj's brothel-school is "a violence sometimes veiled, but always oppressive."[92] Lévi-Strauss describes the Nambikwara as a people "without writing" whose customs prohibit the utterance of proper names; in Derrida's retelling, those customs have led Europeans to impose "ridiculous sobriquets on the natives, obliging them to assume these" in lieu of the proper names that social conventions bar them from revealing.[93] When one little Nambikwara girl—

struck by another—chooses to reveal to Lévi-Strauss the real name of her enemy, prompting the other in turn to reveal *her* adversary's real name, the anthropologist proceeds to "trick" the little girls (as he puts it) into divulging the names of the adults of the tribe, until an elder gets wind of their collusion and puts a stop to the girls' revelations.

In Derrida's analysis, Lévi-Strauss only blames himself—a European—for the betrayal and penetration of Nambikwara society because he refuses to concede that the Nambikwara themselves are capable of violence.[94] What lurks behind Derrida's assessment of Lévi-Strauss's self-imaginings is a question that I have asked elsewhere in this book: can one adequately explain cultural imperialism of the sort that troubles Lévi-Strauss as rape, as *viol*? Derrida suggests otherwise. He rightly critiques Lévi-Strauss's ethnocentric assumption that the agency of the native begins, reactively, when the arrival of the European "unleashes" it. The anthropologist's refusal to imagine the *possibility of violence* among the Nambikwara is of a piece, Derrida argues, with his inability to see Nambikwara society as a *writing* society: for writing in its "common" sense is, to Derrida, but one manifestation of a larger phenomenon he calls *archi-écriture,* or *arche-writing,* which includes speech and gesture and is rooted in the capacity to do violence to presence, to rupture presence by mediating it in and as representation. Arguing that "writing . . . is the originary violence," Derrida locates the origin of that origin in the act of naming: of assigning the "proper" and by so doing obliterating the "property" of the named.[95] (This gesture, I might add, is akin to Benveniste's deixis, for what is a demonstrative like "This is *x*" if not an act of naming?) In Derrida's reading, then, the Nambikwara silence on proper names is nothing if not writing, for it violently "overwrites" and hence overasserts the name, itself the paradigmatic mark of writing and thus of violence.

By rejecting Lévi-Strauss's claim to have "penetrated" Nambikwara society, Derrida daringly dissociates colonial violence from penetration. His analysis shades the landscape of that violence with tints of seduction. Rather than develop the theory of seduction to which his reinterpretation of colonial encounter subtly gestures, however, he merely replaces the assumption of "simplicity" with that of "complicity": the little girls who break their society's secrets collude with the European, are "just as" violent as their European observer. In this analysis Derrida fails to see that complicity, despite its etymological implication of complexity, is merely the double of the simplicity he derides: we have glided too effortlessly from penetration to partnership. Suggesting that the object of the colonial gaze is complicit with the colonizing *I*, he implies that power is reciprocal and commensurable across the divide of colonizer and colonized. Clearly it is not. The colonizing *I* deploys the *illusion* of its equivalence to the *I* of the colonized in order to assert itself *nonmutually, irreciprocally.* Behind the pointer's activation of an illusory reciprocity of *I* and *you* in Faraj's English classroom, after all, the British "ego" is busily writing—obliterating the proper of the naked woman's *you.*

Derrida's discourse, then, ultimately neuters the politics of colonial translation by equating the violence of European expropriation of Nambikwara names with the violence of Nambikwara self-naming. To constitute the Nambikwara as a subject worthy of the name, a writing subject whose experience is as "universal" as the European, Derrida ironically erases Nambikwara claims to the particular, to the "proper." He maintains that the Nambikwara subject is, from birth and irrespective of its freedom from or subjection to European power, brutally written *upon:* marked as soon as another Nambikwara subject affixes to his or her (speechless) infant body a "proper" name that is neither truly "owned" nor—given the double entendre of the French *propre*—truly "clean," purged of the traces of system. In calling oneself by one's "proper" name, one actually presents oneself by representation, which implies self-absence. Self-presence—the "true" proper—is thus an illusion for Derrida, as the body cannot be *thought* outside the system that classifies it: it is "incapable of appearing to itself," he writes, "except in its own disappearance"; it is *"what has never taken place."*[96] Redefining the "proper" (the "native") as "what has never taken place," Derrida suggests that European writing merely exposes the violence of *prior* Nambikwara naming. Revealing the original "so-called proper" native name—the real culprit, he insists, that "has severed the proper from its property"—European writing *denudes* (his word) the farce of that original naming, exposing the fundamental "nonidentity" of the native.[97] A Lévi-Strauss or a Faraj who imagines that he has penetrated the self-determination of those he has colonized, Derrida scoffs, has in fact conquered no one. The colonized who appear to receive "writing lessons" never really have been self-determined anyway; they simply have "exchanged" internal self-erasures for external ones. In Derrida's final articulation of writing-as-violence, "evil, war, [and] rape" share space with the oddly incongruent "indiscretion" (the little girls' revelations to Lévi-Strauss?), not only implicating native betrayals of "property" in foreign transgressions thereof, but also suggesting that those betrayals are commensurable.[98]

I would argue that Derrida's articulation of the violence of writing itself does violence to the traumatic history of colonized and dominated peoples, denying the expropriation of the native by an alien power. Read under conditions of political power, in which the self assumes that it can even *bear* the status of an ego, Derrida's critique of the proper name astutely deconstructs the mythologies of nativism and the writing of hermetic "nation." Read, however, under the unequal condition of colonialism, his claim that "self-presence," or property, is "what has never taken place" appears to explain away colonial expropriations of land, language, and identity by claiming that these last never existed—except in the native's perception. Most disturbing, Derrida suggests that the "native" *needs to be* divested of such illusions of self, and forcibly, by the denuding force of the "writing lesson," defined here as the intrusion of the foreigner. In other words, the colonized *must* be colonized in order to *see* themselves, as, after all, they can only appear to themselves in their disappearance.

If assuming the absolute original "innocence" of the colonized betrays a fundamentally colonial attitude toward those colonized subjects, placing them in the Edenic "first ages" of humankind and Europe in the chronotope of modernity, so too is assuming their absolute original "sin"—as Derrida does here—a potentially recolonizing gesture. Derrida suggests that the virgin little girls who betray their names and, more important, those of their elders to Lévi-Strauss are really, like Ḥamīda in the eyes of Faraj Ibrāhīm and of Maḥfūẓ's narrator, "whores" by instinct. We must interrogate this thesis. What the precolonial subject enjoys, to invoke Antonio Gramsci's citation of Novalis, is the sense of being in "possession of one's transcendental self, of being at one and the same time the self of oneself": the self that has the power to create, and then interrogate, *the lie of itself.*[99] Colonization reconstitutes self-fabricated selves as Other-fabricated selves. And those selves, like the erasures that create them, are not commensurable.

To rethink as seduction the dynamics of the colonial encounters that Lévi-Strauss and Maḥfūẓ describe is, then, to say two things at once. It is to assert the subjectivity and the agency that Derrida would claim for the dominated when he hints that they too play some role in surrendering their sovereignty to their dominator. Yet it is to insist, still, that the dominator commands power by *eliciting* that surrender, by manipulating the attraction of the dominated to a self-image in which she or he appears to occupy the subject position of the dominator. What Derrida's understanding obscures is the way in which the violence of colonial "ex-propriation" he describes might confirm the *self-presence* and sovereignty of the native, not her a priori erasure, in order to erase that self-presence and revoke that sovereignty. ("'You are a princess in a shabby cloak,'" Faraj tells Ḥamīda.) The European who bestows sobriquets on the Nambikwara knows full well that Nambikwara self-presence exists; he is frustrated that the self-presence of the "object" he desires to know does not necessarily make that "object" present to *him*. For in bestowing "ridiculous sobriquets" on the Nambikwara, the Europeans in effect recognize Nambikwara "property" and thus Nambikwara sovereignty; they tacitly submit themselves to the law of ineffability that governs the utterance of Nambikwara names even as they cheapen and undercut it. The little girls who betray their people sense that recognition: when they give up the secret of their people's "proper" names to the European observer, they do so because the European appears *already* to be "in" on that secret.

What the Egyptian woman undergoes in Faraj Ibrāhīm's "department of English" is precisely the sort of colonial denuding, and colonial "writing lesson," that Derrida miscasts as more or less "natural" extensions of native self-writing and self-violence. Here the "forced entry" of the instructor's pointer shapes and reorients, from a foreign view*point*, the intimate space of a naked Egyptian body. Under the colonial violence of Faraj's English lessons, not only are Egyptian women's body parts renamed *in* English and thus divorced from "local" meaning, but even those women's proper names are altered *for* the English. Indeed once he is sure that Ḥamīda has fallen to his seduction, Faraj greets her with a new name: Tītī, a sobriquet as ridiculous as those imposed by Lévi-Strauss's Europeans on the Nambikwara. Having enticed Ḥamīda to his quarters with the prospect of transforming her into the princess he has claimed she already is, he advises her to doff her old name and old life, like old garments both, and take this compound of meaningless monosyllables as a name better in tune with her new identity: "Keep it and forget Hamida, for she has ceased to exist! Names, my darling, are not trivial things, to which we should attach no weight. Names are really everything."[100] Faraj's attitude toward the proper is oddly Derridean. While he initially appears to valorize the "proper"—telling Ḥamīda that names carry material weight, the stuff of which the world is made—he undercuts, in a contradictory move, her very "property." By treating the name "Ḥamīda" as just so many "old clothes" to be "discarded and forgotten," Faraj denudes not only Ḥamīda's body, but also the fiction of its indigenous name: the fiction of a "native" Egypt.[101]

Why this split attitude toward the "proper," this simultaneous affirmation of Tītī's self- (and world-) writing and effacement of Ḥamīda's mark? If names are not trivial things, if names indeed carry weight, on what grounds does Faraj command Ḥamīda to "forget Hamida" and keep "Tītī," unless he has negated the very status of "Ḥamīda" as a name, unless he has stripped Arabic of the authority *to* name?

Faraj's discourse is strategically contradictory. Here the colonial *I*, rechristening the native *you* in its image, infuses the "proper" with political significance, then—realizing that that logic might also impute value to the native's erased original name—disingenuously denies that names matter at all. Pronouncing the colonizer's "proper" meaningful and relegating the native's to meaninglessness, Faraj enables the false exchange of the latter for the former. Ḥamīda herself wonders if "Tītī"—the nickname this Lévi-Straussian stranger to Midaq Alley, this surrogate of the British *I*, has bestowed on her—could be exchangeable with "Ḥamadmad," the nickname that her native foster mother has given her.[102] Yet the incommensurability of the two names is clear. "Ḥamadmad" is a loving, playful spinoff from Ḥamīda's "proper" name; "Tītī," by contrast, is rootless. Ḥamīda recognizes that fact, however vaguely. Confronting Faraj, she questions her new name's meaninglessness. He argues that "a word without meaning can mean almost anything" (*"fal-ismu alladhī lā ma'nā lahu yaḥwī al-ma'ānī kullahā"*; lit., "a name without meaning encompasses all meanings"), lauding "Tītī" as an "ancient name that will amuse Englishmen and Americans and one which their twisted tongues can easily pronounce."[103] This response further complicates the question of naming. Where Faraj earlier argued the "weight" (meaningfulness) of Tītī and the disposability (meaninglessness) of Ḥamīda, he now strategically refigures "Tītī"—the colonial "proper" into which he demands Ḥamīda translate herself—as a *meaningful meaninglessness*, at once like yet unlike the native "proper" of "Ḥamīda." He has chosen the meaningless "Tītī," he says, precisely because it can "mean almost anything"—or, as the original Arabic tells us, because it "encompasses all meanings" and is thus open to every possible investment of sense. Ḥamīda's renaming lampoons the radical exchangeability of language on which al-Ṭahṭāwī earlier predicated European-Egyptian "equivalence," exposing its colonial danger. Like Derrida's proper that has never taken place, Faraj's "word without meaning" is common "property": an empty vessel that can be filled as he wills, and as the British and American soldiers soon to consort with "Tītī" will. It is by disembodying Ḥamīda with the empty name "Tītī," by parodically universalizing her particular, that Faraj and his English-speaking clients can reconstruct her as an object within their power, in the unique instances of copulation that their *Is* command as subjects. "Tītī" is a free-floating signifier—in Benvenistian terms, an empty deictic indicator—to which any signification might attach, depending on whatever *I* happens to sleep with her for the night: she is meant, like the woman in Faraj's English department, for colonial consumption. The English and Americans can easily pronounce "her"; "she" yields no resistance; "she" represents, if anything, a trivializing nickname for Egypt's ancient past (a half-Nefertiti), sundered both from that context *and* from Egypt's present. Associable with anything, she is associable with nothing. Tītī becomes a facile substitution for a complex womanhood and a complex land, ready for the English speaker's taking, or ex-*propriation*.

THE COLONY BEYOND RECOGNITION

Where, on the stage of Egypt's self-loss and self-realization, does Maḥfūẓ's *Zuqāq al-Midaqq* ultimately leave us? Perhaps, paradoxically, with a Derridean assertion, which speaks with uncanny accuracy to a nascent decolonization in 1940s Egypt: "The access to writing is the constitution of a free subject in the violent movement of its own effacement and of its own bondage."[104] For while Faraj appears, initially, the English headmaster triumphant, he is ultimately a headmaster betrayed. By inciting Ḥamīda's "disappearance" and luring her into prostitution, he ultimately enables her to co-opt English and to prostitute it for her own ambitions and Egypt's, thereby inverting—to all appearances—the power relation of colonizer and colonized. Seizing the violences of her erasure and bondage and repossessing these to her own ends, Ḥamīda becomes a provisionally "free" subject.

By the end of the novel, "Tītī" marshals the oscillation between old name and new to manipulate her former fiancé, 'Abbās, into wreaking revenge on Faraj, the very figure of the colonizer. Witness how Maḥfūẓ describes the climactic moment that drives the novel to its tragic end. Crossing Cairo's Opera Square with Ḥusayn Kirsha one day, 'Abbās encounters a carriage carrying a beautiful woman: "She looked somehow familiar. So faintly familiar that his heart, more than his eyes, was the detector."[105] His sudden cry, "Hamida!" answers Tītī's musings as she circles the Opera House, wondering if her former neighbors in Midaq Alley would know her if they saw her. "Would they see Hamida underneath Titi?"[106] When 'Abbās recognizes in the colonial fabrication "Tītī" the trace of an Egyptian "Ḥamīda," he symbolically restores her Arabic name. Intercepting Tītī's journey to the tavern, the site of her prostitution, 'Abbās's shrill "Hamida!" interpellates and reclaims—if even for a moment—the Egyptian Ḥamīda of Midaq Alley by piercing the colonial daydream of "Tītī": a construction whose flimsiness Ḥamīda herself recognizes when she concedes "Ḥamīda's" potential visibility beneath "Tītī's" colonial translation. While the metonymic presence of "Ḥamīda" in "Tītī" is illegible to the British and even to the lazy gaze of Egyptians like Ḥusayn Kirsha—who fails to recognize her—it is legible to the discerning Egyptian eye. 'Abbās recognizes the whisper-thin slippage in her colonial charade—the trace of an occluded Ḥamīda, her ineffable no-body "faintly familiar," legible only to the heart, not to cognition. While Ḥamīda initially is terrified that 'Abbās recognizes her as such and *not* as Tītī, she quickly realizes the strategic value of reclaiming her "proper" name and of disowning its false equivalent. She plays to her advantage the slippage between the hidden "proper" (Ḥamīda, the native Egyptian virgin of Midaq Alley) and the public "improper": Tītī, the anglicized "translation" of Ḥamīda prostituted and paraded in Opera Square, site of the European-style Opera House for which Khedive Ismā'īl—who had declared Egypt "a part of Europe"—had incurred the massive foreign debt that enabled the British occupation of 1882. Holding "Tītī" at arm's length from herself, Ḥamīda turns the "improper" mask that Faraj has bestowed on her "proper" name into a weapon against him. She manipulates the disgust that "Tītī," her prostituted alter ego, evokes in 'Abbās until he becomes the willing instrument of her urge to punish Faraj: an urge motivated not by bitterness over her prostitution but by the sting of Faraj's emotional disinterest, which testifies to her powerlessness to seduce.

In so doing, Ḥamīda rearrogates for herself the role of the seducer and co-opts the pointer of Faraj's department of English, reversing its aim so that it points a finger at headmaster Faraj himself. Her ruse is effective: 'Abbās vows to kill Faraj. Yet events take an unexpected turn when he proceeds too early on the appointed day to the site of the planned duel—the tavern where "Tītī" works. There he spots Ḥamīda in her colonial translation as "Tītī," on the lap of a British soldier, and forgets that "he had any enemy other than her."[107] Crying her name a second time, "Hamida . . . ," he hurls a beer bottle in her face. For this time he effectively recognizes "Ḥamīda" *as* "Tītī." No faint trace of a Ḥamīda who is *not* Tītī peeks from the translation, calling for his heart's interpretation. Seeing Ḥamīda virtually coupled with the British john in whose lap she sits, 'Abbās is no longer content to pierce "Tītī" with a cry. He must physically shatter her made-up mime. His enmity deflected from Faraj to Ḥamīda, 'Abbās no longer avenges his former love, nor the stolen Egypt for which she stands. Suddenly, and strangely, we find the *British* avenging her: mad for "Tītī"—the English "property" their pimp, Faraj, has created—they beat 'Abbās to death.[108] "Tītī" has not quite punished Faraj, but she has, indirectly, killed his power by turning her translation to advantage and thus controlling the British, Faraj's financiers. She even survives the violence that 'Abbās inflicts on her; in the postmurder alley gossip, we overhear the news that the police have taken "the whore off for first-aid treatment."[109] If Ḥamīda's—hence Egypt's—erotic "power" over the British soldiers is such that she can motivate them to kill *for* her, then who is really the colonizer, who the colonized?

While Maḥfūẓ's "England" may think it controls Egypt by translating its bodies and words to satisfy British desires, the Egyptian prostitute in the end exploits the colonizer's cravings by retranslating herself, across the copula, into a seductive power. The novel draws to a close with Shaykh Darwīsh's oracular reminder that all things, including colonial domination, have their end: "[E]verything," he cries, "comes to its *nihaya.*"[110] The British colonial presence may have claimed Ḥamīda and killed 'Abbās, but it too, Darwīsh predicts, will die. This end returns us to Durrell's *Mountolive*; specifically, to the scene in which the former lovers Mountolive and Leila—after years of separation—reunite in an Alexandria taxi in a moment of vexed recognition, strangely reminiscent of 'Abbās's encounter with Ḥamīda-Tītī in the streets of Cairo. Though this meeting, unlike 'Abbās's sighting of Ḥamīda, is planned, the dynamics of the "almost-postcolonial, but not quite" that it inaugurates are no less unsettling:

> Mountolive turned to gaze at the woman beside him. He could very dimly recognize her. He saw a plump and square-faced Egyptian lady of uncertain years. . . . *He did not recognize her at all!* "Leila!" he cried (it was almost a groan) pretending at last to identify and welcome the image of his lover (now dissolved or shattered forever) in this pitiable grotesque . . . [111]

Like 'Abbās, whose eyes do not really recognize Ḥamīda but whose heart detects the wisp of "Ḥamīda-ness" within her colonial "Tītī"—the faint trace of her nonequivalence to the colonizer into which she has otherwise painstakingly translated herself, beyond recognition—

Mountolive struggles to feel out "Leila" with his antennae, hovering on the cusp of recognition and nonrecognition. He knows well, from letters that he and Leila have exchanged over the years, that his long-ago lover cannot possibly look as she once did: cruelly disfigured by smallpox in her prime, she had taken to wearing black veils. Yet Mountolive is oddly shocked to see that Leila has exchanged the British jodhpurs and silk scarf in which she first seduced him for the black dress of the Egyptian peasant, and the small white hands of her heyday for the "chubby and unkempt little hand" that now presses his own.[112] He once had met the unreality of Leila's Ruskinian vision of a still-glorious British Empire with pity and anguish. Now he seems to prefer a Leila "coupled" to a painted image of England, however false, to the unpalatably Egyptian figure she cuts in old age. Her translation into even a prostitution of England, as youthful "mistress of half the earth," is preferable to her almost-postcolonial reconstitution as "an old Arab lady" at this historical moment of Egyptian decolonization. Leila's mingled (largely "Arab," tinged with French) odors of "orange-water, mint, Eau de Cologne, and sesame" repel Mountolive; what saves her is the "dull taint of whisky"—the faint trace of British colonial presence, of the "old" Europhile Leila—that elicits his identification and a flicker of sympathy. This new Leila he barely understands, straining "with all the attention one gives to an unfamiliar language": to an English that no longer strikes the high-empire chords of Ruskin's lecture.[113]

Yet in the very Arabness that Mountolive's imperial aesthetics only sees as "coarse," Leila atones for her earlier prostitutions of self and nation by resuming the role of "a plump and square-faced Egyptian lady of uncertain years." If she is unrecognizable, she is so only because Mountolive does not *wish* to recognize her: to do so would be to acknowledge that the British Empire is truly dead. Rather, he prefers to toe the anxious line that makes him wonder where his colonizing self begins and her colonized Otherness ends, so long as that line points in the direction of Englishness, translating Leila almost beyond recognition as Egyptian. To reverse the vector, to accept a Leila translated almost beyond recognition as *English*, would be to confront the real possibility of his defeat: to confront the suspicion that he and his England might now occupy the position of the once-colonized Egyptian. The prospect worries him. "What might she see upon his face—traces of the feebleness which had overrun his youthful strength and purpose?" he muses. " . . . He eyed her mournfully, with a pitiful eagerness to see whether she indeed really recognized him."[114] Yet Leila has not given up her "painted image of England" after all: "'You have not changed by a day' said this unknown woman with the disagreeable perfume. 'My beloved, my darling, my angel.'"[115] Strangely, she insists on recognizing Mountolive, aging servant of a dying empire, in the unchanged glory of his imperial youth: still her love object. As "Egyptian" or "Arab" as Leila now might be, Ruskin may reoccupy her yet.

That possibility of reoccupation explains why Maḥfūẓ, after intimating imperialism's demise through the voice of Shaykh Darwīsh, feels the necessity of ending *Zuqāq* in English. Why end, otherwise, with the English translation of Arabic's *nihāya*, with Darwīsh spelling an English *end*? Perhaps Maḥfūẓ, writing about 1940s Egypt at the end of World War II—at a time when Egypt is yet to win its definitive independence from Britain—recognizes the precarious status of anticolonial resistance in the face of a colonial power still so stubbornly entrenched. Yet, as much a political as a literary realist, Maḥfūẓ also prophesies with uncanny clarity the persistence of postindependence neocolonialisms and attachments to the former colonizer: a specter that lurks in the figure of Faraj Ibrāhīm, who, after all, still lives at the novel's end, unconquered. To close with English is, perhaps, to temper an affirmation of the subversive power of Egyptian translation, embodied in the character of Ḥamīda, with a suggestion that English may not end, but endure. Maḥfūẓ's *Zuqāq*, then, ultimately stages the British colonization of Egypt as a prostitution and "copulation" of language and identity doomed to repetition after decolonization. Trained (linguistically and sexually) to prostitute herself to English arms, Ḥamīda in the end inspires her Anglo johns to kill *for* her. And her victim is the Egyptian ex-fiancé who hopes to reclaim her *from* prostitution: Ḥamīda supersedes her colonizer only to murder the dream of any possible return to a precolonial sense of "nation." Prostitution becomes the only possible postcolonial relation of the self to itself and of the self to its former colonial Other. On the political horizon Maḥfūẓ can see, Egypt's translation, or conversion, may be irreversible: there may be no real *nihāya*, only an *end*.

CODA

History, Affect, and the Problem of the Universal

I return to Najīb Maḥfūẓ on the relationship of modern Egyptian letters to the West: "Yes, we know Western literature here. In fact, we love it too much."[1] How do we read Maḥfūẓ's assertion? Certainly as confession: we love Western literature passionately; we have surrendered ourselves to its charms. Surely too as indictment: we love Western literature to *excess*, to a fault, more than we should—because it has come to us with the West's "civilizing mission," and that mission has led us to imagine it greater than our own. And perhaps also as testimony to the notion that the postcolony is pre-occupied and thus easily re-occupied by the legacies of colonial history: here the "too much" is the spillage of the colonial-era seduction of Egyptians by Western literature into postindependence cultural consciousness.

This book has set out to answer the question that such a declaration of love begs: why cultural imperialism—as it materializes in the colonizer's "literature"—captivates those it targets, why it does so through translation, why its effects outlive decolonization. If cultural imperialism works, as I have argued, through a translational seduction that lures the colonized into seeing not just their selves but their *best* selves in their colonizers, the upshot of that seduction is a love-of-self-through-the-Other that appears to usurp seduction's very powers. If seduction exerts dominion by turning "equality" to excess, by insinuating the greater-than through the illusion of the equal, its outcome—love—is also always "too much," for it too implies a *dissymmetry* that friendship, for instance, masks. Insisting that the "relationship of domination is asymmetrical"—while reversible, "it can never become reciprocal or equal"— Jessica Benjamin asks, "The relationship of domination is fueled by the same desire for recognition that we find in love—but why does it take this form?"[2] She describes domination (and its corollary, love) in terms not unlike those Jean Baudrillard uses to describe seduction—the reversibility of signs—yet notes that reversibility does not automatically imply a relation of reciprocity, of equal exchange.

For Jacques Derrida, in turn, enmity, friendship, and love contaminate one another: "the enemy," he says, shadows "the friend, the friend, the enemy," and the "two concepts (friend/enemy) consequently intersect and ceaselessly change places," such that "they intertwine, as though they *loved* each other, all along a spiralled hyperbole."[3] In Derrida's double helix of friendship and enmity, love initially appears to be the copula (the messenger RNA?) that translates polarities into metonyms, such that they both haunt one another as parts ("intersect") and eclipse one another as wholes ("change places"): a model that easily could describe the dialectic of self-consciousnesses, Egyptian and French, in Ḥasan al-ʿAṭṭār's *maqāma*—save for the fact that only one party, the "enemy" masquerading as "friend," seems to command the *real* power to haunt and eclipse, to mimic. As if realizing, then, that the concept of the enemy can only "love" that of the friend when a "friend" stands in dissymmetry to the befriended, Derrida decides that he must differentiate love from friendship even while acknowledging the interpenetration of the two: friendship, he argues, "engages translation in the untranslatable" and "supposes a force of the improbable: the *phenomenon* of an appeased symmetry, equality, reciprocity between two infinite disproportions," while love "would raise or rend the veil of this phenomenon . . . to uncover the disproportion and dissymmetry as such."[4] Friendship thus recalls the ecliptic play of appearance/disappearance that Baudrillard associates with seduction: it is the *phenomenon* (appearance) that masks, or eclipses, the inequality between two disproportions, making inequality appear to disappear. Love reveals the inequality so appeased: because it must name its object, it is deictic and thus *directional*, not reciprocal. Echoing Jessica Benjamin, Derrida insists that the locution "'I love you' . . . must remain unilateral and dissymmetrical."[5] "When one names the friend or the enemy," he claims, "a reciprocity is supposed, even if it does not efface the infinite distance and dissymmetry. As soon as one speaks of love, the situation is no longer the same."[6] In the end, it is a copula of *friendship* in Derrida, not love, that makes the concepts "friend" and "enemy" appear deceptively "equal," while love becomes the slash that trumps that equivalence and exposes the ghost of the not-equal that haunts it. What the Derridean distinction *friendship/love* holds apart, the Baudrillardian "feminine"—the oscillatory principle of seduction—conjoins. Its operator is an equal sign that doubles as the slash of the not-equal.

To describe the Egyptian intellectual's relationship to Western literature as *love*, then, may be to admit its birth under the sign of domination and its survival within a regime of political inequality. It is Maḥfūẓ's avowal that Egypt is "in love" with the former colonizer's culture—an avowal of civilizational disproportion—that permits him to see the "too-muchness" inherent in that love: its disproportionate investment in traditions not its own, even inimical in some respects to its own. Yet Maḥfūẓ was not the first to recognize in love—and in the 150-year history of translation that subtends it—both a denial and an index of the historical and political inequality that governs modern Arabic literature's engagements with the West. That recognition, I argue, haunts a 1929 exchange between two of the most important Egyptian intellectuals of the early to mid-twentieth century: ʿAbbās Maḥmūd al-ʿAqqād (1889–1964) and Ṭāhā Ḥusayn (1889–1973).[7] The exchange unfolds across six essays (four by al-ʿAqqād, two by Ḥusayn) published between 9 September and 21 October 1929 in the Cairo weekly *al-Jadīd* (the New). Taken together, the essays probe the psychopolitical motivations of translation: its relationships to war and to love. I choose to conclude this book with an analysis of the ʿAqqād-Ḥusayn exchange because it so powerfully—if indirectly—engages two questions that bear on the seductions of translation in Egypt: First, between the conqueror and the conquered, who translates whom more, and why? Second, is cross-cultural translation motivated by love or by enmity? In this debate, Ḥusayn would espouse a love understood as equality: a universal humanism. By contrast, al-ʿAqqād (prefiguring Derrida) would expose the inequality inherent in loving. Pronouncing love and enmity two sides of a single coin, he critiques the "love-logic" of translation and of the forms of cross-cultural knowledge it engenders. Both al-ʿAqqād and Ḥusayn displace their engagements of translation-as-love-and-war to Western Europe during World War I or to Greek, Roman, Arab, and Persian antiquity. Yet both, I would argue, are preoccupied with the uneasy nexus of translation, empire, and the emerging nation in modern Egypt and thus with Egypt's problematic relation to Europe. That Egypt is barely visible in their debates—that the near is rarely near—is telling. And it tells us precisely where, for two Egyptian thinkers living in the shadow of empire, the greatest malaise of translation might lie.

In the first of these essays, "Ta'āruf al-Shu'ūb" (The Mutual Knowledge of Peoples), al-'Aqqād notes that World War I had sparked an increase in English translations from German and an even greater increase in German translations from English. He ascribes this phenomenon to the struggle for dominance in war, where "human nature" suggests that each party will seek "knowledge of the affairs of his rival."[8] Still, he maintains, "the defeated is fiercer in his concern . . . to probe the causes [that underlie] the power that has won victory over him."[9] In al-'Aqqād's historicized vision of "human nature," the psychodynamics that motivate translation themselves are produced *by* history. These psychodynamics explain why translations from English after World War I outnumber those from German, for nations that do not know the certainty of victory "do not feel the peace of mind of the victor, and they remain in the state of anxiety and wariness that pervades the defeated who struggles to cure himself of the condition of defeat."[10] Thus a political anxiety drives the translation disparity between victors and the vanquished, inclining the latter to know and to supersede their enemy. No better point of departure than this for an analysis of the colonial psychology that had seduced generations of Egyptian intellectuals, from al-'Aṭṭār to Salāma Mūsā, into inclining Egypt toward the West.

If al-'Aqqād argues that the defeated translate the conqueror's texts to better understand their defeat, he also suggests that the seduction of translation lies in the unsettled—and unsettling—promise of seeing oneself sovereign. For the assimilation of the would-be dominator's language into likeness with one's own appears to restore the subaltern language to primacy, to rewrite the "target"—linguistic and military—as "source," as original. This wavering, mirage-like copula of translation is akin to the "neurotic *and*" of comparison that Rey Chow has attributed to "post-European" cultures in their encounters with the hegemonic modern West.[11] Yet al-'Aqqād refuses to restrict the operation of the "neurotic *and*" to the dominated non-Western. He refers its neurosis, rather, to the logic of empire—and especially to the imperial logic of the sovereign nation—as these act both on the strong and on the weak. Certainly, in his schema, the defeated translate to "cure [themselves] of the condition of defeat." Yet so too do major world powers that fear defeat: recognized European nations like Germany and France, which furiously translate one another's texts—and Britain's also—because they sense the fragility of the sovereign, its contingency on supremacy. If such nations translate, how much more so those peoples who remain unsure of their capacity to press their sovereign claims to independence and to supremacy—those suffering ambiguous colonization and ambiguous autonomy, for whom (to reprise the words of Muḥammad al-Sibāʿī) the second *d* of *su'dud* remains suspended in darkness? Indeed, despite his references to anxiety, al-ʿAqqād may not imagine the drive to translate as a "neurosis" at all. Better to call it intoxication: "*tukhāmiru*" ("pervades"), the verb he chooses to describe the way in which anxiety enters the psyche of the defeated and motivates translation, derives from the same root as Arabic *khamr* (liquor). It is thus in a hallucinogenic state that the defeated—or those threatened with defeat—apprehend their "inclinations" toward the knowledge of the victor and their "objectives" in its pursuit. Through the knowledge they gain in translation, the defeated envision themselves empowered (or at least drinking as equal partners from the common "spirit" of the universal), but their pursuit of that knowledge inclines—indeed redirects—them toward the colonizer's objectives. We have come full circle to what al-ʿAṭṭār called "*nashwatu al-adabi,*" the "intoxication of literature."

Although modern Egypt's investment in translation begins in the Mehmed Ali period for precisely the reason al-ʿAqqād suggests—to uncover and recoup the forces that had enabled the French occupation some years earlier—and climaxes in post-1919 efforts to conjure the sovereign Egyptian nation from the British quasi-colony, al-ʿAqqād's analysis elides Egypt. Yet indirectly he diagnoses the logic under which Egypt translates: its tendency to disavow the colonial inequalities that condition its acts of translation and knowledge seeking and to sublimate those acts in the idiom of the universal human—of unconditional love. While al-ʿAṭṭār, Rifāʿa Rāfiʿ al-Ṭahṭāwī, ʿAlī Mubārak, al-Sibāʿī, and Mūsā all place translation under the sign of love, presuming the possibility of transcendental equivalence between the Egyptian and the European and arguing the translatability of the two on that basis, al-ʿAqqād critiques the love-logic of translation and of the universalism that subtends it. To say that knowledge is both the "daughter of enmity" and the "daughter of love," he maintains, is to stake a position "neither contradictory nor divergent."[12] While "the path to love or the path to knowledge . . . appears to us as contradiction in its outward aspect," he writes,

> in its inner aspect it is free of contradiction.
>
> By enmity you sound the power of your Other that turns on selfishness . . .

> And by love you sound the compassionate power of your Other. . . . And both of these probes are essential for the knowledge of one human being by another.[13]

For al-'Aqqād, then, both love and enmity are instruments of measure; he describes the action one undertakes with each with the verb *yasburu*, "to measure, probe, or sound," as when one sounds the depths of a sea to take their measure, and ultimately he calls both affects *misbārayn*, like the probes or echo sounders used to measure water depths. Where al-Ṭahṭāwī chooses to hear only unconflicted "love" between languages—the exchangeability of French and Arabic in the depths of the figurative sea of language that divides, like the physical Mediterranean, Alexandria from Marseilles—al-'Aqqād implicitly calls on his reader to test the waters between Egypt and Europe, to sound them and to listen carefully to the echo they return. Rather than assume the "equivalence" of one's Other to oneself, he suggests, one should measure the proximity or the distance, the altruism or the egoism, that one's Other bears to oneself. While he concedes, then, that all human knowledge is "a mixture of caution and love," it is enmity, not love, that seems more likely to take accurate measure of the Other.[14]

Al-'Aqqād ultimately argues that while love may be the elusive aim of both intercultural translation and knowledge, it cannot be their point of departure. To assume love at the start is to suspend ethical and political judgment; "mutual affection" must originate in "conflict," conflict *precede* love *("al-khilāfu fal-tafāhumu fal-ta'ālufu").*[15] He insists "that love is a great blessing for he who bestows it *if he deserves to bestow it,* and for he who receives it *if he deserves to receive it.*"[16] Only at "the end of the road," when peoples attain "perfect knowledge" of one another, will "the objects of love . . . be distinguished," such that one will know "where it ought to be and where it ought not to be."[17] For al-'Aqqād, then, love is *conditional* both in its extension and in its reception; as a road to cross-cultural knowledge—hence also as an engine of translation—enmity has the upper hand. He tacitly equates knowledge with enmity: notice, earlier, that he opposes the path of "love" to that of "knowledge," substituting the latter for "enmity." By arguing that the paths of love and of enmity/knowledge diverge outwardly but converge inwardly, al-'Aqqād intimates that a love complicated by historicity—not immediately referred to the transcendental human but read in the conditional tense—might look "like" enmity/knowledge. A love that exposes the dissymmetry of human relations and the workings of domination in history—to recall the formulations of Derrida and of Jessica Benjamin—would submit the "universal" to a hermeneutics of suspicion, rephrasing it not as a priori fact but as a directed, and moving, tendency. Knowledge thus becomes a knowledge of to whom one should extend love and from whom one should receive it. A differential praxis of translation, then, best sounds the coercive power of one's Others and feels out their capacities *for* love.

In "Tarjama" (A Translation), the first of two rejoinders by that title, Ḥusayn rebuts al-ʿAqqād's attempts to rehistoricize and "psychoanalyze" the field of intercultural exchange. He divorces translation from nearly all geopolitical motive.[18] Where translation in al-ʿAqqād's essay launches a broader meditation on the conditions of knowledge, translation in Ḥusayn's rejoinder takes theoretical center stage. He argues that "the question of translation and the associated phenomenon of intellectual and artistic rapprochement among peoples is . . . wider in scope" than al-ʿAqqād suggests.[19] By "wider" he means more extensive in time and in space—primordial and universal. For Ḥusayn, translation is cultural exchange at its purest, an elemental expression of human nature. His appeal to "human nature" differs, however, from al-ʿAqqād's. Al-ʿAqqād's reading of the operations of love, hate, and knowledge—hence also the motivations of translation—is historicophilosophical, both materialist and metaphysical. By contrast, the "human nature" that drives Ḥusayn's theory of translation is, like the "proto-Egyptian" Mūsā invokes to secure his theory of Egyptian-British equivalence, effectively prehistorical. According to Ḥusayn, the "true explanation for every translation . . . is human nature, which makes of the human a social animal, as Aristotle says in his *Politics*, and a thinking animal, as Aristotle says in his *Logic*."[20] Although Ḥusayn ultimately will premise translation on the perception and fulfillment of social and epistemological "need," he refuses the historicity of al-ʿAqqād's explanation, referring sociality and knowledge to the biological drives of the human animal.

Thus, while Ḥusayn attacks al-ʿAqqād for too philosophical and too literary an approach to the psychology of translation, insisting that the problem demands rational historical analysis, he invokes history only to deny its impact. "It has not been established," writes Ḥusayn, " . . . that the defeated produce more scientific and literary translations than the victorious; one might say, in fact, that the opposite is true in every way. Thus the victorious translate everything from the defeated . . . , and the defeated translate nothing from the victorious."[21] While al-ʿAqqād interprets the translation drive from the standpoint of the dominated, suggesting that geopolitical inequality engenders a perceived "lack" in the vanquished and thus a perceived "need"—even desire—for self-empowerment through the culture of the dominator, Ḥusayn decouples such need from disempowerment. It is because cultural life was so weak among both the conquering Romans and Arabs, he contends, and their need to "complete" and to "strengthen" their cultures so great, that they translated from the conquered Greeks (in the case of the Romans) and from the conquered Greeks and Persians (in the case of the Arabs). The Greeks and Persians, though defeated, translated nothing.[22] To prove that translation has little to do with power, Ḥusayn turns to European Renaissance translations of the intellectual legacies of ancient Greece and Rome—surely not the result of conquest. "When Europeans discovered the sciences, literatures, and arts of the ancients," he writes, "they sensed their social and intellectual need to 'copy' these," catalyzing "the modern renaissance."[23] Ḥusayn rightly notes that cultural power is not always commensurate with geopolitical dominance, pointing to historical instances in which the colonizer "needed" the culture of the colonized more than the latter did that of the former—and to those in which translation did not issue from conquest at all. Nonetheless, his posture depoliticizes and dehistoricizes the act of translation. Even when he intimates that modernization drives translation—as humans often translate what others innovate (*"yastaḥdithūna"*; lit., "modernize, make new")—he abstracts the will to modernity from empire. Where humans discern a need for the cultural capital of others, he suggests, they will translate, regardless of the geopolitical positions that they (or others) might occupy. Moreover, the status of translation in modernity differs little from that in antiquity. "Social and intellectual need," writes Ḥusayn, "drives translation today, just as it [did] in the ancient and middle ages."[24]

Thus intent on dissociating translation from modern empire, Ḥusayn ultimately posits a counterfactual comparison between the translational activity of the expansionist West and that of the dominated East. Against the evidence of (post)colonial Egypt's hot pursuit—in translation—of Western literature and thought, he maintains that the modern West "needs" and translates the East more than the latter does the former. "It is not possible," he writes,

> for a nation *[umma]* to live alone; thus it is compelled to associate with other nations and to translate from them. Inasmuch as a nation feels this social need, so its share of translation from other nations, and for this reason the English, French, and Germans do not simply translate from one another,

> but translate from the Arabs, Persians, Turks, Russians, and Chinese. Thus the West's share in translation is greater than the East's, because the West's sense of social need today is more acute than the East's.[25]

Ḥusayn goes on to say the same of intellectual need. These assertions press his point that power geopolitical and power cultural are inversely proportional, for here again the dominant alone translate, and the dominated little or not at all. Yet Ḥusayn's abstraction of culture from imperialism—which allows him to impute the victorious West's purportedly avid interest in translation to a depoliticized cultural "need" for the East, on the one hand, and to impute the defeated East's purported disinterest in translation to a depoliticized cultural "claim" over the West, on the other—skirts what is obvious to any reader of nineteenth- and early-twentieth-century history. Like Ḥusayn's native Egypt, virtually all of the Easts he names are under Western hegemony, if not colonial rule, in 1929. Contra Ḥusayn, I would suggest that an acutely political sense of social and intellectual need drove nearly every Eastern people within the orbit of empire—from the Arabs to the Chinese—to translate the texts of the triumphant West. European knowledge production about the East, in turn, served not simply needs social or intellectual, but political: the imperatives of colonial power. By tendentiously defining translation as a politically neutral response to equally neutral social and intellectual need, Ḥusayn can disavow the fact that Western translations of Eastern texts owe their impulse not necessarily to Eastern cultural power but to Western dominance. If anything, such translations create the *illusion* of Eastern power over the West.

Yet Ḥusayn's attempt to decouple translation from power ultimately consumes itself. In the didactic undercurrent of this essay, social and intellectual need and their avatar, translation, are indices of civilizational "advancement" and geopolitical dominion. Interest in translation is the mark of the victor, here the West. To lack a healthy translation drive—as the East supposedly does—is to inhabit the condition of the defeated, to invite regression and thus domination. The East therefore stands accused of an *insufficient sense of its need for Europe.* Underlying Ḥusayn's overt (and apparently apolitical) theses on translation, then, is a tacit prescription to the dominated peoples of the East—Egyptians included—to inhabit other (usually Western) tongues. Translation, he maintains, "is [one] tool for . . . intellectual connection" and production.[26] Yet dependence on translation, he adds, must progress to foreign-language acquisition, for "whoever learns a foreign language translates for himself what the translators could not translate for him."[27]

Indeed, many of the recommendations for Egyptian culture and education that Ḥusayn would articulate in later writings find prior expression in this essay on translation, where Egypt appears nowhere but is in fact everywhere.[28] By "foreign" languages, I would suggest, Ḥusayn means Western languages, ancient and modern, and the learner he has in mind is Egyptian. For the "development" of Egyptian culture through the infusion of Western languages was a leitmotif in his life's work. As minister of culture in the last Wafdist cabinet (1950–52), Ḥusayn would try—unsuccessfully—to introduce Greek and Latin into the Egyptian curriculum, along with Arabic, as foundational languages. Already, in the second of his two rejoinders to al-ʿAqqād—titled "Tarjama" (A Translation) like the first—he explicitly identifies Egypt as the target of his earlier reflections on translation.[29] Arguing that of the many "fertile, productive dimensions of intellectual and human life, Egypt is utterly ignorant," Ḥusayn pronounces a systematic program of translation necessary to the nation's awakening.[30] Comparing, in tones reminiscent of al-Sibāʿī, a tacitly dead Egypt to the "living nations" of Europe—where many are said to command foreign languages and those who do not can avail themselves easily of translations—he writes, "If translation is a tool for the advancement of living nations and for their approximation to the ideal, it is—with respect to us—a tool for life [itself], not for refinement."[31] Large-scale foreign-language acquisition would be a more powerful tool for such renewed "life," although he acknowledges its relative inaccessibility to the masses.

In Ḥusayn's conception, then, foreign-language acquisition is absolute translation. By learning French or English and actively translating those languages into Arabic, as opposed to passively reading French or English in Arabic translation, the ideal Egyptian would become a translated being, become—almost in the sense that Mūsā wished—"French" or "English" and thus elevated to the imperial European. Between Ḥusayn's lines, which prefigure those of the United Nations Development Programme's *Arab Human Development Report 2003*, Egypt stands accused of indifference to foreign texts and tongues: too weak a drive toward translation, partial or absolute.[32] Against this charge stands the inconvenient fact that Egyptian intellectuals had been translating European literature, history, and thought since the early nineteenth century, so avidly that by 1930 at least one Egyptian literary circle—Jamāʿat al-Adab al-Qawmī (Society for National Literature)—

called for a moratorium on translation, arguing that Egyptian imitation had forestalled the evolution of an "original" national literature. Its manifesto of 28 June 1930 argued that Egypt's translational literature was nothing but a "mirror" returning a distorted reflection of Europe.[33]

In two rejoinders of his own titled "al-Tarjama wa Ta'āruf al-Shu'ūb" (Translation and the Mutual Knowledge of Peoples), al-'Aqqād rejects Ḥusayn's near-total identification of the translation drive with the dominator and persistent abstraction of that drive from the sphere of competition.[34] One cannot, he contends, explain the dynamics of translation between two cultures "by the desire for knowledge that Aristotle mentioned alone, without associating with it *[dūna an taqtarina bihā]* . . . the mutual quest for dominance between the two."[35] It is in geopolitical conflict that the desire to know becomes most urgent, for in such conflict desire is "conjoined to competition" *("iqtaranat bi al-tanāfusi").*[36] As competition involves the will to power (and knowledge) of at least two historical actors, so too must translation be more than a one-way, victors-only street: "exchange," he writes, "presupposes the existence of knowledge and intellectual life in *both* parties."[37] Finally, al-'Aqqād maintains that we misunderstand modern translation if we fail to recognize its difference from past formations. Translational activity in antiquity, he argues, cannot be compared to modern translation, for in the past "culture was not global."[38] What makes modern translation "modern" is its logic of exchange, which unfolds within a globality premised on an equally modern politics of national difference. In the past, he writes, "national sentiment often disappeared in the folds of religion"; when the conquered came to share a religion with their conquerors, as in Christendom and Islam, religious unity gradually erased the racial boundaries between them.[39] Domination in antiquity meant total mastery, hence either total dissociation of the conquered from their conquerors or total assimilation of the two. Thus translation disappears. By contrast, modern European peoples enter into translation—as in the English-French-German exchanges of World War I—because each "has a culture steeped in its own color and . . . the characteristics of its nation."[40] Implied is the paradox that the logic of exchange that governs modern translation presupposes the boundaries of the (secular) nation-state. Implied, too, is a corollary thesis: that translation depends on partial conquest—at once distance and assimilation—and thus on the slashed equality of seduction. Against those who see in translation testimony to human equality, then, al-'Aqqād reminds us that one cannot translate sameness—only partial difference.

To prove his point, al-ʿAqqād displaces the problems of history, affect, and the universal in translation to a new chronotope. In his second rebuttal to Ḥusayn, he writes of an experience of *déjà lu*, of reading a Japanese tale and sensing, strangely, that he had read it before. This story involves a girl of extraordinary beauty, raised in poverty by her stepfather, who forestalls the proposals of her many suitors by demanding ever more jewels.[41] Reading a text that bears an ineffable resemblance to one encountered before, al-ʿAqqād suggests, engenders a sensation of half-recognition. Such an experience, he says, is like an encounter with a face that one has seen before yet cannot place, only to slowly recall its features and marvel that one ever forgot it at all, given how "near, near" *("qarībun qarībun")* it was. Literature "translates" to the extent that it is half-recognizable, then fully recognized—universalized. Thus al-ʿAqqād gradually recognizes the Japanese story. Briefly he concedes—then dismisses—the possibility that he once had read a story like it. No, the connection is deeper, more primordial. Asks al-ʿAqqād, "Where had I heard [this] story—or what resembles it—and when did my hearing of it, which preceded all reading and all hearing, occur?"[42] He realizes that the Japanese tale is strangely familiar because very close to home: as a child he had heard its "equivalent" from an old female relation in his native Aswan. "From Japan to Aswan!" he marvels. "How short the distance between human beings and human beings, and how wondrous the translation of ideas and stories from East Asia to the farthest reaches of Upper Egypt in the African continent!!"[43]

Thus al-ʿAqqād initially locates his reception of the "translatable" text not in time but *beyond* time: not only has he heard it—"read" it, if we accept Derrida's contention that writing is intrinsic to speech—before all reading, but he has "heard" it before all hearing, as if in the womb, perhaps even before his conception. He goes on to hypostasize this abstract epiphany of the fundamental likeness of peoples, ideas, and texts in the concrete fantasy of a group of Japanese youths listening to the "same" story at the very moment that he and other Egyptian youths heard it from their foremothers. Further, al-ʿAqqād's rhetoric itself approximates proximity. His locution *"bayna al-nāsi wa al-nāsi"* ("between human beings and human beings") repeats the word *al-nās*, "human beings." This strategy of repetition and nondifferentiation reinforces the notion that the world is one and that its storytellers, audiences, languages, and texts are interchangeable—and it echoes the rhetorical effect of his earlier locution *"qarībun qarībun,"* where the foreign is made "familiar, familiar" or the faraway brought "near, near." Repetition makes the foreign and the faraway more palpable, rhetorically edging them just within reach. So "imagination," writes al-'Aqqād, "brings Japan and Egypt together in the age of childhood before knowledge . . . or history draws the two near."[44] The world precedes its knowledge; if the human is born in innocence *(mawlūd 'alā al-fiṭra),* as Islamic doctrine maintains, so too does the notion of humanity come of age in innocence, in childhood—as inborn instinct rather than learned construct.

Yet this is a slippery text. It begins by flirting with the possibility of a shared human nature that underwrites all texts and makes all languages, stories, and histories exchangeable. Then it retracts that possibility. Witness al-'Aqqād's answer to the question he twice poses himself: "How did this close resemblance between the stories of Japan and the stories of Upper Egypt come to pass?"[45]

> I do not think it a coincidence of ideas, involving no connection between the two sources; rather, I think it most likely that the Turks . . . transmitted these stories from the farthest East of Asia to the deepest reaches of Upper Egypt, for we know of no town in Upper Egypt . . . whose houses do not include a Turkish mother or grandmother or paternal aunt who tells her children such stories, which she [in turn] inherited from mothers and grandmothers. . . . And how did the Turks come by these stories from East Asia? . . . [T]he relationship here is obvious: because the mixing of the Turks, China, and Japan is age-old in the Asian lands, and it is beyond dispute that Japan borrowed from central Asia, and that [central] Asians borrowed from the people of Japan.[46]

Here, similarity (equivalence) and transmission (translation) no longer are mystical quantities, nor are they simply linked to inborn human nature. Rather, they are historical. To find their roots, we must travel their routes: retrace stories through generations of oral transmission by Ottoman Turkish women in Upper Egypt—where empire penetrates the inner sanctum of home and childhood, historicizing the mother figure herself—then through the ancient contact of the Turks across central Asia with Japan. The argument, however, folds on itself again: having said all this, al-'Aqqād assumes the guise of the penitent, one who has focused too much on human differences and now wishes to resurrect the "oneness" of human nature. "Truly spoke he who said that human nature is one in every place," he declares.[47] Yet what does he mean by "human nature"? We might imagine that he has capitulated to Ḥusayn's universal, believing that translation reflects the innate predisposition of all human beings to think and feel "alike" and thus their inherent amenability to exchange. Yet al-'Aqqād's is not a human nature whose universality issues only from the divine zone of *fiṭra* but one whose universality has been created *in* history and *in* story. A "secular" universal, but also a "religious" one. Here, I emphasize, al-'Aqqād is not so much parting ways with a Qur'ānic conception of intercultural knowledge as he is unmasking the duality of that conception within the Qur'ān itself: *al-fiṭra*, inborn human nature—the universal—is both held in advance, a priori, at the moment of a human being's creation, and unfolded in history as peoples come to know one another. The very title of this rebuttal, "al-Tarjama wa Ta'āruf al-Shu'ūb," echoes the Qur'ān: "O humankind! We have created you from male and female and have made you into peoples and tribes that you may know one another *[li ta'ārafū]*" (Qur'ān 49:13). In this worldview "religious" and "secular" visions of the universal human occupy one continuum.

Still, al-'Aqqād can hypothesize "universal" human nature only when he abandons Egypt's colonial-national relation to the West for supra- or subnational relations between East and central Asia and between both Asias and Upper Egypt. By reconsidering the alignments of translation with war and with love on East/East and East/South fronts, he can block war and rethink translation in peacetime, assimilating Turkishness into Egypt (where shared religion trumps the historical fact of Ottoman empire) and Japan to Egypt (where a shared experience of extra-Europeanness replaces shared religion, occluding the possibility of Japanese dominion). War—geopolitical competition—alters the picture.

What al-'Aqqād suggests, then, is that the translational project of the universal human founders in the national world order that European colonialism has engendered, in Egypt as elsewhere. Better to keep your "love" your enemy: better to translate in a way that recognizes rather than mystifies the operations of modern power. He wishes only that translations might widen "the horizons of life" for their readers such that those readers apprehend both "endless types of living beings and warm relationships behind great difference," recognizing that "difference is more conducive to mutual forgiveness and mutual knowledge."[48] Indeed, he emphasizes, we must not marshal translation "to exchange natures and to erase . . . competition and struggle between people."[49] Against the dissolution in "love" of the difference that power makes—against the historical forgetting that drives the ongoing reproduction of the extra-European as Europe's "likeness"—al-'Aqqād calls us to reimagine the politics of translation as *conditional* love. We must, he suggests, allow the world's literatures to tell us when, whether, how, and how much they can or wish to "love" their Others.

Into the love-logic of translation, then, al-'Aqqād's thought enters as interruption—a phenomenon all the more intriguing when we recognize that he came to English through "love." Growing up under British rule in the Upper Egyptian city of Aswan, al-'Aqqād met an English tourist—a Muslim convert—who introduced him to English and gifted him two books: an English translation of the Qur'ān and Thomas Carlyle's *The French Revolution*.[50] Thus, in a pattern by now familiar, al-'Aqqād first experienced Englishness as his "likeness": in the person of an Englishman turned Muslim and in the form of an Arabic book—the holiest book of Islam—turned "English," he witnessed his colonizer's fantastic translation into a seeming "equivalent" of himself. J. Brugman believes it "significant that Carlyle was probably the first English author he read," since al-'Aqqād's later exposure to Carlyle's *On Heroes*—and there the encomium to the Prophet Muḥammad that so seduced his friend al-Sibā'ī—would inspire his later "series about the great men in Islam."[51] Deeply versed in British Romanticism—especially the writings of Carlyle, Samuel Taylor Coleridge, and William Hazlitt—as well as the German thought of Arthur Schopenhauer and Friedrich Nietzsche, which he likely read in English translation, al-'Aqqād clearly did not shun Western influence on Egyptian literature.[52] Indeed, he welcomed it. Yet he was, I argue, perhaps the first to historicize the assumption of "universal" literary translatability in which so many Egyptian intellectuals of his time trafficked. Certainly al-'Aqqād engages Ḥusayn's contention that literature's preoccupations are universal because humans everywhere hold much in common. Ultimately he decides, however, that "translatable" literatures likely owe their commonality to a shared *history* of transmission, thus predicating translatability on travel—physical translation—in time and in space. Rather than refer the "universal" of comparison to a common humanity, then, al-'Aqqād historicizes that universal's emergence. I link this intervention to his acute insistence that translation, comparison, and other modes of intercultural knowledge should proceed from enmity—a hermeneutics of suspicion—to love: his insistence that knowledge is the discernment of where and to what extent love ought and ought not to be directed. According al-'Aqqād a less complicated consciousness, Sayyid al-Baḥrāwī maintains that what he saw as the "advantageous impact" of British cultural imperialism on Egyptian letters, we regard as the "tragedy that befell his generation."[53] Certainly al-'Aqqād fell in love early with English literature, calling for the radical "modernization" of Arabic literature along Western lines. Yet to my mind he sensed—long before we did—the tragedy lurking in that gain.

Love has spoken with a double tongue throughout this book, and so too in these closing pages. At times I have used the term *love-logic* to denote surrender to an imperial universal, as in my discussion of Ḥusayn's view of translation. Elsewhere, however, I have written of love—specifically, of the will to imagine oneself sovereign by imagining oneself as having fallen into love with one's colonizer—as a contestation of empire and its seductions of translation. If, as I have maintained, such surrender and such resistance paradoxically often translate one another, how then to exit this tautology? What politics is possible for those who struggle, even today, to decolonize not only their lands but also their minds? Al-ʿAqqād's invitation to rethink the politics of translation as conditional love suggests one answer. *Conditional love* breaks the circuit in which the self routinely must constitute itself either as equal to or as greater than an Other—must constitute itself in the *I* of that Other. It neither substitutes a new asymmetry for an old nor appeases disproportion in the false symmetry of the universal human. Precisely because conditional love does not seek to install the colonized *I* as sovereign, it does not surrender that *I* to the sovereignty of an Other. Rather, such love—sifted through degrees of enmity—maintains the *I* always on the threshold of the Other, just resistant enough to be "itself" and just porous enough to invite its transformation.

My efforts in this book to reimagine cultural imperialism as a dynamic of translational seduction rather than unilateral imposition, then, in no way neutralize either the cultural or the corporeal violence that domination has visited upon the colonized. Both violences are very real, and both continue to haunt (post)colonial consciousness. Nor does the seduction of the colonized foreclose the possibility of resistance. Quite the contrary. Indeed, I argue, it is precisely by recognizing the seductive face of cultural imperialism that the (post)colonial subject might liberate herself or himself from the sort of colonialism that, in the words of anglophone Egyptian novelist Ahdaf Soueif, "no rebellion can mitigate and no treaty bring to an end."[54] That colonialism is the "too-much" with which the (post)colonial subject often remains in love today, hence also in struggle. To fall *out of* unconditional love and into critical engagement with the enduring legacies of cultural imperialism—as both Maḥfūẓ and Soueif intimate—both the (post)colonial subject and the (post)colony in general must see that they have *fallen into love* in the first place: not simply with the colonizer, but with the delusory "mirror image" of themselves that they have caught, and admired, in the gleam of the colonizer's *I*.

Notes

OVERTURE

The two statements quoted in the epigraph are from Gayatri Chakravorty Spivak, "The Politics of Translation," in *Outside in the Teaching Machine* (New York: Routledge, 1993), 179, 180.

1. See Abdelfattah Kilito, *Thou Shalt Not Speak My Language,* trans. and introd. Waïl S. Hassan (Syracuse, NY: Syracuse University Press, 2008), 4. The original is ʿAbd al-Fattāḥ Kīlīṭū, *Lan Tatakallama Lughatī* (Beirut: Dār al-Ṭalīʿa li al-Ṭibāʿa wa al-Nashr, 2002).

2. Kilito, *Thou Shalt Not Speak,* 4.

3. Ibid.

4. Ibid., 5.

5. Ibid.; Kīlīṭū, *Lan Tatakallama Lughatī,* 9.

6. See Walter Benjamin, "The Task of the Translator: An Introduction to the Translation of Baudelaire's *Tableaux parisiens*" (in German), in *Illuminations*, trans. Harry Zohn (New York: Schocken Books, 1969), 75.

7. See Homi K. Bhabha, "Of Mimicry and Man: The Ambivalence of Colonial Discourse," in *The Location of Culture* (London: Routledge, 1994), 85–92, esp. 86, 88, 91.

8. On the "transcendental signified," see Jacques Derrida, *Of Grammatology* (in French), trans. and pref. Gayatri Chakravorty Spivak, corrected ed. (Baltimore: Johns Hopkins University Press, 1998), 20, 49; on the "transcendental signifier," see 324n9; and Jacques Derrida, "Le Facteur de la vérité" (in French), in *The Post Card: From Socrates to Freud and Beyond*, trans. and introd. Alan Bass (Chicago: University of Chicago Press, 1987), 411–96, esp. 465–66. Critiquing the Lacanian phallus, Derrida dubs it a "transcendental signifier," a "'signifier of signifiers'" that "is therefore also the signified of all

signifieds, . . . sheltered within the indivisibility of the (graphic or oral) letter" (465), whose "indestructibility . . . has to do with its elevation toward the ideality of a meaning" (466). The unbroken Arabic word might be one such illusion.

9. For a critique of the "structural connivance" of postcolonial and poststructuralist theories of translation, see Sathya Rao, "From a Postcolonial to a Non-Colonial Theory of Translation," in *Translation, Biopolitics, Colonial Difference,* ed. Naoki Sakai and Jon Solomon (Hong Kong: Hong Kong University Press, 2006), 73–94, esp. 83–85.

10. Homi K. Bhabha, "Signs Taken for Wonders: Questions of Ambivalence and Authority under a Tree Outside Delhi, May 1817," in *The Location of Culture* (London: Routledge, 1994), 102–22; quotations from 121.

11. See Lisa Lowe, *Critical Terrains: French and British Orientalisms* (Ithaca, NY: Cornell University Press, 1991), 7; and Lydia H. Liu, *Translingual Practice: Literature, National Culture, and Translated Modernity—China, 1900–1937* (Stanford: Stanford University Press, 1995), 25.

12. Liu, *Translingual Practice*, 25.

13. See Lawrence Venuti, *The Scandals of Translation: Towards an Ethics of Difference* (London: Routledge, 1998), 179–86, esp. 184.

14. See Richard Jacquemond, "Translation and Cultural Hegemony: The Case of French-Arabic Translation," in *Rethinking Translation: Discourse, Subjectivity, Ideology,* ed. Lawrence Venuti (London: Routledge, 1992), 139–58, esp. 142. On early translations, see also Carol Bardenstein, *Translation and Transformation in Modern Arabic Literature: The Indigenous Assertions of Muḥammad 'Uthmān Jalāl* (Wiesbaden: Harrassowitz Verlag, 2005). Bardenstein highlights the asymmetrical power relations that subtend nineteenth-century Egyptian translations of French literature into Arabic. For this observation—as for the argument that such translations constitute not a blind Egyptian importation of French texts but an indigenizing, Arabizing, and possibly "resistant" transculturation thereof—her study is an important (and welcome) intervention. Yet in her desire to challenge the uncritical acceptance of European cultural dominance and equally uncritical erasure of European colonial power in mainstream modern Egyptian literary historiography, Bardenstein veers (like Jacquemond) too far in the direction of resistance.

15. See D. J. Taylor, "The Maestro of Middaq *[sic]* Alley," *Sunday Times* (London), 18 March 1990, H8–H9; quotation from H9.

16. See Rasheed El-Enany, *Naguib Mahfouz: The Pursuit of Meaning* (London: Routledge, 1993), 11–12, 42, 246–47n12. See also 18, where the mature Maḥfūẓ is said to have esteemed Leo Tolstoy, Marcel Proust, and Thomas Mann above all writers and to have described "Shakespeare, Kafka, O'Neill, Shaw, Ibsen, and Strindberg as writers 'whom he liked to the point of adoration.'"

17. Bashīr al-'Īsawī, *al-Tarjama ilā al-'Arabiyya: Qaḍāyā wa Ārā'* (Madīnat Naṣr [Cairo]: Dār al-Fikr al-'Arabī, 1996/A.H. 1417), 52.

18. See, e.g., Frantz Fanon, *Peau noire, masques blancs* (Paris: Éditions du Seuil, 1995 [1952]), 51, 179n9; Priya Joshi, *In Another Country: Colonialism, Culture, and the English Novel in India* (New York: Columbia University Press, 2002), 89–91; Christopher L. Miller, *Nationalists and Nomads: Essays on Francophone African Literature and Culture* (Chicago: University of Chica-

go Press, 1998), 56–62; and Gauri Viswanathan, *Masks of Conquest: Literary Study and British Rule in India* (Delhi: Oxford University Press, 1998 [1989]), 20–21, 166–67.

19. I use the term *(post)colonial* to designate both a coloniality that is perpetually interrupted—thus intermittent—and a coloniality that is both finished and unfinished. I concur with Anne McClintock and Ella Shohat, who warn us that the *post-* of *postcolonial* suggests that colonialism (and also, in Shohat's view, anticolonial nationalism) is past, that we have overcome it when in fact it remains very much with us. McClintock further observes that the "post-colonial" not only reinscribes the ideology of progress associated with the colonial but also assumes a uniformly global condition of postindependence. See Anne McClintock, "The Angel of Progress: Pitfalls of the Term 'Post-Colonialism,'" *Social Text,* nos. 31–32 (1992): 84–98; and Ella Shohat, "Notes on the 'Post-Colonial,'" in *Taboo Memories, Diasporic Voices* (Durham: Duke University Press, 2006), 233–49, esp. 236–41.

20. On the pitfalls of Said's Orientalism thesis, see Lowe, *Critical Terrains,* 8.

21. See Abdeslam M. Maghraoui, *Liberalism without Democracy: Nationhood and Citizenship in Egypt, 1922–1936* (Durham: Duke University Press, 2006), xv–xvii, 7–10, 42, 66; quotation from 66.

22. See Maghraoui, *Liberalism without Democracy,* xv–xvii, 3, 5, 36, 47.

23. Stephen Sheehi, *Foundations of Modern Arab Identity* (Gainesville: University Press of Florida, 2004), 35, 34. On translation and the Arab *nahḍa,* especially in Ottoman Syria, see also Laṭīf Zaytūnī, *Ḥarakat al-Tarjama fī 'Aṣr al-Nahḍa* (Beirut: Dār al-Nahār, 1994); and Ibrāhīm Maḥmūd, *al-Ḥanīn ilā al-Isti'mār: Qirā'āt fī Adabiyyāt 'Aṣr al-Nahḍa* (Damascus: Dār al-Yanābī', 2000). Zaytūnī (11–12) echoes al-Bustānī, locating the *nahḍa* in a long-historical cycle of alternating East-West need and exchange; Maḥmūd links the impulses of the *nahḍa* to the imperatives of colonialism.

24. See Thomas R. Trautmann, *Aryans and British India* (Berkeley: University of California Press, 1997; New Delhi: Yoda Press, 2004), 1–27, 62–98; on later Indophobia, see 99–130. Citations are to the 2004 edition.

25. Ibid., 15.

26. Ibid., 18.

27. See Trautmann, *Aryans and British India,* 219–21; quotation from 221. Trautmann relies here on Tapan Raychaudhuri, *Europe Reconsidered: Perceptions of the West in Nineteenth-Century Bengal,* 2nd ed. (New Delhi: Oxford University Press, 2002 [1988]).

28. See Leela Gandhi, *Affective Communities: Anticolonial Thought, Fin-de-Siècle Radicalism, and the Politics of Friendship* (Durham: Duke University Press, 2006).

29. Jean Baudrillard, *Seduction,* trans. Brian Singer (New York: St. Martin's Press, 1990), 22. The original is Jean Baudrillard, *De la séduction* (Paris: Éditions Galilée, 1979), 37. One might compare the Arabic term *fitna,* which conjoins the political to the sexual. While *fitna* connotes erotic seduction, in a specifically Islamic register it also refers to diversion from belief and to religio-political schism, to any ideological split that disrupts the unity of the community by leading it astray from right conduct.

30. On seduction as "war game," see Baudrillard, *Seduction,* 113.

31. See also Naoki Sakai, *Translation and Subjectivity: On "Japan" and Cultural Nationalism*, foreword Meaghan Morris (Minneapolis: University of Minnesota Press, 1997), 11–14. Sakai remarks the *"oscillation or indeterminacy of personality in translation,"* dubbing the translator *"a subject in transit"* (13–14; emphases in the original), as the translator's *I* doubles as that of the original addresser and the translator's *you*—the original addressee—as that of the audience the translator addresses.

32. In referring to the seducer as "she" and to the seduced as "he," I do not intend to correlate these subject positions to biological sex. Baudrillard associates seduction with the "feminine" and (despite problematic lapses into biologism) positions that "feminine" outside the conventional opposition masculine/feminine: beyond the very binary that underpins the regimes of power and of sex.

33. Baudrillard, *Seduction,* 86, 6.

34. Spivak, "Politics of Translation," 179.

35. Ibid., 179, 180.

36. Ibid., 179.

37. Baudrillard, *Seduction*, 39.

38. Ibid., 7.

39. [Evelyn Baring], Earl of Cromer, *Modern Egypt* (New York: Macmillan, 1908), 2:238.

40. Ḥasan ibn Muḥammad al-ʿAṭṭār, "Wa Hādhihi Maqāmat al-Adīb al-Ra'īs al-Shaykh Ḥasan al-ʿAṭṭār fī al-Faransīs," in Jalāl al-Dīn ʿAbd al-Raḥmān ibn Abī Bakr al-Suyūṭī, *Maqāmāt al-Suyūṭī, Mudhayyala bi Maqāma li Ḥasan ibn Muḥammad al-ʿAṭṭār wa Thalāth Nawādir Adabiyya*, ed. Ṣāliḥ al-Yāfī (Cairo, A.H. 1275 [1858/59]), 91–96; hereafter "Maqāmat al-Faransīs"; quotation from 95.

41. ʿAbd Allāh al-Nadīm, "Lā Anta Anta wa Lā al-Mathīl Mathīl," *al-Tankīt wa al-Tabkīt,* no. 10 (15 August 1881): 155–57. On this satire and others criticizing the language politics of the Egyptian elite, see Samah Selim, *The Novel and the Rural Imaginary in Egypt, 1880–1985* (London: RoutledgeCurzon, 2004), 50–54.

42. See [Muḥammad] Ḥāfiẓ Ibrāhīm, "al-Lugha al-ʿArabiyya Tanʿī Ḥaẓẓahā bayna Ahlihā," in [Muḥammad] Ḥāfiẓ Ibrāhīm, *Dīwān Ḥāfiẓ Ibrāhīm,* introd. Muḥammad Ismāʿīl Kānī, ed. Aḥmad Amīn, Aḥmad al-Zayn, and Ibrāhīm al-Abyārī, 2nd ed. (Cairo: al-Hay'a al-Miṣriyya al-ʿĀmma li al-Kitāb, 1980), 1:253–55.

43. On Aḥmad Shawqī's "Wadāʿ Lūrd Krūmir" and other resistance poetry, see Hussein N. Kadhim, *The Poetics of Anti-Colonialism in the Arabic* Qaṣīdah (Leiden: Brill, 2004), 1–84, esp. 1–34.

44. See Muḥammad al-Muwayliḥī, *Ḥadīth ʿĪsā ibn Hishām, aw Fatra min al-Zaman*, introd. ʿAlī Adham (Cairo: al-Dār al-Qawmiyya li al-Ṭibāʿa wa al-Nashr, 1964/A.H. 1383). See also the authoritative new critical edition of the novel—including various chapters in their original serialized forms—in *Muḥammad Ibrāhīm al-Muwayliḥī: al-Mu'allafāt al-Kāmila,* vol. 1, ed. and introd. Rūjir Ālin [Roger Allen] (Cairo: al-Majlis al-Aʿlā li al-Thaqāfa, 2002). The English translation is *A Period of Time: A Study and Translation of Hadith ʿIsa ibn Hisham by Muhammad al-Muwaylihi,* trans. and introd. Roger Allen (Reading, U.K.: Ithaca Press, 1992).

45. On the mutual implication of resistance and domination, see Bhabha, "Signs Taken for Wonders," 110–11.

46. John Tomlinson, *Cultural Imperialism: A Critical Introduction* (London: Continuum, 1991), 94, emphasis in the original.

47. Ibid., 95, 164, 165, emphases in the original.

48. Edward W. Said, "Reflections on American 'Left' Literary Criticism," in *The World, the Text, and the Critic* (Cambridge, MA: Harvard University Press, 1983), 158–77; quotations from 171.

49. Edward W. Said, "The World, the Text, and the Critic," in *The World, the Text, and the Critic,* 31–53; quotation from 45.

50. Ibid.

51. Ibid., 48.

52. Edward W. Said, "Traveling Theory," in *The World, the Text, and the Critic,* 226–47; quotation from 246.

53. Edward W. Said, *Orientalism* (New York: Vintage, 1979 [1978]), 122, emphases in the original.

54. Ibid., 204.

55. Ibid., 25.

56. Edward W. Said, *Culture and Imperialism* (New York: Vintage, 1994 [1993]), xii, emphasis in the original.

57. Ibid., 216, emphases in the original; see also 244.

58. Ibid., 51; quotation from xx, emphases mine.

59. Ibid., 51.

60. Ibid., 109, emphases in the original.

61. Ibid., 262.

62. Ibid., emphases mine; 263–64.

63. Ibid., 110.

64. Timothy Mitchell, *Colonising Egypt* (Cambridge: Cambridge University Press, 1988; Berkeley: University of California Press, 1991), 167. Citations are to the 1991 edition. Jeffrey Sacks, however, argues that Arab-Islamic thought entertained the separation of words from things—the arbitrariness of the sign—as early as the tenth century. See Jeffrey Sacks, "Latinity," *CR: The New Centennial Review* 9, no. 3 (2010): 251–86, esp. 251–52.

65. Mitchell, *Colonising Egypt*, 167.

66. Ibid., 166.

67. Ibid., 167.

68. On the tendency of Egyptian liberal reformers to project "an alien and backward cultural heritage" onto the masses and posit Egypt's true "self-image" as European, see Maghraoui, *Liberalism without Democracy,* 53, 87–92; quotations from 87.

69. Rey Chow, *The Age of the World Target: Self-Referentiality in War, Theory, and Comparative Work* (Durham: Duke University Press, 2006), 79.

70. Ibid., 113n28.

71. Ibid., 77–79; quotation from 89.

72. See Benjamin, "Task of the Translator," 74.

73. See Tejaswini Niranjana, *Siting Translation: History, Post-Structuralism, and the Colonial Context* (Berkeley: University of California Press, 1992),

112–17; Samuel Weber, "A Touch of Translation: On Walter Benjamin's 'Task of the Translator,'" in *Nation, Language, and the Ethics of Translation,* ed. Sandra Bermann and Michael Wood (Princeton: Princeton University Press, 2005), 65–78; and Naomi Seidman, *Faithful Renderings: Jewish-Christian Difference and the Politics of Translation* (Chicago: University of Chicago Press, 2006), 190–98.

74. On this problem, see Liu, *Translingual Practice,* 14–15.

75. See Chow, *Age of the World Target,* 88–89; quotation from 89.

76. Ibid., 89.

77. Ibid.

78. Ibid.

79. Said, *Orientalism,* 201, emphases mine.

80. Ibid., emphases mine.

81. My engagement with the impact of Ottoman rule on translation dynamics in Egypt is limited by the fact that I do not work in Turkish. Of the 804 books translated and printed at Būlāq in the nineteenth century, however, 677 were translations into Arabic and only 117 into Turkish. See 'Āyida Ibrāhīm Nuṣayr, *Ḥarakat Nashr al-Kutub fī Miṣr fī al-Qarn al-Tāsi' 'Ashar* (Cairo: al-Hay'a al-Miṣriyya al-'Āmma li al-Kitāb, 1994), 276, 287. On the history of translation and Westernization in Turkey, see Saliha Paker, "Translated European Literature in the Late Ottoman Literary Polysystem," *New Comparison: A Journal of Comparative and General Literary Studies*, no. 1 (Summer 1986): 67–82; and Şehnaz Tahir Gürçağlar, *The Poetics and Politics of Translation in Turkey, 1923–1960* (Amsterdam: Rodopi, 2008).

82. Eve M. Troutt Powell, *A Different Shade of Colonialism: Egypt, Great Britain, and the Mastery of the Sudan* (Berkeley: University of California Press, 2003), 39.

83. See Powell, *A Different Shade of Colonialism,* 1–25, esp. 12, 22.

84. Cromer, *Modern Egypt,* 2:228.

85. Umberto Eco, "The Roots of Conflict," *CounterPunch* (15 October 2001), www.counterpunch.org/eco1.html (accessed 27 July 2009). The original, "Le guerre sante: passione e ragione," appeared in the Italian daily *La Repubblica* of 5 October 2001.

CHAPTER 1

1. On the production of Napoleon's proclamation, see Ibrahim Abu-Lughod, *Arab Rediscovery of Europe: A Study in Cultural Encounters* (Princeton: Princeton University Press, 1963), 12–13; and Henry Laurens, *L'Expédition d'Égypte, 1798–1801* (Paris: Armand Colin, 1989), 75. Both the French original and the Arabic translation were written aboard *L'Orient,* the vessel on which Napoleon sailed to Egypt. Laurens accurately dates the French to 27 June 1798, followed by the Arabic, and Napoleon's landing to the night of 1–2 July 1798 (75, 78). The printed Arabic bears the incorrect date 13 messidor an VI (1 July 1798).

2. For the ostensible French original of Napoleon's proclamation, see Napoléon Bonaparte, Pièce n° 2723, in *Correspondance de Napoléon 1er, publiée par ordre de l'Empereur Napoléon III* (Paris: Imprimerie Impériale, 1860),

4:269–72; quotation from 270. The *Correspondance*, however, is expurgated. On the tangled history of the proclamation and its translation, see Christian Cherfils, *Bonaparte et l'Islam, d'après les documents français et arabes*, pref. Chérif Abd El-Hakim (Paris: A. Pedone, 1914), 14–17. Cherfils (14) notes a second version of the "original" French proclamation, intercepted by the English and published in London in 1799. Most likely he refers to *Lettres originales de l'armée françoise sous le commandement du général Buonaparte en Égypte interceptées par l'escadre de Nelson et publiées à Londres; avec une carte de l'Égypte* (London: H. L. Villaume, 1799), reprinted in Saladin Boustany, ed., *The Journals of Bonaparte in Egypt, 1798–1801: Intercepted Original Letters* (Cairo: Al-Arab Bookshop, 1971), 10:101–2. This version seems identical to that in the *Correspondance*. Yet another French "original," omitting the preambles of both the standard French "original" and its standard Arabic translation but otherwise matching the Arabic, appears in an official contemporary source; see *Pièces diverses relatives aux opérations militaires et politiques du général Bonaparte* (Paris: L'Imprimerie de P. Didot L'Aîné, An VIII [1800]), 2:233–36.

3. Laurens indicates that Venture de Paradis (1739–99) was the translator. See Laurens, *L'Expédition d'Égypte*, 415n49. See also Jāk Tājir, *Ḥarakat al-Tarjama bi Miṣr khilāl al-Qarn al-Tāsiʿ ʿAshar* (Cairo: Dār al-Maʿārif, 1945), 5–7; and Jamāl al-Dīn al-Shayyāl, *Tārīkh al-Tarjama fī Miṣr fī ʿAhd al-Ḥamla al-Faransiyya* (Cairo: Dār al-Fikr al-ʿArabī, 1950), 45–46. Al-Shayyāl implies that Venture translated the proclamation with the help of Arabic-speaking Muslim former prisoners whom Napoleon had freed on Malta just before his invasion of Egypt.

4. "Manner of meaning" echoes Carol Jacobs's retranslation of Walter Benjamin's phrase "*Art des Meinens,*" which appears as "mode of signification" in Walter Benjamin, "The Task of the Translator: An Introduction to the Translation of Baudelaire's *Tableaux parisiens*" (in German), in *Illuminations,* trans. Harry Zohn (New York: Schocken Books, 1969), 78. See Carol Jacobs, "The Monstrosity of Translation," *Modern Language Notes* 90, no. 6 (December 1975): 755–66; quotation from 762.

5. As elsewhere in the proclamation, the Arabic here is ungrammatical; the end of the quoted clause should read *muslimūna mukhliṣūna.* My source is the original Arabic document, République Française, "Bismillāh al-Raḥmān al-Raḥīm . . . min Ṭaraf al-Jumhūr al-Farānsāwī *[sic]* . . . ," 2 July 1798, TS, British Library, London, shelfmark 1296.h.12(1). This copy was one of thousands distributed in Egypt.

6. See G[eorg]. W[ilhelm]. F[riedrich]. Hegel, *Phenomenology of Spirit* (in German), trans. A. V. Miller (Oxford: Oxford University Press, 1977), 104–19.

7. See Frantz Fanon, *Peau noire, masques blancs* (Paris: Éditions du Seuil, 1995 [1952]), 170–80; quotation from 176, emphases in the original. My translation follows the original more closely. The published English translation is Frantz Fanon, *Black Skin, White Masks,* trans. Charles Lam Markmann (New York: Grove Press, 1967), 217.

8. On sovereign thinking, see Lydia H. Liu, "The Desire for the Sovereign

and the Logic of Reciprocity in the Family of Nations," *diacritics* 29, no. 4 (Winter 1999): 150–77; and Lydia H. Liu, *The Clash of Empires: The Invention of China in Modern World Making* (Cambridge, MA: Harvard University Press, 2004), esp. 5–30.

9. Fanon, *Peau noire*, 175–76.

10. See Homi K. Bhabha, "Signs Taken for Wonders: Questions of Ambivalence and Authority under a Tree Outside Delhi, May 1817," in *The Location of Culture* (London: Routledge, 1994), 102–22.

11. See Homi K. Bhabha, "Of Mimicry and Man: The Ambivalence of Colonial Discourse," in *The Location of Culture,* 85–92; quotations from 89, emphases in the original.

12. Ibid., 90, emphases mine.

13. Fanon, *Peau noire,* 179n9, emphasis mine.

14. Here Fanon writes against the Hegelian climax of the life-and-death struggle for recognition between lord and bondsman; see Hegel, *Phenomenology of Spirit,* 114–19.

15. Napoléon Bonaparte, Pièce n° 2724, in *Correspondance de Napoléon 1er*, 4:272–73; quotations from 273.

16. Napoléon Bonaparte, Pièce n° 2784, in *Correspondance de Napoléon 1er*, 4:323.

17. Napoleon's letter to General Jean-Baptiste Kléber of 30 July 1798 (12 thermidor an VI) argues the need to dissociate French from Crusader. See Napoléon Bonaparte, Pièce n° 2880, in *Correspondance de Napoléon 1er*, 4:388–89. On this letter, see also Juan Cole, *Napoleon's Egypt: Invading the Middle East* (New York: Palgrave Macmillan, 2007), 127.

18. For the original French preamble, see Napoléon Bonaparte, Pièce n° 2723, in *Correspondance de Napoléon 1er*, 4:269. Cherfils and Abu-Lughod also note that the preambles differ in their French and Arabic versions. See Cherfils, *Bonaparte et l'Islam,* 14n2; and Abu-Lughod, *Arab Rediscovery of Europe,* 13n1.

19. See Edward W. Said, *Orientalism* (New York: Vintage, 1979 [1978]), 82.

20. ʿAbd al-Raḥmān al-Jabartī, *Al-Jabartī's Chronicle of the First Seven Months of the French Occupation of Egypt, 15 June–December 1798, Muḥarram–Rajab 1213 / Tārīkh Muddat al-Faransīs bi Miṣr, Muḥarram–Rajab* A.H. *1213, 15 Yūnyū–Dīsimbir* A.D. *1798*, ed. and trans. S[hmuel]. Moreh (Leiden: E. J. Brill, 1975), 42; 11 in the Arabic.

21. al-Jabartī, *Al-Jabartī's Chronicle*, 51, 50; 22–23 in the Arabic.

22. Ibid., 51; 23 in the Arabic.

23. Ibid., 48; 19 in the Arabic.

24. See Laurens, *L'Expédition d'Égypte,* 43–75. My account below of Ottoman influences on Napoleon relies heavily on his research.

25. Ibid., 55–56; see also 408n41; and Henry Laurens, *Les Origines intellectuelles de l'expédition d'Égypte: l'orientalisme islamisant en France, 1698–1798* (Istanbul and Paris: Éditions Isis, 1987), 159–69.

26. ʿAlī Bey al-Kabīr, quoted in the chronicles of Vassif Wassif (Istanbul, 1805), 2:215–16, quoted in Laurens, *L'Expédition d'Égypte,* 58–59.

27. On Egypt and French colonialism in the Americas, see Laurens, *Les Origines intellectuelles,* 179–82.

28. Laurens, *L'Expédition d'Égypte,* 22–29; quotation from 29.

29. See Max Rodenbeck, *Cairo: The City Victorious* (London: Picador, 1998), 71–78.

30. Afaf Lutfi al-Sayyid Marsot, *Women and Men in Late Eighteenth-Century Egypt* (Austin: University of Texas Press, 1995), 18.

31. Ibid., 19.

32. Laurens, *L'Expédition d'Égypte,* 68–69; quotation from 68.

33. Ibid., 69. Laurens relies here on 'Abd al-Wahhāb Bakr, *al-Dawla al-'Uthmāniyya wa Miṣr fī al-Niṣf al-Thānī min al-Qarn al-Thāmin 'Ashar* (Cairo: Dār al-Ma'ārif, 1982).

34. Laurens, *L'Expédition d'Égypte,* 69–70; quotation from 69.

35. Ibid., 70.

36. Ibid. Compare Abu-Lughod, *Arab Rediscovery of Europe,* 21. Abu-Lughod's assessment is not accurate. In *Tārīkh,* al-Jabartī not only notes Napoleon's reference to the "French Republic," which he translates as *"al-jumhūr al-faransāwī,"* but also offers a fairly sophisticated if imperfect analysis of the term. See al-Jabartī, *Al-Jabartī's Chronicle,* 42–43; 11 in the Arabic. Juan Cole also overstates the proclamation's illegibility to "most Egyptians," arguing that it invoked "concepts for which there were no Arabic equivalents"; see Cole, *Napoleon's Egypt,* 30.

37. Marsot, *Women and Men,* 29.

38. Ibid., 70.

39. al-Jabartī, *Al-Jabartī's Chronicle,* 57; 29 in the Arabic.

40. On Bedouin attacks on the fleeing Mamālīk, see al-Jabartī, *Al-Jabartī's Chronicle,* 53, 61–62; 25–26, 34–35 in the Arabic. On inflation, see 58–59; 31 in the Arabic.

41. On French devastation and reconstruction of Cairo's natural and urban geographies, see al-Jabartī, *Al-Jabartī's Chronicle,* 114–15; 88–90 in the Arabic. On the French desecration of al-Azhar, see 100–101; 74–75 in the Arabic.

42. See al-Jabartī, *Al-Jabartī's Chronicle,* 42–47; 10–17 in the Arabic. For other analyses of al-Jabartī's response, see Cole, *Napoleon's Egypt,* 32–34; and Abdeslam M. Maghraoui, *Liberalism without Democracy: Nationhood and Citizenship in Egypt, 1922–1936* (Durham: Duke University Press, 2006), 39–41.

43. al-Jabartī, *Al-Jabartī's Chronicle,* 47; 16 in the Arabic.

44. See al-Jabartī, *Al-Jabartī's Chronicle,* 47; 17 in the Arabic. This translation, however, is mine.

45. See Jacques Derrida, *Politics of Friendship* (in French), trans. George Collins (New York: Verso, 1997), 72.

46. See al-Jabartī, *Al-Jabartī's Chronicle,* 115–17; 90–93 in the Arabic.

47. Edward W. Said, *Culture and Imperialism* (New York: Vintage, 1994 [1993]), 34.

48. See al-Shayyāl, *Tārīkh al-Tarjama fī Miṣr,* 24. Against the argument that al-Jabartī never joined Menou's *dīwān,* al-Shayyāl cites, in the *Courrier de l'Égypte* of 5 frimaire an IX (26 November 1800), the publication of a "friendly

letter" from the new *dīwān* to Napoleon himself in which al-Jabartī's name appears among the undersigned.

49. See Moreh, ed. and trans., in al-Jabartī, *Al-Jabartī's Chronicle,* 23, 25.

50. Napoléon Bonaparte, Pièce n° 2723, in *Correspondance de Napoléon 1er*, 4:269–72; quotation from 270, emphases mine.

51. See Cherfils, *Bonaparte et l'Islam,* 15n1. Cherfils accents Napoleon's insistence on his sincerity as a Muslim.

52. al-Jabartī, *Al-Jabartī's Chronicle,* 42, 47; 11, 16 in the Arabic. See also Cole, *Napoleon's Egypt,* 31. Cole argues that al-Jabartī may have misunderstood French deist unitarianism and "anticlericalism."

53. See Laurens, *L'Expédition d'Égypte,* 47.

54. Ibid., 47.

55. Ibid., 46–48; see also Marsot, *Women and Men,* 17, 20, 24.

56. See Kenneth M. Cuno, *The Pasha's Peasants: Land, Society, and Economy in Lower Egypt, 1740–1858* (Cambridge: Cambridge University Press, 1992), xv, 198.

57. Ibid., 2.

58. Ibid., 46.

59. Ibid., 46, 167, 168.

60. See Cuno, *The Pasha's Peasants*, 167–68.

61. See Khaled Fahmy, *All the Pasha's Men: Mehmed Ali, His Army, and the Making of Modern Egypt* (Cambridge: Cambridge University Press, 1997), 79.

62. Ibid., 80.

63. Ibid.

64. Ibid., 80–81.

65. Douglas Robinson, *Translation and Empire: Postcolonial Theories Explained* (Manchester, U.K.: St. Jerome, 1997), 54.

66. See Ferdinand de Saussure, *Course in General Linguistics,* ed. Charles Bally and Albert Sechehaye (with Albert Riedlinger), trans. and introd. Wade Baskin (New York: McGraw-Hill, 1966), 114–15.

67. Robinson, *Translation and Empire,* 54.

68. Ibid., 55.

69. See Liu, *Clash of Empires*, 13–14.

70. On Castilian (like money) as a "telecommunicative" lingua franca, see Vicente L. Rafael, *The Promise of the Foreign: Nationalism and the Technics of Translation in the Spanish Philippines* (Durham: Duke University Press, 2005), xvii, 10–11, 19–25.

71. See Bhabha, "Signs Taken for Wonders."

72. See Rafael, *Promise of the Foreign*, 23; and Vicente L. Rafael, *Contracting Colonialism: Translation and Christian Conversion in Tagalog Society under Early Spanish Rule* (Durham: Duke University Press, 1993 [1988]).

73. Tejaswini Niranjana, *Siting Translation: History, Post-Structuralism, and the Colonial Context* (Berkeley: University of California Press, 1992), 12–19.

74. See Niranjana, *Siting Translation,* 7–8, 31.

75. Ibid., 10.

76. Ibid., 32.

77. Ibid., 32–33, 10–11.

78. Ibid., 32–33, emphases in the original.

79. Louis Althusser, "Ideology and Ideological State Apparatuses: Notes towards an Investigation" (in French), in *Lenin and Philosophy, and Other Essays,* introd. Fredric Jameson, trans. Ben Brewster (New York: Monthly Review Press, 2001), 85–126; quotations from 118, 121, 123, emphases in the original.

80. Niranjana, *Siting Translation,* 11.

81. Ibid., 32; see also 1–11.

82. See Judith Butler, *The Psychic Life of Power: Theories in Subjection* (Stanford: Stanford University Press, 1997), 95.

83. Lydia H. Liu, *Translingual Practice: Literature, National Culture, and Translated Modernity—China, 1900–1937* (Stanford: Stanford University Press, 1995), 24.

84. Ibid.

85. My theoretical formulation here is indebted to Lydia Liu's theory of the super-sign, which I discuss at length in chapter 5. See Liu, *Clash of Empires,* 13–14.

86. See Natalie Melas, *All the Difference in the World: Postcoloniality and the Ends of Comparison* (Stanford: Stanford University Press, 2007), 92–93.

87. See Melas, *All the Difference,* 92.

88. Ibid.

89. Ibid., 93.

90. Ibid., 93, 92.

91. Ibid., 93, emphases mine.

92. See ibid., 103–12, esp. 108.

93. See Benjamin, "Task of the Translator," 76.

94. See Althusser, "Ideology and Ideological State Apparatuses," 121–23; quotation from 122, emphases in the original.

95. Arguing that *"identification expands the space of the subject:* it is a form of love that tells the subject what it could become in the intensity of its direction towards another (love as 'towardness')," Sara Ahmed implies that identification is a *deictic* love, seeking sovereign subjectivity in futural likeness: it is "the desire to take a place where one is not yet." See Sara Ahmed, *The Cultural Politics of Emotion* (New York: Routledge, 2004), 126, emphases in the original. I complicate that reading. The logic I describe involves not only "the desire to take a place where one is not yet" but also *the desire to take a place where one already was.*

96. See Svetlana Boym, *The Future of Nostalgia* (New York: Basic Books, 2001), xvi.

CHAPTER 2

1. See Jamāl al-Dīn al-Shayyāl, *Tārīkh al-Tarjama fī Miṣr fī 'Ahd al-Ḥamla al-Faransiyya* (Cairo: Dār al-Fikr al-'Arabī, 1950), 31; and Peter Gran, *Islamic Roots of Capitalism: Egypt, 1760–1840,* 2nd ed. (Cairo: American University in Cairo Press, 1999 [1979]), 80.

2. Ḥasan ibn Muḥammad al-'Aṭṭār, "Wa Hādhihi Maqāmat al-Adīb al-Ra'īs al-Shaykh Ḥasan al-'Aṭṭār fī al-Faransīs" (This Is the *Maqāma* of the Foremost

Man of Letters Shaykh Ḥasan al-ʿAṭṭār on the French), in Jalāl al-Dīn ʿAbd al-Raḥmān ibn Abī Bakr al-Suyūṭī, *Maqāmāt al-Suyūṭī, Mudhayyala bi Maqāma li Ḥasan ibn Muḥammad al-ʿAṭṭār wa Thalāth Nawādir Adabiyya,* ed. Ṣāliḥ al-Yāfī (Cairo, A.H. 1275 [1858/59]), 91–96; hereafter "Maqāmat al-Faransīs."

3. Ibid., 91, 93.

4. In summarizing al-ʿAṭṭār's career, I rely heavily on Gran, *Islamic Roots of Capitalism,* 76–91, esp. 78–82; and al-Shayyāl, *Tārīkh al-Tarjama fī Miṣr,* 17–34, esp. 29–32. See also Muḥammad ʿAbd al-Ghanī Ḥasan, *Ḥasan al-ʿAṭṭār* (Cairo: Dār al-Maʿārif, 1968), 20–57.

5. See Gran, *Islamic Roots of Capitalism,* 92–110.

6. Ibid., 123–24.

7. Ibid., 126–30.

8. Ibid., 75. For an annotated bibliography of al-ʿAṭṭār's works, see 197–208.

9. In so choosing, al-ʿAṭṭār was in step with his age; Gran shows that interest in the *maqāmāt* of al-Ḥarīrī reached its peak in the Sufi *majālis,* or assemblies, of eighteenth-century Cairo. Al-ʿAṭṭār joined one such *majlis,* the Wafāʾiyya, in the late 1780s. What sets al-ʿAṭṭār apart is his "novelization" of the *maqāma.* See Gran, *Islamic Roots of Capitalism,* 57–63. On the *maqāma* and its relationship to the modern novel, see Abdelfattah Kilito, "*Maqāmāt,*" in *The Novel*, ed. Franco Moretti (Princeton: Princeton University Press, 2006), 2:138–45.

10. al-ʿAṭṭār, "Maqāmat al-Faransīs," 91–92.

11. See al-ʿAṭṭār, "Maqāmat al-Faransīs," 91; and Elliott Colla, "'Non, non! Si, si!': Commemorating the French Occupation of Egypt (1798–1801)," *MLN* 118 (2003): 1043–69; quotations from 1061–62.

12. République Française, "Bismillāh al-Raḥmān al-Raḥīm . . . min Ṭaraf al-Jumhūr al-Farānsāwī *[sic]* . . . ," 2 July 1798, TS, British Library, London, shelfmark 1296.h.12(1).

13. al-ʿAṭṭār, "Maqāmat al-Faransīs," 92.

14. See Brian Massumi, *Parables for the Virtual: Movement, Affect, Sensation* (Durham: Duke University Press, 2002), 28–34; and Sara Ahmed, *The Cultural Politics of Emotion* (New York: Routledge, 2004), 25, 40n4.

15. Some read al-ʿAṭṭār's feminization of male "beloveds" as evidence of his homosexuality. Wary of imposing twenty-first-century categories on an eighteenth-century life, I am not interested in "outing" al-ʿAṭṭār; I focus on the sexual *form* of his fiction. Gran, however, assumes that al-ʿAṭṭār was homosexual. His strongest evidence is the official notice of al-ʿAṭṭār's appointment as *shaykh al-Azhar,* which notes that "his condition is known" *(wa ḥālu[hu] maʿlūm);* see Gran, *Islamic Roots of Capitalism,* 127, 237n48. Otherwise, his conclusions are speculative; see 81, 129. Gran suggests that the Orientalist of al-ʿAṭṭār's *maqāma* was the translator Remi Raige (1770–1807), noting that both al-ʿAṭṭār and the poet Ismāʿīl al-Khashshāb were "fond of [Raige] to the point of . . . rivalry" (248n3). According to al-Shayyāl, the inspiration for al-Khashshāb's love poetry was not Raige but a higher-ranking Orientalist. ʿAbd al-Raḥmān al-Jabartī describes him as handsome and "eloquent *[faṣīḥa al-lisāni]* in Arabic," having "memorized a great deal of poetry"; thanks to his "affinity" *(mujānasa)* with al-Khashshāb, "the pair became inseparable." ʿAbd al-

Raḥmān al-Jabartī, *'Ajā'ib al-Āthār fī al-Tarājim wa al-Akhbār* (Cairo: al-Maṭba'a al-'Āmira al-Sharafiyya, A.H. 1322 [A.H. 1297]), 4:256, quoted in al-Shayyāl, *Tārīkh al-Tarjama fī Miṣr,* 26.

16. See Rasheed El-Enany, *Arab Representations of the Occident: East-West Encounters in Arabic Fiction* (London: Routledge, 2006), 12–13.

17. Ibid., 12.

18. Ibid., 13.

19. See El-Enany, *Arab Representations of the Occident,* 12.

20. Jūrj Ṭarābīshī, "Tajnīs al-'Alāqāt al-Ḥaḍāriyya," in *Sharq wa Gharb: Rujūla wa Unūtha* (Beirut: Dār al-Ṭalī'a li al-Ṭibā'a wa al-Nashr, 1977), 5–17; quotation from 15–16.

21. See Jean Baudrillard, *Seduction,* trans. Brian Singer (New York: St. Martin's Press, 1990), 42. The original is Jean Baudrillard, *De la séduction* (Paris: Éditions Galilée, 1979), 63.

22. El-Enany, *Arab Representations of the Occident,* 7.

23. Colla, "'Non, non!'" 1064.

24. Ibid.

25. Ibid.

26. Ibid.

27. Baudrillard, *Seduction,* 86.

28. Ibid.

29. Ibid., 6–7, 12, 13. Baudrillard writes of "this *transubstantiation of sex into signs that is the secret of all seduction*" (13, emphases in the original).

30. See Baudrillard, *Seduction,* 68.

31. Baudrillard links seduction to refraction; see *Seduction,* 85.

32. The possessive pronoun *leur* never changes to match the gender of the noun it modifies. Morphologically, however, if a feminine form of *leur* were to exist, it would have to be *leurre.*

33. al-'Aṭṭār, "Maqāmat al-Faransīs," 92–93. Compare 'Abd al-Raḥmān al-Jabartī, *Al-Jabartī's Chronicle of the First Seven Months of the French Occupation of Egypt, 15 June–December 1798, Muḥarram–Rajab 1213 / Tārīkh Muddat al-Faransīs bi Miṣr, Muḥarram–Rajab A.H. 1213, 15 Yūnyū–Dīsimbir A.D. 1798,* ed. and trans. S[hmuel]. Moreh (Leiden: E. J. Brill, 1975), 117; 92 in the Arabic. The thirteenth-century astronomer Naṣīr al-Dīn al-Ṭūsī (1201–74), author of *al-Tadhkira fī 'Ilm al-Hay'a* (Memoir on Astronomy), was the "principal source for [al-'Aṭṭār's] studies on natural science" (Gran, *Islamic Roots of Capitalism,* 161). On *al-Tadhkira,* see George Saliba, "Arabic Planetary Theories after the Eleventh Century A.D.," in *Encyclopedia of the History of Arabic Science,* ed. Roshdi Rashed (London: Routledge, 1996), 1:58–127, esp. 1:93–95. On al-Ṭūsī, see Dimitri Gutas, *Greek Thought, Arabic Culture: The Graeco-Arabic Translation Movement in Baghdad and Early 'Abbāsid Society (2nd–4th/8th–10th Centuries)* (London: Routledge, 1998), 172–73.

34. See Homi K. Bhabha, "Of Mimicry and Man: The Ambivalence of Colonial Discourse," in *The Location of Culture* (London: Routledge, 1994), 85–92. See also Homi K. Bhabha, "Signs Taken for Wonders: Questions of Ambivalence and Authority under a Tree Outside Delhi, May 1817," in *The Location of Culture,* 102–22.

35. On the poem and its reception, see *Al Busiri's* Burda: *al-Burda: The Prophet's Mantle,* trans. and pref. Thoraya Mahdi Allam, rev. M. Mahdi Allam (Cairo: General Egyptian Book Organization [al-Hay'a al-Miṣriyya al-ʿĀmma li al-Kitāb], 1987), 10–13.

36. Bhabha, "Of Mimicry and Man," 91.

37. Colla, "'Non, non!'" 1048–49.

38. See al-Jabartī, *Al-Jabartī's Chronicle,* 117; 92 in the Arabic. The Arabic reads "al-Abūṣīrī," possibly a variant of al-Būṣīrī's name, which derives from that of the village Abū Ṣīr.

39. See Bhabha, "Signs Taken for Wonders," 102–4, 118–21.

40. See Ibrāhīm al-Bājūrī, ed., in [Sharaf al-Dīn] al-Būṣīrī, *al-Kawākib al-Durriyya fī Madḥ Khayr al-Birriyya, al-Maʿrūfa bi al-Burda* (hereafter *al-Burda*), ed. Ibrāhīm al-Bājūrī, rev. ed. and foreword ʿAbd al-Raḥmān Ḥasan Maḥmūd (Cairo: Maktabat al-Ādāb, 1991), 9–10n1; reference from 10. For a bilingual Arabic-English edition, see *Al Busiri's* Burda.

41. al-Bājūrī, ed., in *al-Burda*, 9–10n1; quotation from 9.

42. al-Būṣīrī, *al-Burda,* 9.

43. Bhabha, "Of Mimicry and Man," 90.

44. See Andy Martin, *Napoleon the Novelist* (Cambridge: Polity Press, 2000), 109–11. Martin roots Hegel's understanding of history in his identification with Napoleon.

45. G[eorg]. W[ilhelm]. F[riedrich]. Hegel, *Phenomenology of Spirit* (in German), trans. A. V. Miller (Oxford: Oxford University Press, 1977), 104–19; quotation from 111.

46. Baudrillard, *Seduction,* 13; on duel/dual affinity, see 42; and Baudrillard, *De la séduction,* 63.

47. Hegel, *Phenomenology of Spirit,* 111, emphases in the original.

48. See Lydia H. Liu, "The Desire for the Sovereign and the Logic of Reciprocity in the Family of Nations," *diacritics* 29, no. 4 (Winter 1999): 150–77; and Lydia H. Liu, *The Clash of Empires: The Invention of China in Modern World Making* (Cambridge, MA: Harvard University Press, 2004), esp. 5–30.

49. See Frantz Fanon, *The Wretched of the Earth* (in French), pref. Jean-Paul Sartre, trans. Constance Farrington (New York: Grove Press, 1963), 148–205.

50. Hegel, *Phenomenology of Spirit,* 111, emphases in the original.

51. Ibid.

52. Ibid.

53. Ibid., 114.

54. Frantz Fanon, *Peau noire, masques blancs* (Paris: Éditions du Seuil, 1995 [1952]), 51. My translation follows the original more closely. The published English translation is Frantz Fanon, *Black Skin, White Masks*, trans. Charles Lam Markmann (New York: Grove Press, 1967), 63.

55. Jacques Derrida, *Politics of Friendship* (in French), trans. George Collins (London: Verso, 1997), 220.

56. On symbolic and imaginary identification, see Slavoj Žižek, *The Sublime Object of Ideology* (London: Verso, 1989), 105–6; quotations from 105, emphases in the original.

57. See Edward William Lane, *An Account of the Manners and Customs of the Modern Egyptians, Written in Egypt during the Years 1833, –34, and –35,*

Partly from Notes Made during a Former Visit to That Country in the Years 1825, –26, –27, and –28 (London: Charles Knight, 1836), 1:274–75; quotation from 1:275, emphases mine.

58. al-'Aṭṭār, "Maqāmat al-Faransīs," 93.

59. Ibid.

60. Ibid., 94. To capture al-'Aṭṭār's comparison of the Frenchman to a slender branch, I have taken the liberty of translating *dhawā'ib,* which literally means "locks of hair," as "leaves of hair."

61. Ibid. Al-Shayyāl notes that in Ismā'īl al-Khashshāb's collected poems, which al-'Aṭṭār compiled at al-Khashshāb's death in 1815, is an amatory ode to a "youth in an ornamented black suit of clothes." See al-Shayyāl, *Tārīkh al-Tarjama fī Miṣr,* 26n2. I have located the ode in Ismā'īl al-Khashshāb, *Dīwān . . . al-Khashshāb,* ed. Ḥasan al-'Aṭṭār (Qusṭanṭīniyya [Istanbul]: Maṭba'at al-Jawā'ib, A.H. 1300 [1882]), 350. The language of the ode echoes that of al-'Aṭṭār's *maqāma.* A note to another poem by al-Khashshāb states that it was penned in response to a poem by al-'Aṭṭār, suggesting that the two were at least literary if not amatory "rivals." See al-Khashshāb, *Dīwān . . . al-Khashshāb,* 345–47; citation from 345.

62. Although line 5 of the narrator's poem ends with the word *ta'nīth,* the "grammatical feminine" or "feminine form," al-'Aṭṭār must imply *ta'nīs,* the colloquial Egyptian form of *ta'nīth,* to preserve his rhyme scheme, which ends on the *s* of *sīn,* not the *th* of *thā'.* In standard written Arabic, *ta'nīs* means "putting at ease"; it would reinforce the line's reference to the Frenchman's *luṭf* (friendliness, kindness). Yet al-'Aṭṭār chooses *ta'nīth* both to respect the orthography of literary Arabic and to accentuate the "femininity" with which the Frenchman presents himself.

63. al-'Aṭṭār, "Maqāmat al-Faransīs," 94.

64. While the English *glances*—connoting both the swift look and the graze of a sword or a bullet—beautifully captures the play of seduction and coercion in this text, I am sad to say that it does not hold in the original Arabic, *lafatāt.*

65. Colla, "'Non, non!'" 1055, emphasis in the original.

66. al-'Aṭṭār, "Maqāmat al-Faransīs," 94–95.

67. Colla, "'Non, non!'" 1063.

68. See Silvestre de Sacy, *Le Borda, poème à la louange de Mahomet, traduit de l'arabe de Scherf-Eddin Elboussiri,* in [Joseph Héliodore Sagesse Vertu] Garcin de Tassy, *Exposition de la foi musulmane, traduite du turc de Mohammed Ben Pir-Ali Elberkevi* [Birgilī], *avec des notes, suivie du Pend-Nameh, poème de Saadi, traduit du persan, par le même; et du Borda, poème à la louange de Mahomet, traduit de l'arabe, par M. le Baron Silvestre de Sacy* (Paris: G. Dufour et Ed. d'Ocagne, 1822), 125–48.

69. Silvestre de Sacy, "À Sa Majesté l'Empereur et Roi," dedicatory preface to *Chrestomathie arabe, ou extraits de divers écrivains arabes, tant en prose qu'en vers, à l'usage des élèves de l'École spéciale des langues orientales vivantes* (also titled *Le Compagnon instructif pour l'écolier studieux, et Collection de fragmens de poësie et de prose: Kitāb al-Anīs al-Mufīd li al-Ṭālib al-Mustafīd, wa Jāmi' al-Shudhūr min Manẓūm wa Manthūr*) (Paris: Imprimerie Impériale, 1806), 1:[iii].

70. I thank Muhammad Siddiq for this observation.

71. Allam, trans., preface to *Al Busiri's* Burda, 7.

72. al-Bājūrī, ed., foreword to *al-Burda,* 7.

73. Ibid. Compare Allam, trans., preface to *Al Busiri's* Burda, 9–10. While similar, Allam's account ignores the poetic (and historical) precedent of the *Burda* of Ka'b ibn Zuhayr.

74. See T. Bauer, "Ka'b ibn Zuhayr," in *Encyclopedia of Arabic Literature,* ed. Julie Scott Meisami and Paul Starkey (London: Routledge, 1998), 2:421.

75. al-'Aṭṭār, "Maqāmat al-Faransīs," 93–94.

76. Gran, *Islamic Roots of Capitalism,* 76.

77. Moreh, ed. and trans., in *Al-Jabartī's Chronicle,* 30.

78. According to Sabry Hafez, the unprecedented wave of *maqāma* composition in Egypt, Syria, and Iraq between 1800 and 1900 begins with al-'Aṭṭār's *maqāma.* See Sabry Hafez, *The Genesis of Arabic Narrative Discourse: A Study in the Sociology of Modern Arabic Literature* (London: Saqi, 1993), 109–10. His *maqāma* thus heralds the rise of a hybrid Arabic-European genre in the Egyptian *maqāma*-novels of 'Alī Mubārak (*'Alam al-Dīn*, 1882), Muḥammad al-Muwayliḥī (*Ḥadīth 'Īsā ibn Hishām, aw Fatra min al-Zaman*, 1898–1902), and Ḥāfiẓ Ibrāhīm (*Layālī Saṭīḥ,* 1906), which represent the (post)colonial transformation of Egypt under European influence.

79. al-'Aṭṭār, "Maqāmat al-Faransīs," 95.

80. Ibid., 95–96.

81. See Colla, "'Non, non!'" 1066, for another reading.

82. al-'Aṭṭār, "Maqāmat al-Faransīs," 96.

83. Baudrillard, *Seduction,* 13; Baudrillard, *De la séduction,* 25.

CHAPTER 3

1. Matti Moosa, *The Origins of Modern Arabic Fiction*, 2nd ed. (Boulder, CO: Lynne Rienner, 1997), 94.

2. See Roger Allen, "Rewriting Literary History: The Case of the Arabic Novel," *Journal of Arabic Literature* 38 (2007): 247–60, esp. 250–54; quotations from 252–53, 250–51. See also Roger Allen, "The Post-Classical Period: Parameters and Preliminaries," in *Arabic Literature in the Post-Classical Period,* ed. Roger Allen and D. S. Richards (Cambridge: Cambridge University Press, 2006), 1–21, esp. 6–8. Compare the mainstream accounts of M. M. Badawi and Pierre Cachia, "Introduction," in *Modern Arabic Literature,* ed. M. M. Badawi (Cambridge: Cambridge University Press, 1992), 1–35.

3. Ḥusayn Fawzī al-Najjār, *Rifā'a al-Ṭahṭāwī: Rā'id Fikr wa Imām Nahḍa* ([Cairo]: al-Dār al-Miṣriyya li al-Ta'līf wa al-Tarjama, n.d.), 9. For a critique of the Ottoman decline thesis, see Mehmet Akif Kirecci, "Decline Discourse and Self-Orientalization in the Writings of al-Ṭahṭāwī, Ṭāhā Ḥusayn, and Ziya Gökalp: A Comparative Study of Modernization in Egypt and Turkey" (Ph.D. diss., University of Pennsylvania, 2007), esp. 68–104.

4. al-Najjār, *Rifā'a al-Ṭahṭāwī,* 17.

5. Ibid., 18.

6. Sabry Hafez, *The Genesis of Arabic Narrative Discourse: A Study in the Sociology of Modern Arabic Literature* (London: Saqi, 1993), 18.

7. Ibid.

8. Ibid.

9. Ibid., 10–11, 17–18.

10. Ibid., 38.

11. On Jomard's biography, see Yves Laissus, *Jomard, le dernier Égyptien* (Paris: Fayard, 2004). On the number of Egyptian subjects sent to France, see Anouar Louca, *Voyageurs et écrivains égyptiens en France au XIXe siècle* (Paris: Didier, 1970), 33.

12. Louca, *Voyageurs et écrivains,* 25. On Napoleon's plan to educate Egyptians in France, see Ronald T. Ridley, *Napoleon's Proconsul in Egypt: The Life and Times of Bernardino Drovetti* (London: Rubicon Press, n.d.), 206–7. In the 1820s Mehmed Ali also dispatched Egyptian students to London; see Timothy Mitchell, *Colonising Egypt* (Cambridge: Cambridge University Press, 1988; Berkeley: University of California Press, 1991), 69. Citations are to the 1991 edition.

13. J-m-d [Edme-François Jomard], "Relation de l'expédition scientifique des Français en Égypte en 1798, extrait de l'*Encyclopédie des gens du monde,* Tome XIV, 2e partie, pages 749 et suivantes" ([Paris]: Imprimerie de E. Duverger, n.d.), 12, emphases mine. The *Encyclopédie* appeared between 1833 and 1844. Since more than 115 students were sent to Paris by 1 December 1835 (see Louca, *Voyageurs et écrivains,* 46), Jomard's essay must date to this period.

14. On the recall, see Louca, *Voyageurs et écrivains,* 48.

15. [Edme-François] Jomard, *Coup-d'œil impartial sur l'état présent de l'Égypte, comparé a sa situation antérieure* (Paris: Imprimerie de Béthune et Plon, 1836), 42–44, emphasis in the original.

16. Ibid., 55–56.

17. Ibid., 54, emphasis in the original.

18. Ibid., 50.

19. The original is Rifāʿa Badawī Rāfiʿ al-Ṭahṭāwī, *Hādhihi Riḥlat al-Faqīr ilā Allāh Taʿālā Rifāʿa Badawī Rāfiʿ al-Ṭahṭāwī ilā Diyār Faransā al-Musammāh bi Takhlīṣ al-Ibrīz ilā Talkhīṣ Bārīz, aw al-Dīwān al-Nafīs bi Īwān Bārīs* (Būlāq: Dār al-Ṭibāʿa al-Khidīwiyya, A.H. 1250 [1834]).

20. While al-Ṭahṭāwī was appointed *imām* to the Egyptian mission, a last-minute decree was issued to allow him to study in Paris, where he agreed to master translation; see Jamāl al-Dīn al-Shayyāl, *Rifāʿa Rāfiʿ al-Ṭahṭāwī, 1801–1873,* 2nd ed. (Cairo: Dār al-Maʿārif, [1970]), 26.

21. On al-Ṭahṭāwī's translations in Paris, see Rifāʿa Badawī Rāfiʿ al-Ṭahṭāwī, *Takhlīṣ al-Ibrīz fī Talkhīṣ Bārīz,* ed. Mahdī ʿAllām, Aḥmad Aḥmad Badawī, and Anwar Lūqā (Cairo: Muṣṭafā al-Bābī al-Ḥalabī, 1958 [1834, 1849]), 248–49. On his French education, see 241–46. Among his readings were *Le Port-Royal (Līburtruwāyāl;* i.e., *La Logique de Port-Royal)* and "many of French literature's celebrated works," including works by Voltaire and Racine, "Noël's collection," Rousseau's *Le Contrat social,* and Montesquieu's *L'Esprit des lois* and *Lettres persanes.* He describes this last as "a scale in which Western and Eastern literatures/manners *[al-ādābi al-maghribiyyati wa al-mashriqiyyati]*

are weighed" (243–44). The published English translation is Rifāʿa Rāfiʿ al-Ṭahṭāwī, *An Imam in Paris: Account of a Stay in France by an Egyptian Cleric (1826–1831)*, trans. and introd. Daniel L. Newman (London: Saqi, 2004). All translations, however, are mine.

22. See J. Heyworth Dunne, *An Introduction to the History of Education in Modern Egypt* (London: Frank Cass, 1968), 150. The institution was born in 1836 as the School of Translation before being renamed the School of Languages and placed under al-Ṭahṭāwī's directorship. Compare Albert Hourani, *Arabic Thought in the Liberal Age, 1798–1939* (Cambridge: Cambridge University Press, 1983 [1962]), 71–72; and Ibrahim Abu-Lughod, *Arab Rediscovery of Europe: A Study in Cultural Encounters* (Princeton: Princeton University Press, 1963), 32, 41.

23. Maḥmūd Fahmī Ḥijāzī, *Uṣūl al-Fikr al-ʿArabī al-Ḥadīth ʿinda al-Ṭahṭāwī, maʿa al-Naṣṣ al-Kāmil li Kitābih "Takhlīṣ al-Ibrīz"* (Cairo: al-Hay'a al-Miṣriyya al-ʿĀmma li al-Kitāb, 1974), 26.

24. See Hourani, *Arabic Thought in the Liberal Age*, 72.

25. Rifāʿa Badawī Rāfiʿ [al-Ṭahṭāwī], *Mawāqiʿ al-Aflāk fī Waqāʾiʿ Tilīmāk* (Beirut: al-Maṭbaʿa al-Sūriyya, [1867]).

26. Rifāʿa Rāfiʿ [al-Ṭahṭāwī], *Kitāb Manāhij al-Albāb al-Miṣriyya fī Mabāhij al-Ādāb al-ʿAṣriyya* (Būlāq: al-Maṭbaʿa al-Miṣriyya, A.H. 1286 [1869]); and Rifāʿa Rāfiʿ [al-Ṭahṭāwī], *Kitāb al-Murshid al-Amīn li al-Banāt wa al-Banīn* ([Cairo]: Maṭbaʿat al-Madāris al-Malakiyya, A.H. 1289 [1872]). The English translations of both titles are Hourani's; see Hourani, *Arabic Thought in the Liberal Age*, 72.

27. Al-Shayyāl inscribes al-Ṭahṭāwī's work as a translator within a renaissance project of Egyptian awakening, which seeks to render the Egyptian "like the European in civilization and in refinement." See al-Shayyāl, *Rifāʿa Rāfiʿ al-Ṭahṭāwī*, 26–27; quotation from 27. See also Jābir ʿUṣfūr, "Rifāʿa al-Ṭahṭāwī, Rāʾid al-Tanwīr," in *Iḍāʾāt* (Cairo: al-Hay'a al-ʿĀmma li Quṣūr al-Thaqāfa, 1994), 7–18. ʿUṣfūr describes al-Ṭahṭāwī as "the pioneer of enlightenment, truly the apostle of progress, and indisputably the founder of the modern Arab intellectual renaissance" (7).

28. Al-ʿAṭṭār shaped al-Ṭahṭāwī's interests. See Peter Gran, *Islamic Roots of Capitalism: Egypt, 1760–1840*, 2nd ed. (Cairo: American University in Cairo Press, 1999 [1979]), 185; and Peter Gran, "Tahtawi in Paris," *Al-Ahram Weekly Online*, 10–16 January 2002, http://weekly.ahram.org.eg/2002/568/cu1.htm.

29. On al-Ṭahṭāwī's final examination, held at Jomard's residence on 19 October 1830, see *La Revue encyclopédique* 48 (novembre 1830): 521–23, quoted (with a date of 1831) in Louca, *Voyageurs et écrivains*, 257–58. See also al-Ṭahṭāwī, *Takhlīṣ al-Ibrīz*, 247–51, esp. 250–51.

30. See Ḥijāzī, *Uṣūl al-Fikr al-ʿArabī*, 24.

31. Moosa, *Origins of Modern Arabic Fiction*, 5.

32. Olakunle George, *Relocating Agency: Modernity and African Letters* (Albany: State University of New York Press, 2003), 75.

33. Ibid., emphases in the original.

34. Ibid.

35. Silvestre de Sacy's letters appear in Arabic translation in al-Ṭahṭāwī, *Takhlīṣ al-Ibrīz,* 234–36.

36. See also John W. Livingston, "Western Science and Educational Reform in the Thought of Shaykh Rifa'a al-Tahtawi," *International Journal of Middle East Studies* 28 (1996): 543–64, esp. 554–55.

37. al-Ṭahṭāwī, *Takhlīṣ al-Ibrīz,* 206.

38. Ibid.

39. Egyptian scholars have tended to insist that although al-Ṭahṭāwī's Parisian experience radically altered his patterns of thought, his Islam remained "intact." See, for instance, al-Shayyāl, *Rifā'a Rāfi' al-Ṭahṭāwī,* 30; and al-Najjār, *Rifā'a al-Ṭahṭāwī,* 82–83.

40. al-Ṭahṭāwī, *Takhlīṣ al-Ibrīz,* 206–7.

41. See Pascale Casanova, *The World Republic of Letters* (in French), trans. M. B. DeBevoise (Cambridge, MA: Harvard University Press, 2004), 10.

42. Ibid., 134.

43. Ibid., 133.

44. Ibid., 134.

45. Ibid., 127, emphases mine.

46. Compare Edward W. Said, "Reflections on American 'Left' Literary Criticism," in *The World, the Text, and the Critic* (Cambridge, MA: Harvard University Press, 1983), 171. Said notes that culture is tantamount neither to the state apparatus nor to the forces of corporate capital but is a "separately capitalized endeavor, which is really to say that its relationship to authority and power is far from nonexistent." Casanova deemphasizes that relationship.

47. Casanova, *World Republic,* 154.

48. Ibid., 89, emphases in the original; and Pascale Casanova, *La République mondiale des lettres*, rev. ed. (Paris: Éditions du Seuil, 2008 [1999]), 137.

49. Casanova, *World Republic,* 83.

50. David Damrosch, *What Is World Literature?* (Princeton: Princeton University Press, 2003), 300, 300–301.

51. Ibid., 303.

52. I borrow the phrase "translation zone" from Emily Apter, *The Translation Zone: A New Comparative Literature* (Princeton: Princeton University Press, 2006).

53. Ferial J. Ghazoul, "Comparative Literature in the Arab World," *Comparative Critical Studies* 3, nos. 1–2 (2006): 113–24; quotation from 114, emphasis in the original.

54. See Lydia H. Liu, "The Question of Meaning-Value in the Political Economy of the Sign," in *Tokens of Exchange: The Problem of Translation in Global Circulations,* ed. Lydia H. Liu (Durham: Duke University Press, 1999), 13–41; quotation from 21.

55. Ibid., 21.

56. al-Ṭahṭāwī, *Takhlīṣ al-Ibrīz,* 127–28.

57. Liu, "Question of Meaning-Value," 19.

58. Ibid., emphases in the original.

59. See Nadia Al-Bagdadi, "Registers of Arabic Literary History," *New Literary History* 39, no. 3 (Summer 2008): 437–61, esp. 440–41; quotation from 441.

60. See Abdelfattah Kilito, *Thou Shalt Not Speak My Language,* trans. and introd. Waïl S. Hassan (Syracuse, NY: Syracuse University Press, 2008), 8; and ʿAbd al-Fattāḥ Kīlīṭū, *Lan Tatakallama Lughatī* (Beirut: Dār al-Ṭalīʿa li al-Ṭibāʿa wa al-Nashr, 2002), 12–13.

61. Kilito, *Thou Shalt Not Speak,* 9.

62. Ibid.

63. See Damrosch, *What Is World Literature?* 281–84.

64. Kilito, *Thou Shalt Not Speak,* 15; Kīlīṭū, *Lan Tatakallama Lughatī,* 21.

65. [François-Joseph-Michel] Noël and [Guislain-François-Marie-Joseph] de La Place, eds., *Leçons françaises de littérature et de morale . . . ,* 7th ed., 2 vols. (Paris: Le Normant, 1816).

66. See René Wellek, "The Name and Nature of Comparative Literature," in *Discriminations: Further Concepts of Criticism* (New Haven: Yale University Press, 1970), 1–36; citation from 10; see also Susan Bassnett, *Comparative Literature: A Critical Introduction* (Oxford: Blackwell, 1993), 12.

67. Casanova, *World Republic,* 46.

68. See Casanova, *World Republic,* 53–54; quotation from 53, emphases in the original.

69. See Casanova, *World Republic,* 64–67.

70. [François-Joseph-Michel] Noël and [Guislain-François-Marie-Joseph] de La Place, eds., *Leçons de littérature et de morale, ou Recueil, en prose et en vers, des plus beaux morceaux de notre langue, dans la littérature des deux derniers siècles . . . ,* 2 vols. (Paris: Le Normant, An XII/1804), 1:i.

71. Ibid., 1:vi.

72. Ibid., 1:vii.

73. al-Ṭahṭāwī, *Takhlīṣ al-Ibrīz,* 124.

74. Lawrence Venuti, *The Translator's Invisibility: A History of Translation* (London: Routledge, 1995), 17, emphases mine.

75. Ibid., 18.

76. al-Ṭahṭāwī, *Takhlīṣ al-Ibrīz,* 128. On the three Arabic works al-Ṭahṭāwī names here (*al-Muṭawwal*, *al-Aṭwal*, and *Saʿd*), see Newman, trans., in *An Imam in Paris*, 184–85n2, 185n3, 185n4.

77. On al-Ṭahṭāwī's construction of "likeness" between Egypt/Arabic and France/French, see also Amina Rachid, "Regards croisés sur la France et l'Égypte: Rifâʿa al Tahtawi et Suzanne Voilquin: idéologie et conscience de classe," in *Le Miroir égyptien,* ed. Robert Ilbert and Philippe Joutard (Marseilles: Éditions du Quai, 1984), 225–38, esp. 232–37; Myriam Salama-Carr, "Negotiating Conflict: Rifāʿa Rāfiʿ al-Ṭahṭāwī and the Translation of the 'Other' in Nineteenth-Century Egypt," *Social Semiotics* 17, no. 2 (June 2007): 213–27, esp. 218–19; and Mohammed Sawaie, "Rifaʿa Rafiʿ al-Tahtawi and His Contribution to the Lexical Development of Modern Literary Arabic," *International Journal of Middle East Studies* 32 (2000): 395–410, esp. 404–5.

78. See Walter Benjamin, "The Task of the Translator: An Introduction to the Translation of Baudelaire's *Tableaux parisiens*" (in German), in *Illuminations,* trans. Harry Zohn (New York: Schocken Books, 1969), 69–82; quotations from 75.

79. Ibid., 74, emphases mine.

80. Ibid., 72. Compare Tejaswini Niranjana, *Siting Translation: History, Post-Structuralism, and the Colonial Context* (Berkeley: University of California Press, 1992), 112–14. Niranjana insists that "The Task of the Translator" be read through the prism of Benjamin's later theories of historicity. While I agree that "in Benjamin's later work the task of the translator becomes the task of the historical materialist" (114), I maintain that "The Task of the Translator" is less interested in the historical than Niranjana might wish it to be. Niranjana ascribes the "intentions" of Benjamin's future works to those of his past.

81. Benjamin, "Task of the Translator," 80.

82. al-Ṭahṭāwī, *Takhlīṣ al-Ibrīz,* 207.

83. See al-Ṭahṭāwī, *Takhlīṣ al-Ibrīz,* 207; and Mitchell, *Colonising Egypt,* 142–43, 151–53.

84. Antoine de Rivarol, *De l'universalité de la langue française* (1784; Paris: Obsidiane, 1991), 39, quoted in Casanova, *World Republic,* 72.

85. al-Ṭahṭāwī, *Takhlīṣ al-Ibrīz,* 129.

86. Casanova, *World Republic,* 126–27.

87. al-Ṭahṭāwī, *Takhlīṣ al-Ibrīz,* 129.

88. Ibid.

89. Ibid., 132.

90. See Antoine-Isaac Silvestre de Sacy, *Discours prononcé par M. Silvestre de Sacy en faisant hommage au Corps Législatif de son ouvrage intitulé* Grammaire arabe, à l'usage des élèves de l'École spéciale des langues orientales vivantes, *séance du 5 mars 1810* ([Paris?]: Hacquart, [1810]), 4–5.

91. Ibid., 4.

92. Ibid., 5.

93. Ibid., 4.

94. See Kilito, *Thou Shalt Not Speak,* 15–16; see also Frantz Fanon, *Peau noire, masques blancs* (Paris: Éditions du Seuil, 1995 [1952]), 170.

95. See Edward W. Said, *Orientalism* (New York: Vintage, 1979 [1978]), 123–30.

96. Joseph Agoub, *La Lyre brisée, dithyrambe, dédié à Madame Dufrénoy,* in *Mélanges de littérature orientale et française, avec une notice sur l'auteur par M. de Pongerville, de l'Académie française* (Paris: Werdet, 1835), 310–16. Citations are to this edition. The original is Joseph Agoub, *La Lyre brisée, dithyrambe, dédié à Madame Dufrénoy, par M. Agoub* (Paris: Dondey-Dupré, 1825).

97. For one exception, see Aḥmad Aḥmad Badawī, *Rifā'a Rāfi' al-Ṭahṭāwī,* 2nd ed. ([Cairo]: Lajnat al-Bayān al-'Arabī, n.d.), 199–203. Badawī observes that al-Ṭahṭāwī's introduction to the poem testifies to the translator's forcing of sign to signification, to his struggle to balance the formal demands of Arabic poetry with the affective effusions of Agoub's French (200).

98. On Agoub and the Egyptian francophone tradition, see Jean-Jacques Luthi, *La Littérature d'expression française en Égypte (1798–1998),* rev. ed. (Paris: L'Harmattan, 2000), 89–91, 241.

99. Louca, *Voyageurs et écrivains,* 26.

100. See Joseph Agoub, *Coup-d'œil sur l'Égypte ancienne et moderne, ou Analyse raisonnée du grand ouvrage sur l'Égypte,* in *Mélanges de littérature orientale et française,* 173–301; and Joseph Agoub, *Discours historique sur*

l'Égypte, in ibid., 123–70. The three chapters collected as *Coup-d'œil* first appeared as J[osep]H. Agoub, "Description de l'Égypte," *La Revue encyclopédique* 12, no. 35 (novembre 1821): 360–73; J[oseph]. É[lie]. Agoub, "Description de l'Égypte," *La Revue encyclopédique* 21, no. 61 (janvier 1824): 111–35; and J[oseph]. Agoub, "Description de l'Égypte," *La Revue encyclopédique* 29, no. 85 (janvier 1826): 100–29. The *Discours* first appeared in stand-alone form as Joseph Agoub, *Discours historique sur l'Égypte, par M. Agoub, membre du Conseil de la Société Asiatique* (Paris: Imprimerie de Rignoux, 1823).

101. al-Ṭahṭāwī, *Takhlīṣ al-Ibrīz,* 135.

102. Ibid.

103. Ibid.

104. Ibid., 137.

105. [Rifāʿa Rāfiʿ al-Ṭahṭāwī], trans., *Naẓm al-ʿUqūd fī Kasr al-ʿŪd: La Lyre brisée, dithyrambe de M. Agoub, traduit en vers arabes par le cheykh Réfaha* (Paris: Dondey-Dupré, A.H. 1242/1827), 7.

106. A preface to a posthumous republication of Agoub's collected works describes him as "born in Cairo, cultivating our literature in Paris, become French by his labors"; see M. de Pongerville, "Notice," in Agoub, *Mélanges de littérature orientale et française,* iii. Agoub, however, sees himself as an Egyptian "attached to France by admiration . . . and recognition"; see Agoub, *Coup-d'œil sur l'Égypte,* 174.

107. Agoub, *La Lyre brisée,* 310.

108. Ibid., 311.

109. Ibid.

110. Ibid.

111. Ibid.

112. Ibid., 312.

113. Ibid., 313.

114. [al-Ṭahṭāwī], *Naẓm al-ʿUqūd,* 17.

115. Ibid., 18.

116. al-Ṭahṭāwī, *Takhlīṣ al-Ibrīz,* 105. *Miṣr* (Egypt) is also an epithet for Cairo.

CHAPTER 4

1. [Evelyn Baring], Earl of Cromer, *Modern Egypt* (New York: Macmillan, 1908), 2:238.

2. Ibid., 2:235–36, emphases mine.

3. Thomas Babington Macaulay, "Minute on Indian Education," in *Speeches by Lord Macaulay with His Minute on Indian Education*, introd. G. M. Young (London: Oxford University Press, 1935), 345–61; quotations from 345–46. Macaulay's address installed English as the official language of education in India. See also Charles E. Trevelyan, *On the Education of the People of India* (London: Longman, Orme, Brown, Green, and Longmans, 1838), 167–68, which invokes Mehmed Ali's Egypt as a model for the British "enlightenment" of India.

4. Cromer, *Modern Egypt,* 2:236.

5. Macaulay, "Minute," 359.

6. On the 1820s London mission, see Timothy Mitchell, *Colonising Egypt* (Cambridge: Cambridge University Press, 1988; Berkeley: University of California Press, 1991), 69. Citations are to the 1991 edition. By contrast, more than 115 Egyptians had studied in Paris by 1835; see Anouar Louca, *Voyageurs et écrivains égyptiens en France au XIXe siècle* (Paris: Didier, 1970), 46.

7. Cromer, *Modern Egypt,* 2:236–38, emphases mine. See also Edward W. Said, *Orientalism* (New York: Vintage, 1979 [1978]), 211–12. In Said's view, Cromer invokes this passage to contrast the actuality of British colonialism in Egypt to the ephemerality of the French. I suggest that Cromer yearns to take a page from French seduction.

8. Cromer, *Modern Egypt,* 2:236–37.

9. Ibid., 2:238, emphasis mine.

10. Ibid., 2:257, emphasis mine.

11. Compare Ashis Nandy, *The Intimate Enemy: Loss and Recovery of Self under Colonialism* (Delhi: Oxford University Press, 1983), 4, 7. While Nandy contends that British colonialism rested on a denial of "bisexuality," Cromer predicates its success on a "bisexual" or hermaphroditic gendering of power.

12. On Dinshawāy and its impact on Egyptian nationalism, see Afaf Lutfi Al-Sayyid, *Egypt and Cromer: A Study in Anglo-Egyptian Relations* (New York: Praeger, 1969), 169–75.

13. Cromer had served in Egypt twice before: from 1877 to 1879, as commissioner on the Caisse de la Dette Publique, and again in 1879 as controller; see Al-Sayyid, *Egypt and Cromer,* 54–55.

14. Cromer, *Modern Egypt,* 2:525. Here Cromer cites Macaulay's stance on India in a speech the latter delivered before the House of Commons on 10 July 1833.

15. See Robert L. Tignor, *Modernization and British Colonial Rule in Egypt, 1882–1914* (Princeton: Princeton University Press, 1966), 348.

16. Cromer, *Modern Egypt*, 2:525, emphases mine.

17. Ibid., 2:228. Cromer elaborates on the present character and political potential of the "Europeanised Egyptian," 2:228–34.

18. On the etymology of *culture* and its roots in cultivation, see Raymond Williams, "Culture," in *Keywords: A Vocabulary of Culture and Society,* rev. ed. (New York: Oxford University Press, 1985), 87–93, esp. 87.

19. Cromer, *Modern Egypt,* 2:527.

20. One might argue that a more utilitarian translation—from French, not English—paved the way for al-Sibāʿī's intervention. In 1899 Aḥmad Fatḥī Zaghlūl, brother of the Egyptian nationalist Saʿd Zaghlūl, published an influential Arabic translation of Edmond Demolins's *À quoi tient la supériorité des Anglo-Saxons* (Paris: Firmin-Didot, 1897), which probed the growing dominance of the British in the world. See Aḥmad Fatḥī Zaghlūl, *Sirr Taqaddum al-Inkilīz al-Sāksūniyyīn, ta'līf Idmūn Dīmūlān* (Cairo: Maṭbaʿat al-Shaʿb, 1908 [1899]). On the impact of Zaghlūl's translation in Egypt, see Mitchell, *Colonising Egypt,* 110–11.

21. Thomas Carlyle, *On Heroes, Hero-Worship, and the Heroic in History* (London, 1841), translated by Muḥammad al-Sibāʿī as "al-Abṭāl wa ʿIbādat al-Buṭūla," *al-Bayān* 1, nos. 2–3 (30 Ramaḍān/30 Shawwāl A.H. 1329 [1911]),

81–121. Excerpts of al-Sibāʿī's translation first appeared in this journal, where an editor's note refers to the publication of the full volume by the house of *al-Bayān*; see "al-Abṭāl wa ʿIbādat al-Buṭūla," 82. Unless otherwise indicated, however, my quotations refer to the full volume, Muḥammad al-Sibāʿī, trans., *al-Abṭāl, ta'līf al-Faylasūf al-Akbar Tūmās Kārlayl*, 3rd ed. (Cairo: al-Maṭbaʿa al-Miṣriyya bi al-Azhar, 1930/A.H. 1349 [1911]).

22. Muḥammad al-Sibāʿī, "Kalimat al-Mutarjim" (Translator's Foreword), in *Qiṣṣat al-Madīnatayn, ta'līf Sharlz Dikinz* (Charles Dickens), trans. Muḥammad al-Sibāʿī (Cairo: Maṭbaʿat al-Bayān, 1912), 1:*alif* [i].

23. See Frantz Fanon, *The Wretched of the Earth* (in French), trans. Constance Farrington, pref. Jean-Paul Sartre (New York: Grove Press, 1963), 148–248; and Partha Chatterjee, *Nationalist Thought and the Colonial World: A Derivative Discourse?* (London: Zed Books, 1986).

24. See Trevelyan, *On the Education of the People of India,* 36. Trevelyan's ideas prefigure Charles Darwin's thesis that a "host" nation is fortified by selective adaptation to a foreign invader; the first edition of Darwin's *On the Origin of Species* would not appear until 1859.

25. Walter Benjamin, "The Task of the Translator: An Introduction to the Translation of Baudelaire's *Tableaux parisiens*" (in German), in *Illuminations,* trans. Harry Zohn (New York: Schocken Books, 1969), 69–82; quotation from 71.

26. ʿAlī Bāshā Mubārak, *ʿAlam al-Dīn* (Alexandria: Maṭbaʿat Jarīdat al-Maḥrūsa bi al-Iskandariyya, A.H. 1299/1882), 4 vols. On the publication of the first volumes, see *al-Muqtaṭaf* 6, no. 10 (Ādhār [March] 1882): 640; *al-Muqtaṭaf* 7, no. 1 (Ḥuzayrān [June] 1882): 63.

27. See Mitchell, *Colonising Egypt,* 71; and Gilbert Delanoue, *Moralistes et politiques musulmans dans l'Égypte du XIXe siècle (1798–1882),* vol. 2, bk. 5 ([Cairo]: Institut Français d'Archéologie Orientale du Caire, 1982), 494.

28. Mubārak held various posts under the khedives ʿAbbās I (1848–54) and Ismāʿīl (1863–79), including those of minister of religious endowments *(awqāf)* and minister of military affairs. He also founded the Khedival Library, known today as the Egyptian National Library. See Wen-chin Ouyang, "Fictive Mode, 'Journey to the West,' and Transformation of Space: 'Ali Mubarak's Discourses of Modernization," *Comparative Critical Studies* 4, no. 3 (2007): 331–58, esp. 335–36.

29. On Mubārak's transformations of Egyptian education and urban space, see Mitchell, *Colonising Egypt,* 63–69, 74–80.

30. Muḥammad ʿImāra conjectures that Mubārak began writing *ʿAlam al-Dīn* around 1858; Wadad al-Qadi concurs. See Muḥammad ʿImāra, ed. and introd., *al-Aʿmāl al-Kāmila li ʿAlī Mubārak* (Beirut: al-Mu'assasa al-ʿArabiyya li al-Dirāsāt wa al-Nashr, 1979), 1:19–308; citation from 1:84. See also Wadad al-Qadi, "East and West in ʿAli Mubarak's *ʿAlamuddin,*" in *Intellectual Life in the Arab East, 1890–1939,* ed. Marwan R. Buheiry (Beirut: American University of Beirut, 1981), 21–37; citation from 23. Yet Mubārak himself says he began the novel "during his stint as Minister of Education," a post he would not occupy until 1867–68. See ʿAlī Bāshā Mubārak, preface to *ʿAlam al-Dīn,* 1:5–8; quotation from 7. For Mubārak's autobiography, see ʿAlī Bāshā Mubārak, *al-*

Khiṭaṭ al-Tawfīqiyya al-Jadīda li Miṣr al-Qāhira wa Mudunihā wa Bilādihā al-Qadīma wa al-Shahīra (Būlāq: al-Maṭba'a al-Kubrā al-Amīriyya, A.H. 1304–6 [1886–89]), 9:37–61.

31. See Mitchell, *Colonising Egypt,* 63.

32. While 'Alam al-Dīn's travels are modeled on those of al-Ṭahṭāwī and the Syro-Lebanese intellectual Aḥmad Fāris al-Shidyāq (1804–87), his fictional friendship with the English lexicographer likely is patterned on the friendship between the Egyptian Azharite Ibrāhīm al-Dusūqī (1811–83) and the British Orientalist Edward William Lane; see Ouyang, "Fictive Mode," 336–37. Al-Dusūqī's biography in Mubārak's *Khiṭaṭ* quotes an account by al-Dusūqī himself of his association with Lane; see Mubārak, *al-Khiṭaṭ al-Tawfīqiyya,* 11:10–13. Al-Dusūqī helped Lane compile his Arabic lexicon, *Madd al-Qāmūs,* an expansion of the dictionary *Tāj al-'Arūs,* itself based on *Lisān al-'Arab;* see Geoffrey Roper, "Texts from Nineteenth-Century Egypt: The Role of E. W. Lane," in *Travellers in Egypt,* ed. Paul Starkey and Janet Starkey (London: Tauris Parke [I. B. Tauris], 2001), 244–54, esp. 248–49. Roper notes that al-Dusūqī's autobiography in Mubārak's *Khiṭaṭ* puns on the Arabic transliteration of Lane's name—*layyin* (gentle)—to emphasize his kindness (253n21).

33. The *Lisān al-'Arab* of Ibn Manẓūr, completed in 1290, was printed at Būlāq in the late nineteenth century.

34. Mubārak, *'Alam al-Dīn,* 1:70.

35. Ibid., 1:71.

36. Ibid.

37. Ibid.

38. Ghislaine Alleaume, "L'Orientaliste dans le miroir de la littérature arabe," *Bulletin (British Society for Middle Eastern Studies)* 9, no. 1 (1982): 5–13; quotation from 7.

39. See Mubārak, *'Alam al-Dīn,* 1:356 and 4:1214; quotation from 1:354.

40. Ibid., 1:352.

41. Ibid., 1:356.

42. Ibid., 1:358, 359.

43. On the young Briton's account of his travels in Africa, see Eve M. Troutt Powell, *A Different Shade of Colonialism: Egypt, Great Britain, and the Mastery of the Sudan* (Berkeley: University of California Press, 2003), 58–62.

44. Mubārak, *'Alam al-Dīn,* 1:320. The reading itself unfolds in the novel's twentieth chapter, "al-'Arab" (The Arabs); see 1:321–39. Louca suggests that this "prooftext" is taken from L. A. Sédillot, *Histoire des Arabes* (Paris, 1854; 2nd ed., 1877), of which Mubārak would publish an abridged translation in 1891. See Louca, *Voyageurs et écrivains,* 88, 88n4, 98; see also Alleaume, "L'Orientaliste," 12n9.

45. Mubārak, *'Alam al-Dīn,* 1:339.

46. Ibid., 1:340. The opening of this passage, *"Falammā qaṣṣa 'alayhi mā qaṣṣa,"* mimics the style of a Qur'ānic verse: *"[F]alammā jā'ahu wa qaṣṣa 'alayhi al-qaṣaṣa . . . "* (Qur'ān 28:25).

47. Alleaume argues that Mubārak relied on Orientalist texts to represent entire facets of medieval Arab-Islamic culture in his *Khiṭaṭ;* see Alleaume, "L'Orientaliste," 12n10.

48. Ouyang, "Fictive Mode," 338.
49. Ibid.
50. Ibid.
51. Ibid.
52. Emily Apter, *The Translation Zone: A New Comparative Literature* (Princeton: Princeton University Press, 2006).
53. Ouyang, "Fictive Mode," 348.
54. Mubārak, *'Alam al-Dīn,* 3:1077–78.
55. Ibid., 3:1078.
56. Ouyang, "Fictive Mode," 350. Here Ouyang notes 'Alam al-Dīn's lecture on Arabic poetry before members of the "Oriental Society"; see *'Alam al-Dīn,* 4:1153–79.
57. This fictional Frenchman may be a composite of the historical figures Jean-Michel Venture de Paradis, who died in Egypt around 1799, and Edme-François Jomard, who died in 1862. In this scene 'Alam al-Dīn, in turn, approximates 'Abd al-Raḥmān al-Jabartī.
58. Ouyang, "Fictional Mode," 348.
59. Mubārak, *'Alam al-Dīn,* 3:1079. By "the Muḥammadan family" *("al-'ā'ilati al-Muḥammadiyyati"),* it is not clear if Mubārak means the family of the Prophet Muḥammad (which Islamic sources call *ahl al-bayt*) or the community of the Muslim faithful. The latter usage would be startling. While Orientalist writings (see 1:320) often used the terms *Mohammedan* and *Muslim* interchangeably, the former is generally repugnant to Muslims.
60. Ouyang, "Fictional Mode," 349; see also 350.
61. Mubārak, *'Alam al-Dīn,* 3:1079–80.
62. Ibid., 3:1080.
63. Ibid., 3:1081.
64. See Rasheed El-Enany, *Arab Representations of the Occident: East-West Encounters in Arabic Fiction* (London: Routledge, 2006), 27.
65. Mubārak, *'Alam al-Dīn,* 3:1082.
66. Ibid.
67. Ibid.
68. Ibid., 3:1082–85.
69. Ibid., 3:1085.
70. Ibid.
71. Ibid., 3:1093–1120.
72. Ibid., 3:1093.
73. Ibid., 3:1095.
74. Ibid.
75. Ibid. This historicist comparison of religions recalls the work of Ernest Renan (1823–92).
76. See e.g., Mubārak, *'Alam al-Dīn,* 3:1106.
77. Ibid., 3:1096–98.
78. Ibid., 3:1099.
79. Ibid.
80. Citing at least one Egyptian contemporary, Delanoue suggests that Mubārak may have abetted the 1882 British invasion of Egypt—a painful pos-

sibility that Egyptian nationalist history elides. See Delanoue, *Moralistes et politiques,* vol. 2, bk. 5, 518–19.

81. On this point, see also al-Qadi, "East and West," 34n10.

82. Indeed, the British already "ruled" Egypt, having seized control (with the French) of its finances in the 1870s to ensure repayment of Ismāʿīl's massive debts to European creditors.

83. Nandy, *Intimate Enemy,* ix.

84. Ibid.

85. Michael K. Goldberg, in Thomas Carlyle, *On Heroes, Hero-Worship, and the Heroic in History,* introd. Michael K. Goldberg, ed. Michael K. Goldberg, Joel J. Brattin, and Mark Engel (Berkeley: University of California Press, 1993), 257.

86. Talal Asad, *Formations of the Secular: Christianity, Islam, Modernity* (Stanford: Stanford University Press, 2003), 222.

87. See Matti Moosa, *The Origins of Modern Arabic Fiction,* 2nd ed. (Boulder, CO: Lynne Rienner, 1997), 99. English became the primary language of instruction around 1900; see Tignor, *Modernization and British Colonial Rule,* 326.

88. Naẓārat al-Maʿārif al-ʿUmūmiyya [Ministry of Public Instruction], *Barnāmij Madrasat al-Muʿallimīn al-Khidīwiyya: al-Madrasa al-ʿĀliya* (Cairo: al-Maṭbaʿa al-Amīriyya, 1913), 3–6, esp. 6.

89. Tignor, *Modernization and British Colonial Rule,* 347.

90. See Anwar al-Jindī, *Taṭawwur al-Tarjama fī al-Adab al-ʿArabī al-Muʿāṣir* (Cairo: Maṭbaʿat al-Risāla, n.d.), 49.

91. On al-Sibāʿī's graduation, see ʿAlāʾ al-Dīn Waḥīd, *Muḥammad al-Sibāʿī: al-Adīb Alladhī Sabaqa ʿAṣrah* ([Cairo]: al-Hayʾa al-Miṣriyya al-ʿĀmma li al-Kitāb, 1982), 19. The translations I cite are Muḥammad al-Sibāʿī, trans., *Tshāyild Hārūld* and "ʿArūs ʿAbdūs," in *Abṭāl al-ʿĀlam . . . al-Lūrd Bayrūn* (Cairo: Majallat al-Bayān, n.d.), 49–87, 95–120; *Riwāyat Dhāt al-Thawb al-Abyaḍ, li Wāḍiʿihā al-Kātib al-Qiṣaṣī al-Inkilīzī al-Shahīr Kūlins,* 4 vols., *Musāmarāt al-Shaʿb* 6, nos. 114–17 [1909?]; *Qiṣṣat al-Madīnatayn, taʾlīf Sharlz Dikinz,* 3 vols. (Cairo: Maṭbaʿat al-Bayān, 1912); *Rubāʿiyyāt ʿUmar al-Khayyām* (Cairo: Maṭbaʿat Dār Iḥyāʾ al-Kutub al-ʿArabiyya, n.d.); *al-Tarbiya, li al-Faylasūf Sbinsir* (Cairo: Maṭbaʿat al-Jarīda, 1908); and *Riwāyat Yūlyūs Qayṣar, taʾlīf Shāksbīr* (Cairo: Maṭbaʿat Maktabat al-Wafd, n.d.). On al-Sibāʿī's translations, see also J[an]. Brugman, *An Introduction to the History of Modern Arabic Literature in Egypt* (Leiden: E. J. Brill, 1984), 104–6; al-Jindī, *Taṭawwur al-Tarjama,* 47–51; and Moosa, *Origins of Modern Arabic Fiction,* 100, 108. After 1919 he translated more French and Russian works, especially those of Guy de Maupassant and Anton Chekhov.

92. See Waḥīd, *Muḥammad al-Sibāʿī,* 31–32, 48–49.

93. Ibid., 15, 13.

94. Ibid., 17.

95. Ibid., 14.

96. Ibid., 101.

97. Al-Sibāʿī made his debut in *al-Jarīda* on 23 November 1907; see Brugman, *An Introduction,* 99. Al-Jindī and Moosa give the date as 1908; see al-

Jindī, *Taṭawwur al-Tarjama,* 50; and Moosa, *Origins of Modern Arabic Fiction,* 108. For al-Sibā'ī's eulogy to Zaghlūl, see Muḥammad al-Sibā'ī, "Ilā al-Rāḥil al-'Aẓīm: Fī Dār al-Khulūd," *al-Balāgh al-Usbū'ī* 1, no. 41 (2 September 1927/6 Rabī' al-Awwal A.H. 1346): 24–25.

98. Al-Sayyid, *Egypt and Cromer,* 193.

99. Ibid., 188–94; quotation from 189.

100. al-Sibā'ī, "Ilā al-Rāḥil," 24.

101. Waḥīd, *Muḥammad al-Sibā'ī,* 101.

102. See Sameh F. Hanna, "Hamlet Lives Happily Ever After in Arabic: The Genesis of the Field of Drama Translation in Egypt," *Translator* 11, no. 2 (2005): 167–92; and Sāmiḥ Fikrī [Ḥannā], "Ṭāniyūs 'Abduh wa Riwāyat Hāmlit al-Tamthīliyya: Fī Madīḥ al-Khawana al-Nubalā'," *Akhbār al-Adab,* 12 February 2006, www.akhbarelyom.org.eg/adab/issues/657/0600.html (accessed 25 June 2007).

103. According to Hanna, 'Iffat's preface to this translation indicates that Shaykh Muḥammad 'Abduh, the celebrated Islamic reformist, had encouraged its publication; see Sameh F. Hanna, "Decommercialising Shakespeare: Mutran's Translation of *Othello,*" *Critical Survey* 19, no. 3 (2007): 27–54; citation from 36. 'Iffat also published a translation of *Macbeth* in 1911, as did Aḥmad Muḥammad Ṣāliḥ; see Hanna, "Decommercialising Shakespeare," 31. On Shakespeare translations, see also Ferial J. Ghazoul, "The Arabization of *Othello,*" *Comparative Literature* 50, no. 1 (Winter 1998): 1–31.

104. The Dīwān school drew its name from the title of a book by two of its major exponents that attacked modern Arabic neoclassicism. See 'Abbās Maḥmūd al-'Aqqād and Ibrāhīm 'Abd al-Qādir al-Māzinī, *al-Dīwān: Kitāb fī al-Naqd wa al-Adab,* 2 vols. (Cairo: Maktabat al-Sa'āda, 1921).

105. See Muhammad 'Abdul-Hai, *Tradition and English and American Influence in Arabic Romantic Poetry: A Study in Comparative Literature* (London: Ithaca Press, 1982), 20–23; quotation from 20.

106. 'Abbās Maḥmūd al-'Aqqād, quoted in Yūsuf al-Sibā'ī, "Kāna Abī," introduction to Muḥammad al-Sibā'ī, trans., *100 Qiṣṣa* ([Cairo?]: Dār al-Jumhūriyya li al-Ṭibā'a, n.d.), n.p.

107. Ṭāhā Ḥusayn, "Muqaddima," introduction to *al-Faylasūf,* by Muḥammad al-Sibā'ī, 2nd ed. (Cairo: al-Sharika al-'Arabiyya li al-Ṭibā'a wa al-Nashr, 1963), 5–6.

108. Brugman, *An Introduction,* 345.

109. See 'Abbās Maḥmūd al-'Aqqād, "Muqaddimat al-Ṭab'at al-Ūlā," in 'Abbās Maḥmūd al-'Aqqād, *'Abqariyyat Muḥammad,* 2nd ed. (Cairo: Maṭba'at al-Istiqāma, 1942/A.H. 1361), 5–16; the reference to Carlyle appears on 6–8. Al-'Aqqād does not name al-Sibā'ī here. Elsewhere, however, he reports that he and the publisher of *al-Bayān* urged al-Sibā'ī to translate *On Heroes;* see 'Abbās Maḥmūd al-'Aqqād, "Muṣṭafā Luṭfī al-Manfalūṭī Kamā 'Araftuh," *al-Majalla* 6, no. 70 (November 1962): 2–6; see 3–4.

110. See al-'Aqqād, "Muqaddimat al-Ṭab'at al-Ūlā," 7.

111. Ṭāhā Ḥusayn, quoted in Yūsuf al-Sibā'ī, "Kāna Abī," introduction to Muḥammad al-Sibā'ī, trans., *100 Qiṣṣa* ([Cairo?]: Dār al-Jumhūriyya li al-Ṭibā'a, n.d.), n.p.

112. Muhsin J. Al-Musawi, *Islam on the Street: Religion in Modern Arabic Literature* (Lanham, MD: Rowman and Littlefield, 2009), 23–24.

113. Ibid., 23–24; quotation from 23.

114. Thomas Carlyle, *On Heroes, Hero-Worship, and the Heroic in History*, introd. Michael K. Goldberg, ed. Michael K. Goldberg, Joel J. Brattin, and Mark Engel (Berkeley: University of California Press, 1993), 38–39, emphasis in the original. All citations are to the 1993 edition.

115. Muhammed A. Al-Da'mi [Muḥammad al-Da'mī], *Arabian Mirrors and Western Soothsayers: Nineteenth-Century Literary Approaches to Arab-Islamic History* (New York: Peter Lang, 2002), 84–91.

116. A. J. Arberry, trans., *The Koran Interpreted* (London: Allen and Unwin, 1955; New York: Touchstone, 1996), 2:126. Citation is to the 1996 edition.

117. On Ernest Renan's 1883 Sorbonne lecture "L'Islamisme et la science" and Jamāl al-Dīn al-Afghānī's rebuttal thereof in the *Journal de débats* of 18–19 May 1883, see Albert Hourani, *Arabic Thought in the Liberal Age, 1798–1939* (Cambridge: Cambridge University Press, 1983 [1962]), 120–23; Stephen Sheehi, *Foundations of Modern Arab Identity* (Gainesville: University Press of Florida, 2004), 138–41, 143–49; and Margaret Kohn, "Afghānī on Empire, Islam, and Civilization," *Political Theory* 37, no. 3 (2009): 398–422, esp. 406–16.

118. al-Sibā'ī, "al-Abṭāl wa 'Ibādat al-Buṭūla," 84; reprinted in al-Sibā'ī, *al-Abṭāl*, 54.

119. Arberry, *Koran Interpreted*, 2:126. Al-Sibā'ī's intended effect registered well beyond Egypt. In 1912 the Damascus monthly *al-Muqtabas* (the Quoted), edited by Muḥammad Kurd 'Alī, praised al-Sibā'ī's *al-Abṭāl* for introducing Arab readers to Carlyle, who had written of the Prophet with a "power that no Westerner, in our estimation, has matched." See "al-Abṭāl," *al-Muqtabas* 7 (1912/A.H. 1330), 148–49; quotation from 148.

120. Carlyle, *On Heroes*, 148, emphases in the original.

121. Compare al-Sibā'ī, *al-Abṭāl*, 128, 142; Carlyle, *On Heroes*, 85, 95–96.

122. Carlyle, *On Heroes*, 95.

123. Ibid., 96–97.

124. Ibid.

125. al-Sibā'ī, *al-Abṭāl*, 143.

126. Ibid.

127. One should note, however, that by the early twentieth century, *umma* had undergone a semantic shift toward the latter. See Asad, *Formations of the Secular*, 196–98.

128. Gauri Viswanathan, "Secularism in the Framework of Heterodoxy," *PMLA* 123, no. 2 (2008): 466–76; quotation from 468; see also 473.

129. Ibid., 466. On British mobilizations of "secular" English literature to insinuate Christianity into colonial India, see Gauri Viswanathan, *Masks of Conquest: Literary Study and British Rule in India* (Delhi: Oxford University Press, 1998 [1989]), 63–93, esp. 85–88.

130. Muḥammad al-Sibā'ī, "Kalimat al-Mu'arrib" (Arabizer's Foreword), in *al-Abṭāl, ta'līf al-Faylasūf al-Akbar Tūmās Kārlayl*, 3rd ed. (Cairo: al-Maṭba'a al-Miṣriyya bi al-Azhar, 1930/A.H. 1349 [1911]), *lām–mīm* [xii–xiii].

131. Asad, *Formations of the Secular,* 196–7; see also 196n21.

132. Carlyle, *On Heroes,* 154, emphasis in the original. Carlyle repeatedly lambastes the eighteenth century as a time of unbelief; see 147–52.

133. Ibid., 148. While al-Sibāʿī must have noted Carlyle's comparison of Bentham to the Prophet Muḥammad, his translation omits the comparison; see al-Sibāʿī, *al-Abṭāl,* 228–30.

134. See M. K. Gandhi, *Indian Home Rule* (Madras: Ganesh, 1922), 30–39.

135. Carlyle, *On Heroes,* 140, emphasis in the original. See also 138.

136. Ibid., 141. Here Carlyle misappropriates the thought of the German philosopher Johann Gottlieb Fichte (1762–1814). On this point, see Elizabeth M. Vida, *Romantic Affinities: German Authors and Carlyle* (Toronto: University of Toronto Press, 1993), 117–21. For Fichte, heroes cannot be worshiped, only admired, for worship is directed to God alone; further, the human is the organ that unfolds the "Divine Idea," not its symbol (117, 118).

137. Carlyle, *On Heroes,* 140, emphasis in the original.

138. On the Qur'ān's dialectical relationship to pre-Islamic literary forms, see Naṣr Ḥāmid Abū Zayd, *Mafhūm al-Naṣṣ: Dirāsa fī 'Ulūm al-Qur'ān* (Cairo: al-Hay'a al-Miṣriyya al-'Āmma li al-Kitāb, 1990), 155–78, esp. 161–64.

139. See Carlyle, *On Heroes,* 4–12; quotations from 11, 9.

140. Ibid., 4.

141. Although his first biographer, Richard Garnett, argues the contrary; see Richard Garnett, *Life of Thomas Carlyle* (London: Walter Scott, 1887), 168.

142. Carlyle, *On Heroes,* 11.

143. Ibid., 19, emphasis mine; and Benjamin, "Task of the Translator," 80. On the "world-tree," see Carlyle, *On Heroes*, 32.

144. Carlyle, *On Heroes,* 19.

145. See Benjamin, "Task of the Translator," 71, 73. Benjamin does not invoke images of growth in any commonplace sense. "Life" is the effect of history, not of nature. I would suggest that Carlyle too does not so much compare history to life as historicize life: the leaves and boughs of his world-tree resemble biographies and histories, not the other way around.

146. Carlyle, *On Heroes,* 19.

147. Ibid., 20, emphasis in the original.

148. Ibid.

149. See *The Last Khedive of Egypt: Memoirs of Abbas Hilmi II* (in French), ed. and trans. Amira Sonbol (Reading, U.K.: Ithaca Press, 1998), 172, 230; quotation from 230.

150. Ibid., 174.

151. Carlyle, *On Heroes,* 30, emphasis in the original.

CHAPTER 5

1. Ibrāhīm 'Abd al-Qādir al-Māzinī, "al-Ustādh al-Sibāʿī wa Adabuh," introduction to Muḥammad al-Sibāʿī, *al-Ṣuwar* (Shubrā [Cairo]: Sharikat Fann al-Ṭibāʿa, 1946), 3–9; quotation from 4.

2. Ibid.

3. Frantz Fanon, *The Wretched of the Earth,* trans. Constance Farrington, pref. Jean-Paul Sartre (New York: Grove Press, 1963), 39.

4. Muḥammad Sayyid Kīlānī, *Tirām al-Qāhira: Dirāsa Tārīkhiyya, Ijtimā'iyya, Adabiyya* (Cairo: Maṭba'at al-Madanī, 1968), 32.

5. See Partha Chatterjee, *Nationalist Thought and the Colonial World: A Derivative Discourse?* (London: Zed Books, 1986).

6. Ibid., vii.

7. Ibid.

8. Lawrence Venuti, "Local Contingencies: Translation and National Identities," in *Nation, Language, and the Ethics of Translation,* ed. Sandra Bermann and Michael Wood (Princeton: Princeton University Press, 2005), 177–202; quotation from 180.

9. Ibid.

10. Ibid.

11. Ibid., emphases mine.

12. Antony Easthope, *Englishness and National Culture* (London: Routledge, 1999), 5, quoted in Venuti, "Local Contingencies," 180.

13. On the nation as limited, sovereign community, see Benedict Anderson, *Imagined Communities: Reflections on the Origin and Spread of Nationalism,* rev. ed. (New York: Verso, 1991), 7.

14. Naoki Sakai, *Translation and Subjectivity: On "Japan" and Cultural Nationalism*, foreword Meaghan Morris (Minneapolis: University of Minnesota Press, 1997), 50.

15. Ibid., 163.

16. Ibid.

17. Joseph Agoub, *Discours historique sur l'Égypte*, in *Mélanges de littérature orientale et française, avec une notice sur l'auteur par M. de Pongerville, de l'Académie française* (Paris: Werdet, 1835), 123–70; quotation from 126.

18. With 'Abbās Maḥmūd al-'Aqqād, al-Māzinī was an exponent of the influential Dīwān school, which called for a radical "reform" of Arabic poetry based on the aesthetics of British Romanticism.

19. Ibrāhīm 'Abd al-Qādir al-Māzinī, "al-Qawmiyya al-'Arabiyya," *al-Risāla* 3, no. 112 (27 Jumādā al-Ūlā A.H. 1354/26 August 1935): 1363–64; quotation from 1363. This issue commemorated the eighth anniversary of the death of the Egyptian nationalist Sa'd Zaghlūl.

20. Timothy Mitchell, *Colonising Egypt* (Cambridge: Cambridge University Press, 1988; Berkeley: University of California Press, 1991), 141–42. Citations are to the 1991 edition.

21. Ibid., 148–49. Mitchell's analysis relies on Monçef Chelli, *La Parole arabe: une théorie de la relativité des cultures* (Paris: Sindbad, 1980), 35–45.

22. See al-Māzinī, "al-Qawmiyya al-'Arabiyya," 1363.

23. Like al-Māzinī, Bakhtin insists on the unity of "form and content" in discourse and thus on the radical sociality of very utterance. See M[ikhail]. M[ikhailovich]. Bakhtin, "Discourse in the Novel" (in Russian), *The Dialogic Imagination: Four Essays by M. M. Bakhtin,* ed. Michael Holquist, trans. Caryl Emerson and Michael Holquist (Austin: University of Texas Press, 1981), 259–

422; quotation from 259. Written in 1934–35, the essay was first published in Moscow in 1975.

24. Bakhtin, "Discourse in the Novel," 270–71, emphases in the original.

25. al-Māzinī, "al-Qawmiyya al-'Arabiyya," 1363.

26. Lydia H. Liu, *The Clash of Empires: The Invention of China in Modern World Making* (Cambridge, MA: Harvard University Press, 2004), 37.

27. Ibid., 13.

28. Ibid.; see also 14.

29. Ibid., 14.

30. Muḥammad Ḥusayn Haykal, "Iḥtiḍār al-Jumūd wa al-Fawḍā—Kayfa Yattasiq al-Niẓām al-Jadīd," *al-Jadīd* 1, no. 2 (6 February 1928): 4–6.

31. Aḥmad Ḥasan al-Zayyāt, "Fī al-Adab al-'Arabī," *al-Jadīd* 1, no. 2 (6 February 1928): 19–20.

32. These twin poles "bookend" twenty theses on translation in Emily Apter, *The Translation Zone: A New Comparative Literature* (Princeton: Princeton University Press, 2006), xi–xii.

33. Rifā'a Badawī Rāfi' al-Ṭahṭāwī, *Takhlīṣ al-Ibrīz fī Talkhīṣ Bārīz,* ed. Mahdī 'Allām, Aḥmad Aḥmad Badawī, and Anwar Lūqā (Cairo: Muṣṭafā al-Bābī al-Ḥalabī, 1958 [1834, 1849]), 299.

34. Mitchell, *Colonising Egypt,* 78.

35. Ibid., 79.

36. Ibid., 79–80.

37. Ibid., 82.

38. Arthur Goldschmidt Jr., "al-Hilbawi, Ibrahim," in *Biographical Dictionary of Modern Egypt* (Boulder, CO: Lynne Rienner, 2000), 78.

39. Haykal, "Iḥtiḍār al-Jumūd," 4.

40. Ibid.

41. Ibid.

42. On 'Adlī Yakan Pasha, see Arthur Goldschmidt Jr., "Yakan, 'Adli," in *Biographical Dictionary of Modern Egypt,* 229. As minister of education from 1917 to 1919, Yakan had presided over the Arabization of Egyptian primary and secondary schools, enforcing Arabic as the primary language of instruction.

43. Haykal, "Iḥtiḍār al-Jumūd," 4.

44. The term may have been less unusual in Arab Christian or Jewish usage, however. In 1914 the Syrian Christian *mahjar* (émigré) writer Nasīb 'Arīḍa, writing under the pseudonym Mālik, published an essay in the New York journal *al-Sā'iḥ* (the Traveler) titled "Rasā'il min Burj Bābil" (Letters from the Tower of Babel); see Mālik [Nasīb 'Arīḍa], "Rasā'il min Burj Bābil," *al-Sā'iḥ* 2, no. 145 (16 March 1914): 4–5.

45. "Fawḍā al-Azyā' fī Miṣr," *al-Siyāsa al-Usbū'iyya* (4 December 1926): 19.

46. Anderson, *Imagined Communities*, 24–26.

47. James Jankowski, however, contends that Haykal was a staunch "Easternizer" by the 1920s. See James Jankowski, "The Eastern Idea and the Eastern Union in Interwar Egypt," *International Journal of African Historical Studies* 14, no. 4 (1981): 643–66, esp. 645–48. Haykal's pro-Westernization pronouncements in "Iḥtiḍār al-Jumūd" might complicate this view. While Haykal was a member of al-Rābiṭa al-Sharqiyya (the Eastern Society), which promoted

the Easternization of Egypt and the formation of an Eastern cultural and political bloc, he was also a Pharaonicist in virtually the same period and thus espoused a Westernizing view of Egypt.

48. See Maḥmûd Ṭâhir Ḥaqqî, *The Maiden of Dinshway,* in *Three Pioneering Egyptian Novels,* trans. and introd. Saad El-Gabalawy (Fredericton, NB: York Press, 1986), 36; Maḥmūd Ṭāhir Ḥaqqī, *'Adhrā' Dinshawāy,* introd. Yaḥyā Ḥaqqī (Cairo: al-Dār al-Qawmiyya li al-Ṭibā'a wa al-Nashr, 1964 [1906]), 52–53. On the cologne as colonial and class signifier, see Samah Selim, *The Novel and the Rural Imaginary in Egypt, 1880–1985* (London: Routledge-Curzon, 2004), 98.

49. Selim, *Novel and the Rural Imaginary,* 98.

50. See Abdeslam M. Maghraoui, *Liberalism without Democracy: Nationhood and Citizenship in Egypt, 1922–1936* (Durham: Duke University Press, 2006), 103–6.

51. Selim, *Novel and the Rural Imaginary,* 98. I would put pressure, however, on Selim's assumption of a "natural" complicity between colonial authority and the native professional elite. This book attempts to theorize a complicity that Marxist theory might too easily naturalize.

52. Haykal, "Iḥtiḍār al-Jumūd," 5–6.

53. Ibid., 6.

54. Rey Chow, *The Age of the World Target: Self-Referentiality in War, Theory, and Comparative Work* (Durham: Duke University Press, 2006), 88–89, emphasis in the original.

55. Jacques Derrida, "Onto-Theology of National-Humanism (Prolegomena to a Hypothesis)," *Oxford Literary Review* 14, nos. 1–2 (1992): 3–23; quotation from 11, emphasis in the original.

56. Ibid., 10.

57. On translation of the foreign "into an element of oneself," see Vicente L. Rafael, *The Promise of the Foreign: Nationalism and the Technics of Translation in the Spanish Philippines* (Durham: Duke University Press, 2005), 14.

58. See Derrida, "Onto-Theology," 11–20, esp. 19.

59. Derrida, "Onto-Theology," 19.

60. Lydia H. Liu, "The Desire for the Sovereign and the Logic of Reciprocity in the Family of Nations," *diacritics* 29, no. 4 (Winter 1999): 150–77; see 169.

61. Henry Wheaton, *Elements of International Law*, 3rd ed. (1846; Oxford: Clarendon Press, 1936), 28–29, quoted in Liu, "Desire for the Sovereign," 169.

62. Liu, "Desire for the Sovereign," 170–71, emphasis mine.

63. Ibid., 171.

64. Rafael, *Promise of the Foreign*, xvi.

65. Ibid., xvi, xvii.

66. Ibid., xvii.

67. Ibid., 15.

68. Ibid., 2, emphases mine.

69. Ibid., 14.

70. Ibid., 5.

71. Ibid.

72. Ibid.

73. Derrida, "Onto-Theology," 19.

74. Haykal, "Iḥtiḍār al-Jumūd," 5.

75. al-Zayyāt, "Fī al-Adab al-'Arabī," 19–20.

76. Ibid., 19.

77. Ibid., 19–20.

78. Edward W. Said, *Beginnings: Intention and Method,* Morningside ed. (New York: Columbia University Press, 1985 [1975]), xvii.

79. On Mūsā's life, see Salāma Mūsā, *The Education of Salāma Mūsā,* trans. L. O. Schuman (Leiden: E. J. Brill, 1961). The original is Salāma Mūsā, *Tarbiyat Salāma Mūsā* (Cairo: Dār al-Kātib al-Miṣrī, 1947).

80. Salāma Mūsā, "Ilā Ayyihimā Naḥnu Aqrab: al-Sharq am al-Gharb?" *al-Hilāl* 35, no. 9 (1 July 1927/2 Muḥarram A.H. 1346): 1072–74; quotation from 1072.

81. Ibid., 1073.

82. Ibid., 1073–74.

83. Rudyard Kipling, "The Ballad of East and West," in *Ballads and Barrack-Room Ballads* (New York: Macmillan, 1892), 3–11; quotation from 3. Mūsā ignores the rest of Kipling's refrain, which suggests that power levels hierarchies of geography, race, and class.

84. Thomas Babington Macaulay, "Minute on Indian Education," in *Speeches by Lord Macaulay with His Minute on Indian Education,* introd. G. M. Young (London: Oxford University Press, 1935), 359.

85. Salāma Mūsā, "al-Miṣriyyūn Umma Gharbiyya," *al-Hilāl* 37, no. 2 (1 December 1928/18 Jumādā al-Ākhira A.H. 1347): 177–81; quotation from 177.

86. Ibid., 177, 178.

87. G[rafton]. Elliot Smith, *The Ancient Egyptians and the Origin of Civilization,* rev. ed. (London: Harper, 1923), vii–ix. The title page identifies Smith as professor of anatomy at the University of London. On Mūsā's debts to Smith, see also Omnia El Shakry, *The Great Social Laboratory: Subjects of Knowledge in Colonial and Postcolonial Egypt* (Stanford: Stanford University Press, 2007), 60–66. On Mūsā's interest in colonial Egyptology and role in Egyptian Pharaonicism, see Elliott Colla, *Conflicted Antiquities: Egyptology, Egyptomania, Egyptian Modernity* (Durham: Duke University Press, 2007), 155–56, 243.

88. Smith, *Ancient Egyptians,* 66–67.

89. Ibid., 58.

90. Ibid., 58–60, 62. *Armenoid,* which came into use in the early twentieth century, designated a racial type understood as "white" (originally "Alpine," or central European) and said to inhabit the lands between Europe and Asia, especially West Asia. See Carleton Stevens Coon, *The Races of Europe* (Westport, CT: Greenwood Press, 1972 [1939]), 293, 625, 628–30.

91. Smith, *Ancient Egyptians,* 61.

92. Ibid., 65; see also 67–68.

93. Ibid., 68.

94. See Maghraoui, *Liberalism without Democracy,* 78–79; quotation from 79. Interestingly, Maghraoui misquotes Smith's analysis of ancient Egyptian

representations of the Arabs, replacing Smith's "Armenoid" with "Negroid" (see 79).

95. See Mūsā, "Ilā Ayyihimā," 1072.

96. See Lillian Eichler, *The Customs of Mankind, with Notes on Modern Etiquette and the Newest Trend in Entertainment* (London: William Heinemann, 1924), 132–33, quoted in Mūsā, "al-Miṣriyyūn Umma Gharbiyya," 179–80. Eichler's Egyptian-English word table derives from an extensive lexicon in Gerald Massey, *Egyptian Origines in the British Isles,* vol. 1 of *A Book of the Beginnings, Containing an Attempt to Recover and Reconstitute the Lost Origines of . . . Religion and Language, with Egypt for the Mouthpiece and Africa as the Birthplace* (London: Williams and Norgate, 1881), 49–81. The work's subtitle originates language in Africa, whose "mouth" is Egypt. Yet the title of its first volume, *Egyptian Origines in the British Isles,* registers precisely the ambiguity Mūsā exploits to posit affinities between Egypt and England. For while Massey originates Britain in Egypt, this title seems also to originate Egypt in Britain.

97. Mūsā, "Ilā Ayyihimā," 1074.

98. Ibid.

99. Ibid.

100. Derrida, "Onto-Theology," 10.

101. I borrow the words of the Martinican poet-philosopher of decolonization Aimé Césaire, describing the German anthropologist Leo Frobenius's revaluation of African cultures. See Aimé Césaire, *Discourse on Colonialism* (in French), trans. Joan Pinkham (New York: Monthly Review Press, 2000), 53.

CHAPTER 6

1. Lawrence Durrell, *Mountolive* (New York: Penguin, 1991 [1958]), 28.

2. Ibid., 28–29.

3. Ibid., 41. My reading of *Mountolive*'s Leila is indebted to Roger Bowen's analysis of Durrell's treatment of British Orientalism in *The Alexandria Quartet,* as well as to his contention that the quartet represents an elegy to the idea of British Empire. See Roger Bowen, *"Many Histories Deep": The* Personal Landscape *Poets in Egypt, 1940–45* (Madison, NJ: Fairleigh Dickinson University Press, 1995), 162–85, esp. 167.

4. Durrell, *Mountolive,* 29. I quote only a portion of Leila's recitation, which reproduces most of section 28 of John Ruskin, "Lecture I: Inaugural," in *Lectures on Art Delivered Before the University of Oxford in Hilary Term, 1870* (Oxford: Clarendon Press, 1870), 23–24. Durrell's rendering contains one error: Ruskin's original reads "mistress of Learning and of the Arts"; see 24. On the Ruskinian resonances in Durrell, see Anne R. Zahlan, "Rhodes, Ruskin, and the Myth of Empire: Imperial Intertextuality in Durrell's *Mountolive,*" *Deus Loci: The Lawrence Durrell Journal,* n.s. 8 (2001–2): 226–30.

5. William Shakespeare, *Richard II,* in *William Shakespeare: The Complete Works,* ed. Stanley Wells, Gary Taylor, et al., 2nd ed. (Oxford: Oxford University Press, 2005), 2.1.40. Reference is to act, scene, and line.

6. Ruskin, "Lecture I," 24–25.

7. John Milton, "Lycidas," in *John Milton: The Complete Poems,* ed. John Leonard (New York: Penguin, 1998), line 109.

8. Ruskin, "Lecture I," 25–26.

9. See Edward W. Said, *Culture and Imperialism* (New York: Vintage, 1994 [1993]), 102–4; quotation from 104, emphasis in the original.

10. See "On *The Works of Sir Joshua Reynolds, Knight*, edited by Edmund Malone, 3 volumes (1798)," in *Blake's Poetry and Designs,* ed. Mary Lynn Johnson and John E. Grant (New York: W. W. Norton, 1979), 439. Compare "A Public Address to the Chalcographic Society," in *Blake's Poetry and Designs,* 420.

11. Ruskin, "Lecture I," 24.

12. Hala Youssef Halim Youssef [Hala Halim], "The Alexandria Archive: An Archaeology of Alexandrian Cosmopolitanism" (Ph.D. diss., University of California, Los Angeles, 2004), 256.

13. Ibid., 260–61.

14. On Sigmund Freud's *unheimlich* (uncanny) and Homi Bhabha's related notion of "mimicry" in the context of Durrell's *Mountolive*, see Youssef, "The Alexandria Archive," 232–41.

15. See "Persuading the World to Tap the Source of Laughter in Itself," in *Lawrence Durrell: Conversations*, ed. Earl G. Ingersoll (Madison, NJ: Fairleigh Dickinson University Press, 1998), 71.

16. Durrell, *Mountolive,* 29–30, emphasis in the original.

17. Ibid., 29–30.

18. See Jonathan Bolton, *Personal Landscapes: British Poets in Egypt during the Second World War* (New York: St. Martin's Press, 1997), xiv. Durrell arrived in Egypt in June 1941 and left in the late spring of 1945; see Bowen, *"Many Histories Deep,"* 15, 39, 141–42.

19. Maḥfūẓ's *Zuqāq* was not translated into English until 1966, so Durrell could not have read it before he published his *Quartet.* For Maḥfūẓ, Durrell's *Quartet* is intriguing "but about foreigners," not Egyptians; see D. J. Taylor, "The Maestro of Middaq *[sic]* Alley," *Sunday Times* (London), 18 March 1990, H8–H9; quotation from H9.

20. See Amira el-Azhary Sonbol, *The New Mamluks: Egyptian Society and Modern Feudalism,* foreword Robert A. Fernea (Syracuse, NY: Syracuse University Press, 2000), 110–11.

21. "New Alliance," in *The* Times *Book of Egypt, Reprinted from the Egypt Number Published on 26 January 1937* (London: Times Publishing Company, n.d.), 1–4; quotation from 1.

22. "Anglo-Egyptian Treaty [of Alliance]," 26 August 1936, quoted in *The* Times *Book of Egypt,* 15.

23. Ibid., 16.

24. Ibid.

25. Ibid., 16–17, emphases mine.

26. Ibid., 26. The addendum qualifies Article 2 of the treaty.

27. On the "boy-to-schoolmaster" relation between Fārūq and Lampson, see Artemis Cooper, *Cairo in the War, 1939–1945* (London: Hamish Hamilton,

1989), 25. See also Lampson's entry of 21 April 1944 in *The Killearn Diaries, 1934–1946: The Diplomatic and Personal Record of Lord Killearn (Sir Miles Lampson), High Commissioner and Ambassador, Egypt,* ed. Trefor E. Evans (London: Sidgwick and Jackson, 1972), 298.

28. Bowen, *"Many Histories Deep,"* 164. In Memlik Pasha, another character in Durrell's *Mountolive,* Bowen identifies a Fārūq lookalike (179–80).

29. On Fārūq's place in Easternist and Islamist movements of the 1930s, see Israel Gershoni and James P. Jankowski, *Redefining the Egyptian Nation, 1930–1945* (Cambridge: Cambridge University Press, 1995), esp. 158–63.

30. Trevor Le Gassick's translation inverts the name Faraj Ibrāhīm to read Ibrahim Faraj. In the Arabic, the name appears once (erroneously) as Ibrāhīm Faraj; see Najīb Maḥfūẓ, *Zuqāq al-Midaqq* (Cairo: Maktabat Miṣr, n.d. [1947]), 259.

31. In the persona of Faraj Ibrāhīm, Maḥfūẓ may have conflated King Fārūq and his barber and confidant, the Italian Rafael, who was rumored to be a pimp. Rafael's "other half" may be the barber 'Abbās al-Ḥulw, Ḥamīda's jilted fiancé and Faraj's nemesis.

32. Such representations of Egypt as a woman—by turns traditional, by turns Europeanized—have circulated since the beginnings of the Egyptian nationalist press. See Beth Baron, *Egypt as a Woman: Nationalism, Gender, and Politics* (Berkeley: University of California Press, 2005), 57–81. See also Lisa Pollard, *Nurturing the Nation: The Family Politics of Modernizing, Colonizing, and Liberating Egypt, 1805–1923* (Berkeley: University of California Press, 2005), 166–204. *Al-Kashkūl*'s backing by the palace explains the anti-Wafdist tenor of the cartoon in question; see Baron, *Egypt as a Woman,* 69.

33. "Miṣr wa 'Uṣbat al-Umam" (Egypt and the League of Nations), *al-Kashkūl* 9, no. 437 (27 September 1929): 1.

34. "Istiqlāl Miṣr wa al-Nuqṭa al-'Askariyya al-Inkilīziyya" (The Independence of Egypt and the Position of the British Military), *al-Kashkūl* 9, no. 468 (2 May 1930): 28.

35. Compare this uncertainty to the political confidence of Egyptian nationalism in an earlier cartoon that Pollard cites. Published in August 1920, while Sa'd Zaghlūl was in London negotiating an end to the British Protectorate, this cartoon depicts an elegant Egyptian female diner—face unveiled and sporting European high heels—asking an English waiter for a "platter of independence." Writes Pollard, "This is not the image of a clumsy, backward, colonized entity seeking entrance into the league of refined, modern nation-states: this woman—while obviously not European—asks for what she wants with all the ease of a Western counterpart." See Pollard, *Nurturing the Nation,* 183–84.

36. Prostitution was a hot-button issue in early- to mid-twentieth-century Egypt. On its history, see Margot Badran, *Feminists, Islam, and Nation: Gender and the Making of Modern Egypt* (Princeton: Princeton University Press, 1995), 192–206. At the 1944 Arab Feminist Conference in Cairo, Bahīja Rashīd—representing the Egyptian Feminist Union—called for a ban on legalized prostitution in all Arab countries (205–6). This event coincides with the time in which Maḥfūẓ's novel is set. Yet associations of prostitution with colonialism in Egyptian literature and politics date at least to the turn of the

nineteenth century; Muḥammad al-Muwayliḥī's *maqāma*-novel *Ḥadīth 'Īsā ibn Hishām* (1898–1902; 1907), for example, links the new theaters of Cairo to brothels and both European "imports" to imperialism. Further, as Marilyn Booth contends, many European fictions translated into Arabic during the *nahḍa* featured "fallen women," anticipating a flurry of first-person memoirs by Egyptian prostitutes published during the 1920s. See Marilyn Booth, "Un/safe/ly at Home: Narratives of Sexual Coercion in 1920s Egypt," *Gender and History* 16, no. 3 (November 2004): 744–68. Booth argues that the "presence of Britain's imperial troops in Cairo gave prostitution more pervasive social visibility and political controversiality" (750). Noting that Egyptian feminists "attacked the state for continuing the colonial apparatus of legalised prostitution after Egypt's 1923 partial independence" (751), she implies that these women read prostitution as testimony to the ongoing—and unacceptable—coloniality of the supposedly "independent" Egyptian nation. I argue that Maḥfūẓ's *Zuqāq* elaborates this notion.

37. See 'Abd al-Muḥsin [Ṭāhā] Badr, *Najīb Maḥfūẓ: al-Ru'ya wa al-Adāt* (Cairo: Dār al-Thaqāfa li al-Ṭibā'a wa al-Nashr, 1978), 1:408n1. Contra Ghālī Shukrī, Badr argues that Maḥfūẓ's *Zuqāq* unfolds between 1944 and 1945. I concur with Badr, though I would suggest that the novel also reflects a long memory of prior decades.

38. On Shaykh Darwīsh and his translations, see Shaden M. Tageldin, "'Dignity is the most precious . . . deformity there is!': Language, Dismemberment, and the Body Colonized in Naguib Mahfouz's *Zuqaq al-Midaqq*," *Critical Sense* 7, no. 1 (Winter 1999): 11–53, esp. 18–32, 50–52n27.

39. See Naguib Mahfouz, *Midaq Alley*, trans. Trevor Le Gassick, 2nd U.S. ed. (Washington, DC: Three Continents Press, 1989), 11–12; Najīb Maḥfūẓ, *Zuqāq*, 15–16.

40. See Mahfouz, *Midaq Alley*, 3; 7 in the Arabic, which reads, "*yartadī jilbāban dhā banīqatin mawṣūlin bihā rubāṭu raqabatin mimmā yalbasuhu al-afandiyyatu.*"

41. See Joseph A. Massad, *Desiring Arabs* (Chicago: University of Chicago Press, 2007), 277–78; quotation from 278.

42. See Rajā' al-Naqqāsh, *Udabā' Mu'āṣirūn* (Cairo: Maktabat al-Anjlū al-Miṣriyya, 1968), 83–87; quotations from 83, 85, 86.

43. See Badr, *Najīb Maḥfūẓ*, 414.

44. Ibid., 412.

45. Ibid., 411.

46. See Rasheed El-Enany, *Naguib Mahfouz: Egypt's Nobel Laureate* (London: Haus, 2007), 57–58.

47. Ibid., 59.

48. Ibid., 59, emphases in the original.

49. Muhammad Siddiq, *Arab Culture and the Novel: Genre, Identity, and Agency in Egyptian Fiction* (London: Routledge, 2007), 57.

50. Ibid. See also Tageldin, "'Dignity,'" 38.

51. Mahfouz, *Midaq Alley*, 190–91; Maḥfūẓ, *Zuqāq*, 218–19.

52. Ibid., 191; 219 in the Arabic.

53. See Emile Benveniste, *Problems in General Linguistics* (in French),

trans. Mary Elizabeth Meek (Coral Gables: University of Miami Press, 1971), 217–30.

54. Ibid., 226.
55. Ibid., 219–20.
56. Ibid., 226.
57. Ibid., 220, emphases mine.
58. Ibid., 225.
59. On sovereignty and deixis, see also Lydia H. Liu, *The Clash of Empires: The Invention of China in Modern World Making* (Cambridge, MA: Harvard University Press, 2004), 17.
60. Benveniste, *Problems in General Linguistics,* 225.
61. Mahfouz, *Midaq Alley,* 190; Maḥfūẓ, *Zuqāq,* 218.
62. Ibid., 191; 219 in the Arabic.
63. Ibid.
64. See Mona Takieddine-Amyuni, "Images of Arab Women in *Midaq Alley* by Naguib Mahfouz, and *Season of Migration to the North* by Tayeb Salih," *International Journal of Middle East Studies* 17, no. 1 (February 1985): 25–36; esp. 31, which argues that Ḥamīda undergoes such a commodification.
65. Mahfouz, *Midaq Alley,* 187; Maḥfūẓ, *Zuqāq,* 214.
66. Ibid.
67. Ibid., 2; 6 in the Arabic.
68. Ibid., 177–78; 202 in the Arabic.
69. Ibid.
70. Ibid., 2; 6 in the Arabic.
71. Takieddine-Amyuni notes that Ḥamīda's prostitution is only the most obvious in Maḥfūẓ's *Zuqāq,* whose "sexual and political go-betweens are all forms of the prostitution of the self and the nation"; see Takieddine-Amyuni, "Images of Arab Women," 31.
72. 'Abbās's departure for the camps, located at al-Tall al-Kabīr, is symbolically freighted. As Takieddine-Amyuni notes, this was the site at which the British defeated the forces of Aḥmad 'Urābī in 1882—and a base for British operations in Egypt in the 1940s. See Takieddine-Amyuni, "Images of Arab Women," 36n6.
73. Maḥfūẓ, *Zuqāq,* 156.
74. This nuance, mistranslated in the English, is crucial. Compare Mahfouz, *Midaq Alley,* 137, and Maḥfūẓ, *Zuqāq,* 156.
75. Ibid., 219, emphases mine; 253–54 in the Arabic.
76. But not raped. Ḥamīda will insist on losing her virginity *consensually* to Faraj, well before she learns English or consorts with its speakers, thus defying his suggestion that she save it for the Americans who would "gladly pay fifty pounds for virgins." See Mahfouz, *Midaq Alley,* 192.
77. Maḥfūẓ, *Zuqāq,* 254, translation mine. Compare Mahfouz, *Midaq Alley,* 219, which reads, "for the love of the consequent battle."
78. Mahfouz, *Midaq Alley,* 157; Maḥfūẓ, *Zuqāq,* 179.
79. Ibid.
80. Mahfouz, *Midaq Alley,* 157; Maḥfūẓ, *Zuqāq,* 179–80.
81. Ibid.

82. Jean Baudrillard, *De la séduction* (Paris: Éditions Galilée, 1979), 63; and Jean Baudrillard, *Seduction,* trans. Brian Singer (New York: St. Martin's Press, 1990), 42.

83. Mahfouz, *Midaq Alley*, 143; Maḥfūẓ, *Zuqāq*, 164.

84. Baudrillard, *Seduction,* 105.

85. Compare Mahfouz, *Midaq Alley,* 219, and Maḥfūẓ, *Zuqāq*, 254.

86. Mahfouz, *Midaq Alley,* 171, emphases mine; 196 in the Arabic.

87. Ibid., 166; 190 in the Arabic.

88. See also Mahfouz, *Midaq Alley,* 172; 197 in the Arabic.

89. Mahfouz, *Midaq Alley,* 166; 190 in the Arabic.

90. Ibid., 169; 193–94 in the Arabic.

91. Ibid., 220, emphases mine; 255–56 in the Arabic.

92. See Jacques Derrida, *Of Grammatology,* trans. Gayatri Chakravorty Spivak, corrected ed. (Baltimore: Johns Hopkins University Press, 1997), 95–118; quotation from 107. The original is Jacques Derrida, *De la grammatologie* (Paris: Éditions de Minuit, 1967).

93. Ibid., 113.

94. Ibid.; 166–67 in the French.

95. Writes Derrida, "For writing, obliteration of the proper classed in the play of difference, is the originary violence itself"; see *Of Grammatology,* 110.

96. Derrida, *Of Grammatology,* 112, emphases mine.

97. Ibid.

98. Ibid.

99. Gramsci cites this reflection by Novalis on "the supreme problem of culture" in "Socialism and Culture," published under the pseudonym Alfa Gamma in *Il Grido del Popolo,* 29 January 1916. I refer to the version reprinted in David Forgacs, ed., *The Gramsci Reader: Selected Writings, 1916–1935,* introd. Eric J. Hobsbawm (New York: New York University Press, 2000), 56–59; quotation from 56.

100. Mahfouz, *Midaq Alley,* 186–87; Maḥfūẓ, *Zuqāq*, 213.

101. Ibid.

102. Ibid.

103. Ibid., 187; 214 in the Arabic.

104. Derrida, *Of Grammatology,* 132.

105. Mahfouz, *Midaq Alley,* 225; Maḥfūẓ, *Zuqāq*, 262.

106. Ibid., 224; 261 in the Arabic.

107. Ibid., 241; 282 in the Arabic.

108. Ibid., 241–42; 283 in the Arabic.

109. Ibid., 243; 285 in the Arabic.

110. Ibid., 246; 287 in the Arabic.

111. Durrell, *Mountolive,* 281, emphases in the original.

112. Ibid., 280.

113. Ibid., 280–81.

114. Ibid., 281–82.

115. Ibid., 282.

CODA

1. See D. J. Taylor, "The Maestro of Middaq *[sic]* Alley," *Sunday Times* (London), 18 March 1990, H8–H9; quotation from H9.

2. Jessica Benjamin, *The Bonds of Love: Psychoanalysis, Feminism, and the Problem of Domination* (New York: Pantheon, 1988), 51–84; quotations from 62.

3. Jacques Derrida, *Politics of Friendship* (in French), trans. George Collins (London: Verso, 1997), 72, emphasis mine.

4. On friendship as that which "engages translation in the untranslatable," see Derrida, *Politics of Friendship*, 166. All other references are to 220.

5. Ibid., 220.

6. Ibid., 221.

7. On ʻAbbās Maḥmūd al-ʻAqqād, see Shawqī Ḍayf, *Maʻa al-ʻAqqād* (Cairo: Dār al-Maʻārif, 1964). On Ṭāhā Ḥusayn, see Jābir ʻUṣfūr, *al-Marāyā al-Mutajāwira: Dirāsa fī Naqd Ṭāhā Ḥusayn* (Cairo: al-Hay'a al-Miṣriyya al-ʻĀmma li al-Kitāb, 1983); and ʻAlī Shalash, *Ṭāhā Ḥusayn: Maṭlūb Ḥayyan wa Mayyitan* (Cairo: al-Dār al-ʻArabiyya li al-Ṭibāʻa wa al-Nashr wa al-Tawzīʻ, 1993); in English, see Pierre Cachia, *Ṭāhā Ḥusayn: His Place in the Egyptian Literary Renaissance* (London: Luzac, 1956); and Abdelrashid Mahmoudi, *Ṭāhā Ḥusain's Education: From the Azhar to the Sorbonne* (Richmond, Surrey: Curzon, 1998).

8. ʻAbbās Maḥmūd al-ʻAqqād, "Taʻāruf al-Shuʻūb," *al-Jadīd* 2, no. 33 (9 September 1929): 4–5; quotation from 4.

9. Ibid.

10. Ibid.

11. Rey Chow, *The Age of the World Target: Self-Referentiality in War, Theory, and Comparative Work* (Durham: Duke University Press, 2006), 89.

12. al-ʻAqqād, "Taʻāruf al-Shuʻūb," 4.

13. Ibid., 4–5.

14. Ibid., 5.

15. Ibid., 4.

16. Ibid., 5, emphases mine.

17. Ibid.

18. See Ṭāhā Ḥusayn, "Tarjama," *al-Jadīd* 2, no. 34 (16 September 1929): 4–5. The second rebuttal appears in Ṭāhā Ḥusayn, "Tarjama," *al-Jadīd* 2, no. 38 (14 October 1929): 4–5.

19. Ḥusayn, "Tarjama" (16 September 1929), 4.

20. Ibid.

21. Ibid.

22. Ibid., 4–5.

23. Ibid., 5.

24. Ibid.

25. Ibid.

26. Ibid.

27. Ibid.

28. One such articulation is Ṭāhā Ḥusayn, *Mustaqbal al-Thaqāfa fī Miṣr*, introd. Aḥmad Fatḥī Surūr, 2nd ed. (Cairo: Dār al-Maʻārif, 1996 [1938]).

29. See Ṭāhā Ḥusayn, "Tarjama," *al-Jadīd* (14 October 1929): 4–5, esp. 5.

30. Ibid., 5.
31. Ibid.
32. See United Nations Development Programme, Regional Bureau of Arab States, *Arab Human Development Report 2003: Building a Knowledge Society* (New York: UNDP/RBAS, 2003), 66–68, 129, 176.
33. See "Da'wa ilā Khalq al-Adab al-Qawmī," *al-Siyāsa al-Usbū'iyya* (28 June 1930): 7; responses appear in "al-Da'wa ilā Khalq al-Adab al-Qawmī," *al-Siyāsa al-Usbū'iyya* (5 July 1930): 24–25, followed by a clarification in Muḥammad Zakī 'Abd al-Qādir, "Da'wat al-Adab al-Qawmī: Bayān," *al-Siyāsa al-Usbū'iyya* (12 July 1930): 14. On the society, see Israel Gershoni and James P. Jankowski, *Egypt, Islam, and the Arabs: The Search for Egyptian Nationhood, 1900–1930* (New York: Oxford University Press, 1987), 194, 201.
34. See 'Abbās Maḥmūd al-'Aqqād, "al-Tarjama wa Ta'āruf al-Shu'ūb," *al-Jadīd* 2, no. 36 (30 September 1929): 4–5; and 'Abbās Maḥmūd al-'Aqqād, "al-Tarjama wa Ta'āruf al-Shu'ūb," *al-Jadīd* 2, no. 37 (7 October 1929): 4–5. The final essay in the exchange, following Ḥusayn's second rejoinder of 14 October 1929, is 'Abbās Maḥmūd al-'Aqqād, "Bayna al-'Aqqād wa Ṭāhā Ḥusayn Munāqasha," *al-Jadīd* 2, no. 39 (21 October 1929): 4–5.
35. al-'Aqqād, "al-Tarjama wa Ta'āruf al-Shu'ūb" (30 September 1929), 4.
36. Ibid. Here (and elsewhere) al-'Aqqād uses the verb *iqtarana,* "to conjoin," which derives from the same root as the Arabic for "conjunction" or "marriage," *qirān;* "comparison," *al-muqārana;* and the *comparative* of "comparative literature," *al-adab al-muqāran.*
37. Ibid., emphasis mine.
38. Ibid.
39. Ibid., 5.
40. Ibid., 4–5.
41. al-'Aqqād, "al-Tarjama wa Ta'āruf al-Shu'ūb" (7 October 1929), 4.
42. Ibid.
43. Ibid.
44. Ibid.
45. Ibid.
46. Ibid.
47. Ibid.
48. Ibid., 5.
49. Ibid.
50. See 'Abbās Maḥmūd al-'Aqqād, *Anā* (Cairo: Dār al-Hilāl, n.d.), 51; and J[an]. Brugman, *An Introduction to the History of Modern Arabic Literature in Egypt* (Leiden: E. J. Brill, 1984), 122.
51. Brugman, *An Introduction,* 122.
52. See M. Hammond, "al-'Aqqād, 'Abbās Maḥmūd," in *Encyclopedia of Islam, Three,* ed. Gudrun Krämer et al., Brill Online, www.brillonline.nl/subscriber/entry?entry=ei3_COM-0020 (accessed 27 April 2009); Sayyid al-Baḥrāwī, *al-Baḥth 'an al-Manhaj fī al-Naqd al-'Arabī al-Ḥadīth* (Cairo: Dār Sharqiyyāt li al-Nashr wa al-Tawzī', 1993), 17–33; and David Semah, *Four Egyptian Literary Critics* (Leiden: E. J. Brill, 1974), 1–65.
53. al-Baḥrāwī, *al-Baḥth 'an al-Manhaj,* 30.
54. Ahdaf Soueif, *In the Eye of the Sun* (New York: Vintage, 1992), 512.

Index

Italicized page numbers refer to illustrations.

'Abbās I, Khedive, 27, 114, 312n28
'Abbās II, Khedive, 194
'Abduh, Ṭāniyūs, 176–77
'Abqariyyat Muḥammad (al-'Aqqād), 177, 316n109
al-Abṭāl (Carlyle; al-Sibā'ī, trans.), 180, 186–87, 311–12n21, 317n119. See also *On Heroes . . .* (Carlyle)
"al-Abṭāl wa 'Ibādat al-Buṭūla" (Carlyle; al-Sibā'ī, trans.), 180, 186–87, 311–12n21
Abu-Lughod, Ibrahim, 45, 294n1, 296n18, 297n36
'Adhrā' Dinshawāy (Ḥaqqī), 216
'Adlī Yakan, 213, 320n42
affect/affective relations, 4, 9–10, 13, 17, 25–28, 31, 57, 244, 278, 284. *See also* enmity; friendship; love; in *'Alam al-Dīn* (Mubārak), 160, 163, 165–67, 171; in "Maqāmat al-Faransīs" (al-'Aṭṭār), 71, 104–5; and al-Ṭahṭāwī's translation theory, 120, 122–23, 309n97
al-Afghāni, Jamāl al-Dīn, 180
Africa: African Sphinx, 121; in *'Alam al-Dīn* (Mubārak), 162; and al-'Aqqād, 284; and George, 115–16; and Ismā'īl, Khedive, 160; in *La Lyre brisée* (Agoub), 145, 147–48; and nation/nationalism, 201, 229–30, 236, 323nn96,101; in *Peau noire, masques blancs* (Fanon), 36
Agoub, Joseph: and nation/nationalism, 201–2, 211–12, 214; and al-Ṭahṭāwī's translation theory, 29, 116, 122, 141–49, *142–43*, 154, 309n97, 310n106
Ahmed, Sara, 71, 299n95
'Ajā'ib al-Āthār fī al-Tarājim wa al-Akhbār (al-Jabartī), 47, 54
'Alam al-Dīn (Mubārak), 29, 55, 159–72, 180, 182, 188, 304n78, 312nn26,30, 313nn32–33,44–46, 314–15nn56–57, 59,80
Alexandria, 34, 39, 42, 44–45, 159, 223, 240, 270, 278
The Alexandria Quartet (Durrell), 237, 323n3, 324n19
Alexandrowicz, C. H., 219–20
'Alī Bey al-Kabīr, 43–44
Alleaume, Ghislaine, 161, 163, 165, 313n47
Allen, Roger, 108–9
Althusser, Louis, 29, 57, 59–63, 67, 76, 89
The Ancient Egyptians and the Origin of Civilization (Smith), 229–31, 232, 233, 322n87
Anderson, Benedict, 215, 319n13
Anglo-Egyptian Treaty (1936), 242–44
anticolonialism, 21, 46; in *'Alam al-Dīn* (Mubārak), 164, 167–70; and 1919 Egyptian revolution, 30–31, 176, 196,

anticolonialism (*continued*) 200, 206, 227; and al-Sibā'ī, 175–76; in *Zuqāq al-Midaqq* (Maḥfūẓ), 245, 272
antiquity, 121–23, 135–37, 163, 201–2, 223–24, 231, 235–36, 275, 280, 283
Apter, Emily, 165, 307n52, 320n32
al-'Aqqād, 'Abbās Maḥmūd, 31, 177–78, 275–79, 283–88, 316n109, 319n18, 330nn34,36
Arab Feminist Conference (Cairo, 1944), 325–26n36
Arab Human Development Report 2003, 31, 282
"Arabic book," 57–58, 82, 163, 287
Arabic language/literature, 1–5, 15–16, 29, 275, 289–90nn8,14; in *'Alam al-Dīn* (Mubārak), 160–67, 170, 314n56; and al-'Aqqād, 287; complexity of, 135; and de Sacy, 23, 29, 98–99, 116, 122–24, 137–41, 144; grammar of, 46–55, 125–26, 138, 224; and Ḥusayn, 280–83; and al-'Īsawī, 5–6, 22, 27; in "Maqāmat al-Faransīs" (al-'Aṭṭār), 15, 66–67, 79–84, 89–92, 95–104, 167, 303nn60,62,64, 304n78; and al-Māzinī, 201–11, 214, 220, 225, 319–20nn18–19,23; and Moosa, 108–9; and al-Najjār, 109–10; and Napoleon's proclamation, 14–15, 28–29, 33–58, *35*, 63, 78, 80, 82, 84, 89, 170, 294–95nn1–3,5, 296n18, 297n36; and nation/nationalism, 195–96, 200–202, 206–7, 209–11, 214, 217, 224–26, 231–36, 234, 320n42; and Romanticism, 141–42, 319n18; and al-Sibā'ī's translation of Carlyle, 173–91, 194–96, 316n104; and al-Ṭahṭāwī's translation theory, 29, 108–51, 143, 161, 200, 211, 278, 309n97; in *Tārīkh Muddat al-Faransīs bi Miṣr* (al-Jabartī), 80–81; and al-Zayyāt, 210–12, 224–26; in *Zuqāq al-Midaqq* (Maḥfūẓ), 247–57, 261, 267, 269, 272
Arab-Islamic cultural heritage, 2, 5–10, 19, 31–32; in *'Alam al-Dīn* (Mubārak), 161, 164–72; and decline thesis, 108–9, 304n3; and Ḥusayn, 280; in *al-Khiṭaṭ al-Tawfīqiyya al-Jadīda* (Mubārak), 313n47; in "Maqāmat al-Faransīs" (al-'Aṭṭār), 80–84, 98–99, 102–3; and *al-Mu'allaqāt*, 83; and Al-Musawi, 30, 178; and *nahḍa* (renaissance) ideology, 4–5, 8, 15–16, 102, 109–10, 114, 127, 177, 197, 207, 227, 291n23, 306n27, 325–26n36; and al-Najjār, 109–10, 307n39; and Napoleon's proclamation, 14–15, 34, 36–37, 57; and nation/nationalism, 203, 207, 209, 223–24; and order/disorder, 22–23, 210–18, 224, 226; rejection of dualism of sign/signification, 22–23, 293n64; and al-Sibā'ī's translation of Carlyle, 29–30, 176–84, 188; and al-Ṭahṭāwī's translation theory, 29, 109, 116–18, 121–28, 131, 133, 135–40, 144; in *Tārīkh Muddat al-Faransīs bi Miṣr* (al-Jabartī), 80–81; and al-Zayyāt, 210–12, 224–26
Aristotle, 228, 279
Armenoid, 229, 322–23nn90,94
"'Arūs 'Abdūs" (Byron; al-Sibā'ī, trans.), 175, 315n91
Asad, Talal, 30, 174, 187–88
Asia, 44, 99, 101, 173, 201, 227–29, 235–36, 281, 284–86, 322n90
assujetissement (subjectification/subjection), 60
atheism. *See* belief/unbelief
al-'Aṭṭār, Ḥasan, 15, 29, 66–107, 274, 300n9. *See also* "Maqāmat al-Faransīs" (al-'Aṭṭār); activity as writer, 67–68, 102, 304n78; and al-'Aqqād, 276–77; as Azharite, 67, 99, 101; biography of, 67–68; and homosexuality, 300–301n15; and al-Khashshāb, 300–301n15, 303n61; Lane's encounter with, 95; and al-Ṭahṭāwī's translation theory, 113, 125, 127, 151, 306n27; and *Zuqāq al-Midaqq* (Maḥfūẓ), 259–61
"Die Aufgabe des Übersetzers (Benjamin). *See* "The Task of the Translator" (Benjamin)
"autocolonization," 29, 59–63
Les Aventures de Télémaque, fils d'Ulysse (Fénelon), 114
awakening. See *al-nahḍa*
al-Azbakiyya, 68–70, 84–87, 89, 106
al-Azhar/Azharites, 2, 28, 46, 55, 80, 82; in *'Alam al-Dīn* (Mubārak), 160, 166, 313n32; and al-'Aṭṭār, 67, 99–100, 113–14, 306n27; and nation/nationalism, 210, 213, 228; and al-Sibā'ī's translation of Carlyle, 177–78; and al-Ṭahṭāwī, 109, 113–14, 117–18, 132, *143*, 306n27

Babel narrative, 25, 30, 200, 210, 213–14, 225, 320n44

Badī' al-Zamān al-Hamadhānī, 68
Badr, 'Abd al-Muḥsin Ṭāhā, 251–52, 326n37
Al-Bagdadi, Nadia, 127
al-Baḥrāwī, Sayyid, 287
al-Bājūrī, Ibrāhīm, 82, 101
Bakhtin, Mikhail, 30, 204–5, 319–20n23
al-Balāgh al-Usbū'ī (The Weekly Report), 175–76
"The Ballad of East and West" (Kipling), 228, 322n83
"Bānat Su'ād" (Ka'b), 101
Bardenstein, Carol, 290n14
Baring, Evelyn. *See* Cromer, Earl of (Lord)
Baudrillard, Jean, 13; and *'Alam al-Dīn* (Mubārak), 166; and "Maqāmat al-Faransīs" (al-'Aṭṭār), 29, 74–79, 83, 86, 89, 91, 93–94, 96–97, 105; and nation/nationalism, 197–98; and seduction, 11–13, 74–79, 83, 86, 91, 93–94, 96–97, 105, 154, 197–98, 255, 260, 274–75, 291n29, 292n32, 301nn29,31; and al-Sibā'ī's translation of Carlyle, 178; and *Zuqāq al-Midaqq* (Maḥfūẓ), 255, 260
al-Bayān (the Explication), 180, 186, 311–12n21, 316n109
beginnings, 14, 227, 235–36. *See also* origins/original
Beginnings (Said), 227
belief/unbelief: in *'Alam al-Dīn* (Mubārak), 171; and Casanova, 118, 120; in "Maqāmat al-Faransīs" (al-'Aṭṭār), 70; and Napoleon's proclamation, 48, 70; and al-Sibā'ī's translation of Carlyle, 173, 179, 187–93, 318nn132–33; and al-Ṭahṭāwī's translation theory, 116–18, 120, 144, 150
Bengal: and Aryan idea, 9; autocolonization in, 57–59; and "Minute on Indian Education" (Macaulay), 228; and politics of translation, 8–12, 58–59
Benjamin, Jessica, 31, 274, 279
Benjamin, Walter, 2, 25, 29, 63, 91, 133–36, 158, 192–93, 225, 295n4, 309n80, 318n145
Bentham, Jeremy, 181, 189–90, 211, 318n133
Benveniste, Émile, 18, 30, 255–56, 259–60, 263
Bhabha, Homi, 17, 19, 29; and "English book," 57–59, 81–82; and hybridity, 3; and mimicry, 2–3, 37–40, 57, 80, 83, 85, 88, 228
Bible, 25, 57, 81, 223
binarism/binary oppositions, 6–7, 17, 19, 57, 64, 203, 292n32
Blake, William, 239
Booth, Marilyn, 325–26n36
Bowen, Roger, 244, 323nn3–4, 325n28
Boym, Svetlana, 64
"The Bride of Abydos" (Byron), 174–75
British colonialism, 4–7, 10, 13–17, 20, 26, 28; in *'Alam al-Dīn* (Mubārak), 29, 160–65, 167, 169–72, 314–15nn80,82; Anglo-Egyptian Treaty (1936), 242–44; and al-'Aqqād, 276–77, 287; and civilization, 158, 163, 181–82; and Cromer, 14, 16, 30, 152–59, 311nn7,11,13; and Dinshawāy affair, 155, 212, 216, 321n48; Dual Control, 27–28; and educational missions, 20, 153, 305n12, 311n6; Egypt as protectorate, 28, 176, 194, 196, 230, 325n35; and Egypt as woman, 30, 245–47, 248, 249, 250–62, 264, 266–70, 272, 325–26nn32,35–36; and Entente Cordiale (1904), 194; and Ḥusayn, 279; in India, 9–10, 57–60, 81–82, 152–53, 155, 158, 174, 183–84, 194, 205–6, 209, 228, 230, 311n14; invasion/occupation of Egypt, 27–29, 153, 159, 164, 243–44; al-'Īsawī's views on, 5–6, 22, 27; in *Mountolive* (Durrell), 30–31, 237–47, 271–72, 323n3; and nation/nationalism, 30, 176, 195–96, 200–201, 205–7, 209–10, 212, 217, 227–31, 235–36, 323n96; and Shawqī, 16; and al-Sibā'ī's translation of Carlyle, 29–30, 157–58, 173–94; in *Zuqāq al-Midaqq* (Maḥfūẓ), 30–31, 242–69, 272, 325–26n36, 327nn72,76
Brugman, J., 177, 287
Būlāq presses, 112–13, 136, 313n33
al-Burda (The Mantle), 15, 66–67, 79–85, 89, 96, 98–102, 302n38, 304n73
al-Būṣīrī, Sharaf al-Dīn Abū 'Abd Allāh Muḥammad ibn Sa'īd, 80–81, 83, 99–101, 302n38, 304n73
al-Bustānī, Buṭrus, 8, 291n23
Butler, Judith, 60
Byron, Lord, 174–75, 315n91

Cairo. *See also* al-Azbakiyya; al-Azhar/Azharites: Cairo Opera House, 27; in *Ḥadīth 'Īsā ibn Hishām* (al-Muwayliḥī), 16, 325–26n36; and Heliopolis,

Cairo (*continued*)
195–96; and Ismā'īl, Khedive, 16, 269; and Jomard, 111; in "Maqāmat al-Faransīs" (al-'Aṭṭār), 66–67, 69, 82, 86, 95; Metro tram, 195–97, 277; and Mubārak, 159; and Napoleon's proclamation, 39, 42, 45–47; and nation/nationalism, 212, 228–29; and al-Sibā'ī, 157, 173–74, 176, 180, 195; and al-Ṭahṭāwī, 113, 149–51; in *Zuqāq al-Midaqq* (Maḥfūẓ), 247–48, 252, 258–59, 268–70
Carlyle, Thomas, 29–30, 157, 159, 164, 171, 173–94, 287, 316n109, 317n119, 318nn132–33,136,141,145. See also *On Heroes . . .* (Carlyle)
Casanova, Pascale, 29, 118–24, 129, 132, 136, 307n46
Castilian Spanish, 57–58. *See also* Philippines
Catholicism, 48–49, 58, 169–70
center/periphery model, 119–21, 127
Chatterjee, Partha, 30, 157, 197–200
Childe Harold's Pilgrimage (Byron), 174, 315n91
Chow, Rey, 24–27, 218, 276
Chrestomathie arabe (de Sacy), 99
Christianity: in *'Alam al-Dīn* (Mubārak), 162–63, 169–72, 314n75; and al-'Aqqād, 283; and Babel narrative, 320n44; Christian Trinity, 86; Coptic Christians/Copts, 176, 223, 237, 240; and Cromer, 30, 155–56; crusades, 40–41, 44, 48, 113, 139, 241, 296n17; in *Mountolive* (Durrell), 238–39; and Napoleon's proclamation, 14, 33, 40–41, 48–49, 55, 82; and nation/nationalism, 223; in Philippines, 58; and al-Sibā'ī's translation of Carlyle, 173, 176, 178–82, 186–89; and al-Ṭahṭāwī's translation theory, 137–39, 141
civilization, Egyptian, 145, 147–48, 163–64, 190, 223–24
civilization, Western, 14–16, 59, 152–53, 181; in *'Alam al-Dīn* (Mubārak), 163–65, 167; Maḥfūẓ's view of, 4–5, 252–54, 273, 275, 290n16; in "Maqāmat al-Faransīs" (al-'Aṭṭār), 70, 73–74, 77, 89, 92–93, 104; *mission civilisatrice*, 110, 149, 273, 275; and nation/nationalism, 212–13, 215, 222–24, 228, 230; and al-Sibā'ī's translation of Carlyle, 158, 181–82; and al-Ṭahṭāwī's translation theory, 93, 109–15, 124, 132, 135, 149, 306n27
Colla, Elliott, 69–70, 75–76, 80–81, 97–98
collaboration, 20–21, 52, 70, 97–98
Collins, Wilkie, 175, 315n91
commensurability/incommensurability, 25, 30; in *'Alam al-Dīn* (Mubārak), 169; in "Maqāmat al-Faransīs" (al-'Aṭṭār), 84, 90, 94, 104; and Napoleon's proclamation, 37–38, 50–51; and nation/nationalism, 201, 204, 219, 230; and al-Sibā'ī's translation of Carlyle, 183, 190; and al-Ṭahṭāwī's translation theory, 116, 122, 125, 131, 133–37, 149, 161; in *Zuqāq al-Midaqq* (Maḥfūẓ), 260, 262, 264, 267
comparative literature, 24, 27, 115, 121, 123–41
conquerors/conquered: in *'Alam al-Dīn* (Mubārak), 169–70; and al-'Aqqād, 31, 275–77, 283; and Ḥusayn, 31, 275, 279–83; in "Maqāmat al-Faransīs" (al-'Aṭṭār), 69, 74, 76; and Napoleon's proclamation, 14, 33, 40, 42, 49
"consecration," 119–21
Le Contrat social (Rousseau), 305–6n21
Copts/Coptic Christians, 176, 223, 237, 240
copula/copulation, 13–14, 27, 30, 274; and al-'Aqqād, 276; and deixis, 197, 210, 255, 259–60, 263; and "Maqāmat al-Faransīs" (al-'Aṭṭār), 78, 86, 90, 94, 99; and *Modern Egypt* (Cromer), 155; in *Mountolive* (Durrell), 240; and Napoleon's proclamation, 37–39, 49–50, 55, 58; and al-Sibā'ī's translation of Carlyle, 181, 183; and al-Ṭahṭāwī's translation theory, 113, 123, 151; in *Zuqāq al Midaqq* (Maḥfūẓ), 248, 254–56, 262, 268, 270, 272
Coup-d'œil impartial sur l'état présent de l'Égypte (Jomard), 111–13
Coup-d'œil sur l'Égypte ancienne et moderne, ou Analyse raisonnée du grand ouvrage sur l'Égypte (Agoub), 142–43
Cromer, Earl of (Lord), 14, 16, 30, 152–59, 170, 174, 194, 311nn7,11,13–14
Crusaders, 40–41, 44, 48, 113, 139, 241, 296n17
cultural imperialism, 2, 6–22, 28–29, 31–32, 109–10, 161, 173, 263, 273, 288

Culture and Imperialism (Said), 19–22
Cuno, Kenneth, 53–54
The Customs of Mankind (Eichler), 231–35, 234, 323n96

Damrosch, David, 29, 121, 128
Dante, 184, 188
Darwin, Charles, 158, 227, 312n24
decline thesis, 108–9, 304n3
decolonization, 7, 16, 19–21, 26–27, 36, 108, 115, 121, 273, 288, 323n101; in *'Alam al-Dīn* (Mubārak), 164; in *Mountolive* (Durrell), 30, 247, 271; and al-Ṭahṭāwī's translation theory, 121; in *Zuqāq al-Midaqq* (Maḥfūẓ), 30, 247, 268, 272
deictic indicators, 197, 210, 255, 259–60, 263
De la grammatologie (Derrida), 262
de La Place, Guislain-François-Marie-Joseph, 123–24, 129–31, 137, 139
De la séduction (Baudrillard), 11
De l'universalité de la langue française (Rivarol), 135
Demolins, Edmond, 311n20
denial of difference, 121–23
Derrida, Jacques, 3, 30, 289–90n8; and al-'Aqqād, 275; and enmity/friendship/love, 31, 47, 94, 274–75, 279; and nation/nationalism, 207, 209, 218–20, 222, 235; and the "proper," 218, 263–64, 266–67; and "transcendental signified," 3, 55–56, 87, 204, 207, 209, 219, 222, 230; and "transcendental signifier," 3, 207, 209, 289–90n8; and writing-as-violence, 30, 262–68, 328n96; and writing/speech, 284
de Sacy, Silvestre, 23, 29, 98–99, 116, 122–24, 137–41, 144, 165
Description de l'Égypte (Institut d'Égypte), 111; and Agoub, 142, 309–10n100
Dhū Salam. *See* Medina
dialectic, Hegelian, 13, 34, 36, 38, 86–92, 97, 259; and Fanon, 13, 34, 36, 38–39, 67, 73, 85, 88–95, 259, 296n14; and Sheehi, 8; and Ṭarābīshī, 73–75
Dickens, Charles, 4, 157–58, 175, 226, 315n91
Dinshawāy affair, 155, 212, 216, 321n48
Discours historique sur l'Égypte (Agoub), 143
Dithyrambe sur l'Égypte (Agoub), 141
dīwān: (anthology), 113, 177; (council), 47, 297–98n48; (historical record), 127
Dīwān school, 177, 316n104, 319n18
dominance/domination, 3–10, 12–24, 28, 31, 273–75, 288, 290n14; in *'Alam al-Dīn* (Mubārak), 161, 165–66, 168; and al-'Aqqād, 276, 279–80, 283, 286; and Benjamin, Jessica, 31, 274, 279; and Casanova, 118–23, 136–37; and El-Enany, 72–73; and Fanon, 7, 73, 139; and Hegel, 8, 73, 88; and Ḥusayn, 279–80, 282–83; in "Maqāmat al-Faransīs" (al-'Aṭṭār), 68, 70, 72–76, 80; in *Mountolive* (Durrell), 238–41, 243–44, 246; and Napoleon's proclamation, 14–15, 33–34, 49–50, 57, 62; and nation/nationalism, 196–97, 199, 209–10, 215, 221–22, 224, 227; and Niranjana, 59–60, 63–64; and al-Sibā'ī's translation of Carlyle, 173, 179, 183, 193; and al-Ṭahṭāwī's translation theory, 116, 118–25, 133–34, 136–37, 139, 141, 147; and Ṭarābīshī, 74–75; in *Zuqāq al-Midaqq* (Maḥfūẓ), 243–44, 246, 252, 255, 265, 270
Drovetti, Bernardino, 110–11
dualism, 3, 23, 34, 203, 293n64. *See also* binarism/binary oppositions; duel/dual affinity, 74, 86–88, 260; mind-body, 22
Dufrénoy, Adélaïde-Gillette Billet, 141
Dunlop, Douglas, 175
Durrell, Lawrence, 30–31, 237–45, 247, 251, 256, 258, 270–72, 323nn3–4, 324nn18–19, 325n28
al-Dusūqī, Ibrāhīm, 313n32

Easthope, Antony, 198–99
Eco, Umberto, 31
École des Langues Orientales (Paris), 113–14
École Égyptienne de Paris, 111–12, 114, 116, 159, 211
École Militaire Égyptienne (Paris), 159, 211
Education (Spencer), 175
education, Egyptian, 22; and *'Alam al-Dīn* (Mubārak), 159, 162, 312n30; and Cromer, 152–53, 155–57, 174, 315n87; educational missions, 20, 22, 110–18, 152–53, 159, 305–6nn12–13,20–21, 311n6; and French reeducation project, 111–13, 136; and Haykal, 210–15; and Ḥusayn, 282; and Jomard, 110–14, 116, 118, 151, 305n13; and nation/nationalism, 211–13, 215, 222, 320n42; and al-Sibā'ī's translation of

education, Egpytian (*continued*)
Carlyle, 174–75, 186, 194, 315nn87,91; and al-Ṭahṭāwī's translation theory, 113–15, 117–18, 124, 211, 253, 306n22; in *Zuqāq al-Midaqq* (Maḥfūẓ), 248–58, 262, 264, 266, 268–69
Egyptian Feminist Union, 325–26n36
Egyptian Ministry of Public Instruction, 175, 315n88
Eichler, Lillian, 231–35, 234, 323n96
Elements of International Law (Wheaton), 220
El-Enany, Rasheed, 72–75, 168, 252
Empain, Édouard, 195
English colonialism. *See* British colonialism
English language/literature, 5–6, 9–10; in *'Alam al-Dīn* (Mubārak), 29, 160–62, 188; and al-'Aqqād, 276, 283, 287; and Cromer, 153–54, 157, 315n87; "English book," 57–61, 81; homology with ancient Egyptian, 30, 231, 233–34; and Ḥusayn, 280–82; and Macaulay, 152–53, 155, 183, 228, 237, 311n14; in "Maqāmat al-Faransīs" (al-'Aṭṭār), 15; in *Mountolive* (Durrell), 237–42, 247, 258, 271; and Mūsā, 200–201, 227–36, 234, 276–77, 279, 282, 322nn83,87, 323n96; and nation/nationalism, 195–96, 200, 207, 209–10, 217, 227, 231–36, 234; and Romanticism, 319n18; and al-Sibā'ī's translation of Carlyle, 157–58, 173–96, 315nn87,91; in *Zuqāq al-Midaqq* (Maḥfūẓ), 247–62, 266–69, 272
enlightenment, Egyptian, 109, 197. See also *al-nahḍa*
enlightenment, French, 50–51, 70, 101, 118, 172–73, 189
enmity, 14, 288; and al-'Aqqād, 31, 275, 277–79, 286–88; and Derrida, 31, 47, 94, 274–75, 279; and Ḥusayn, 31, 275; in *Zuqāq al-Midaqq* (Maḥfūẓ), 270
Entente Cordiale (1904), 194
equivalence, 6, 8–10, 12–15, 18, 23, 27, 273–75; in *'Alam al-Dīn* (Mubārak), 160–63, 170, 172; and al-'Aqqād, 275, 277–78, 283–85, 287–88; and Benjamin, 25, 134–35; and Casanova, 118–19; and Fanon, 63, 88–89; and Ḥusayn, 275, 279; in "Maqāmat al-Faransīs" (al-'Aṭṭār), 74, 78, 80, 82–84, 87–92, 97–98, 104–6; in *Modern Egypt* (Cromer), 157; in *Mountolive* (Durrell), 240, 242–44; and Napoleon's proclamation, 14–15, 33–34, 37–38, 48–51, 57, 63; and nation/nationalism, 197–98, 205–6, 208–9, 214, 219–20, 222, 227, 235; and Niranjana, 64; and al-Sibā'ī's translation of Carlyle, 174, 179–83, 190, 193–94, 196; and al-Ṭahṭāwī's translation theory, 115–16, 118–19, 122–28, 133–37, 140–41, 161, 200; in *Zuqāq al-Midaqq* (Maḥfūẓ), 242–44, 248, 250–51, 255–56, 259, 261–62, 264–65, 269–70
erotic *and*, 24–32, 250. *See also* "neurotic *and*"
eroticism, 26–27, 57; and Colla, 75–76; in "Maqāmat al-Faransīs" (al-'Aṭṭār), 15, 66, 75–76, 93–94, 154; in *Modern Egypt* (Cromer), 153–55, 157, 170; in *Peau noire, masques blancs* (Fanon), 93–94, 154; and al-Ṭahṭāwī's translation theory, 123, 145, 148–49; in *Zuqāq al-Midaqq* (Maḥfūẓ), 250
L'Esprit des lois (Montesquieu), 305–6n21
European imperialism, 4–10, 14–17, 19–32, 160, 288. *See also* British colonialism; cultural imperialism; French colonialism; in *'Alam al-Dīn* (Mubārak), 159–66, 170–72; and al-'Aqqād, 275–78, 286–87; and Ḥusayn, 275–76, 280–83; and al-Manfalūṭī, 1–2, 4, 28; in *Modern Egypt* (Cromer), 152–54, 156; and Napoleon's proclamation, 55, 57; and nation/nationalism, 30, 196–201, 203, 205–7, 209–18, 220, 222–24, 226–36, 232, 233, 234, 321n48; post–9/11 resonances of, 31–32; Renaissance Europe, 138–39; and al-Sibā'ī's translation of Carlyle, 174–84, 189, 193–94; and al-Ṭahṭāwī's translation theory, 29, 108–16, 120–24, 127–28, 131–33, 135, 137–40, 145, 147; in *Zuqāq al-Midaqq* (Maḥfūẓ), 30, 245–47, 248, 249, 250–69, 325–26nn32,35–36
exchangeability, 13, 274; in *'Alam al-Dīn* (Mubārak), 160–62, 164; and al-'Aqqād, 283–86; and nation/nationalism, 209, 220; and al-Sibā'ī's translation of Carlyle, 174, 182–83, 185, 189, 193; and al-Ṭahṭāwī's translation theory, 29, 113, 115–16, 118–19, 123–25, 133, 137–38, 149, 161, 278; in *Zuqāq al-Midaqq* (Maḥfūẓ), 248, 254, 256–61, 264, 267

Fahmy, Khaled, 27, 53–54
Fanon, Frantz, 7, 29, 63, 75, 139, 154, 157; and *'Alam al-Dīn* (Mubārak), 166; and nation/nationalism, 196, 207; *Peau noire, masques blancs*, 36–39, 93–94, 154, 296n14, 302n54; rewriting of Hegel, 13, 34, 36, 38–39, 67, 73, 85, 88–95, 259, 296n14; and *Zuqāq al-Midaqq* (Maḥfūẓ), 259
"A Farewell to Lord Cromer" (Shawqī), 16
Fārūq, King, 196, 242–45, 325n28, 325nn30–31
"Fawḍā al-Azyā' fī Miṣr" (cartoon), 214
fear: in *'Alam al-Dīn* (Mubārak), 167; in "Maqāmat al-Faransīs" (al-'Aṭṭār), 67–71, 77, 84–86, 89, 103, 167; and Napoleon's proclamation, 39–40; in *Zuqāq al-Midaqq* (Maḥfūẓ), 261
the feminine/feminization, 149; and Baudrillard, 12–13, 74–79, 93–94, 154, 275, 301nn29,31; and Damrosch, 121–22; and El-Enany, 72–75; and Fanon, 93–94; in "Maqāmat al-Faransīs" (al-'Aṭṭār), 15, 66, 71–79, 90–91, 94, 96–98, 100, 102–3, 105–6, 154, 300–301n15, 303n62; in *Modern Egypt* (Cromer), 154–55, 170; and Napoleon's proclamation, 78; and Said, 72–73; and al-Ṭahṭāwī's translation theory, 146, 148; and Ṭarābīshī, 73–75; of the West, 72–79; in *Zuqāq al-Midaqq* (Maḥfūẓ), 250
Fénelon, François de Salignac de La Mothe-, 114
"Fī al-Adab al-'Arabī" (al-Zayyāt), 224–26
FitzGerald, Edward, 175
Foucault, Michel, 9, 18
French colonialism, 3–7, 10, 13–17, 20, 26, 290n14; in *'Alam al-Dīn* (Mubārak), 29, 165–72, 180, 188, 314nn56–57,59, 315n82; in Algeria, 5, 34; and al-'Aqqād, 276–77, 283; and civilization, 14–16, 59, 70, 73–74, 77, 89, 92–93, 104, 109–15, 124, 135, 149, 152–53, 165, 167, 306n27; and de Sacy, 98–99, 116, 122–24, 137–41, 144, 165; Dual Control, 27–28; and educational missions, 20, 110–14, 152–53, 159, 305–6nn12–13,20–21, 311n6; and Egypt as woman, 30, 245–47, *248*, 325–26nn32,35–36; end of in Egypt, 28, 108, 130, 141; and Entente Cordiale (1904), 194; al-'Īsawī's views on, 5–6; in "Maqāmat al-Faransīs" (al-'Aṭṭār), 15, 29, 66–107, 145, 151, 160, 167; in *Modern Egypt* (Cromer), 152–55, 157, 311n7; Napoleonic invasion/occupation of Egypt, 5–7, 14–15, 27–29, 33–58, *35*, *41*, 63, 66–67, 80, 95, 98–99, 107–12, 114, 121–22, 140–41, 145, 151, 159, 277, 294–95nn1–3,5, 296n17; and nation/nationalism, 201, 205–7, 210, 212, 217, 245–46; and al-Sibā'ī's translation of Carlyle, 173, 181, 187–90; and al-Ṭahṭāwī's translation theory, 29, 108–51, 161, 306n27; in *Zuqāq al-Midaqq* (Maḥfūẓ), 250
French language/literature, 3–6, 10, 14; clarity of, 135; and de Sacy, 98–99, 116, 122–24, 137–41, 144, 165; and *grammaire*, 125–26, 129, 132, 135; and Ḥusayn, 280–82; and *Leçons françaises de littérature et de morale* (Noël and de La Place), 123–24, 129–31; in "Maqāmat al-Faransīs" (al-'Aṭṭār), 15, 66, 76–77, 79–82, 86, 89, 91, 95, 98–99, 103; in *Modern Egypt* (Cromer), 153–54, 159; and Napoleon's proclamation, 15, 33–34, 38–40, 43, 46–48, 50–51, 58, 77; and nation/nationalism, 200, 207, 210, 217; and Romanticism, 141–42; and al-Sibā'ī's translation of Carlyle, 159, 190, 315n91; and al-Ṭahṭāwī's translation theory, 29, 111–51, *143*, 161, 200, 211, 278, 309n97
French Republic, 44–45, 53, 297n36; seal of, 34, *35*, 40
French Revolution, 12, 45
The French Revolution (Carlyle), 287
friendship: in *'Alam al-Dīn* (Mubārak), 160–63, 165, 172; and Anglo-Egyptian Treaty (1936), 242–43; and Derrida, 31, 47, 94, 274–75, 279; and Gandhi, Leela, 10; versus love/enmity, 31, 47, 94, 274–75, 279; in "Maqāmat al-Faransīs" (al-'Aṭṭār), 70, 80, 89, 94; in *Modern Egypt* (Cromer), 154; and Napoleon's proclamation, 33, 48, 70, 80
Fu'ād, King, 196, 245

Gandhi, Leela, 10
Gandhi, Mohandas, 190
George, Olakunle, 115–16
Germany/Germans, 219, 276, 280–81, 283, 287
Ghazoul, Ferial, 124

Glissant, Édouard, 62
Grammaire arabe, à l'usage des élèves de l'École spéciale des langues orientales vivantes (de Sacy), 138–39
grammatical theory: and ambiguity of Arabic, 46–48, 125–26, 135, 138, 224; and clarity of French, 135; and *grammaire* (grammar), 125–26, 129, 132, 135; and *nisba*, 149–51; and science of Arabic/Arabic sciences, 125–26
Gramsci, Antonio, 59, 62, 265, 328n100
Gran, Peter, 102, 300–301n15
Greek language/literature, 39, 55, 223, 231, 275, 282; in *'Alam al-Dīn* (Mubārak), 163; and Ḥusayn, 280; and al-Ṭahṭāwī's translation theory, 122–25, 127, 129–32, 135, 138–41, 144, 146

ḥadīth, 68, 106
Ḥadīth 'Īsā ibn Hishām, aw Fatra min al-Zaman (al-Muwayliḥī), 16, 292n44, 304n78, 325–26n36
Hafez, Sabry, 110, 304n78
Haitian Revolution, 44, 130
al-Ḥalabī, Sulaymān, 54
Halim, Hala, 240
Hamlet (Shakespeare), 177
Ḥaqqī, Maḥmūd Ṭāhir, 216
al-Ḥarīrī, Abū Muḥammad al-Qāsim ibn 'Alī, 68, 137–38, 300n9
Haykal, Muḥammad Ḥusayn, 30, 200–201, 210–18, 222–24, 226, 320–21nn47–48
Hegel, G. W. F., 8, 60, 88, 166, 302n44; Fanon's rewriting of, 13, 34, 36, 38–39, 67, 73, 89–95, 259, 296n14; and "Maqāmat al-Faransīs" (al-'Aṭṭār), 29, 85–95, 302n44; and recognition, 85–86, 90–94, 97, 261
Heliopolis, 195–96
hero/heroism worship, 186–89, 191–92, 318n136
heteroglossia, 204–5, 208
hieroglyphs, 152, 227, 235–36
Ḥijāzī, Maḥmūd Fahmī, 113, 115
hijra, 53, 82, 128
al-Hilāl (the Crescent), 227
al-Hilbāwī, Ibrāhīm, 212–16, 321n48
Histoire des Arabes (Sédillot), 313n44
Ḥizb al-Aḥrār al Dustūriyyīn, 212
Ḥizb al-Umma, 175–76
al-Ḥizb al-Waṭanī, 176
Homer, 125, 127, 150, 239
homoeroticism, 75, 93
homosexuality, 250, 300–301n15
human nature, 276, 279, 285–86
Ḥusayn, Ṭāhā, 31, 177–78, 275–76, 279–85, 287–88, 329n28

Ibn Manẓūr, 160, 313n33
Ibrāhīm, Ḥāfiẓ, 16, 304n78
Ibrāhīm Bey, 42, 45
identificatory meaning, 33, 94–95, 104, 183; imaginary identification, 94; symbolic identification, 94–95
'Iffat, Muḥammad, 177, 316n103
"Iḥtiḍār al-Jumūd wa al-Fawḍā—Kayfa Yattasiq al-Niẓām al-Jadīd" (Haykal), 212–18, 222–24, 226, 320–21n47
"Ilā Ayyihimā Naḥnu Aqrab: al-Sharq am al-Gharb?" (Mūsā), 227–28
illusion, 11, 13, 15, 273, 288; in *'Alam al-Dīn* (Mubārak), 157, 166; and Ḥusayn, 282; in "Maqāmat al-Faransīs" (al-'Aṭṭār), 74, 76, 78–79, 89–93; and Napoleon's proclamation, 36, 38, 56; and nation/nationalism, 202, 209, 227, 236; and al-Sibā'ī's translation of Carlyle, 178, 183, 190; in *Zuqāq al-Midaqq* (Maḥfūẓ), 256, 260, 264–65
Imagined Communities (Anderson), 215
imām, 47, 52, 113, 305–6nn20–21
An Imam in Paris: Account of a Stay in France by an Egyptian Cleric (1826–1831) (al-Ṭahṭāwī), 305–6n21, 308n76
imposition, 3, 7, 17–19, 21, 204–5, 243, 288
independence, 27–28; and al-'Aqqād, 277; and Egypt as woman, 247, 248, 249, 325–26nn35–36; in *Mountolive* (Durrell), 241–42, 245, 247; and nation/nationalism, 196–97, 213–15, 220, 222; and al-Sibā'ī's translation of Carlyle, 176; in *Zuqāq al-Midaqq* (Maḥfūẓ), 242, 245, 247, 250, 272
India, 9–10, 57–60, 81–82, 152–53, 155, 158, 174, 183–84, 194, 205–6, 209, 228, 230, 311n14. *See also* Bengal
inequality. *See* commensurability/incommensurability; equivalence
Inferno (Dante), 184
Institut d'Égypte, 46, 111, 305n13
intention/Intention, 18, 25, 134, 137, 144–45, 178, 188, 192, 194; and nation/nationalism, 198, 208–10, 225

"interpellation," 29, 57, 59–65, 67, 194, 269; and "dissimilation," 29, 55–65; and translational seduction, 29, 55–65
The Intimate Enemy (Nandy), 172–73, 311n11
intoxication, 15, 67–68, 79, 85, 98, 102, 104, 106–7, 277
intranational translatability, 201, 204, 210–11, 214–15, 218, 224
al-'Īsawī, Bashīr, 5–6, 22, 27
Islam. *See also* Arab-Islamic cultural heritage: and al-Afghāni, 180; in *'Alam al-Dīn* (Mubārak), 162–72, 182, 314n75; and al-'Aqqād, 283, 285–87; and *bida'*, 117; and *al-fiṭra*, 286; five pillars of, 70; and "fundamentalism," 31–32; and *ḥadīth*, 68, 106; Islamic calendar, 128; Islamic law, 103, 106, 252; and al-Jabartī, 81; and al-Jazā'irlī, 45; and Ka'b ibn Zuhayr, 101; in "Maqāmat al-Faransīs" (al-'Aṭṭār), 68, 70, 79–83, 101, 103; in *Modern Egypt* (Cromer), 156–57; and Al-Musawi, 30, 178; and Napoleon's proclamation, 14, 40–53, 55–58, 80, 157, 172, 298n51; and nation/nationalism, 223–25, 245; and Renan, 179–80; and *shirk*, 186; and al-Sibā'ī's translation of Carlyle, 29–30, 173–93; and al-Ṭahṭāwī's translation theory, 114, 116–18, 121, 127–28, 137–38, 144, 149–51, 307n39; in *Tārīkh Muddat al-Faransīs bi Miṣr* (al-Jabartī), 80–81; in *Zuqāq al-Midaqq* (Maḥfūẓ), 252
Ismā'īl, Khedive, 16, 27, 114, 159–60, 235, 269, 312n28, 315n82
Istanbul, 42–43, 45, 52

al-Jabartī, 'Abd al-Raḥmān, 40–43, 45–49, 54, 297–98nn36,48,52; and *'Alam al-Dīn* (Mubārak), 172, 314n57; and al-'Aṭṭār, 80–81; on inspiration for al-Khashshāb's love poetry, 300–301n15; lively realism of, 102
Jacquemond, Richard, 3–4, 290n14
al-Jadīd (the New), 212, 224, 275
Jamā'at al-Adab al-Qawmī (Society for National Literature), 282–83
Jankowski, James, 320–21n47
Japan/Japanese, 199–200, 245, 284–86
al-Jarīda (the Newspaper), 175–76
al-Jazā'irlī, Ḥasan Pasha, 45
al-Jindī, Anwar, 174, 315–16n97
Johnson, Samuel, 188, 190–91
Jomard, Edme-François, 110–14, 116, 118, 140, 142, 149, 151, 156, 305n13, 314n57
Jones, William, Sir, 58–60
Julius Caesar (Shakespeare), 174

Ka'b ibn Zuhayr, 101, 304n73
Kāmil, Muṣṭafā, 10, 176
al-Kashkūl, 245, 248, 249, 325n32
al-Khashshāb, Ismā'īl, 300–301n15, 303n61
al-Khiṭaṭ al-Tawfīqiyya al-Jadīda (Mubārak), 159, 313nn32,47
Kīlīṭū, 'Abd al-Fattāḥ (Abdelfattah Kilito), 1–2, 4, 28, 29, 127–28, 139
kinship, 8–9; in "Maqāmat al-Faransīs" (al-'Aṭṭār), 104; and nation/nationalism, 202, 208, 230–31, 236; and al-Ṭahṭāwī's translation theory, 116, 122–23, 128, 134, 137, 140–41, 150
Kipling, Rudyard, 228, 322n83
Kléber, Jean-Baptiste, 47, 54, 296n17
knowledge: in *'Alam al-Dīn* (Mubārak), 160, 162–68; and al-'Aqqād, 275–79, 283–87; and Ḥusayn, 280–82; in "Maqāmat al-Faransīs" (al-'Aṭṭār), 73–75, 77, 80–81, 87, 91, 97–98; and Napoleon's proclamation, 50–51, 55–56, 77; and nation/nationalism, 206–7, 223; and al-Sibā'ī's translation of Carlyle, 175, 189–90; and al-Ṭahṭāwī's translation theory, 108–9, 113–14, 116, 118, 123–27, 129, 138, 253; in *Tārīkh Muddat al-Faransīs bi Miṣr* (al-Jabartī), 80–81; in *Zuqāq al-Midaqq* (Maḥfūẓ), 253
kufr, 188–89. *See also* belief/unbelief

"Lā Anta Anta wa Lā al-Mathīl Mathīl" (al-Nadīm), 16
Lamartine, Alphonse de, 141–42
Lampson, Miles, Sir, 242–45
Lane, Edward William, 95, 313n32
Lan Tatakallama Lughatī (Kīlīṭū), 1
Latin, 122–23, 129–32, 138–41, 223, 231, 275, 282
Laurens, Henry, 43–45, 49, 294–95nn1,3, 296n24
League of Nations, 243, 245–46, 248
Leçons françaises de littérature et de morale (Noël and de La Place), 123–24, 129–31, 137, 139

Lettres persanes (Montesquieu), 305–6n21
Lévi-Strauss, Claude, 262–67
Liberal Constitutionalist Party, 212
Lisān al-ʿArab (Ibn Manẓūr), 160, 313n33
Liu, Lydia, 3, 30, 56, 61, 88, 124–26, 137, 207–9, 220–21, 299n85
Louca, Anouar, 311n6, 313n44
love, 4, 6–7, 9–10, 17, 26–27, 31, 273–75, 288; and Ahmed, 71, 299n95; in *ʿAlam al-Dīn* (Mubārak), 29, 159–60, 162–67, 170–72; and al-ʿAqqād, 31, 275, 277–79, 286–88; and Benjamin, Jessica, 31, 274, 279; and *al-Burda* (The Mantle), 83; and Casanova, 119; conditional love, 277–79, 286, 288; and Derrida, 31, 47, 94, 274–75; versus friendship/enmity, 31, 47, 94, 274–75, 279; and Gandhi, Leela, 10; and Ḥusayn, 31, 275, 288; love-logic, 6, 9, 89, 166, 275, 277, 287–88; in "Maqāmat al-Faransīs" (al-ʿAṭṭār), 29, 69–73, 75–76, 78, 83–85, 89, 91–97, 99–100, 103–7, 300–301n15; in *Mountolive* (Durrell), 243, 247, 270–72; and Nandy, 173; in *Peau noire, masques blancs* (Fanon), 93–94; and al-Sibāʿī's translation of Carlyle, 183; and al-Ṭahṭāwī's translation theory, 119, 142, 144–50, 278; as upshot/contestation of seduction, 26–27, 92–94; in *Zuqāq al-Midaqq* (Maḥfūẓ), 243, 251, 257–59, 261–62
Lowe, Lisa, 3, 291n20
"al-Lugha al-ʿArabiyya Tanʿī Ḥaẓẓahā bayna Ahlihā" (Ibrāhīm), 16
La Lyre brisée (Agoub), 29, 141–49, 142–43, 309n97

Macaulay, Thomas Babington, 152–53, 155, 183, 228, 237, 311n14
Madrasat al-Alsun (Cairo), 113–14, 306n22
Madrasat al-Muʿallimīn (Cairo), 174–75
Magallon, Charles, 44
Maghraoui, Abdeslam, 8, 216, 230, 322–23n94
Maḥfūẓ, Najīb (Naguib Mahfouz), 4–5, 30–31, 242–70, 272–73, 275, 288, 290n16, 324n19, 325–26nn30–31,36–37, 327nn64,71–72,76
Mamlūk/Mamālīk (Mameluke/Mamelukes), 42–47, 49–53, 94, 102, 167–69
Manāhij al-Albāb al-Miṣriyya fī Mabāhij al-Ādāb al-ʿAṣriyya (al-Ṭahṭāwī), 114
al-Manfalūṭī, Muṣṭafā Luṭfī, 1–2, 4, 28
"manner of meaning," 33, 295n4
maqāma, 16, 66, 68–70, 94, 102, 106, 137, 300n9, 304n78. *See also* "Maqāmat al-Faransīs" (al-ʿAṭṭār)
"Maqāmat al-Faransīs" (al-ʿAṭṭār), 15, 29, 66–107, 274, 300n9; and *ʿAlam al-Dīn* (Mubārak), 160, 167; and Baudrillard, 29, 74–79, 83, 86, 89, 91, 93–94, 96–97, 105; and Bhabha, 29, 80–83, 85, 88; and Fanon, 13, 29, 34, 36–39, 63, 67, 73, 75, 85, 88–95, 296n14, 302n54; and Hegel, 29, 85–95, 302n44; and al-Jabartī, 80; and *Modern Egypt* (Cromer), 154; Napoleon's proclamation in, 15, 67, 69–72, 76–78, 80, 82; and al-Ṭahṭāwī's translation theory, 145; and Ṭarābīshī, 29, 73–75; and Žižek, 29, 94–95, 97; and *Zuqāq al-Midaqq* (Maḥfūẓ), 259–61
Marsot, Afaf Lutfi al-Sayyid, 44, 46
Marxism, 25, 59, 321n51
the masculine/masculinization, 7, 13, 15; in "Maqāmat al-Faransīs" (al-ʿAṭṭār), 72–76, 78, 80, 91, 93–94, 103, 106; in *Modern Egypt* (Cromer), 154–55; and al-Ṭahṭāwī's translation theory, 146; and Ṭarābīshī, 73–74; in *Zuqāq al-Midaqq* (Maḥfūẓ), 254
Massad, Joseph, 250
Massey, Gerald, 323n96
Massumi, Brian, 71
master/mastery, 8, 11, 24; in *ʿAlam al-Dīn* (Mubārak), 166, 169; and al-ʿAqqād, 283; and Bhabha, 88; and Damrosch, 122; and Fanon, 36–39, 67, 75, 88–89, 92–95, 296n14; and Hegel, 36, 38–39, 67, 87–94, 259; in "Maqāmat al-Faransīs" (al-ʿAṭṭār), 66–67, 75–77, 81, 87–92, 94; and Napoleon's proclamation, 36–39, 43, 58, 67; and al-Sibāʿī's translation of Carlyle, 183, 193; and al-Ṭahṭāwī's translation theory, 133
Mawāqiʿ al-Aflāk fī Waqāʾiʿ Tilīmāk (Fénelon; al-Ṭahṭāwī, trans.), 114
al-Māzinī, Ibrāhīm ʿAbd al-Qādir, 30, 195, 201–11, 214, 220, 225, 319–20nn18–19,23
McClintock, Anne, 291n19
Mecca, 53, 128, 185
Medina, 53, 82–83, 85, 128
Mediterraneanness, 223, 229–30, 236
Mehmed Ali, 27–28, 108, 277; in *ʿAlam*

al-Dīn (Mubārak), 160, 167, 314n59; and al-'Aṭṭār, 67; and Būlāq presses, 112; and Cuno, 53–54; death of, 114; descendants of, 27, 196; educational missions of, 20, 110–13, 116, 152–54, 159, 305–6nn12–13,20–21; and Fahmy, 54; and Shawqī, 16; and al-Ṭahṭāwī, 113–16, 147, 151
Melas, Natalie, 29, 56–57, 62–64
memory, cultural, 16, 84, 113, 127–28
Menou, Jacques 'Abd Allāh, 47, 297–98n48
metempsychosis, 56
Midaq Alley (Mahfouz). See *Zuqāq al-Midaqq* (Maḥfūẓ)
mimicry: and Bhabha, 2–3, 37–40, 57, 80, 83, 85, 228; in "Maqāmat al-Faransīs" (al-'Aṭṭār), 74, 79–80, 82–83, 85, 91, 94, 97–98, 100, 104, 106, 274; in *Mountolive* (Durrell), 240; and Napoleon's proclamation, 34, 36–40, 45, 48–49, 57
"Minute on Indian Education" (Macaulay), 152–53, 228
mirror images, 77, 120, 288; in "Maqāmat al-Faransīs" (al-'Aṭṭār), 77–78, 80; in *Mountolive* (Durrell), 241; and Napoleon's proclamation, 55, 77; and al-Sibā'ī's translation of Carlyle, 174; in *Zuqāq al-Midaqq* (Maḥfūẓ), 242, 260–62
"al-Miṣriyyūn Umma Gharbiyya" (Mūsā), 229
Mitchell, Timothy, 22–23, 27, 30, 56, 135, 159, 203, 206–7, 211–12
Modern Egypt (Cromer), 14, 152–59
modernity, 5, 14, 16, 30, 74; in *'Alam al-Dīn* (Mubārak), 159, 164, 167–69; and al-'Aqqād, 283, 286–87; and Casanova, 119–22, 136; and Damrosch, 122; and George, 115–16; and Ḥusayn, 280; and Jomard, 112; in "Maqāmat al-Faransīs" (al-'Aṭṭār), 81–82; and *Modern Egypt* (Cromer), 152–53; and nation/nationalism, 195–96, 200–203, 212–18, 221–24, 226, 230–31, 236; and Shawqī, 16; and al-Sibā'ī's translation of Carlyle, 174, 177–78, 180–82, 186–87, 190, 192; and al-Ṭahṭāwī's translation theory, 109–10, 115–16, 119–23, 127–28, 136–37; in *Zuqāq al-Midaqq* (Maḥfūẓ), 252, 259, 265
Montesquieu, 305–6n21
Moosa, Matti, 108–10, 115, 315–16n97
Morant Bay massacre (Jamaica), 155
Moreh, Shmuel, 47, 102
Mountolive (Durrell), 30–31, 237–47, 251, 256, 258, 270–72, 323nn3–4, 324n19, 325n28
al-Mu'allaqāt, 83, 103
Mubārak, 'Alī, 22, 29, 55, 159–73, 180, 182, 188, 211, 277, 304n78, 312nn28,30, 313n47, 314–15n80
Muḥammad, Prophet: in *'Alam al-Dīn* (Mubārak), 167, 314n59; biographies of, 177; and *al-Burda* (The Mantle), 15, 66–67, 79–82, 99, 101, 167; and *ḥadīth*, 68, 106; and *hijra*, 53, 82, 128; in "Maqāmat al-Faransīs" (al-'Aṭṭār), 66–67, 79–82, 99, 101, 167; and Napoleon's proclamation, 41, 43, 47–48, 53; and al-Sibā'ī's translation of Carlyle, 29, 173, 175, 177–85, 187–88, 190–91, 193, 287, 316n109, 317n119, 318n133; and al-Ṭahṭāwī's translation theory, 117, 133
Muḥammad 'Alī. *See* Mehmed Ali
al-Muqtabas (the Quoted), 317n119
al-Muqtaṭaf (the Selection), 176, 312n26
Murād Bey, 42, 45
al-Murshid al-Amīn li al-Banāt wa al-Banīn (al-Ṭahṭāwī), 114
Mūsā, Salāma, 30, 200–201, 227–36, 232, 233, 234, 276–77, 279, 282, 322nn83,87, 323n96
Al-Musawi, Muhsin, 30, 178
Muslims. *See also* Islam; *names of Muslims*: in *'Alam al-Dīn* (Mubārak), 160–64, 167–71, 314n59; and al-'Aqqād, 287; and Cromer, 30, 156; in al-Manfalūṭī's questions, 28; in "Maqāmat al-Faransīs" (al-'Aṭṭār), 77, 80–81, 89, 91, 104, 106; and Napoleon's proclamation, 14, 33–34, 36–37, 40, 43–53, 57–58, 77, 295n3, 298n51; and nation/nationalism, 223–24; post–9/11 position of, 31–32; and al-Sibā'ī's translation of Carlyle, 173–93; and al-Ṭahṭāwī's translation theory, 117, 144; in *Tārīkh Muddat al-Faransīs bi Miṣr* (al-Jabartī), 80–81
Mustaqbal al-Thaqāfa fī Miṣr (Ḥusayn), 329n28
al-muthāqafa (fencing/transculturation), 73–74
al-Muwayliḥī, Muḥammad, 16, 304n78, 325–26n36

al-Nadīm, ʿAbd Allāh, 16
al-nahḍa, 4–5, 8, 15–16, 102, 291n23; and Allen, 108–9; and nation/nationalism, 197, 207, 227; and prostitution, 325–26n36; and Sheehi, 8; and al-Sibāʿī's translation of Carlyle, 177; and al-Ṭahṭāwī's translation theory, 109–10, 114, 127, 306n27
al-Naḥḥās, Muṣṭafā, 242, 245–46
al-Najjār, Ḥusayn Fawzī, 109–10, 307n39
Nambikwara Indians of Brazil, 262–66
Nandy, Ashis, 172–73, 178, 311n11
Napoleon Bonaparte (Napoléon Bonaparte). *See also* Napoleonic proclamation: in *ʿAlam al-Dīn* (Mubārak), 163, 166–72; Code Napoléon, 114; *Correspondance de Napoléon*, 48; defeat at Waterloo, 131; invasion/occupation of Egypt, 5–7, 14–15, 27–29, 33–58, *35*, *41*, 63, 66–67, 80, 95, 98–99, 107–12, 114, 121–22, 140–41, 145, 151, 159, 166–72, 277, 294–95nn1–3,5, 296n17; in "Maqāmat al-Faransīs" (al-ʿAṭṭār), 15, 67, 69–72, 76–78, 80, 82, 84, 89, 98–99, 101, 151, 302n44; in *On Heroes* . . . (Carlyle), 188, 191; and al-Ṭahṭāwī's translation theory, 140–41
Napoleonic proclamation, 14–15, 28–29, 33–65, *35*, 294–95nn1–3,5, 296nn17–18, 297–98nn36,48,51; in *ʿAlam al-Dīn* (Mubārak), 163, 168, 170–72; and Althusser, 29, 57, 59–63; in "Maqāmat al-Faransīs" (al-ʿAṭṭār), 67, 70, 77–78, 80, 82, 84, 89; and Melas, 29, 56–57, 62–64; and Niranjana, 29, 56–61, 63–64; and Rafael, 29–30, 57–58, 61; and *Zuqāq al-Midaqq* (Maḥfūẓ), 260–61
naql (transport/translation), 195–96, 216–18, 222
al-Naqqāsh, Rajāʾ, 51
nation/nationalism, 4, 30–31, 195–236; in *ʿAlam al-Dīn* (Mubārak), 169, 314–15n80; and al-ʿAqqād, 275–76, 283; and Bakhtin, 30, 204–5, 319–20n23; and Casanova, 121; and Chatterjee, 30, 197–200; and Derrida, 207, 209, 218–20, 222, 235; Eastern nationalisms, 197–98, 205–10, 227–28, 231, 233, 235–36, 320–21n47; and Haykal, 30, 200–201, 210–18, 222–24, 226, 320–21n47; and Ḥusayn, 275–76, 280–81; and Liu, 30, 207–9, 220–21; and Maghraoui, 8; and al-Māzinī, 30, 195, 201–11, 214, 220, 225, 319–20nn18–19,23; and Mitchell, 30, 203, 206–7, 211–12; in *Mountolive* (Durrell), 245–47; and Mūsā, 30, 200–201, 227–36, *232*, *233*, *234*, 322nn83,87, 323n96; and al-Najjār, 109; and Napoleon's proclamation, 49, 52–53; and national universal, 201, 205, 215; and 1919 Egyptian revolution, 31, 176, 196, 200, 206, 227; and particularism/universalism, 30, 198–202, 205–7, 209–10, 212, 215–16, 218–20, 222, 224, 226, 235–36; and Rafael, 30, 220–22; and Sakai, 30, 199–200, 207; and al-Sibāʿī's translation of Carlyle, 157–58, 175–76, 178, 184–85, 187, 194; and al-Ṭahṭāwī's translation theory, 114, 121, 123, 141, 146–47, 253, 306n27; and Venuti, 30, 198–99; and al-Zayyāt, 30, 210–12, 224–26; in *Zuqāq al-Midaqq* (Maḥfūẓ), 245–47, 250–53, 327n71
Naẓm al-ʿUqūd fī Kasr al-ʿŪd (Agoub; al-Ṭahṭāwī, trans.), 29, 141–49, *142–43*, 309n97
neighborliness, 69, 77, 79, 82–85, 99
"neurotic *and*," 25–27, 123, 218, 276
Niranjana, Tejaswini, 25, 29, 56–61, 63–64, 309n80
nisba, 149–51
Noël, François-Joseph-Michel, 123–24, 129–31, 137, 139
Novalis, 265, 328n100

Odin, 188, 191, 193
Of Grammatology (Derrida), 262
"Of Mimicry and Man" (Bhabha), 37, 80
On Heroes, Hero-Worship, and the Heroic in History (Carlyle), 29–30, 157, 159, 173–94, 287, 316n109, 317n119, 318nn132–33,136,141,145; and hero worship, 186–89, 191–92, 318n136; and Muḥammad, Prophet, 29, 173, 175, 177–85, 187–88, 190–91, 193, 287, 316n109, 317n119, 318n133; and secularism, 173–93, 317n127; and Shakespeare, 29, 173–74, 176–77, 184–85, 188, 191–93, 315n91, 316n103
On the Education of the People of India (Trevelyan), 158, 312n24
On the Origin of Species (Darwin), 312n24
order/disorder, 22–23, 210–18, 224, 226
L'Orient (ship), 34, 39, 294n1

Orientalism, 7–9, 15, 19–24, 26, 29; in *'Alam al-Dīn* (Mubārak), 159–72, 188, 313n47, 314n59; and British colonialism, 29–30, 58–60; in "Maqāmat al-Faransīs" (al-'Aṭṭār), 72, 74–75, 81, 89–92, 98, 102, 104, 300–301n15; in *Mountolive* (Durrell), 323n3; and Napoleon's proclamation, 55, 58; and *On Heroes . . .* (Carlyle), 173, 179; and al-Shayyāl, 300–301n15; and al-Ṭahṭāwī's translation theory, 115–16, 122–23, 137–41
Orientalism (Said), 9, 19, 72–73
origins/original, 2–3, 5, 12, 16, 25; and *'Alam al-Dīn* (Mubārak), 168–69, 172; and al-'Aqqād, 276; in "Maqāmat al-Faransīs" (al-'Aṭṭār), 99–101; and Napoleon's proclamation, 33–34, 37, 40, 48–49, 55, 99; and nation/nationalism, 197–98, 200–202, 220–21, 224–36, 232, 233, 234, 322nn83,87; and Niranjana, 56, 59–60; and al-Sibā'ī's translation of Carlyle, 178, 180–82, 185–86, 188–89, 192–94; and al-Ṭahṭāwī's translation theory, 29, 122–23, 127–29, 132–35, 138–41, 144, 146–47, 149–50
Other, 8–9, 12–13, 23–24, 273; and al-'Aqqād, 277–79, 286, 288; and Fanon, 93–94; and Hegel, 86–94; in "Maqāmat al-Faransīs" (al-'Aṭṭār), 74, 79, 82, 84, 86–95, 97, 102; in *Mountolive* (Durrell), 247, 271; and Napoleon's proclamation, 34, 36–37, 49, 64; and nation/nationalism, 198–99, 203, 205, 217, 219; supersession of, 87–94, 145; and al-Ṭahṭāwī's translation theory, 120, 131, 137, 139–40, 145; in *Zuqāq al-Midaqq* (Maḥfūẓ), 247, 251, 272
Ottoman Egypt, 16, 20, 27–28, 294n81; in *'Alam al-Dīn* (Mubārak), 159, 165, 169; and al-'Aqqād, 286; and Entente Cordiale (1904), 194; in "Maqāmat al-Faransīs" (al-'Aṭṭār), 67, 69, 77, 101; and Napoleon's proclamation, 42–46, 49, 52–55, 77; and nation/nationalism, 195–96, 200–201, 214, 223–24; and pan-Islamism, 176; and al-Sibā'ī's translation of Carlyle, 175–76, 183, 194; and al-Ṭahṭāwī's translation theory, 108–9, 113–14, 122, 133, 140, 147
Ouyang, Wen-chin, 164–67, 314n56
Paris: in *'Alam al-Dīn* (Mubārak), 159, 165, 169; as Bārīz, 136, 149–51; and Casanova, 120–22, 132, 136; Egyptian educational mission in, 20, 22, 29, 110–18, 305–6nn13,20–21; and Napoleon's proclamation, 52; and al-Sibā'ī's translation of Carlyle, 173; and al-Ṭahṭāwī, 22, 29, 54, 113–18, 121–24, 129, 131–32, 136–37, 141, 146, 149–51, 159, 305–6nn20–21
particularism: and nation/nationalism, 199–200, 202, 205–7, 209–10, 219, 222, 224; and al-Sibā'ī's translation of Carlyle, 193; and al-Ṭahṭāwī's translation theory, 118–19, 123, 125–26, 128, 133–35; in *Zuqāq al-Midaqq* (Maḥfūẓ), 264, 268
Peau noire, masques blancs (Fanon), 36–39, 93–94, 154, 296n14, 302n54
Persian language/literature, 138–40, 275, 280–81
Phänomenologie des Geistes (Hegel), 34
Pharaonic cultural heritage, 5, 8, 202, 223, 237
Phenomenology of Spirit (Hegel), 34, 86, 89
Philippines, 57–58, 61, 63, 220–21
philoxenia, 10
physiognomy, 171, 201–2, 226, 231
Politics of Friendship (Derrida), 47, 329n4
"The Politics of Translation" (Spivak), 11–12
Politiques de l'amitié (Derrida), 47
Pollard, Lisa, 325n35
Le Port-Royal (La Logique de Port-Royal), 305–6n21
Powell, Eve Troutt, 28
precolonial self, 14, 23–24, 64; in *'Alam al-Dīn* (Mubārak), 164; in "Maqāmat al-Faransīs" (al-'Aṭṭār), 67, 90; and Napoleon's proclamation, 14, 37, 67; and nation/nationalism, 203; and al-Sibā'ī's translation of Carlyle, 180, 183; and al-Ṭahṭāwī's translation theory, 137; in *Zuqāq al-Midaqq* (Maḥfūẓ), 262, 265, 272
presses, 39, 168; of Būlāq, 112–13, 136, 313n33
pronominality, 57, 67
prophecy, 60–61, 177, 191, 194
prostitution, 241–42, 244–45, 247, 251–62, 264–66, 268–72, 325–26nn31,36, 327nn71,76

proto-Egyptians, 229–31, 232, 233, 279, 322–23nn90,94
"pure language," 25, 133–35, 144–45, 225

al-Qadi, Wadad, 164
Qāḍī 'Iyāḍ ibn Mūsā, 79, 81
qaṣīda (ode), 16, 225
Qiṣṣat al-Madīnatayn (Dickens; al-Sibā'ī, trans.), 157, 175, 315n91
"Qu'est-ce qu'une nation?" (Renan), 220
Qur'ān: in *'Alam al-Dīn* (Mubārak), 168, 171, 313n46; and al-'Aqqād, 285–87; and *ḥadīth*, 68, 106; in "Maqāmat al-Faransīs" (al-'Aṭṭār), 81; and Napoleon's proclamation, 14, 40, 43–44, 47–48, 50, 58; and nation/nationalism, 214, 223; and al-Sibā'ī's translation of Carlyle, 173, 179, 181, 185, 189, 191; and al-Ṭahṭāwī's translation theory, 117, 124, 132, 151; in *Tārīkh Muddat al-Faransīs bi Miṣr* (al-Jabartī), 81

race/racial types, 8, 49, 104, 170, 322n90; and Agoub, 201–2; and al-'Aqqād, 283; and Cromer, 156–57; and nation/nationalism, 211, 225, 227–33, 232, 233, 235–36
radical translatability, 30, 135, 138, 173
Rafael, Vicente, 29–30, 57–58, 61, 220–22
rape, 26, 74, 170, 263–64, 327n76
reason: in "Maqāmat al-Faransīs" (al-'Aṭṭār), 67, 69–70, 96, 105–6; and Napoleon's proclamation, 50–51; and al-Sibā'ī's translation of Carlyle, 177, 180, 190; and al-Ṭahṭāwī's translation theory, 116, 118–19, 135
reciprocity/irreciprocity, 8, 274; in *'Alam al-Dīn* (Mubārak), 160–62, 164, 172; and Fanon, 36, 38, 90; in "Maqāmat al-Faransīs" (al-'Aṭṭār), 73–74, 80, 90, 94, 97–100, 104; in *Mountolive* (Durrell), 243; and Napoleon's proclamation, 36, 38; and al-Ṭahṭāwī's translation theory, 113, 116, 134, 161; in *Zuqāq al-Midaqq* (Maḥfūẓ), 243, 255–56, 259, 264
recognition: and al-'Aqqād, 284; and Benjamin, Jessica, 274; and Casanova, 119–21; and Hegel, 85–86, 90–94, 97, 261; in "Maqāmat al-Faransīs" (al-'Aṭṭār), 94, 97, 101; in *Mountolive* (Durrell), 247, 270–72; and nation/nationalism, 205, 220; and al-Ṭahṭāwī's translation theory, 119–21; in *Zuqāq al-Midaqq* (Maḥfūẓ), 247, 261–62, 266, 268–70
refraction, 78, 90, 120, 128, 166, 242, 259, 301n31
"Relation de l'expédition scientifique des Français en Égypte en 1798" (Jomard), 111, 305n13
renaissance, Egyptian. See *al-nahḍa*
Renaissance Europe, 138–39, 280
Renan, Ernest, 179–80, 220, 314n75
La République mondiale des lettres (Casanova), 118
resemblance, 34, 38–40, 46–49, 52, 78, 80–82, 84–85, 124
resistance, 3–4, 7–8, 12, 16–22, 24, 64, 288, 290n14; in *'Alam al-Dīn* (Mubārak), 164–65, 168–70, 172; and Bhabha, 88; and El-Enany, 72–73; and Glissant, 62; in "Maqāmat al-Faransīs" (al-'Aṭṭār), 69–70, 72–74, 76; in *Mountolive* (Durrell), 245; and Napoleon's proclamation, 47, 52, 55, 57; in *Zuqāq al-Midaqq* (Maḥfūẓ), 245, 250, 268, 272
al-Risāla (the Message), 210
Rivarol, Antoine de, 135
Riwāyat Dhāt al-Thawb al-Abyaḍ (Collins; al-Sibā'ī, trans.), 175, 315n91
Riwāyat Hāmlit (Shakespeare; 'Abduh, trans.), 177
Riwāyat Qalb al-Asad (Scott; Ṣarrūf, trans.), 176
Riwāyat Rūmiyū wa Jūlīt (Shakespeare; 'Abduh, trans.), 176–77
Riwāyat Yūlyūs Qayṣar (Shakespeare; al-Sibā'ī, trans.), 174, 315n91
Robinson, Douglas, 55–56
Roman antiquity, 55, 123, 129, 139, 223, 275, 280. *See also* Latin
Romanticism, 141–42, 287, 319n18
Romeo and Juliet (Shakespeare), 176–77
Rousseau, Jean-Jacques, 191, 305–6n21
Rubáiyát of Omar Khayyám (FitzGerald, trans.), 175
Rubā'iyyāt 'Umar al-Khayyām (FitzGerald; al-Sibā'ī, trans.), 175
Ruskin, John, 237–41, 244, 247, 256, 258, 271–72, 323n4

Said, Edward, 7, 9, 17–24, 26, 28, 40, 47, 72–73, 140, 227, 239, 307n46, 311n7
Sa'īd, Khedive, 114
Saint-Domingue, 44, 130
Sakai, Naoki, 30, 199–200, 207, 292n31

Sanskrit, 9, 58–59, 61. *See also* Bengal; India
Ṣarrūf, Ya'qūb, 176
Saussure, Ferdinand de, 56
al-Sayyid, Aḥmad Luṭfī, 175–76
scepticism, 181, 189, 191
School of Languages (Cairo), 113–14, 253, 306n22
science. *See also* knowledge; modernity: in *'Alam al-Dīn* (Mubārak), 160, 162–64, 168; and de Sacy, 139; and George, 116–17; and Ḥusayn, 280; and al-Jabartī, 80–81; and Jomard, 111–12; and "Maqāmat al-Faransīs" (al-'Aṭṭār), 68–69; in *Modern Egypt* (Cromer), 152–53; and Napoleon's proclamation, 50, 53; and al-Sibā'ī's translation of Carlyle, 180, 190; and al-Ṭahṭāwī's translation theory, 111–13, 115–17, 124–27, 135
Scott, Walter, Sir, 4, 176
secularism, 29–30; in *'Alam al-Dīn* (Mubārak), 160, 169; and al-'Aqqād, 283, 286; in *Modern Egypt* (Cromer), 156; and Nandy, 173–74, 178; and Napoleon's proclamation, 40–41, 50, 53, 55; and nation/nationalism, 210, 213; and al-Sibā'ī's translation of Carlyle, 173–93, 317n127; and al-Ṭahṭāwī's translation theory, 116–18, 120, 124; and Viswanathan, 186; in *Zuqāq al-Midaqq* (Maḥfūẓ), 250
Sédillot, L. A., 313n44
seduction, 2–4, 7, 9–15, 17, 19, 26–28, 273, 288. *See also* translational seduction; in *'Alam al-Dīn* (Mubārak), 160–61, 164, 166–67, 170, 172; and al-'Aqqād, 275–76, 283; and Baudrillard, 11–13, 74–79, 83, 86, 91, 93–94, 96–97, 105, 154, 197–98, 255, 260, 274–75, 291n29, 292n32, 301nn29,31; and *fitna*, 291n29; and Ḥusayn, 275; versus "interpellation"/"dissimilation," 29, 56–65; in "Maqāmat al-Faransīs" (al-'Aṭṭār), 15, 66, 68–70, 72–79, 82, 85, 88–100, 103, 106–7, 151, 303n64; in *Modern Egypt* (Cromer), 14, 154, 157, 311nn7,11; in *Mountolive* (Durrell), 240–44, 246–47, 271; and Napoleon's proclamation, 14–15, 34, 37–39, 49, 51–52, 55, 57–58, 170, 261; and nation/nationalism, 30, 197–99, 205, 210, 215, 235; and Said, 21–22, 311n7; and al-Sibā'ī's translation of Carlyle, 157–58, 181, 183, 189, 193–94, 287; and al-Ṭahṭāwī's translation theory, 111, 115, 117, 120, 123–24, 137, 141, 145–51; in *Tārīkh Muddat al-Faransīs bi Miṣr* (al-Jabartī), 80; in *Zuqāq al-Midaqq* (Maḥfūẓ), 242–44, 246–47, 251–52, 255, 257–66, 269–70
Seduction (Baudrillard), 11
self, 6, 8–9, 12–13, 16, 21–25, 28, 273; and al-'Aqqād, 277–79, 288; and Fanon, 34, 36, 38–39, 93; and Hegel, 8, 13, 34, 36, 38–39, 85–92; and al-Manfalūṭī, 2, 4; in "Maqāmat al-Faransīs" (al-'Aṭṭār), 79, 84–92, 94, 96–98, 102, 106; in *Mountolive* (Durrell), 247, 271; and Napoleon's proclamation, 34, 36–39, 49, 52, 61; and nation/nationalism, 198–99, 205, 219, 221–22, 226–27; and al-Ṭahṭāwī's translation theory, 145; in *Zuqāq al-Midaqq* (Maḥfūẓ), 247, 251, 258–62, 265–67, 272, 327n71
Selim, Samah, 216, 321n51
Sève, Joseph (Süleyman Pasha), 54
shahāda, 41, 179
Shakespeare, William, 174, 176–77, 290n16; in *Mountolive* (Durrell), 237–38; in *On Heroes . . .* (Carlyle), 183–84, 188, 191, 193; and al-Sibā'ī's translation of Carlyle, 29, 173–74, 177, 183–85, 188, 192, 315n91, 316n103
Shawqī, Aḥmad, 10, 16
al-Shayyāl, Jamāl al-Dīn, 47, 295n3, 297–98n48, 300–301n15, 303n61, 306n27, 307n39
Sheehi, Stephen, 8
al-Shidyāq, Aḥmad Fāris, 128, 313n32
Shohat, Ella, 291n19
al-Sibā'ī, Muḥammad, 29–30, 157–59, 173–94, 287, 311–12nn20–21, 315–16nn91,97,109, 317n119, 318n133. See also *On Heroes . . .* (Carlyle); and *'Alam al-Dīn* (Mubārak), 164–65; and al-'Aqqād, 277; biography of, 174–77, 315–16n97; and Cromer, 30, 157–59, 174, 194; and Egyptian education, 174–75, 186, 194, 315nn87,91; and heroism, worship of, 186–89, 191–92, 318n136; and Ḥusayn, 282; on Metro tram, 195–96, 277; and nation/nationalism, 226
Siddiq, Muhammad, 253, 304n70
signifier/signified, 3–4, 12, 22, 56, 59, 87, 131; and nation/nationalism, 201,

signifier/signified (*continued*)
203–10, 214, 216–17, 219, 221–22, 230, 235, 321n48; and al-Sibāʿī's translation of Carlyle, 186, 193–94; in *Zuqāq al-Midaqq* (Maḥfūẓ), 250, 268
"Signs Taken for Wonders" (Bhabha), 37, 81
al-Siyāsa (Politics), 210
al-Siyāsa al-Usbūʿiyya (Politics Weekly), 210
slaves: in *ʿAlam al-Dīn* (Mubārak), 169; in *La Lyre brisée* (Agoub), 146; Mamālīk as, 44, 169; master-slave dialectic, 36–39, 87–95, 169, 259, 296n14
Smith, Grafton Elliot, Sir, 229–31, 232, 233, 235, 322–23nn87,94
"Smūking," 212, 215–17, 222, 226
Soueif, Ahdaf, 288
sovereignty, 8–9, 17, 21, 218, 220, 288; and Ahmed, 299n95; in *ʿAlam al-Dīn* (Mubārak), 160, 165–68; and al-ʿAqqād, 276–77, 288; and Baudrillard, 11, 13, 76–78, 197–98; as cognate of empire, 197, 206; and deixis, 197, 210, 255, 259–60, 263; "desire for the sovereign," 88; and Fanon, 63, 67; and Liu, 88, 220; in "Maqāmat al-Faransīs" (al-ʿAṭṭār), 67, 75–78, 87–95, 97–98, 105; in *Modern Egypt* (Cromer), 155; in *Mountolive* (Durrell), 241–42, 246; and Napoleon's proclamation, 14, 36–37, 40, 45, 51, 53, 57, 63, 65; and nation/nationalism, 30, 195–200, 205–6, 209, 218, 220, 222; in *Peau noire, masques blancs* (Fanon), 93–94; and al-Sibāʿī's translation of Carlyle, 178, 183–84; and Tagalog speakers, 61; and al-Ṭahṭāwī's translation theory, 116, 123, 132–33, 136, 145–46; in *Zuqāq al-Midaqq* (Maḥfūẓ), 242, 246, 250–51, 256, 258–62, 265–66
"Spanish book," 57–58, 61, 63
Spencer, Herbert, 175
Spivak, Gayatri Chakravorty, 2, 11–13, 24, 26
students, Egyptian: in London, 20, 153, 212–13, 215, 222, 305n12, 311n6; and nation/nationalism, 212–13, 215, 222; in Paris, 20, 22, 29, 110–18, 152–53, 159, 305–6nn13,20–21, 311n6; al-Sibāʿī as, 174–75, 315nn87,91
subalternity, 12, 98, 116, 119–21, 123, 136, 146, 221–22, 276
Sublime Porte, 42–43, 45, 52
Sudan, 28, 54, 114, 246
Suez Canal, 27, 243–44, 246
Süleyman Pasha (Joseph Sève), 54
supersession of the Other, 87–94, 145
"super-sign," 207–10, 217, 221, 299n85
supplementarity, 24–25, 90, 133–34, 192–93, 225
surrender, 1, 3–4, 10–12, 22, 288; and Ḥusayn, 288; in "Maqāmat al-Faransīs" (al-ʿAṭṭār), 70, 76, 78, 85, 92, 94, 100, 103; and Napoleon's proclamation, 39, 52; Spivak's views on, 4, 11–12, 24; in *Zuqāq al-Midaqq* (Maḥfūẓ), 261, 265
surrogacy, 11, 101, 146, 149, 154–55, 194, 250, 255, 257, 259, 267
Syria/Syrians, 8, 28, 54, 141, 176, 304n78

"Taʿāruf al-Shuʿūb" (al-ʿAqqād), 276
Tagalog, 57–58, 61. *See also* Philippines
al-Ṭahṭāwī, Rifāʿa Rāfiʿ, 22–23, 29, 54, 108–51, 154; and Agoub, 29, 116, 122, 141–49, *142–43*, 211, 309n97; and *ʿAlam al-Dīn* (Mubārak), 161–62, 313n32; and al-ʿAqqād, 277–78; as Azharite, 113–14, 117–18, 132, *143*, 306n27; and Benjamin, 29, 133–36, 309n80; and Casanova, 29, 118–24, 136, 307n46; and Damrosch, 29, 121, 128; death of, 114; and de Sacy, 23, 29, 116, 122–24, 137–41, 144; exile to Sudan, 114; head of School of Languages (Cairo), 113–14, 306n22; as *imām*, 305–6nn20–21; and Kilīṭū, 29, 127–28, 139; and nation/nationalism, 200; and Paris, 22, 29, 54, 113–18, 121–24, 129, 131–32, 136–37, 141, 146, 149–51, 159, 305–6nn20–21; and al-Sibāʿī's translation of Carlyle, 173, 190, 192–93; translation theory of, 108–51, *142–43*, 306n27, 307n39; in *Zuqāq al-Midaqq* (Maḥfūẓ), 253
Takhlīṣ al-Ibrīz fī Talkhīṣ Bārīz, aw al-Dīwān al-Nafīs fī Īwān Bārīs (al-Ṭahṭāwī), 29, 113–18, 123–38, 143–45, 149, 211
Takieddine-Amyuni, Mona, 327nn64,71–72
The Tale of ʿĪsā ibn Hishām; or, A Period of Time (al-Muwayliḥī), 16
A Tale of Two Cities (Dickens), 157, 175, 226

The Talisman (Scott), 176
Talleyrand, 44
Ṭarābīshī, Jūrj, 29, 73–75
al-Tarbiya (Spencer; al-Sibāʿī, trans.), 175
Tārīkh Muddat al-Faransīs bi Miṣr (al-Jabartī), 41–43, 46–47, 54, 80–81, 102, 297n36
"Tarjama" (Ḥusayn), 279, 282
"al-Tarjama wa Taʿāruf al-Shuʿūb" (al-ʿAqqād), 283, 286
"The Task of the Translator" (Benjamin), 25, 133–35, 295n4, 309n80
Tawfīq, Khedive, 200
Teachers' College (Cairo), 174–75
"telecommunication," 29, 57–58
The Tempest (Shakespeare), 177
terror. *See* fear
Thou Shalt Not Speak My Language (Kilito), 1
Tignor, Robert L., 174
time: and al-ʿAqqād, 284, 287; and Gregorian calendar, 127–28; and Islamic calendar, 128; and Kīlīṭū, 127–28; in "Maqāmat al-Faransīs" (al-ʿAṭṭār), 67, 82; and Napoleon's proclamation, 53, 57; and nation/nationalism, 214–15, 217, 224, 231; and seduction, 26, 64; and al-Sibāʿī's translation of Carlyle, 184; and al-Ṭahṭāwī's translation theory, 127–28
Tomlinson, John, 17
"transcendental signified," 3, 55–56, 87, 204, 207, 209, 219, 222, 230
"transcendental signifier," 3, 207, 289–90n8; of the native, 209
transculturation *(muthāqafa)*, 73–74, 290n14
translational seduction, 9–10, 13–14, 17, 27–28, 273, 288. *See also* seduction; in *ʿAlam al-Dīn* (Mubārak), 160–61, 164, 166–67, 170, 172; and al-ʿAqqād, 275–76, 283; and Ḥusayn, 275; in "Maqāmat al-Faransīs" (al-ʿAṭṭār), 88–92; and *Modern Egypt* (Cromer), 157–58; in *Mountolive* (Durrell), 240, 243; and Napoleon's proclamation, 29, 56–65, 170, 261; and nation/nationalism, 205, 210, 235; and al-Sibāʿī's translation of Carlyle, 157–58; in *Zuqāq al-Midaqq* (Maḥfūẓ), 243, 255, 261
"translation zone," 122, 165, 307n52
translatio studii et imperii, 55–56, 123
transubstantiation, 60, 78, 86, 136
transvestite state, 105–6, 154
transymmetry, 18–19, 255
Trautmann, Thomas, 8–9
Trevelyan, Charles, 158, 312n24
Tshāyild Hārūld (Byron; al-Sibāʿī, trans.), 174–75
Turco-Circassian ruling class, 175, 200
Turkey/Turks, 28, 112–13, 175, 281, 285–86, 294n81
al-Ṭūsī, Naṣīr al-Dīn, 79, 301n33

unitary language, 203–5, 208, 319–20n23
United Nations Development Programme, 31, 282
universalism, 24–25, 224; in *ʿAlam al-Dīn* (Mubārak), 161, 164; and al-ʿAqqād, 275, 277, 279, 284, 286–88; and Ḥusayn, 275, 279, 287–88; in *Mountolive* (Durrell), 244; and Napoleon's proclamation, 55; and nation/nationalism, 30, 198–202, 205–7, 209–10, 212, 215–16, 218–20, 222, 224, 226, 235–36; and al-Sibāʿī's translation of Carlyle, 179–82, 184, 192–93; and al-Ṭahṭāwī's translation theory, 118–29, 131–33, 135–37, 144, 146, 149; in *Zuqāq al-Midaqq* (Maḥfūẓ), 244, 264, 268
ʿUrābī, Aḥmad, 10, 200
Utilitarianism, English, 181, 189–90, 211

Venture de Paradis, Jean-Michel, 33, 295n3, 314n57
Venuti, Lawrence, 3–4, 30, 131, 198–99
violence, 6–7, 26, 32, 288; in *ʿAlam al-Dīn* (Mubārak), 167, 170; and Derrida, 30, 262–68, 328n96; in al-Jabartī, 80; in "Maqāmat al-Faransīs" (al-ʿAṭṭār), 80, 84–85, 95; and Napoleon's proclamation, 52, 80; and al-Sibāʿī's translation of Carlyle, 179; and al-Ṭahṭāwī's translation theory, 131; and *Zuqāq al-Midaqq* (Maḥfūẓ), 30, 247–48, 250–51, 253–54, 256–57, 262–68, 270, 272
Viswanathan, Gauri, 30, 186
Voltaire, 187–90, 305–6n21

"Wadāʿ Lūrd Krūmir" (Shawqī), 16
Wafd Party, 175–76, 245, 282, 315–16n97, 325n32
al-Waqāʾiʿ al-Miṣriyya (Egyptian Events), 67
Wheaton, Henry, 220
woman, Egypt as, 30, 245–47, 248, 249,

woman, Egypt as (*continued*)
250–62, 264, 266, 268, 270, 272, 325–26nn32,35–36
The Woman in White (Collins), 175
The World Republic of Letters (Casanova), 118
The World, the Text, and the Critic (Said), 18
World War I, 275–76, 283
World War II, 241–42, 247–48, 251–54, 257–58, 272, 326n37, 327nn72,76

Zaghlūl, Aḥmad Fatḥī, 311n20
Zaghlūl, Sa'd, 175–76, 311n20, 315–16n97, 319n19, 325n35
Zawba'at al-Baḥr (Shakespeare; 'Iffat, trans.), 177, 316n103
Zaynab (Haykal), 210
al-Zayyāt, Aḥmad Ḥasan, 30, 210–12, 224–26
Žižek, Slavoj, 29, 94–95, 97
Zuqāq al-Midaqq (Maḥfūẓ), 30–31, 242–70, 272, 324n19, 325–26nn30–31,36–37, 327nn64,71–72,76

TEXT
10/13 Sabon Open Type

DISPLAY
Sabon Open Type

COMPOSITOR
Modern Language Initiative

TEXT PRINTER AND BINDER
Odyssey Publications

INDEXER
Sharon Sweeney

www.ingramcontent.com/pod-product-compliance
Lightning Source LLC
Chambersburg PA
CBHW022008300426
44117CB00005B/84
9780520265523